In Armageddon's Shadow:
The Civil War and Canada's Maritime Provinces

The United States had important and long-standing economic, social, and kinship ties with Nova Scotia, New Brunswick, and Prince Edward Island that were profoundly shaken by the Civil War. In this engaging and accessible account, Greg Marquis explores the shadow cast on the Maritimes and its people by America's bloodiest conflict.

In Armageddon's Shadow chronicles events as they unfolded and highlights the very real threat of conflict between Britain and the United States. Major crises such as the highjacking of the *Chesapeake* by Confederate partisans and the destructive cruise of the CSS *Tallahassee* – the only Confederate warship to reach a mainland British North American port – in addition to Halifax's growing importance as a communications link for the South and the Maritimes' involvement in blockade running are recounted in detail.

Marquis also explores the impact of the Civil War at a more personal level. He highlights Maritimers' growing support for the beleaguered Confederacy, despite the colonies' official neutrality, and the grave implications this had for local race relations. He describes the impact of refugees, crimping, and recruiting on Maritimers' attitudes and recounts the experiences of some of the thousands of men born in New Brunswick, Nova Scotia, and Prince Edward Island who served in the Civil War.

Drawing extensively on newspaper reports, personal papers, and local histories, Marquis captures the drama of events as they unfolded, effectively putting the reader into the thick of the action and into the minds of the individuals involved. *In Armageddon's Shadow* is a must read for anyone with an interest in the American Civil War or the history of the Maritime provinces.

GREG MARQUIS teaches history at Saint Mary's University.

In Armageddon's Shadow

The Civil War and Canada's Maritime Provinces

GREG MARQUIS

Gorsebrook Research Institute for Atlantic Canada
Studies, Saint Mary's University · Halifax

McGill-Queen's University Press
Montreal & Kingston · London · Ithaca

© McGill-Queen's University Press 1998
ISBN 0–7735–1792–8

Legal deposit fourth quarter 1998
Bibliothèque nationale du Québec

Printed in Canada on acid-free paper

McGill-Queens' University Press acknowledges
the financial support of the Government of Canada
through the Book Publishing Industry Development
Program for its activities. We also acknowledge
the support of the Canada Council for the Arts for
our publishing program.

Canadian Cataloguing in Publication Data

Marguis, Greg
   In Armageddon's Shadow: The Civil War and Canada's
   Maritime Provinces

   Includes bibliographical references and index.
   ISBN 0–7735–1792–8

   1. Maritime Provinces – History – To 1867. 2. United
States – History – Civil War, 1861–1865. 3. United States
– History – Civil War, 1861–1865 – Participation,
Canadian. 4. Canadians – United States – History – 19th
century. I. Title.

FC2032.M37 1998   971.5'02   C98–900645–X
F1035.8.M36 1998

For Donna

Contents

Acknowledgments

The topic of the Civil War and the Maritimes first came to my notice in the early 1980s. A dozen years later, a bout of unexpected (and unwanted) free time provided the perfect opportunity to explore this neglected subject in detail. What I discovered about the 1860s Maritime colonies provoked both surprise and excitement.

This book would not have been possible without the assistance and support of many individuals and organizations. These include Henry and Agnes Marquis, Frank Jones, Ed MacDonald, Ethel Nepveux, Dr. Allan Marble, Edward Sloan, Colleen Murphy, Gilles Deveau, CBC Radio (Halifax, Saint John, and Moncton) and the Royal Nova Scotia Historical Society.

Special thanks to Tom Brooks and Ed Milligan for generously supplying information from the National Archives and Records Administration in Washington on Maritimers who served in the war. Tom's regular "dispatches" from Gravenhurst provided many insights for the final version of this manuscript. To my family, who purchased a computer on my behalf to assist with my writing, I owe a large debt of gratitude.

It has been a pleasure to work with editor Aurèle Parisien and the rest of the team at McGill-Queen's University Press; Dr. Colin Howell, Saint Mary's University; Jackie Logan, Gorsebrook Research Institute; and Douglas Beall, copy-editor.

Researching the Civil War as a part-time instructor based in Halifax presented a number of challenges; these were offset by the assistance rendered by the staff of the Public Archives of Nova Scotia; the Public

Archives of New Brunswick; the New Brunswick Museum Archives; the Killam Library at Dalhousie University; the Patrick Power Library at Saint Mary's University; the Mount Saint Vincent University Library; the Vaughan Library at Acadia University; and the Maritime Museum of the Atlantic.

Finally, I want to thank my wife, Donna, for her understanding and support.

List of Illustrations

Preface

In Halifax's historic Camp Hill Cemetery a little-known unmarked grave contains the remains of Major J. Smith Stansbury of the Confederate States Army. Stansbury, a native of Maryland, a border slave state that did not secede from the Union in 1861, was born in Louisiana in 1820 and was descended from a Southern family that had distinguished itself in the Revolution and the War of 1812. Graduating from the prestigious United States Military Academy at West Point in 1841, five years prior to the war with Mexico, he served in the Regular Artillery. Twenty years later, Stansbury, like most Southerners with military training, threw in his lot with the Confederate States of America. He joined the Provisional Artillery as an ordnance specialist, working in what became the most successful branch of the Confederate supply effort. By the summer of 1862, Captain Stansbury commanded the Richmond Arsenal on Byrd Island, where his duties included attending to artillery and small arms captured by the Army of Northern Virginia during the Peninsular campaign. The arsenal and armoury were equipped with machinery removed from the Harper's Ferry Arsenal. Nearby on the Kanawha canal were the famous Tregedar Iron Works. Promoted to the rank of major, he next was appointed to a board examining officer candidates in the Confederate capital. In December of 1862 the Marylander examined ordnance officer candidates in Charleston, South Carolina, and Mobile, Alabama.[1]

In the spring of 1864, Stansbury and his wife arrived in Halifax from the British colony of Bermuda, where he had been stationed to oversee ordnance procurement through the Union naval blockade. Nova Scotia's temperate climate was supposed to benefit the Confederate's deteriorating health, but he became increasing ill and succumbed to "disease of the liver" on 26 April. The rebel officer died far from home, but among friends and sympathizers, which was some comfort to his grieving widow. According to his death notice, Stansbury had been distinguished by "his studious habits and fondness for scientific research." The highly respectable funeral procession was a who's who of local supporters of the Confederacy, including prominent citizens and officers of the blockade-running steamers that periodically visited the port. Reverend William Bullock of Saint Luke's Anglican Cathedral and Dr. W.J. Almon preceded the corpse to the graveyard situated west of the Public Gardens.[2] Almon's own son, who had volunteered as a military surgeon in distant Virginia, would be interred in Camp Hill in 1867. A long line of carriages, one containing the Roman Catholic archbishop of Charleston, South Carolina, closed the melancholy scene. Major Stansbury had not only attracted considerable attention in death; his final resting place was the family plot of a prominent merchant and politician, Benjamin Wier. When Wier died four years later, a senator of the Dominion of Canada, he was buried within feet of the Southern artillery officer, a poignant tribute to a lost cause that had stirred public opinion in Nova Scotia and its neighbouring colonies in the early 1860s.[3]

The day of Stansbury's passing, another soldier was laid to rest in Holy Cross Cemetery several blocks to the south. Richard Wall, described in the burial register as a twenty-two-year-old law student, had joined the 91st New York Regiment of the Army of the Potomac. This regiment, organized at Albany in 1861, had seen service in Florida and Louisiana. Following the siege of Port Hudson in 1863, it was posted to garrison duty at Fort Jackson, below New Orleans. On 13 April 1864, Wall died in Boston, either from wounds or disease. He was buried, with little community recognition, in a markerless plot in Halifax's Roman Catholic graveyard. Yet he was one of hundreds of Maritimers who had enlisted to defend the Union from rebellion.[4]

The Civil War was the bloodiest conflict in American history. The fighting and its associated disease and famine consumed over 600,000 lives. The "war of the rebellion" degenerated into a total war in which civilian property and infrastructure were considered fair game, not just by common soldiers but by the high command. The most valuable property of the secessionist South were the 3.5 million black slaves who formed the backbone of plantation agriculture. Although three-quarters of white Southerners owned no slaves, most were prepared to defend the "peculiar institution" from Yankee interference. The inner turmoil of a powerful nation that was half slave and half free naturally attracted the attention of the outside world. Friends and rivals looked on in fascination, from the growing crisis of the 1860 election to the Confederate surrender at the Appomattox courthouse in 1865. Civil war had actually begun in "Bleeding Kansas" in the mid-1850s after national legislation left the slavery issue up to local opinion in the territory. In 1861, combat became a spectator sport and Lee, Jackson, Grant and Sherman became household names, their photographs collected like modern sports cards. The conflict was immediately recognized as significant for both North America and the world. It abolished slavery in the United States, revolutionized naval and army technology and tactics, and modernized American society. The struggle, despite the triumph of the "free soil" states, also bequeathed a troubled legacy of race relations.[5]

From the first cannonade in Charleston harbour to the execution of the conspirators in Lincoln's assassination, the events of 1861 to 1865 reverberated loudly in the colonies of British North America.[6] They contributed in no small measure to the formation of the Dominion of Canada in 1867, or so the textbooks tell us.[7] But in 1861, or even 1864, Confederation was not a foregone conclusion. In the meantime the events and personalities of the Civil War had a dramatic and immediate impact on the lives of Canadians, New Brunswickers, Nova Scotians and Prince Edward Islanders. If the battles were distant, the shockwaves were felt nonetheless. British colonists enjoyed, through newspapers, the telegraph, personal letters and word of mouth, a ringside seat for one of history's most important military struggles. To a degree that we have forgotten, Confederation was not an all-consuming issue in the Maritimes prior to 1865. The war seemed to foretell the future of not only the colonies but also the entire Western Hemisphere.

The crisis brought out intense feelings that revealed much about colonial society. Everyone had an opinion, most of them governed by emotion and folk belief, not reason. A farmer on the Maine–New Brunswick border told a reporter that Confederate General Stonewall Jackson was "a mity smart feller," who had "chawed them Northerners up about slick." Thomas Parker of Deer Island named his fishing boat *Jefferson Davis* in honour of the president of the Confederacy; yet the Saint John built and manned boat that won the 4 July 1863 Boston Regatta was called the *George B. McClellan*, after the popular Union general and future Democratic presidential candidate. In late June of 1863, heavy betting was reported in Saint John on whether the Confederates could hold the fortress of Vicksburg. Wesleyan minister John Brewster of Charlottetown asserted that "there was nothing in the cause of the South to command the sympathy of wise and good men." The local debating society thought otherwise and decided that the Confederacy should be recognized as a nation.[8]

Nova Scotians also were affected. The 1865 class at King's College, Windsor, registered its displeasure with the new American President by singing "We'll Hang Andrew Johnson from a Sour Apple Tree" during the graduation procession. At Tusket, Nova Scotia, in August 1864, young John C. Hamilton, who had served with the Confederacy and lost a hand, was enraged by the anti-Southern remarks of Daniel Benson, an immigrant sawyer who worked in local shipyards. The two men came to blows and the one-handed veteran stabbed Benson in the thigh and lower torso. He died the following day and Hamilton was sentenced to three years in the penitentiary.[9] The war provided ample opportunity for ministers, lecturers, politicians, small-town journalists and amateur poets to comment on both American and Maritime society. Northern journals produced detailed, biased and often inaccurate accounts of the week's military campaigns; Southern newspapers, which arrived in Saint John and Halifax courtesy of sea captains and steamer passengers, rebutted enemy claims in equally exaggerated fashion. British publications, the true intellectual trendsetters in the colonies, tended to support the Southern underdogs. The *Index*, the Confederacy's effective English propaganda organ, could be purchased in Halifax for six pence. Another important source of information came from the actual participants. Maritimers serving with the Blue and the Grey sent home letters describing camp life, endless marching, the glories and horrors of combat, and the miseries of prison or hospital. These missives ranged from high-minded compositions sprinkled with classical and Biblical allusions to crude and sometimes bitter narratives.[10]

Noncombatants also recorded history in the making, describing the mood in the Carolinas prior to secession, jubilant war preparations in the deep South, the mobilization of volunteers in Boston and New York, ruthless guerrilla warfare in Missouri, New Orleans under occupation by the troops of Benjamin "The Beast" Butler, and the fall of Savannah to Sherman. Merchants and shipowners also followed the war and its numerous repercussions: the fluctuating price of gold and cotton; the blockade of Southern ports; the annoying passport regulations; the profits to be made by running the blockade via the West Indies, Bermuda and Mexico. During the heated debate over Confederation from 1865 to 1868, more than one observer made use of Civil War analogies for local politics. A Halifax journal, for instance, warned readers to "pause before we rush into a Confederation from which we cannot even cut ourselves free by the sword hereafter, lest Halifax may be as Richmond, Ottawa may be as Washington."[11]

The Maritime colonies, although British possessions and officially neutral, had important and longstanding economic, social and kinship ties with the United States. Canadians, Newfoundlanders and Maritimers would constitute the fourth largest immigrant group in the U.S. in 1870. In the northeastern states their presence was even greater. Few of the region's 670,000 inhabitants, whatever their race or ethnicity, had no friends or relations south of the border. The words of a Fredericton woman writing in the 1850s rang just as true for most Maritime communities a decade later: "of the few young men of the place, all are leaving to try to make it somewhere else."[12]

Hundreds of former Bluenoses toiled in workshops, stores, lumber camps, factories and homes in New England. Others had migrated to Western states such as Ohio and Wisconsin and to the California goldfields, and not a few were established in the mid-Atlantic and Southern regions. In the colonies, American influences were noticeable in religion, journalism, education and social movements such as temperance and women's rights. U.S. consular officials, facilitating American shipping and commercial interests, were stationed in most ports. American capital and know-how helped develop New Brunswick's forestry sector and Nova Scotia's mining industry. Capitalists in Maine and New Brunswick dreamt of a rail link between New England and the Gulf of St. Lawrence. The rail line that eventually linked the port of Saint John with the Northumberland Strait bore the grandiose title of European and North American. Steamship connections fostered a nascent tourism industry as Americans arrived to fish, hunt and soak up the romantic atmosphere of Longfellow's "Land of Evangeline." Prince Edward Islanders supplied American boats which had long frequented the fishing grounds and bays of the region. Maritimers consumed Yankee provisions and manufactured goods. And the relationship was reciprocal, with Maritimers sharing catches on Gloucester fishing schooners, felling timber in the Maine woods and crowding dozens of Yankee harbours with their own shipping and products such as fish, coal and gypsum.[13]

Despite these close connections, colonial patriotism was based on homage to the British connection and a healthy scepticism towards the successes of the American republic. Britain, after all, had gone to war with the upstart Americans in 1812, and both sides had indulged in sabre rattling in the late 1830s in a dispute over the valuable timberlands of the Maine–New Brunswick border. Colonials, caught up in a shift from mercantilism to free trade within the Empire, had looked upon American expansionism in the 1840s with both envy and fear. The Americans annexed Texas, defeated Mexico and added California and Oregon to their national territory, the last at Britain's expense. The future status of the added territories threatened to upset the balance between free and slave states. In the early 1850s, relations soured over the question of American access to the fisheries of the Maritime region, a situation ameliorated by the 1854 Reciprocity Treaty, which also gave natural products from the colonies duty-free entry into the U.S. America appeared to relish Britain's rough handling by the Russians during the Crimean War, and in 1857 the U.S. secretary of state and Senate had protested British searches of suspected slave-carrying vessels as a violation of sovereignty. Whether it was the genteel but cruel plantation owner or the wily Yankee out of the pages of Thomas Chandler Haliburton's Sam Slick stories, Maritimers had mixed feelings about Americans. They were to be ridiculed or admired, but never totally trusted.[14]

The perceived instability, excess and corruption of American politics contributed to this feeling of ambivalence. "Brother Jonathan" was blessed with an abundance of land, resources, wealth and ingenuity; his public facilities, voluntary associations and charitable institutions were second to none. European immigrants, seeking economic, religious and political freedom continued to flock to America. Yet the political system, even the entire society, was deeply flawed, or so argued Philip Carteret Hill, lawyer, future mayor of Halifax and future premier of Nova Scotia, in a public lecture in 1859. Describing a recent tour of the States, Hill praised its material progress but excoriated its moral and social decay. Slavery was legal in the Southern states and national legislation authorized the apprehension of slaves who managed to flee to free soil. Hill recalled that upon first encountering slaves on a riverboat, "I sighed for the air of that glorious Empire which no slave can breathe." American politics were "rampant with bribery, jobbery, incapacity and brutality unequalled in the world."[15] The agrarian slave states were in conflict with the more urban, industrial North over the future status of the territories west of the Mississippi. This festering dispute, which ultimately tore the republic apart, proved to Maritimers that the American republicanism was inherently self-destructive. Hill reminded his listeners that they "may well rejoice that we are under the rule of Britannica and have a nobler flag to repose under than the Stars and Stripes."[16]

The first sign of potential conflict between the colonies and Civil War America came late in 1861 when the U.S. Navy insulted the British flag by intercepting the steamer *Trent* on the high seas and removing two Confederate diplomats. John Bull rushed troops, arms and supplies to North America and instructed the Royal Navy to prepare for war, until diplomacy settled the matter. Potential conflict again arose two years later when an American steamer was commandeered in the name of the Confederacy by armed passengers. On a cold winter night off the coast of Cape Cod, one crewman, an American citizen, was killed, two others were wounded and the vessel's course was altered to the Bay of Fundy. The voyage of the *Chesapeake* tied together not only the communities the pirates visited – Grand Manan, Saint John, Yarmouth, Lunenburg, Petite Riviere, Sambro and Halifax – but also much of the region. By this time, in the aftermath of Gettysburg and Vicksburg, the balance had tipped in favour of the North, yet Confederate apologists abounded in Britain and her colonies.

The diplomatic crisis of late 1861 had caused Maritimers to contemplate the very real possibility of war with the North. It also highlighted Halifax's strategic importance and the vulnerability of the New Brunswick frontier. The *Chesapeake* incident, which brought American warships under British guns at Halifax, made the region a focal point in relations between the United States and Britain at a time when the former was flexing newly developed military muscles. The highjacking of the steamer by British subjects and its cruise up the Bay of Fundy and along Nova Scotia's south shore did not create the same degree of international tension as the *Trent* dispute had, but it did incur the wrath of anti-British politicians and journalists in the North. It also revealed the full range of colonial opinion on the war. Depending on their predisposition towards Abraham Lincoln and Jefferson Davis, Maritimers viewed the *Chesapeake* captors as either daring raiders conducting legitimate warfare or cowardly murderers and pirates deserving the noose. Largely because of romantic ideals surrounding Southern society, many Maritimers, wishing to see the Confederacy achieve its independence, suspended their normally sobre attachment to fair play and British justice. The blundering of the American gunboat commander who violated Nova Scotia neutrality at Sambro caused British blood to boil and engendered support for the quixotic mission of John C. Brain and his men. And so did the howls of an antagonistic Northern press.

The cruise of the Confederate raider *Tallahassee*, which reached Halifax in 1864 after a destructive foray along the northeastern coast, also focused attention on Britain's Maritime colonies. The refuelling of the raider at a time when the port sheltered steamers involved in the Confederate supply effort confirmed all the worst anti-British suspicions of the North. When the Fathers of Confederation visited Halifax, the harbour hosted several British and Southern blockade

runners. The 1863 piracy, the 1864 raid, fisheries patrols and sur-
veillance of blockade runners brought unprecedented numbers of
Union warships into the waters of a region whose population regarded
British naval supremacy as a matter of course.

In the early 1860s the people of the Maritimes sensed that they
were at a crossroads in the history of North America. The Reciprocity
Treaty of 1854, which was thought to have stimulated prosperity,
was already under attack in American business and political circles.
Once the rebellion had begun, Britain had decided that its colonies
would follow a policy of neutrality. For sympathizers of both the
Union or Confederacy, the controversy generated by the *Chesapeake*
and *Tallahassee*, the enlistment of colonials in both armies, and Halifax's
links to Confederate supply raised fundamental questions: Why did
the supposedly enlightened British North American colonies seem
to support the "slaveocracy" of the South? Could the colonies be
defended in the age of ironclads and rifled artillery? Was neutrality
really possible when one's neighbours were in the throes of a life
and death struggle? Were Richard Wall, William Bruce Almon II
and the thousands of Bluenoses who took up arms in the conflict
nothing better than mercenaries? For the historian a particularly
intriguing question is how the debate on slavery and race related
to the place of the disadvantaged black minority in Maritime society.

This is the first study to examine the impact of the Civil War
on the Maritimes. The war was not only a catalyst for change (trade,
shipping, defence, Confederation) but also a mirror on which colonial attitudes were projected on a wide range of topics, notably
republicanism, national self-determination, the morality of war, slavery
and race relations. The Civil War, which still supports a large
publishing industry south of the border, holds a special interest for
a growing number of Canadians, who are realizing that it was not
only part of the American experience but of their own history as
well.

1 The War Next Door

"God is putting a great nation through a course of discipline."
— Halifax *Citizen*, 23 January 1864

In late November of 1860 the Boston steamer brought disturbing news to Halifax: South Carolina had all but broken away from the Union, Southern militia units were drilling, Federal officers were resigning their commissions, rumours abounded of slave conspiracies and the New York stock exchange was swept by panic.

The British colonies had been aware of trouble brewing in the American republic for some time.[1] In 1859 the Maritime press had reported on John Brown's raid on the U.S. arsenal at Harper's Ferry, Virginia, and his subsequent execution. While colonial opinion could understand the fiery abolitionist's hatred of slavery, it could not condone Brown's violence or his plan to foment a slave insurrection. The year 1860 had brought news of the fragmentation of the Democratic party, the election of a Republican to the White House and the beginning of what many regarded as a second American Revolution. To the independent-minded states of the lower South, the election of the relatively unknown Abraham Lincoln as president was a slap in the face. Many Republicans strongly opposed the institution of slavery, protected for eight decades by political compromise, and vowed to block its extension into the West. For many white Southerners the issue was not slavery but the rights of individual states versus the hostile power of a Yankee-dominated national government.[2]

Before the outbreak of the Civil War, British North American opinion tended to side with the free-soil North rather than the slave states. Britain's colonies considered themselves progressive and enlightened. Most colonists would have supported the assertion of a Maine newspaper that slavery was "a plague spot" that "makes fiends out of men."[3] The abolition of slavery within the British Empire, an achievement still celebrated by blacks in Halifax and Saint John in the 1860s, was trumpeted as one of the age's great reforms. Maritime newspapers, editorials and letters denounced the mild policies of lame-duck President James Buchanan in 1860 as protective of slavery and an encouragement of Southern treason. Most colonists who expressed an opinion adopted a centrist, anti-slavery view of the American political system and stressed the cultural and institutional linkages between Britain and New England.[4] A New Brunswicker writing home from New York at the outbreak of the rebellion explained that Canada and the Lower Provinces shared with the Northern states a love of "order, liberty and humanity."[5]

Maritimers had followed the deteriorating political situation for some time. In November 1860 the local press carried stories of se-cessionist meetings, drilling by Southern "minutemen" and plans for Southern tariffs on Northern goods. Militant South Carolina withdrew from the Union before Christmas, an act that New Bruns-wick Provincial Secretary Samuel L. Tilley described to a Sons of Temperance colleague in the South as "precipitate, not to say rash and foolish."[6] By early 1861 the *Novascotian* was predicting a "bloody revolution." In January a Bluenose in Mobile wrote describing Southern war fever: state forces had occupied naval and port facilities, patriotic ladies were making bandages and sandbags, and the Lone Star flag floated over the customs house where vessels leaving port were cleared by "the independent state of Alabama." In February the Southern Convention, with delegates from seven seceded states, met in Montgomery, Alabama, and formed a Confederacy with its own constitution. The *Acadian Recorder* of Halifax commented: "This looks like business."[7]

Another Nova Scotian touring the South at this time was sus-pected in New Bern, North Carolina, of being an abolitionist and was arrested, threatened by a hostile crowd and fined $130. He was struck by the fact that even temperance supporters, Sunday school teachers, church deacons and ministers were "ultra slavery." He heard secessionist speeches in Richmond and then left by train for Norfolk, Virginia. Conscious of being suspected as "a Northern man," he primed his revolver. At Baltimore he witnessed street fighting, the result of anti-Northern hostility towards volunteer troops from Massachusetts and Pennsylvania. Washington, D.C., was an armed camp, but New York was in a festive mood, the principal thoroughfares crowded with flags, banners and volunteers.[8]

Captain Thomas Vaughan, Jr. of Saint John was less fortunate. According to a letter to his firm, a mob in Savannah, Georgia, a timber port where colonial vessels picked up naval stores, had accused the New Brunswick skipper of "entertaining a negro at his table." The captain had allowed a black stevedore to eat breakfast at his own table, a violation of the local racial code. When on shore, Vaughan was seized and taken to the outskirts of town where he was partially stripped and had his hair cropped. The vigilantes then applied tar and cotton to his head and released him. Despite this humiliation, the captain was not seriously injured and his vessel returned to sea.[9]

Perhaps the saddest case of a Maritimer caught in the South at the war's outbreak was that of Laughlan McLean of Pugwash, Nova Scotia. A stevedore in Richmond in April 1861, McLean was accosted by a recruiting sergeant who inquired if he, like most able-bodied men, would be joining the Confederate army. The Scot brusquely told the sergeant to mind his own business and the two scuffled. The Virginian pulled out a pistol and shot McLean in the knee. Making it back to his boarding house, he hid, fearing that he would be taken as a Northern spy. The wound deteriorated and McLean went to hospital, where he was treated by student doctors. The injured leg had to be amputated above the knee and continued infection necessitated a further amputation. The crippled Nova Scotian languished in hospital for months until his case came to the attention of the British consul, who arranged his repatriation. Under a flag of truce, McLean was taken into Union lines and sent north to Boston. As Reverend John Munro of Wallace informed the provincial secretary, McLean's parents and relatives were too poor to look after him. A Cunard steamer carried McLean to Halifax, where the mayor, assisted by the North British Society, presented him with a pair of crutches and a small sum of money. The railway company arranged a free passage to Truro, and McLean was reunited with his brothers and sisters in Cumberland County.[10]

A SOUTHERN TOUR

Daniel McNeil Parker, a Halifax physician, left behind a vivid account of a nation on the brink of war. In March 1861, Dr. Parker, together with father and son William J. and John Stairs, sailed for Boston on the Cunard line. In New York they toured Barnum's museum and, like most middle-class Victorians, they also visited charitable institutions and churches. William J. Stairs, of the prominent Halifax hardware and ship chandlery firm, was a former alderman who would sympathize with the Confederacy.[11] Twelve-year-old John, who as an adult would serve as a member of Parliament and give a boost to the career of Max Aitken (Lord Beaverbrook), wrote his mother that Yankee troops encountered at Washington were "dressed in blue something like the French soldiers uniform. They do not look like English soldiers one bit but more like a lot of big boys with whiskers."[12]

Parker sought relatives in the vicinity of Fayetteville, North Carolina, and the Stairs had kin in Georgia. In a letter to his wife, Dr. Parker concluded that the South "is irretrievably gone" and that the two sections "are at this moment, and will be forever, distinct nations." His slave-owning relations were desirous of avoiding war but refused to be coerced by the North. The U.S. government, without a large navy or standing army, was "as helpless as a child." As for the men of the South, they were "an honourable, honest people; but the hot weather, especially in these times, makes their blood hot, and they become excitable and hot-headed." The plantation owners encountered by Parker discussed their slaves as Bluenose farmers would horses and cattle. The bondmen were described as childlike, "respectable, quiet and orderly" in the presence of whites, and "happy in the evenings with their music and their games."[13]

During the Nova Scotians' tour, rebel batteries in Charleston harbour opened up on the Federal garrison in Fort Sumter. News of the action stirred Virginia and three other states to join the new Confederacy. Lincoln, who had refused to fire the first shots, could now argue that the Southerners had started the war. Prior to the attack, South Carolina gunners had also attacked the vessel *Star of the West*, which had been attempting to relieve Sumter's garrison. Parker and his travelling companions, arriving in Charleston by train on the eve of the bombardment, saw signs of military preparations. Early in the morning of 12 April they heard the boom of artillery. Young John wrote that he had "seen shot and shell in earnest." He also described the flag of the new Confederacy.[14]

The continued shelling of the fort by surrounding batteries shook their hotel to its foundations. Dr. Parker recorded that "all, even the ladies, are anxious that the existing state of things should be terminated, even at the sacrifice of human blood." At a Presbyterian church, Parker heard a minister preach on the South's just and righteous cause. Writing from Georgia a few days later, Stairs described the scene in Charleston harbour: "Crowds of people were on the wharves, or any place where a view could be obtained, looking at the fort with spy glasses, and cheering loudly when a shell went in." The mood in the city following the fort's capitulation was jubilant. Parker even caught a glimpse of the surrendered commander, Major Robert Anderson, on the street. At Savannah the Bluenose tourists visited a Yarmouth vessel and noted several New Brunswick craft loading pine. Dr. Parker prayed that the world would be "saved the pain of witnessing a long and bloody war of brethren of the Anglo-Saxon race." On the return north the travellers passed the ruins of the naval yard at Norfolk, razed by retreating Union forces, and were questioned by Northern soldiers. Their travelling companions below and above the Mason-Dixon line were citizen soldiers armed with bowie knives, pistols and muskets.[15]

News of the bombardment of Fort Sumter reached Halifax by telegraph on 13 April 1861. The colony's legislature, normally caught up in the rough and tumble of politics based on personality, patronage and ethno-religious disputes, recognized the historic significance of the moment. Provincial Secretary Joseph Howe proclaimed that the shots fired at Charleston were "injurious to the interests of the civilized world." Another speaker suggested the propriety of an official expression of regret that would avoid taking sides. The legislature went on record as lamenting that "those who speak their language and share their civilization should be shedding each other's blood."[16] The P.E.I. Legislative Council tabled a similar resolution but fussy British diplomats refrained from forwarding it to the U.S. secretary of state on the grounds that it violated neutrality and protocol. New Brunswick was more preoccupied by an election campaign. In the weeks following the lowering of the Stars and Stripes at Fort Sumter, wild rumours abounded. A Halifax merchant received a letter stating that Washington, the capitol, was surrounded by pro-secessionists. Another report predicted an attack on the Brooklyn navy yard. Yet fans of the North confidently argued that the rebellion would be crushed by the Fourth of July.[17]

EARLY REACTIONS

In the early summer of 1861 the American conflict began to hit closer to home. Geography and commerce were drawing the colonies, indirectly perhaps, into the war. Word arrived that two Nova Scotia schooners bound for Norfolk had been ordered off by blockading vessels. The Saint John brig *Hiawatha* was captured off Richmond after being warned by the U.S. Navy and was taken to New York for prize adjudication. Mysterious cannonading was heard off the Maritime coasts. Rumours, false as it turned out, spread of the presence of Confederate privateers cruising in colonial waters for

Yankee fishing schooners. From the waters of Labrador to the Bay of Fundy there was not a single Union warship. This panicked the crews of Northern vessels loading deals at Pugwash, on the Northumberland Strait. Especially worried were black crewmen, who feared being sold into slavery if captured.[18]

Not all Maritime newspapers were overwhelmed by the events of the spring and early summer of 1861. The *Acadian Recorder*, commenting on the vulgar displays of patriotism, bombastic speeches and overly optimistic military expectations of the North, described the war in May as little more than a bluff.[19] The weeks between Sumter and the first major battle in Virginia, like the Phoney War period of World War II, lulled foreign observers into a state of cynical incredulity. By mid-May, Union fatalities amounted to only a half dozen and most of these were incurred when Baltimore mobs clashed with Union troops passing through Maryland. Prior to First Bull Run, the war was fought largely in the minds of politicians, journalists and amateur soldiers. Yet "braggart campaigners" in the North were predicting that the hostilities would soon be ended. Generals were becoming "as thick as blackberries" as part of the newest quest for political honours. With the exception of some skirmishing, action in the eastern theatre was confined to the parade square, the banquet room and the political rostrum.[20]

BULL RUN

Then came news of the encounter at Bull Run, or Manassas Junction. The Union army under McDowell, pushed on by political pressure, attacked Beauregard's Confederate forces in Virginia on 21 July, but the last-minute arrival of reinforcements saved the day for the Southerners. The results were disastrous for the North; and the propaganda defeat was even more serious, turning neutral and even pro-Northern opinion towards the Confederacy. The actual battle was a draw; the Northern troops had been on the offensive during most of the day. The real Union disgrace came when panic turned a retreat into a disorderly rout. The Pictou *Colonial Standard* dubbed the action "the run away of the bullies." A Halifax journal compared the conflict to the battle of Bunker Hill during the American War of Independence.[21] Union politicians and generals became figures of ridicule, and the bravery and military skill of Yankee citizen-soldiers was now suspect. The Charlottetown *Examiner* doubted whether the North, despite its superior resources, could mount an effective war effort. The proud American eagle, Edward Whelan wrote, "cannot reasonably be expected to soar his wonted flight, having lost one of his wings and the other being badly wounded at Bull Run." Soon after the battle, the *Examiner* published the lyrics of the secessionist anthem "Maryland, My Maryland," which exhorted Southerners to "avenge the patriots' gore" by battling the "Northern scum."[22]

Maritime journalists praised Southern panache while mocking the bumbling cowardice of the Union regiments. An exception was made for Irish and Scots immigrants serving in units such as the 69th and 79th New York regiments, who, according to reporters of Irish and Scots descent, served with gallantry: "The Irish and Scotch regiments fought more in accordance with the monarchial principles taught at Agincourt or Fontenay than with the democratic principles of ninety-day regiments." Yankee soldiers obviously were no match for the British troops "who knelt in square at Waterloo or charged the Russian batteries at Balaclava." The retreat to Washington, in the minds of critics, was symbolic of a decadent Yankee society.[23]

Maritimers were treated to Southern, Northern and British accounts of the Bull Run campaign, as well as those of eyewitnesses from their own region. A young New Brunswicker who had lost his job in a Boston factory and joined a New Hampshire infantry regiment informed a Saint John paper that the Union troops had fought like tigers but had run out of ammunition. He estimated the Southern army to have numbered 90,000 (the armies were evenly matched at 35,000). Several Maritimers participated in the engagement, at least three on the Confederate side. Twenty-two-year-old Jonas Howe of Saint John was a member of Company A, Hampton Legion, a unit of infantry, cavalry and artillery raised and led by a wealthy South Carolina planter. The Hampton Legion suffered frightful casualties at Manassas.[24] Among the Union dead was George W. Gray of New Brunswick. Thirty-year-old Thomas Roome was killed by a rebel bullet, but fellow Haligonian Henry Anderson survived. William Hayes of Windsor, Nova Scotia, James E. Cameron, formerly of Fredericton, and Colin Shaw, an ex-Islander, were present in the ranks of the 11th Massachusetts Volunteers. A Bluenose member of the 5th Massachusetts survived and returned home in August with battle trophies–a revolver and Bible belonging to a dead Georgian.[25] At nearby Blackburn's Ford, scene of skirmishing, the ranks of the 2nd Michigan Infantry included a New Brunswick woman, Sarah Emma Edmonds, disguised as a male soldier, Frank Thompson. Her regiment would help cover the humiliating Union retreat to Washington.[26]

Charles M. McFadden, of Pictou Co., Nova Scotia, formerly a member of a Halifax volunteer rifle company, fought as a sergeant

"Awkward Squad"

in the 69th New York "Highland" Regiment, many of whose members were of Scots birth or descent. The Highlanders wore kilts as their dress uniform but trousers in the field. Before the brigade went into action, McFadden and his companions had made out their wills (the practice did not originate in World War I). After charging enemy lines, capturing a number of guns and wading Bull Run creek under fire, the attackers were raked by short-range artillery: "The roaring of the cannon and the shrieks of the wounded men and horses, many of the latter running about the fields riderless," he wrote, "made up a scene I will never forget. The ground became slippery with blood and covered with the dead and wounded." McFadden also described the terrifying charge of the Rebel Black Cavalry led by J.E.B. Stuart. McFadden was nearly sabred by a Rebel horseman, who was then shot by another infantryman. McFadden's regiment laid down to let the cavalry pass over them. The survivors slept in the open before beginning the long retreat through Centreville. At one point as McFadden stopped to aid a wounded bugler, the injured soldier was pulverized by an artillery projectile. This first inglorious campaign made the Nova Scotian "heartily sick of the way in which Uncle Sam treats his soldiers. Nothing but crackers and water will weaken any man in a warm country, with plenty of marching to do."[27]

BROTHER JONATHAN VS. JOHN BULL

Bull Run is not the only factor that can explain the shift in colonial opinion away from the Union cause. Northern berating of Britain and her colonies, the result of Britain's proclamation of neutrality, irked lukewarm supporters as poor sportsmanship. Washington was disturbed by Britain's recognition of the Rebels' belligerent rights on the high seas. To the British, Lincoln's initial refusal to abolish slavery, in the hopes that he could win back slave-holding states of the upper South, was hypocritical.[28]

In the Maritimes, public displays in favour of the Union became rare and Southern partisans more daring. The *New Brunswick Reporter* noted the irony of the American government, which professed to be battling for freedom and democracy while retaining its "slave code" even after "the autocrat of Russia" had abolished his.[29] In Charlottetown, pranksters cut down the U.S. consul's flagstaff. On 4 July 1862, Saint John firemen celebrated Southern victories by hoisting a Confederate flag over one of their engine houses. A few months later, the office of John S. Hay, the proprietor of the *St. Croix Herald* of St. Stephen, was vandalized. The editor claimed that pro-Southern New Brunswickers were responsible. An outspoken supporter of Lincoln's government, he relocated his journal to Calais, Maine, an abolitionist stronghold. Hay later enlisted in the 9th Maine Regiment. The Halifax News Room, where merchants gathered to peruse journals and discuss current events, became a "secesh" hotbed that ostracized pro-Union individuals.[30]

Maritimers, members of the world's greatest empire, could not help pondering the rebellion's possible impact on international relations. Halifax, an Imperial garrison town and naval base, was especially interested in such geopolitical questions.[31] In a lecture on the constitutionality of secession, Haligonian George F. Kenny argued that the American crisis was merely the latest example of an historic pattern, that of powerful, proud empires or nations rising to prominence, then being destroyed by conquest or inner turmoil and corruption. Some predicted the permanent disruption of the American republic and its reconstitution into two or even three new entities. Perhaps the West, the more raw and energetic region, would rise to dominate the continent, free of the sectional issue of slavery.[32] Others argued that a disunited States would benefit Britain and her colonies strategically and economically. Fewer Imperial troops and ships would be required to safeguard the colonies, and Yankee industrial and shipping competition would abate. An independent South would value economic links with British possessions. Others warned that an aggressive Southern slave empire would be a destabilizing force and threaten not only Mexico and Cuba but also British interests. Perhaps neither side would prevail and both the North and South would nurture revenge and maintain large military establishments, turning the Western Hemisphere into one large armed camp.[33]

Maritimers influenced by Calvinism interpreted the war as divine judgement on a republican political system that had tolerated slavery. For this sin, the people of both the South and North would now suffer as had the ancient Hebrews. The "First New Nation" would either be purified by fire and the sword or fade into obscurity. Reverend William Wilson, a Wesleyan preacher who had authored a small book arguing that the Crimean War fulfilled Biblical prophecy, informed a Woodstock audience that the American crisis was the "retributive judgement of God."[34]

The disruption of the American republic also had an impact on popular culture. Maritime newspapers printed song lyrics and original war poetry, most of it forgettable, by local enthusiasts. Sheet music for songs such as "The Bonnie Blue Flag" and "The Battle Cry of Freedom" was purchased for parlour sing-alongs. A Saint John printer attempted to profit from this vogue by publishing sheet music for "When This Cruel War Is Over." The *New Brunswick Minstrel*, a book of musical arrangements, included "The Southern Marseillaise" and "Just Before the Battle, Mother." In Charlottetown a hurdy-gurdy man attracted large crowds by playing "Dixie," a popular air in both the North and South. Minstrel shows, which amused audiences of all classes with caricatures of Southern blacks and raucous banjo music, were a hit. One troupe touring P.E.I. was praised for portraying "the real plantation negro." Instant books on the war circulated, such as the popular series by Edward A. Pollard, a Virginia journalist. Charles Hallock's brief biography of Stonewall Jackson was reprinted in Halifax in 1863 after the popular Confederate's death.[35] Merchants exploited the war to sell their wares, such as a powder that conquered bedbugs. In 1863, LaRue's War Show toured the region, offering models, dioramas and reenactments of Civil War battles. In Halifax an artist displayed watercolours of graceful blockade runners. Soldiers sent home their photographs and returned, on leave or discharged, with uniforms, weapons and assorted trophies of war. The revival of the militia in New Brunswick, Prince Edward Island and Nova Scotia, although partly the result of Imperial defence concerns, owed something to the militarization of American society in the early 1860s. Then there were the lecturers, either local amateurs or Confederate émigrés and the rare Yankee, who gave talks on the war for profit or charity. Mrs. H. Nina Smith, formerly principal of the Western Missouri Female College, lectured at the Saint John Mechanics Institute on "Southern Women" and "The Revolution."[36]

COLONIAL DEFENCE

War seemed the order of the day in the early 1860s, fitting punishment for the vain pronouncement of an earlier generation who had declared that commerce and industry would abolish large-scale conflict. The Maritime colonies, like Canada, had no "defence policy" and little defensive capability. In fact, with the exception of Halifax and possibly Quebec City, the North American colonies were more of a strategic liability. Military matters, like foreign affairs, were in the hands of the Imperial authorities, acting through local commanders and the governors. The latter, traditionally ex-military types, were in charge of the militia, such as it existed. But the first line of defence for the colonies was Imperial–the Royal Navy on the seas and British redcoats on land. By 1858 the garrison of the Nova Scotia command, which included New Brunswick, was costing British taxpayers one quarter of a million pounds yearly. Colonial politicians, such as New Brunswick's ruling "Smashers," were not interested in paying for local defence.[37]

The commander of Her Majesty's forces in North America was a Nova Scotian by birth, Sir Fenwick Williams, a Colonel Blimp type who had won minor fame by defending (and eventually surrendering) Kars, in Turkish Armenia, during the Crimean War. Born in 1800 at Annapolis Royal, Fenwick Williams (who may have been the illegitimate son of the Duke of Kent) attended Woolwich military academy and then served in various garrisons throughout the Empire. He was made a baronet in recognition of his services to the Turkish government and appointed commandant of Woolwich. He next left for British North America to serve as General Commanding the Forces. General Williams arrived in Halifax, which he regarded as the key to the defence of the colonies, in June of 1859. Two years later, with America split by civil war, Britain declared itself neutral and sent token reinforcements to North America. Williams personally saw war with the North as inevitable. British North America's frontiers, natural barriers such as rivers and lakes, and garrison towns suddenly took on a heightened significance. Like most British officers and members of the upper classes, he sided with the Confederates, who appeared not only more refined but also more professional in the art of war. As late as the winter of 1864–65, Williams, whose forces could never have seriously contested an American invasion of Canada West and much of Canada East, was confident, in spite of all rational evidence to the contrary, of a Southern victory.[38]

THE ROYAL NAVY

That the Royal Navy, Britain's "wooden walls," was key to colonial defence gave Maritimers, or at least Nova Scotians, great comfort. Halifax, with its superb sheltered harbour and basin and its temperate climate, was the summer and fall base of the North America and West Indies Squadron. Founded as an Imperial outpost against the French in 1749, the city was described by Nova Scotia's lieutenant-governor in 1864 as "a creation of English blood and treasure . . . the only strategic possession in British North America."[39] During the Civil War period, the "Warden of the North" ranked with Gibraltar and Bermuda in strategic importance. This base was relatively easy to defend from sea and land attacks, enjoyed rail and telegraph links and, importantly, had access to coal, which had become central to naval operations. The Admiralty preferred high-quality Welsh coal, but it was reassuring that its North American squadron could rely on indigenous supplies in emergencies. The squadron's duties were not so much to protect the Maritime colonies as to remind the Americans that John Bull was in the neighbourhood. The navy policed the Newfoundland fisheries, provided internal security in the West Indies, watched for slavers who had eluded patrols off the coast of Africa, kept an eye on the French and American navies and protected British interests in the Caribbean, Mexico and Central America.[40]

In 1861 the Royal Navy's commander in the western Atlantic, Vice-Admiral Sir Alexander Milne, K.C.B., was saddled with grave responsibilities. Britain and its colonies had an immense merchant marine and important trade ties with the Southern states. Yet Lincoln had proclaimed a blockade of Rebel ports and was gradually providing armed vessels for its enforcement. By late 1861 the Union navy had more than 260 ships. Milne's forbearance in the face of American bluster and aggressive patrols enforcing the blockade was mistaken by hard-core Southern supporters in the colonies as timidity or favouritism towards the North. They longed for a fighting admiral who would shoot first and ask questions later. Yet the task of safeguarding British interests and maintaining workable diplomatic relations with the Americans was one of great delicacy. Milne knew Halifax well, having served on the post as a midshipman, a mate and a lieutenant commander. Now, for at least part of the year, Sir Alexander and Lady Milne occupied the Admiral's House near the Halifax waterfront. From here and from his flagship, the seventy-eight-gun *Nile*, the "cool-headed Scot" attempted to protect British neutrality.[41]

Although the growing U.S. Navy outnumbered Milne's squadron, many of the American vessels were converted merchantmen propelled by sail and manned by inexperienced officers and crews. Britain's North America and West Indies Squadron was steam-powered. Milne also benefited from the senior service's professionalism and reputation for invincibility. In the summer of 1861, armchair admirals began to speculate that the Royal Navy, assisted by France, would break the Northern blockade in order to secure badly needed cotton for Europe's mills. A Halifax journal commented: "There is something ominous in the number and the class of English men of war that are arriving in these waters." Britain, together with France and Spain, was about to intervene not in the South but in Mexico, to collect the debts of foreign creditors. The allies landed troops at Veracruz before year's end. Royal Marines who had taken ill in Mexico were later brought to Halifax to recover.[42]

The annual arrival and departure of the squadron at Halifax was an impressive sight, and to older Haligonians brought back memories of the War of 1812, when the HMS *Shannon* had bested the USS *Chesapeake* off Boston and American prisoners of war had been kept on Melville Island on the Northwest Arm. On a beautiful day in May 1862 a large number of citizens left work to gather on the wharves in expectation of the fleet's arrival. They were treated to the glorious sight of ten British warships, with flags flying and bands playing, entering the harbour. The Citadel boomed a welcoming salute. The vessels, including fast frigates and black-hulled sloops, were all under steam, but for effect they glided in with royal and top gallant yards across. British ensigns floated from stores, shops and warehouses, and merchant vessels displayed bunting in honour of the Admiral. The pomp and ceremony continued on shore, with the landing of a four-thousand-man naval brigade of marines and artillery which proceeded from the dockyard to the Commons for field exercises. The brigade then paraded to Point Pleasant where many of the bluejackets adorned themselves with spruce boughs for the march back to their ships.[43]

The fleet added to the general rhythms of the harbour and waterfront. Teams of horses carried supplies and foodstuffs to the dockyard on Water Street, which contained workshops, a careening dock, a slipway, sail loft and mast pond, and other facilities for repairing naval vessels, plus a hospital. Anchored in the harbour or tied up at the dockyard were massive ships of the line with innumerable gunports, speedy frigates and corvettes, paddle-wheel sloops and gunboats, and dispatch boats. Darting among the warships were bumboats which sold fruit, candy and other luxuries, and pleasure craft and rowboats conveying sightseers and visitors. In the harbour and beyond, jack tars busied themselves with scrapping, painting, polishing and scrubbing and with boat, gun, spar and sail drills. The Royal Navy was converting to steam, but traditional exercises such as bending and unbending and shortening sails and shifting topsails were still important. Individual vessels would cruise to outports or quiet harbours for gunnery practice. In the fall of 1861 the navy disturbed peaceful slumberers by "firing broadsides in the middle of the night" in Bedford Basin.[44]

THE IMPERIAL GARRISON

After years of attempting to scale down its North American military establishment, Britain, in the months following the capitulation of Fort Sumter, sent three infantry battalions and an artillery battery to the colony of Canada, some on the giant steamer *Great Eastern*. However, the seaboard colonies received no reinforcements. Halifax was the main garrison town of the Maritime region and a small detachment was found at Fredericton. Tiny Fredericton was blessed with redcoats because of its status as a colonial capital and its strategic location along the Saint John River valley, the land route between the Maritimes and Canada East. The port of Saint John was described as having "no local defences." Fenwick Williams found Prince Edward Island to be completely undefended in 1859.[45] At Charlottetown there had been little danger of enemy attack but considerable agitation over the land question. British troops on the island had served as a security force on behalf of the local authorities troubled by tenant farmers who defied landlords, land agents and bailiffs. But by the mid-1850s, Charlottetown, as well as Windsor and Annapolis, Nova Scotia, were no longer military posts. Sydney had also lost its small garrison, another slight to a town that had once been the capital of the separate colony of Cape Breton, yet the local coal industry, and shipping communications with Newfoundland, gave the community a certain strategic value.

Halifax was garrisoned by infantry and detachments of engineers and artillery. The main inner harbour defences were the Citadel and the batteries of George's Island, both hundreds of yards from the city's wharves. In 1861 the main ship channel was protected by fortifications on Point Pleasant in the city's south end, which included a Martello tower and an elevated battery, and by two outer works, a tower on McNab's Island, and York Redoubt, on a height of land south of the Northwest Arm. Ideally, these positions could project converging fire on attacking warships and the garrison could repel landings. The eastern passage into the harbour was protected by shoals between McNab's Island and the mainland and by Fort Clarence, a battery in the adjacent town of Dartmouth. British taxpayers had poured significant sums of money into Halifax's Citadel over the past thirty years. It was an extensive, sunken fortification containing barracks, bombproofs and stores, protected by sloping earth ramparts and a deep ditch. The fort bristled with cannon yet by 1861 it was all but obsolete; none of its ninety-eight guns were rifled. Improvements in artillery and naval construction, specifically the development of rifled, breech-loading guns and experimental ironclad warships, were causing the British to rethink coastal defence and naval tactics. Long-range artillery meant that the Citadel, located in the heart of the city, was no longer the harbour's defensive bulwark. Outlying gun batteries and more powerful artillery would be the way of the future.[46]

The military presence was politically reassuring and economically beneficial, but not without controversy. As one Haligonian wrote, "the presence of the Army and Navy cannot add greatly to the improvement of our morals."[47] The visit of the squadron was designed to give officers, sailors and marines what the Admiral termed "some reasonable recreation on shore." The two thousand libertymen who hit Halifax in May of 1862 were particularly high spirited. And they had money to burn, most of it in the city's many groggeries. The press reported that British tars were "running wild," promenading up and down Granville Street wearing steel-hooped skirts, petite bonnets and other finery of the fairer sex. A carnival atmosphere pervaded the town, and horse and coach rentals were brisk. Rum drinking was the favourite pastime and one that Haligonians were ready to accommodate, but at times the groggeries threatened the health and discipline of armed forces personnel. Vice-Admiral Milne complained to the governor in 1862 that "a large number of petty officers, sailors and marines" had fallen into disgrace because of the sale of adulterated, "unwholesome spirits."[48]

Soldiers and sailors also patronized houses of ill repute, which did a flourishing trade during visits of the fleet. In 1863 an altercation at the notorious Blue Bell near the foot of Citadel Hill led to rioting by soldiers, who the next night attacked officers, policemen and civilians with sticks, stones, slingshots and belts. A large number of windows were smashed before military pickets and special constables restored order. Following the riot, garrison personnel were temporarily banned from the red light district on Albermarle and Barrack streets. Another riot took place in 1864, this time between redcoats and bluejackets. The navy attempted to keep its libertymen in order with shore patrols by marines. Servicemen also seemed to be involved in innumerable brawls, fights and individual disputes, most involving liquor and/or women. The area frequented by off-duty servicemen was one where, according to a Protestant missionary, "the lower classes are steeped in irreligion and abandoned habits." A Royal Artillery officer wrote that "Halifax has its St. Giles, larger than it might be for causes that require no explanation."[49] Relations between the military and civilians, even in sedate Fredericton, were not always rosy. In 1863, when officers of the 15th Regiment took liberties with respectable women there, they were pelted with stones by outraged bystanders.[50]

Another problem was desertion. The Civil War, with its manpower needs and enlistment bounties, provided incentives to would-be military deserters in Nova Scotia and New Brunswick. Yet the North American station had long been plagued by desertion among both branches of the service. Low pay, long terms of service, strict discipline and monotony, combined with easy access to an entire continent where wages were high and opportunities greater than in the Old Country, tempted many soldiers and sailors. Civilians sympathized with fugitives and aided in their flight, providing clothing, food, shelter and transportation, often for a price. The Imperial authorities had cited desertion and the lack of a competent civil police as the reasons behind the withdrawal of the P.E.I. garrison in 1854. In 1861 an entire infantry detachment was transferred from Fredericton to Nova Scotia to remove it from the nearby border with Maine after some of its members had been tempted to desert. The outbreak of fighting in the South also brought a rise in naval desertions. Men jumped ship at Sydney, Saint John and Halifax. The navy was convinced that Sydney had a well-organized ring of crimps, an allegation local magistrates hotly contested. In one period seventy sailors disappeared from HMS *St. George* alone, and most of them probably shipped out on Yankee schooners. In response, Milne posted the HMS *Pyramus*, an old receiving ship, off Maugher's Beach, near Halifax, to stop and search departing merchant vessels suspecting of harbouring deserters. Merchants, shipowners and the U.S. consul protested this action as interference with trade. A compromise, whereby the navy inspected vessels before they sailed, appeared to stem the tide of footloose seamen.[51]

Army desertions continued throughout the early 1860s and influenced postings. A British officer reported in 1860 that "men of the line" in Saint John tended to become intimate with the locals, who "corrupted" them and encouraged them to desert. In 1864 ten privates of the 10th Regiment stationed at Mount Fordham, New

Bunswick, absconded with their rifles. They were arrested, court-martialed and sentenced to be branded with the letter D before a period a penal servitude. In the North American command, the risk of desertion was a disincentive to maintaining scattered garrisons and stationing naval vessels at Halifax year-round.[52]

For the most part, given the security, status and profits to be derived from the military, Haligonians tolerated the vices associated with the garrison and navy. Any negatives were also offset by the contributions of navy and army officers to community and social life. Military types were enthusiastic sportsmen, and the class background of mid-Victorian officers guaranteed their patronage of cultural events. Thus the military in Halifax and, on a smaller scale, Fredericton, took part in church services, concerts, receptions, dinners, bonnet hops, bazaars, cricket matches, sleighing parties and amateur theatricals. In Halifax, "society," such as it existed, revolved around the admiral and his lady, the lieutenant-governor and the senior officers of the garrison. The result was that the city had a more visibly British, aristocratic tone than "Yankee-fied" Saint John, where status was based on commercial acumen. Halifax belles were aware of the latest Paris fashions and read French novels, and the local "bloods" rode fast horses and dog carts. The belles also studied the army and navy lists, and much was made in the press of British officers marrying the daughters of rich Bluenose merchants. According to a touring French nobleman, the ladies of Sydney remembered its garrison years "as a golden age, and it still makes some of them sigh."[53]

THE MILITIA

If faced with invasion, the governor of a colony would, in theory, call out the militia, an old but, by 1861, not very respected institution. Nova Scotia's first militia law, enacted in an age of warfare with the French and the Mi'kmaq, authorized the enlistment of all males between the ages of sixteen and sixty. New Brunswick's militia tradition began in the 1780s with the founding of the colony by Loyalists, including those who had served in provincial regiments during the Revolutionary War. Particularly after the War of 1812, which had not involved any land action in the Maritime colonies, the reassuring presence of the Royal Navy and British regulars undermined the need for militia. In New Brunswick, tensions along the international border, which climaxed in the 1838–39 Aroostook War, helped revive the institution. A series of disputes across the border and the mobilization of Maine volunteers had caused the governor to call out militia companies to protect Fredericton and Saint John and place a detachment of regulars at Woodstock. The Pine Tree state, in a fit of anglophobia, had seemed ready, in the words of New Brunswick's militia commander, "to go the whole hog." A posse of Maine volunteers had ventured into disputed territory and seized a number of colonists. In the end, the only real action in the war was a brawl in a Houlton tavern.[54] Yet the legacy of the land and timber disputes of the 1820s and 1830s, together with the occupation of eastern Maine during the War of 1812, ensured an anti-British tone in the state's politics.[55]

Over the years, militia officers continued to be appointed, largely for political and social reasons, but by the 1850s the annual musters were sparsely attended, the drill was slipshod and weapons were nonexistent. Most descriptions of the militia in this period were satirical, but some at least complimented the citizen soldiers for their physical capabilities, if not their military value. At an 1863 muster in Fredericton, officers contented themselves with merely forming companies and calling roll. The two thousand class B and C men of Saint John's Queen's and Sydney wards who mustered on tidal flats in 1864 had no uniforms, so officers used chalk to mark stripes and numbers on their clothing. The institution's social functions–for the men, playing pranks, carousing and drinking, and for the officers, attending banquets, making speeches and drinking–superseded its martial functions. In 1863 the four Prospect companies of the 9th Regiment of the Halifax Militia, after attending battalion drill, were rewarded with a meal, while the officers retired to a Halifax hotel for a formal banquet. The *Carleton Sentinel*, a supporter of temperance, equated the old-fashioned militia with dissipation and immorality. The class B and C men of Saint John in 1863, reflecting the paternalistic role of traditional militia officers, demanded to be treated at the nearest dramshop.[56]

Militia efficiency faced a variety of obstacles other than lack of military ardour. Many of its officers, appointed for reasons of patronage, were not suitable. Others were old and decrepit. This was particularly so in the rural areas, where the bulk of the population dwelled. The lieutenant-governor of Nova Scotia wrote of the institution in 1861: "There is no ground work to start with and the officers are generally speaking totally ignorant of their duties and most of them are unfit for the service in the consequence of their age."[57] Similar problems existed in New Brunswick, where some officers were in their seventies and eighties. Furthermore, there were no adjutants or staff, or uniforms or weapons, even for the officers. The vintage artillery of the British North American militia tended to be in storage, and it was of the small-calibre, smooth-bore variety. In theory, the New Brunswick militia of 1861 consisted of 41,000 men in forty-eight regiments, but they were armed with only two hundred rifles. The population's economic pursuits were another obstacle, especially in a seasonal agrarian and resource economy; summer and fall militia musters clashed with the labour needs of farming and fishing. Even with the war scares of the Civil War and the reform of Nova Scotia's militia beginning in 1862, by 1865 in the Annapolis Valley drill was "generally looked upon by the people as a nuisance." Enrolling and drilling the scattered rural population was a challenging task. Much depended on the popularity of their officers. Few could motivate their once-a-year soldiers to march fourteen miles on poor roads to attend drill, then march home, as did the forty-eight men of the Sambro Company, 9th Halifax Regiment, in 1863. The men of the village of Hillsburgh certainly resented having to travel even farther to attend battalion drill in Annapolis.[58]

Politics was another barrier to an active and efficient militia. The force was commanded by the lieutenant-governor, but colonial legislatures were not lavish in voting militia appropriations, at least not until the fighting started. In 1854 the legislatures of New Brunswick and Nova Scotia had promised Britain, then stripping its garrisons to fight Russia, that the colonies could defend themselves. Yet militia budgets remained minuscule. Politicians valued militia commissions as a reward for the party faithful, not as tools for building a citizen army. In 1863 Nova Scotia Provincial Secretary Joseph Howe, a master at the game of patronage, requested the lieutenant-governor to reserve a number of commissions for Acadians from Clare and other districts. The Acadians were "a part of the population who will make fine soldiers and whose loyalty is undoubted." In other words, the Acadians had votes and expected recognition from Halifax.[59] The Earl of Mulgrave reported in 1861 that the Nova Scotia legislature was not keen on militia expenditures, viewing defence as a responsibility of the motherland. The total militia appropriation, for a drill instructor and practice ammunition, was two thousand pounds. The adjutant general of militia reported in 1863 that, although the militia had "sunk into obscurity from neglect," the fighting potential or "temper" of the "original settlers" remained. In New Brunswick, Lieutenant-Governor Gordon encouraged the assembly to vote increased sums for the militia.[60]

THE VOLUNTEERS

If the militia circa 1861 existed mainly on paper, the Imperial authorities expected much from the volunteer movement. Volunteers formed their own rifle or artillery companies, elected their officers, chose their uniforms and equipment, and trained as a sort of semi-permanent militia. They were motivated not only by patriotism and an interest in military affairs, but by social considerations. Membership in a volunteer company brought community recognition and business contacts. Like participation in the Freemasons, the Orange Association or a temperance society, it also helped pass the long winter nights. Pictou merchant W.N. Rudolf belonged to a company that drilled three evenings a week in 1862. The drill sergeant, whose salary was paid by the provincial government, was a capable British NCO whose "previous training and habits," Rudolf regretted, did not "allow him to become a Son of Temperance."[61]

The volunteer movement had originated during the Crimean War when civilians had organized volunteer units to relieve British infantry and artillery regiments shipped off to fight the Russians. The embers of Imperial patriotism were fanned by the Indian Mutiny of 1857, which was widely reported in the Maritime press. Volunteering spread to British North America in 1859, encouraged by Imperial officials and governors. Patriotism and paranoia were enhanced by the "French war scare," when Britain and its colonies had been swept by panic as a result of a military and naval buildup by the French emperor, who was fighting a war in Italy against Austria, and by disputes over the Newfoundland fishery. Recalling, no doubt, the glorious age of Trafalgar and Waterloo, in 1861 Lieutenant R.G. Haliburton (later a member of the intellectual movement Canada First) of the Halifax Scottish Volunteers gave a lecture entitled "War and Its Lessons," wherein he warned the audience not of the Russian Bear or Brother Jonathan, but of France. This ancient foe, he argued, was watching Nova Scotia and would surely attack "Acadia" in the event of war with Britain. In this scenario, the colony's several hundred volunteers would be helpless against the powerful ironclads of Napoleon III.[62]

Despite Haliburton's fanciful remarks, France was more of an ally than an enemy. French warships made regular visits to Halifax and Sydney as part of their Newfoundland fishery patrols and other operations in the Western Hemisphere, and French officers were honoured guests. Early in the American war, which coincided with French military adventurism in Mexico, Halifax was visited by the Prince Napoleon Jerome and Princess Clothilde (who also toured

British Reinforcements: 63rd Regiment crossing New Brunswick's Nerepis Valley as a result of the Trent Crisis.

New York, Washington and even the Confederate headquarters beyond the Potomac).[63]

In 1859, Nova Scotia's lieutenant-governor, the Earl of Mulgrave, in view of the sorry state of the militia, encouraged the formation of volunteer artillery and infantry companies in strategic spots such as Pictou. The impending visit of the Prince of Wales in 1860 sparked a wave of patriotism and volunteering, which in the words of the Halifax *British Colonist* was "indispensable to the formation of national character."[64] When the Prince arrived in Halifax that summer to dedicate the Parker-Welsford monument near Government House, local volunteers were in attendance. By 1860, Nova Scotia had thirty volunteer companies stretching from Cape Breton to Yarmouth. A similar number were training in New Brunswick, where Lieutenant-Governor Manners-Sutton had encouraged volunteering in the late 1850s. New Brunswick's volunteers were tutored by twelve British drill sergeants who, unlike the individual in Pictou, were "cold water" men. The Imperial authorities even equipped the volunteers with modern Enfield rifled muskets, the large-calibre weapon common among Confederate soldiers. Governor Gordon later complained that some New Brunswick volunteers had abused their government rifles by using them as shotguns. In addition to rifles, the authorities had several thousand smoothbore muskets in storage.[65]

Volunteering continued to grow, but it was largely an urban, middle-class phenomenon. A number of commentators worried that the movement was merely a fad whose novelty would fade. The Charlottetown *Examiner* ridiculed P.E.I.'s small but enthusiastic force of "holiday soldiers," pointing out that a single enemy warship could subdue the entire island, the Prince of Wales Rifle Corps notwithstanding. Edward Whelan, hostile to the big landowners, called upon the British government and the proprietors to pay the costs of defence. In early 1861, Whelan warned that the volunteers could be employed to quell riots and collect rents from rebellious tenant farmers. Catholics feared that volunteer companies contained large numbers of antagonistic and armed Orangemen. The Summerside Rifle and Artillery Company, despite several months of drilling, numbered only thirteen men by October 1861. A number of Summerside gentlemen, proud of the local volunteer fire company, were keen on forming a corps of Fire Zouaves, modelled on the red-trousered volunteer soldiers from New York who fought at Bull Run. The community of St. Eleanors enthusiastically welcomed its triumphant volunteer company back from a rifle match in Charlottetown where it had proved itself "the crack regiment of the colony."[66]

By March 1862, Nova Scotia had 2,500 active volunteers. On the Queen's birthday that year the Lunenburg Volunteers paraded and fired a feu de joie from Blockhouse Hill. In Halifax they had organized by "nationalities": the Chebucto Greys for those of English descent; the Irish Rifles; the Scottish Rifles; and the Victoria Rifles for African Nova Scotians, who were "not behind their fellows in shewing their loyalty and willingness to defend their homes." In February of 1861 the "coloured" company mustered on the Grand Parade and then, headed by the fife and drums of the 63rd Regiment, proceeded to Government House to present a loyal address. A similar address was given to the commander of the garrison and then the Victoria Rifles paraded through the principal streets, followed by a large crowd unaccustomed to seeing blacks in uniform. That evening the company attended a lecture at Dalhousie College. Several Halifax-Dartmouth area volunteer units were later consolidated into the Halifax Volunteer Battalion, but the Victoria Rifles and one or two others were passed over and eventually faded from the scene.[67]

THE *TRENT* CRISIS

In late 1861 questions of defence and possible involvement in the American war became more than matters of conjecture. Relations had already soured between Washington and London, largely as a result of Britain's neutrality policy, which seemed to favour the "insurgents," as the Southerners were called by Secretary of State Seward. Both sides were also dissatisfied with the blockade. Now news arrived via telegraph of an incident on the high seas involving a British mail steamer and an American warship. The *Trent* affair started as a relatively minor maritime dispute but almost led to war between the two powers. Early one November morning Captain Charles Wilkes of the USS *San Jacinto* stopped the SS *Trent* in the Bahama channel and removed, as contraband, two Confederate envoys travelling to Europe. The prisoners were taken to Fort Warren, Boston. Given its performance on the battlefield, the North was badly in need of good news and Wilkes became a national hero for twisting the tail of the British Lion.[68] Most Maritime journals reacted patriotically. A Saint John newspaper opined that a war with the Americans would "stir the blood, unite us more closely together, provide for us the beginning of a noble history, and attach us more closely to Great Britain." It took almost three weeks for the intelligence to reach England, where the reaction of the public was bellicose to the extreme. Wilkes had merely practised what the Royal Navy had made routine during the Napoleonic Wars, but by challenging the rights of neutral British vessels on the high seas he hit a raw nerve.[69]

The British government instructed Lord Lyons, its minister at Washington, to present the Americans with an ultimatum: release the envoys or prepare for war. Britain's five thousand regulars in North America were put on alert, but to a large extent the threat was sheer bluster. Given their small numbers and limited artillery, and the poor state of the colonial militia, Canada West, part of Canada East and perhaps western New Brunswick were vulnerable, especially by summer. New Brunswick had only a handful of redcoats, fifty companies of volunteers, several thousand old flintlocks stored for militia use and only eleven rounds for each musket. Major General Trollop, commander of the forces in the region, had several thousand percussion-cap, smoothbore muskets for the Nova Scotia mi-

Volunteers respond to the Imperial call for preparedness: The Sydney Mines
Volunteer Rifles, 1859.

litia. The most important role would be played by the navy; Britain
would go on the defensive on land, attempting to hold Montreal,
Quebec and Halifax.[70]

STRATEGY AND LOGISTICS

From Britain, Nova Scotia Liberal leader Joseph Howe, who seemed
to be an expert on everything, wrote to advise the Earl of Mulgrave
on defence strategy. Howe, who had favoured the North at the
outset, now threw his moral support behind the Confederacy, largely
because of Wilkes' insult to the flag. A prominent journalist and
politician, Howe had stirred up considerable controversy during
the Crimean conflict by attempting to recruit a British "foreign legion"
in the United States. Now he was in London attempting to find
support for an intercolonial railway. Given that the water route
into Canada would be frozen over, British troops would have to
march overland after the onset of winter, a practical demonstration
of the need for a rail link. "This mortal blow, aimed at our national
honour," Howe wrote, "gives of course importance to our mission."
He expressed doubt "that the mob of New York will permit the
men to be given up." [71] The colonies, therefore, should gird their
loins for battle. He urged the lieutenant-governor to call up the
entire militia. One of Halifax's two regiments of foot could reinforce
New Brunswick or Canada while local volunteers performed garrison
duties. He also suggested the fitting out of privateers, a successful

tactic during the Revolutionary War, the struggle with France and the War of 1812:

If war breaks out, letters of marque should be issued promptly both to Nova Scotia and New Brunswick [so] that the enemy will not get the start on us. Any privateers will give the Eastern States enough to do. The ice will defend our Gulf ports. Our Eastern harbours will not be attacked. Halifax will be cared for seaward by the squadron, and landward by a few regiments of county militia, accustomed to field work, and hard work, concentrated in the rear of Halifax, Liverpool and Yarmouth. [This] would probably be sufficient to defend the Western seaports and a few Armstrong guns, if you have them, would not be out of place at Lunenburg, Liverpool and Yarmouth.[72]

Privateering–Howe's enthusiasm aside–was out of the question. Britain had signed an international convention in 1856 abolishing the use of private armed vessels in warfare. A correspondent to the Halifax *Morning Chronicle* was less optimistic than Howe, noting that the North had mounted a successful joint operation against Hatteras Inlet which proved that it could, with proper planning, land troops at Windsor or St. Margaret's Bay and attack Halifax from the rear. The Americans, it turned out, were far too preoccupied with the rebels to seriously consider attacking the Maritimes. Lincoln cautioned his advisers that they could fight only one war at a time. The colonial authorities knew this and refrained from calling out the militia.[73]

The Queen's ultimatum arrived in Halifax via steamer and was dispatched by warship to Washington, D.C., reaching Lord Lyons by 19 December 1861. Meanwhile, ships, troops, artillery and supplies were being organized on the other side of the Atlantic in expectation of a spring campaign. Florence Nightingale advised the government on proper clothing for the harsh Canadian winter. Steamers were chartered to carry troops and baggage, but none were able to reach the St. Lawrence before the ice set in. One vessel made it as far as Bic, Canada East, but was forced back by rough weather and ice. It stopped at Sydney before arriving in Halifax with the Scots Fusilier Guards. The first battalion of the Rifle Brigade landed in Halifax on Boxing Day. The Grenadier Guards, "the flower of the British Army," disembarked, paraded before the citizens and then climbed back on board the troopship for New Brunswick. From Liverpool came two artillery companies and thirty thousand stand of arms. From Queenstown, Ireland, came the Hospital Corps, cavalry and more artillery. The 63rd Regiment of Foot, stationed at Halifax since 1856, also was off to New Brunswick. The 62nd Regiment took part in a similarly emotional farewell, parading to popular airs such as "Auld Lang Syne" and "The Girl I Left Behind Me." The regiment was shipped by steamer to St. Andrew's, then on by rail and sleigh to Canterbury, Woodstock and Fredericton.[74]

In the port city of Saint John, the authorities, under Gordon's direction, were making last-minute preparations for the transhipment of several thousand troops to Canada via the Saint John River valley and Lake Temiscouata. The operation continued even after word arrived on 28 December that the Southern envoys had been released and immediate war averted. HMS *Rinaldo*, the frigate that picked up Mason and Slidell, the Confederate diplomats, and took them to England, was known on the Halifax station. There was no guarantee that relations with the Americans would not deteriorate once again and the British government remained determined to bolster its North American defences. Saint John, which was not a major garrison town, was determined to show that it could outdo its rival, Halifax, in terms of hospitality. Redcoats were quartered in barracks, public buildings and the car shed of the European and North American Railway. A journalist described the Grenadier Guards repairing and cleaning their equipment and generally "musing upon the chances of war with the Northerners." A number of troops were put on report for consuming too much of the local "white eye." Sleds hauled straw, fuel and provisions through the streets. Volunteers performed fatigue duties such as unloading stores and prepared for possible action.[75]

The troops were taken, eight men to a sled, by civilian teamsters to Fredericton and on to Riviere du Loup, where the Grand Trunk Railway would carry them to Quebec City and Montreal. Before the journey, which one reporter likened to "one long sleighing party," the British soldiers were feted by the citizens of Saint John. The *Illustrated London News* depicted the men as having to trudge on foot through a bleak winter wilderness. In reality the passengers were bundled up in the sleds and fed and warmed in shelters at regular intervals. They also received "a gill of spirits" at each stop. Little wonder that only seven men deserted.[76]

As of 3 January 1862, there were roughly five thousand regulars in New Brunswick and Nova Scotia. By the end of March, 5,500 officers and men had passed through the Timber Colony, hauled by 840 teams of horses. An additional sixty-four teams had carried artillery, which had encountered some difficulty in the deep snow because of poorly designed English sleds. As an exercise in logistics and a display of political will, the winter reinforcement was impressive, but the force sent to Canada was little more than a trip wire. At the time of the *Trent* outrage the Northern armies had grown to 700,000 men. And by 1862, more casualties were being incurred in individual battles in Virginia than there were troops in British North America. If war came, the colonies looked to the Royal Navy to save the day.[77]

In late 1861, Vice-Admiral Milne, erroneously warned by Lord Lyons months earlier to expect war, was advised to avoid dispersing his forces. The Royal Navy was outnumbered by the Americans six to one in the western North Atlantic, but the British had many more vessels in other parts of the globe. Vice Admiral Milne would concentrate his ships at Bermuda and Havana, leaving communications open with the Gulf of St. Lawrence, Halifax and Washington. Immediate reinforcements gave Milne a "very respectable" strike force of forty steamships, including eight ships of the line and thirteen frigates and corvettes. The British were confident that their new Armstrong guns would perform well. There was no evidence in December 1861 of any contemplated alliance with the Confederacy, but Milne regarded it as a practical ally if hostilities commenced. Some colonial newspapers envisioned British men of war providing covering fire for Confederate troops along the Potomac. The navy's strategy was simple: find and destroy the American blockading squadrons off the coasts of Florida, the Carolinas and Virginia, and then impose a British blockade on the North. The Admiralty, in preparation, forwarded large supplies of Welsh coal to Halifax,

Bermuda and the West Indies. Milne did not favour raids on Yankee ports; like many commanders he had a healthy respect for artillery in fixed positions. At any rate, Maine was not a Royal Navy priority. Thirty additional vessels were steaming to North America and more were available if needed. The Royal Navy did possess two powerful ironclads, but they were not suitable for coastal and blockade work. If war had been declared and lasted until the summer, British block-aders might have been caught off guard by the USS *Monitor*. [78]

THE FRONTIER

The frontier was not exactly bristling with American bayonets. A lieutenant-colonel of the 62nd recorded that Houlton, Maine, across from Woodstock, was protected by only a few dozen volunteers "whom I saw marching in the town without arms, to the inspiring air of Yankee Doodle playing on a solitary fife accompanied by a big drum." He determined that the Maine militiamen would have been easy pickings for the regulars. The mayor of Woodstock, a community normally enjoying cordial relations with its Yankee neighbours, portrayed the American crisis as the revenge of the Loyalists. The disruption of the republic vindicated the loyalty and wisdom of the Loyalist forefathers who had settled the Saint John valley. For a time the small community housed nearly eight hundred officers and men of the 62nd Regiment. Although marked by a couple of attempts to entice desertion, the presence of the British troops was Woodstock's social highlight of the year. Even Houlton got into the spirit of things when a number of its citizens visited the redcoats and were honoured with a serenade by the regimental band.[79]

New Brunswick's long, exposed frontier, it was felt in London, was vulnerable to small forces who could easily disrupt commu-nications with Canada. The British government discussed the expediency of reviving a successful strategy of the War of 1812: an occupation of eastern Maine. During the later stages of the earlier conflict, the British, taking advantage of naval superiority and the docility of New England, had launched a joint operation that captured Eastport, Castine, Belfast, Bangor and Machias. British troops had then occupied and administered a portion of Maine east of the Penobscot River for several months, and large numbers of Americans had sworn allegiance to George III. In 1814 the British had also landed an expedition in Chesapeake Bay and marched on Washington and burned the capitol. After being blocked at Baltimore, the redcoats had sailed back to Halifax.[80]

In late 1861, Maine was understandably anxious about British intentions. The state had over one hundred harbours, most of them completely defenceless. Now the British, because of a relatively trivial incident at sea, seemed ready to seize Portland and its magnificent harbour. Republican Governor I. Washburn, Jr. addressed the state assembly on the subject of defence, declaring that the unjust boundary settlement had deprived Americans of valuable timberlands and pointing to the remote, undefended border with Canada to the North and New Brunswick to the east. He also spoke of the "deep and bitter hostility" borne by many British colonists against the people of Maine.[81]

As Portland's defences were in a sorry state, heavy guns were sent to Forts Scammel and Preble. Larger ordnance was sent to Fort Knox at the Bucksport Narrows, on the Penobscot, the river that twice had served as a British invasion route. Two new Maine volunteer regiments were instructed to remain in Augusta. The Eastport *Sentinel* called for new fortifications along the border, the occupation of Campobello Island to protect Eastport on Moose Island, and the placing of a battery at Robbinston to menace St. Andrew's and guard the approach to Calais up the St. Croix River. The governor called on the federal authorities to make Portland harbour a Gibraltar or Sebastapol.[82]

The people of Maine, however, had little cause for alarm even if fighting had erupted. Although Sir Charles Hastings Doyle, the military commander of the Maritimes, argued for a pre-emptive strike, the Royal Navy was cool to the scheme. Early in 1862, Governor Gordon sent a confidential agent into the Pine Tree State to examine the condition of fortifications and learn of troop movements. B. Robinson found the people of the state "warlike," vengeful and boastful. Although Maine was all but denuded of troops and the border posts Forts Fairfield and Kent were little more than decrepit shacks, a Yankee officer warned Gordon's spy that "the thrashing Scott gave the Mexicans wouldn't be a patch to the greasing we'd get."[83] Unlike the authorities in Maine, who feared British aggression, the secretary of state in Washington adopted what one historian describes as a "nonchalant" attitude towards the arrival of Imperial troop reinforcements, even offering the British the right of passage through Maine on the Grand Trunk Railway's Portland to Montreal line.[84]

Fortunately for all parties concerned, apart from the Confederates, the American government agreed to release the envoys and the British war footing in North America was ended. The squadron, which had left Halifax for the season, returned to routine duties.

During the crisis, more than ten thousand troops had passed through the Maritimes. The growl of the British Lion, to paraphrase New Brunswick's lieutenant-governor, had echoed across the Atlantic. Throughout the remainder of 1862, the South, with the exception of the Battle of Antietam, continued to outfight the North, or so the headlines suggested. This removed the fear of imminent invasion in British America, but neither the British nor the colonial governments remained complacent on defence questions. The *Trent* incident had contributed to a greater sense of collective identity and common destiny among the colonies, but it had not overcome decades of parochialism. After the war scare, Nova Scotia and New Brunswick, for example, did not link up their fledgling railway systems, separated by a gap from the Bend of the Petticodiac River to Truro.[85]

NEW TECHNOLOGY

The possible local implications of developments in the American war, particularly if they involved new tactics or technology, were no longer ignored. Maritime journalists were fascinated by the famous Battle of Hampton Roads between the ironclads CSS *Virginia* (or *Merrimack*) and USS *Monitor* in 1862. The smaller Union ironclad had prevented the giant *Virginia* from destroying the Chesapeake blockading squadron. More importantly, both sides had demonstrated to the world the fighting value of protected "monitors" capable of ramming larger men of war and shelling coastal forts at point-blank range. The battle heralded a new age of naval warfare based on armour, rifled artillery and powerful steam engines. As the Nova Scotia *Provincial Wesleyan* noted, "The endurance and power of each vessel proves that iron-clad vessels may be constructed so as to pass the strongest forts with impunity and lay cities and dockyards in ashes and destroy shipping at will–a terrible revelation to all the nations of the world."[86]

The long-term significance for the defence of colonies dependent on the Royal Navy was disturbing. The North America and West Indies Squadron mounted hundreds of guns but possessed not a single ironclad. If American ironclad and "tinclad" river gunboats and mortar schooners were proving so useful on inland waters, how secure were the Great Lakes and the St. Lawrence and Saint John valleys? Perhaps even the defences of Halifax, which the citizens had regarded as impregnable, and the new coastal batteries planned for Saint John harbour, were already obsolete. The Federal capture of New Orleans in April 1862, effected largely by naval power, added to these anxieties. Admiral Farragut had run his flotilla of wooden ships past two masonry forts that mounted eighty guns and had not lost a single vessel.[87]

The battle of the ironclad monsters was described in detail by Thomas Foley to his parents at South Shore, P.E.I. Foley's Massachusetts regiment, encamped at Newport News, had been ordered to prepare for action once the *Virginia* appeared out of the Elizabeth River. The Union infantry supported shore batteries that took part in the ensuing battle. *Ross's Weekly* reported that Foley shared a rifle pit with a corporal who was killed, "having his head knocked clean off, and the blood and the brains of the deceased dashed all over him." After ramming and raking the gundeck of the U.S. *Congress* with its forward gun, the Confederate vessel rammed a second hole below the water line. The Union sailors, who knew that their ship was going under, continued to load and fire their remaining guns:

The decks were slippery with blood and arms and legs and chunks of flesh were strewn about. The *Merrimac* (*Virginia*) laid off at easy point blank range discharging broadsides alternating at the *Cumberland* and *Congress*. The water by this time had reached the magazines of the *Cumberland*. The men, however, kept at work, and several cases of powder were passed up, and the guns kept in play. Several men in the shell room lingered too long in their eagerness to pass up shells and were drowned.[88]

Foley credited the Union sailors with unflinching courage in the face of an unbeatable foe. The men of the doomed *Cumberland* were "as brave a crew as ever walked a deck." The rebel ram and its consorts set the *Congress* ablaze with concentrated artillery fire. The vessel blew up hours later. When the *Virginia* returned the following day, hoping to finish off the stranded *Minnesota*, it "met with something that knocked her 'higher than a kite'," USS *Monitor*. As the rebel vessel closed in on the helpless frigate, the smaller Union ironclad, with its single revolving turret, steamed directly for the enemy. *Monitor* was outgunned, but because of superior manoeuvrability it was able to probe the enemy's defensive armour of wrought iron, and save the squadron.[89]

DEFENCE IMPROVEMENTS

The war scare of 1861–62 also reinvigorated the colonial militia. The colonies, according to one newspaper, had to become more military if they were to survive. Prince Edward Island, which had several hundred volunteers by 1863, conducted a general muster of its militia. On the Queen's birthday in 1862 the Island volunteers staged a field day at Charlottetown's Barrack Square. New Brunswick legislation in 1862 created two classes of militiamen: the sedentary (all males between eighteen and forty-five) and the active (up to one thousand volunteers who promised to drill six days each year). Logistical difficulties persisted. As Gordon noted in 1861, the Timber Colony's population was scattered over an area the size of Ireland. To counter this, the government experimented with a summer training camp for select volunteer and militia companies. The 1865 camp of instruction at Fredericton attracted one thousand officers and men. Yet apathy, lax enforcement of the militia law and the needs of the economy presented difficulties to building a citizen soldiery. When two battalions of Saint John militia were enrolled in the fall of 1865 only a third of the men turned out. Portland parish enjoyed greater success, but at the cost of a considerable disruption in the work day.[90]

The Nova Scotia Militia Act of 1862 allowed the governor to call out a levee en masse in time of emergency and to place it under strict discipline. The annual muster period was increased to five days and drill to four hours each day. Yet in 1863 the Halifax militia was still described as possessing "a laughable appearance," and in Yarmouth a public meeting protested the mandatory nature of the militia law.[91] Officers, many of them drawn from the volunteers, were required to drill twenty-nine days each year. The legislature also increased its militia budget. The revived militia eventually eclipsed the volunteers and became an integral part of defence strategy, for example, in manning the forts and guns of Halifax. By May of 1863, 37,000 had been enrolled and several hundred officers were being trained. In February of 1864, Lieutenant-Governor Hastings Doyle reported that more than 46,000 had been enrolled in the militia and more than 2,300 in the volunteers.[92]

Loyalty was not found wanting. Tracadie, Clare, Meteghan, Tusket and Pubnico mustered companies of Acadians; the militia company of St. Andrew's, Nova Scotia, was made up of Gaelic-speaking Highlanders. Most of the men in each category had been drilled and inspected, a decided improvement over earlier times, but firearms still were in short supply. By the end of the Civil War, Nova Scotia's governor, expecting trouble with the Americans, was urging the training of militia artillery units in Halifax County. The militia artillery manned thirty-two-pounders at Pictou. Guns also were mounted at Digby and Granville Township to command Digby Gut, and at Sydney Mines (where British troops were stationed briefly in 1864 to break a strike by coal miners).[93] The militia revival would serve the colonies well in 1866 with the threat of attack by Fenians, Irish nationalists based in the United States.

The American war also caused the Imperial authorities to study the overall problem of North American defence. The reinforcement of Canada through snowbound New Brunswick had highlighted the need for improved communications. The American struggle was proving the value of railroads for transporting troops, munitions and foodstuffs; the Confederates, for example, had rushed last-minute reinforcements to Manassas by rail. In 1862 the British government offered to help finance an intercolonial railway, a project valued by colonial politicians more for its economic advantages than its military purposes. A series of reports on colonial defence pointed to the need to fortify and rearm Canada and to protect the Saint John River, which commanded the Bay of Fundy and provided communications with Canada East.[94]

Saint John's rudimentary harbour defences, it was recommended, should be expanded and equipped with modern weapons. Special attention was to be paid to Partridge Island in the mouth of the harbour, which British authorities had been interested in fortifying since the French scare of the late 1850s.[95] In late 1863 a civilian contractor, under the supervision of the Royal Engineers, began construction of an eight-gun battery at Red Head, an often fog-bound point to the east of the harbour. The purpose of this fortification, a newspaper explained only half jokingly, was to repel Yankee monitors. A year later, work began on a larger coastal battery at Negro Head in Carleton, to the west of the city. Saint John's new defences were to be manned by local volunteer artillerymen. A report by an officer of the Royal Engineers concluded that western New Brunswick had little to fear from Maine, given the state of transportation and sparse settlement along the frontier, but that the waterborne threat was legitimate. He suggested a force of gunboats for the Saint John River.[96]

The experts advised that neither Windsor, which had a tidal harbour, nor ancient Annapolis Royal should be refortified, but that Sydney required a few rifled guns and trained volunteers. Prince Edward Island, which had neither a permanent garrison nor fortifications, did not even enter into the discussion. The volunteer artillery at Charlottetown continued to train with its small brass field guns. British regulars did return to the Island in 1865, but their presence had nothing to do with external threats; two companies of the 16th Bedfordshire Regiment arrived at the request of the colony's administrator late that summer to assist the civil power in controlling protests and resistance by tenant farmers.[97]

The defence panic of the early 1860s led to the extensive rebuilding and rearming of Fortress Halifax, which continued to be valued as an Imperial base. After the *Trent* incident the British military began a construction program that brought Halifax into the age of the rifled gun and the ironclad. Following a survey of coastal defences, it was decided to ring the harbour with rifled muzzle loaders (RMLs). George's Island's defences were modernized between 1864 and 1870, and a new fort was constructed at Ive's Point on McNab's Island to enable crossfire on attacking vessels or enemy siege batteries. Dartmouth's Fort Clarence was improved, and decayed York Redoubt, with its superb view of the western channel, was rebuilt starting in 1863. The Cambridge battery at Point Pleasant was rearmed with RMLs, and the nearby Martello tower served as a defensible magazine. Much of this work was not finished by the time the Civil War ended, yet enough had been completed by November 1864 to make the harbour, in the words of the governor, "almost impregnable."[98]

ANTI-YANKEEISM

The most immediate impact of Wilkes' action and the British response was to increase animosity in the colonies towards the North.[99] Three decades later, the New Brunswick poet and writer Charles G.D. Roberts recalled that colonists at the time appreciated the "poetic justice" of Southern secession. The Confederates justified their actions on the same principles "so rudely insisted upon in 1776" when the British Empire had been dismembered. A New Brunswick merchant wrote an English relative in 1862 that he had "thought it quite possible that England and these colonies would have to give the Yankees a whipping to learn them to be civil."[100] Joseph Howe, corresponding with a British member of Parliament a year after the *Trent* imbroglio, argued that the achievements of the South, like those of small but independent states such as Holland and Switzerland, were an inspiration for Nova Scotia's future. The Confederacy proved that "a highly-spirited, determined people, fighting on their own soil, against fearful odds and vastly superior numbers, could triumph." These were not the words of a neutral observer; by 1862 the North was a foil for Howe's Nova Scotia patriotism. Although public opinion was never static, for many these hostile feelings lasted until the war's end. The colonies were in no immediate danger in late 1862 when the Confederates were pummelling the Union forces at Fredericksburg, but Howe remained haunted by the spectre of invasion: "our cities would be captured, our fields laid to waste, our bridges blown up, our railways destroyed." Worst of all, Howe feared, would be the fate of British North American women, who were "as remarkable for their beauty as for their purity of heart." The womenfolk "would become a prey to a soldiery largely drawn from the refuse of society in the old world and the new."[101]

The fear of invasion was less strong in Nova Scotia or New Brunswick than in Canada. The British ambassador at Washington reported that many colonists supported British recognition of the Confederacy in order to prevent the reunification of a powerful United States which might turn its hostile gaze northwards. As Alabama politician Clement C. Clay, appointed "commissioner" to Canada in 1864, wrote to the Confederate secretary of state: "I do not know if the British subjects of the Bermudas, Nova Scotia, New Brunswick and the Canadas love us better, but they certainly hate the Yankees, and cordially rejoice in our triumphs over them." A Confederate courier to France, in a letter to Atlanta, described Halifax as "a hot Southern town–they hate the Yank as bad as we do."[102]

The growing sympathy in the colonies for the South was negatively linked to the North's sinking esteem. This feeling was summed up by Bluenose author and former chief justice Thomas Chandler Haliburton, who had always suspected American republicanism at heart. His wily Yankee character Sam Slick had once described Southern whites as "a kind-hearted, hospitable, liberal race." Now a British member of Parliament, he had dined with one of the Confederate commissioners seized from the *Trent*. Haliburton approved of neither "the ungodly and unchristian way in which they [the North] carried on the war in which they were at present engaged, nor in their utter disregard of all International law."[103]

2 The Commerce of War

It turns out that with our fish and plaster and our "unblenched cotton" trade we have been aiding and abetting, supporting and sustaining one of the most fearsome curses that has ever stained our sin-cursed globe.
                    —"Malachi," *Christian Messenger*, 9 April 1862

The initial economic impact of the war on the Maritimes was negative, for the region's economic life was integrated with that of the United States. Because of a decline in imports from the United States for 1861–62, the Nova Scotia government feared it would have to raise tariff levels to offset losses in revenues.[1] Merchants in the three colonies expected a commercial depression. Saint John businessmen, who had been mostly pro-North, began to resent the blockade and general disruption of trade. Fishermen, many of them destitute and heavily in debt, were discouraged by the closure of the Southern market for salt fish, a dietary staple of the slaves. Fishers from Ragged Islands, Nova Scotia, for example, took cod and herring off Labrador, preserved their catches in salt and supplied Halifax merchants who marketed the product to the West Indies and the American South. One journal estimated that the colony had exported fifty thousand barrels of fish to the Southern states each year. The fishery, which also was hurt by a series of poor harvests, would not recover until 1863. Nova Scotia's gypsum (used for fertilizer) and plaster industry, which laid off several thousand workers as the bottom fell out of the American market, suffered and truckmen and longshoremen were also affected. Rumours of high wages drew large numbers of Maritime sojourners and immigrants to the Northeast, but not all were successful in finding employment. Back home, Maritimers paid higher prices for American imports such as flour and manufactured goods.[2]

STAPLES INDUSTRIES

Three decades earlier, merchants and shipowners had debated whether the abolition of slavery in the British West Indies would harm or benefit regional producers of fish and lumber products and consumers of sugar, molasses and rum.[3] Similar ethically charged trade questions now arose. As much as one-seventh of Britain's population depended, in one way or another, on cotton imports. Aside from shipowners and one Saint John manufacturer, Maritimers did not directly benefit from the transatlantic cotton trade, but as loyal British subjects they resented the raw materials famine induced by both the Union and Confederate governments. The Union naval blockade, for many colonists, was in essence a war against the industrial and commercial interests of Great Britain. Millions of British men, women and children suffered with the closure of cotton and textile mills and the people of Halifax, Yarmouth, Saint John, Fredericton, Charlottetown and other Maritime communities raised funds for distressed factory operatives.[4]

On balance, the Civil War was more of a blessing than a curse. Nova Scotia exports to the U.S. doubled in value between 1861 and 1865. Although shut out of Southern markets, Maritime lumbermen, farmers, fishermen and miners benefited from the voracious demands of the Northern economy, which experienced rapid industrialization after 1861. The lumber camps, mills and ports of New Brunswick were busy getting out sawn lumber deals (planks) and other forestry products from the colony and from northern Maine.[5] The bay shore villages of the Annapolis Valley shipped out apples, cheese, butter and other agricultural exports. Large quantities of sheep, oxen and livestock were exported from Nova Scotia to Bermuda, a market normally supplied from New York, to feed the Confederate armies, benefiting ports such as Port Williams. The crisis gave a boost to prices and demand for P.E.I. agricultural exports, which had enjoyed good days since the 1854 Reciprocity Treaty.[6]

Mining also advanced because of outside interest. Gold fever first hit the Ovens, near Lunenburg, then Wine Harbour, Tangier, Sherbrooke and other areas of Nova Scotia; and coal fever hit Pictou County and Cape Breton. The end of the General Mining Association's monopoly made coal particularly suitable for development by American capital. New mines were opened, communities were founded and existing facilities were expanded. The Block House Mine on Cape Breton shipped largely to New York in American vessels. Coal shipments from Lingan increased to the point where the lieutenant-governor appointed an American consular agent. The

Confederate invasion of Pennsylvania in 1863, which cut rail links
to vital coalfields, brought more business to Pictou County mines.
In 1863, Albion Mines shipped nearly 200,000 tons. More than seven
hundred vessels, many of them heading for Northern ports, loaded
at South Pictou that year. American colliers were constant visitors
to Pictou harbour in the summer months. By 1865, coal constituted
one-third of Nova Scotia's exports by value, and most of it went
to the U.S. The Londonderry iron mine shipped several loads to
Northern ports during the 1864 season. Nova Scotia even supplied
grindstones, for sharpening swords and bayonets, to the Union
armies.[7]

Shipbuilding and shipowning were two bright spots for the
Maritimes during the war years. Increasingly the trend was to not
only build wooden vessels for sale abroad but to operate them for
profit. The three colonies launched more than 260 vessels in 1861;
the New Brunswick craft were larger, averaging five hundred tons
displacement each. By 1863, New Brunswickers of all classes were
investing in shipping on a share basis. The colony registered close
to a thousand vessels in 1864, three-quarters of them in Saint John.
Shipyards, employing sawyers, shipwrights, caulkers and other
skilled workers, boomed, and not only in the Timber Colony.
Maitland, at the mouth of Nova Scotia's Shubenacadie River, was
a beehive of activity, with twenty vessels on the stocks at one point
in 1863. "From Canning upwards to Truro," a journalist reported,
"the whole shore is speckled with shipyards." The Minas Basin shore
from Noel Shore to Five Mile River built thirty-five vessels – brigs,
brigantines, barques and schooners – in 1863 and 1864. In 1865,
the last year of the war, more than 560 vessels came out of Maritime
shipyards.[8]

Saint John, the region's chief shipowning centre, specialized in
deep-sea, long-haul voyages. Its square-rigged ships ranged the
North and South Atlantic, the Indian Ocean and the Pacific. Nova
Scotia's ocean-going fleet was owned in the outports. Yarmouth in
1861 had a fleet of more than 150 vessels over twenty-five tons.
Over half of them were schooners, the rest an assortment of
brigantines, brigs, barques and ships.[9] Every outport or river outlet
had its coasting vessels which sailed to Newfoundland, Maine, Massachusetts or the West Indies. The shallow-draught schooner,
employed in fishing, the West Indies trade and coasting runs, was
the region's workhorse, the nineteenth-century equivalent of the
tractor-trailer. In a region with only a few hundred miles of railway,
many passengers preferred to go by water. Because wooden-hulled
sailing vessels were cheap and efficient, locally owned steamships

were a rarity. Halifax, for example, did not own a single ton of ocean-going steam shipping in 1861.[10]

FLIGHT FROM THE FLAG

One unanticipated benefit of the war was a "flight from the flag" that drove hundreds of American merchant vessels into British registry. Most of the sales and transfers took place with deepwater vessels; coasters were considered safer investments. New Brunswick merchant and shipowner W.H. Harrison wrote in 1864 that "vessels have been a very good property in the last few years . . . as our Yankee neighbours are still trying to conquer their Southern brothers but do not accomplish anything but the destruction of property." The American fishing fleet also shrunk, although for a number of reasons not directly related to the war.[11]

Confederate privateers and commerce raiders such as the CSS *Alabama* captured and destroyed or bonded dozens of Northern ships. The American government later sent the British, whose shipyards, chandlers and arms merchants had equipped a number of the Confederate raiders, a bill for nineteen million dollars. Historians argue that the *Alabama* and seven other Confederate cruisers effectively crippled the Northern merchant marine by driving up freight and insurance rates. Others suggest more complex explanations. Another reason behind the drying up of Northern shipping was that the Union government was confiscating and hiring merchant steamers, ferries and tugs for war service, and shipyards were converting to naval production. The steamer *New Brunswick*, for example, was chartered to evacuate troops from the James Peninsula in 1862. The *Empress*, which carried passengers, mail and freight between Saint John, Windsor, Digby and Annapolis, was hired as a troopship in 1863.[12]

The fruits of the cruise of the Alabama, launched in May 1862, were immediately tangible in the Maritime colonies. The Eastport *Sentinel* regarded British toleration of Confederate commerce raiders as a conspiracy to undermine the Union's high-seas merchant marine. Maine, which had dominated the American fishery by sending hundreds of schooners to the Nova Scotia banks, the Gulf of St. Lawrence, the Newfoundland banks and Labrador, had cause for complaint. American vessels and cargoes were charged higher marine insurance rates, so the market found a solution. A Saint John vessel chartered by a Boston firm to replace a Yankee ship on a transatlantic run signalled the trend: American owners were transferring their vessels to the protection of the British flag. In

1863 they signed over eighty-six craft – ranging from three-hun-
dred-dollar fishing boats to deep-sea carriers worth $45,000 – to
owners in New Brunswick, P.E.I. and Nova Scotia. Yarmouth
residents picked up seventeen of the transfers, whose names usually
were changed, and Saint Johners bought a dozen. A number of
the new "owners" no doubt were operating the vessels on behalf
of the original owners as a ruse to avoid Confederate raiders. One
wonders if this was the case with Annie Kidley, an English spinster
residing at St. Andrew's, who suddenly came into possession of
several American merchantmen.[13] This shift hurt Maine shipbuild-
ers; not only were close to ninety Maine-built vessels captured or
destroyed by the Confederates, but the state registered less than
150 new craft from 1861 to 1864.[14]

Although often benefiting from the destructive cruises of the Confederate rovers, Maritimers had mixed feelings about the *Alabama*
and similar raiders that preyed upon defenceless cargo carriers and
fishing vessels. By war's end, nearly 260 Northern merchant ships
and whalers had been destroyed. The pro-Union Halifax *Sun*
applauded the sinking of the *Alabama* off the coast of France by
USS *Kearsage* in 1864, dismissing Confederate Captain R. Semmes
as a "notorious freebooter." P.W. Craighen, a Bluenose in the Union
army, wrote from Washington that Semmes was nothing more than
"a base, cringing, cowardly sea robber." Other Maritime journals
defended the legality of commerce raiding and reminded readers
that the Americans themselves had launched public armed vessels
against British shipping in two previous wars.[15]

In the war's early months, Rebel privateers lurked in the shallow
waters off the Carolinas.[16] One of the Confederacy's first raiders,
the brig CSS *Jefferson Davis*, had a Maritime connection. Its captain
Louis M. Coxetter, regarded by Rear Admiral S.F. Dupont as "the
most skilful man on the coast," had been born in Nova Scotia in
1818 and had a brother on the Saint John Common Council. Prior
to the rebellion, Coxetter had served as a master of transport during
the war with Mexico and skippered the steamer *Everglades* between
Florida and South Carolina. In 1858 a Baltimore-built vessel under
the name *Echo* had been captured off Cuba carrying slaves. In June
of 1861 it was commissioned as a private armed vessel, a privateer,
by the Confederacy and armed with five old British guns. The crew
of seventy, including marines, was issued with cutlasses and firearms. The "*Jeff Davis*" left Charleston on a seven-week cruise that
caused panic as far north as the Gulf of Maine. Its captain and
crew were denounced in the North as pirates who deserved the
gallows. Coxetter, described as "a thick-set, gentlemanly mariner

of middle age with a florid complexion and round face set off by a mustache and goatee," was as ruthless as he was determined. According to the memoirs of a "rebel reefer," during one pursuit he threatened to shoot an engineer if the steam engine malfunctioned and the vessel was captured. A contemporary account was more flattering: "He is a determined looking man, and one who would fight to the death, and probably sink rather than surrender."[17]

As a privateer, Louis Coxetter captured several Northern vessels, releasing three of them, including the brig *Mary E. Thompson* of Searsport, Maine. The brig *John Welsh* from Bangor was taken off Hatteras carrying sugar and sent into Charleston as a prize. Another victim was the schooner *S.J. Waring*, later recaptured through the efforts of a black crewman who killed three members of the prize crew in their sleep rather than be taken to South Carolina and probable slavery. The *Jefferson Davis*, sailing under false colours, ranged to within one hundred miles of Nantucket shoals and encountered a number of neutral vessels. One was the brig *Ada* out of Walton, Nova Scotia. The Yarmouth brigantine *Ann Lovett* was boarded at latitude 29°, 45', longitude 67°. A week later the *Jeff Davis* arrived off St. Augustine, Florida, in a gale. The ex-slaver attempted to enter the harbour but struck a bar and was wrecked. Its captain was given a hero's welcome in St. Augustine and Charleston. According to an American diplomat in Britain, Coxetter was on the *Trent* when it was overhauled by Captain Wilkes later that year. He went on to captain blockade runners.[18]

THE BLOCKADE

The Union blockade proclaimed in April 1861 was a major cause in British North America of growing support for the Confederacy. Nearly 3,600 miles of Rebel coast contained nearly two hundred harbours and navigable inlets.[19] Early in the conflict the naval screen did not appear to conform to international law, and Thomas Annand's Halifax *Morning Chronicle* proclaimed it "of doubtful character." The inability of the North to immediately close all Rebel ports caused many Maritimers to support British intervention to break the blockade. One journal suggested that the Royal Navy organize convoys into Southern cotton ports. Prior to the war, Nova Scotian sailing craft ran "into almost every bay, river and inlet along the whole seaboard from Eastport to New Orleans," carrying fish, lumber, plaster and potatoes. Many Maritime shipowners and exporters considered the blockade a violation of the 1854 Reciprocity Treaty, under which natural products entered the United States duty-free.[20]

To add insult to injury, in late 1861 the U.S. Navy attempted to seal up Charleston harbour by sinking a "stone fleet," an incident captured in verse by Herman Melville. A number of old whalers, loaded with stone and manned by special crews, were scuttled in an attempt to impede navigation by blockade runners and enemy gunboats. News of the sinking of the stone fleet arrived at a time when the Nova Scotia government was announcing that the block-ade had materially affected trade and provincial customs revenues. A naval blockade could be lifted, but a harbour, once ruined, could not be rebuilt. Colonial journals accused the North of violating the rules of war. Woodstock's *Carleton Sentinel* pronounced the action a threat to the rights of neutrals, principally Britain.[21]

Maritimers naturally pondered the war's impact on future eco-nomic relations. Some saw Southern independence as an economic boon. The ruling Republicans in the North, it was pointed out, were a high-tariff party, unlike the Southerners who were an agricultural people. Southern apologists such as Donald Currie of Charlottetown even believed that the tariff, not slavery, had been the cause of the war.[22] There were predictions that the U.S. Congress, no longer saddled with the free-trade South, would terminate the Reciprocity Treaty with the British colonies, endangering the long-term pros-perity of the Maritimes. On the other hand, there were new markets to be exploited south of the Mason-Dixon line. The pro-Southern Halifax *Morning Journal*, William Penny proprietor, explained that an independent Confederacy would open its coasting trade and markets to colonial merchants (the Reciprocity Treaty had contin-ued an earlier exclusion of Maritime "coasters" between American ports). Southerners, a Haligonian wrote from Maryland, were "not strictly a mercantile nor a manufacturing people." And neither were they a maritime people, thus they would need their goods carried to world markets. Perhaps enterprising Bluenoses could displace the now-despised Yankees, not only in shipping but in supplying manufactured goods. S.H. Holmes of Pictou's *Colonial Standard* pointed out that the Confederacy was a market of ten to twelve million and that Nova Scotians, like Southerners, "have been hewing wood and drawing water for the Yankees quite long enough."[23]

The condemnation of the blockade was based more on principle than sound economics. Most American trade was with the North before and during the war. The flight from the flag did little to stop the growth of trade with Northern ports. Joe Howe explained to a business audience in Detroit in 1865 that for every ton of goods shipped from British North America to the South, fifty were sent to the North. Half the vessels clearing Nova Scotia harbours were destined for the United States; almost as many of the ships entering the colony sailed from American ports.[24] School teacher E. Roche, addressing the Charlottetown YMCA, warned that Prince Edward Islanders should lend moral support to "our best customers," the Northern states. The war did present business opportunities. Early in the rebellion, for example, officials from Maine purchased blankets in Saint John for military volunteers, and the Mispeck Woolen Factory filled orders for the Northern army. The Acadia Powder Company, with powder works at Waverley, Nova Scotia, starting in 1862, probably shipped black powder to the North. Customs records indicate that far more vessels arrived in Nova Scotia from, and sailed to, the Northern states during the war than to the West Indies, the linchpin in blockade running. A Nova Scotian wrote in 1863 that "to the United States we are indebted for much of our present prosperity as a province, and are linked to them by all the ties of trade and commerce."[25]

One student of the era concludes that "the arrival of a single ship from the South," combined with tales of huge profits from blockade running, captured far more attention "than the arrival of a hundred ships from Boston" and explains why Halifax merchants, who controlled most of Nova Scotia's imports and much of its exports, increasingly believed "that their commercial future lay with the Confederacy." Outside observers such as London's *Steam Shipping Gazette* repeated exaggerated claims of Nova Scotia's trade with the South. However, colonial merchants actually had more to gain from a prolonged war than from Southern independence. The molasses and sugar trade was a case in point. New York and Boston merchants normally imported these products directly from the West Indies. But during the war sugar and molasses were transhipped through Halifax in secure British bottoms, enriching local merchants.[26] The result was that this port became "a more important distribution centre for West Indies products" in peacetime.[27]

In 1862, as the Union forces captured Southern ports and coastal territory in order to better enforce the blockade, Maritime vessels gradually resumed legal trade with occupied ports. In early 1864, Captain Rufus F. Cutten of the brig *Gorilla* wrote his brother from Union-controlled Louisiana. The locals in New Orleans had little good to say about the Yankees: "The Southern ladies are very bitter in their hostility." Cutten journeyed up the Mississippi on a riverboat and saw the former Confederate strongholds of Port Hudson, Vicksburg and Island No. 10. He also witnessed devastated plantations and incredible suffering among soldiers and former slaves alike. Unable to secure a cargo of precious cotton, the Bluenose skipper left New Orleans with a load of corn for Mexico.[28]

BLOCKADE RUNNING

One of the more dramatic and romantic aspects of the Civil War at sea was running the blockade. Maritimers participated in this activity, but never to the extent alleged by Northern critics. The Union naval cordon tightened each month, but the business of blockade breaking was extremely profitable. The Confederates were prepared to pay large sums for munitions, arms, medicine and other items, and European industrialists were hungry for the Southerner's expensive exports. The price of naval stores, for example, increased one thousand percent from 1860 to 1863 because of the blockade.[29] Most of the supplies shipped out of Halifax were not locally produced but imported from the United States and Britain; the port served as more of a clearing house and was never of primary importance in the rebel supply effort.

The Northern press cried foul when British subjects were captured in Confederate service or when British goods were intercepted. Yet Maritimers involved in blockade running were not acting out of political ideals so much as continuing the smuggling tradition, one that was common among border people. This same enterprise and daring would later make fortunes for Maritimers during American Prohibition. More than one journal explained that all seafaring people would attempt to bypass a blockade if profits were to be had. This was particularly so of the British, the world's most nautical race. The U.S. consul at Saint John wrote caustically that

Halifax Waterfront, c. 1870: Halifax merchants such as Benjamin Wier dominated Nova Scotia's export-import trade.

smuggling was "by no means inconsistent with what they know of the Bluenose mentality." The details of Maritime involvement in the overall Confederate supply effort are obscure, but it appears more extensive than Howe claimed. The capital for large ventures probably came from the Confederacy, Britain or even the North. In other words, local merchants, shipowners and sea captains may have acted for silent partners or employers. In its early months, smuggling was not highly organized but a decentralized business involving owners of small sailing craft who were not intimidated by the thinly deployed U.S. Navy. In 1861, 90 percent of the blockade runners, usually small vessels entering unguarded creeks and coves, succeeded in their mission, but their carrying capacity was too limited to make much of an impact on the rebel supply effort.[30]

Most of the early, amateur blockade runners from Nova Scotia sailed out of Halifax, but there were also vessels from Yarmouth and outports along the Fundy shore. Dozens of schooners, many of them British, entered and cleared Wilmington, North Carolina, which had rail links to Virginia and South Carolina. In August 1861, three schooners reached Halifax from North Carolina, two of them consigned to B. Wier and Co., an outfit that came to play an important role for Confederate interests in Nova Scotia.[31] Vessels from other colonies such as Bermuda or the Bahamas arrived in the Maritimes to load clothing, blankets, shoes and boots, tools, pig iron and other cargo obviously destined for the Confederacy. Late in the summer of 1861 a fisherman from Gloucester, Massachusetts, witnessed the return of four blockade runners to Halifax. Big profits were to be had, he wrote, in fish and in return cargoes such as turpentine, tar and pitch. Some vessels actually sailed south in ballast simply to pick up these valuable commodities. Bluenoses believed "that

the Reciprocity Treaty guaranteed them access to all American ports." The schooner *Emery*, after carrying fish and pork into Savannah, eluded the blockading squadron in a gale and returned to Halifax in November 1861 with a cargo consigned to merchant S.F. Barss. Barss risked the sixty-one-ton schooner *Beverly* and a cargo of Newfoundland salt fish on a voyage to Wilmington, North Carolina.[32]

A correspondent to the Philadelphia *Ledger* in the fall of 1861 reported that small Nova Scotia craft were clearing for the West Indies but sailing directly to the Southern coast. Once the Union had secured Hatteras Inlet, such ventures became more hazardous. The copper-fastened, clipper-built topsail schooner *Spitfire*, William Grant master, allegedly shipped a cargo that included rifles and bullet molds. The captain boasted that he would "shoot any Yankee that block[ed] his path" with his six-pounders. The Yarmouth schooner *Harmony*, destined for Key West, Florida, was captured by the USS *Gemsbok* off North Carolina.[33] The Yarmouth brig *Napier* departed from Havana in ballast in September 1861 and then seemed to disappear. Its master later explained that he had been forced to take shelter in the Cape Fear River and was detained for several weeks by Confederate authorities. The *Napier* sailed in the company of a British ship through the blockade, arriving in Liverpool, Nova Scotia, early in 1862. The *Thomas Killam* of Yarmouth was reported as carrying arms from Britain to Halifax. The *Albion*, purchased in South Carolina (after the promulgation of the blockade) by prominent Yarmouth shipowner Nehemiah K. Clements, left Cuba bound for Halifax but was stopped near North Edisto, South Carolina. The schooner, owned and registered by a British subject, manned by Southerners and skippered by a Maine seafarer, carried arms and foodstuffs.[34]

According to the American consul and a Boston newspaper, even the former consul at Halifax, Albert Pilsbury, was involved in the contraband trade. He was rumoured to have purchased an old vessel to smuggle gunpowder secreted in barrels of fish. Those involved planned to beach the vessel on the Southern coast and sell the cargo. A loyal Northerner residing in Halifax reported that Pilsbury had loaded the contraband at his place of business on the Dartmouth side of the harbour.[35] According to family lore, Captain William Henry Pye of Pye's Head, near Liscomb, Nova Scotia, ran the blockade in his Port Medway–built schooner *Agility* and operated for a time out of New Orleans. The owners of the Nova Scotia–built brigantine *Standard* supposedly ran into difficulties of an unexpected nature. *Ross's Weekly* reported that after he had reached a Florida port the captain was induced to scuttle the craft at the urging of Confederate authorities who feared that it would fall into the hands of the enemy.[36] The owner of the Halifax-based schooner *Fairplay*, used as a packet to Digby, gambled by conveying New Brunswick lumber and fish to South Carolina in the spring of 1862. In April 1863 the Bluenose schooner *Mary Jane*, hauling salt and coffee from Nassau, was intercepted off New Inlet, North Carolina (the eastern entrance to the mouth of the Cape Fear River.)[37] According to the Halifax shipping register, it was owned by master mariner William A. Fraser of Pictou.[38]

Captain William Fraser was involved in at least two attempted smuggling voyages. Early in the war he succeeded in delivering contraband to the South for Pictou merchants. In January 1862 he was at Nassau with the *Magnet*, which he intended to take to the American coast and into Wilmington. The schooner had been blown off course and reached the Bahamas for repairs. One of the voyage's backers, Pictou merchant William Norman Rudolf, confided to his diary that he and his associates planned to keep Fraser "in the trade." A few days later, Rudolf learned that the *Magnet*, despite its leaks, had arrived in the Confederacy in early February and Fraser was expected to return to Halifax. "He is a bold fellow," Rudolf recorded, "and ready for anything yet thoroughly honest and upright." The schooner, unfortunately for its owners, was seized by U.S. Marines during the capture of Fernandina, Florida, in March 1862. According to an officer on the USS sloop *Pawnee*, the abandoned vessel had been loaded with coal. Rudolf later wrote that Fraser was caught in a second smuggling operation organized by Halifax partners. In late 1863, W.A. Fraser embarked on the better-known part of his career, as skipper of the mission vessel *Day Spring*, a fast barquentine built by Carmichael and Co. of New Glasgow. After signing on a crew that promised to abstain from liquor, tobacco and profanity, Fraser, along with his wife and Presbyterian minister Donald Morrison, departed for the distant New Hebrides via the Cape of Good Hope and Australia. Until his return in 1872, the former smuggler commanded *Day Spring* in its voyages supplying Protestant missionaries in the South Pacific island chain.[39]

NEW BRUNSWICK AND
PRINCE EDWARD ISLAND

Normally, New Brunswick shipped little to the West Indies other than lumber. In fact, the press chided the mercantile community for neglecting the West Indies market. Much like Halifax, Saint John was suspected to be a major blockade-running port, but it never lived up to the reputation. Almost half of the vessels entering New Brunswick ports arrived from the United States, and a third or more of the colony's clearances were for American ports.[40] According to a censorious New York *Herald*, the Loyalist city was little more than "a group of huts, many of them inhabited by rogues who have made a few pennies since the war broke out by lending their names to blockade runners." Early in the war, Saint John vessels, or ships loading cargo at the port, attempted to smuggle contraband in and out of Southern ports. The *Volga* of Saint John returned from Cherrystone, Virginia, during the *Trent* crisis, its captain claiming not to have seen a single blockader. U.S. Consul J.Q. Howard telegraphed intelligence on shipping to the State Department and the Department of the Navy in Washington. In 1862 and again in the summer of 1863 he boasted that no vessel sailing from the port had succeeded in breaking the blockade. Howard also proposed that he buy large quantities of gunpowder on the local market to keep it out of enemy hands.[41]

On one occasion a local American businessman, Andre Cushing, wired the authorities about the suspicious movements of the schooner *Kate Hale*, arrived from Georgetown, South Carolina, with a cargo consigned to W. and R. Wright. Originally the *H. and J. Neild* built at Baltimore, this vessel had been commissioned as the privateer *Dixie* earlier in the year and had taken three Union prizes before returning to Charleston in August. The collector of customs, worried that entering this vessel was tantamount to recognizing the Confederate States, corresponded with the governor.

Consul Howard also notified Washington of the *Judah*, which cleared port with two Southern pilots and a load of tin, lead and quicksilver. This schooner succeeded in reaching Florida by late summer of 1861. Before it could be fitted out as a privateer on the lines of the *Jefferson Davis* it was cut out and burned by Union raiders at Pensacola. *Kate Hale*, renamed *Success*, cleared for Nassau with fish, butter, oakum, pig iron and quinine. It was captured near Georgetown, South Carolina, in April 1862. The British brig *Mystery*, which loaded ice at Saint John, was suspected of attempting to enter Charleston for a cargo of pitch pine; blocked by naval patrols, it sailed for Cuba but was later intercepted.[42]

Saint John gained added notoriety because of the presence of the *Alliance*, a British-registered steamer anchored at adjacent Carleton and flying the palmetto flag of South Carolina. Its captain, according to a New York journalist, was a former slaver, and its cargo of pig and sheet iron, mackerel, wine and quicksilver had been purchased by the Rebel government. The ship itself was rumoured to belong to the English firm Fraser, Trenholm and Co., a subsidiary of a South Carolina company heavily involved in blockade running and Confederate supply. The *Alliance* cleared for Havana on August 14, 1861, and, as American officials predicted, pierced the blockade off North Carolina. It was made a prize when Union forces overran Beaufort, North Carolina, in May 1862. The New York *World* accused the Saint John collector of customs of malfeasance for authorizing the transfer of registry. At this time Howard reported the presence of J.B. Lafitte, a Georgian shipping agent who worked for John Fraser and Co. of Charleston. Washington was also alerted of the schooner *Julia* and the brigantine *Gold Hunter*, which both loaded blockade goods in September 1861. In 1864 the *Globe*, a staunch supporter of Lincoln, reported that Saint John commercial interests had refused to enter into blockade running on any significant scale. In the winter of 1865 the Saint John schooner *Halatia*, carrying lumber to Matamoras, Mexico, met a storm and was abandoned, its crew presumed lost. Large quantities of musket percussion caps were found between decks and hidden among the official cargo. New Brunswick merchants and shipowners, although not deeply involved in direct contraventions of the blockade, did take part in the indirect trade through the Bahamas and Bermuda.[43]

One writer has suggested that economic considerations made Saint John and vicinity pro-South, in contrast to Fredericton and the upper Saint John River valley, which were pro-North.[44] Yet public opinion often was divorced from trade patterns: most of the colony's trade was with Britain and the North, and pro-Southern sentiments were found in Woodstock. Lumbering, milling and manufacturing along the St. Croix River were international activities and the attitude of Charlotte County residents towards the war were as ambivalent and vacillating as any in the region. Northern sailing vessels crowded New Brunswick harbours at peak seasons of the year. Saint John merchants were notoriously "Yankee" in manners and taste, yet the Loyalist city developed a pro-"secesh" reputation after 1861. New Brunswick was more dependent upon U.S. imports than Nova Scotia and P.E.I., but its inhabitants held multifaceted views on the war.[45]

Prince Edward Island was noted for its seafarers but not for links to blockade running, largely because there were ready markets for agricultural products in neighbouring colonies and Northern states. The Island's navigation season (May to December) was also shorter because of the presence of ice in the Gulf of St. Lawrence and Northumberland Strait. Most clearances from P.E.I. ports were for

New Brunswick, Canada and Nova Scotia, yet America was not terra incognita. Charlottetown was a port of registry for a considerable hinterland.[46]

The U.S. consul, New Yorker James Sherman, although vigilant, found no widespread smuggling out of P.E.I. Lieutenant-Governor George Dundas reported in 1864 that there had been no significant reshipment of goods via the colony to Southern ports or the British West Indies. But Islanders were far-ranging seafarers and at least one of their ships ended up in prize court in New York City. Sherman was momentarily agitated by rumours that the fast, shallow-draught steamer *Heather Belle*, built and owned by James Duncan, was about to be purchased by Halifax merchants involved in Confederate supply. Launched at Duncan's Water Street yard in 1862, the *Heather Belle* was a 108-foot paddle-wheeler propelled by a powerful Glasgow-built engine. A work party was hired to chop a channel in the ice of Charlottetown harbour to allow the steamer to depart, but the deal fell through. Consul Sherman later asked his superiors whether he should make a bid on the vessel for use by the navy. The reply was negative: paddle-wheelers were not suitable as gun or patrol boats.[47]

NOVA SCOTIA

Not every smuggling voyage met with success. The Yarmouth schooner *Argonaut*, with fish from Westport, Nova Scotia, was captured when standing in for Hatteras Inlet on 13 September 1861. The vessel's papers listed its destination as Union-held Key West. A boarding party from the USS *Susquehanna* discovered a cargo that included shoes, soap, cotton goods and tea. The fall of Forts Hatteras and Clark on 27 August, the U.S. consul reported, had discouraged Nova Scotia vessels from approaching the inlet. The Union navy was slowly choking off the coastal trade of the Carolinas. The *Revere* out of Yarmouth, carrying salt and herring, was stopped off Beaufort, North Carolina, well off course to Key West. The Nevis craft *Susan Jane*, loaded in Halifax and formerly registered in the South, was intercepted carrying dry goods, tools and hardware off Hatteras Inlet on September 10. The previous day, blockaders had impounded the Lunenburg schooner *Louisa Agnes*, Captain Nickerson, for deviating from its official course to Baltimore.[48]

Bluenose forwarders and shipowners involved in sail-powered smuggling gradually learned, to their cost, of the Union navy's growing effectiveness. The Nova Scotia schooner *Ariel* was run aground near the mouth of the Cape Fear River in November of

1862. A Yankee gunboat fired a few shells to prevent the crew from unloading the cargo of salt and later put the vessel to the torch. The schooner *Adelso* of New Brunswick was returning with naval stores from North Carolina when heavy weather forced it into Newport, Rhode Island. Revenue officers seized both vessel and cargo. Contraband ships and cargo usually were sent to prize court and auctioned off in public, and the crews of blockade runners were released if they were neutrals.[49] The crews of the North and South Atlantic blockading squadrons which intercepted Maritime smugglers, or vessels that had visited Halifax, Yarmouth or Saint John, included Maritimers. Norman Wade of Granville Ferry, Nova Scotia, wrote that he had fired two cannon rounds at the Lunenburg schooner *Native* while serving on the steam barque USS *Young Rover*.[50]

A blockade, according to international law, had to be not only proclaimed but effective. In 1861 and 1862 there were doubts as to that effectiveness. A number of Maritime journals declared that Galveston, Texas, was an open port because blockading vessels had been temporarily driven off. In early 1863, when Richmond announced that it had broken the blockade outside Charleston, the *Acadian Recorder* predicted that Nova Scotia merchants would soon be shipping goods into the South Carolina port. The U.S. Navy, however, returned in force. The tightening naval screen was disappointing to Maritime merchants and skippers, but there were still safe profits to be made in hauls to the West Indies.[51] And for the more adventurous, a single round trip "might allow profits enough to pay for both cargo and the vessel."[52]

Increasingly aggressive American interpretations of the blockade placed Bluenose vessels in the centre of a number of diplomatic rows. Union cruisers began to stop, search and seize neutral vessels far from Southern shores. Thomas Chandler Haliburton declared that the judges of the Northern prize courts who sat in judgement of colonial vessels nabbed by the U.S. Navy "were generally chosen for political objects" and were "beneath contempt."[53] In 1862 a Halifax mercantile house protested to Vice Admiral Milne that the USS *Rhode Island* had stopped a brigantine in the Gulf of Florida carrying sugar from Mexico and had put the vessel, cargo and crew at considerable risk because of heavy weather. A year later, Nova Scotia merchants were astonished by the arrest of the brig *Isabella Thompson*, returning to Halifax from Nassau with cotton and turpentine, having landed lumber and fish. The vessel, owned by Master Mariner James McDaniel, and its freight, consigned to Wier and Co., were taken as prizes to New York City. The Yarmouth schooner *Glen*, supposedly on a run from Matamoras to Nassau, was seized for being several hundred miles off course.[54]

Nova Scotia trade with Matamoras, in the Mexican state of Tamaulipas, was growing at this time, largely because of the war. Matamoras, near Brownsville, Texas, had become an important, if roundabout, supply point for the Confederacy. After the secretary of the treasury banned American clearances for Matamoras in August 1861, Nova Scotia merchants began to pay more attention to the Mexican market. The first reported shipment of Texas cotton directly from Matamoras arrived in Halifax on the schooner *Oasis* in the spring of 1862. A correspondent to the Halifax *Morning Chronicle* visited the town in its heyday, sailing into the Rio Grande and over the bar to the shantytown port of Boca del Rio, known as Baghdad to gringos. Riding at anchor while lighters carried cotton, food and munitions through the pounding surf were dozens of neutral merchantmen. The Nova Scotia visitor landed at Baghdad, where most of the dingy buildings were devoted to gambling and liquor, and took a wagon to Matamoras where Mexican officials levied contributions on goods crossing into Confederate Texas. Nearby Brownsville, it was noted, had recently been commanded by a Colonel Sweet, a New Brunswicker. The correspondent's tale contained the obligatory descriptions of Mexican corruption, gambling, cockfighting and pretty senoritas.[55]

Incidents stemming from the blockade continued. In 1862 the Yarmouth schooner *Will o' the Wisp* was boarded at the mouth of the Rio Grande by the USS *Montgomery*. The ship was seized after its cargo, owned by Halifax merchants including Salter and Twinning and J.G.A. Creighton and Co., was landed by lighters and the loading of cotton had begun. Rough weather had delayed the schooner's departure for weeks. *Will o' the Wisp* was taken to Key West where a prize court ruled the capture illegal (even though the cargo had included gunpowder and percussion caps in casks marked "fish"). The supercargo, left ashore when the schooner was boarded, returned home on his own. The backers of the voyage had expected to pick up a return cargo for sale in New York and were now out of pocket, so compensation was demanded. The vessel's charter, they explained, had prohibited the captain from entering interdicted ports. In the spring of 1864 the master of the brigantine *Sarah Crowell*, which had put in at Halifax in May, was mistreated at Boston. It was hauled to by a revenue cutter and ordered to drop anchor. Then a shot was fired across the ship's bows. Following a boarding the ship's papers were confiscated; then, on clearing port, it was seized and the captain was subjected to a stiff fine. When the Union authorities opened Beaufort, South

Carolina, to legal trade in 1862, it gave smugglers an excuse for being in the general area. Captain Charles A. Russell of Perryville, Nova Scotia, in charge of the sloop *Racer*, out of Abaco, was nabbed off Bull's Bay, South Carolina, supposedly on a voyage to Beaufort.[56]

By 1863, small sailing craft were less successful in getting into the main blockaded ports of the South. At year's end the U.S. Navy had seized over one thousand vessels since the outbreak of the war.[57] As the blockaders became more numerous and effective, the business of smuggling became more organized and specialized. Fast, low, shallow-draught steamers, many of them purpose built, were the solution. One or two voyages into the beleaguered Confederacy could produce profits; several meant a fortune for owners and captains. London insurance companies, factoring the risks of accident or capture, provided loss coverage for these craft. The chief entrepôts for blockade breakers were Nassau, Bermuda and Havana. Nassau, on New Providence Island, now a busy port for cruise ships and duty-free shopping, was once a rendezvous of buccaneers. Because a steamer leaving Nassau could make Wilmington or Charleston in three days, it became the boom town of the blockade. "All of the business of this place," a Nova Scotia journalist reported in 1864, "is in furnishing goods to the rebels." Steamers crowded the harbour, a small dry dock was in operation and merchants stockpiled goods for the Southern market. The smaller vessels, constantly loading and unloading, plied between the Bahamas and Florida. Nova Scotia West Indiamen were also common sights at New Providence and other Bahamian islands. Bermuda contained similar sights, according to a Halifax reporter. "Long lines of cotton bales lie piled upon the shore," he wrote, "and gangs of stalwart blacks are rolling others from ship to shore." The harbour of St. George's contained sleek, lead-coloured steamers flying the British ensign or the Southern cross. Wilmington was just over 670 miles away. Shopkeepers, tavern owners, labourers and even idlers were greatly interested in Confederate supply; songs such as "Dixie" and "The Bonnie Blue Flag" were heard in the streets; and every home, however humble, had a photograph or memento of the Confederacy. The South, it was reported, was enriching Bermuda, "just as her trade will one day enrich the citizens of these provinces when her ports are open."[58]

WATCHING THE WATERFRONT

The dispatches of the U.S. consul at Halifax, who kept a close watch on the waterfront, reveal that the Nova Scotia capital was of some importance to the Confederate supply effort, if only in a secondary capacity. Joseph Howe later contended that only a few commission agents had speculated in smuggling and that most of the capital invested was actually British or American. Nonetheless, the colonial press and public lent moral support to the Southern cause by surrounding the blockade runners with an aura of glamour and respectability. When the steamer *Ella* left Saint John, for example, it was cheered by a crowd on the wharf. From Halifax, Consul Mortimer Jackson was able to report suspected smugglers to Washington by telegraph, a fact which made the Nova Scotia capital less attractive to large-scale smugglers. In 1861, Jackson reported that a Yarmouth-based vessel had returned from North Carolina to Halifax and then sailed again, ostensibly for Mexico, under an American master familiar with the Southern coast. Suspicious transfers of ownership were also logged. The ship *Consul*, originally from Maine, took out British papers in 1861; and the Delaware-built steamer *France* and its cargo were purchased at Halifax in 1864, probably for a smuggling venture. In 1863, Jackson worried that the Brooklyn, New York, built steamer *Ella*, registered in New Brunswick, was destined for the Nassau-to-Charleston run. The 150-foot sidewheeler, purchased by the Rebel government at Wilmington, was intercepted by a Union gunboat despite lightening its load. In late 1863, Halifax brewer Alexander Keith, Jr. purchased the 503-ton, Quebec paddle-wheeler *Caledonia*. Later certified to be sold at Charleston, the vessel was "lost" in an accident before the registry could be transferred. The consul at Saint John filed a warning after the *Caledonia* took on coal at Shediac, New Brunswick.[59]

The consul also relayed information on British runners and blockade supply vessels which put in at Halifax. The American authorities derived intelligence advantages if smugglers touched at the Nova Scotia port. The British steamer *Sunbeam*, captured by a gunboat off New Inlet in September 1862, had refuelled at Halifax, where loose-tongued sailors in taverns had revealed the vessel's destination.[60] In early 1863 the iron propeller craft *Princess Royal*, carrying a Charleston pilot, left Halifax, allegedly with munitions from Britain. Northern newspapers announced its departure from Nova Scotia and described both the ship, owned by Fraser and Trenholm and Co., and cargo. The Richmond government had planned to employ the *Princess Royal* to ship valuable machinery. Beneath its hatches were two steam engines, six artillery pieces, gunpowder, munitions, drugs, hardware, shoes, clothes and dry goods. It was surrounded near Charleston by watchful Northern cruisers, run aground and captured. Because the engines were intended for ironclads, this was "possibly the war's most important single cargo of contraband." Rebel dispatches were also found on board.[61]

Many of the well-known blockade runners that entered Halifax in 1863 and 1864 were not discharging or picking up cargo, but seeking water, fuel or repairs. The steamer *Cossack*, for example, reached port early in 1864, coaled at Cunard's wharf and then continued on to Liverpool with its valuable freight. The Chebucto Marine Railway, patronized by merchant vessels and the Royal Navy, specialized in refitting hulls damaged by the heavy swells of the North Atlantic. Its superintendent, American engineer H.I. Crandall, had designed bilge and keel blocks to operate in conjunction with the marine railway, which hauled ships out of the water. The Dartmouth firm's principal investors included former U.S. consul Albert Pilsbury, Robert Boak of Boak, Taylor and Co., and John Wylde of Wier and Co. The marine railway repaired blockade runners such as the *Boston* (built at Quebec), *Little Hattie* (ten successful trips) and *City of Petersburg* (sixteen successful trips) in 1863–64.[62]

The steam-powered blockade runner became a familiar sight in Halifax, and to a lesser extent Saint John, about midway through the war. The *Spaulding* had formerly been the blockade runner *Saint John* captured by the Union navy in April 1863. Sold as a prize in Boston, it was purchased by Northern businessmen and fitted out as a blockade runner in New Brunswick, where it was registered to Saint John businessman William Miller M'Lean. The 350-ton sidewheeler had been rebuilt at Savannah in the 1850s. The American consul described it as "an old, dingy-looking craft, slow, [that] sails low in the water." It steamed to Nassau and then slipped into Charleston where it loaded cotton. The *Spaulding*, despite its age, made at least two successful runs before being captured on the Georgia coast in October 1863.[63] The steamers *Flushing* and *Laura Jane* were both registered and outfitted in Saint John for smuggling purposes. The former, a small sidewheeler constructed at Brooklyn, New York, was painted black in Saint John and renamed *NanNan*. Its new owners explained that it was intended for legitimate trade between St. Thomas, Barbados and other island ports. It pierced the naval screen at least eleven times before its capture near the Savannah River in 1864.[64]

In September of 1863, smuggling activity by locals was reported to be a "dead letter" in Halifax, but a few weeks later the business was livelier, supposedly in the hands of "young men, not regular traders in the town."[65] The captains, officers and crew of the steamer fleet tended to be Confederate or British, but a few Maritimers were involved. One New Brunswicker left for Nassau where he caught "cotton fever" and shipped on a smuggler to Wilmington, where he was almost conscripted into the Confederate army. On his next inward voyage his vessel was stopped by the USS *Rhode Island* off Grand Bahama Bank and made a prize of war. The crew was landed on the island of Abaco and the New Brunswicker returned to Nassau, survived a bout of fever and then boarded a schooner to the Maritimes. John McWhinnie of Granville Ferry, Nova Scotia, a mariner since 1855, served on blockade runners for three years. After the war he became a sea captain and commanded the schooner *Leona* and the barques *E.D. Bigelow* and *Glen Afton*.[66]

On occasion, British subjects were captured as passengers on blockade runners. Among those detained in November 1863 were three Royal Artillery officers stationed in Halifax who had booked passage as a lark. Three mariners jailed in 1864 on suspicion of being American citizens serving on blockade runners insisted that they were British subjects: John McKenley argued that he was a Nova Scotian; New Brunswicker William Miller, captured on the Anglo-Confederate Trading Company's *Banshee*, had made the run past the blockading squadron six times; and John Temple, who said he was from Saint John, was held in the New York county jail on suspicion of being a naturalized American. The steel-hulled *Banshee* had been built "from the keel up" as a smuggler. The sidewheeler, which had visited Halifax, was taken in November 1863 near Cape Fear when burning highly visible soft coal.[67]

A number of famous Confederate supply vessels entered Halifax in 1863 prior to the *Chesapeake* affair. In July the *Harriet Pinckney*, on its return voyage to Britain, discharged cargo, including six hundred bales of cotton, at the Wier and Co. wharf. Previously it had carried supplies from London to Bermuda. Built at Middlesborough, Great Britain, in 1862, this screw steamer was owned by the Confederate government. It was not a blockade runner but a consort that specialized in shipping freight between Britain and the West Indies. Cotton formed the bulk of Southern exports to Halifax during the war; the remainder consisted of naval stores such as turpentine, tar and pitch. A correspondent to a New Brunswick journal noted that schooners continued to load blockade goods for the West Indies.[68] The *Acadian Recorder*, although anti-Yankee, labelled local efforts in supplying the South as "mercenary aid to a fratricidal war, which, without outside intervention, would have long ago ended."[69]

Another 1863 arrival was the *General Banks*, formerly the *Scotia*, a swift mailboat on the Dublin to Hollyhead route. According to a New York *Post* correspondent, the sidewheeler was owned by a company of Rebel sympathizers, the chief of them Halifax merchant Benjamin Wier. Another rumour was that the steamer's real owners resided in New York. Built in 1847 for the Chester and Holyhead Railway Co., the iron steamer had been converted into a runner by a Liverpool firm. Seized in Bull's Bay near Charleston in 1862, it was condemned in the Boston prize court and auctioned to Massachusetts interests. The owners sent it to Saint John where the consul concluded that it had been purchased by "Nassau funds."[70] Renamed the *General Banks*, the vessel cleared for Halifax where it took on a valuable cargo, worth $400,000 in the Confederacy, and departed under a new name for a neutral port. It soon returned, officially because of engine trouble, but caution may have been induced by lurking Union warships. The *Post*'s correspondent predicted that "Halifax is destined to be a nest of blockade runners, like Nassau. If the *Scotia* should succeed, two or three more fast steamers will put to sea on the route, and your blockading squadron will have plenty to do." At Halifax the steamer was registered as the *Fannie and Jennie*, under the name of Benjamin Wier and his partner Levi Hart. The certificate of registry indicates that Hart intended to sell the vessel in the West Indies, but this might have been a ruse to deceive the Union authorities. Other sources suggest that Charleston merchant John Fergusson and other Southerners were partners in the *Fannie and Jennie*, which completed at least two smuggling runs.[71]

York Redoubt, Halifax Harbour.

Another celebrated vessel in maintaining the South's lifeline was the *Robert E. Lee*, formerly the *Giraffe*, a Scottish-built steamer capable of twenty knots. The Confederate army transport, flying British colours, arrived in Halifax from Wilmington in October 1863 after only five days. While heading for sea the *Lee* had been fired upon and one crewman seriously wounded. One of the war's most established smugglers, with twenty-one successful trips to its credit, the steamer landed five hundred bales of cotton (worth forty pounds sterling each), tobacco and fifty barrels of turpentine consigned to Wier and Co. Much to Consul Jackson's ire, one reporter described the *Lee* as "a beautiful specimen of naval architecture," flying the Confederacy's "handsome banner." One journal noted that "disciples of Jeff Davis" congregated on "the Confederate wharf," where they gave three cheers for the Rebel flag and "three groans" for Abe Lincoln. The *Lee* also brought special passengers on a secret mission, Confederate sailors assigned to liberate the inmates of a prison camp on an island in Lake Erie. The captain of the Quebec packet at Pictou was offered a handsome reward if he delayed sailing to allow the Confederates to reach Northumberland Strait. The presence of Southerners en route to Canada was an ominous sign, but trouble, when it came, would be much closer to home.[72]

3 The Race Question

The republic, Sir, was begotten in Sin and brought forward in
iniquity, and its end will assuredly be disastrous in the
extreme.

– Martin Wilkins, *Novascotian*, 5 June 1854

Slavery, the great issue of the Civil War, was of more than passing
interest to the racially conscious majority of the Maritime colonies.
Their reactions to the war, and sympathies for either South or North,
revealed much about local race relations. These revelations, sadly,
challenge the traditional perception that Canadians were less racist
than Americans. The black minority of New Brunswick, Nova Scotia
and Prince Edward Island were primarily descendants of American
slaves who had arrived after the Revolutionary War or the War
of 1812. In 1861 many were only one generation away from slavery
and a number of the elderly had been born into bondage. The
seemingly alien ways of this minority, combined with their inferior
socio-economic status, appeared to prove to the white majority, not
just supporters of the Confederacy, that blacks required direction
and control by whites, a type of trustee relationship later personified by white colonialism. So engrained were these prejudices that
they were shared by some of the best educated and socially prominent individuals of colonial society.[1]

WHITE-BLACK RELATIONS IN
THE MARITIMES

Although the French at Louisbourg had had slaves in the eighteenth
century, the first major influx of Afro-Americans into the Maritimes
had come as part of the Loyalist migrations of the 1780s. Three
thousand free black men, women and children landed in Nova Scotia,

many of them ending up in the Shelburne area. Others went to Annapolis and Guysborough. In addition to these recently freed slaves, a number of bonded servants arrived with their white masters. One Loyalist landed at Port Roseway (the original name for Shelburne) with fifty-seven slaves. William Schurman, the founder of Bedeque, P.E.I., brought two slaves, who were liberated in 1790. Lieutenant-Governor Edward Fanning possessed four "negro servants" in the 1780s. The elite founders of Loyalist New Brunwsick owned slaves, and so did clergy, such as Reverend James Scovil of Kingston.[2]

Despite their loyalty to the Crown, black Loyalists were not treated fairly by the authorities or by white refugees. Two-thirds of black families acquired no title to land, and those who did received small holdings more fitting peasants than yeoman farmers. For many, indentured servitude under white farmers and artisans was only one step above slavery. A race riot erupted in Shelburne in 1784 during which white vigilantes expelled the "free negroes" from town, allegedly because of their labour competition. Fifteen hundred black refugees congregated in nearby Birchtown, a bleak, rocky coastal area hemmed in by thick woods.[3]

White racism, economic hardship and official interest in resettlement led to an exodus of Nova Scotia and New Brunswick blacks in 1792. Loyalist emigration was not unique, but the destination of the black migrants was peculiar. Nearly twelve hundred, one-third of the black population of the two colonies, agreed to embark on ships for the new promised land, Sierra Leone, in Africa. Fifteen vessels departed from Halifax early in the year. The expedition not only depopulated Birchtown and other communities, it also removed a number of black leaders, such as David George, a former South Carolina slave turned Baptist preacher who had been assaulted during the Shelburne riot.[4]

Four years later, several hundred Jamaican Maroons, fiercely independent descendants of escaped slaves who had battled white rule, were resettled by the British authorities in Halifax and vicinity. These martial non-Christians were a flamboyant presence in Halifax and they reportedly looked down on the black Loyalists. They worked on the building of the Citadel and hired themselves out to farmers from their base at Preston. The Trelawny Town Maroons also defied Governor Wentworth's attempts to civilize them, practising polygamy and African burial customs. Like many of the Loyalist blacks before them, the Jamaicans were temporary residents. In 1800 a second Sierra Leone settlement expedition was arranged, this time for 550 Maroons whose support from the Jamaican government had ended in 1798.[5]

A third and more long-lasting influx of blacks began in 1813 with the arrival of liberated slaves from the Chesapeake Bay area and Georgia's Cumberland Island. By 1816, two thousand African-American "Refugees" freed by the British military during the War of 1812 had been shipped to Nova Scotia. The New Brunswick government reluctantly agreed to accept five hundred in 1815, settling them on marginal land east of Saint John. In the Timber Colony the minority clustered in and around Saint John and in the rural counties of York, King's and Sunbury. Because the Refugee blacks remained dependent upon government rations, the authorities encouraged no further immigration of this type. In 1820 the Imperial government offered to transport the Nova Scotia and New Brunswick Refugees to Trinidad, but less than one hundred consented.[6]

The two principal settlements for Refugees near Halifax were Preston and Hammonds Plains. Both communities were remote, situated on rocky land and had small farming lots. As was the case near Saint John, blacks tended to drift into town to sell handicrafts and products such as barrels, to seek labouring jobs or to beg. Early journalistic and literary depictions of Nova Scotia blacks stressed their servile status.[7] By 1861, Preston's population was over six hundred; nearly eight hundred resided at Hammonds Plains. A smaller number of blacks were settling along Bedford Basin, forming the basis of the later community of Africville. Several hundred lived within Halifax city limits, and a like number lived in rural Guysborough County. Charlottetown's small black population at this time eked out a modest existence in the Bog, a poor area in the town's west end.[8]

Most Maritime blacks were free by 1815, but conditions did not greatly improve for them. Many settlers in the pioneer era initially were dependant on the "King's Bounty," yet the Refugees, largely for reasons beyond their control, were not able to reach the stage of self-sufficiency. The combination of poor land, official and unofficial discrimination, isolation and inferior educational opportunities condemned a majority of Maritime blacks to the status of a semi-permanent underclass. An 1818 court case, where a Refugee was charged with assault and battery for resisting white hunters who had trespassed on his land in Dartmouth, indicates that the legal system was stacked against persons of colour. In this instance the suit of Fuller, a former slave, was dismissed and he was incarcerated for assault. The court warned that further misbehaviour might result in all Africans being deported back to the United States.[9]

Individuals still managed to rise to prominence within their communities. Reverend Richard Preston, born into slavery in Virginia, was known as the "Black Father" to Afro–Nova Scotian Baptists and helped to build a religious institutional base for the minority community. Following his manumission, Preston had journeyed to the colony seeking his mother, a Refugee. After training under a white preacher, he was named the first black delegate to Nova Scotia's Baptist Association in 1821. He was licensed to preach two years later and by 1833 had organized an African Chapel for Halifax blacks. Preston's United African Baptist Association focused on Refugees and had fifteen congregations by the eve of the Civil War.[10] One African Nova Scotian who died in 1863 owned and operated a schooner, an investment beyond the capabilities of many whites, along the eastern shore. A handful of blacks achieved prominence beyond their own race. One was Nova Scotian William Hall, son of a Refugee, who had served in the American Navy in the 1840s, and then the Royal Navy. Hall was awarded the Victoria Cross for valour during the Indian Mutiny of 1857, ironically helping to subdue unruly natives for white colonial masters. Overall, as Jim Hornby writes of nineteenth-century P.E.I., the region's blacks continued to be "largely invisible" in public affairs.[11]

MARITIME SLAVERY

Contrary to popular belief in the Victorian age, the institution of slavery had existed in the Maritime colonies in the late eighteenth and early nineteenth centuries. Charles Dixon, a Yorkshireman who had settled the Chignecto area in the 1770s, was a follower of the teachings of John Wesley. Yet conversion to Methodism did not prevent him from purchasing the slave Cleveland for sixty pounds. During the Loyalist era, newspapers advertised rewards for runaway black servants, an euphemism for slaves.[12] By the time of the War of 1812, slavery's legal status was on the wane. Either out of guilt or because of community feeling, masters began to pay their slaves wages. Prince Edward Island's Supreme Court confirmed the validity of a slave sale in 1802, but during this period a number of slaves were given their freedom. In 1825 the P.E.I. legislature abolished chattel servitude. Twenty-eight Annapolis County residents, who claimed to possess a total of eighty-two slaves, petitioned the Nova Scotia legislature in 1808 for "recovery of their property in their Negro servants" or "if such property is to be sacrificed to the public good," compensation from the government. The following year a provincial assemblyman proposed a bill to regulate "Negro servants." Under Thomas Ritchie's proposal, slaves would have been freed following a period of indentured labour (four years for bondsmen in their twenties). This regulated gradualism, typical of anti-slavery legislation in the Northern states between 1784 and 1804, had also been adopted by Upper Canada in 1793.[13]

By 1833, the year the British Parliament voted to abolish slavery in the Empire, in the Maritime colonies the institution, although it had involved only a small number of people, was a recent memory. West Indian slavery subsidized Maritime consumers of sugar products and provided a market for ships, lumber products, agriculture and fish, particularly prior to the 1830s when American vessels had been excluded from the British island colonies. Rural Southern slave culture no doubt continued to influence the lives of free blacks of the region. One 1840s Halifax journalist, for example, portrayed a young Afro–Nova Scotian as using the term "massa" while seeking alms. The recently arrived Chesapeake Refugees, it was noted in 1815, reserved the Sabbath for visiting one another, a common practice among slaves in the West Indies and American South.[14]

SLAVERY'S TAINT

The Maritime press occasionally offered encouragement to local blacks, especially when they aspired to self-help and other respectable endeavours, but the minority was constrained by segregation and discrimination. Even "friends of the negro" such as Halifax's *Morning Sun* were smugly racist in their attitudes towards allegedly weaker races. The journal, a lonely supporter of the Union cause in Halifax, was edited by A.J. Ritchie, a Nova Scotian who had learned his trade in Chatham, New Brunswick. The *Sun* observed that "the free nigger is proverbially sassy."[15]

Journalists, clergy and politicians declared that local blacks were protected by British institutions, but further immigration of persons of colour was discouraged. In 1834 the Nova Scotia legislature, fearing that recently freed West Indian slaves would swamp the colony, enacted a law to "Prevent the Clandestine Landing of Liberated Slaves," a discriminatory measure that was struck down by the Imperial government later in the decade. Popular culture was equally uncharitable. Even anti-slavery editors and journalists referred to "niggers" and "darkies," and all newspapers carried examples of Negro humour, often in the form of dialect.[16]

Social segregation was a fact of life. Blacks, as in the Northern states, were shut out of the professions and most non-service, non-labouring jobs. White school children shunned their dark-skinned classmates, a situation that eventually produced segregated schools in Halifax. Waiting rooms on the Halifax-Dartmouth ferry excluded blacks and the city's early conscript nightwatch legally exempted Africans, not out of charity but because white citizens would have refused to serve with or obey them. James McArthur, a "sable brother" ordained as a Congregational missionary at Sheffield, New Brunswick, in 1858, was prevented from patronizing the dining room on a riverboat from Saint John. In 1862 an educated black Jamaican visiting Halifax was turned away from hotels and respectable boarding houses because of his colour. In 1865 a black property owner and Freemason was refused admission to the speaker's gallery of the Nova Scotia legislature, until the members intervened.[17]

Educated, "respectable" blacks were more likely to protest and elicit white sympathy, but their lower-class counterparts encountered discriminatory attitudes and treatment on a regular basis. Both editor J.B. Cooper of Charlottetown's *Monitor* and one of his correspondents in 1862 repeated the widely held folk belief that blacks, free or slave, gave off an offensive odour. These attitudes would persist into the twentieth century, even amongst the educated. One commentator explained that "negrophobia" was characteristic of the "meanest classes in the Northern states and the mean whites of the South," but in Nova Scotia well-educated, wealthy colonists were just, if not more, as mean-spirited.[18]

As in the United States "north of slavery," custom often was a more formidable barrier than law in the Maritimes. Blacks were excluded from jury duty and public office, but minority voters in the Halifax area formed organizations in the 1840s associated with the Tories and Reformers.[19] The militia was another public institution where racial discrimination was evident. It seems that where blacks were enrolled in the militia, as in 1790s Halifax or Digby County, or mid-nineteenth-century York County, New Brunswick, they formed separate companies. During a general muster of citizen soldiers in Saint John's south end in 1864, blacks who attempted to join white companies were turned away and forced to form their own "awkward squad." The militia in nearby Lancaster parish included an "African" company.[20]

The best-known African military unit in the Maritimes in the early 1860s was Halifax's Victoria Rifles. In October of 1861 these enthusiastic volunteers encountered racial discrimination at a provincial rifle match. A sergeant of the elite Chebucto Greys, whose quartermaster was Alexander Keith, Jr. and whose honourary members included M.B. Almon, Benjamin Wier and J.W. Ritchie (all strong supporters of the Confederacy), spoke rudely to members of the Rifles. The white commander of the Victoria Rifles protested, and resigned when a court martial refused to find fault. White volunteer militiamen in Nova Scotia, like most white soldiers in the Union armies, did not want to march, drill or fight alongside blacks. As an elite Haligonian later observed of the Rifles: "The other companies would not allow them to come near them, to mingle with them, in the event of any united movement rendering it desirable to equalize the companies – they must be kept at a distance." Racism prevented the Victoria Rifles from becoming part of the Halifax Volunteer Battalion, much like it kept Canadian blacks from joining the army during World War I.[21]

The moral, intellectual and biological inferiority of blacks was taken for granted by most white colonists in the 1860s. However sympathetic to their plight, whites tended to believe that blacks were a permanent pauper class. Degradation was a common theme; in the racial pecking order the decendents of slaves were regarded as beneath the Mi'kmaq and the Maliseet. They were also associated with crime – the press always noted the racial status of minority offenders. The Victorian clergyman who authored a history of Yarmouth described descendants of slaves in that county as utterly destitute and dependent upon charity. One township inhabited by blacks, according to Reverend J.R. Campbell, "had not been ornamental to the county, and scarcely useful." A resident of Liverpool who resented the behaviour of some local blacks cautioned advocates of emancipation to look at the ex-slaves in Nova Scotia, who in his estimation were inferior to whites. An article in the Halifax *Bullfrog*, an anti-Confederation sheet published in 1865, argued that the role of blacks as a cause of the Civil War was ironic, given that whites had nothing but "profound contempt" for these people "who have no country and no history."[22] Charles Hallock, a renegade Yankee journalist who supported the Confederacy, described Halifax blacks as indolent and Preston and Hammonds Plains as "odorous."[23] Edward Willis's Saint John *Morning News* was equally contemptuous of the descendants of the War of 1812 Refugees:

These people never came to any good in Halifax. Uninured to the hardships of civilized life, or rather to the responsibilities of making a living for themselves, they were unable to keep pace with the drag put upon their energies, and so they dwindled away to a miserable, effete population in the localities provided for them, and where their descendants, not much better off without them, are at this day, not far from Halifax.[24]

One thing is clear: Maritimers shared assumptions about the so-called "lesser races" that differed from the views of Southern slaveowners only by degree. T.C. Haliburton's *Rule and Misrule of the English in America* (1851) examined American history and politics, commented on the constitution and society, yet made no mention of slavery, perhaps taking it as a given. Haliburton, a giant of early Canadian literature, also reflected contemporary North American racist caricatures in his humourous writings, which were a favourite of Abraham Lincoln and tens of thousands of fans on both sides of the Atlantic after 1835. In London during the Civil War, Haliburton was on the organizing committee of the Southern Independence Association, dedicated to recognition of the Confederacy by Britain, the gradual extinction of slavery and the "preservation of property."[25]

Former Halifax resident Hugo Reid, a cultured Englishman, in his 1861 *Sketches in North America*, indicated that pseudo-scientific European racism, influenced by Darwin's theories about survival of the fittest, was finding advocates in British North America. Reid, who had served as principal of Dalhousie College in the 1850s, wrote that although Halifax contained a few polite and gentlemanly "coloured" men, others were neither pleasant nor mild in disposition and appeared to possess more savage features. The forbidding appearance of the latter, according to Reid, suggested that Southern slaveholders and their families awaited a terrible fate.[26] Reid also employed phrenological observation – the characterization of personality and behaviour according to the size and shape of the head – in his discussion of race:

The small, contracted forehead, generally found in the negro race, appears to indicate but moderate intelligence, and though some have evinced considerable mental capacity, such cases are rare and there can be little doubt of the great natural inferiority of the negro to the white race. This seems to be the general conviction of the most intelligent of those friends of the negro in North America who have had the best opportunities of judging his powers.[27]

Other traits of supposedly inferior peoples, whether Irish, French-Canadian or African, were cheerfulness and "earthiness." Describing black passengers on the Dartmouth ferry travelling to Halifax to sell berries, handicrafts and their labour, Reid resorted to another racial stereotype: "They seem a light-hearted and cheerful people, always laughing and making merry." Such were the racial views of one of the best-educated and most cosmopolitan Haligonians of the late 1850s.[28]

VIEWS OF AMERICAN SLAVERY

Despite widespread evidence of racial prejudice among all classes, the Maritime colonies prided themselves on being free societies. This was no contradiction by the standards of the day. Abolitionism was never organizationally vibrant, but individuals, usually Protestant ministers and evangelical laypersons, spoke and wrote against slavery. The rise of anti-Northern feeling after the battle of First Bull Run meant that Maritime critics of American slavery often were voices in the wilderness. Enemies of bondage paid tribute to Britain's efforts at enlarging freedom and tolerated American abolitionists despite their extremism. The Charlottetown *Examiner* described slavery as "a bane wherever it exists."[29]

The Baptist *Christian Messenger* declared that the "black spot of slavery casts a gloom over the meteor flag of the neighbouring republic."[30] The Free Will Baptist *Religious Intelligencer* regularly reprinted anti-slavery items and news.[31] In the opinion of the Saint John *Globe*, slavery had "inflicted untold miseries upon millions." Prior to the Civil War the "chivalrous" Southern slaveowner had had few defenders in the British colonies. "It is impossible for the haughty, labour-despising slaveholder," wrote the Halifax *Citizen*, "to respect the industrious, hard-working men of these British Provinces." According to historian W.S. MacNutt, the American Fugitive Slave Act shocked the puritanical morals of Protestant New Brunswickers in the 1850s. Stories of fugitive slaves who attempted to reach the safety of Canada West evoked great interest and sympathy. The case of John Anderson, who killed a white man in order to effect his escape to Canada, and whose extradition was demanded by the United States, received wide press coverage in the Maritimes. Yankee journals such as the *Maine Farmer*, which circulated in the colonies, helped to spread the anti-slavery message.[32]

A number of fugitives arrived in Nova Scotia from Massachusetts through the aid of Yankee abolitionists, although to speak of an underground railroad into the region is misleading. As many or more blacks left the Maritimes as arrived there prior to the Civil War. One of the freedom seekers was Jesse Coleman, who fled Baltimore and settled in Halifax in 1839 where he became a founder and preacher at the Zion Methodist Church. One of Saint John's most successful black residents was Robert J. Patterson, born a slave at Richmond, Virginia. He fled first to New York City by ship in the 1840s and worked for several years in Boston. Fearing bounty hunters after the passage of a new Fugitive Slave Act in the early

1850s, Patterson travelled to New Brunswick where he established a viable catering business.[33] Haliburton's fictional character Scippy had been "inveigled away by the mate of a Boston vessel that was loading at his master's estate." Patterson and other fugitives, in contrast, were not passive emigrants but active participants in planning and carrying out their escapes. According to Sam Slick, Scippy, although free, was unhappy because of Nova Scotia's severe climate, hard labour and the lack of the plantation's "community of interests."[34]

One of the few fugitive slave narratives with Nova Scotia connections is John William Robertson's "The Book of the Bible Against Slavery," a pamphlet probably printed in Halifax in the 1850s. The document, in rough English, begins with a religious argument against slavery and then proceeds to recount the author's escape from bondage in the Chesapeake. The narrator lived with his master in Virginia until 1852 when his "spirits became brightened by God." Proceeding to the coast, Robertson stole a boat and rowed and drifted to a small town in Maryland where he posed as a free sailor. Hired on an oysterman, he eventually arrived in Baltimore where he was questioned by a constable in search of a fellow fugitive. The narrator confidently responded that he had been manumitted at twenty-one and refused to exhibit his "freedom papers" unless taken before the mayor. The bluff worked. Falling in with a second captain, Robertson shipped out for the port of Philadelphia. There he jumped ship to search for another "soft hearted captain" to carry him further north. The resourceful runaway's final job was as a steward on a schooner. Taking his leave at Hadford, Massachusetts, Robertson went to Boston where acquaintances assured that he was beyond the reach of bounty hunters. Yet Robertson pressed on, arriving in Halifax on the vessel *Sir John Harvey*. In Nova Scotia he worked as the servant of an officer in the garrison, who taught him to read and write (95 percent of American slaves were illiterate c. 1861).[35]

The region's other surviving slave narrative was written by, or more accurately, for Thomas H. Jones, born in bondage near Wilmington, North Carolina, in 1806.[36] Jones, like Robertson, had aspired to freedom as a result of religious conversion and the patient and often risky acquisition of literacy. Jones's *Experience* recalled his happy early childhood with his parents, from whom he was painfully parted. At nine years of age he was sold to a planter and storekeeper named Jones. Working first as a domestic and cook, Thomas graduated to working in the master's store, where the presence of a youthful white clerk first turned his thoughts to learning. At considerable personal risk, and despite repeated beatings, he learned the alphabet and basic reading comprehension. Jones also was attracted to "coloured" Methodist prayer meetings and services. Despite his master's wishes, he attended meetings whenever possible and eventually became a member. In his twenties he "married" Lucilla Smith, who bore him three children. When Lucilla's mistress moved to another locale, the family was torn apart. Jones found a new spouse, Mary R. Moore, and a new mission. By selling his labour in off hours over a period of years, he was able to purchase his wife's manumission – a tremendous achievement given the rising price of slaves in the 1840s – and a small cabin.[37]

Fearing that his family would be reenslaved, Jones, himself still a slave, sent his wife and children on to Brooklyn, New York. Plotting his own escape, he corresponded regularly in plain, earnest prose. Bribing a ship's steward, Jones stowed away on a vessel bound for New York City where he had a joyous reunion with his family. He lectured in Protestant churches in New York and New England and was befriended by abolitionist clergymen.[38] Threatened by bounty hunters in the early 1850s, Jones proceeded to safe British territory, using Saint John as the base of his anti-slavery activities. He planned to travel to England on a speaking and fundraising tour but appears to have confined his anti-slavery activities to Nova Scotia and New Brunswick. Writing Reverend Daniel Foster, a Garrisonian abolitionist, in 1851, he described Saint John as "full of true, warm generous Christians" who had received the fugitive "in the spirit of brotherhood."[39] Two years later Jones returned to Massachussetts to rejoin his family and further the abolitionist cause. His poor treatment by the crew of the steamship *Eastern City* on the return voyage made headlines.[40]

Anti-slavery discussions in the Maritimes were usually refracted through an Imperial lense. Before, during and after the Civil War, blacks in Saint John and Halifax gathered to celebrate Emancipation Day, 3 August, the anniversary of the abolition of slavery in the British Empire. The Charitable African Society of Halifax marked the day in 1846 with a parade and picnic and a loyal address to the governor that praised Nova Scotia, "where all are free to enjoy equal rights." That year Richard Preston, who had heard the great British abolitionist orators such as Wilberforce, founded an abolition society whose membership appears to have been confined to blacks.[41] Robert Patterson helped organize an emancipation society in Saint John in the 1850s. Publicizing the plight of American slaves became part of its program. In 1863, local blacks celebrated 3 August with a picnic, a hotel banquet and an evening of speeches and toasts, "almost all the most industrious and respectable of the coloured people being present." Prominent white politicians addressed the boisterous assembly, congratulating them for their "improvement." Yet Irish Catholic journalist Timothy Warren Anglin, with an eye perhaps to the Irish situation, insisted on reminding the audience that "there were millions of white men in Europe in worse bondage than that of the slavery of the South." Significantly, the gathering also wished success for Union arms, suggesting that for colonial blacks with roots in the South, like refugee slaves in Canada West, the American Civil War was important to the future of their own communities and the fortunes of blacks in general.[42]

THE CHURCHES AND SLAVERY

Religious concerns, not attachment to human rights, continued to motivate most anti-slavery commentary. The Nova Scotia *Presbyterian Witness*, commenting on the outbreak of the Civil War, explained that the price of liberty was blood and called on that price to be paid. One journalist writing in 1864 theorized that Pictou County's sympathy with the Northern cause was attributable to the predominance of Presbyterianism, a denomination which, in Nova Scotia, shared "great hatred" towards slavery.[43] The *Witness* was shocked at the ease with which Southern divines found scriptural authority for the peculiar institution. The Free Will or Christian Baptists, a presence in New Brunswick, forbade slave-owning communicants in the United States.[44] The Halifax *Sun* mocked the Confederate delusion that bondage was the natural condition of the African, declaring the institution a sin against God and humanity. William Sommerville, a Reformed Presbyterian minister at Cornwallis, Nova Scotia, produced a pamphlet, "Southern Slavery Not Founded on Scriptural Warrant," which argued that modern slavery was far worse than the benign system of the ancient Hebrews.[45] The *Eastern Chronicle* similarly attacked the religious hypocrisy of slaveholders and their supporters amidst the flood of praise for Confederate leader Stonewall Jackson. The British and colonial press gushed over the late general's Christian qualities, but the Pictou journal doubted that Christianity had "influenced a man who would lay down his life for a war to perpetuate and extend negro slavery." Another correspondent denounced the tendency to compare the South's military genius to that grim Christian warrior, Oliver Cromwell. The latter had fought for freedom; Jackson was simply a "rebel, slaveholding, slavery defending traitor."[46]

Maritime Protestants – at least some of them – employed the issue of the Civil War to preach racial equality. Wesleyan Methodist

Reverend J.R. Narraway confessed to his Saint John audience that he was "a black Republican, and an admirer of William Seward and Lincoln." These were radical and unpopular statements in 1862. John Brewster, a Wesleyan divine who had been posted to all four Atlantic colonies, also held advanced views on the war. Such opinions, the *Wesleyan* noted, lost the Englishman many friends. The secretary of the Charlottetown YMCA, in his annual report for 1862, asked members to pray "for their dark-skinned compatriots" and that God "take away their yoke, never to be imposed again." The local Evangelical Alliance, in one of its prayer meetings in 1864, asked for the end of hostilities and the abolition of slavery. T.M. Lewis of Yarmouth argued that a true British subject could only abhor the institution of slavery.[47]

Reverend William Wilson of Woodstock, preaching in aid of the distressed factory operatives of Lancashire, declared, in Calvinist fashion, that British cotton-mill owners and workers now had to suffer for having benefited from slave labour. Reverend Professor Hensley, of the Anglican King's College in Windsor, lectured that slavery "retarded and sometimes destroyed civilization."[48] A former student of Reverend E.A. Crawley, president of Acadia College in the 1850s, recalled that he often was "grandly eloquent in his denunciations of the United States for holding so many millions in bondage." Reverend John Mockett Cramp, the English Baptist who also served as president of Acadia, was more active in temperance work and anti-Catholic propaganda, but was proud to have shaken the hand of Abraham Lincoln, who had signed the Emancipation Proclamation. Editor of the *Abstainer* and a leader of the international Sons of Temperance, Cramp met the president as part of a temperance delegation, one of whom reported that the president was a big fan of "Sam Slick." The minister of Halifax's Grafton Street Chapel preached in 1865 that the war was not pointless if it succeeded in lifting the chains of slavery.[49]

Given the pervasive racism of colonial society, individuals who opposed slavery on principle were not advocating the social equality of the races. In fact, many disliked slavery and blacks at the same time. The abolitionist movement, historians agree, did little to ameliorate conditions for British North American blacks.[50] In the Maritimes, devotion to social hierarchy was strong and inhibited racial tolerance. The region had no "movement" and only the most conservative abolitionist stances were respected. Even sympathetic opinion was tinged with racial paternalism. Charlottetown's *Ross's Weekly*, a supporter of emancipation, reasoned in 1861 that American slavery could be ended only in stages, because bondsmen, having been kept in a state of ignorance and brutality, were "not capable of providing for the ordinary wants of human nature." They would perish miserably if freed at once, "and while perishing would inflict ruin upon the country." Pictou journalist S.H. Holmes expressed similar opinions. The abolitionist Halifax *Sun* stated that blacks, whether free or enslaved, were "naturally lazy" but deserved freedom all the same.[51]

Nova Scotian T. Knight published a pamphlet in 1864 which argued that complete emancipation was an "impracticability" because Southern slaves were thriftless, ignorant and numerous. Instead he advocated British mediation to end the war and the passing of humane laws to soften slavery's harshest edges. Marriages could be legitimized and slave families kept intact. Punishments should be limited and education provided until the slaves were prepared to accept the obligations of freedom. Sam Slick offered the same advice to his Bluenose narrator in the 1830s: reform that would make bondage "nothin' more than sarvitude in name, and something quite good in fact." Similar opinions were recorded by Dr. Daniel McNeil Parker of Halifax in notes made during his American tour of 1861. To Knight and other moderate or theoretical abolitionists, the ultra-anti-slavery activists of the North were unrealistic fanatics. Another school of thought was more cold-blooded, interpreting slavery not as degradation of a vulnerable minority but a threat to free, white labour. If emancipated slaves failed to adjust to freedom, according to this reasoning, it was only the working out of racial destiny.[52]

ABOLITIONISM EXAMINED

Maritime views of the American abolition movement, like every other aspect of the Civil War and its causes, were complex. Most commentators were far from flattering in their assessments of radical emancipationists and "black Republicans." Despite the pro-Northern utterances of a few liberal clergymen, most evangelical clergy in the region were not ardent abolitionists and were far more concerned with temperance and church politics.[53] Nathaniel Gunnison, a Universalist minister from New Hampshire who would be at the centre of the *Chesapeake* affair, thought that the ministers of Halifax were about "fifty years behind the clergy of New England."[54] Of the opinions of Catholic clerics we can only guess, but the American Roman Catholic hierarchy was hostile towards abolitionists, many of whom were either ultra-Protestants or anticlericalists. Thomas L. Connolly, Archbishop of Halifax, warmly sympathized with the Confederacy and mocked abolitionists such as Wendell Phillips as one of the peculiarities of "Yankeeland," to be ranked with P.T. Barnum.[55] One Nova Scotia journalist lambasted Yankee "war preachers" for their ferocity in advocating the slaughter of their fellow Christians. T.W. Anglin's *Freeman* blamed Phillips, William Lloyd Garrison and other activists for driving the South into rebellion. A native of Nova Scotia's south shore denounced the famous New England preacher Henry Ward Beecher "and his crowd of negro worshippers."[56]

After witnessing the attack on Fort Sumter, Dr. McNeil Parker and William Stairs returned to New York where they attended an evening service in Beecher's Brooklyn Tabernacle. In the words of Parker's son, the Nova Scotians were disgusted by "the mountebank preacher and savage abolitionist," who took up a collection to buy revolvers with which to kill Southerners. The sermon was "a brutal, blood thirsty, blasphemous tirade against the Confederacy, in which the spirit of the evil one himself would appear to have usurped the pulpit."[57] The *Christian Messenger* chastised the abolitionists for arrogantly declaring that God was on their side, an assumption that flew in the face of traditional Calvinism. One journal remarked that abolitionist Gerrit Smith had once been in a madhouse. The *Provincial Wesleyan* disapproved of the violence of the abolitionist onslaught on occupied Maryland, Kentucky and Tennessee. Editors, reporters and correspondents more openly hostile to the North predicted that once the blacks of the South became the total responsibility of the Northern government, the racial hypocrisy of Yankees and Westerners would be exposed to the world.[58] A New Brunswicker writing from Boston condemned "the nigger-worshipping Excellency Gov. John Albion Andrew" and claimed that Massachusetts "is coloured, root, stock and branch. The people in the rural districts in this vicinity have a particular divinity, St. Sambo, whom they worship, but exclude from their pews." Hugo Reid wrote in 1861 that few of his Bluenose acquaintances who had visited the South or the West Indies supported the "abolition party." Some endorsed Southern extremism, most deplored slavery in principle but doubted the success of emancipation "and saw no prospect of freedom for the slaves without some fearful convulsion."[59]

Many middle-class British North Americans were stirred by the publication in the early 1850s of Harriet Beecher Stowe's sentimental and fictional *Uncle Tom's Cabin*. First serialized in newspapers, the work became an international bestseller. In 1863 a visiting clergyman representing the English Emancipation Society addressed a Congregational assembly in Saint John and praised Beecher Stowe's novel for aiding the freedom movement. Yet a number of Maritime journals remained unimpressed by the book. The Charlottetown *Islander* found the story excessively romantic and not typical of the slavery experience. A New Brunswick reviewer, although no fan of slavery, felt little sympathy for "colonial negroes" who were deficient in "morality, intelligence and cleanliness." During the Civil War a number of Nova Scotia journals referred to Beecher Stowe as a fanatic, but her popular tale was a favourite dramatic presentation of touring companies.[60]

More sensational in its impact was the raid on the U.S. arsenal at Harper's Ferry in 1859 by the fanatical abolitionist John Brown. A veteran of guerrilla war in Kansas who was financed by Northern abolitionists, Brown led a party of whites and blacks, including Canadian residents, in an attack that killed several citizens in the Virginia hamlet and threw the South into a panic. Harper's Ferry was less than sixty miles from Washington, where the streets were patrolled in anticipation of an uprising by blacks. The *New Brunswick Reporter* announced that "an old crazy gentleman named Brown" had fomented a slave insurrection and that white Southerners were taking the threat seriously. Editor James Hogg predicted that the failed raid was the beginnings of emancipation. He also warned of the bloodthirstiness of Virginia's chivalry.[61]

Three of Brown's backers fled to Canada, and one of his wounded men, who later died, was Stewart Taylor of Canada West, facts that caused anti-British resentment in the South. Prior to the execution of Brown and his assistants, a large public meeting was convened in Montreal, but sympathies for the would-be liberator were muted because of his aggressive violence. According to Hugo Reid, Brown had plotted bloody revolution and had stirred Southern patriotism and militarism to the brink of rebellion. George Coles, a leading P.E.I. Liberal, and a Southern sympathizer in the 1860s, later concluded that Brown was guilty of rebellion and murder and deserved to die.[62]

Brown's trial and execution excited great curiosity in British North America, where journalists were impressed by his resolve and dignity in his final hours. Saint John's *Morning News* judged his crimes to be of great magnitude. Ten raiders had been killed at Harper's Ferry, and six would join Brown at the gallows. The Fredericton *Headquarters* reported: "The old man died as firm as a rock." A correspondent to Nova Scotia's Baptist journal described Brown's pivotal role in American history. New England did not regard him as an unblemished martyr, given his excesses in Kansas, but Brown had evoked the compassion of thousands in the North. When the war clouds gathered in 1861, a writer to the Yarmouth *Tribune* declared that John Brown was speaking from the grave, "calling for vengeance on oppression and freedom to the oppressed."[63]

In the wake of the trial and execution of the Harper's Ferry raiders, a strange story arose in the bordertown of Woodstock, New Brunswick. Local blacks and their white supporters were convinced that George L. Raymond had taken a black youth, William Hoyt, to Virginia where he had been sold into slavery. Public meetings and petitions requested that the attorney general investigate. Hoyt had accompanied Raymond and his son on a trip to Maine, Massachusetts and Virginia. Arriving in Richmond at the height of the South's panic over slave uprisings, Raymond was told to report with his black travelling companion to the mayor. Raymond advised Hoyt that it would cause less difficulty if he pretended to be Raymond's slave. With Southern paranoia rampant, all strangers had to prove to the authorities that they did not plan on tampering with slavery. Hoyt spent four days in jail until he confessed that he was a free British subject. He was sent, under confinement, back to Boston by steamer, accompanied by the Raymonds, with whom he later parted company. At New York City, Hoyt fell in with another black and together the two shipped out on a merchant vessel, spending the next few months visiting ports on both sides of the Atlantic. Months later, when his Woodstock compatriots feared that he was in bondage in Virginia, Hoyt was sighted in Boston in the company of a well-known crimp, a boarding-house keeper who illegally recruited seafaring labour.[64]

RATIONALIZATIONS FOR SLAVERY

By 1861, Maritimers were not unfamiliar with pro-slavery opinions, and as the Civil War progressed many who opposed the institution in theory began to make excuses for it in practice. Maritimers had prospered indirectly from slavery and there were rumours that certain Nova Scotians derived income from American cotton plantations. By 1860, white Southerners had developed an articulate response to abolitionist critiques. Slavery, once regarded as a "necessary evil," was now defended as a "positive good." In a letter from Maryland in 1861, a Baptist told the *Christian Messenger* that slavery had to be tolerated for climatic and racial reasons and warned that if large numbers of slaves managed to escape to British territory, then racial attitudes in the colonies would harden. A letter from Charlotte, North Carolina, to another Nova Scotia newspaper stated that Southern whites were no worse than Northerners or

British subjects; indeed they had inherited slavery as part of their British ancestry. Southern refugees and visitors promoted these arguments in the Maritime press during the war. A Georgia subscriber to a Woodstock journal criticized it for daring to suggest that blacks deserved equality with whites.[65] A "Southerner" attacked a Halifax newspaper in 1864 for not comparing plantation slaves to the labouring poor of all nations:

It is the position in which it has pleased Divine Providence to place the poor and feeble in all ages, and almost all countries of which he has recognized and established of which as a form of social life, and the regulation of which, if duly regarded, secure to the slave all the benefits, physical, moral and religious, which the labouring poor can ever hope to command.[66]

Not all pro-slavery pronouncements came from Southern visitors or correspondents. Donald Currie, in response to Reverend John Brewster, lectured the Charlottetown YMCA and Literary Institute that the Confederacy's slaves were better off than blacks in the free states. M.S. Hall, a New Brunswicker who had lived in the South, went so far as to argue that the slaves were comfortable, happy and loyal and that "he had never known a slave to be illtreated except when he deserved it." The pro-Confederacy *Novascotian* was convinced in 1864 that Southern blacks were "the happiest labouring class on the face of the earth."[67]

These opinions did not go unchallenged. The correspondent "Africanus" lampooned the argument that Nova Scotia should promote itself as a hospitable tourist destination for Southern gentlemen and their families. The arrival of large numbers of these "secesh" gentleman, Africanus reasoned, would necessitate the passing of a provincial Fugitive Slave Act in order to secure the human property of the distinguished visitors. Enterprising merchants would import, for the use of Southern bloods, "bowie knives, daggers, pistols, and those innocent weapons which are in daily use in the South: bales of feathers and barrels of tar."[68]

SLAVERY AND THE CIVIL WAR

As colonial public opinion shifted away from the North in 1861, the initial consensus that slavery was the cause of the war eroded. But a minority of anti-slavery commentators stuck to their guns. The Halifax *Morning Sun* blamed the crisis on the sheer greed of slave owners. T.M. Lewis of Yarmouth, in a public lecture, singled out "God-dishonouring slavery" and explained that Southerners had plotted against the U.S. Constitution for thirty years. The editor of the Liverpool *Transcript*, born a Maine Yankee, wrote that every slaveholder was "sleeping on a volcano," so unjust was the Confederate cause. The Saint John *Telegraph*, the *Carleton Sentinel* and the Fredericton *Headquarters* all agreed that slavery was the fundamental cause of the rebellion. The *Globe*, reviewing an American publication on the African race in North America, concluded that the institution had survived because it had enriched individuals and gratified "the innate love of power." The *Provincial Wesleyan* of Nova Scotia rejoiced in the "unholy and profane" South being visited by divine retribution but reminded readers that Northern capitalists were equally culpable in sustaining the sin of human bondage.[69]

The argument that the North, through unsavoury compromises such as the Fugitive Slave Act, had to share in the blame was attractive to those who distrusted Yankee war aims. Even pro-Northern spokespersons such as Reverend T.B. Smith and Reverend J.R. Narraway, who lectured to the Saint John public on the war in 1862, questioned the constitutional right of the Union government to abolish slavery unilaterally. Lincoln's initial inaction on slavery, his refusal to give the war a higher moral purpose, dismayed fence sitters in the British colonies. The *Wesleyan* called Lincoln's 1861 inaugural address a pro-slavery speech. Other critics pointed out that the Union government was in effect fighting to preserve slavery where it existed. John Charles Fremont, Union commander of the Western Department in 1861, embarrassed Lincoln by declaring martial law in Missouri and stating that all slaves owned by rebels were now free. When the president countermanded this policy, cynicism in British North America reached new levels. The Halifax *Reporter* stated that the North's toleration of slavery in 1861 was earning it "the scorn of the civilized world."[70]

Enemies of slavery were heartened by one advance in 1862, the abolition of slavery in the District of Columbia. For the *Reporter* this indicated that the Lincoln administration had accepted the inevitability of emancipation and had committed itself to nothing less than total victory. Yet the *Reporter*, no advocate of egalitarianism, also explained that "Englishmen have never mixed freely with inferior races," implying that free blacks could expect little improvement in their situation.[71] As the former principal of Dalhousie College wrote in 1861, Northern whites exhibited "repulsion" towards blacks and the situation in Canada was no different. In the British colonies slavery was a thing of the past, but blacks were "despised and shunned – treated as an inferior race – mortified, degraded and deprived of many opportunities of evincing their capabilities and improving their situation."[72] The Halifax *Express*, a Conservative, pro-Southern organ, declared that the Northern black was "a sort of human leper." Repeating a common Victorian social theory, this journal reasoned that a weaker race could not exist in a state of equality with a superior one. The nearly four million slaves of the South, if left to their own devices, would begin to vanish, like the North American Indians. The anti-draft riots of the summer of 1863, when New York City mobs assaulted and murdered blacks in the streets as a protest against conscription, seemed a portent of a coming race war. Racial animosities were also visible in Boston, Philadelphia, St. Louis and other "free" cities.[73]

A string of Confederate victories and Union blunders in 1862, combined with the appeal of a romantic vision of a stable, chivalrous plantation society in the South, made many Maritimers more and more tolerant of slavery. By the time of Lincoln's Emancipation Proclamation, anti-Northern feelings in the British colonies were quite strong. The proclamation, issued after the battle of Antietam, where Union forces halted a Confederate incursion, stated that as of 1 January 1863 all slaves found in enemy territory would be considered free. British and colonial journalists pounced on the inconsistency of this policy. What about slaves in Union-controlled territories? How could the Union exercise authority over the condition of blacks behind enemy lines? The Halifax *Morning Journal* declared that Honest Abe would never rise "above the scope of a mere, pettifogging third-rate country lawyer."[74] The *Acadian Recorder*, recalling that Lincoln recently had proposed shipping American blacks to Central America, doubted his sincerity. The *Novascotian* reminded readers that Washington had not gone to war to liberate the slaves. The Halifax *Reporter* predicted that the proclamation "will not create any additional sympathy for the North abroad."[75] James Hogg of the *New Brunswick Reporter* deemed the policy useless, motivated not by morality but military expediency. To the *Christian Messenger* the proclamation was "a piece of sheer humbug."[76]

One fear was that Lincoln's proclamation would unleash a race war far worse than the Indian Mutiny. The *Provincial Wesleyan* concluded that "it is the bosom of enfeebled age, and guileless infancy, of the wife and mother, that is to receive the mortal blow." The Halifax *Evening Express* feared that slave uprisings would convert a fair region into "a howling wilderness." Another Nova Scotia journal predicted "savagery, murder, lust and rapine." Pictou's *Colonial*

Standard worried not for slaveholders but for rebellious slaves who would be annihilated in senseless insurrection.[77] Nova Scotia's Anglican publication, the *Church Record*, condemned the North's "sham philosophy"; breaking the bond between master and slave, it warned, would subject blacks to far greater hardship. Despite this torrent of abuse, the policy did have local supporters, including New Brunswick's *Colonial Presbyterian* and *Carleton Sentinel*, P.E.I.'s *Ross's Weekly* and Nova Scotia's *Morning Sun*.[78]

Maritime critics of the North delighted in listing the many faults of the "contrabands," or liberated slaves, and the inadequacies of "coloured" troops in Union service. These stereotypes were shared by many white Northerners, particularly in the Democratic camp. The *British Colonist* contrasted the white freeman of the South with the "ignorant European immigrant" and the "half-savage negro" soldiers of the North.[79] Halifax's *Morning Journal* reported caustically that white occupation soldiers had become the servants of the blacks at Beaufort, South Carolina. The *Novascotian* described the New Orleans area in 1864, where thousands of "contrabands" had perished from disease and starvation since Federal occupation. This supposedly proved that the African was unfit for self-government: "Physiology proves that he is utterly ungovernable by men of his own race." Following the Union failure to take Richmond in 1864, one Nova Scotia journalist opined that only white soldiers could be relied upon "in crises that demand the utmost bravery and good conduct."[80]

Bluenoses who took part in the war left behind a mixed record of attitudes towards contrabands and black soldiers (the latter eventually constituted one-tenth of the Union armies). A combat-weary Haligonian whose regiment had been reduced to 350 men rejected immediate emancipation as a war aim: "I have seen enough of slavery to know that the slaves are not so badly off. The idea of setting them free at once is wrong, for they don't know how to take care of themselves." New Brunswicker Patrick O'Kane, a Union soldier, in a 1862 letter, expressed little enthusiasm for fighting to end slavery: "I wish to God this war was conducted for 'the Union as it was and the Constitution as it is.' I would be willing to lose my life for these principles, but the continual niger, niger (sic)."[81]

Others were more charitable. Sarah Emma Edmonds of New Brunswick, author of *Nurse and Spy in the Union Army*, argued that "contrabands" of both sexes were rational beings and faithful to the Union. Although her bestselling book was more patriotic in tone than abolitionist, Edmonds welcomed the miltary contribution of blacks and pitied "the poor, down-trodden descendants of Africa."[82]

C.W. Hall, an Islander serving with a Massachusetts regiment that had been stationed in New Bern, North Carolina, offered a positive, if somewhat patronizing assessment of black military ability:

The negro is fast proving to mankind his ability to fight; regiments of blacks are forming all along the shores of the Atlantic and the Gulf. Two were filled up at New Bern before we left, and finer men, physically, I never saw. Quick to comprehend an order, swift to obey, of undaunted courage and great strength and endurance, these "Sepoys" of the New World will, in all human probability, form the main reliance of our army in the great future before us.[83]

Always faithful to the Union cause, the Halifax *Sun* admitted that although white troops resented fighting alongside blacks, this "grateful and loving race" was proving itself on the battlefield. Likewise, the Halifax *Express* conceded that negroes could be trained to fight well. To date little has been discovered on how Maritimers who fought for the Confederacy rated the fighting capacity of blacks. One former resident of the region recorded that his unit had skirmished with "Terry's negro troops" near Charleston in 1863, but mentioned little else.[84]

Scores of blacks from Canada West, including former slaves who had escaped north on the "Underground Railroad," were recruited for "negro regiments" such as the famous 54th Massachusetts or the U.S. Colored Troops. Less is known about Maritime blacks in the Northern ranks. Two New Brunswick–born blacks were located in a study of recruiting in seven representative New York counties; another researcher has found several Maritime-born blacks in regiments of U.S. Colored Troops. One Afro–Nova Scotian who served for the Union was Ben Jackson, from Lockhartville, Nova Scotia. Using the name Lewis Saunders, Jackson joined the U.S. Navy in 1864, which, unlike the regular army or volunteer regiments, was not closed to blacks. Indeed a large minority of the navy's rank and file was African-American, one of the most overlooked aspects of the war effort. Over one thousand foreign blacks were enrolled in the navy. Although blacks were not officers, it seems that saltwater and riverboat sailors accepted a rough racial equality. From one-third to one-half of the crews were foreign-born, so Jackson may have served with other Maritimers. He first sailed on the brig *Chalerodonia* from Horton at the age of sixteen in 1851. During his stint with the navy, "Lewis Saunders" served on the frigate USS *Potomac*, the *Richmond* and the *Carolina*. He saw action in the attack on Fort Morgan and was wounded while posted to the *Richmond*

during an attempt to remove an explosive mine from the Mississippi. He appears to have served as a gun captain on the 2,700-
ton steam sloop. This Bluenose sailor was treated at Pensacola,
Florida, and at the Brooklyn naval base hospital before his honourable discharge in 1865. He returned to Nova Scotia's Annapolis
Valley, where a road outside of Hantsport bears his name.[85]

RECONSTRUCTION

Maritime reaction to the racial dimensions of Reconstruction following the Confederate surrender revealed contemporary colonial
attitudes on race relations. The *Eastern Chronicle*, in predicting a
Union victory in 1863, surmised that rebellious Southerners would
be relocated and replaced with "the hardy men of the North." For
another Nova Scotia journal, emancipation of the "sluggish, timid,
unskilled" Africans would lead to starvation on a mass scale; slavery
had at least offered protection to these "childlike" people. William
Drake, a Federal soldier in the forces of occupation, wrote to his
family in Prince Edward Island late in 1865, explaining that Southern blacks had been better off as slaves, "for the men are too lazy
to work, so that I feel you can't trust them any more." "Without
a boss over them," Drake continued, "they are nowhere."[86]

The *Casket*, a Nova Scotia journal, explained that the Northern
states had abolished slavery not because of morality or religion,
but for reasons of "domestic economy" – free labour was more
efficient. The *Provincial Wesleyan* deemed it appropriate to elevate
the slaves to all the privileges of citizenship, yet it cautioned that
the African-American would require a period of temporary servitude "to introduce him to the blessings of advanced Christian civilization." Abolitionists and radical Republicans proposed not temporary servitude but freedom, accompanied by the ballot, the school-
house and the Bible – the program worked out by the Port Royal
Experiment in occupied South Carolina. Yet few Northerners, or
British colonists, expected the legal and political reforms of Reconstruction to produce social equality. Even the abolitionist Halifax
Sun declared that God had "made the race lower than ours, morally
and intellectually, and they can never rival the white man." The
Sun, to reassure conservative readers, denounced "amalgamation,"
or miscegenation, the sexual mingling of the races, as "unnatural
and revolting."[87]

Reverend Charles Henry Corey, who had been born and raised
in "one of the back settlements of New Brunswick," took a prominent role in Reconstruction, first as an employee of the United States

Christian Commission in the occupied South, then as president of the Richmond Theological Seminary. Corey obtained his B.A. from Acadia College in 1858 and then studied theology in New Hampshire. From 1861–65 he was pastor of a Baptist church in Seabrook, New Hampshire. Then he felt the pull of war, joining the United States Christian Commission (USCC), a missionary organization that tended to the spiritual needs of dying, wounded and hospitalized soldiers and helped them contact family and friends. During his stint with the USCC, Corey was posted at New Orleans; Indianola, Mississippi; and Brownsville, Texas; Alexandria and Port Hudson, Louisiana; and Morris Island, off Charleston harbour. He became involved in preaching to and teaching black soldiers and helped meet the religious needs of newly liberated slaves following the capture of Charleston in February of 1865. The New Brunswicker was present at the ceremony marking the restoration of the Stars and Stripes at Fort Sumter and heard speeches by William Lloyd Garrison and Henry Ward Beecher.[88] Following the end of hostilities, he returned to Richmond, accompanied by his wife, under the sponsorship of the American Baptist Home Missionary Society. "The regime of the lash had gone," he wrote, "the regime of the spelling book had come." The mission was dedicated to assisting South Carolina blacks, who were without "self-reliance" or "guidance or counsellors." Corey helped to establish new Baptist congregations for blacks and whites and ordained ministers. Following a posting in Georgia, he returned to Richmond where for three decades he was president of the theological seminary. In a history of the institution published in 1895, Corey praised the former slaves for their advances and defended them from their many detractors.[89]

In the immediate aftermath of the American war, Maritime newspapers that had supported the Confederacy – and there were many – looked for any evidence of black ingratitude, irresponsibility or treachery in the South. Many announced with great satisfaction that the former slaves had become a millstone around the neck of the Federal government. The Freedmen's Bureau and the army fed thousands of Southerners, black and white. One Bluenose journalist concluded that Southern blacks, once completely free, could not be made to work. The evidence? The "decline" of the blacks of the British West Indies since their emancipation in the 1830s. Halifax merchant William Stairs, who had witnessed the bombardment of Fort Sumter, confided to his journal in 1865 that in the South "the Freeman became a slave and the slave became a freeman."[90] Other disappointed pro-Confederate commentators predicted widespread violence as Southern soldiers returned home destitute to encounter former slaves

flaunting their new status under the protection of Northern bayonets. The Halifax *Reporter* envisioned an apocalyptic scenario in which
white Southerners would exterminate freed blacks by the thousands.[91]

This racial pessimism was countered somewhat in Baptist circles,
although many white practitioners in Nova Scotia were spared such
debates because of the existence of segregated churches. In 1865,
Massachusetts abolitionist J.D. Fulton addressed a Baptist convention at Berwick and a public meeting in Saint John. Both talks
promoted the work of the Freedmen's Bureau. The aim of the war,
he explained, had been simple: to give Southern blacks their
"manhood." Fulton praised British liberty and assured his audience
that "in every slave cabin in the South the name of the English
queen is spoken with blessing." British libertarian rhetoric by colonial
politicians, journalists, petitioners and judges often paid homage
to Imperial emancipation as a major event in world history, but
the colonial elite was not willing to translate abstract racial freedom
into a social equality of the races.[92]

A rebellion in Jamaica in late 1865, an aftershock of the liberation
of the South, proved to opponents of abolition the treacherous and
ungrateful nature of former slaves. Prompted by educated leaders,
the rebels slaughtered a number of whites before the revolt was
put down with great brutality by troops, militia and Maroons. There
were scores of summary executions, hundreds of floggings and more
than one thousand houses were burned. Troops of the 17th Regiment were sent from Halifax on the HMS *Duncan*. The Halifax
Reporter blamed the rebellion not on grinding poverty among the
island's blacks but on "their disinclination to work." Jamaica, formerly a well-run British colony, was "rapidly receding into a savage
state," the journal continued, which could only be remedied with
a return to "involuntary service" for "illiterate and half-savage
Africans." In a parting shot aimed at American emancipation, the
editor speculated that the rebellion had been sparked by Reconstruction, which threatened to place "the white man beneath the
feet of the blacks, wherever the latter are in the majority."[93]
Charlottetown's *Examiner*, anxious over the local land question,
reported that the "diabolical and unprovoked" uprising was "now
happily crushed." For the *Novascotian*, Jamaica was "the Ireland of
the Western seas" whose people were barbarians. Saint John's *Freeman*
was more openly critical of Jamaica's governor, who had been aware
of the deteriorating economic situation: having ignored the warning
signs, the British rulers, aided by their "savage allies" the Maroons,
had ended the revolt with extreme violence.[94]

The Civil War, although taking place on American soil, illuminated the issue of race relations at a time when the white majority of the Maritimes colonies had all but forgotten that slavery had once existed in their own region. By 1871, more than one-third of Canada's blacks lived in the Maritime provinces, yet their numbers were small. According to the census, persons of African descent were less than 2 percent of the Nova Scotia population and an even smaller proportion in New Brunswick, hardly sufficient to develop the eventual political clout of a minority such as the Acadians.[95]

If Maritime whites seemed unconcerned or cynical about the plight of Southern blacks, it was largely because they had little under-standing of the underprivileged minority in their own community, which was depicted in the press almost exclusively in terms of de-rision. The Jamaica planter elite, like white Southerners, viewed blacks as ignorant, lazy, childlike, dependent and immoral. White Maritimers of all classes, blinded by similar stereotypes, tended to agree. The Civil War was an opportunity not for self-examination on racial issues but for testing the achievements and failures of the American republican experiment. Racial equality, even among evangelicals, seems to have been left at the church door; as in neighbouring Maine, the major churches took no stand on the issues of slavery and abolition. Despite their deep roots in the region, blacks were regarded as aliens. If the Civil War's twin achievements of emancipation and Reconstruction inspired black Maritimers, the descendants of Southern and Caribbean slaves, they did little to alleviate their burdens, which in some respects, such as social segregation, actually became more onerous as racial attitudes hardened in the late Victorian period.[96]

4 Refugees, Crimps, Spies and Skedaddlers

Our streets swarm with suspicious-looking characters—fellows of the cut-throat species – men accustomed to handle "blood money" and but a slight degree higher than the assassin in morals.
– Saint John *Telegraph*, 20 July 1864

Steamer and sailing ship routes and overland connections with Canada made the Maritimes, particularly Halifax and Saint John, important stopping points for Confederate soldiers and civilians seeking to avoid the hostile Northern states.[1] Given Britain's reputation as a refuge for foreign political offenders, local Union partisans had few objections to providing asylum for Southerners, provided they did not violate neutrality by plotting violent deeds from British soil. By 1864, a Halifax drug store even sold Confederate postage stamps for newspapers and letters sent on blockade runners. In time, Southerners patronized favourite hotels, boarding houses and watering holes. The visitors included not only stranded tourists but also escaped prisoners of war, and officers and diplomats assigned to duties in Europe, Canada or the West Indies. Despite the high regard Southerners came to enjoy, before the war they had been an unknown commodity. The South, a Confederate resident of Nova Scotia wrote, "was a region as unfamiliar to the people of the Provinces as the unexplored portion of Africa."[2]

One of the war's ironies was that grandsons of Loyalists flocked to preserve the republican union that had severed the British Empire. Another was that British colonies felt an affinity with the Confederacy despite a history of ambivalent relations. Virginia had been one of the centres of revolution. Imperial troops had passed through, fought over and evacuated Southern centres such as Savannah, Augusta, Charleston, Wilmington and Richmond. Cornwallis had surrendered at Yorktown in 1781, having conducted operations on territory that would see fighting between 1861 and 1865. One-quarter of the Loyalists who fled to Nova Scotia in the 1780s were Southerners, as were almost all of its black immigrants (also part of the Loyalist wave). More recently, Southern "War Hawks" had pushed the republic into war with Britain in 1812, and Southern politicians had viewed British abolitionism with dismay in the 1820s and 1830s.[3]

NORTH AND SOUTH IN CONTRAST

As one student of the era observed, the Confederate refugees, officers and officials who passed through the Maritimes and received so much press coverage were part of the Southern elite – educated, cosmopolitan, articulate and skilled in social graces. Frances Monck, wife of Canada's governor general, confided in her journal: "All the nicest, bravest and most gentlemanly men belong to the South."[4] The Saint John *Telegraph*, discussing the influx of Southerners and anti-war Northerners, was reminded of an earlier migration in protest of republican extremism, that of the Loyalists: "As a general rule they belong to the more refined and intelligent class of Americans. They are liberal in their views, and know nothing of prejudices, religious, social or political."[5] Even the pro-Union Halifax *Sun* was impressed by the fact that most Southern gentlemen and their families seeking hospitality in British North America had conducted themselves with discretion. They mingled freely with the colonial elite, some of whom appear to have subscribed to the 'moonlight and magnolias' image of plantation society. The U.S. consul at Halifax reported that Southerners of this class had attempted to sway public opinion before the war broke out. They also supplied local editors with highly prized newspapers from Richmond, Charleston and Savannah.[6]

In contrast, Northerners in the Maritimes, although more numerous, were less exotic. One New Brunswicker in twenty-five was American-born. "Nine-tenths of all the floating population in all the provinces," one newspaper article explained, "were Yankees, on tours of pleasure; who thronged the hotels and boarding houses and filled the travelling conveyances." Maritime houses were filled with clocks, pictures, dry goods and bric-a-brac purchased from enterprising Yankee pedlars. Halifax was connected with the American telegraph network by 1849, and Yankee books, periodicals and newspapers were common in the region. Familiarity possibly bred contempt. The Northern press was diverse politically and accessible to the people of British North America, thus more was known about the Union war effort, successes as well as failures, unity as well as dissension.[7]

The distant, beleaguered Confederacy presented to outsiders an appearance of unaniminity and resolve.[8] Although pro-Northern journals such as the Saint John *Globe* spoke of the "grinding despotism of Jefferson Davis," most of the region's press saw only a government of reasonable gentlemen casting off the Northern yoke, much like the Italians were doing with the Austrians or the Poles with the Russians.[9] Within the British world there was a tendency to deny that slavery was the war's main cause. Another point to consider is that Northerners were not unanimous on aspects of the war such as conscription, civil liberties, emancipation and peace negotiations. Some were strong Union supporters, other lukewarm "Copperheads" who disapproved of abolition and of militarily defeating the South. Peace Democrats, for example, were a strong force in Maine state politics.[10]

In the early stages of the war, before public sentiment shifted against the North, Maritimers appear to have entertained negative opinions of Southerners, who were viewed as self-indulgent, uncouth and violent, despite their thin veneer of civility. Hugo Reid, who encountered Southerners in Washington after leaving Halifax in 1859, noted that "when aroused, they are impatient and fiery, reckless of life and vindictive, and ever ready, for a mere trifle, with the bowie knife or the revolver."[11] John Boyd, editor of the *Casket*, published in Halifax and Antigonish in the 1860s, noted that the majority of American army and naval officers were Southerners "who despise peaceful pursuits." The *Acadian Recorder* commented on the "coarseness and brutality" of Confederate leaders. This was a far cry from the ideal of restrained manhood that was so respected in the Protestant culture of both the North and the British colonies. The culprit was the Southern code of honour, which demanded that a gentleman seek satisfaction not in the law courts but with his fists or, if necessary, weapons.[12]

As Maritimers grew more hostile towards Yankees after Bull Run and the *Trent* affair, Southern hotbloodedness became an admirable quality. It reminded colonial journalists of the traditional English aristocracy, addicted to horses, blood sports and violence. Elite Southerners, and foreign observers, liked to think of the planter class as an aristocracy. One Nova Scotia journal theorized that the South had inherited "the haughty, high-born spirit of the Cavaliers"; the North was "the exponent of Puritanism."[13] In another allusion to England's own civil war, reporters contended that Rebel cavalry chief Jeb Stuart and his troopers were the heirs of Prince Rupert and his dashing cavaliers. The military competence of the outnumbered and outgunned Southern armies also appealed to educated colonists who endorsed the liberal ideal of national self-determination. The Southerners appeared to possess a distinct culture and territory and a history of grievances against an outside oppressor. Charles Pilsbury, a New Englander and son of the former U.S. consul for Nova Scotia, wrote that the Rebels were "a struggling people" who would conduct a punishing guerrilla war long after the fall of their cities. The *British Colonist* admired General Robert E. Lee not only for his military skill but for his modesty and composure, which was reminiscent of the "old Roman model" of self-abnegation.[14]

ANTI-NORTHERN FEELING

Given their natural sympathies with the underdog, and the presence of Southern gentlemen in their major cities, many Maritimers were predisposed to think the worst of Yankees. This explains why Northern accounts of Confederate atrocities, such as the massacre of black troops at Fort Pillow, Tennessee, or Quantrill's bloody raid on Lawrence, Kansas, were downplayed or ignored in the local press, while stories of Northern war crimes were highlighted. Benjamin Butler, who had ordered his troops to treat insolent Confederate ladies at New Orleans as "women of the town," shocked Victorian sensibilities. One New Brunswick journal surmised that the Confederates accused of the Fort Pillow atrocities had been "goaded into retaliation" by Union excesses. Island journalist J.B. Cooper, discussing the Union war effort, asked how British subjects could sympathize with "a people who are the fawning admirers of despotism."[15] The conservative *Colonial Standard* labelled the republic a "cesspool," the repository of "all the filth and offscourings of all the other populations of the earth."[16]

The Northern atrocity story that captured the most attention in the Maritimes was the execution of fifteen Rebel guerrillas by Missouri Union forces in late 1862. Although legal according to the rules of warfare, this stern measure was all the more outrageous because it had been ordered by a former Nova Scotian, John McNeil, a St. Louis hat maker turned state militia leader. McNeil had learned the trade in Halifax, departing in his early twenties for further training in Boston. After operating a retail outlet in New York, he migrated to Missouri, where he became involved in state politics. At the start of the 1861 crisis he mobilized a loyal Union militia.[17]

The war in Missouri, involving large numbers of irregular troops and guerrilla operations, was particularly nasty, marked by bushwacking, looting and summary executions.[18] The fifteen prisoners captured in battle at Kirksville in August 1862 had previously signed paroles promising to refrain from taking up arms for the Confederacy. One of the condemned partisans allegedly rode to the execution site with his young son. McNeil, thereafter known as "the Butcher of Palmyra," had supporters in the Maritimes, but as in Britain most commentators were outraged by the executions. Nova Scotia's *Provincial Wesleyan* portrayed the former colonist as a "monster of inequity." The London *Times* denounced the act as beyond the rules of civilized warfare; Jefferson Davis placed a price on McNeil's head.[19]

CONFEDERATE VISITORS AND EXILES

Confederates who reached the Maritime colonies during the war often were treated as celebrities. Among those passing through on official business was Commodore Matthew Fontaine Maury, the well-known hydrographer and "sailor's friend," who arrived in Halifax on Cunard's SS *Delta* from Bermuda in late 1862. Maury, who had steamed past the blockade in Louis Coxetter's slow but elusive steamer *Herald*, had been cashiered from the U.S. Navy. He became the director of the Confederacy's "naval submarine battery service." Naval mines, or "torpedoes," developed by this arm destroyed or disabled over thirty Union vessels by the end of the war and helped protect harbours and rivers from enemy gunboats. Maury, who was visited by distinguished citizens during his sojourn at the Halifax Hotel, was on his way to Europe to help outfit Confederate commerce raiders. According to James Morris Morgan, then a young Rebel naval officer, Maury was received by the governor, the admiral and the garrison commander. Recently the London *Herald* had published one of his letters which explained and justified the Southern cause.[20]

Other Rebel naval officers followed, including Commodore George T. Sinclair, travelling to Britain to confer with James Bulloch, the Confederacy's foreign agent. Sinclair claimed to have given the order to blow up the ironclad CSS *Virginia* (*Merrimac*) before it could fall into enemy hands (the responsibility actually rested with Josiah Tattnall, a Confederate naval officer who lived in Dartmouth, Nova Scotia following the war). The U.S. consul noted the presence of other Confederate officers, whom he suspected were planning to take charge of steam rams being built for the enemy in Britain. Lieutenant Thomas Dornin, CSN, was known in Halifax, probably because of a sojourn on the way back from Europe, where he had been first officer on CSS *Rappahannock*. A private letter that arrived on a blockade runner in 1865 relayed the news that Tom Dornin had been seriously wounded or killed by the bursting of a gun during an attack on Fort Fisher, North Carolina.[21]

Sydney, somewhat off the beaten track for Southern émigrés, in 1863 was visited by S.F. Cameron, an army chaplain en route to Britain from Jamaica, whose mission was to obtain medicines and books for the Southern war effort. Cape Bretoners tended to lean towards the South, but the editor of the *Cape Breton News*, James P. Ward, sympathized with the North. Nevertheless, the journal's interview with Cameron, who had escaped from prison in Maryland, was respectful and positive in tone: "He was a good specimen of a Southern gentleman, and a most agreeable acquaintance." The Episcopalian chaplain had stopped in Sydney because his steamer was seeking coal. "We liked him much," the *News* wrote, "and although differing widely from him, felt constrained to sympathize for the many sufferings of his fellow citizens." It was noted that Cameron, although a man of the cloth, had commanded a troop of cavalry "during all the engagements from Manassas to Antietam."[22]

Southerners with business or family in Canada, or who were fleeing Union prison camps, did travel overland through Ohio, Michigan, New York and other states. But considerable numbers of Confederate military personnel also passed through the lower provinces.[23] The Saint John *Telegraph* announced in 1864 that some of the Southerners in that city were "determined looking fellows who might think nothing of burning Calais, Eastport or any other Maine town." Late in 1863, New Brunswick was stirred by reports that a party of Southern officers, escapees from Northern prison camps, was travelling via Woodstock from Quebec. Among those rumoured to be among the party was the celebrated cavalry leader John Hunt Morgan, a Kentuckian who staged widely publicized raids into enemy territory before being captured in July 1863. The rumour proved to be false, as Morgan had escaped from Ohio directly into Confederate territory. Likewise, despite press speculation, the "Colonel Wheeler" frequenting Saint John in late 1863 was not a Confederate officer and definitely not Major-General "Fighting Joe" Wheeler, commander of cavalry of the Army of the Mississippi, then too preoccupied with the Chattanooga campaign and its aftermath to be spending time in distant New Brunswick.[24]

The Southerners who travelled down the Saint John River valley in early December were described as "intelligent and bold-looking, somewhat rough in speech, though careful in their conversations before strangers not to say anything about their intentions, and heavily laden with silver and gold." The latter suggests that the party contained members of the aborted mission to free the prisoners on

Johnson's Island, Lake Erie, which was returning via Lower Canada. The governor general of Canada had alerted the Americans of impending trouble. The raiders, although successful in commandeering the *Philo Parsons*, lost heart when they sighted the fourteen-gun steamer *Michigan*. The mission had indirectly involved Lieutenant John Wilkinson, CSN, recently captain of the successful blockade runner *Robert E. Lee*. The officers passed on to Halifax, no doubt to sail to Nassau or Bermuda. A certain Captain Atkins, who spent the day socializing with three British officers, ended up in small claims court for refusing to pay a cabman for the hire of his rig.[25]

In the spring of 1864, Patrick Niesen Lynch, the Roman Catholic archbishop of Charleston, South Carolina, was a guest of the diocese of Halifax. Lynch had gained international attention as a result of published correspondence with the archbishop of New York in which he had blamed the war on fanatical abolitionists. In 1864 he had additional reasons for disliking the North: Union siege guns had destroyed both his cathedral and residence. Lynch had arrived from Bermuda on the *Delta* and rested before sailing to Europe to argue the Confederate cause before Catholic governments and pay a visit to his native Ireland. While in Halifax the South Carolina archbishop preached a sermon at St. Mary's Cathedral, attended the funeral of Major Smith Stansbury, CSA, and was entertained by the local pro-Confederate coterie.[26]

Lynch's host, Reverend Thomas Connolly, was a kindred spirit. Best remembered for his active role in promoting Confederation among Maritime Catholics, Connolly warmly supported the Rebels and even wrote letters of introduction to smooth the way for Southern envoys travelling to Canada. One testimonial, for Clement C. Clay of Alabama, described the Confederate cause as commanding "the respect and sympathy of the world." Clay, a land and slave owner who held a Confederate congressional seat, left for Montreal by stage. In his opinion, many of the British colonists who criticized British policy towards the Confederacy were Roman Catholics (the same constituency who in the North supported the Democratic party). In 1864, Connolly apparently expressed a willingness "to traverse the U.S. as an advocate of peace, or to do something to promote that end that was compatible with his duty to his Church and Queen." Somewhat ironically, in 1861 the Bluenose archbishop had toured Washington and the front lines across the Potomac in the company of a French admiral and three foreign officers in McClellan's staff.[27] On another occasion he visited Hamilton, Bermuda, where he was received by the local Confederate agent, Major Norman Walker, and his socialite wife, who left behind a glowing account of the anti-Yankee cleric:

He warmly espouses the Southern cause. What a glorious man he is! . . . a cordial and elegant man, very learned, and understands thoroughly the South, in all its aspects. . . . He looks every inch a "Lord" and his red stockings, gold shoe buckles and emerald rings, the size of a partridge egg, set in diamonds, dazzled *my* delighted eyes. I would vote for him for Pope tomorrow.[28]

Georgiana Gholson Walker described Halifax, where she and her husband resided during the fall of 1864 and winter of 1865, as a "land of snow and ice – another temporary home for us 'poor wandering rebels,' as the Yankee would call us." The autumn weather was cold and dismal, in contrast to "the hearts of the people" who welcomed the Confederates. Arriving on the blockade runner *Falcon*, and surviving an outbreak of yellow fever that killed the pilot and eight others, the Walkers were greeted by Gustave Alexandre, a clerk in Confederate service, and prominent merchant Benjamin Wier. The Walkers were received by Alfred Jones, Dr. William J. Almon and other social leaders. For a few months Georgiana and the children visited Britain but returned to winter in Nova Scotia, where her fourth child was born on 30 November 1864.[29]

A particularly distinguished Confederate to travel through the Maritimes was General William Preston, who crossed the Bay of Fundy from Saint John to Windsor in November 1864 with his wife and daughter, private secretary and black servant. Arriving on the train from Windsor, Preston left his luggage and servant at the Richmond station, to the north of Halifax, in order to secure lodgings. The servant immediately decamped with the trunks and was reported to the police. The Preston ladies were put on a steamer to Boston (where they were regarded as spies and escorted to the Canadian border) and the general attempted to get back to the South. Early in the new year he was almost captured when the blockade runner *Chameleon* ran into Fort Fisher at the mouth of the Cape Fear River after it had fallen to the enemy. The captain, meeting no response to his signals, fled to Nassau. Preston, although appointed a diplomat, ended up entering Texas through Mexico.[30]

A number of prominent Confederate civilians were rumoured to have been in the Maritimes during the war. Halifax papers, for example, were convinced that one of the Southerners in the city in 1861 was none other than J.C. Breckenridge, a Kentucky native who had been vice-president under Buchanan and the presidential candidate for the Southern Democrats in the 1860 election, where he had captured almost one-fifth of the popular vote. Breckenridge, as a senator, had also been one of the last secessionist politicians expelled from Washington. Breckenridge actually was busy fleeing from Kentucky and taking up a commission as a Confederate brigadier general at this time. The U.S. consul was more sure about the notorious George N. Sanders of Kentucky, the former consul at Liverpool, who turned up in Halifax early in 1863. Sanders, who would be involved in planning the St. Alban's raid and organizing the raiders' legal defence, had escaped to Canada and was on his way to England.[31]

Southern exiles also came to the public's attention between 1861 and 1865, although most kept a low profile. A number were renegade Northerners, or Britons who had thrown their support to the Rebels. Reverend John Tovell was a British subject who had taught at a Baptist college in Montreal. When the war broke out, he was editor of the *Tennessee Baptist* in Nashville, where he became critical of Union troops who had occupied the border slave state. Suspected of being "secesh," he was sent to the state prison for a few months, and then parted from his property and family by being sent into Confederate lines. Embittered, Tovell booked passage on a blockade runner out of North Carolina to Nassau, then sailed to Halifax, where he was befriended by pro-Southern activists. In one of his letters to the *Christian Messenger*, describing blacks in the West Indies, Tovell wrote that he understood why Southern masters could lose their tempers. In 1864 he lectured in Halifax, Saint John and Woodstock on the brutalities of Yankee occupation. His presentation focused on Butler, McNeil and radical Unionist Parson Brownlow.[32]

More controversial was Charles Hallock, a Northerner whose father had edited the New York *Journal of Commerce*. During the early part of the war, he ran a paper in Georgia, where he had espoused the Rebel cause. In 1863, after visiting the West Indies and writing freelance pieces about the blockade, Hallock surfaced in Halifax, where he contributed to the pro-Southern *Journal*. His story "Aroostook and Madawaska," published by *Harper's*, portrayed northeastern Maine as an economic and social extension of New Brunswick. Soon after his arrival he published a Halifax edition of his small book *Sketches of Stonewall Jackson*, in honour of the military genius who had conducted the Shenandoah Valley campaign. Jackson, who had been accidentally wounded by friendly fire, died of pneumonia in 1862. Hallock's work repeated all the hallowed myths associated with Southern chivalry and duty, praising Jackson as the "father of his country . . . the hero, the soldier, the Christian, whose character and achievements have placed him high in the list of immortal conquerors." The Confederates were compared to the heroic Spartans of old, fighting the Persian hordes. In a Temperance Hall speech on the causes of the war, Hallock "brought down the house" with his conclusion that Nova Scotia's future prosperity lay with an independent Confederacy. Previously he had described the Emancipation Proclamation as a "monstrous edict" that would result in the removal or extermination of the white race. He later relocated to Saint John, where he was a staff writer for the *Telegraph* and editor of "a spicy little sheet" known as the *Humourist*.[33]

Another renegade Northerner to visit Nova Scotia was Mrs. Henry Grinnell, "the Florence Nightingale of America." The daughter of Sir John Musgrave, this Englishwoman served with Nightingale in the Crimea, then married Grinnell, a New York merchant. With the outbreak of war, both sided with the Confederacy, the husband raising a company of troops, the wife working in the hospitals of Richmond. A Mrs. Nicholson, a native of Canada but a resident of Louisiana, arrived in Halifax in 1863, supposedly banished by Union occupation forces for collusion with the Confederates. She told sympathetic hearers "a pitiful tale of hardships endured" and, from a residence on Bedford Road, solicited assistance in the form of "medicines, quinine, opium, articles of clothing or articles suitable for hospital use," presumably for the Confederacy. A letter from North Carolina to Halifax in March 1864 confirmed that Mrs. Nicholson, "an indefatigable heroine," had safely arrived back in Wilmington, through the blockade.[34]

Despite the ease with which Southerners appeared to journey from Wilmington and Charleston to Nova Scotia, deep-sea steamship travel was not for the faint of heart in the 1860s. An account of a passage on the Cunard liner *Alpha*, which left Halifax weekly for Bermuda, suggests that even first-class passengers had to endure overcrowding, seasickness and poor sanitary conditions. The packet had only seven first-class staterooms and two dozen first-class berths, which meant that many passengers had to sleep in the first-class saloon, which doubled as a sitting and dinning room. The handful of stewards and stewardesses had their hands full with the many passengers, including women and children, who were constantly seasick. The deck was crowded with cattle and sheep. The author of the account doubted whether there were sufficient lifeboats on the steamer to accommodate passengers and crew. Yet the Royal mail steamers, after the *Trent* incident, at least were safe from Union naval patrols.[35]

The Maritimes was a travel corridor for two well-known anti-war

Northern politicians, Clement Vallandigham and Fernando Wood. Congressman Vallandigham was an Ohio "Peace Democrat," or Copperhead, and a newspaper editor whose anti-Lincoln statements had incurred the wrath of Union loyalists. In what was regarded as a despotic act in the British colonies, he was arrested by orders of General Burnside and banished beyond Union lines. He proved no more popular in the Confederacy, where he was suspected as a spy and sent packing. The anti-abolitionist was lionized by Southern partisans in British North America, but he was not a pro-Confederate. He disembarked at Halifax from Bermuda early in the summer of 1863, reportedly "afraid to step out of his hotel room." Vallandigham travelled on to Canada and was feted in Quebec, Montreal and Toronto. His base became the border town of Windsor, from where he directed anti-Republican strategy in the lead-up to the 1864 election. Part of this involved the shadowy group the Sons of Liberty, which spread through the Midwest. Fernando Wood, a former Tammany Hall mayor of New York, was a Peace Democrat leader in Congress who landed at Halifax in 1863, travelled to Saint John and booked passage to New York. Both Wood and Valladigham spoke at the 1864 Democratic convention and led the peace wing of the party in an effort to derail Lincoln.[36]

Hindsight suggests that the frequent appearance of Southerners in Nova Scotia and New Brunswick was a temporary abberation. Yet there were those who thought of the region as a playground for Southern tourists after the war. The Halifax *Morning Journal* wrote gushingly about the area's potential as a "watering place" for Confederates once hostilities ceased. The independent Southerners, it reasoned, would no longer feel comfortable at Newport, Rhode Island, Saratoga, New York, the resort hotels of Vermont's White Mountains or other upscale vacation spots. Southern plantation families would prefer "the bracing atmosphere of Nova Scotia" to these Yankee-infested locales. One Southern visitor known to the *Journal* estimated that thousands of his countrymen would flock to Nova Scotia to enjoy yachting, hunting, fishing and British hospitality. Weekly steamship connections, it was predicted, would be introduced between Richmond and Halifax. A New Brunswick journal, although pro-South, sounded more of a warning note, cautioning readers to beware of "so-called Confederates" in Saint John and Halifax who took advantage of sympathies and hospitality "to line their pockets by a system of deception and false promises." Halifax, in particular, because of its status as an international way station, was vulnerable, its citizens taking Confederates into their homes and paying their steamship passages, boarding-house bills and even tailor's accounts. The Halifax *Sun* warned that Southerners were flattering and cajoling gullible Bluenoses. Even the generally anti-North journals reminded readers that Southerners were slaveholders and in this sense fundamentally different from Nova Scotians. Another criticism crept in towards the latter part of the rebellion: how could Confederates residing in New Brunswick or Nova Scotia take part in the war?[37]

SKEDADDLERS AND CRIMPS

A further manifestation of the American conflict was the "skedaddler" or draft dodger. An estimated 200,000 men deserted from Union forces and 16,000 failed to show for draft processing. One was John Adams, a Nova Scotian who had lived in Maine prior to enlisting in an infantry regiment late in the war. He deserted at Washington during the summer of 1865.[38] According to the press, not a few of these individuals arrived in the Maritimes by foot, schooner or steamship. Maritime journals tended to look down upon draft dodgers as cowards. Rather than wait to be conscripted, these individuals fled to the sanctuary of British territory. A number worked in the lumber camps of New Brunswick, and others were thought to be sheltering in the fishing fleets that touched shore at Canso and other historic New England gathering places. Early in 1865, justices of the peace and citizens in the Port Mulgrave area petitioned the Halifax government for assistance in dealing with problems arising out of the annual visit of fishing fleets, whose crews contained "the scum of all nations, with a good sprinkling of skedaddlers, etc., from the American states." New Brunswick's immigration officer reported, for 1863, the arrival of "considerable numbers" of Americans and British subjects formerly living in the States to the "upper counties." One pioneer community that sprang up east of the border town of Weston, Maine, was "Skedaddlers' Ridge," in the vicinity of McAdam, a rough settlement of fifty individuals by late 1863. Other new settlements allegedly including skedaddlers included Gordonville, Glassville and Knowlesville. Almost any Yankee living or travelling through the provinces came under suspicion. The Charlottetown *Monitor* identified travelling salesmen, "peddling harpies from Yankeedom," as a type of skedaddler. The Eastport *Sentinel* and other border journals commented on their movements into British territory.[39]

Not all of the commentary on skedaddlers was unsympathetic, particularly as Bluenoses became more critical of the Northern war effort. Conscription was antithetical to British traditions, being a hallmark of authoritarian states or corrupt republics such as revolutionary France. Edward Willis of the Saint John *Morning News* opined that enforced military service was a denial of civil liberty. A resident of Little Falls, New Brunswick, sympathized with Maine border dwellers who contended that the draft was unfair to small communities. As a result, many were seeking asylum on "this side of the Potomac." Woodstock, St. Stephen, Saint John and Halifax were their favourite points of entry.[40] Other commentators offered a broader perspective: the arrival of Americans was part of the intermingling of the North American peoples. An American journalist noted that a large number of Northerners were sojourning in New Brunswick "to avoid the draft and other burdens at home." This influx of people and capital was part of the "inevitable drawing of the two countries together." He predicted that the British provinces would first join into a colonial union, then apply to become part of the United States.[41]

Another character type produced by the Civil War was the crimp, or freelance recruiting agent. Enlistment in a foreign war, voluntary or not, was a highly charged issue in Maritime society and so were the activities of recruiters. Crimps, often seeking workers for "civilian" jobs, were known to be active in the border areas of New Brunswick, the ports of Nova Scotia and the émigré communities of Boston and New York.[42] Under the British Foreign Enlistment Act, it was illegal to recruit on British soil for foreign military service. Yet given the big profits to be had in signing up men for Uncle Sam, this deterrent was insufficient. By 1864, with town and state governments offering large bounties for volunteers or substitutes for those who had been drafted, "bounty brokers" stood to make considerable gains. In 1863, expecting the draft, the town of Houlton voted to raise three hundred dollars for each volunteer or substitute. Municipal governments in Massachusetts alone raised $13 million for bounties. A New Brunswick journal castigated "the Yankee prowler, in our province, who lies in wait to trap the innocent and unwary with promises of great bounties and who rush the youngsters into recruiting offices."[43]

The most obvious targets of recruiters were British soldiers and sailors who were accustomed to military life and already possessed sufficient reasons to desert.[44] In the spring of 1861 an American attempted to recruit thirty members of a detachment of the 62nd Regiment at Fredericton. The American war offered higher pay, slacker discipline, improved chances of promotion, and the very real possibility of action. The Militia Act of 1862 had authorized conscription, but it had pressured so many Northerners into volunteering that no draft had been enacted. In 1863 Lincoln cancelled the commutation option in response to cries that the struggle had become a poor man's war, and enlistment and substitute bounties went through the roof, to as high as $1,500. This explains why British infantry- and artillerymen stationed in New Brunswick and Nova Scotia, despite the risk of being imprisoned and branded, attempted to reach Maine by foot or boat.[45]

Crimps met redcoats and British tars at taverns, eateries, street corners and wharves and promised them "civvies," transportation across the border and a large bounty (most of which was destined to remain in the hands of the crimp). In 1863 an American who claimed to be a discharged veteran of the 7th New York Cavalry was fined heavily for attempting to entice soldiers to desert from the Saint John garrison. John Newman, arraigned in 1863 for enticing a redcoat at Cuniff's tavern, was discharged for being of unsound mind; he claimed to have been wounded on the Union side at the Battle of Fair Oaks. On another occasion a tippling soldier was told that he would be promoted to captain within weeks in the Union army. The Fredericton mayor's court sentenced Daniel Murphy to eighteen months in penitentiary for a similar offence in 1863. Murphy, a veteran of the British army, claimed to have served in the Southern ranks at Bull Run. Lorenzo "Bony" Fields of Woodstock received four months for a like crime.[46] Two soldiers of the 17th Regiment in Halifax said nothing when Michael Gallagher offered them $100 to board a ship and join "the Yankee Army." In the British army, he explained, they were only "half paid and half fed." The men continued drinking, but when the Queen was called "a bloody whore," they took Gallagher to the police station.[47]

Civilians also were fair game. Refined methods for crimping sailors for the merchant marine proved to be effective. Reports surfaced in Fredericton and Halifax that recruiters were after young boys. A number of victims or near victims of the recruiters claimed that they had been drugged or intoxicated when they had signed on. In 1864 there was a rare case of a crimp who attempted to kidnap a colonist from the British side of the line. The village of Digby was thrown into an uproar when word circulated that a Bridgetown youth had been drugged and placed aboard a Boston-bound schooner by "enlisting agent" John McGucken. A party of men – vigilantes, except for the fact that they had procured a warrant from a justice of the peace – sailed to catch the vessel and take the offender into custody. A Digby correspondent noted that the men had been drinking, and that "one more bottle of rum would have tarred and feathered McGucken on Friday night."[48]

Overall, the Foreign Enlistment Act was not effective in controlling crimping and desertion. When a newspaper published in St. Stephen ran a recruiting notice for the 15th Maine Regiment that promised "higher pay for better work," $14–22 per month, clothing, medical care, "abundant" food and a $100 exit bounty, the governor complained that "no provincial jury" would register a conviction. A British officer added that New Brunswick police and civilians were not prepared to help secure convictions of tavern keepers and others who assisted in this human traffic.[49]

Mi'kmaq Ben Christmas, who for part of the war was the assistant to Reverend Silas Rand's mission to the Indians, was rumoured to have become a freelance bounty broker among First Nations people in Maine and the Maritimes. Christmas, who had been baptized in 1857 and had assisted Rand in his translation of parts of the New Testament into Mi'kmaq, had broken with the mission in 1860. Other journals declared that he had joined the Union army. Given their mobility, interaction with Native peoples in Maine, familiarity with New England, participation in other wars, and experience in joining the American armed forces this century, other Maritime Native warriors, some of them no doubt victims of crimps, fought in the 1860s.[50] One was John Ward, a twenty-two-year-old Mi'kmaq who joined the 12th New York Cavalry at Buffalo in 1863.[51]

The Nova Scotia, New Brunswick and Imperial authorities were aware of the problem of recruiting. The issue brought back unpleasant memories of Joe Howe's controversial scheme to recruit Yankees to fight for John Bull in the Crimea. Lieutenant-Governor Gordon reported to London that, anti-Yankee feeling aside, it was impossible to convince independent-minded colonists as to the impropriety and illegality of "taking part in the existing war." The Foreign Enlistment Act was being broken on a daily basis, he wrote in 1864. Early in the war the newly appointed governor had been loath to prosecute those who enticed desertion from Her Majesty's forces, as it would generate "considerable excitement" and threaten relations with Maine.[52] The British consul in Boston failed to cooperate with a businessman who wanted to recruit three or four hundred colonials to work in a brick factory; a Halifax *Citizen* correspondent warned that such men would "sell themselves into slavery worse than the negro slavery of the South." Most of the reported crimping was for the Northern forces, but in Halifax in 1864, individuals were seen wearing Confederate grey, supposedly recruited by "the unrecognized consul" of the Rebels.[53]

Most crimping of Bluenoses, folklore aside, was carried out in the United States, beyond the reach of British law, and most clients were willing victims. According to New Brunswicker Charles Humphrey, Jr., Maritimers in Boston did not need the inducement of crimps and bounty brokers because they were constantly reminded about military enlistment by posters, newspapers and official recruiters. Given the poor job prospects of many Bluenose newcomers, "the only business doing in Boston" was recruiting for the army and navy. In Humphrey's street alone there were four recruiting offices.[54] The correspondent "J.H." visited the "conscript camp" on Boston's Long Island and reported to the *Freeman*: "I was sorry to observe among the substitutes no less than five persons – young men – from Saint John. They did not inform me, if any opportunity presented itself, whether they intended to battle for the Union or skedaddle for the East." Another correspondent, touring Camp Readville, was surprised at the large contingent from the British provinces. In his estimation, a colonist who joined for pay was nothing but a hired assassin; if for the love of fighting, a "blood thirsty murderer." J.H., in a second report, blamed Boston's boarding house keepers and their runners for taking advantage of reckless individuals "unable to earn an honest living." The victims were led to believe that they could skedaddle after signing up and obtaining their bounty payment. "Bounty jumping" could be profitable but dangerous. According to one rumour, a Saint John man who allegedly enlisted and deserted four times was sentenced to be executed by firing squad at Fort Independence (the rumour was false). Boarding house keepers, loafers, gamblers, conmen, and even the police were involved in the recruiting business in Portland, Boston and New York. British subjects and other foreigners were arrested for minor offenses, real or imaginary, and then offered the chance to defend the Union.[55]

One of the more disturbing aspects of crimping stories was that many of the recruiters encountered in Boston or New York on steamers or in border areas were Maritimers. Cyrus Stevens of Stewiacke attributed his troubles to such an individual. Stevens had been illegally drafted into a cavalry regiment but fled to Kentucky where he worked under an assumed name. Drafted again, he went back to Boston where he was tricked into volunteering by a Saint John man, "one of the organized set of villains who infest every state in the Union."[56] A New Brunswicker residing in Massachusetts warned young travellers to avoid "recruiting doctors" who promised but rarely delivered substantial sums to enlistees. "Stavely," writing in a Nova Scotia journal in 1864, reported that men were arriving from the provinces daily to join the army. The Charlottetown *Monitor* relayed a tale of a Nova Scotia machinist who was conveyed, by means of a drugged drink, on board a naval receiving vessel and sent off to a distant station.[57]

Letters to the Saint John press warned provincialists to avoid former colonists who now lived in Boston and preyed on vulnerable economic migrants. Several of these characters were reported to be visiting Saint John, flashing greenbacks and wearing fancy clothes. Albert Melvin, a young watchmaker travelling in the U.S. without a passport, wrote home to Bridgewater that he had been tricked into joining the 2nd Massachusetts Heavy Artillery for three months. In this case the culprits were army officers on his train to Philadelphia. To avoid being taken for naturalized immigrants, a number of Bluenoses in the United States sought official "British protection," documentation to prove nationality. In the wake of the 1863 draft rioting in New York and Boston, two brothers in the latter city wrote Nova Scotia to secure proof of their nationality. One wrote that the British consul was of little use in securing such protection, because "thear (sic) is so many coming to him every day for the like that he don't know British subjects from American."[58]

ESPIONAGE AND INTELLIGENCE

Another figure who received press attention during the Civil War was the spy. The Saint John *News* fretted that Southern refugees would attract Federal spies on steamships and at hotels and railroad stations. A Halifax paper reported in 1862 that locals had sent two such individuals on a wild goose chase to Windsor. The issue of spying, with its connotations of European despotism, definitely damaged American prestige in English-speaking societies, where such practices were an anathema. The large communities of Southern refugees in British North America were worth watching. The Union authorities, for purposes of military intelligence, border control and general security, appointed detectives and special agents who obtained information from informers. In response to the threat of border incidents, and as a form of diplomatic pressure, the Union government, early in the war and again in late 1864, began to enforce passport regulations, until then unheard of in North America. Maritimers regarded this as not only inconvenient but uncivilized. Even Frederick William Seward, who assisted his father at the State Department, later admitted that the system of passports, port surveillance and frontier guards was "vexatious."[59] The New Brunswick government, under pressure in 1865 to follow the Canadian example by enacting alien control legislation, refused on the grounds that it would be viewed as political extortion. In addition, both the

Tilley and Smith administrations feared that troublesome Confederate visitors would simply cluster in neighbouring colonies.[60] The
privacy of communications also became a concern; many feared that
postal inspectors were opening the mail and that U.S. officials were
monitoring telegraph communications, not to mention censoring telegraphic and press reports. Confederate ciphers used in British North
America were easily broken and the mail of individuals such as
Benjamin Wier of Halifax was intercepted.[61]

Critics of the North's war effort seized upon spying and other
actions such as the suspension of habeas corpus as proof that the
Union was deteriorating into a military dictatorship. The peace wing
of the Democratic party, which proposed a negotiated settlement of
the war, shared these assumptions. That a republic would arrest
fifteen thousand of its citizens on suspicion of disloyalty seemed to
harken back to the dark days of the French Revolution. New York
resident Daniel Lord, writing Nova Scotia Chief Justice William
Young, expressed confidence in the North's just cause but regretted
"the army of spies and informers that now swarm the land."[62] To
most British subjects, spies were "a class of persons who are among
the most ignoble and despicable of beings everywhere."[63]

The *Novascotian* advised no one to leave the province without a
passport and cautioned that "every steamer and railway out of the
United States is watched by policemen." A number of Maritimers
encountered difficulties on steamers to Maine and New York. Even
prominent lawyer and politician John Hamilton Gray of New Brunswick was nervous about travelling in the United States without protection papers. In the early months of the war, two Bluenoses, William
Patrick, a resident of New York, and James Leguire, who was attempting to visit his brother in Tennessee, were arrested as suspected Confederate sympathizers. Young Leguire had foolishly carried his Halifax Scottish Rifles uniform in his luggage, which had
given the appearance that he was on his way to Nashville to enlist
in the Confederate forces. Patrick, originally from Merigomish, was
imprisoned in Fort Lafayette by order of the secretary of war. He
had a business partner in Mobile and had married a Southern belle
(and had forced her to sell her slaves before the wedding). A police
official reminded Patrick that Andrew Jackson had once executed
two British subjects "for meddling in our affairs." Both Patrick and
Leguire were released after the intervention of British authorities. Colonial commentators interpreted the Northern suspension of habeas
corpus as an unprecedented attack on popular rights and called Lincoln a tyrant. Pro-Southern journals argued that the Confederacy did
not incarcerate women, shackle its press or suspend habeas corpus.[64]

Each of the three colonial capitals had American consuls, paid by fees, whose dispatches are an important source for examining the war's impact on the region. Washington's chief operative in Halifax for most of the war was Judge Mortimer M. Jackson, who arrived from New York several weeks after First Bull Run. Albert Pilsbury, who had held the post since 1855, had been displaced by the Republican administration.[65] An interim appointee, J.E. Vinton, had not met with the approval of Congress, although he had kept track of suspicious vessels and Southerners. Jackson, a good Republican, had practised law in pioneer Wisconsin before being elected to the bench. In the 1850s he had run without success for state attorney general and for the U.S. Senate. Most of Wisconsin had opted for the Republican candidate in the 1860 election, and Lincoln's cabinet had a long list of party faithful to reward. Josh Giddings, an Ohio anti-slavery activist with no diplomatic experience and little money, was named consul for Canada East. James Q. Howard of Ohio, who had worked on Lincoln's campaign, replaced the incumbent Collins Whittaker in Saint John despite the protests of his supporters. Howard became a social acquaintance of the local police magistrate, a relationship that proved beneficial.[66] Albert Caitlan, the consul for P.E.I., according to Vinton, in 1861 was "a secessionist . . . continually talking against the government." Caitlan took a loyalty oath and was backed by such luminaries as William Pope and T. Heath Haviland but was purged nonetheless by the State Department. The consul at Pictou was the popular Major B. Hammant Norton, whose elegant sandstone house is now an historic guest inn. Norton, an American expansionist who was well respected in eastern Nova Scotia, had a son in the Union army during the war.[67]

Robin Winks has concluded that the consuls, not spies, proved to be "the most valuable listening posts" in the provinces during the war.[68] In peacetime they administered the Reciprocity Treaty, issued documents to American vessels, assisted distressed citizens and reported on general economic conditions and policies affecting trade. During the Civil War their duties became more devoted to national security. And none was more dedicated or effective than Judge Jackson in Halifax, who dipped into his own savings to pay for information of strategic importance. He reported on the Royal Navy and British troop movements, the gold fields of the colony and the presence of blockade runners and Southern émigrés. His "detectives" were more in the style of amateur informers. Jackson recommended new consular agents for Digby, Annapolis, Barrington, Yarmouth, Windsor and Shelburne, all of them American citizens except John C. Wade of Digby, a provincial assemblyman "friendly to the Union cause." This network, connected to Halifax by telegraph, would prove indispensable during the hunt for the captured *Chesapeake*. Through his observations, personal contacts, paid informers and newspaper clippings, Jackson performed an effective intelligence role in Nova Scotia even if at times he was excessively alarmist. He also helped local militiamen and British officers secure commissions in the United States' service. Jackson's reports could reach Washington within minutes on the American-owned telegraph system. In 1862 the *Evening Reporter* announced that the consuls, formerly regarded as gentlemen, were engaged in "political espionage" by reporting on "all Southerners who arrive in our midst."[69]

A New Brunswick contemporary asserted that the consuls sought popularity in Washington by portraying the colonies in as bad a light as possible. It dismissed consul Howard of Saint John as little more than "a petty commercial agent, permitted to reside here by our people for better facilitating commercial transactions between this port and the United States." Yet the same official allegedly employed "pimps listening to your conversation" to gather information on blockade running and Confederate activity.[70]

Given the enormity of Northern intelligence and security problems, it is unlikely that the opinions and actions of a few people in the Maritime colonies were of much concern in Washington. There were exceptions. In February of 1864, after the *Chesapeake* highjacking, the secretary of the navy passed information from Halifax on to the North Atlantic Blockading Squadron. Consul Jackson had reported the arrival of the suspicious British screw steamer *Will o'the Wisp* and warned that several wanted persons, including ex-Marshall George F. Kane of Baltimore (a police official implicated in secessionist activities in 1861), two Confederate escapees from Johnson's Island, a deserter from the Union army and a number of Maryland refugees would soon leave Halifax for Bermuda with the hope of evading the blockade. This information was confirmed by War Department detectives, a sign that Halifax was recognized as a port deserving surveillance. *Will o'the Wisp*, owned by the Anglo-Confederate Trading Company, would complete a dozen trips through the blockade before running aground in 1864, and Kane and several other Southern gentlemen were entertained at the new Halifax Club before departing for Nassau.[71]

5 Bluenoses in Arms

These deluded men are seeking the bubble reputation at the cannon's mouth in a cause and on a field where there is neither glory to be gathered nor laurels to be reaped nor even prize monies to be pocketed.

– *Colonial Farmer*, 4 April 1863

A principal reason that the Maritime colonies were fascinated by the American war was that scores of their sons were participants. The reasons for this were diverse and not always easy to fathom, for few left behind diaries or letters to explain their motives. The most important factor was the Bluenose presence in New England, particularly Maine and Massachusetts, and in the Mid-Atlantic states, principally New York. Few of the Maritimers who ended up in American military service in 1861–65 travelled stateside expressly for this purpose; those who did risked being regarded as mercenaries back home. It was principally the expatriate Maritimer and those visiting or living in the Northern states for other reasons who enlisted. Some had moved with their parents at an early age and by 1861 their only links with the Maritimes were kinsfolk. Others migrated in search of work or to study. Colonel Thomas Cass, of the famed 9th Massachusetts Regiment, an Irish unit, had lived in Saint John as a youth. His regiment contained other men with New Brunswick connections. Wentworth Dow, born at Kingsclear, New Brunswick, in 1829, had resided at East Brighton until 1856, whereupon he migrated to the Wisconsin frontier to work as a lumberman. A naturalized American by 1861, he joined the 16th Wisconsin Volunteers and recorded his war experiences in a diary. General John McNeil, the Missouri militia officer who gained notoriety by ordering the execution of Confederate guerrillas in 1862, had lived in Halifax as a youth.[1]

NUMBERS AND MOTIVATION

Historians and commentators have debated the numerical representation of British North Americans in the Civil War armed forces since the late nineteenth century.[2] In the 1950s, Robin Winks attempted to refute the often-quoted estimate of fifty thousand British North Americans in the Union armies by raising the questions of domicile and citizenship. That is, most "Canadian" recruits were residents of the United States, and in many cases naturalized citizens, when they signed up for the army or navy. Ties with Canada and Britain, in other words, were weak. More recent research, all of it in progress, suggests that the "mythical" fifty thousand may be close to the truth, going by place of birth alone. This author, for example, estimates that the number of Maritimers and former Maritimers in the American forces was as high as ten thousand. I also have argued, in response to Winks, that this military participation by brothers, sons and friends, however distant from 'home,' had significance for attitudes in the colonies.[3]

The question of motivation is both straightforward and mystifying, for statistics and social history hypotheses can never explain the individual decisions of thousands of men in time of war. Opportunity was a dominant factor in explaining enlistments. Men and women were the Maritimes' most valuable exports to the United States. Many Bluenose warriors had married, settled down, taken out citizenship and voted in American elections. These individuals volunteered out of patriotism or at least sympathy with the cause of the Union, which explains why married men with children cheerfully relinquished peaceful pursuits in 1861. Former Islander F.L. Cooper was sufficiently influential to be able to raise a company of infantry in New Jersey, and three years later he commanded his regiment. John J. MacDonald, born at Lot 47, P.E.I., joined the 28th Massachusetts Regiment in 1861, not to fight slavery but to defend the republic. He also saw the rebellion as a chance for New England Catholics, the subject of discrimination in the 1850s, to prove their mettle as citizens.[4]

Maritime émigrés and sojourners, particularly if they were Protestant and possessed a skilled trade, found New England, the Mid-Atlantic states and the West to be congenial environments. Although a fifth of Boston's gainfully employed British Americans in 1850 worked as domestics or labourers, others were clerks, artisans and tradesmen. In both Boston and New York, and their surrounding communities, Maritimers rarely ended up in the criminal courts, jails or almshouses. On the island of Manhattan in 1860, British

Americans constituted a cross-section of the workforce; one-fifth of the gainfully employed were found in the building and marine trades. Maritime-born women were dressmakers and domestics – immigration brought equal numbers of young men and women. By 1865, Boston and Cambridge each housed more British North Americans than German- or English-born immigrants.[5] Although immigrants, in the Northern states Maritimers were culturally acceptable; they in turn accepted much of American culture, including republican political ideology and abstractions such as the sanctity of the Union.

The eradication of slavery, at least early in the war, was not a priority for recruits. In time most Bluenose warriors came to accept emancipation on military or political, if not social, grounds. "Free soil" ideology was prevalent in a number of letters from Maritimers in the Union forces. A former Yarmouth resident serving in Western Virginia in 1861 predicted that superior Northern civilization would crush "the half-clad and poorly-fed conscriptionists" motivated by "Southern fanaticism." A society built on slavery could not stop the "heavy and stalwart" men of the North, "inured to labour and blest with the broadest intelligence."[6] Regional chauvinism aside, few Union volunteers expressed sympathy with either slaves or abolitionists. John J. MacDonald, for example, was hostile to "that fanatical tribe" of abolitionists and admired Lincoln for refusing in 1861 to fight "an abolition war."[7]

Not a few were drawn into Union ranks for economic reasons, although this is probably truer of the period 1864–65 than earlier, and truer of the navy than the army. War-related production also offered employment opportunities: the Brooklyn navy yard had seven thousand workers by 1864. Yet the streets of Boston and New York, particularly if one lacked a trade, capital or connections, were not paved with gold. As a Nova Scotian wrote from Boston, "A great many Bluenoses have enlisted, principally from necessity."[8] British North Americans had joined the U.S. Army regulars before the war. The Union soldier and sailor were relatively well paid and the work, if hazardous for the former, was steady.[9]

Medical students took advantage of the war's widening demand for surgeons, either as contract physicians or commissioned officers who served in urban military or battlefield hospitals or on board ship. John Leander Bishop (b. 1820), educated at Nova Scotia's Horton Academy and Acadia College, had studied medicine in Halifax. He had migrated to Philadelphia to continue his education and turned to writing. Enlisting as an acting surgeon with a Pennslyvania regiment in 1862, he tended the wounded at Second Bull Run,

Nova Scotian Robert Campbell, in
the Union Army, 1865.

Fredericksburg and the Wilderness. Dr. C.H. Giberson of New Brunswick was a federal surgeon in occupied New Orleans. Although
he recognized that the question of emancipation had divided Northern opinion, he came to support abolitionism during the war.[10] In
addition to physicians, the Northern armies required chaplains, and
several Maritime clergymen served in this capacity.

British North Americans also enlisted out of restlessness or a
yearning for adventure, a factor in immigration history not easily
quantifiable. The typical volunteer, in his late teens or early twenties, was not saddled with the responsibilities of family, career or
property. Robert Alder McLeod was lured to South Carolina in the
fall of 1860 "by the prospect of stirring times."[11] Militarism, or interest in things military, does not seem to have been a primary
consideration. One exception was John Beardsley of Grand Falls,
New Brunswick, who joined the 10th Maine Regiment, as he explained to New Brunswick's governor, "for the purpose of acquiring
a practical knowledge of the art of war." Against the backdrop of

the *Trent* crisis and concerns about British neutrality, Gordon removed Beardsley's name from the list of Victoria County volunteer militia officers.[12]

One minority that does not appear to have participated in the American war in significant numbers is the Acadians, over 15 percent of New Brunswick's population in 1871. A handful of Nova Scotia Acadians (some with anglicized names) have been linked to the war, but the topic of Maritime francophone involvement in the conflict awaits detailed study. Acadians had not started to migrate southwards in large numbers prior to 1861, but this would change after Confederation. New Brunswick Acadians, oriented to the Gulf of St. Lawrence, feared enforced military service during the Confederation debates of the 1860s. Most francophones in the Union forces, and there were thousands, hailed from Quebec or from the growing Franco-American communities of New England. The Maine border counties, especially in the Madawaska region, appear to have had low enlistment levels. Maine's Franco-American volunteers tended to be recruited in southern communities such as Lewiston or Portland. Familiarity with English-speaking, urban culture or the existence of ethnic support networks in industrializing New England probably were the major determinant of Franco-American mobility and enlistment. The Acadians of the Maritimes lacked these characteristics prior to 1865.[13]

Another possible factor is the low participation rate of Acadians in the militia. Historically the Acadians shunned military pursuits and probably did not strongly identify with an English-language institution.[14] In New Brunswick, higher posts went to anglophones; the militia reforms of the Civil War era, which included a literacy test and examinations in English, saw the number of Acadian officers fall to less than thirty. In Madawaska, with its history of border tensions with Maine, prominent Acadians were more likely to be active.[15]

Ongoing research is uncovering Civil War service by British North American–born blacks such as Ben Jackson of Nova Scotia. As discussed in Chapter 3, the North's "sable arm," which consisted mainly of Southern blacks, also contained scores of Canadian blacks and dozens of Maritime-born blacks. The contribution of the African-American soldier, although controversial at the time, was impressive and burdensome; one in three died of wounds or disease, largely because of inferior diet, medical care and shelter. Maritime-born blacks who entered the Union army or navy, such as Nelson Owen of Yarmouth or George Crosby of P.E.I., like their white counterparts, had probably cut many of their ties to the region.[16]

UNDER THE BONNIE BLUE FLAG

Geography and trade, not ideology, dictated that few colonists would serve under the Rebel flag.[17] The limited numbers of Maritimers who fought for the Confederacy tended to be living and working in the South prior to 1861. Given the region's remoteness to the British colonies, the barrier of the military front, and the ever-tightening blockade, it was difficult and expensive for colonists to reach the Confederacy once the fighting started. Southerners had been spoiling for a fight since the John Brown raid, and patriotism was a heady brew among the Rebels. Former Maritime residents who enlisted under the Confederate banner tended to reflect this ideological commitment in their letters home. One former New Brunswicker wrote to his sister in 1863 that he was "as mad a secessionist as any Southern man" and vowed to fight "until the Confederacy is acknowledged a nation or conquered and the army dispersed." But many were probably victims of circumstance with little choice but to take up the Rebel cause. Few left the Maritimes to do so. Those such as William Bruce Almon II, a young Halifax physician who ran the blockade in 1863 in order to offer his services to the Confederate medical authorities, were rare.[18] There were other Maritimers in Confederate service, but they were very much the exception. John Stoop, intending to pursue a career as an artist, left Saint Andrew's, New Brunswick, for Virginia in 1860. He was commissioned a lieutenant in the Confederate artillery in 1861 and was later promoted to captain. In 1864–65 he commanded a battery in the defence of Richmond, where he died from dysentery before the war's end.[19] P.E.I.'s Alexander MacIntosh, who migrated to Texas in the 1850s, rode with the Confederate cavalry, was wounded and ended up as a prisoner of war. Richard McCully, from Truro, Nova Scotia, also was living in the South when the war broke out. In May 1862, at Fort Darling on the James River south of Richmond, he commanded a gun in a battery that helped block the ironclads *Monitor* and *Galena*. While attempting to clear debris from his cannon, McCully was mortally wounded by a shell fragment. The Halifax *Express* justified McCully's war participation on the grounds that he had been residing in a country that was being invaded, unlike other Bluenoses who, like Hessian or Swiss mercenaries of old, had accepted blood money to fight on foreign soil. Anti-Yankee journals were particularly troubled by the fact that Bluenoses who enlisted in Northern ranks swore loyalty to the Union.[20]

Another Maritimer who helped repulse the Yankees at Fort Darling was Robert Alder McLeod, born at Bedeque, P.E.I. His father was a Wesleyan Methodist minister who later edited the *Wesleyan Anthenaeum* in Halifax; one grandfather was a Yorkshire pioneer in Chignecto, the other a Scottish soldier who had battled the Patriots at Cowpens during the Revolutionary War. Robbie had attended Mount Allison Academy before the family moved to Baltimore where his father edited a Methodist journal. The family embraced Southern nationalism; McLeod's mother, described as a "fine Southern lady," published a poem on Stonewall Jackson. At the age of sixteen, Robbie moved to Charleston hoping to work towards his education. He witnessed the attack on Fort Sumter and then joined the Washington Light Artillery for three months. In 1862, before the action at Fort Darling, his unit signed up for "the duration." He was at the Battle of Secessionville that summer where John J. MacDonald was killed, and he spent several days in Fort Wagner, Morris Island, before it was evacuated on 6 September 1863. McLeod, a member of the 23rd South Carolina Regiment, was one of the last soldiers out of Sumter when it was temporarily abandoned in late 1863; he sent his sister a fragment of the fort's tattered flag. Other engagements that year included Swift Creek, Mechanicsville, Cold Harbour and Petersburg. During the siege of Petersburg, the regiment spent two months in the trenches without relief.[21]

Promoted to sergeant, McLeod was wounded outside enemy breastworks on the Weldon and Petersburg Railroad. His Yankee captors took him to hospital at City Point, from where he wrote one of his brothers. A few days later, in a Philadelphia hospital, a surgeon amputated the Rebel's shattered arm. The pain was countered by liberal doses of brandy, punch and porter. After a partial recovery, McLeod and other prisoners of war, experiencing considerable hardship, were shipped to Savannah. McLeod's letters to his family first were examined by Southern provost marshalls and then sent via steamer to Havana to be forwarded to friends in the colonies or Northern states. Replies, understandably, were long in coming. He particularly appreciated family photographs and a sprig of mignonette.[22]

PRESERVING THE UNION

As colonial newspapers began to print obituaries of fallen Bluenoses, and as embalmed bodies were shipped back to New Brunswick, Prince Edward Island and Nova Scotia from Union military hospitals, few communities remained untouched by the spectre of death. Even journals that supported the North, such as the *Cape Breton News*, regretted that so many young provincialists were risking their lives and health and causing their families such great suffering for a foreign war. Commenting on the tragic case of Alexander Musgrave of Little Bras d'Or and his cousin Thomas Musgrave, who had succumbed to typhoid fever without having seen combat, the *News* regretted their "mistaken zeal." Similarly, the pro-Northern *Globe* of Saint John cautioned the young men of the provinces to reconsider before travelling to the United States to enlist. As long as the Rebels appeared to have the upper hand, as in 1861 and 1862, or when the military situation appeared to be inconclusive, as in 1863 and parts of 1864, many in the Maritimes resented the use of their young men as Yankee cannon fodder. Yet Bluenoses served with distinction in all theatres of the war and in all branches of the armed services. Some led companies or even regiments, others commanded gun batteries and naval vessels, but most were the common infantry soldiers who actually won the war.[23]

Although not a Nova Scotian by birth, Frederick George Strasser, alias Baron or Count D'Utassy, was a former Halifax resident who later commanded a colourful regiment of "foreigners," the 39th New York Volunteers. Strasser was one of the war's great impostors. He eventually ended up in New York's Sing Sing Prison, not for having passed himself off as a Hungarian nobleman but for having defrauded the government. The diminutive but debonair "D'Utassy" claimed to have received an officer's commission in Austrian service in 1843 and to have participated in the Revolution of 1848 and the Crimean War. Armed with a bogus degree from an Italian university, the multilingual confidence artist was engaged as a master of modern languages by Dalhousie College in 1855. He had met Principal Hugo Reid while in London, where he had claimed to have experienced Bohemian life in Paris. While in Nova Scotia D'Utassy published a small book, *Biographical Sketches of the Leading Characters of Piedmont*. His polished manners, continental sophistication and skill in languages, fencing and horsemanship endeared him to Halifax's snobbish elite. D'Utassy became the personal tutor to the family of the lieutenant-governor. In February of 1860, following the temporary closing of the college, the board of governors decided not to renew his contract. For a time he studied medicine with Dr. W.J. Almon, but eventually he moved to New York's greener pastures.[24]

A year later, in the flurry of volunteering following the attack on Fort Sumter, D'Utassy organized a regiment of Italians, Swiss, Germans, Hungarians, French and Iberians which marched to revolutionary tunes and wore stylish uniforms. The unit was dubbed the Garibaldi Guards in honour of the famed Italian patriot. Its colonel was lionized by New York journalists and politicians and showered with gifts and praise. A master publicist, D'Utassy, in imitation of French regiments, even recruited a couple of *vivandières*, young women in uniform who sold liquor and refreshments to the regiment. The officers of the "Garibaldians" enjoyed the finer things in life and the regiment looked superb on the parade ground. Its motto was "Victory or Death."[25]

In 1861 the Garibaldians took part in the ill-managed Bull Run campaign, acting as a reserve unit in the rear guard on the road from Manassas to Alexandria and Washington. D'Utassy came under official investigation in 1862 following the Union debacle at Harper's Ferry, prior to the bloody encounter at Antietam. At Harper's Ferry the Union commanders allowed themselves to be surrounded by Rebel forces on nearby bluffs, resulting in the surrender of twelve thousand men. Even more serious was the fact that Stonewall Jackson's divisions were able to push on to Sharpsburg, or Antietam. D'Utassy, commanding a brigade, later testified that he had questioned his commanding officer's order to abandon Maryland Heights. An investigating commission exonerated D'Utassy, who had been placed under military arrest, and noted that he had expressed a desire to fight his way out rather than surrender. He also had ordered the regiment's rifles to be destroyed rather than fall into enemy hands and had saved the regimental flags in his luggage. The Halifax *Express* opined that the count was serving in "a bad cause" and that his elite Halifax friends would have preferred to have seen "the gallant Colonel's military experience and energy as heretofore on the side of those who are struggling for freedom and independence" (an allusion to D'Utassy's claim that he had supported Kossuth in the 1848 Revolution in Hungary).[26]

Critics of D'Utassy's extravagance suggested that he was an impostor, a Hungarian Jew who had operated a pawn shop and sold horses to the army. In the end it was not his invented title and accomplishments, but peculation, defrauding the United States government for personal gain, that landed him in hot water. The Garibaldi Guard, it seemed, had not only served the ego of this consummate showman but had also lined his pockets. Halifax supporters of the count were shocked. He was cashiered from the army and sentenced to penitentiary for one year. Typically, the former Haligonian insisted on receiving special treatment in prison on the grounds that he was a gentleman, possessed a university education and could speak eleven languages. When last heard from, Strasser, or D'Utassy, was in the photography business at Delaware Gap.[27]

UNION NURSE, SOLDIER AND SPY

An even more intriguing story involving a former Maritime resident and the Civil War is that of Sarah Emma Edmunds (or Edmonson), who had been born in Maguadavic, York County, New Brunswick, circa 1840. It reads like the folk tale of the young woman who disguises herself as a man in order to follow her true love to war, but with a twist. Unlike the girl in the folk story, Emma donned men's clothing not to follow a lover but to give expression to her own free spirit and questioning of restrictive gender roles. Of pioneer Scottish and Irish stock, she worked briefly in a store in Salisbury, New Brunswick, and may have fled parental authority because of plans for an arranged marriage. Either before or after leaving the colony, she began to disguise herself as a man, Frank Thompson, a travelling book salesman who was considered an eligible bachelor. Enjoying the independence of male garb, the "beardless boy" travelled westward and settled in Flint, Michigan.[28]

In the wave of local patriotism in 1861, "Frank" volunteered for a unit that became part of the 2nd Michigan Infantry, bluffing her way past the medical examination. The regiment participated in the Bull Run campaign. As a member of Company F, Edmunds was present at several important engagements, including Fair Oaks, Williamsburg, Malvern Hill and Fredericksburg. She constantly feared discovery and was the butt of jokes about her small boots and girlish features. For a time "Frank" helped out as a male nurse, a duty she later claimed to have preferred over soldiering. He/she also served as regimental postmaster and dispatch rider.[29]

After 1862, Edmunds' story becomes somewhat hazy. After the regiment was posted to Kentucky in 1863, Frank Thompson deserted and resurfaced as a female nurse tending the sick and wounded. Many of the details in Edmunds' 1865 memoirs, *Nurse and Spy in the Union Army*, written to raise money for medical relief, probably are fictional, yet the book is exceedingly entertaining and places the protagonist at most of the key events of the war, including First and Second Bull Run, Williamsburg, Seven Oaks, the Seven Days battles, Antietam and Fredericksburg. One American reviewer compared the volume, which also was written to raise morale, to the tales of Baron Munchhausen. Edmunds claimed to have volunteered for dangerous spying missions behind enemy lines, disguised as both men (black and white) and women. She supposedly met a former sweetheart, now in Union blue, who did not recognize her in masculine garb. Another story has the heroine, having confiscated supplies from a Rebel house, shooting and torturing a "secesh" woman after surviving an assassination attempt. Emma later explained her desertion as being motivated by her fear of being found out. Having injured her leg while riding on a mule, and being denied a medical discharge, she went absent without leave, convalesced in the North and worked for the U.S. Sanitary Commission.[30]

In her 1865 book, written before the war had ended, Emma spoke of her "adopted home" not as Michigan but New England. News of the war broke as she was in the West, waiting to travel east. Edmonds claimed to have left her rural home in New Brunswick in search of "Foreign Missionary" work. She now vowed to aid "the most happy and prosperous nation the sun ever shone upon" by becoming a nurse: "It is true, I was not an American – and I was not obliged to remain here during this terrible strife – I could return to my native land where my parents would welcome me to the home of my childhood, and my brothers and sisters would rejoice at my coming." Unable to decide the proper course, she "carried this question to the Throne of Grace, and found a satisfactory answer there": she would volunteer as a field hospital nurse "and partici- pate in all the excitement of the battle scenes."[31]

Visiting New Brunswick after the war, Emma met, or possibly was reacquainted with, lumberman Linus Seelye. Courtship ensued and the pair was married. At first they resided in Cleveland, Ohio. For the next thirty years the Seelyes were on the move, living in Michigan, Ohio, Missouri and Kansas. For a time they were "car- petbaggers" running an orphanage for black children in Louisiana. In 1882, Frank Thompson revealed his true identity; having deserted during the war, Emma was not entitled to any pension. Two years later she was reunited with former regiment members. Former of- ficers, overcome by chivalry, praised Emma's war service and fought the desertion charge. She became the first woman to receive a regu- lar army pension and the first woman to be inducted into the Grand Army of the Republic, a veterans' organization. Edmunds passed away at La Porte, Texas, in 1898, at age fifty-seven. None of her adopted children survived her.[32]

Emma Edmunds' war participation was an exception for Maritime women; most were affected only indirectly by the war. Mothers, sisters and spouses coped with separation and loss and supported absent warriors with prayers, letters and care packages from home.

The teenaged sister of one Nova Scotian recruit in the Union army admonished her brother not to neglect "the precious blood of Christ before it is too late." Maritime women who had migrated to New England headed households when husbands were absent in the army or navy; others laboured in traditional sectors such as domestic service or the needle trades or in textile and shoe factories as industry converted to the war effort.[33] Not all Bluenose warriors were young or single: William Henry Charlton's wife had nine children before he joined Company D of the 30th Maine Regiment at forty-two in 1863. He returned to Halifax, fathered more children and worked as a stone cutter.[34]

CHRISTIAN WARRIOR

Another perspective on the war is found in the experience of Colin Shaw, born in Elliot River, P.E.I., the grandson of Scottish immigrants. One of eight sons, several of whom supposedly enlisted in the American war, Shaw was married with children and living in Salem, Massachusetts, in 1861, having emigrated to New England as a youth.

Shaw followed the trade of cabinetmaker and gave vent to his intense spirituality through the Baptist Church and the Sons of Temperance. In early June 1861, out of patriotism for his adopted home, he enlisted in the 11th Massachusetts Volunteers, a unit that also contained a number of British deserters. The regiment departed for Washington and reached Virginia in time to participate in the fight at Manassas. His pastor later recalled that, at Bull Run, Colin had "waded shoe deep in blood in taking one of the enemy's batteries," yet afterwards, in the midst of a panicked retreat, had calmly returned to a corner of the field to fetch his canteen and knapsack. Shaw allegedly told his curious company commander that he believed God was watching over him.[35]

Next came an interlude that reveals much about Shaw's motivations. The regiment spent several months at Budd's Ferry, Maryland, and there Shaw revealed a rare quality in a Union soldier at that point in the war: compassion for slaves. "He regarded the Christian life as warfare," his eulogist recalled, "and this earth a glorious field of labour." This included the slaves and former slaves whom most Northern troops despised. Posted as a guard on a nearby plantation, he angered its mistress by teaching slaves to read and write and reading them Scripture. "I begin at one cabin," Shaw wrote, "and go through the whole, reading a chapter to every family." He comforted an aged bondsman on his deathbed and performed a ceremony for a small child who was about to be buried like a dog. When ordered by the plantation's mistress to desist in his preaching, he threatened to withdraw his guard services. Shaw also distributed tracts and other religious publications among his military comrades.[36]

Colin Shaw experienced over one dozen battles, several of which became household names for a generation. He was wounded only twice. At Fair Oaks he felt protected by divine intercession after a bullet pierced his coat sleeve and shrapnel ruined his rifle. He next survived "the slaughterous retreat from Richmond," marching for several days under the burning sun. At the Second Battle of Bull Run (29 August 1862) the former Islander was wounded in the side by a musket-ball. In a fierce twenty-minute encounter, the 11th Massachusetts, "the battalion of direction," had fired one volley, then attacked uphill with bayonet and rifle butt through two lines of Confederates. The brigade was halted by a third line of Rebels and fell back under artillery fire. Weakened by loss of blood, Shaw was prostrate for twenty-four hours then evacuated by wagon, an excruciatingly painful ordeal for the wounded. Two days later, either abandoned or overtaken by Confederate patrols, he was made a prisoner of war. Despite his wounds, he was kept for ten days with no medical treatment on a hard floor. Fortunately, Shaw was released and was able to recuperate in Fairfax Hospital in Alexandria. The recovery took four months, time Shaw spent in evangelical work, attempting to convert lapsed Christians to a life of personal piety. He turned down an offer by the head surgeon to remain in hospital as a nurse; his duty was with his regiment.[37] A few weeks after his release from hospital, the regiment was on the field at Fredericksburg, where a smaller but well-positioned Confederate army of over seventy thousand looked down from entrenchments across the Rappahannock River. The Federals crossed the river on pontoon bridges but failed to drive Longstreet from Mayre's Height and Jackson from Prospect Hill.[38] Assaulting on the Confederate left, the 11th Massachusetts lost one-third of its effective strength on the first day of the battle. On the second day it was pulled out of the lines to catch its breath. Shaw took his canteen and water dipper to the wounded and dying, quenching their thirst and making them as comfortable as possible under the circumstances. After the battle he wrote, "How tired and sick we all are of such work. If it were not plain for all the world that we are engaged in a just and holy cause, I would die before I would discharge a gun at anyone, but God helping men I am willing to do all I can to put down this wicked rebellion and if it costs me my life, I say God's will be done."[39]

Another Maritimer, W.R. Snow, of Woodstock, recorded his experience of the battle. He was on orderly duty with General Gordon G. Meade of Reynold's corps. As the Pennsylvania troops approached the Rebel right, they were hit by fire from well-concealed batteries:

By Moses if the shell and solid shot did not hum around us, cutting the trees on the side of the road, smashing rails, tearing up the ground and raising the duce generally. After that all was noise and confusion; the cheers of the men, the commands of the officers, the groans of the wounded and dying, the thundering of artillery and the rushing of the infantry are all easier imagined than experienced.

As Meade's orderly, Snow was in the thick of the fighting; Meade's hat was pierced by a bullet, his horse was killed underneath him and his personal aide was shot dead.[40]

Next came the decisive battle of Gettysburg. After a forced march, the 11th Massachusetts was ordered into arms at dawn on the second day, which climaxed with the 20th Maine's defence of Little Round Top. As part of the 3rd Corps, Shaw's regiment was in position to meet the Confederate attack on the Peach Orchard and Wheat Field. Between three and eight in the afternoon the regiment absorbed a charge from an Alabama regiment and countered with two of its own. At some point in the action, Shaw was hit in the leg above the knee and fell to the ground. He lapsed into unconsciousness while the battle surged around him and remained on the ground for two days and nights, cannon-balls ploughing up the earth nearby and musket-balls whizzing by his ears. The Islander lay helpless as the Union forces routed Pickett's charge, and during the battle he wrote his wife a long letter. He was carried from the field to hospital where the wounded leg probably was amputated. The low-impact, large-calibre bullets of the 1860s tended to shatter the bone, making delicate surgical repairs unpractical. The surgeons also knew little, or cared little, about antiseptic safeguards. Although the pain was countered by morphine, infection set in and Colin Shaw expired a month after the battle. Prior to his death he was visited by his brother Neil, who shared his strong religious faith. According to his nurse, Shaw's final words were "How easy it is for a Christian to die." The Colin Shaw story, along with the equally sad news of his wife's death within a few months of his own, was relayed to Islanders in the pages of the *Protestant and Evangelical Witness*.[41]

CAVALRY SOLDIER BOY

The memoirs of William Charles Archibald, published forty-five years after the Confederate surrender, provide a rare glimpse into the motivations of British North Americans who served under the Stars and Stripes. Of colonists who ended up enlisting after journeying to the States during the war, his case is probably most typical because he did not leave rural Halifax County intending to become a soldier. Rather, he had been drawn to the States by a combination of wanderlust, ambition and curiosity that has lured generations of Maritimers to "go down the road." But Archibald's experience is atypical in one sense: unlike most British Americans who entered the Union army, he returned home after the war. His first loyalties were with Nova Scotia and, later, the Dominion of Canada. Yet this Bluenose trooper firmly supported the Union cause and for eighteen months took part in some of the heaviest action of the war.[42]

Born in 1842, Archibald grew up in the Musquodoboit Valley of Halifax County. A member of a large rural family, as a boy he eagerly followed the exploits of the British military in the Crimean War and other theatres. With the death of his father in 1860, William Charles inherited the responsibilities of the man of the household, but he grew restless. After contemplating a trek to distant California, he opted for New England. Thousands of his fellow colonists, male and female, had settled in or were temporarily working in the northeastern states, part of a mass movement that was to gain increased momentum after the Civil War and eventually attract previously sedentary groups such as the Acadians. Maine was the first stop for Maritimers looking for work amongst the Yankees, with hundreds of Bluenoses labouring in the fishery alone. In the fall of 1863, Archibald joined this outmigration by embarking on a steamer from Windsor to Portland, Maine.[43]

For a time he laboured on an uncle's farm at Cape Elizabeth. This branch of the family had left Nova Scotia in 1849. Working as a teamster at Oxford a few months later, he first encountered a recruiting agent offering large bounties to volunteers. In Maine, British subjects were beyond the jurisdiction of the British Foreign Enlistment Act and British colonists were found in most military units recruited in the Pine Tree State. Archibald was still unsure. But the death of his cousin, a member of a Maine infantry regiment, stirred his sympathies. Other young Maritimers were drawn into the conflict by stages; Hugh Munro of Pictou County also worked in a Maine lumber camp before volunteering. After some reflection Archibald travelled to Portland where he enlisted in the 1st District of Columbia Cavalry, which was mustered into service at Augusta on February 8, 1864. By this time the superior industrial, naval and manpower resources of the North had turned the tide of the war, but in the eastern theatre Union soldiers still maintained a healthy respect towards the Army of Northern Virginia.[44]

Back in Nova Scotia, Archibald's family very much opposed his enlistment in a foreign cause. The dutiful and guilt-ridden son sent his mother his initial enlistment bounty, a sum equivalent to a labourer's yearly wages, in goods and cash: a Singer sewing machine and barrels of flour and sugar found their way up the Bay of Fundy and by train and wagon to the homestead at Poplar Grove, courtesy of Uncle Sam, and further payments probably were sent as remittances. "Willie" also wrote his mother weekly or more often, and forwarded poetry, a lock of his hair and a photograph of the "cavalry soldier boy" in uniform. His mother wrote back that his going to war was "the greatest trial I have ever had." In a letter written in August 1864, she revealed that Nova Scotians closely followed the war:

I fear you will have a hard time of it. The North expects to meet the rebels, and oh, what is to be expected then? Bloodshed such as has not been since the war commenced. Yes, the ensuing summer, the writers say, will be fearful beyond description.

Years later Archibald concluded that no amount of money, gifts or correspondence could have compensated for the family's emotional sufferings caused by his enlistment. Even neighbours wept when his mother read his regular letters aloud at the farm.[45]

The family enlisted the aid of a cousin, Reverend Eliakim Archibald, to persuade the errant son to return. (The Archibalds were a religious clan, and several children had been named after missionaries.) "Willie's" response indicates that he was motivated by a combination of wanderlust, political support for the American republic and a belief in divine providence:

The Yankees are a go-ahead people. Living on the farm is too quiet for me. I want my blood warmed. My childish fancy often pictured daring exploits. I like the word hero. Well you say, I enlisted for fame. No, not altogether. I am doing something for this Union, as I think the North is doing right and will finally subdue. . . . When I was in Nova Scotia, nothing could have tempted me to enlist, but His way is not our ways. I hope that it will be all for the best. There are as many as ten thousand Nova Scotians and Canadians in the war.[46]

These views would have clashed with majority opinion in the Maritime provinces in 1864, when public opinion was still with the South, if only because of the anti-British tone of the Yankee press. Archibald's letters, preserved in his 1910 memoirs, *Home-making and its Philosophy*, suggest that he was a typical Union volunteer in that he did not enlist to fight slavery so much as Southern secession.

Indeed, slavery is only incidental to the memoir.[47]

The 1st D.C. Cavalry, also known as Baker's Mounted Rangers, went by rail to Washington where it trained at Camp Baker. Archibald mentioned little about training and horsemanship, but as a young farmer he would have had, in the words of Canadian military authority Colonel George T. Denison, "a good seat on a horse and a general knowledge of the use of the rifle." The recruits were issued with sabres, revolvers and sixteen-shot Henry rifles, which according to the Confederates could be loaded in the morning and fired all day. Possession of this rapid-firing weapon, in Archibald's words, "made our numbers appear quadrupled."[48]

The regiment, without horses, was shipped in May 1864 to Fortress Monroe, near the mouth of Chesapeake Bay, then up the James River to Bermuda Hundred, a neck of land between the enemy strongholds of Richmond and Petersburg. At this time General Benjamin "The Beast" Butler was bottled up at Bermuda Hundred after being repulsed on the way to Richmond. The 1st District of Columbia Cavalry relieved an infantry division along the Union position and came under fire for the first time. Archibald recalled that the cannon-balls "made a sound very much like a pigeon's wings swiftly cutting the air, some screaming overhead, others tearing up the ground." Much of this first campaign was the classic military routine of "hurry up and wait" – monotonous picket duty near fortified positions. Casualties were light. But in early June the Maine troopers, serving as dismounted infantry, were attacked by a South Carolina regiment which announced its intentions "with a shrill yell we were beginning to know." The 1st District of Columbia met the rebel yell with rifle fire. Nearby gun batteries sprayed the "Johnnies" with short-range canister and grape shot and the Union line held. The regiment, still lacking mounts, next took part in operations against Confederate earthworks outside of Petersburg, a position that stubbornly held out until 1865.[49]

Five days after receiving their horses, the troopers were ordered to the James River to participate in a classic cavalry mission: a raid into enemy territory. The cavalry enjoyed a glamorous reputation, but the war had produced few large cavalry engagements; artillery, rifled muskets and defensive positions had increased the importance of the foot soldier. Mounted troops served as scouts, pickets, foragers and mobile skirmishers. During the first two years of the conflict the Union cavalry's performance was less than inspiring, but by 1864 the North was emulating the effective mounted arm of the enemy by launching destructive raids. Archibald described the regiment's preparations: "There were many raw recruits who had never sat in the saddle before, and of course no time for their training; in fact they could not put their saddles together without assistance, but they were plucky fellows and had to learn quickly. Three hours later we started on the celebrated Wilson's Raid."[50]

General James Wilson's targets were the Southside and the Richmond and Danville railroads, lifelines to the besieged cities of Petersburg and Richmond. On 23 June 1864 the raiders, five thousand strong, crossed the Petersburg and Weldon Railroad at Reams's Station, south of Petersburg, and moved inland. For the next few days Archibald participated in the burning of bridges, railway stations and rolling stock and the destruction of gristmills, sawmills and supplies of cotton, feed and food.[51] Rail lines were pulled up, ties burned and track twisted into odd shapes. Local slaves, viewing the men in blue as liberators, began to follow the Union columns. Soon entire families of refugee blacks, with appropriated cattle, horses and wagons, were trailing behind the invaders, who levied "contributions" from the larders of "secesh" farmers. Cavalrymen adopted a broad interpretation of foraging. One New Brunswicker entered a plantation house to forage "ten dollars worth of sheet music" as well as corn and other supplies.[52]

The punishment of enemy civilians, supposedly alien to British military principles, became an important part of the Union war effort by 1864. A number of Maritime volunteers were involved in this despoliation, which was intended to deny supplies to enemy regular forces. The confiscation and destruction of civilian property was also part of operations against guerrillas harboured and supported by the rural populace. Charles McGill of Yarmouth, a member of the 1st Massachusetts Heavy Artillery, described one antipartisan operation in Virginia:

Some of our number gave out on the way, and were murdered and stripped by the Guerillas. As soon as General Warner found out that they had been murdered, he issued an order to burn all buildings within two and one half miles of the road. This provided some sport, setting fire to anything and everything that would burn, some nice houses were destroyed and their occupants made to have an awful time. It did the soldiers good to see their comrades avenged. We found a great many of our soldiers had been shot by the farmers and their negroes.

McGill's letter continued:

You ought to see a crowd of us sally into a house and go through and sack it high and low, tear down and stave up! I got a few trophies but

William Charles Archibald, 1st
Maine cavalry, at age 21.

could have got a cartload. We destroyed some millions of dollars worth
and done what they call a big thing. We must obey orders.[53]

A Nova Scotia surgeon attached to a Union infantry regiment reported that his unit had the reputation of being able to "march
further, fight harder and steal more" than any other regiment in
the Army of the Potomac.[54]

Although screened by enemy cavalry and occasionally fired upon
by field artillery, Archibald's brigade met no serious opposition until 24 June when it was ordered to capture a railroad bridge over
the Staunton River. The enemy's Home Guard had positioned
skirmishers on the near shore and held the high ground behind
the bridge, which the 1st D.C. was detailed to capture and burn.
Archibald recalled: "The undertaking was a very perilous one, the
wisdom of doing so was questioned and yet the order was given
to charge across the level ground in the face of Rebel batteries."

Musket and cannon fire killed four and wounded twenty-two of the attackers and the bridge remained intact. The regiment was ordered to withdraw. Acting as rearguard, it covered eighty miles over the next thirty-six hours. Superior Rebel forces, having been drawn northward as part of a diversionary movement, were closing in.[55] At Stony Creek Station the two Union divisions were blocked by artillery and troops under Confederate General Wade Hampton. After a severe but indecisive firefight, the raiders, having abandoned their ambulance wagons and wounded, pushed on to Reams's Station, which was supposed to be in Union hands. Instead of relief forces they found an enemy infantry division and three divisions of cavalry, one of them under Lee's son Fitzhugh. Things looked grim for the trainwreckers after the Confederates managed to separate Wilson's division from Archibald's, which was commanded by General August Kautz. Fortunately, Kautz led a successful retreat through a swamp made passable by a recent drought and the 1st D.C. Cavalry reached Union lines more or less in one piece. But one-third of the raiders had been captured and all their wagons, artillery and supplies had been lost. The enemy, using slave labour, was able to repair the damage to its supply line within weeks.[56]

After a period of rest, the regiment took part in a feint north of the James River in late 1864 as part of the interminable Petersburg campaign. An account by a New Brunswicker in a Massachusetts infantry regiment indicates that, by the summer of 1864, life in the system of rifle pits, trenches and forts that snaked around the town had settled into routine:

The enemy's advance line of rifle pits is about forty feet distant from ours in one part of the line and very often the men of each side barter and trade with the other. I was talking to a rebel officer on Sunday last. I met him halfway between the lines and exchanged papers with him. We gave each other our names and parted, to all appearances on good terms and as good as friends as could be found. We do not fire on each other on this side of the line except [when] one party or the other attempts to advance.[57]

Crossing a pontoon bridge in the extreme Virginia heat, Archibald wrote, was one of the most gruelling experiences of the war. This stage of the campaign ended with the disastrous Battle of the Crater, where Northern troops undermined enemy earthworks and detonated four tons of gunpowder beneath two enemy regiments but failed to penetrate Petersburg's defenses. Archibald next was back along the Weldon railroad, which the Union forces had permanently cut despite the dangers of a counterattack. In late August his regiment took part in a series of skirmishes and battles in and around Reams's Station, where once again it encountered Hampton's Legion. Two infantry divisions, a cavalry division and Archibald's brigade were detailed to tear up track south of the station. According to Archibald, the Rebels, despite their bravery, were no match for disciplined troops armed with repeaters. Yet at Reams's Station the Confederates won the day, capturing two thousand prisoners. The 1st District of Columbia suffered sixty-five casualties. Soon after these engagements, several companies of the regiment, including Archibald's, were transferred to the 1st Maine Cavalry, a veteran unit whose flags were stitched with the names of dozens of battles. The 1st D.C. had been recruited principally in Maine and had fought alongside the 1st Maine, yet the merger caused resentment in the ranks. The Pine Tree State regiment, nicknamed "The Puritans," was replenished with veteran cavalrymen just prior to the mustering out of its three-year volunteers. William Charles Archibald was assigned to Company H, under Captain John D. Myrick of Augusta. He was now part of Gregg's cavalry division, Army of the Potomac.[58]

Before the transfer could be completed, Archibald suffered his only serious wound of the war. When preparing to mount for picket duty, he caught his rifle's trigger on a tree branch, causing the weapon to discharge. The bullet literally parted his hair and creased his skull, rendering him unconscious. While recovering he had the good fortune to catch a glimpse of Abraham Lincoln, who was touring the hospital, and was impressed by the president's sympathetic behaviour. The hospital interlude was doubly fortuitous. In mid-September the Confederates attacked the lightly defended camp of the 1st D.C. Cavalry at Sycamore Church, south of the James River. Dismounted Confederate cavalry drove off over two thousand head of cattle for Lee's starving army and seized over 150 members of the regiment. Some of the captives, including Archibald's close friend Samuel Elliot of Cornwallis, Nova Scotia, would perish in Southern prison camps.[59]

Archibald's initial test with the 1st Maine came during the Battle of Hatcher's Run, also known as the Boydton Plank Road, in late October. The road ran from Petersburg parallel to the Appomattox River and the Southside Railroad. Over forty thousand Union troops were deployed to cut the railroad and choke off Petersburg. Gregg's division, including the 1st Maine Cavalry, reached Boydton Road by noon on 27 October, accompanied by part of Winfield Scott Hancock's Second Corps. Fighting beside cavalry regiments from New York and Pennsylvania, the Maine soldiers once again tangled with Hampton's division when the Confederates attempted to dislodge the attackers. Archibald described his regiment's role in the battle:

We were under a heavy fire and knew ourselves to be in a tight place, and were afterwards awarded much praise. Had this brigade given way, the Second Corps would have gone also; but the position was held until dark, and we retired in the night. We lost of the First Maine at Boydton Plank Road (the boys called it "Bull Pen") eleven killed, sixty-two wounded and eight missing.

He later wrote that he never "once felt any danger of being shot" (by the enemy), believing his life to be under divine protection. Archibald does not appear to have suffered from any of the war's many diseases, which were far more efficient killers than the Minié bullet or bayonet.[60]

Maritimers serving on both sides paid tribute to God's providence in preserving their lives. Both armies were composed largely of evangelical Protestants; even if they were not church members, Protestant Maritimers were steeped in a religious culture that provided a world view and moral rules for personal conduct.[61] Nathan Huestis of Yarmouth, Nova Scotia, attributed the hand of God to his surviving a sharp engagement with Mosby's partisan cavalry. A former Queen's County, Nova Scotia, resident, a member of the Union signal corps, wrote a friend from a ship in the invasion fleet off Rebel-held Port Royal in 1861. He confided that he feared neither death nor the possible lack of Christian burial in combat situations: "We fear not the transit, having a clear conscience towards both God and man." Maritimers in Confederate service also wrote of heavenly protection. Robert Alder McLeod confided that he put his trust in God; "The Lord of Hosts" favoured not only "the nation" and "the cause" but individual Confederates in battle.[62]

With the exception of some skirmishing and a raid on a railroad bridge at Stony Creek Station, Archibald's regiment spent the next few months in winter quarters. Here the usually mobile troopers, accustomed to sleeping in the saddle or on the ground without tent or blanket, constructed more permanent shelters and attempted to obtain extra supplies and luxuries. Many of Archibald's anecdotes reflect the Yankee soldier's obsession with food. In camp, the "marching rations" of hardtack (dried biscuit, often crumbled in hot coffee), salt pork and beans were supplemented with rice, soap and candles, packages from home and expensive canned meat, fruit and vegetables purchased from civilian sutlers. Cavalrymen on patrol were expert in foraging or "liberating" milk, hens, eggs and produce from Rebel farmers. In November of 1863 the Puritans enjoyed a Thanksgiving dinner of turkey and sweetmeats, courtesy of the people of Maine. Another feature of camp life were the ubiquitous body lice, which according to army lore enlisted "for three years or during the war."[63]

Winter camp afforded opportunities for rest, socializing and contemplation. Many soldiers in the largely Protestant armies of the North seem to have appreciated the presence of regimental chaplains and religious publications supplied by the Christian Commission. Amongst the 1st Maine Cavalry, in Archibald's recollections, the vices of camp life – swearing, drinking, gambling and whoring – were rare, and religion was a comfort to men surrounded by death:

The general observation has been that men show less of the spirit of profanity in war than in civilian life. Of course the recklessly profane are there, but they disgust far more than they attract. In the Civil War there was a strong grade of men who lived daily at best, amid scenes of carnage which they regarded as necessary. It is a fair statement that almost every man had his Bible or Testament with him, perhaps given by a mother, wife or sister whom he loved and who was writing letters, often weekly, and which were very strong factors for good in the soldier's life.

The reality probably was less pristine.[64]

The Army of the Potomac was addicted to mail from home. One New Brunswick soldier was cheered when his wife sent him a pair of socks. Hometown newspapers were highly prized. Outgoing correspondence blended Victorian sentimentality with high realism. Some of it was sent to colonial newspapers, which were much freer than Northern journals to print letters criticizing the war effort. A Saint John native on duty in the trenches outside Petersburg in 1864 wrote of the typical themes of duty, sacrifice and discipline: "Soldiering is a rigid school but a good one. It makes a man dependent upon himself, and if there is any man in his makeup it will bring it out." W.R. Snow of Woodstock made no attempt to whitewash the conduct of his own troops who got drunk and looted the town on the eve of the battle of Fredericksburg. The initial carnival atmosphere contrasted with the carnage of the following day; Snow described headless and legless bodies, horribly wounded horses and corpses stacked three deep awaiting burial.[65]

In the spring of 1865 the war of attrition in Virginia resumed. Archibald's regiment was roused out of winter quarters when the Confederates attempted to puncture the Petersburg siege lines by capturing Fort Stedman. The Federals struck back in force, and the 1st Maine became part of Sheridan's campaign to encircle and capture Petersburg. Fighting as infantry near Dinwiddie Court House on the Boydton Plank Road, the regiment ran out of ammunition in the middle of an enemy attack. It was relieved by a cavalry division under Brigadier-General George Armstrong Custer. Archibald recalled how during a lull in combat the two sides fought with music, the Confederate bands playing "Dixie" and "Bonnie Blue Flag," and the Union musicians responding with "Yankee Doodle" and "The Star-spangled Banner." Prior to the engagement, Archibald and his comrades had sewn their money into the linings of their uniforms in case they were taken prisoner or left wounded on the field.[66]

When the Rebels charged across the creek near Dinwiddie Court House on 31 March 1865 the 1st Maine formed the third or reserve line of battle. Archibald did not know it at the time, but the famous Appomattox Campaign had begun. In ten days his regiment would lose one-third of its enlisted men and half its officers. The second stage of the battle, at Five Forks, was decisive. Sheridan routed Pickett's forces on the enemy right, took four thousand prisoners and opened the road to Petersburg. Richmond, seat of the Rebel government, was also doomed. Robert E. Lee retreated up the Appomattox River, intending to link up with Johnston's army in North Carolina. Both Petersburg and Richmond were evacuated by 3 April.[67]

After the battle of Five Forks, Archibald's unit was part of the force pursuing the weakened Army of Northern Virginia. Even in defeat, Lee's troops were capable of delivering punishing counterattacks, so the 1st Maine habitually fortified its nightly position with breastworks of earth, fence rails and trees. At Jetersville the regiment was sent in to capture Lee's baggage train but was prevented from doing so by swampy ground. On 7 April the Maine troopers bore the brunt of the fighting at Farmville, driving the enemy from town until meeting a formidable rearguard which burned the bridges. Reaching Appomattox Station on 8 April, Archibald's brigade was placed across the main road to Lynchburg, Virginia. If Lee could force this route, he possibly could reach Johnston's Army of Tennessee and prolong the war. Archibald recorded that the road to Appomattox Station had been clogged with cast-off equipment, horses and dead men. The 1st Maine threw up another breastwork and awaited the dawn. Archibald was awakened by the rumbling of enemy artillery. A Confederate assault drove the Union troops from their position, but superior forces halted the attack. Later that day, Lee, his supplies exhausted and famed army melting away, surrendered to Ulysses S. Grant at Appomattox Court House.[68]

Following a brief stint in camp in Virginia, the 1st Maine Cavalry was sent home. The men were "told off" in August at Augusta. The regiment had covered itself in honour, but not without cost. No other Union cavalry regiment had lost so many men in action or from mortal wounds. In addition, more than 340 had succumbed to diseases such as typhus and malaria. Archibald, promoted to corporal before his honourable discharge, proudly returned home with his "war accoutrements," including his prized Henry rifle. A steamer from Portland to Halifax, a train to Shubenacadie, a stage-coach to Musquodoboit and he was back at his beloved Poplar Grove. Archibald had left the colony as an inexperienced youth with a thirst for adventure. He now returned in his mid-twenties a veteran soldier. Like Cincinnatus of ancient Rome, upon reaching home he went back to his fields, arriving in time to help with the hay harvest. Months of bivouacking in tents or under the stars left Archibald unable to enjoy a regular bed. For a week he slept on the floor. The "cavalry soldier boy" of 1864 appears to have later adjusted to civilian life, securing a position in a business firm and enrolling in a school of commerce in Halifax. He would marry twice and produce fourteen offspring. Years later, in his memoirs published in Boston, he described a reunion with a former officer of the 1st Maine: "There came back to us, as we talked, the old tie of comrade-ship, and although I live in Canada and love my country best, we are comrades and friends for life. Ties and friendship such as these are worth much between the nations, and have their peace value."[69]

IN THE UNION NAVY

Given the region's economy of wood, wind and water, Maritimers naturally were part of a wave of several thousand British North Americans who gravitated to the Civil War navies. The U.S. Navy, which possessed less than fifty vessels prior to the war, was as-signed a herculean task: a blockade of dozens of harbours, neu-tralization of Confederate commerce raiders and penetration of the vast river systems of the South. As the navy expanded, experienced mariners were in high demand. Sailors, unlike army recruits, were not paid a bounty but were entitled to a share of prize money. At the close of the rebellion the saltwater and freshwater navy consisted of over 51,000 officers and men. Two-thirds of total personnel were "landsmen."[70]

Maritimers who served in the USN included John Webster of Pictou, engineer on the gunboat *Penguin*; New Brunswicker David

Patterson, killed on board the armoured corvette *Galena* when it attacked Fort Darling in 1862; and William K. Connell of P.E.I., stationed on the powerful ironclad frigate *New Ironsides* in operations against the harbour defenses of Charleston. J.C. Richards of Greenwich, New Brunswick, graduated from Columbia Medical School and then was appointed surgeon on the ninety-day gunboat *Aroostook* Islanders Edward Briggs, forty-five, and Edward Moss, twenty, joined the ship's company of USS *Nahant* at Boston.[71]

Discipline on board the saltwater navy was stricter than on the river gunboats, but blockade duty was not overly dangerous. Although Du Pont's flagship *New Ironsides* was subjected to a torpedo attack by one of the Rebels' "David" craft, the heat was a more intense enemy. Sailors shared in prize money and were well fed by the standards of the day. Onboard the *Ironsides*, for example, they were treated to ice, fresh fruit and, prior to and following major action, rum. American tars were more likely to die in falls from masts or drown than to be killed in action. John Martin of Halifax, of the barque *Restless*, drowned in Bull's Bay, South Carolina, when his boat capsized during the capture of a blockade runner. Norman Wade, of Granville Ferry, Nova Scotia, a sailor on the propeller barque USS *Young Rover* on blockade duty off Florida, fell to his death in 1862. Disease took its toll as well. John Boyd Harbell of Saint John and James R. Young of Prince Edward Island succumbed to consumption.[72]

Life for the saltwater sailor in Uncle Sam's navy became more precarious when ships were sent in against fortified positions. A Saint John native, a printer by trade, wrote home to describe the capture of Fort Fisher, the massive sand fortress that guarded the entrance to the Cape Fear River and under whose rifled guns blockade runners nestled.[73] The first attack, launched in late December 1864, was poorly planned and executed. His vessel, the screw sloop *Brooklyn*, engaged the enemy batteries for several hours. Union troops, behind schedule, were landed under sniper fire on the beaches. The New Brunswick sailor, crew on a cutter, assisted in the hazardous landing, which was called off after only two thousand troops waded through the surf. The sailor, risking musket fire, now had to help evacuate the tired, demoralized and nearly mutinous infantrymen. His letter criticized on the Union military commander, "old goggle-eyed Ben" Butler and senior officers in general: "No wonder the war continues with such men as Butler commands."[74]

The *Brooklyn* returned with the North Atlantic Squadron on 15 January 1865. This time the New Brunswick native was in the first line of attack, shielded only by four Union ironclads. A further letter described the second and final assault on the fort: "I must overhaul my jaw tackle," he wrote, "and spin you a yarn about the fight." A fleet of more than forty vessels began the assault by pounding the main fort for two days. The gun crews poured on a murderous fire, one that was returned by the obstinate defenders: "They did stand to their guns, though, and like heroes, if they *are* rebels." This time the sailors were landed as part of a two-thousand-man naval "boarding party" which included marines whose task was to sweep over the fort's seaward defences. When the steam whistles sounded, the sailors, armed with cutlasses and revolvers, charged up the beach. Many were pinned down, but others scrambled to the ramparts: "The gallant tars charged headlong with a yell to the very ramparts of the fort, and the stars and stripes were almost planted on the parapet. But it was impossible for any mortal to live amid the hail of grape and canister which plunged like hail down the side of the mountain." The fighting became intense and hand-to-hand: "It was the fairest whipped fort that was ever taken. We bent them clean out of it, and they disputed every inch of it as though their very hopes of heaven depended on its capture." The tide of battle turned when the army, assigned to attack from the landward side, breached the defences. The joint operation took Fort Fisher, Fort Columbia and Battery Buchanan and forced the "Johnnies" to blow up nearby Fort Caswell.[75]

John C. Allen was one of the few Maritimers to receive a naval command during the war. Born in Saint Andrew's in 1836, he relocated across the Bay of Fundy to Yarmouth where at age twelve he went to sea. As a young man he was in partnership with another Yarmouthian, possibly as a vessel owner. After entering the USN as an ensign in 1861, Allen was promoted to acting master of the USS *Portsmouth* of the West Gulf Blockading Squadron. During the Battle of Mobile Bay the Bluenose officer served on the fourteen-gun sloop *Lackawanna*, one of several vessels to engage the rebel ram *Tennessee*. Prior to the appearance of the ironclad, *Lackawanna*, in the centre of the Union battleline, exchanged fire with Fort Morgan. The fort scored a direct hit on one of Allen's rifled guns. "Blood and mangled human remains," the captain's journal read, "for a time impeded the working of the 150-pounder." USS *Tecumseh* hit a mine and sank, drowning over ninety men. During the fight with the *Tennessee*, *Lackawanna* fired at the ram point-blank. The two vessels were so close, Allen later reported, that the Rebels had thrown a spittoon and a holystone at the Union sailors. In the confusion, Allen's vessel rammed Admiral David Farragut's flagship, the

John C. Allen, formerly of Yarmouth, served on the USS *Lackawanna* during the battle of Mobile Bay.

Hartford. The Rebel ram, its rudder disabled, surrendered and the Federals eventually gained control of Mobile Bay. The *Lackawanna*'s hull had been penetrated several times, its sails and rigging shot away, and the crew had suffered thirty-nine casualties. Early in 1865 Allen led a boat expedition from the *Lackawanna* to the approaches of Galveston harbour in order to destroy a beached blockade runner. The Union raiders were driven off by fire from the vessel, the beach and nearby Fort Magruder. For bravery in action at Mobile Bay, Allen was promoted to command the USS *Selma*, a captured wooden gunboat mounting six guns that had operated as a picket off Mobile. He resigned his commission in 1866 and embarked upon a career as a shipmaster and owner.[76]

In the end, there is no single explanation for why large numbers of Maritimers answered the call of war in the 1860s. Like Canadians who fought in Vietnam a century later, their motives were not well understood and their contribution was often ignored in the land of their birth. The international border was a fluid concept and it is possible to hold multiple national loyalties. In her propagandistic and semi-fictional potboiler *Union Nurse and Spy*, Emma Edmonds penned a telling anecdote about national allegiance. Although acknowledging the United States as her adopted home, she (allegedly) visited Washington, where her latent but deeply rooted attachments to "John Bull" surfaced within a matter of seconds. After viewing paintings of the surrender of Cornwallis to Burgoyne in 1781, she departed with "feelings of humiliation and disgust."[77] Most

Bluenose warriors were already on their way to becoming American, a process the war hastened. Peter Welsh, born at Charlottetown in 1830, ended up in Boston where he married an Irish woman, and then they moved to New York. Although a British subject by birth, the Catholic Welshman resented England's Irish policies. Against his wife's wishes, and following a bout of unemployment and heavy drinking, he volunteered. The crisis of the Union gave this Maritime immigrant a sense of purpose. Like Islander John J. MacDonald, another member of the 28th Massachusetts Regiment, he saw the rebellion as a proving ground for Catholic Americans, earlier the target of political nativism. Neither man survived the war.[78]

As was the case with William Charles Archibald, most who enlisted after crossing the border probably did so spontaneously and sought their justifications later. Few were as certain as Emma Edmonds, who in 1865 wrote that she had enlisted for "Truth, Right and Liberty."[79] They came to see themselves as soldiers of liberty, a freedom that did not necessarily extend to the slaves of the South; indeed, the typical Bluenose warrior, like white Maritimers in general, rejected radical abolitionist assumptions about racial equality. The minority who served with the Confederacy fought for another version of freedom, although Southern dwellers had fewer options. Maritimers who sympathized with the Confederacy or preached strict neutrality viewed Bluenose combatants in the Northern forces as either cold-blooded soldiers of fortune or unfortunate dupes of the wily Yankee. The reaction to the enlistment of provincialists constantly fluctuated, depending on the course of the war and the context of their participation. Joseph Howe, for example, in a crowd-pleasing speech to Detroit businessmen, praised his son Fred for having joined the 23rd Ohio Infantry and having served with Sheridan in the Shenandoah Valley. Among the actions of this regiment was South Mountain, or Boonsboro, where the 23rd were deployed as skirmishers. In private, Howe worried over his son's safety and on more than one occasion expressed sympathy for the Rebels.[80]

The military participation of Maritimers, mostly in Union ranks, indicates that the colonies were never of one mind on the Civil War. There were many layers of public opinion, and at least one was strong for the Union. Successes such as New Orleans and Gettysburg also rehabilitated the North's reputation in the British colonies. The initially critical or factual and then increasingly positive reporting of Bluenoses serving with the North as soldiers, sailors or military surgeons is important evidence of a subtle shift in colonial opinion towards a view that a Confederate defeat was both inevitable and desirable.[81]

6 The *Chesapeake* Pirates

Both on the land and the sea they fight against such odds so
bravely that we must heartily admire their manly valour.

Halifax *Citizen*, 5 November, 1863

The stirring events surrounding the capture of the steamer *Chesapeake*
in late 1863 crystallized the arguments of pro-Confederate and pro-
Union opinion in the Maritime provinces. Like the *Trent* incident,
it caused politicians, merchants and journalists to ponder the region's
future relations with the United States. In Nova Scotia that year,
politics were almost exclusively internal in their focus; the spring
election had been waged on the issue of the electoral franchise.
In New Brunswick the issue was railroads. P.E.I. politicians and
journalists pondered colonial union, but disgruntled farmers organized a Tenant League after the Imperial government vetoed land
reform legislation.[1]

The revelation that most of the "Confederates" who highjacked
the vessel were not Southern irregulars but New Brunswickers further soured Northern opinion of British neutrality. The military situation was still uncertain, even after the Northern victories at
Gettysburg and Vicksburg. The most recent news was the Confederate retreat from Tennessee, their tactical victory at Chickamauga
and the decisive battles for Chattanooga in late November. Most
Maritimers, even the minority who were pro-Union, expected, if
not a Confederate victory in the field, at least a truce that would
end the fighting and concede Southern independence. Rebel partisans, lacking detailed knowledge of the war and blinded by their
romantic image of the Confederate rebellion, tended to exaggerate
and glamorize any Rebel success, however marginal its contribution
to the war effort. In the case of the *Chesapeake* affair, many were

prepared to excuse cowardly piracy as a brave and necessary act of war.[2]

PRECEDING EVENTS

The *Chesapeake* operation has several strands. The first begins far to the south in the Caribbean in early 1863 when CSS *Retribution*, a black-hulled privateer schooner, was spreading panic among Yankee merchant vessels in the vicinity of the Danish island of St. Thomas. In peacetime the vessel had been a steam-powered tug, the *Uncle Ben*, on Lake Erie and around New York. In April 1861 the tug was chartered by the Federal government as part of the expedition to relieve Fort Sumter. Captured by the Confederates on the Cape Fear River, its engines had been removed and it had been converted into a private, armed vessel with the addition of a small gun. Early in 1863 the U.S. consul reported that the *Retribution* had chased two American ships back into port at St. Thomas. USS *San Jacinto*, under Commander Edward T. Nichols, was sent to the area. According to Nichols, cruising off the coasts of Puerto Rico in pursuit of the raider, *Retribution* had employed a consort, the schooner *Dixie*, to secure heavier armament at a remote island. The privateer was said to be swift and armed with three nine-pounder rifled cannons.[3]

The *Retribution*'s captain was of Maritime origins, although this was unknown to the Federal authorities at the time. Vernon Guyon Locke was born in 1827 at Sandy Point, Shelburne County. The family name was well known in the county; one important fishing community later bore the name of Lockeport. According to his brother Eben, Locke had left the Ragged Islands area in the early 1840s to work and live in the United States. By 1860 he was based in Fayetteville, North Carolina, but he had previously sailed out of New York and Cape Cod and was familiar with not only the waters of the northeast but also the West Indies. Diarist William Norman Rudolf, who attempted to profit from the blockade, wrote that Locke had also sailed out of Pictou in a vessel called *Vernon*, built by Captain D. Donald for a Boston firm. According to the shipping register for the port of Pictou, a 265-ton brigantine *Vernon* had been constructed at Merigomish in 1856 for a Boston owner. Four years later it was wrecked and then sold. The *Eastern Chronicle* reported that Locke had been well known in Pictou County as master of the *Senora* and the *Vernon*. He also was reported to have captained the *Enchantress* out of Newburyport, Massachusetts. During the *Chesapeake* crisis Rudolf wrote of Locke: "He is said to be a great scamp, and a very plausible one."[4]

With the advent of rebellion, Locke offered his services to the South. He secured the *Retribution*'s letter of marque from its most recent owner, Thomas Power, and appropriated an alias, John Parker, as a cover for his privateering activities. The Confederacy, with its infant navy, had placed great hopes in privateers but their performances were disappointing. Far more effective were commerce raiders manned by regular naval officers. In January of 1863, Locke captured the Northern schooner *Hanover*, bound for Boston, and took the prize to Fortune Island in Crooked Island Passage, where it was run aground and its cargo unloaded for sale in Nassau. The schooner, under Captain Case of Provincetown, had encountered the privateer off Santo Domingo, flying a Union flag. The *Retribution* raised the Confederate banner, ran out its guns and sent a boarding party to take the *Hanover*. Case later landed at Haiti where he met several former crew of the *Retribution* who had left the ship when they had discovered it was to be a privateer, not a blockade runner. They suggested that Locke, despite his naval uniform, was more of a pirate than an officially commissioned privateer. According to a U.S. Navy source, Locke refloated the *Hanover*, loaded it with salt and attempted to run it through the blockade.[5]

Retribution next captured the brigs *Emily Fisher* and *J.P. Ellicott*. The *Emily Fisher*'s shares were owned mainly in Eastport and Portland. It was taken off Castle Island in the Bahamas, three of the crew defecting to the privateer. The captain and crew spent a few hours in irons before being landed with their personal property on Acklin's Island. The privateer seemed to be working in conjunction with two wrecking schooners. The captain protested against the unloading of the cargo of sugar in British territory. He recognized the *Retribution*'s master, who went by the name John Priestly, as a Captain Locke who possibly belonged to Calais. The sailors of the *Ellicot*, from Bucksport, Maine, were able to overpower the seven-man prize crew and retake the ship. Early in March the *Retribution* put into Nassau, where it was condemned as unseaworthy and seized by the authorities. Locke's brother Eben, another seafarer, visited Nassau that spring and met Vernon in command of a privateer flying the flag of the Confederacy. Vernon, who was using the name John Parker, showed his brother his commission and letters of marque. On learning that "Parker" had violated British neutrality and revenue laws by selling captured cargo in the Bahamas, the local authorities, under considerable pressure from the U.S. State Department, placed him under arrest. The Bluenose privateer posted bail and was released from custody. He promptly vanished, whisked away by one of the dozens of sailing vessels that plied the waters of the Caribbean. Locke subsequently turned up in New Jersey where he supposedly met his chief collaborator in the plot to seize the *Chesapeake*.[6]

The second strand in the story is the vessel itself. The 460-ton *Chesapeake* had first come to the attention of the Maritime public in the summer of 1863 as the result of a remarkable cruise by a Confederate commerce raider. The *Tacony*, a 296-ton American barque travelling in ballast from Port Royal, South Carolina, to Philadelphia in early June, 1863, was intercepted by the Rebel brig *Clarence* under the command of Lieutenant Charles W. "Savez" Read, CSN. Read had been in charge of a gun on the ram *Arkansas* when it had battled its way through the Union fleet to reach Vicksburg on the Mississippi in 1862. The famous CSS *Florida* under J.N. Maffitt had taken the *Clarence* in early May as it had been carrying a load of coffee from Brazil to Philadelphia. The *Florida*, one of the controversial steam-powered raiders built for the Confederacy in Britain, would go on to capture and burn more than three dozen prizes, including several from Maine. In April of 1864 it boarded the Granville, Nova Scotia schooner *Belle*, heading for a port in eastern Brazil. Confederate raiders unable to take their captures into Southern prize courts normally set the vessels on fire. But Read suggested an intriguing strategy. The young officer wanted to take the *Clarence*, under a small crew, into Hampton Roads, where Northern merchant vessels would raise few suspicions, and destroy shipping at Fortress Monroe. A prize crew was arranged and the new raider was armed with a lone, twelve-pound howitzer.[7]

Sailing northwards the Confederates encountered and captured a barque, a schooner and a brig. Read, who kept a journal of the cruise, decided that Fortress Monroe was too heavily defended; instead the *Clarence* would sail the waters of New England looking for prizes. He next captured the barque *Tacony* and two more schooners, bringing his individual prize total to six. To confuse pursuers and secure a faster sailer, the Confederates transferred their stores and arms to the *Tacony* and set the *Clarence* ablaze. The cruise of the *Tacony*, which the twenty-one-man prize crew renamed the *Florida II*, began on 12 June and lasted less that two weeks. In this period, which coincided with unrest over the military draft in New York, the port towns and ship owners of the northeast were thrown into an uproar and Washington was swamped with angry letters and telegrams as the *Tacony* captured and destroyed over a dozen additional vessels. Yankee fishermen, whose boats in Maritime waters numbered several hundred at the peak of the summer season, feared the worst. Gloucester fishing interests demanded a Federal gunboat to patrol the waters between Cape Sable and Canso, Nova Scotia, and a second for the Gulf of St. Lawrence. As usual, rumours grew like topsy. These alarms were false, but the Confederate raid was no figment of the imagination. Read stopped the Pictou schooner *Arabella* and invited its captain to dinner. In keeping with his successful modus operandi, Read transferred his command to the small prize schooner *Archer* and burned the *Tacony*.[8]

By this time the U.S. Navy was scouring the New England coasts. The patrols did not save the *Shamtemuc*, which was about to speak tothe *Tacony* when a shot was fired across its bows. An armed boat crew took possession of the Maine vessel and transferred its passengers, without their luggage, to a neutral ship that eventually landed them at Saint John. After intercepting the ninety-ton fishing schooner *Archer* near Portland, Maine's largest city, Read steered toward the port. Securing two local fishermen as pilots, and not revealing their own identity, the Confederates took the vessel into Portland harbour on 26 June to attempt the most audacious feat of the voyage. At dockside lay the revenue cutter *Caleb Cushing*, a fine sailer armed with two guns: a thirty-two-pounder and a twelve-pound Dahlgren mounted on a pivot. Its captain had died that very day of heart failure. Read's men stole aboard the cutter during the early hours of 27 June, overpowered the watch and placed the crew below decks in irons. Originally Read had hoped to burn two gunboats being constructed at Portland. Instead he decided to leave on the evening tide, sail beyond the reach of the local gun batteries, and sit astride the entrance to Portland's busy harbour in order to inflict as much destruction as possible upon Northern shipping. Timing was crucial, so two small boats manned by Confederate oarsmen began to pull the prize seaward, exiting through the channel that was not covered by artillery. But at dawn the *Caleb Cushing* was still within range of the Federal shore guns, so Read made for the open sea and a rendezvous with the *Archer*.[9]

The raiders'extraordinary luck began to turn. The winds died, giving the citizens of Portland sufficient time to organize a pursuit force. Within an hour of the discovery of the disappearance of the revenue schooner, the collector of customs, Jedediah Jewett, had enlisted the aid of four steamers carrying Regulars from Fort Preble, members of the 7th Maine Volunteers, armed citizens "of all ages and colours" and a few field guns. The lead vessel was *Forest City*, a sidewheeler coaster well known to New Brunswickers. It was assisted by the small steamer *Casco* and a steam tug. The propeller *Chesapeake*, owned by H.B. Cromwell of New York, was getting up steam at the time of the alarm, so it was pressed into service. Originally known as the *Totten*, the three-masted steamer had been rebuilt circa 1860. It had once plied between Savannah, Charleston, Baltimore and New York. Now it was on the coastal run between New York and Portland, the eastern terminus of the Grand Trunk Railroad. Its skipper was Isaac Willett, a thirty-year veteran who resided in Brooklyn. The *Chesapeake*, protected with bales of cotton, sporting two small guns from the Maine arsenal and carrying a party of the 7th Maine and civilian volunteers, soon approached the fleeing cutter. Much to their dismay, after clearing for action, the Southerners found their ordnance supply was limited. The Rebels several times fired round shot in the direction of the *Forest City*, which kept its distance, not because of the wishes of the military commander on board, but because it contained a large number of civilians who viewed the chase as a pleasure excursion.[10]

After conferring with the *Forest City*, the officers on the *Chesapeake* decided to try to ram the cutter, which was tacking and firing at the steamer. Twenty miles out to sea, having exhausted all available ammunition – (Read was unable to find the ammunition storage locker which contained several dozen more round shot) – the Confederates put their prisoners into a boat and threw them the key to their handcuffs. The Rebels took to two small boats and set a fuse near the vessel's magazine. The *Forest City*, no longer facing artillery, bore down upon the Southerners, who "frantically displayed white handkerchiefs and masonic signs" and were spared. The *Caleb Cushing* blew up and sank, the final victim of the *Clarence-Tacony-Archer* raid. The little fishing schooner was recaptured at sea.[11] Despite the capture of the Confederates, the people of Portland remained jittery. On 29 June they awoke to vague rumours of an attack. The church bells rang and men, women and children "ran hither and thither in aimless fright."[12]

The third strand of the saga was John Clibbon Brain, a mysterious and slightly shady Englishman who was at the centre of the plot. Historians are unsure of the exact details of Brain's personal life, motivation and Civil War activities; even his letters to kinsfolk in England must be approached with suspicion, given his penchant for bragging and lying.[13] One of the many unsubstantiated rumours surrounding Brain was that he had been a mate on the *Retribution*. Born at Ball's Point, Islington (a London suburb), in 1840, Brain emigrated to the United States with his parents on a Liverpool packet a decade later. His early life is obscure. According to the heroic version, repeated in the biography *The Last of the Confederate Privateers*, he was living in the South when the rebellion began and trained as a Confederate gunner. Brain then allegedly transferred to the navy and served aboard CSS *Jamestown*, a steamer in the James River Squadron. The *Jamestown* was a consort to the *Virginia* in its 1862 attack on the Union fleet at Hampton Roads. In May 1862 its guns and gunners were placed in the earthworks at Drewery's Bluff. Brain's biography, without documentary proof, next has the hero operating in the North as a spy and member of a secret society the Knights of the Golden Circle. It is here that he runs afoul of Federal authorities and is imprisoned for several months. But Brain's early war years were far less heroic and honourable.[14]

Brain's early war years were in reality less heroic. According to a letter, by his own hand, sent to the British consul at Boston in early 1862, he was arrested as a security risk in Michigan City, Indiana, on 18 August 1861, leaving his wife stranded without money or friends. Soldiers of the 9th Indiana Volunteers had taken him into custody on a charge of furnishing arms to the Rebels. Brain had explained that his father lived in Virginia and his mother resided in Ohio. Brain junior, who was still a British subject, had left Nashville in May to seek work as an engraver and commercial artist in Louisville, Kentucky. When arrested in Indiana he had been preparing a map of the Michigan Central Railway, supposedly for a guidebook. He spent over one month in prison in Indiana and then was transported in irons to New York. His final destination was Fort Warren, in Boston harbour, from where he appealed to the British authorities for his release. He denied any connection to the Confederacy and stood on his rights as a subject of the Queen. In February 1862 he swore an oath that he would not involve himself in insurrection against the American government and was liberated a month later.[15]

Brain's whereabouts for the next year are unknown. He may have returned to England as his biography suggests, or he may have continued his habit of drifting from town to town, leaving unpaid bills in his wake. Financially strapped and broken in health upon his release as a political prisoner, he no doubt harboured great hostility towards the Union, oath or not. The prison interlude made it impossible for Brain to have served on the Jamestown or in the defence of Drewery's Bluff. Neither is he likely to have been a member of the 2nd Kentucky Regiment, as newspaper sources later claimed. Rather he became part freelance guerrilla acting in the cause of the South, part confidence artist. In the summer of 1863 he visited Halifax as the prospective publisher of a "mercantile statistical work and business directory" for Canada and the provinces, a project purported to be under the patronage of the Grand Trunk Railway.

By this point he probably had already met Vernon Locke and possibly planned an irregular operation against Northern shipping. Perhaps they were inspired by the voyage of the *Tacony* and the relatively undefended nature of the waters of Maine. Brain, repeating a similar con he had worked in Canada East and the United States, solicited subscriptions from a number of businessmen and promptly disappeared. In late 1863 a New Brunswick journal reported that Haligonians had been victimized by a well-dressed "vile swindler" carrying a carpet bag and a lady's portmanteau. In his next manifestation in the Maritimes, John C. Brain would adopt a more swashbuckling appearance.[16]

CAPTURE

On the fourth and fifth of December 1863, the steamship *Chesapeake*, lying at Pier 9 on the North River – part of the Hudson between New York and New Jersey – loaded cargo for Maine. The freight, consigned to various merchants, including some in Canada East and New Brunswick, consisted of sugar, cotton, wine, flour, leather and dry goods, all worth up to $100,000, more than the vessel itself. Everything pointed to a routine cruise to Portland, a trip thatnormally took thirty-six hours. Captain Willett, on Saturday, 6 December, noted that several passengers had not secured tickets in advance but had paid their fare on board. The late arrivals had missed the steamer at Pier 9 and had hadto be rowed out to it in midstream after it had cast off. Willett wrote their names on a slip of paper and gave it to the stewardess who arranged their berths. The crew rarely paid much attention to the passengers on these coasting runs; they included the usual assortment of young labourers, mariners and businessmen of various nationalities. Some no doubt were soldiers on leave. One of the passengers announced himself as "Colonel" John C. Brain. The second mate recognized the Englishman because he had previously travelled on the *Chesapeake* with a woman and a child (presumably his family). Brain, representing himself as the agent of a British steamboat company, had secured a complimentary pass. The vessel steamed down the North River, leaving America's busiest port in its wake. A number of the passengers, individually or in small groups, seemed to take an inordinate interest in the vessel's layout and operation.[17]

By midnight on Sunday the cold night air cut like a knife and the deck was covered with ice. The passengers and most of the crew were snug in their cabins. The *Chesapeake*, having passed Nantucket Island, was roughly twenty miles north-north-east of Cape

Cod. Second engineer Orin Schaffer had taken over in the engine room; there were few other signs of activity. Sometime after midnight (crew members remembered it as just after either 1 or 2 a.m.) Captain Willett was awakened by the chief mate, who informed him that a member of the crew had been shot. Was it murder or mutiny? At this point piracy seemed out of the question. The captain had small arms in the room but gave them no thought. Leaving his cabin near the engine room on the main deck, he was shot at by unknown parties. As a number of pistol balls whizzed by, Willett noticed the second engineer lying on the deck apparently dead, his head resting in blood. The captain proceeded to the pilot house where the nature of the attack started to become clear. One of the passengers, who identified himself as "First Lieutenant" H.A. Parr, collared Willett, put a pistol to his face and announced that he was now a prisoner of the Confederacy. Parr, an apprentice apothecary, was one of the few genuine Southerners on board. The highjackers appeared to be numerous, determined and well-armed. Willett was handcuffed and confined in his cabin for an hour until the high-jackers secured their prize. The pirates had even wanted to "iron" his twelve-year-old son.[18]

Patrick Connor of New York, fireman, later testified that he had been on duty in the fire room at 2 a.m. when four armed men had entered, fired pistols andthen placed him in irons. One of the guns had been so close that Connor was burned by the powder flash. At this point, second engineer, Schaffer had come up on the grating from oiling the engine. An American citizen born in North River, New York, he was described as "a stout, able man" roughly forty years of age. Entering the fire room, he demanded to know what was happening. A shot was fired and Schaffer fled, covering his face with his hands and yelling for the captain. Connor was ignorant of what next befell the second engineer because he was held captive in the fire room and engine room for the next hour and a half. Once the fires burned low and the steam pressure fell, he was released from his handcuffs and told to attend to the furnace. Under guard, Connor would continue to stoke the fire until his rescue by the U.S. Navy. George Ames, the cabin boy, was sleeping in the lounge with the cook when they heard noises. which the cook took to be the crew taking in sail. This was followed by pistol shots and groans. Minutes later, at the companionway, they were ordered to surrender "to the Southern Confederacy." Their captors informed them that they would not be harmed if they behaved, and that the second engineer had been killed and his body thrown overboard. The Confederacy had claimed its first fatal casualty in

New England waters.[19]

Daniel Henderson, the second mate, a native of Portland, was also taken by surprise. Finishing his watch at midnight, the veteran seaman retired to his cabin adjoining the pilot house. Prior to leaving the pilot house he had caught a glimpse of passenger Brain on deck braving the cold and rain squalls. An hour and a half later, four intruders brandishing guns broke open his door and ordered him to get dressed. As he was ironed at the wrists, he was informed that he was a prisoner of the Confederacy. Henderson asked to see the captain but was refused and locked in his room. Later he was escorted to the pilot house where he sat, fearing for his life, in a corner. He noticed that "a big, tall fellow, with sandy coloured whiskers" was at the helm.[20]

James Johnston, born in Ireland but a naturalized American, held the important post of chief engineer. He had worked on the *Chesapeake* for three years. Johnston had been in charge of the engine room until midnight, whereupon he retired to his room. Awakened by what sounded like gunfire, he went on deck to discover Schaffer lying prone, with his feet down the hatchway leading to the engine room. Schaffer appeared to have been shot before crawling up the ladder that led to the house on the hurricane deck, where he expired. Descending the hatchway, Johnston met an armed passenger, David Collins. Collins levelled his weapon at the engineer's head, but Johnston grabbed the assailant's arm, calling "Hold on!" A second highjacker, standing beside Collins, discharged a small-calibre pistol, wounding Johnston in the chin. In the confusion the Irishman left the scene, spoke to a third passenger who did him no harm, and then met the mate, Charles Johnston, who had been wounded in the knee and arm.[21]

Mate Charles Johnston later filed an affidavit in Portland that recounted his experience. The Brooklyn native had been on watch with Albion Oslin and Thomas Hudkins. Going below to warm himself with a coffee he heard a loud noise in the engine room. Suddenly a man entered and fired a pistol in his direction, the shot striking part of the engine. Schaffer appeared hollering that he had been wounded, and was shot two more times as he started up the ladder. The pirates discharged their weapons "as rapidly as boys firing crackers." Charles Johnston, with one bullet in his left arm and another in his right knee, retreated to the kitchen. The two Johnstons retreated to the kitchen through a hatchway and sheltered there for a half hour. None of their wounds was serious. From there they saw the body of their unfortunate comrade Orin Schaffer being tossed over the side.[22]

The cook, followed by one of the captors, George Robinson, a New Brunswicker who was sailing master (navigator) of the pirate crew, entered the kitchen. Unlike the other pirates, Robinson, sometimes called Sears on board, appeared to be unarmed. He escorted chief engineer James Johnston, who was still in his night-shirt, to his cabin to dress and then to the captain's cabin. Captain Willett remained in irons. Henry A. Parr, the Confederates' "surgeon", removed a pistol ball from the hand of one of the highjackers and tended the wounds of mate Charles Johnston. He lacked the skill or instruments needed to extract the bullet from the chin of James Johnston. The stewardess, Mary Burgoyne of Jersey City, New Jersey, had also been awakened by noises. She had seen mate Charles Johnston go into the pantry and heard "a great number of pistol shots." The cook knocked on her door and asked if she was frightened. "I said no", Burgoyne recalled, "and I asked if all hands were killed." The cook replied in the negative, informing her that they were the captives of Confederate raiders who promised to treat them well if they cooperated. Presently, Captain Willett, still in irons, entered Burgoyne's cabin to assure her that she would be safe. The chief engineer repeated this intelligence. Parr, who seemed to be one of the pirate leaders, reassured them that they would be released at the first harbour they reached; he also seemed quite concerned about James Johnston's wounds. The highjackers, although they had killed one unarmed man and wounded two more, appear to have been chivalrous in their conduct towards the stewardess. Until they were released, the remaining passengers and crew were confined to the main cabin.[23]

The significance of the highjacking began to dawn upon the crew and passengers of the *Chesapeake*. The plot, on behalf of the Confederacy, had involved sixteen insurgent passengers, most of whom were now brandishing six-barrelled revolvers. Their guns and handcuffs had been secreted in their luggage. Whether obstructed or not, they had murdered the second engineer and wounded two of the crew. Equally serious was the fact that the raiders had committed piracy on the high seas. The Rebels demanded paint with which to obscure the vessel's signboard and seized Willett's coasting licence and other papers, and his small arms. Their leader, "Lieutenant" John C. Brain, went out of his way to explain the legality of the capture under the rules of war, issuing Willett a copy of his orders issued by Captain John Parker of the privateer CSS *Retribution*. The document instructed Lieutenants Brain and Parr, 2nd Lieutenant David Collins, sailing master George Robinson and crew to board the steamer at New York, to capture it and take it to the island of Grand Manan.[24] A New York journal later dismissed the document as "a fabrication of a smart and clever cut throat." Although the pirates claimed to be in Confederate service, they did not possess a Southern flag. A number of the pirates conversed with the prisoners, who were informed that most of the expedition had been hired in New Brunswick. Parr, a Canadian who had lived in the South, claimed to have escaped from prison with Confederate general Morgan.[25]

FLIGHT

The captured vessel steamed up the coast of Maine firemen Patrick Connor, R. Tracy and John Murphy, chief engineer James Johnston and his assistant A. Striebeck forced to tend the boilers and engine under armed guard. As the highjackers stood watch, one of their party polished brass fixtures, an incongruous example of routine under the circumstances. One of the passengers, Robert Osburn, who had sailed out of Saint John as master of the *Fellow Craft* and was well acquainted with the Bay of Fundy, was forced to act as pilot. They steamed parallel with the Maine coast, passing Isle du Haut and Swan's Island.[26]

After sighting Mount Desert Island, a landmark for generations of navigators, Osburn, at Brain's order, took the steamer to Seal Cove Harbour on the New Brunswick island of Grand Manan, off Quoddy Head, Maine. The cliff-ringed island, centre of a rich herring and cod industry, had become officially British only in 1817. It was inhabited by an independent race of Loyalists and Yankees who excelled at fishing, seamanship and evading revenue officers. On the way the highjackers spotted a barque and a schooner. The captors appeared to be following a pre-arranged plan, but witnesses told conflicting stories. One version of events was that three or four men went ashore in a boat at Seal Cove early Tuesday morning and returned with a man referred to as "Captain" – Vernon Locke, alias Captain Power – who assumed command. Second mate Henderson later testified that the captain boarded two to three hours after they had left Grand Manan's southwestern coast. The plan seemed to be to secure coal supplies and head for the open sea as soon as possible, and somehow get the prize to the confederacy. In 1863, blockade running steamers still had a 75 per cent success rate in reaching their destinations. Fuel would be essential as the vessel's small sails were intended for auxiliary power only.[27]

Continuing up the Bay of Fundy, the *Chesapeake* encountered George Mulherrin's pilot boat *Simonds*, possibly near Dipper Harbour or Musquash, to the west of Saint John. Again, the testimony is confusing. To some of the captives this seemed no accidental meeting. Charles Johnston believed that the pilot boat was the *Robert R. Wilson*, responding to a distress signal. One group of witnesses, including Osburn, claimed that Locke came on board at this point, opposite Point Lepreau. The steamer towed the pilot boat to within five to seven miles of Saint John, and then put the captain, most of the crew and the five passengers who were not part of the conspiracy on board. Willett, for some reason, had been permitted to keep his navigational instruments, which suggests that the raiders did not contemplate taking their prize to sea. Osburn was allowed to go ashore near the city.[28]

Again, the specific details of the evening are conflicting. One journal asserted that Brain briefly went ashore at Partridge Island, site of the celebrated steam-powered fog horn. Another contended that the captured craft communicated with a second vessel off the island. James Johnston swore that "Parker," Brain, Parr and a fourth pirate went ashore. The *Chesapeake* hovered off Saint John on the evening of 8 December and then set a course southward in the wee hours of the morning. If the Saint John visit had been to secure coal, it was a failure. Captain Willett, four of the crew and two passengers, having acquired a boat from a vessel at Partridge Island near the mouth of the harbour, reached Saint John at 4 a.m. on 9 December. The rest of the party reached shore a few hours later. The captives working the engine – three firemen, the chief engineer and the oiler – remained on board.[29]

News of the piracy created a sensation in Saint John, while remaining passengers and crew eventually were sent back to Portland. Observers had been predicting an incident of this type for some time. During the *Tacony* scare, the steamer *New Brunswick*, about to leave on the return route to Portland and Boston, had been detained. In the aftermath of the Brain escapade, extra security measures were put in place on the other "Boston boat," the *New England*. With the approval of Saint John's mayor and the police magistrate, but much to the ire of the local press, passengers who wished to board were searched for concealed weapons. For the Saint John *Freeman*, this was tantamount to being "under the despotic rule of Abe Lincoln himself." Early in the New Year it was revealed that undercover Boston police had been accompanying the steamer to New Brunswick. Tensions along the border were heightened. The town of Calais enrolled volunteers to guard bridges leading to New Brunswick and the police in Portland enforced a late-night curfew to round up possible raiders. Newspapers in Maine were circulating a theory that the *Chesapeake* plot had been hatched not in New York but in Saint John, another sign that their Bluenose neighbours could not be trusted. In Halifax, as mentioned in an earlier chapter, suspicious characters had been gathering, possibly Confederates planning an expedition. News of the foiled Confederate plot to liberate prisoners of war on Johnston's Island, Lake Erie, and the recent return of Rebel officers and men from Canada to Halifax made conspiracy theories attractive for newspapers on both sides of the border.[30]

U.S. consul James Q. Howard reported to the secretary of state the disturbing news that the majority of the pirates were "British subjects, composed of the dregs of society and rotted rubbish that collect at sea port towns." According to Howard's sources, the plot had been forged in Saint John by men bankrupt in "morals, money and reputation."[31] Some of the conspirators apparently had voyaged from Saint John to Boston on the *New England*. The conspiracy had been well planned with one exception: two engineers hired to board the *Chesapeake* at New York had gotten drunk and had been left behind. Seven of the desperadoes hailed from Carleton, a village across the harbour from Saint John. The pro-Union *Globe* described the locals involved in murder and piracy on the high seas as "roughs . . . two of them the very worst species of 'roughs' at that, regular jailbirds." A knowledgeable source described the expedition's leader as a young man possessing good manners and a prepossessing appearance. The editor of the *Colonial Presbyterian* had been a passenger on the steamer to Eastport when he noticed strangers, possibly some of "Morgan's men" rumoured to be conspiring against "Federal commerce." He was surprised to see an acquaintance among the group travelling under an assumed name. The unnamed individual, who had been imprisoned earlier when caught on a blockade runner, probably was George Robinson from St. Stephen, New Brunswick.[32]

Most American commentators were quick to condemn the seizure and to point an accusatory finger at Johnny Bluenose. News of the capture, when announced in New York's theatres and other public places, produced great excitement. At first it was thought that Confederates had staged the highjacking entirely out of New York. Once the details of the plot and the events surrounding the recapture of the *Chesapeake* were circulated, anti-British nationalism filled the pages of the Northern press. John Bull had built and equipped commerce raiders for the Rebels and allowed British merchants and ship owners to break the blockade; now Rebel operations were being plotted on his soil. The Milwaukee *Sentinel* described the people of Saint John as "mere pimps of Jefferson Davis and his fellow traitors." The New York *Herald* excoriated Bluenoses as "men with [the] cold blood and feeble circulation of reptiles."[33]

For their part, most Maritime journals, even those with Southern leanings, condemned Brain's expedition as cold-blooded murder and wanton piracy. P.E.I.'s influential *Ross's Weekly* argued that most of the regional press disapproved of the crime. The Pictou *Eastern Chronicle* described the highjacking as "beyond the pale of civilized warfare." Halifax's pro-Rebel *Evening Express* labelled the operation piratical, a "ruffianly and cowardly" act; the "Confederates" went on to advertise themselves at a half dozen places, and at the first sign of trouble they would flee like "fools and dastards." The *New Brunswick Courier* agreed that the seizure was "a base and cowardly act" perpetrated by "a band of desperadoes" and "sordid mercenaries." To T.W. Anglin's *Freeman* the highjackers were "little better than pirates." Another Saint John publication opined that legitimate privateering was "infinitely preferred to this mode of injuring an opponent."[34]

Not all colonial journals refused to condone the capture. Nova Scotia's *Colonial Standard* concluded that the action was compatible with international law. Edward Willis's Saint John *News* argued that Brain had acted under proper authority and that commandeering a civilian steamer at midnight was no less civilized than destroying Confederate tanneries and salt works, burning farmers' barns in Virginia or pouncing on defenceless blockade runners. The *New Brunswick Reporter*, although describing the plot as cowardly, was unable to distinguish between the *Chesapeake* raiders and British subjects who enlisted in "the Army of the Potomac to kill Southerners." Colonists' opinion would change as the courts examined the action in light of international law. A Canadian paper concluded that the fate of the fugitives depended on whether they were genuine privateers acting under orders. Without an official commission and letters of marque, Brain and his men were mere pirates who deserved "short shrifts" and "long ropes."[35]

On the afternoon of 9 December, roughly sixty hours after the highjacking, and several hours after the landing of the passengers and crew at Saint John, the Navy Department in Washington received its first notice of the affair. Telegrams came from the collector of customs at Portland, the consul at Saint John and the governor of Massachusetts. The latter warned that the Confederates were likely to seize a second steamer at Portland. Consul Howard reported that the pirates had "received two officers" at Saint John and had departed before dawn. All Secretary of the Navy Welles knew for

certain by Wednesday afternoon was that the steamer was somewhere in the Bay of Fundy or off the tip of Nova Scotia. Naval
commanders at Philadelphia, New York, Boston, Portsmouth and
Portland were contacted and urged to respond. Twenty-four hours
after his first cable, Howard wired a report that the *Chesapeake* had
been in the vicinity of Pubnico Harbour, near Cape Sable, Nova
Scotia. The sources suggest that the Navy Department was not well
prepared to suddenly organize a pursuit operation in and around
the waters of the Maritimes. Geographic knowledge was imprecise;
for example the commandant of the New York Navy Yard had to
correct basic information about the navigability of the Minas Basin–
Shubenacadie River area. Other problems arose. One of the vessels
closest to the area, the USS *Acacia*, was prevented from leaving Portland because of extensive leaks which might have been caused by
sabotage. But eventually several American warships were ordered
to steam towards Nova Scotia.[36]

The United States Navy was not totally unfamiliar with the waters of Atlantic Canada. In the early 1850s, prior to the Reciprocity
Treaty, disputes had arisen over American and British interpretations of the 1818 Commercial Convention regulating the fisheries.
In 1852, following the seizure of several American schooners in colonial waters, the secretary of the navy had dispatched Commodore
Matthew C. Perry to investigate the problem and show the flag.
Perry, brother of the War of 1812 hero, had helped establish Liberia
in Africa, patrolled against slavers and commanded the Gulf squadron in the war with Mexico. The commodore steamed to Saint John,
travelled upriver to meet the colonial administrator, and then continued to Halifax to confer with naval and civil authorities.

The U.S. consul reported that Perry's arrival at Halifax on the
steam frigate *Mississippi* had caused a sensation. The *Mississippi*
cruised the coast of Cape Breton, the Magdalens, Chaleur Bay and
the north shore of PEI, all historic fishing grounds of New England.
In a report that reflected older, mercantilist naval strategy, Perry
valued the estimated 27,500 cod and mackerel fishermen frequenting the region as a "nursery of seamen" for the republic's defence.
In 1853 a follow-up cruise by Commodore W.B. Shubrick brought
the USS *Princeton, Fulton* and *Decataur* into Maritime waters.[37]

The Civil War made Halifax visits by the "Northern" navy extremely controversial. Edward F. Devens, volunteer lieutenant in
command of the wooden U.S. gunboat *Howquah* in 1863, was so
incensed by his rude reception in Nova Scotia's capital that he was
compelled to write the secretary of the navy. USS *Howquah* was
a schooner-rigged screw steamer, a 460-ton merchant vessel con-

verted into a warship by the addition of two thirty-pound, rifled Parrott guns and two twelve-pounders. The recently commissioned gunboat, on a cruise to protect New England fishermen from the *Tacony*, put into Halifax for coal and was immediately surrounded by curious and hostile civilians. The locals, in small boats, subjected the officers and crew to insults and language "unfit for publication in any respectable journal." One critic noted that the hecklers were not from the lower orders but "gentlemen and others who would scorn to be associated with the working class." A crowd gathering on the water and on shore waved Confederate flags and sang secessionist songs. As the *Howquah* coaled at Cunard's wharf, a few less hostile Haligonians toured the ship and conversed with the officers. Devens "spoke pretty freely about the Southern sympathies of the Provinces" and "guessed the North could fight as long as the South could." The *Acadian Recorder*, accustomed to the smartness of the Royal Navy, commented on the crew's general lack of discipline. As the gunboat weighed anchor, two men jumped ship, one of them diving overboard. The officers managed to catch one of the deserters but were obstructed by a hostile crowd which cheered Jefferson Davis and the Rebels. So ended the Halifax visit of the *Howquah*, which went on to participate in the blockade off the coast of North Carolina.[38]

Other Maritime ports were affected by the foreign naval presence. Union naval vessels made nearly 230 visits to British home and colonial ports during the war; only 25 official Confederate visits were recorded. Yet American diplomats later accused the British of extending excessive hospitality to Confederate warships such as the *Alabama*. One Nova Scotia journal complained that an American man of war disturbed the sabbath by conducting small-arms practice in a harbour along the Eastern shore.[39]

On 18 September 1864 the *Flamingo*, recently in Halifax, entered Pictou harbour, a rare visit by a blockade runner to a Gulf of St. Lawrence port. A purpose-built smuggler, the three-masted steamer had been purchased in Scotland by Commodore James D. Bulloch, CSN. It was operated not by private interests but the Confederate navy. The steamer had arrived in North Carolina in early August and then successfully sailed for Bermuda a week later. Its Nova Scotia visit probably was part of a voyage to Britain. William Norman Rudolf noted that the day after the *Flamingo* left Pictou, the port was visited by "a dark coloured Federal gunboat." American Consul Norton, who had a son in the Union army, had gone aboard and been saluted by a broadside. Rudolf complained that the Yankee gunboat had remained at Pictou for over twenty-four hours

– a violation of the Queen's proclamation regarding belligerent vessels in Imperial ports.[40]

The cruise of the *Tacony*, the *Tallahassee* and other Confederate raiders resulted in an increased American naval presence in the Gulf of Maine and Maritime waters, but never to the strength demanded by the fishing ports of Massachusetts. Although hundreds of Yankee schooners roamed the waters of the Gulf of St. Lawrence, Newfoundland and Labrador, from 1862 to 1866 the tonnage of the total American fishing fleet dropped by half. As a result of the Reciprocity Treaty of 1854, Yankee fishermen were a frequent presence on the Gulf shore of P.E.I., where they landed for bait, supplies and shelter, and they were followed by American gunboats. In October of 1863 the barque USS *Ethan Allen* and the mortar schooner USS *George Mangum*, converted merchantmen, paid an official visit to Charlottetown. The barque carried a complement of 130 and sported nine guns. Although Tom Harris wrote that the American vessels were far from impressive, they would have outgunned the typical Rebel privateer. The governor was absent, but the naval officers were informed by the deputy colonial secretary, J.W. Morrison, that neutrality regulations dictated that the vessels could stay in port for only twenty-four hours. Acting Commodore Pennell and Captain Collins and their staff offered champagne and wine, which Morrison regretfully declined, being a member of the Sons of Temperance.[41]

A few weeks later the two vessels visited the village of Georgetown, in eastern P.E.I., where their reception was radically different, possibly because one of the naval officers hailed from the locale. The cutter *George Mangum* had visited the port in August. Now its officers, along with those of the *Ethan Allen*, were warmly received by the citizens. It was noted that the clergy, magistrates and villagers in general presented them with a flattering address, one to which they responded. Both vessels saluted the American consular agent, A.A. McDonald. The Americans, who were appreciated for their "kindness and urbanity," even engaged in a friendly target-shooting competition with the locals. As a parting gesture they presented a sum of money to Georgetown's Catholic and Anglican churches. The visitors, in the words of the *Protestant and Evangelical Witness*, had greatly advanced "Union sentiment" in King's County. Union warships continued to be a regular sight off the Island during fishing season. Later in the war the USS *Iosco*, a "double-ender" steamer, lent assistance to a P.E.I barque, towing it against a head wind into Malpeque harbour.[42]

THE HUNT OF THE *CHESAPEAKE*

One of the first vessels to put to sea in search of Brain and his crew was the USS *Ticonderoga*, under Captain Charles Steedman. The wooden-hulled sloop, carrying eleven guns, had been launched at the New York Navy Yard in 1862. Its cruise against the *Chesapeake* met with little success, reminding us that, even in the age of steam, sea travel was unpredictable. The vessel left Boston on the morning of Friday 11 December, heading for Pubnico Harbour, a long narrow inlet on the tip of Nova Scotia that points to New England. At midnight Steedman encountered a snowstorm that continued for ten hours, followed by dense fog that refused to lift until midnight the following Monday. Steering southeasterly by the direction of the pilot and the reckoning of the sailing master, the captain, trying to avoid the dangerous coast, knew by soundings that he was close to land. As the fog lifted, the Steedman found himself in the vicinity of Yarmouth, well to the north of his intended position. Having doubts about the abilities of both sailing master and pilot, and "dreading the influences of the strong currents sweeping into the mouth of the Bay of Fundy", the captain pushed off to the southwest. That evening the vessel was seized by a gale. A heavy sea ran for twenty-four hours, and when Steedman was finally able to find his location the *Ticonderoga* was two hundred miles from Nova Scotia. Concluding that the pirates would be long gone from Cape Sable, he pointed his bow in the direction of Boston.[43]

The wooden frigate *Niagara*, which departed from Gloucester on 10 December and reach Pubnico only with difficulty.[44] After clearing the Massachusetts coast, the frigate met easterly winds and heavy fog and was unable to make landfall at Pubnico Harbour until the afternoon of 13 December. Commodore Thomas Craven communicated with shore but could learn nothing about the *Chesapeake*. The weather situation deteriorated: "We were detained riding out a gale on a lee shore," he recorded, "until the morning of the 17th."[45]

Meanwhile, the *Chesapeake*, with Locke acting as both captain and pilot, skirted Brier Island, cruised past Yarmouth and the Tusket Islands, rounded Cape Sable and made Shelburne forty hours after leaving Saint John, despite rough weather. The fugitives had reached Nova Scotia's south shore, whose coastal folk toiled at fishing, seafaring, shipbuilding, farming and lumbering. At Shelburne on the evening of 10 December and the next morning, the insurgents announced that their vessel was the blockade runner "*Jane*" from Wilmington, bound to Bermuda from Halifax and short on coal. They remained nearby overnight, illegally landed part of the cargo into a vessel that came alongside and shipped a few tons of coal and some wood. One report was that four new crewmen, two of them named Snow and Smith, joined the expedition at Shelburne. When the steamer left the harbour, the Confederate flag flew at the main peak.[46]

On 11 December, the day the *Chesapeake* left Shelburne, Lord Lyons, the British representative at Washington, had telegraphed Nova Scotia's administrator, Sir Charles Hastings Doyle, requesting his government to take all measures compatible with international and municipal law in dealing with the missing steamer. Doyle's response revealed how little the Nova Scotia government knew at this point; he promised to impound the vessel if it reached any port in the colony.[47] Locally, Consul Gunnison contacted Provincial Secretary Dr. Charles Tupper and Attorney General J.W. Johnston, asking them to treat Brain's crew as pirates and murderers and to detain the *Chesapeake* if it were found within colonial waters. He informed the authorities that the steamer was at Shelburne, but they required more evidence before arrest warrants could be issued. The consul later opined that this initial reluctance probably stemmed from "secession proclivities" on the part of the Nova Scotia government.[48]

By the time they had reached Nova Scotia waters, the *Chesapeake* highjackers had lost the element of surprise. Although aided by a sympathetic population and the weakness of the colonial government, their situation was critical. Neutrality regulations forbade the bringing of prizes into British waters, and their coal supply problem had not been solved. There were more than a dozen major harbours, many inlets and innumerable islands between Cape Sable and Halifax, but the coastal ports of the colony contained American consular agents and American citizens and sympathizers who were able to contact the consul in Halifax.

The consular agent at Yarmouth, J.M. Merrill, reported to the Halifax consulate that the *Chesapeake* was "hovering along shore east of Shelburne Saturday night [12 December]." Cornelius White, the agent at Shelburne, first recognized Captain Parker as Vernon G. Locke of Ragged Islands. A.F. Farrar of Barrington telegraphed on 14 December that the vessel was behind Blue Island, at the head of Jordan Bay, discharging cargo into lighters.[49]

The *Chesapeake*, like the *Flying Dutchman*, was reported in several places at the same time. It left Jordan Bay and steamed past the historic port of Liverpool, settled by New Englanders a century earlier. For a time the highjackers sheltered in the beautiful La Have River, where the arrival of a large steamer was a novelty. According to the captive chief engineer, the pirates had evaded an unknown steamer at the mouth of the river. The cold weather had arrived, overland travel would soon be difficult and rural Nova Scotians were settling in for a long, dull winter. The *Chesapeake* may have been the first steamer on the La Have, an area noted for its saw mills. The "Southerners" made themselves popular in short time. A resident of the village of Bridgewater reported to the Protestant publication *The Burning Bush* that on Monday, 14 December, a large "Confederate" steamer, *Retribution*, had anchored a few miles downstream at Conquerall Bank, opposite William McKenny's wharf. One of the captured stokers recalled that they had spent two nights "abreast a large church." Captain Parker was visited by the Lunenburg collector of customs, who at first did little to stop the landing of cargo. Twenty-five bales of cotton, three hundred barrels of port wine, and a church bell valued at one hundred dollars had been landed. A Halifax journal reported that the bell, intended for a congregation in Maine, had been given, along with a cask of wine, to the managers of a church in Lunenburg County (probably the Church of the Redeemer which was being built at Conquerall Bank).

The *Chesapeake* highjackers gave a bell to the Church of the Redeemer on the La Have River, Nova Scotia.

Wine was distributed to everyone on board, including the prisoners. Tilley Spearwater of Mahone Bay obtained four hogsheads of sugar. Prominent Irish trader William McKenny supposedly purchased a substantial portion of the cargo at one-third its value.[50]

Once word got around that the mystery vessel was none other than the *Chesapeake*, and that merchandise was being unloaded into a schooner to raise funds for the voyage, the collector of customs, John Harley, forbade the further landing of goods. Harley later reported that he stayed on the vessel for two days, along with a trusted assistant, who remained to collect lighthouse dues.[51]

Brain supposedly left the ship at Shelburne and rejoined it at the mouth of the river, which the French had settled two hundred years earlier. He then took a trunk, went ashore and was not seen again, according to one of the original crew members working the engine. There were suggestions that he had absconded with a sizeable amount of cash.[52]

The acting U.S. consul at Halifax, Reverend Nathaniel Gunnison, telegraphed the missing vessel's position to Washington on 14 December. Halifax supposedly was "thronged with Southern refugees." The regular consul, Judge Jackson, was absent but Gunnison proved to be an able stand-in.[53] Gunnison telegraphed Dr. Joseph Davis, the former U.S. consular agent at Liverpool, who purported to have met Brain on shore and conversed with him about the capture. Davis, asked to come to Halifax as a witness, reached the city on 15 December. He claimed to have followed Brain to Petite Riviere, a small settlement ten kilometres southwest of La Have, where he had attempted his arrest. Brain had shown him his Confederate naval commission, letters of marque and instructions to capture the *Chesapeake*. According to Davis, "The citizens interfered and prevented me from taking him and holding him a prisoner." He also reported that parties from Grand Manan, Musquash, Saint John, Yarmouth, Shelburne and Halifax were implicated in the plot. One account suggests that Davis had mistakenly encountered not Brain but H.A. Parr, who had left the ship in search of his comrade.[54]

On 15 and 16 December telegrams were sent to Halifax by customs officers at Lunenburg and Bridgewater stating that the *Chesapeake* had identified itself as the Confederate steamer "*Retribution II*" and had been prevented from landing goods.[55]

The USS *Dacotah*, a propellor-driven sloop of the pre-war navy, had cast off from Portsmouth, New Hampshire on 13 December. The bark-rigged vessel, which had been launched at Norfolk in 1859, carried roughly 150 officers and men and mounted a battery that included a one-hundred-pounder Parrott rifle. Earlier in the year, the *Dacotah* had been on blockade duty off Forts Fisher and Caswell, North Carolina. Its captain, Albert G. Clary, was an experienced officer who had captured several blockade runners in and around Bahamiam waters. Within months he would be reporting that the craft was unfit for ocean duty. The commandant of the Portsmouth Navy Yard hastily furnished the undermanned sloop with firemen, coal heavers and other personnel. On the first day of its cruise to Nova Scotia, the sloop was delayed by the storm that battered its sister vessels. It spoke to the American ship *Argo* from Saint John, which reported that the *Chesapeake* had left the Bay of Fundy. Commander Clary, studying the charts and making an educated guess, set a course for the Loyalist community of Shelburne, which he reached three days later. The Rebel steamer "*Jane*" had been there but was now gone.[56]

The fast side-wheeler USS *Ella and Annie*, leaving the Boston Navy Yard, had arrived at Eastport on 12 December, stopping only long enough to receive a telegram reporting the pirates in St. Margarets Bay. It also picked up an experienced "Down East" pilot, John Diggins. The captain was Acting Volunteer Lieutenant J. Frederick Nickels of Searsport, Maine. His officers had all volunteered for the mission, some of them having just returned from a two-year tour on USS *Santiago de Cuba* without seeing their loved ones. Others were on leave while their vessels were in drydock.[57]

The *Ella and Annie* had reached Cross Island at the head of Lunenburg Bay on the early evening of 13 December. The cruise from Maine, Lieutenant Nickels wrote, had been cold and stormy; now the weather was preventing the gunboat from touching shore. Low on coal and light in ballast, it was difficult to manoeuvre in the rolling sea. Unable to proceed into Lunenburg, Nickels headed for Halifax. Nickels was not able to make land until the afternoon of 15 December, when he hastily proceeded to pick up 136 tons of coal and a coastal pilot. Learning from Consul Gunnison that the *Chesapeake* was in the La Have River, the gunboat left Halifax harbour before midnight, without paying respects to the colonial executive.[58]

On the morning of 16 December, the *Chesapeake* left its La Have anchorage, "carrying with the heartiest sympathies and 'God-speeds' of the people to whom they had endeared themselves with their many kindnesses." The people along the river "admired the daring show in the capture of the boat." Harley sent a constable to follow the vessel in a horse and wagon, to prevent it from landing cargo. But at some point it took a schooner in tow and loaded it with freight near the river's mouth. The *Ella and Annie* entered the mouth of the La Have River on the afternoon of 16 December. Here Nickels learned that "the pirate" had reached Lunenburg, twenty-five miles to the east.[59]

According to one interpretation, within hours, a Federal gunboat appeared in the La Have, stalking its prey, "but the bird had flown to Lunenburg." This seafaring and fishing town, settled by Germans and other "foreign Protestants" in the eighteenth century, lay to the east. The *Chesapeake* supposedly set out for Lunenburg but stopped after sighting an unknown vessel and extinguished its lights. Fortunately for the fugitives, as Locke no doubt knew, the numerous islands at the mouth of the La Have offered ideal cover from the prying eyes of the U.S. Navy. A skilful pilot allegedly directed the steamer in behind the Spectacle Islands, situated between Mosher's Bay and Mosher's Island. According to this account, as the Union gunboat (probably the *Ella and Annie*) chugged upstream, the *Chesapeake* cleared the estuary and made for open water.[60]

Meanwhile, Commander Clary of the *Dacotah* telegraphed Yarmouth, Liverpool and Halifax but received no reply until Wednesday, 16 December at 11 a.m. The pirates had been sighted at La Have, sixty miles to the east. The *Dacotah* got up steam and reached La Have by late afternoon, only to hear from the keeper of the outer lighthouse that the *Chesapeake* had departed that morning heading east. Clary could do nothing that night, but neither could the pirates because they lacked fuel.[61]

The *Chesapeake* was in desperate need of both fuel and engine oil. Leaving the approaches to Lunenburg, it had entered Mahone Bay and then possibly passed between Little Tancook Island and the Aspotogan peninsula to St. Margarets Bay. With the coal taken on at Shelburne all but gone, on Wednesday 16 December, Locke steamed into Mud Cove harbour at Sambro, a rugged fishing community several miles to the west of Halifax. The area was situated on an inlet sheltered by an island on which stood the Sambro Light, a navigational aid that had operated since 1758. The vicinity of Sambro with its dangerous hidden reefs was a death trap to ships, particularly in foggy weather. The British military maintained signal guns on Sambro Island to warn vessels of navigational hazards and to alert signal stations at Camperdown and York Redoubt of approaching warships. According to a visiting American yachtsman, even a dozen years later, Nova Scotia's south shore was dotted with shipwrecks and "strangely deficient in buoys and lights." Behind the lighthouse was Inner Sambro Island, just off Cape Sambro. The main settlement was located on a curved finger of land adjacent to the small inlet of Indian Harbour; nearer to the west lay the coastal villages of Peggy's Cove and Prospect. Sambro and the other little seafaring communities that stretched along the coast to Halifax were home to expert boatmen and pilots essential to the operation of the port. From this vantage point the highjackers could

Britain's wooden walls: HMS Duncan, flagship of Vice-Admiral Sir James Hope, at Halifax 1864.

observe any vessel cruising east or west along the coast.[62]

Locke, wasting little time, set out by land for Halifax to secure a quadrant, two qualified engineers and a schooner-load of coal. He promised James Johnston that he would soon be released from his labours in the engine room. A newspaper account claimed that the captain of the first schooner Locke contracted balked when heavily armed men attempted to board her. Eventually master mariner Thomas Holt, owner and operator of the small Halifax schooner *Investigator*, was engaged to carry a load of coal and the engineers to Sambro, a distance of sixteen miles. Perhaps not coincidentally, until July the small two-masted craft, built at La Have, had been owned by B. Wier and Co. Holt left Halifax an hour before midnight on Wednesday, 16 December, reaching Mud Cove harbour four hours later. He sighted the steamer lying in the mouth of the cove, "a harbour inside of Sambro headlands," three hundred yards from shore "in a situation conspicuous to vessels passing into or out of the harbour of Halifax." The *Investigator* came alongside the captured vessel and commenced the dirty and arduous task of transferring coal into its bunkers.[63]

The two new engineers, William and Alexander Henry, were Scottish immigrants and Halifax residents who recently had returned from sea. They had emigrated in the early 1850s and worked on land as well as the water, in Nova Scotia and the United States. On Wednesday an acquaintance had advised them that employment was to be had on a steamer at Sambro. Whether the Scots had previous experience on blockade runners is unknown. They embarked on the schooner for the night voyage and reached a vessel they understood to be the *Chesapeake*. Neither seems to have been overly concerned that it was a captured merchantman being hunted by the U.S. Navy or aware that part of the original crew was being held against its will. The engineers were allowed to sleep in a state room while the crews of the steamer and schooner transhipped the coal.[64]

The Yarmouth *Herald* would report on the seventeenth, accurately as it turned out, that the pirates were somewhere on the coast between Lunenburg and Halifax, in search of fuel.[65]

At Lunenburg Lieutenant Nickels of the *Ella and Annie* landed to send a cable to Halifax. Judge J.M. Owen of Lunenburg remembered years later that H.A. Parr was in town at the time attempting to purchase coal. Part of the lore of the *Chesapeake*'s visit to the south shore was that the telegrapher and postmistress, Mrs. William Randolph, sheltered the Confederate pirate in one room while waiting on the American naval office in another.[66] In Lunenburg the determined Nickels learned that the *Chesapeake* was at Sambro.[67]

At daylight on the seventeenth, the *Dacotah* cruised in the direction of the provincial capital Halifax, looking in each bay and inlet. The *Chesapeake* had been on the run for ten days, but the hounds were closing in.[68]

Just as Captain Locke, abandoned by Brain and Parr, had succeeded in securing coal, engineers and a quadrant and appeared on the verge of successfully taking his prize to open sea, the pirates met their nemesis. Early on 17 December, William Henry was roused by a man bearing news of the arrival of a gunboat. A pilot informed Locke that a warship was entering the harbour. From the *Chesapeake*'s deck William Henry spied a steamer to the leeward side of Sambro Island, three miles distant. Having been ordered to get up steam, Henry went below and shut the furnace door; the fire had been burning but was not dampened. Returning to deck a few minutes later, he discovered that the captain and crew, who had been preparing to disembark in small boats, had vanished. Before abandoning ship, Locke ordered captive chief engineer Johnston to scuttle the craft. Locke secured some last-minute plunder and then took to one of the boats. The crew of the *Investigator* also saw the warship bearing down. Captain Holt had first observed a steamer off Sambro, "but as soon as she had opened the harbour she bore North and stood right in and toward" the "*Retribution II*" and the schooner. The crew of the former "made their escape to the shore, having put a number of chests and a quantity of loose clothing and other articles on board the schooner."[69]

Locke's men, who disappeared into the woods, were taking few chances. Whether the strange gunboat was American or British, they were in no mood for confrontation. One source suggests that the intelligence that the fugitive vessel was at Mud Cove harbour had reached the U.S. consulate through J.F. Lewis, an acquaintance of Locke's. Lewis, who had boarded at one of the south shore stops under the guise of friendship, later applied for a reward for his services to the North, but Consul Gunnison dismissed the claim. A Halifax merchant involved in blockade running, in a letter to the Confederate agent at Bermuda, repeated the theory that Locke had been betrayed by a "Federal spy." If a trap had been sprung, it would have been difficult to find a more suitable place than Sambro. Eben Locke, who arrived at Mud Cove a half an hour after the pirates had decamped, hired a horse and wagon to carry his brother back to Halifax. Given that he would have been easily recognized, Vernon Locke did not remain long in town and possibly departed for Sherbrooke, a river village along the eastern shore.[70]

Lieutenant Nickels, unable to secure a pilot until dawn, had been waiting outside of Sambro for hours. On the way in, the Yankee sailors mounted their guns on the starboard, the side from which Nickels planned to launch his boarding party. Remembering that the *Chesapeake* mounted two small signal guns and fearing it was manned by experienced Confederate sailors such as those who had cut out the *Caleb Cushing*, the bluejackets expected resistance. Nickels, in his haste to retake the vessel, was not allowing details such as international law to interfere with his mission. Spotting the approaching warship, Captain Holt wisely hauled his vessel off four hundred yards further into the harbour and dropped anchor. About fifteen minutes later one of the *Chesapeake*'s original crew ran up the Stars and Stripes "Union down," the signal for vessel in distress. A number of men who were still on board told William Henry that they were part of the crew captured off Massachusetts. At 7:50 a.m. the *Ella and Annie* hove to, lightly struck the stranded steamer and sent away armed boarders. Below deck, Alexander Henry, who had slept through the commotion, was confronted by an American naval officer, cutlass in hand, who ordered him topside. There the two engineers were interrogated by Lieutenant Nickels. Despite their insistence that they were British subjects and Halifax residents who had not taken part in the highjacking (information that was cor-

The USS *Malvern* [*Ella and Annie*] recaptured the *Chesapeake* at Sambro, Nova Scotia.

roborated by the original crew), the Henry brothers were immediately ironed at the wrists and ankles and taken into custody.[71]

About one hour after the recapture a boat load of armed men
boarded the *Investigator*, a clear violation of British sovereignty since
the British schooner was within Nova Scotia territorial waters. A
junior officer, Acting Master William M'Gloin, commanded Captain
Holt to open his hatches; the skipper demanded to see his authority
for a search. According to Holt the Yankee "placed his hand upon
his pistol and replied, "This is my authority." Three sailors levelled
guns at Holt who grudgingly obeyed. Part of the boarding party
remained on deck, others went below and "ransacked the Schooner,
and took away a large number of trunks, bags and loose clothing
and any other articles they could find that they supposed belonged
to the men who had been on board the *Chesapeake*." The impounded
property included the bags and sea chests of the Henry brothers.
The American sailors, turning over a buffalo robe in one of the
berths, found something of greater value: George Wade, a New
Brunswicker who had been part of Brain's gang. Holt had not been
aware of any highjackers remaining on board. Whether Wade had
been left behind by accident or because he was ill (or hungover)
is not clear. Along with the Henrys, Wade was carried away as
a prisoner of Uncle Sam. When Captain Holt protested, he was
warned to be silent least he himself were arrested and taken to
Boston as a witness. Pilot John "Jock" Flemming, who would be
involved in the *Tallahassee* affair of 1864, and seaman George Tanner
later corroborated Holt's version of the events of that morning.[72]

The short-lived career of CSS *Retribution II*, which might have
become a blockade runner, was over. A Nova Scotia journal summed
it up best: "Steamers and their machinery do not lend themselves
readily for adventure." In the end it was the telegraph that had
doomed Brian's expedition to failure. Southern sympathizers later
criticized the highjackers for dawdling along Nova Scotia's south
shore, but neither the fuel situation nor weather was conducive
to any other course of action. Their inability to secure a sizeable
load of coal until it was too late suggests that the pirates had not
given much thought about what would happen to their prize once
it had been seized.[73]

Once Nickels had secured his prisoners and sufficient coal and
supplies had been put on board the *Chesapeake*, preparations were
made for the voyage back to Massachusetts. Wade and the Henrys
were destined to be held incommunicado on the gunboat for more
than fifty hours, "in close confinement and heavily ironed." As Nickels
was about to set a course for home, Commander A.G. Clary ap-

peared in the sloop *Dacotah* which had been reconnoitring to the west. The arrival of the senior officer was timely. Upon hearing the details of the events at Sambro and understanding the diplomatic implications of the affair, he ordered the *Ella and Annie* to Halifax "to legalize the capture." Before leaving Mud Cove, Commander Clary sent a telegram to inform Washington of his intentions.[74]

HALIFAX: CHRISTMAS WEEK

At noon on Thursday, 17 December, the director of signals at the Citadel received a message that Federal gunboats were entering the harbour. Crowds rushed to piers, wharves and Citadel Hill to get a better look. In steamed the *Chesapeake*, under a prize crew, followed by *Ella and Annie* and *Dacotah*. Lieutenant-Governor Hastings Doyle, an Irish soldier who had been sworn in as provincial administrator in the fall, was immediately informed. Doyle had enlisted in the British army in 1819 after training at Sandhurst, purchased an officer's commission and served in the Quebec garrison during the turbulent 1830s. Several years later he had bought his lieutenant colonelcy. During the 1850s Doyle had served in the Crimean War and as inspector of militia for Ireland. His command of British North America's Atlantic region had begun in 1861. At the time of the *Trent* crisis, Doyle had advocated the aggressive occupation of strategic border points in Maine. Now he was in charge of resolving a diplomatic issue of considerable sensitivity.[75]

Doyle had no time to seek advice from London; the transatlantic telegraph cable had ceased to function within months of its completion in 1858. The lieutenant-governor could consult with Lord Lyons in Washington, but with the exception of his legal and political advisors he was on his own. Relations between the North and Great Britain had stabilized, but memories of the *Trent*, the blockade dispute and the depredations of Confederate commerce raiders maintained a reservoir of ill will on both sides. Since September the Baltic fleet of Russia, an enemy of Britain's, had been paying a goodwill visit to the Northern states, a move that diplomats interpreted as a slight against London. William Henry Seward, the American secretary of state, was somewhat forceful; he asked Lyons if Brain and the rest of the "pirates" could be detained by colonial authorities before formal affidavits allowing criminal charges arrived from the United States. Seward also wanted the *Chesapeake* immediately returned to its rightful owners and the captured "pirates" kept in the custody of the navy.[76]

Halifax was garrisoned by British infantry, artillery and engineers, but its security was not up to full potential. First of all, none of the new Armstrong guns had been mounted in the city's fortifications. The older smooth-bore cannon which ringed the harbour had an effective range of only sixteen hundred yards. Largely as a result of the *Trent* crisis, the British military had decided to rearm Halifax with rifled artillery with a range of from two to three miles. The army's deputy director of works had toured the defences just months before the *Chesapeake* incident, noting that none of the new cannon had been installed. In fact, the rifled muzzle loaders would not arrive until after the Civil War terminated. The second defence problem was on the water – to Hastings Doyle's embarrassment, not a single ship of the Royal Navy remained on station. The squadron, following custom, had departed weeks earlier for warmer climes. the only armed vessel the Nova Scotia government had at its disposal was the revenue schooner *Daring*. The harbour, meanwhile, sheltered first two, then four and finally five American warships.[77]

Ella and Annie, Dacotah and prize anchored at roughly 2:30 p.m. but made no attempt to communicate with the authorities. Nickels sent a message ashore to be telegraphed to the American Navy Department. By suppertime the lieutenant-governor, a stickler for protocol, forwarded a letter through Provincial Secretary Tupper inquiring into the purpose of the visit. Commander Clary immediately went ashore with a government clerk who had visited the sloop. Before Clary could reach Government House, one of his junior officers arrived with the U.S. consul. Clary apologized for his tardiness and for the failure of the *Ella and Annie* to officially report during its earlier visit. That evening Tupper received an official communiqué from Clary explaining that the U.S. Navy wished to comply with "all the proprieties required in British ports" and intended to deliver the *Chesapeake* into the hands of the British authorities or "to the owners, upon faith." The commander promised restitution if any diplomatic or legal difficulties had arisen. *Ella and Annie*, he explained, had entered British waters because of the distress signal, to find the missing steamer in control of five of the original crew. At this point Clary made no mention of the fact that three British subjects – one New Brunswicker and two Nova Scotians – were being detained on one of his vessels in the harbour.[78]

On land that day the story of the *Chesapeake* took another of its bizarre twists. Acting Consul Gunnison instructed his lawyer to attempt to secure a warrant for the arrest of John Brain and company. The colonial authorities, anxious to maintain good relations with the Northern government, were not unreceptive to this request. On the evening of 16 December, Gunnison sent the provincial secretary a requisition for the pirates' arrest. A preliminary warrant bearing the signature of the lieutenant-governor and Attorney General James William Johnson was issued at one in the morning. Chief Justice Young added his signature at three in the morning, which suggested that the authorities were not as anti-Yankee as Gunnison claimed. The warrant, for the arrest of Henry alias John Brain and ten others, was placed in the hands of county constable James Montieth, who was instructed that Brain was in the vicinity of Sambro. At the request of Charles Tupper the constable was accompanied by officers Hutt and Power of the Halifax police.[79]

The peace officers encountered a suspect near Sambro whom they assumed was the infamous Brain. As they attempted to make the arrest, the individual, probably not Brain but Henry A. Parr, was surrounded by a "desperate looking set" of men, presumably pirates fleeing Mud Cove, who "continuously discharged pistols into the air" and resisted the officers. The constables, lacking sufficient force to execute the warrant, returned to Halifax empty-handed. A frustrated Gunnison wrote to the State Department: "Braine, the captain of the pirates, boasted that he was perfectly safe in Halifax." Gunnison also contended that Brain and other wanted parties had flaunted the law by openly appearing in town.[80]

On Friday morning, 18 December, the Nova Scotia government lowered the diplomatic boom, informing Clary that it would not consent to the steamer's departure until the entire matter had been investigated. The lieutenant-governor also forbade the departure of the warships. Soon after, the Nova Scotia authorities learned more about the events at Sambro, partly through Dr. W.J. Almon, who had engaged a lawyer to assist certain parties. After receiving communications from Susan Henry, wife of one of the engineers, and Captain Holt, Tupper and Hastings Doyle were made aware of the boarding of the *Investigator* and the illegal seizure of three British subjects. A second, more stern note was sent to the *Dacotah*, accusing the U.S. Navy of not only violating British sovereignty, but withholding information about the arrests. Irrespective of the details surrounding the retaking of the *Chesapeake*, American sailors had committed a "forcible entry" on a Nova Scotia schooner.[81]

One hour later, Clary, although displeased, agreed to release both the *Chesapeake* and the three prisoners at 1 p.m. the following day.[82] The *Diary of Gideon Welles* relates that the Secretary of the Navy, upon being informed on 17 December that the steamer had been captured at Sambro, immediately wired the Halifax consulate that it must be handed over to the colonial authorities. The message was not delivered until the following day. Clary explained that neither he nor Consul Gunnison had been cognizant of all of the facts of the case. Given the rapidity by which events were unfolding, this was entirely credible; Clary believed, for example, that the "pirate" captured on the *Investigator* was Vernon Locke. But the commander was guilty of attempting to cover up the rashness of Lieutenant Nickels. In his explanation to the lieutenant-governor, Clary stressed that the Union gunboat had entered Mud Cove "to afford relief" after spying the distress signal. Yet in his official report, the commander of the *Ella and Annie* made no mention of the signal and explained that he had approached the steamer and schooner soon after they had been sighted. The affidavit of the *Investigator*'s captain's explained that the flag had been run up when the Union sidewheeler was only one hundred yards away. Sir Charles Hastings Doyle's note lectured the Americans that "a grave infraction of international law" had been committed.[83]

There is no indication that the Americans ever seriously considered attempting to leave port, but the government's ultimatum was followed by increased tension. A correspondent to a New Brunswick journal declared that the city's defences, for the first time since the War of 1812, had "assumed a hostile attitude," with artillerymen confined to barracks. According to a biography of Charles Tupper, Doyle had raised the possibility that the Americans would refuse to hand over the three prisoners and try to steam out of the harbour. Tupper allegedly remarked that Doyle would then have to order the batteries to open fire. Evidence is slight that Halifax forts were put on special alert on 18 December although a local merchant recorded that the lieutenant-governor ordered "all the harbour batteries doubly manned and prepared for the worst."[84]

Even when the U.S. Navy's firepower increased substantially on Saturday, with the arrival of the crack frigate USS *Niagara* which mounted over a dozen one-hundred-pound rifled guns and twenty eleven-inch smoothbores, Citadel gunners were more concerned with firing salutes. For some reason the *Niagara* delayed its salute until later that afternoon; then the Citadels' signal battery boomed back a twenty-one-gun welcome. The American naval presence had been building since Thursday, and two additional gunboats, the *Cornubia* and *Acacia*, arrived on Friday. The latter, in expectation of criminal proceedings, carried witnesses, members of the *Chesapeake*'s crew.[85]

The consul's lawyer, W.A.D. Morse, advised that the steamer should be handed over to the colonial authorities. But Morse added that criminal charges could be levelled against George Wade once

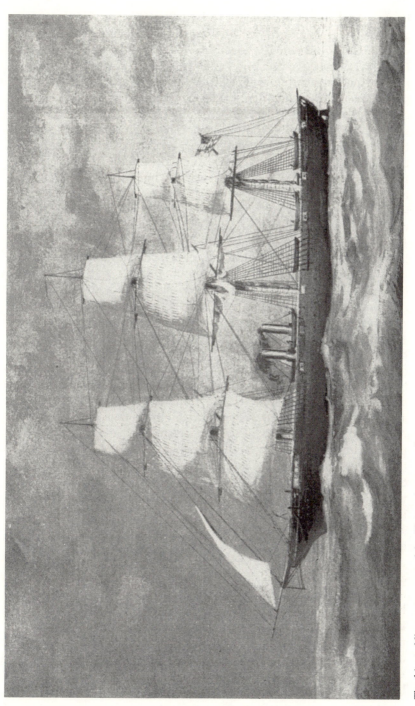

The frigate *Niagara* was part of the *Chesapeake* pursuit force.

he was released from the American gunboat. The consul hurriedly applied for a new warrant, this time from a justice of the peace, which would facilitate extradition to the United States. Mayor P.C. Hill, the city's chief magistrate, after viewing affidavits from members of the *Chesapeake*'s original crew, issued a warrant to the city marshall. In the event Brain and his crew surfaced in Halifax, the city police were kept out in the streets all night during severe winter weather. The authorities had only one likely candidate for extradition, Wade, who gave his name as Wilson. A reporter for the pro-Union Halifax *Sun* who had been allowed to tour the *Ella and Annie* on Friday noted that Wade was strongly suspected of being implicated in the murder of Schaffer. The Nova Scotia government told the U.S. authorities that, once released, Wade would be "amenable to the action of any persons desirous to proceed against him." The American government was under pressure to apprehend the culprits. One New York journal said of Schaffer's murder: "As a deed of unmitigated atrocity, it is scarcely possible to find a parallel in the annals of crime." The New York *Mercury*, pandering to popular Anglophobia and mistaking Nova Scotia for part of Canada, snapped "we might as well have open war with the colony at once."[86]

The transfer and release of the prisoners was to take place on the Queen's wharf, a site selected by Sheriff J.J. Sawyer of Halifax County. The Henrys, who could not be charged with murder, would be delivered into the custody of the sheriff and released. Wade would be allowed to walk around for a few minutes (a suggestion of Consul Gunnison) and then arrested for the murder of Orin Schaffer. Although the mayor, who as chief magistrate was in charge of the police, later claimed that he had been unaware of the details of the transfer, the warrant's execution would be in the hands of the city marshall, Irishman Garrett Cotter. One of Cotter's assistants was Constable Lew Hutt, later described as having had "a chequered and interesting history."[87]

Halifax's pro-Confederate group, in the meanwhile, had not been inactive. Two of them, Dr. Almon and Alexander Keith, would be on the Queen's wharf that day. William Johnson Almon, M.D., was at the centre of the social set that befriended, sheltered and entertained Southern officers, refugees and officials who passed through Halifax, either on the way to or from Canada, Britain or the West Indies. These men were well into middle age or older, wealthy, respected and politically connected. Almon was described as an old-style Tory. Born at Halifax in 1816, the son of William Bruce Almon, a British military surgeon who had served in the Revolutionary War, he had attended King's College before studying medicine in Edinburgh and Glasgow. Obtaining his M.D., W.J. Almon had returned to Nova Scotia and taken over his father's medicine and drug store, and his post as medical superintendent of the poor's asylum. In 1849 Almon had married Elizabeth Ritchie. Earlier in his career he had challenged journalist Joseph Howe to a duel. Several years later, Almon pioneered the use of chloroform as an anaesthetic in British North America. In the mid-1850s, along with Dr. Daniel McNeill Parker, he had opened a private hospital. Almon served as president of the provincial medical society and later was a founder of Dalhousie's faculty of medicine. After Confederation, he entered Dominion politics as a Conservative.[88]

During the Civil War, Almon went to considerable expense in aiding Confederates who reached Halifax. His commitment to the Confederacy was not financial but intensely personal, like that of his own son, William Bruce, who entered the Rebel medical service. Another son, Charles M., a supercargo on two blockade runners, fittingly was given a position in the Nova Scotia customs department by Premier Charles Tupper. W.J. Almon, like other colonial supporters of the rebellion, no doubt viewed Southern society as one built on honour, patriotism and order. In 1863 he instituted a prize at the elite King's College in Windsor for the student who composed the best ode, in Latin and English, to the memory of Stonewall Jackson. The Almon scrapbook in the Provincial Archives of Nova Scotia reflects the family's close ties with the Confederacy. Its collection of photographs is a who's who of Rebel generals and statesmen. The Almon papers hint at intrigue involving Confederate envoys and escaped POWs and suggest that Almon played a behind-the-scenes role. In 1862, Dr. Luke Blackburn, a Southerner in Montreal, wrote to introduce Almon to two Confederate officers on their way to Halifax. Blackburn passed on regards to noted local Confederate sympathizer Reverend Thomas Connolly and promised: "I will be down in a few weeks to see Fields. I will bring Welsh and money with me."[89]

Benjamin Wier, of the import-export firm Wier and Co., was the second leader of Halifax's pro-Southern group. Wier and Co., with its extensive experience and contacts in the New England trade, became involved in the Confederate supply effort, servicing blockade runners and acting as local business agent for the Confederate authorities. The West Indies became its field of opportunity. Wier's involvement may have been more financially motivated, but he appears to have shared the political views of the pro-Southerners with whom he had close personal ties. He was born at Newport, Hants County, of Rhode Island "Planter" stock – his grandfather was an original grantee of the township in 1761. In the 1840s, as a whole-saler and owner of coasting schooners, Wier, with a warehouse on Lower Water Street, specialized in trade with the northeastern states. He supported the incorporation of Halifax in the early 1840s and served as Liberal member of the assembly for Lunenburg from 1859 to 1863 following an earlier stint on the executive council. Wier was appointed to the cabinet again from 1860 to 1863 as a supporter of William Young and Joe Howe. In 1862, he represented the colony as a business delegate to the Inter-Colonial Railway conference in London. As a cabinet member, he had been embroiled in a conflict of interest in connection with the land speculation and gold mining. The year 1863 had been a busy one for Wier: he had contested, and lost, a seat for the Liberals in Hants County, purchased one-quarter of the shares in the new sailing vessel *Atalanta* and built an impressive Italianate residence on Hollis Street, beside the new house of Alexander Keith, Jr. In 1862 and 1863, Wier, whether personally or through his trading house, was involved in the sale of one ship and two schooners on the West Indian market.[90]

When John Wilkinson, CSN, had arrived in Halifax in October 1863 on the blockade runner *Robert E. Lee*, he had carried a letter to Wier and Co. The firm sold the *Lee*'s cargo to raise money for boots and other supplies for the Confederacy. According to Wilkinson's memoirs, the cargo, although officially listed as belong-ing to private parties, was the property of the Southern govern-ment. The balance of the profits was held as credit. One of Wier's letters to a Confederate official in Bermuda, dated January 1864, contains an intriguing suggestion, one difficult to confirm, that the *Chesapeake* conspiracy may have involved a wider circle than John Brain and Vernon Locke: "Captain Wilkinson left me with $720 to purchase coals and otherwise assist in getting the *Chesapeake* away from our coasts. A portion has been expended in various ways. The coals, of course, were lost." Had Wilkinson, who settled in Halifax after the war, plotted in advance with Brain or Locke? If he had, he made no mention of these men, or of the highjacking, in his memoirs.[91]

Alexander Keith was a sixty-eight-year-old Scot who had im-migrated to Nova Scotia following the Napoleonic Wars. Rightly or wrongly, he was identified by the American consul as a leading aider and abettor of the Confederacy.[92] The full reasons behind this involvement are unknown; many Scots abhorred slavery and up-held the Union. Keith had left Caithness-shire in northeastern Scot-land as a youth to study the brewing trade in England. After reach-ing Halifax, he had worked as head brewer for Charles Boggs and then became the establishment's proprietor. The Keith brewery, on Lower Water Street and later Hollis, was well known for its India pale ale. In 1863, to match the new home of his friend and neighbour Benjamin Wier, he built Keith Hall, a residence in the "Renaissance palazzo style, with baroque adornments." It was connected to the brewery by means of a tunnel. Keith, in addition to amassing a fortune from quenching the thirst of Nova Scotians, invested in banking, utility companies and fire and life insurance. He was socially prominent as a leading Freemason. His political credentials were equally impressive: Halifax city councillor from 1841 to 1852, legislative councillor in the 1840s and mayor in 1853 and 1854. A supporter of Confederation, in 1867, like Wier, he was promised a senatorship, a plumb he passed over in favour of the position of "president of the council" in the provincial government.[93]

Portrayed by modern brewing interests as a purveyor of Maritime hospitality, Keith's chief endeavour was making money. He profited from the American rebellion, buying foodstuffs in the Northern states for reshipment via Nassau or Bermuda through the blockade. In August of 1864, for example, he authorized his New York agent to purchase several hundred barrels of pork – ideal military rations – to be shipped to Boston and on to Halifax. But the schooner carrying the cargo was detained in New York and boarded by the city marshall. When it reached Boston the cargo was seized by Federal authorities and Keith was out $24,000. As mentioned earlier, from December 1863 until the following April, Keith owned the paddle-wheeler *Caledonia*, which was to have been sold to parties in the South.[94]

As Saturday arrived, the various parties prepared for the delivery of the prisoners. Lieutenant-Governor Doyle's instructions to the military were revealing; he ordered that only "peace officers and respectably dressed citizens" should be allowed past the guard. It would have been wiser, as it turned out, to screen people for their political views rather than social status. As the appointed hour approached, the sheriff and other officials assembled on the lower end of the wharf. Most bystanders, including the curious lower orders Doyle feared, were kept to the rear by the military piquet. Joining Acting Consul Gunnison were the provincial secretary, Dr. Tupper, and Solicitor General William A. Henry, an Antigonish-based lawyer-politician.[95]

Prior to the landing of the prisoners from the gunboat, onlookers were distracted by the arrival of the frigate U.S.S. *Niagara*, whose commander outranked A.G. Clary. Would the prisoners be released as planned or would Commodore Craven overrule the understand-

ing agreed to by the *Dacotah*'s captain? A dispatch boat flitted between the frigate and the *Dacotah*, and another came to the wharf.
At last *Ella and Annie*'s boat, containing the three prisoners, approached the transfer point. George Wade was described as a thin,
ragged individual whose appearance suggested "hard usage." He
sported "an immense shaggy beard of light, yellowish-gray tint,"
which suggests that he might have been the person who took over
the helm of the *Chesapeake* during the capture.[96]

Minutes after the American boat touched the wharf, a junior officer, Ensign Coghlan, brought the captives forward to be identified
by the sheriff and then unlocked their manacles. As the sheriff announced that the men were free to go, a whaler, manned by two
sturdy rowers, approached the wharf from the direction of the fish
market. Wade was jostled into the boat as it bumped against the
pilings; the Henry brothers were left unmolested. The city marshall
cried: "Who is in that skiff?" The American consul replied: "That's
Wade, that's Wade!" A boat of bluejackets from the *Dacotah* and
a boat belonging to the Ordnance Department were nearby, but
their crews made no attempt to interfere as the whaler was pulled
out through the other boats. As the boat rounded the corner, a man
in a slouched hat and overcoat ran to the edge of the wharf. This
individual, who produced a Colt revolver and commanded:
"Gallagher, stop, I want that man," was Constable Hutt, in plain
clothes. As Hutt raised his arm to aim the weapon he was seized
by three bystanders – Dr. Almon, Alexander Keith and Dr. Peleg
Wisiwell Smith. The rowers hesitated until someone cried, "Pull on,
pull on, you're all right" and were soon out of sight. As bystanders
laughed and cheered, Wade stood in the boat and yelled three times:
"For God's Sake, thank the Queen for my liberty."[97]

The authorities seemed paralysed by this bold rescue, which suggested to pro-Union opinion that Bluenose officialdom was hostile
towards enforcing the law against Southern partisans. The men who
had grabbed and disarmed officer Hutt were not waterfront toughs
but respectable members of the local elite. The vessel at the centre
of the controversy, however, was secure. Within the hour the
Chesapeake was handed over to revenue officers to await adjudication in the colonial Admiralty court. The American vessels, their
mission accomplished, began to take their leave. Prior to departing,
Commodore Craven of the *Niagara* paid his respects to the lieutenant-governor, who personally promised that the pirates would
be arrested and brought to trial. But the warrants issued in Nova
Scotia, either because the suspects had left the colony or were
sheltered by sympathizers, remained outstanding. As one Halifax

journalist pointed out, neither the colonial nor municipal government exerted themselves in tracking down the gang. No "hue and cry" was issued and no reward was posted. From afar, this lack of official action appeared not as inefficiency or procrastination but pure anti-Yankee feeling, further indication of Bluenose support for the Rebels.[98]

Although Bostonians and New Yorkers did not realize it, many Maritime journals condemned the Queen's wharf affair. Some directly blamed Almon, Keith and Smith, others censured the authorities for poor planning and lax security. Whatever the political implications of the Wade escape, British subjects, it was argued, had besmirched the Queen's name by interfering with the lawful execution of a warrant. The *Eastern Chronicle* expressed surprise that a man of Almon's status would be involved in interfering with the police. The incident on the wharf, the *Chronicle* continued, was not indicative of British fair play; Keith, Smith and Almon, furthermore, did not represent true Nova Scotian feeling on the matter. Yet others argued that the authorities had gone too far by catering to the whims of a foreign government whose navy had transgressed on British sovereignty. In the *Colonial Standard*'s opinion, Almon and his colleagues had been motivated not by pro-Southern feeling but pro-British sentiment, by "the sight of a British subject in irons on a British wharf" who had been an unauthorized prisoner on a foreign warship. Another newspaper objected to the whole province being made "a police" for the U.S. government. The telegraph system, it was noted, was American-owned, and constable Lew Hutt, who had pulled the revolver, had once sworn loyalty to the American republic.[99]

John Brain not only refused to immediately disappear, but attempted a final headline-grabbing adventure before vanishing from the region. Incredibly, he showed up in Saint John, which he most likely reached my boat, just before Christmas. He spent a relaxing holiday at the Lawrence Hotel and passed the time visiting saloons, stores and photographic studios where he was treated like a celebrity. Many New Brunswickers were still predisposed towards the Southern cause.[100]

Always a shrewd publicist, the pirate leader consented to be interviewed by the *Morning News*, predictably defended his reputation and offered his own interpretation of recent events. Little of his account matched the testimony of witnesses to date. Brain attempted to establish the legitimacy of the operation, which critics were dismissing as a criminal attack on unsuspecting, helpless civilians. The mission, he reiterated, had been planned in New York, not the colonies, and had been carried out by Southerners, not British subjects. Most of the pistol shots, Brain contended, had been fired as a warning; his men had been ordered to use restraint. The second engineer, he regretted, had fired three times at the highjackers and attempted to scald them with hot water from the boiler. Schaffer had been shot in self-defence, not cold blood. Brain also denied that Captain Willett had been ironed for most of the voyage and told of discovering a plot to recapture the vessel. As for his Nova Scotia adventures, Brain stated that "Pitcher," an ex-consular agent (and actually named Dr. Joseph Davis) who had followed and accosted him at Petite Rivière, had been armed. After a local magistrate had refused to issue a warrant against Brain, so the story went, "Pitcher" pulled out a revolver, which caused sympathetic locals to intervene. Lastly, Brain denied ever having been near Sambro or having resisted constables who attempted his arrest.[101]

Brain's New Brunswick sojourn abruptly ended on 26 December. The colony's young governor, Arthur Hamilton Gordon, under pressure from the American consul, issued a warrant for the arrest of Brain and the gang on charges of piracy and murder. A series of delays (the warrant was issued in Fredericton) gave the Confederate partisan time to make his escape. Typically, "Lieutenant" Brain left without paying a tailor for a fine new uniform of Confederate grey. He travelled eastward on the European and North American Railway as far as the Bend (Moncton), pursued by Saint John police officers. The police were much ridiculed for failing to ferret out their prey in Westmoreland County, where Brain was sheltered by sympathizers. The pro-Southern Saint John *Telegraph* mocked the abilities of Saint John's finest, whose detective techniques in Westmoreland amounted to interrogating old ladies and small children. One of the officers went as far as Sackville, missing Brain in Dorchester. From the Bend, across the Nova Scotia border to the railhead at Truro, Brain would have had to proceed by wagon or sleigh. From here he could try to ship out of Pictou, travel on to Cape Breton or head back into the lion's den to Halifax.[102]

In Halifax the American counsul's lawyer informed Mayor Hill that the fugitive planned to arrive from Truro by train on the evening of 29 December. Two Halifax policemen were sent ahead to board the train at Truro while the mayor applied to the government for a strong military force to aid the civil power. Hill feared that, if the police attempted to apprehend Brain at the end of the line outside Halifax, a mob scene would ensue. The British military commander was requested to send two companies of redcoats to surround Richmond Station. But when the evening train pulled in to meet a strong party of police and troops, the fugitive had vanished. Rumour had it that a lone individual, probably Brain, had left the train at Bedford Station outside of Halifax. Over the next few weeks the press speculated as to the pirate's whereabouts. Was he still in Nova Scotia, or had he sailed to Bermuda or the West Indies? British justice had stretched out its long arm, but Brain was either too wily or had too many abettors among the local populace. Early in 1864, Josh Giddings, the U.S. consul for Canada East, reported that the culprit was in Montreal, on his way to Windsor, the rendezvous for Confederate spies, Southern refugees and Northern copperheads.[103]

Both the American and British governments had diplomatic grounds for complaint. Secretary of State Seward had disavowed any assumption of authority by U.S. naval officers within the territorial waters of Her Majesty's government, thus admitting Nickels' two blunders; but the Nova Scotia authorities had failed to execute an arrest warrant against a suspected murderer and pirate as he had stepped onto a closely guarded wharf in broad daylight. Although the officials directly responsible for the botched arrest were civic and not provincial, the American press and public made no such distinction, blaming the Halifax "mob" for a blatant failure of justice and disregard of international law. The *Saint Croix Herald* described the neighbouring colonies as "a refuge for pirates and murderers."[104]

The *Chesapeake* pirates, in the words of one commentator, had defied the power of two empires. American papers denounced the actions of Haligonians in freeing George Wade; in Washington, Lord Lyons initially attributed the interference not to locals but to "rebels, secessionists, of whom there are great numbers in Halifax." The affair on the wharf displayed a degree of spontaneity, but there was evidence of prior planning. Dr. W.J. Almon must have known that Wade would be arrested once released by the Americans. According to an account penned three decades later, Almon had orchestrated the entire escape. The initial plan, abandoned because security was too tight near the wharf gate, involved whisking Wade away in a fast horse and carriage. The second relied on two well-known champion oarsmen, Jerry Holland and Bernard Gallagher, who were promised a generous reward if they assisted; such was the level of popular resentment against the U.S. Navy after the events at Sambro that the two Ketch Harbour residents, despite the danger of arrest, agreed. Wade, in William Dennis's account, was rowed to Ketch Harbour, near Sambro, and then taken by carriage to Hantsport, on the Avon River. From there he presumably caught an outward-bound vessel to New Brunswick or another destination. In the end, it had taken only three of Halifax's respectable residents, and two local boatmen to effect the escape.[105]

7 The *Chesapeake* Pirates and the Courts

The pious folk at sweet La Have
May weep and sigh in vain
To see their cruizer of the waves
Come back to them again;
And bring them something for their church,
To ring a peal or knell,
For Tupper's left them in the lurch
And ta'en away their bell.
They cry and sob and cry again,
"Bring us another, Captain Braine!"
– Soft Soder, Halifax *Sun*, 28 April 1865

For a brief time the *Chesapeake* incident threatened to hamper relations between two of the world's most powerful nations. Starting in January 1864, colonial merchants importing goods from New York were forced to post bonds for double the value of the invoice to guarantee that cargoes would not be reshipped or sold for eventual use by the Rebels. The new policy, which provoked protests, had more to do with abuses in the New York Customs House than with the *Chesapeake* affair, but many interpreted it as punishment for colonial sympathy with the Confederates.[1] From Washington, Lord Lyons reported to London that Lincoln's administration was determined to keep matters from developing into a crisis on the scale of that which followed the *Trent* incident. The secretary of state was afraid "of the excitement which the affair and the Confederate schemes in Canada appear to be producing in the public."[2]

DIPLOMATIC AND OTHER REACTIONS

John Hay, the president's private secretary, visited the State Department to find Secretary Seward "very busy over the complications arising from the Chesapeake piracy." Also present was Republican Senator Charles Sumner, chair of the foreign relations committee. Sumner, who had pro-annexation leanings, exclaimed gleefully: "This proves my position to be correct that England was wrong in conceding belligerency to those people," to which Seward replied, "Of course, but how the devil does that help the matter?" Once Lord Lyons read Lieutenant-Governor Doyle's detailed report on the incident, he understood its potential damaging effect on Anglo-American relations. "I don't think it would be prudent to pass over it lightly," he wrote, "because if we give the United States Junior Officers an inch in such matters, they will be apt to go to such lengths, as to force us into a quarrel at last. I should be very loathe to make any specific demand without instruction."[3]

Lyons skilfully avoided making an official complaint over the events at Sambro and Halifax, anticipating that the Americans would meet him halfway. Seward reluctantly tendered an official apology for the conduct of the *Ella and Annie*'s officer, who had acted out of "patriotic and commendable zeal." Nickels, it was promised, would be reprimanded. But the State Department was far from satisfied with the conduct of the British authorities. The Secretary of State believed that several of the captors were Nova Scotians; he wondered to Lyons if Washington "would have to adopt extraordinary precautions with respect to intercourse with the colony."[4]

Seward considered sending a protest through his minister in Britain, Charles Francis Adams, over Nova Scotia's decision to put the *Chesapeake* into Admiralty court, but Lyons advised him such an action would be unwarrantable and "ungracious." In a letter to Adams, Seward concluded that the highjacking, the escape of the pirates and other "border incidents" were the result of Britain's "premature toleration of the anomalous insurgent." In the British House of Commons, former Bluenose Thomas Chandler Haliburton, who sympathized with the Confederacy, questioned the foreign secretary if it was true that an American gunboat had nabbed a steamer flying the Confederate flag "under the guns of the fort" at Halifax. The foreign secretary replied that Her Majesty's government was satisfied with the outcome of the incident.[5]

Back in the Maritimes, a large body of public opinion, ever flexible, was gravitating towards the highjackers. Colonists began to rationalize the highjacking and murder in terms of the wider context of a war for national survival. The fact that most of the pirates were local men also changed the equation.[6]

A number of Nova Scotians, nonetheless, were embarrassed by the colony's growing notoriety as a nest of Rebel sympathizers. In the midst of the crisis a number of prominent Haligonians who sympathized with the Union cause, and to date had been relatively silent, openly challenged the pro-Southern clique by organizing a memorial to Abraham Lincoln. One of the leaders behind this controversial document was Irishman John Tobin, Liberal assemblyman for Halifax West in the 1863 election that had swept in the Conservatives. Born in Kilkenny, Tobin had relocated to Halifax and established a mercantile firm dealing in liquor, tea and foodstuffs. Unlike members of the Anglican elite, he was a self-made man. By the early 1860s, Tobin was a leading Catholic layperson in Halifax and controlled the votes of several of his co-religionists in the assembly. The memorial, signed by visitors to a store kept by Donald Ross (who wrote pro-Union letters to the press), was criticized by opponents for violating the spirit of British neutrality, but similar messages of support had been forwarded by municipalities and other organizations in England. The document was presented to the American consul, who sent it on to Washington.[7]

Much like the individuals who supported the Confederacy, the men whose signatures accompanied this document belonged to no one class, religion or political party. Prominent signatories in addition to Tobin included Reverend John Pryor, a Baptist minister who had been head of Horton Academy and president of Acadia College, and merchants James Cochran, John Gibson and George McKenzie. John Young was a wealthy West Indies merchant with a well-known house on Hollis Street. Other signatories included barrister Alexander James, Ward Six alderman and magistrate Joseph Jennings and dozens of other "merchants, mechanics and labourers." The memorial was strongly pro-Union, pro-Lincoln, pro-Republican and anti-slavery, attributes guaranteed to raise eyebrows and tempers in Halifax. One merchant who signed had visited South Carolina, where he had learned about slavery firsthand. The memorialists professed themselves to be allied "in race, language, literature, commerce and civilization, as well as in geographical proximity, to the great American nation." They pronounced slavery "a foul blot upon your country and Constitution." Lincoln was congratulated for recent military successes against the Rebels and strides towards the eradication of bondage. The message went far beyond the spirit of British neutrality:

Your memorialists rejoice in the advent to power of the great republican party, through whose anti-slavery policy these great and beneficial changes have been inaugurated; and they are fully convinced that the sympathies of all real lovers of liberty and of humanity, whether in Great Britain or in the British colonies are due to that noble struggle on your part to maintain intact the Union, while determinedly resisting the infamous and insidious encroachments of the slaveholding faction in the rebel states.[8]

The document repudiated all sympathy with slaveholders and

wished for the speedy termination of the war. Britain, it was noted, had prevented the future sale of steam rams to the Confederacy for use against Northern shipping. Victory could best be secured "by withholding all aid and sympathy from the rebels of the South, the authors of all theses calamities, and lending all possible moral influence and strengthening in every possible fashion the executive government at Washington." The memorial concluded that the war's only acceptable outcome was a peace with restoration of the Union and the total destruction of slavery.

For pro-Confederates the message was inflammatory, the work of meddlesome Yankees and unpatriotic British subjects. For those of neutral opinion it was an injudicious deviation from British policy. One of the more outspoken critics was Halifax's *Journal*, edited by the son of former U.S. Consul Charles Pilsbury. The elder Pilsbury, although not a Southerner, continued to earn the scorn of pro-Unionists in Halifax. Reverend N. Gunnison, philosophically and theologically opposed to capital punishment, was prepared to make an exception in the case of Pilsbury's treasonable beliefs and activities. The ex-consul not only speculated in blockade goods but was an investor in the Dartmouth marine works which repaired blockade-running steamers. He had been among the notables allowed on the Queen's wharf in December 1863. The *Journal* run by the younger Pilsbury, according to a contemporary, was "less judicious than a paper published in Richmond" and its young editor "a renegade loafer from Maine."[9]

THE AUTHORITIES ACT

Although Brain and Locke were out of harm's way, their expedition's legal ramifications would continue until the final month of the war. The affair would produce three criminal proceedings in New Brunswick, and one criminal and one Vice-Admiralty case in Nova Scotia. By year's end of 1863 the focus of the *Chesapeake* affair had turned to New Brunswick where three of Brain's crew had been arrested by the Saint John police. On 22 December 1863, Consul James Howard had applied for an arrest warrant under the 1842 Ashburton Treaty between Britain and the United States. Prior to the recapture of the vessel at Sambro, Howard, who probably had consulted a lawyer, advised the State Department that Washington could demand the fugitives "if the piratical character of the vessel is established." Howard was correct; article 10 of the treaty allowed for the extradition of those charged with murder, attempted murder, piracy, arson, robbery and forgery. But extradition was a political act, in that the final decision rested with the "proper executive authority" or government of the particular country.[10]

In response to Howard's request, Lieutenant-Governor Gordon consulted the attorney general and solicitor general but wondered "how he could order the arrest of persons who are not even alleged to be in this province." Gordon's warrant authorized all magistrates and justices of the peace to detain the named parties. The governor's warrant named eleven: John C. Brain, "John Parker Locke," H.A. Parr, H.C. Brooks, David Collins, Robert Clifford, Linus Seely, George Robinson, Gilbert Cox, Robert Cox and James McKinney. All but the first three were New Brunswickers, most of them from Saint John County. The magistrate's warrant, issued on Christmas Day, did not include Parker/Locke. Missing from both warrants were highjackers George Wade, a mysterious individual named MacDonald, and Isaac Treadwell, a thirty-six-year old Saint John native. As mentioned above, delays in issuing Gordon's warrant and sending it down river to Saint John allowed John Brain to escape to the Nova Scotia border between Christmas and New Year's Day.[11]

Three of Brain's local associates, who had eluded the authorities in Nova Scotia, were not so fortunate in New Brunswick. On 27 December the chief of the Saint John police, John Marshall, a Northern sympathizer, arrested David Collins, the *Chesapeake* expedition's "second lieutenant," and James McKinney at the home of the father of George Wade at Loch Lomond, in rural Simonds parish east of the city. Brain had recruited both men locally. Collins' father, an Irishman, was a respected local farmer and Wesleyan lay preacher who lived in the area. Collins had a brother in the Confederate army who had escaped from imprisonment, returned briefly to New Brunswick and then supposedly gone back to the South.[12]

McKinney, who hailed from Spurr's Cove in Portland parish on the northern edge of Saint John, had a brother on the police force. Both prisoners were described as respectable; in the words of the *Freeman*, "they did not look cold-blooded or reptile-like." Collins, who was about thirty, had a balding head and stooped shoulders. McKinney was the same age with red hair, whiskers and moustache. The prisoners had no trace of uniforms or equipment but wore ordinary workingman's clothing. Chief Marshall, recently appointed by the Liberal "Smasher" government in Fredericton, was viewed by Confederate sympathizers as pro-Northern because of his professional contacts with police departments in New England. Marshall also arrested a third highjacker, Linus Seely, who arrived on a trading schooner from Windsor, Nova Scotia. Unlike his two colleagues, Seely was a known jailbird who had served time in penitentiary. One journal predicted that the Carleton resident would come to "a bad end." The prisoners were lodged in the dingy police lockup, under Marshall's authority, to await their examination by the police magistrate, who had issued his own warrant for the arrest of the pirates.[13]

LEGAL PROEEDINGS AT SAINT JOHN

Magistrate Humphrey T. Gilbert, brother of a Westmoreland County politician, was a fifty-nine-year-old barrister from Dorchester who had been appointed stipendiary magistrate by the provincial government in the mid-1850s as part of the reform of the local police and courts. Gilbert's normal duties were examining and punishing drunks, brawlers, petty thieves and vagrants. Now he would be ruling on a matter of considerable legal and diplomatic complexity. Local feeling seemed to be running with the prisoners. Extradition for piracy could result in the imposition of the death penalty on British subjects. In mid-January, as Gilbert's examination dragged on, the lieutenant-governor informed the Colonial Office that he feared an attack on the gaol if the subjects were convicted.[14]

Gilbert would not be trying the prisoners but determining whether there was sufficient evidence to warrant extradition. This was the first case of extradition before the courts of New Brunswick. The examination which began on 4 January attracted considerable public attention. The press noted that the police court, a favourite resort of the idle and the poorer classes ("the great unwashed"), was crowded with curious respectable citizens.[15] The *Chesapeake* examination, unlike the typical case before the court, also attracted eminent legal counsel. The prosecution was handled not by the Crown but by Andrew Rainsford Wetmore, Q.C., and William H. Tuck, who appeared "on behalf of the Federal authorities." Their services no doubt were engaged by the U.S. consul. Wetmore, born in Fredericton in 1820, was the scion of a Loyalist legal family. A prominent criminal lawyer, prior to the *Chesapeake* case he had not been actively involved in politics. Later, in 1865, when the Tilley government ran on a platform of Confederation, Wetmore was elected as a member of Albert J. Smith's "Anti" government and was responsible for the memorable remark about the pro-Confederationists selling out New Brunswickers for "eighty cents a head. " He later defected to Tilley and served as the province's first premier and attorney general under Confederation. In 1870 he would be appointed to the province's Supreme Court. Tuck, an important organizer in Saint John County for Tilley's Liberals, would also receive an appointment to the bench for his political services.[16]

The prisoners were represented by prominent barristers John Hamilton Gray, Q.C., and Charles Weldon, who stated dramatically that they had been retained by the Confederacy. In reality the Richmond government had no direct ties with the New Brunswick lawyers. Gray, who led the defence, had one local contact, William H. Turlington, who corresponded with a North Carolina resident with political connections in Richmond, but the Confederacy had no consul or permanent agent in the Loyalist city. Turlington, described by the U.S. consul as a Wilmington native who acted as informal Southern agent in New Brunswick, wrote that the young men in custody were natives who "went into the affair with spirit" and deserved the protection of the Southern government. The defence of Collins, McKinney and Seely in all likelihood was arranged by Saint John and Halifax sympathizers. The impending Vice-Admiralty proceedings in Nova Scotia, which would determine the lawful ownership of the *Chesapeake*, would explore legal issues similar to those to be examined in Saint John. Gray asked Turlington if the Confederacy would "recognize" the highjacking as an act of war and admitted that the informality of the transfer of the *Retribution*'s letter of marque and Locke's use of an alias would create difficulties for the defence.[17]

Given his background and views on the American situation, John Hamilton Gray probably offered his services to the defendants out of principle. Born in Bermuda in 1814, he had been educated at King's College, Nova Scotia, before taking up law. Politically active, Gray was a member of the New Brunswick executive council, or cabinet, for most of the 1850s and a member for Saint John city and county until 1867. In 1860 he had represented the Imperial government on the Prince Edward Island Land Commission. Although a Conservative by background, Gray's support for colonial union and railways had drawn him close to the Tilley government. Early in 1863, in a lecture at the Mechanics's Institute, he had concluded that the Civil War had been inevitable and would result in the permanent disruption of the Union. A member of the Tilley government in 1864–65 who attended the Charlottetown and Quebec conferences, Gray earned distinction as a "Father of Confederation." In the spring election of 1865, he would be defeated in a county seat by Timothy Warren Anglin, editor of the *Freeman*. The correspondent of the Charlottetown *Monitor* described Gray as "a valiant, skilful champion, one who had shivered many a lance" in the court room. Following the *Chesapeake* case, he was known as "the Honourable member from Richmond."[18]

Gray sympathized with the Confederates for political as well as personal reasons. His brother, a Confederate engineering officer, had been killed in action at Fort Pillow, on the Tennessee bank of the Mississippi north of Memphis. Captain A.B. Gray had been responsible for supervising the construction of fortifications and the positioning of batteries on Island No. 10, at a strategic bend of the Mississippi near New Madrid, during 1861 and 1862. His workforce had consisted of slaves, Irish navvies and military sappers. In August he recommended the occupation of Columbus, Kentucky, the gateway to the interior of Tennessee. Gray completed land batteries on the island, a floating battery and supporting batteries on the Tennessee shore. Following the Confederate withdrawal from Columbus, Island No. 10 was reinforced. During the attack by gunboats and troops under Major-General John Pope in the spring of 1862, Gray worked under fire to repair damage to the Confederate works and supervised the sinking of a steamer in the channel as an obstruction. After the battle of Shiloh and the surrender of Island No. 10, Captain Gray was sent to survey defensive positions between Fort Pillow and Port Hudson, but he was killed at the former site before his mission could be completed.[19]

At the initial examination the prisoners appeared before the magistrate and were read the governor's warrant and the deposition of Captain Isaac Willett. One journal reported that the court's atmosphere was "a degree less oppressive than in the Black Hole of Calcutta." The defence began by challenging Gilbert's authority to examine prisoners on the charge of piracy. It was absurd, they claimed, to try such an important case in a lowly police court. The prosecution, Gray contended, had first announced that it would proceed on the charge of murder, but then decided to start with piracy. Gray considered this irregular and reminded the court that Imperial law required a special commission for the trial of piracy. A further objection was that the warrant issued by the lieutenant-governor was poorly framed and insufficient to meet the requirements of the extradition section of the Ashburton Treaty. He demanded copies of all documents relating to extradition proceedings. Gray even wrote Arthur Hamilton Gordon, intimating that the defence was prepared to subpoena the lieutenant-governor unless the papers were forthcoming. This no doubt confirmed the lieutenant-governor's worst suspicions about the backwoods colony's lack of manners and deference. Lastly, the defence argued that the warrant listed two distinct offenses, murder and piracy, and that the authorities had failed to issue a warrant for each. The police magistrate publicly admitted that he now had doubts as to his jurisdiction in the matter but decided to continue with the examination.[20]

A.R. Wetmore, for the prosecution, presented copies of President Lincoln's 1861 proclamation declaring privateering to be piracy, acts of Congress dealing with piracy, the American Shipping Act and Brain's orders that had been left with Captain Willett of the *Chesapeake*. The prosecution called two witnesses on the first day, Captain Willett and second mate Daniel Henderson. Brain's interview with the press had created sympathy for the expedition with the suggestion that Orin Schaffer had offered violent resistance to the "Confederates." Brain contended that the second engineer had been armed and had fired on the intruders. Wetmore and Tuck attempted to discredit this notion and to show that the captors had employed excessive force. According to the law of the sea, the use of any force against the master of a vessel was a serious offence. Willett, whom the press considered an entertaining witness, modified his story somewhat, claiming that he had been shot at, by unknown parties, only three times. "He appeared a good humoured sailor," one reporter recorded, "who, without a trace of ill feeling, related what he saw happened and showed no over eagerness to secure a conviction." Parr, he repeated, had put a pistol to his head before placing him in irons. The pirates, he recalled, were eleven in number. They had seized his double-barrelled shotgun, his rifle, six handguns and three of his coats. The passengers were not plundered of their belongings. He remembered Brain, Brooks, Robinson, Seely, Collins, McKinney, Parr and Captain Parker. Willett did not witness Schaffer's body being dumped overboard. The second mate, wounded in arm and leg, was in pain for the duration of the voyage and had to lay prone on a bed until placed on the pilot boat near Saint John. Henderson saw Collins and McKinney standing watch after he had been roused from his cabin by four armed men. The second mate denied the defence counsel's explanation that the murdered engineer had attempted to scald the raiders with hot water from an engine room hose. Such an undertaking, Henderson contended, was not possible.[21]

On 8 January the prosecution called Chief Engineer James Johnson, forced to remain with the captors until liberated by U.S.S. *Ella and Annie* at Mud Cove Harbour. Johnson repeated the testimony in his deposition, describing how he discovered the dead engineer after responding to the sound of gunfire. He recalled how he had been confronted by an armed Collins and fired at by an unknown person, perhaps H.C. Brooks (the defence had this comment struck from the record). Brooks, recruited in Saint John, was wounded in the hand, probably by one of his comrades. Johnson also insisted that Parker and MacDonald had boarded the *Chesapeake* after it had left Grand Manan. MacDonald is something of an enigma. He allegedly told the engineer that he would be held for only forty-eight hours. Johnson told the court that he had encountered MacDonald again; the two had actually travelled together from Halifax as far as the Bend. Schaffer, he testified, was not known to carry a pistol; indeed Johnson had disputed with Brain the charge that the murdered man had fired shots at the highjackers. Johnson later accompanied Henry A. Parr, one of the pirates, to Schaffer's cabin where they found a pistol in a drawer.[22]

THE DEFENCE

The first witnesses for the defence were three residents of Carleton, across the harbour, who had attended meetings organized by the plotters in Saint John's Lower Cove district. W.H. Turlington had written to his political contact in the Confederacy on 4 January with the news that Vernon Locke had arrived in Saint John early in November and to find Brain and "other Southerners" anxious to raid Northern shipping. Turlington believed Brain's story about having served in the 1st Kentucky Regiment. Brain's father, furthermore, who lived near Holly Springs, was supposedly an officer in a Mississippi regiment.[23]

The testimony of defence witnesses corroborated the theory that the plot had originated in Saint John. Charles Watters of Carleton, who knew both Seely and McKinney, recalled how he had met these individuals and two Cox brothers, all members of the expedition, at a house in Lower Cove where "the captain" had promised shares for the men if the steamer was captured for the Confederacy. The meeting took place in a workshop at the rear of the house. Captain Parker (Vernon Locke) had read aloud his commission from the Rebel authorities and proposed to raise men "for the Confederate service." Watters, who later saw McKinney and Seely depart on the American boat, testified with some reluctance. John Ring, who was acquainted with Seely and McKinney, had attended two of the meetings; he remembered Brain but could not identify the captain; Parr had not been present. Ring testified that the expedition's organizers had displayed a "commission" for the *Retribution*. The third witness, James Trecartin, claimed that he had been present at the final meeting and remembered seeing the captain's authority bearing the signature of Jefferson Davis and a diamond-shaped stamp. Trecartin had heard rumours that an expedition would be organized to capture an American steamer. George and Robert Cox of Carleton had also attended the second meeting. George Robinson urged "the boys" to sign up for the mission; when asked about its location, he replied that they would find out when they reached their destination.[24]

The next set of witnesses appeared on 30 January, the day they arrived from travelling down the Saint John River valley. The testimony of four Southerners, three of them escaped prisoners of war, added an exotic dimension to the proceedings. The defence had employed the Confederates hoping to establish the validity of Locke's orders to Brain. Dr. Luke Blackburn, who had journeyed from Canada to Halifax, testified that he had recognized the signatures of Jefferson Davis and the Confederate minister of war on Parker's commission. One reporter described the physician as "a person whose bearing bespoke the true gentleman." Blackburn, a native of Kentucky who had been state medical director for Mississippi, claimed to be intimately connected with President Davis, with whom he corresponded. He also knew and recognized the handwriting of Secretary of State Benjamin. The Natchez resident added that the Confederacy had issued letters of marque to privateers.[25]

Alonzo G. Coleman, a Confederate soldier, told the court that it was the practice of field commanders to delegate authority to subordinates for particular missions. An Alabamian whose family had "large estates" (and slaves), Coleman was a gentleman who had enlisted as a lowly private. In response to Gray's question he stated that Confederate officers appointed in the field were treated as officers when captured in battle. Captain T.H. Davis, a Virginian captured at Gettysburg after Pickett's bloody charge, had escaped from prison in Ohio. Davis had volunteered early in the crisis, serving at Fort Moultrie during the bombardment of Fort Sumter in 1861. He had gone on to fight in Longstreet's corps. Davis had escaped from Johnson's Island prison on New Year's Eve, walking over one hundred miles to the safety of Canada. He confirmed Coleman's assertion that the Confederate military frequently delegated authority to junior and non-commissioned officers. Ephraim Tom Osborne, a Kentuckian and former member of Morgan's cavalry, offered similar opinions.[26]

Gray and Weldon continued in their attempt to prove the belligerent status of the expedition and their three clients. Eben Locke, the Nova Scotia sea captain, testified that he had encountered his brother, using the name John Parker, in Nassau in 1863 in command of the *Retribution*. The brothers had not met in twenty years. Eben, who had been to Wilmington, possibly as a blockade runner, had requested to see his brother's authority for operating as a privateer; this same document, he testified, was now entered as evidence before the court. Other witnesses were called to identify Vernon Locke's handwriting on the order to Brain and a commission for Collins and to establish the authenticity of the transfer of the letter of marque from the original captain to Parker. The document submitted by the defence bore the signature of a South Carolina customs official. By comparing the handwriting to one on a second document in the possession of a local shipping company (a certificate of transfer for a Southern schooner to British registry), the defence alleged that the transfer of the letter of marque had, according to the rules of war, been legal. The hoped-for documents from Richmond never arrived, so Gray and Weldon were grasping at straws.[27]

If Gilbert ruled in favour of extradition and was backed up by the New Brunswick government, the American authorities would face the thorny problem of how to proceed. The *Chesapeake* incident appeared to be without precedent, but a number of other cases involving privateering or piracy, guerrilla warfare and sabotage behind the lines seemed to be relevant. At the outset of the war the Lincoln administration had threatened to treat all Rebel privateers as pirates, but in practice it became impossible to execute prisoners of this type for two reasons. First, the United States, which had benefited from privateering in past wars with both Britain and France, had refused in 1856 to sign the Declaration of Paris whereby the European powers had placed privateering beyond the rules of warfare. Secondly, the Rebel government forced the North to treat privateersmen as prisoners of war by threatening retaliation against Union officers captured at Bull Run. The incident that sparked this policy was the trial of the *Savannah* pirates, who had been captured and condemned by a New York court in 1861. The *Savannah*, a pilot boat outfitted as a privateer by eight Charleston businessmen, had captured the Maine brig *Joseph* en route to Philadelphia and sent it into Charleston as a prize in 1861. The privateer was captured by U.S.S. *Perry* and its crew lodged in New York's Toombs prison.[28]

About the same time that the fate of the *Savannah* pirates was being decided, the authorities in Philadelphia were trying the prize crew of the *Enchantress*, captured by the privateer *Jefferson Davis*. In February of 1862 the American government, in the face of Confederate threats, began to treat the pirates as prisoners of war. Another case was that of the *Chapman* pirates, Confederates in California who had attempted to convert a schooner into a commerce raider. They were captured in San Francisco harbour, sent to Alcatraz and put on trial for piracy. In December of 1863, as

news was breaking of the *Chesapeake* highjacking, the president
pardoned the three leaders of the *Chapman* crew convicted of piracy.
A more recent case that involved British jurisdiction was that of
the Boston-owned schooner *J.L. Gerrity*. A party of Confederate
sympathizers (including one Canadian) had boarded the vessel at
a neutral Mexican port, captured it at sea and set the crew adrift
in small boats. The highjackers sailed the schooner to British
Honduras where it entered port as the blockade runner *Eureka*.
Months later, three of the leaders were arrested in Britain on piracy
charges but acquitted.[29]

Another point to consider is that enemy troops caught behind
the lines in civilian garb could be executed as spies or saboteurs
– and they were. In April of 1862, for example, two dozen Union
soldiers volunteered to cut the rail link between Marietta, Georgia,
and Chattanooga, Tennessee, and steal a locomotive. The so-called
Andrews Raiders captured a train but ran out of fuel near Graysville.
They fled on foot but were all captured. Andrews and seven of
his men were executed in Atlanta as saboteurs. Then there was
the case of Virginian John Yates Beall, a master in the Confederate
navy who was captured at the head of a party of raiders, in civilian
clothing, on the Chesapeake. Beall earlier had attacked Northern
gunboats on the Rappahannock River, lighthouses and enemy
transport vessels. The Union officer who reported the capture of
Beall's raiders described them as a band of outlaws who should
be tried either by military tribunal or the civil courts, not treated
as prisoners of war. Beall, who later made Canada West the base
of his guerrilla activities, was recaptured in New York as a saboteur
and executed in 1865, becoming a martyr for colonial sympathizers
of the Confederacy.[30]

The New York *Times*, under the impression that the *Chesapeake*
prisoners were being tried in Halifax, predicted that if they were
charged with piracy and murder after being extradited the only
result could be the death penalty. The *Times* hoped that the government would see the case through to the bitter end: "They are
of no earthly use to us as prisoners of war. We can get more and
better prisoners of war and easier in Georgia or Mississippi or
Virginia than in Halifax." Washington had to demand the extradition of the prisoners, or take some kind of retaliation, otherwise
"we virtually concede to Semmes, Maffitt and the rebel rovers the
right to murder the crews of prizes they capture, or spare them
at their option."[31]

On the day of Gilbert's decision the prisoners exhibited "a wan,
haggard appearance." The police magistrate's ruling went very much

against public opinion, as did his pronouncement that the capture had been "the work of a coward and a villain, which ought to be considered against all law – Human or Divine." Gilbert declared that the self-defence argument had no bearing on the case because captains and crews had the right to use force in order to safeguard their vessels, passengers and cargo. Any authority to seize the steamer would have been derived from Locke and his status; Gilbert ruled that the letter of marque was irregular, that the document referred to John Parker, not Vernon G. Locke, and that the original commander had been Thomas Power. It was unlikely, therefore, that Locke possessed authority to recruit sailors or soldiers for Confederate service. Thus the seizure of the steamer, the murder of Schaffer and the wounding of the two other men were not acts of war. In terms of jurisdiction, Gilbert argued that the Ashburton Treaty and Imperial law gave magistrates the right to examine and try piracy. Authorities in international law held that vessels on the high seas were the equivalent of national territory; a crime committed on a Yankee vessel, therefore, fell under American jurisdiction. The taking of the *Chesapeake* was not *jure belli* but piracy justiciable in the United States. The prisoners were ordered committed to gaol to await extradition.[32]

Gilbert's decision produced, in the words of the *Telegraph*, "intense feeling in the community." The journal's editor was outraged that two respectable British subjects, McKinney and Collins, could possibly be sent to their deaths on the ruling of a mere police magistrate (there was less concern about Seely's fate). A Nova Scotia journalist reported widespread dissatisfaction with the verdict. On the evening of the judgement the prisoners were detained in the watch house, without a bed to lay on, while the police magistrate laboured on a warrant to confine them to gaol. The county gaol keeper knew nothing of their whereabouts and many feared that the police would cooperate with the U.S. consul and spirit them away on board an American warship. Thursday passed and the three men still had not been placed in the custody of the sheriff. Eventually Gilbert completed the document and they were sent to the gaol on the east side of King Square. Gray and Weldon announced that they would seek the release of the prisoners on a writ of habeas corpus. To do so they had to apply to one of the justices of the provincial supreme court.[33]

In a move that proved to be somewhat presumptuous, on 3 March the U.S. revenue cutter *Miami* was dispatched from New York to Saint John to bring the fugitives back to American justice. Two U.S. marshals prepared to receive the prisoners from the British authori-

ties. After stopping in Saint John, the cutter was scheduled to steam
for Halifax to escort the *Chesapeake*, freed by the Vice Admiralty
court, back to its owners. As far as the New York *Times* was
concerned, the actions of Britain's colonial courts had been "so
satisfactory that our own Government will hardly find cause in it
for complaint." In a related development, the Saint John *News*
reported that "MacDonald," one of Brain's men, had been arrested
in Bangor after arriving from Saint John. Apparently a detective
in the employ of the U.S. War Department was involved in the
arrest.[34]

In the midst of the New Brunswick court deliberations, a curious
legal notice appeared in three Virginia papers. The district attorney
of the eastern district court of the state served notice for all parties
involved in the disposition of the *Chesapeake* and cargo to appear
in Richmond by 22 March 1864 where the steamer would be condemned as a Confederate prize. Secretary of State Benjamin had
instituted the proceedings upon the receipt of dispatches from
Bermuda. According to the notice, "John C. Bruine," "Henry A. Pare"
and "divers other citizens of the Confederacy" had captured the
steamer as a legitimate act of war. District Attorney P.H. Aylett
not only asserted that Brain and crew were bona fide Confederates,
he also proclaimed that Parker's letter of marque for the *Retribution*
was legitimate and transferable. The New York *Times* dismissed
this example of "rebel prize law" as an absurdity.[35]

THE RULING REVIEWED

The Supreme Court justice approached by the defence was William
Johnston Ritchie, brother of the Halifax barrister acting on behalf
of the Confederacy. Like the Halifax Ritchie, the New Brunswick
judge was a brother-in-law of Dr. W.J. Almon, the key defendant
in the Wade escape trial. The two families were closely intertwined.
W.B. Almon, the banker, had married an aunt of W.J. Ritchie. Ritchie
had trained in law and set up a practice in New Brunswick. Unlike
his Tory brother, he gravitated to Reform, winning a seat in the
legislature in 1849. Prior to his nomination to the bench in 1855,
Ritchie was a member of the Fisher-Tilley Liberal government.
Political historian and journalist G.E. Fenety considered Ritchie, who
was destined for an important judicial career, "the ablest lawyer
that this province has ever known."[36]

Ritchie ordered the pertinent documents and began reviewing
the appeal on 27 February. Gray and Weldon challenged the earlier
proceedings by stating that the United States authorities had not

properly initiated extradition and that the consul's authority was insufficient under the treaty. Second, the arrest warrant had been vaguely worded, failing to indicate that legal proceedings had begun or were pending in the States. The defence repeated its argument that the two nations shared jurisdiction over piracy on the high seas and that the British authorities should be trying the prisoners. But given that Britain recognized the belligerent status of the Confederacy, a colonial court, they argued, would be unlikely to convict the prisoners on piracy. The defence further argued that the expedition, organized in neutral territory, might have violated British neutrality, but this could not affect the prisoners' status vis-à-vis the United States. Lastly, Gray and Weldon suggested that the prisoners, having entered the military service of a nation at war, were not accountable for actions carried out against the enemy. The negotiators of the 1842 treaty between Britain and American had not contemplated civil war. In short, McKinney, Seely and Collins, although possibly guilty of violating British law, were not fugitives from American justice.[37]

At this point, Judge Ritchie hinted at the direction of his decision by commenting that the police magistrate should have dealt with the case as he would have an offence triable in New Brunswick. Wetmore countered that the American consul's letter to the provincial government was a valid requisition and that the lieutenant-governor had conformed to the treaty by issuing his warrant. "The question of the parties holding a valid commission from the Confederate states," the prosecution argued, "should be settled by an American court." The legality of the transfer of the letter of marque to Locke had not been proved beyond a doubt. But the last word went to Gray: "Surely a person calling himself a United States Consul cannot by merely writing a letter to the Lieutenant Governor, have a warrant, calling on all magistrates to arrest any number of her Majesty's subjects the Consul may choose to name?"[38]

On the morning of 10 March the streets buzzed with speculation about the fate of the captives. The excitement was increased, according to one account, by "the report that two U.S. officials were in town for the purpose of receiving the men after they had been given up, and absurd reports of Yankee gunboats, ironclads and flotillas filled the air." At the appointed hour the judge's chambers, in Ritchie's Building, were jammed to capacity "while the queue of anxious expectants trailed down three flights of stairs to the street where a large crowd was gathered. The audience assembled was a motley one and included several citizens of the Confederate and United States." The crowd, which sympathized with the prisoners and viewed their crime as a political act, sensed that Gilbert's decision would be overturned but not that the men would be liberated. A hush fell over the room as the judge began to carefully read his decision.[39]

Ritchie began by reviewing the opposing arguments. He was careful to condemn the highjacking by British subjects who had travelled into the territory of a friendly neighbouring power intent on doing violence. "The scheme and seizure were," he concluded "to say the least, a very questionable proceeding." The ruling rested on four main points. The first was that the lieutenant-governor's warrant had been issued under improper circumstances. The U.S. government, not one of its local consuls, was the proper authority to initiate extradition. Consul Howard was not authorized to make this request, and furthermore the charges listed in his two requisitions had been vague. The government of which extradition was requested "must have reasonable prima facie evidence of the guilt of the party, submitted to it, as well as the demand of the Executive authority." Another problem was that no charges had been laid against the captors on the American side of the border, a necessary precursor to extradition.[40]

Ritchie next pointed out that the alleged pirates and murderers had not been in American territory since the offence was committed, so they were not subject to the jurisdiction of American courts. Piracy was recognized by the law of nations and punishable by all nations, therefore the prisoners could be tried in New Brunswick. The Colonial Office, as we shall see, had come to this same conclusion.[41]

The third grounds for release was that the police magistrate, as the defence had argued, was not empowered to examine suspects on charges of piracy on the complaint of Captain Willett.

Fourth, Gilbert, by omitting a key phrase declaring the evidence sufficient to have justified the arrest and committal of the prisoners under New Brunswick law, had issued a "bad" warrant. The affidavits of the captain and second mate, sworn before the magistrate, were ruled to be "wholly extra judicial." Gilbert should have proceeded under the governor's warrant rather than issuing his own. A justice of the peace was not authorized to receive an information on the charge of piracy or examine such a charge if cognizable in New Brunswick. This procedural error was crucial because it meant that the prisoners examined in January had not answered charges under the governor's warrant but on the complaint of the *Chesapeake*'s captain.[42]

Ritchie declared that the authenticity of Locke's commission, his orders to Brain and his commission appointing Collins second lieutenant were all open to question. His opinion of this evidence varied little from the police magistrate's. The judge noted that "John Parker," a British subject, had issued a Confederate commission to another British subject in one of the Queen's dominions. At this point the judge admonished those who contravened the Empire's neutrality policy and the Foreign Enlistment Act and assailed those who took advantage of the hospitality of a friendly power. Careful to note that the provincial government had acted promptly in the matter (but not promptly enough for the lieutenant-governor), Ritchie expressed the hope that both governments would continue to honour extradition under the treaty. But his understanding of the law dictated that habeas corpus would be granted.[43]

Once Ritchie's remarks had concluded, those present attempted to get up a cheer, but this was suppressed by the decorum-conscious judge. The crowd outside the door passed the news down to the street and a message was sent to the gaol, where the mood of the prisoners instantly passed from dejection to relief and joy. The men were not immediately freed because the sheriff was out of town and his deputy feared he lacked the authority to do so. After a telegram arrived from the sheriff, the cell door was opened and McKinney, Collins and Seely walked out free men. They were met by an escort who hurried them through the crowd.[44]

The released captives were not immune from further prosecution. The provincial authorities, intent on preserving the rule of law and sensitive to the needs of diplomacy, had made provisions for such a decision. Governor Gordon, following the advice of the Colonial Office, had contacted his attorney general three days before the judgement. He asked that two different warrants be prepared. If Ritchie released the prisoners as bona fide belligerents, they would be rearrested under the Foreign Enlistment Act.[45] If Seely, Collins and McKinney were ruled to be beyond the jurisdiction of the American courts, they would be apprehended under a charge of piracy and put on trial in New Brunswick.[46] On 8 March the governor was informed by the provincial secretary that his instructions had been carried out. But in keeping with the entire tenor of the *Chesapeake* affair, Gordon's request was not given top priority by New Brunswick Attorney General John Mercer, who offered "no explanation of why the order to rearrest was not executed." According to historian W.S. MacNutt, the governor, who had considered the legal proceedings irregular, was not surprised by the attorney general's delay. Although the men were now wanted under the Foreign Enlistment Act, prima facie evidence suggested that they also could have been charged with piracy.[47]

Once again the Americans had grounds for complaint. The bellicose New York *Herald* ridiculed the colonial judge as a "saw-log lawyer" who had improperly disclosed information to the defence counsel. Ritchie also was accused of allowing family ties to cloud his judgement and of refusing to order the immediate rearrest of the accused. His judgement, cheered by the Saint John "mob", supposedly had set aside "the authority of the entire provincial government and its legal advisers." J.Q. Howard wrote, in the heat of the moment, that a criminal could now murder the governor of Massachusetts, travel to the provinces and "walk the streets of Saint John for twenty days with impunity." The New York *Times* was disappointed but not surprised by the verdict. The Revenue Cutter Service yacht *Miami* had been sent on a "fool's errand." Yet the *Times*, which persisted in the belief that the trial had taken place in Nova Scotia, noted that the colonial judge had suggested that the prisoners probably were guilty of piracy triable in a colonial court. The problem was that public opinion in the colonies was strongly against such action. At any rate, the point was moot, for Seely, Collins and McKinney, on the advice of their supporters, promptly disappeared. Seward, after reading Ritchie's printed judgement, wrote Lord Lyons: "The reasons referred to seem to be so erroneous and inconclusive and so much at variance with the intentions of the parties of the treaty of Washington [Ashburton Treaty] that it is to be hoped that the proceedings adverted to may not be final." Seward feared that if the prisoners had been extradited and not severely punished, their example would have given rise to other highjackings.[48]

The colonial response was mixed. Anti-Northern journals welcomed the decision. The Saint John *Telegraph*, a noted Southern partisan, explained that Ritchie had freed the men because they had been ignorant of the mission for which they had volunteered. The decision was "very elaborate and admirable, one of the most important ever rendered by a New Brunswick judge." Yet the pro-Confederate *Telegraph* agreed with Ritchie's condemnation of colonists who launched belligerent acts from British soil: "If these parties desire to engage in warlike operations against the Northern States, let them at once go South where they will find a field large enough to satisfy the most vaulting ambition."[49] The *Telegraph* queried why Seely, the jailbird, had not been arrested under the Foreign Enlistment Act, as he had been seen recently in town. The journal also rejoiced in the news that MacDonald, one of Brain's crew, had been arrested in Maine. The anti-Southern Saint John *Globe* reasoned that "ignorant, thoughtless and, in some cases reckless Bluenoses" had been duped by outsiders. "A swindling book peddlar and an apothecary's apprentice," the *Globe* concluded, "were the leaders, backed up perhaps by one or two cowardly schemers, among whom Mr. Vernon G. Locke, alias Parker, was the principal." Yet not all Maritime journalists were satisfied by the successful appeal. Halifax's *Express* concluded that the judge's arguments "may be perfectly correct literally, but socially or morally we should say they are not calculated to promote the comity of nations."[50]

NOVA SCOTIA VICE-ADMIRALTY

The Nova Scotia executive council had decided to place the *Chesapeake* in Vice-Admiralty court because of the U.S. Navy's violation of British sovereignty. The attorney, or advocate, general had ordered the "arrest" of the steamer upon receiving depositions from several individuals. The *NovaScotian* wondered why the vessel had not been made a droit of the Admiralty earlier, given that it had been in the hands of the Nova Scotia government since 19 December. Sir Charles Hastings Doyle explained: "The council (and I agree) believed to hand over the vessel after such action would have not comported with the national dignity or deference due to the Queen's Government." As for the assertion that the steamer had been captured in the name of the Confederacy: "The Attorney General and Solicitor General did not believe it lay within the Provincial government either to determine the validity of that pretext or the consequences to be attached to the infraction of neutrality by the bringing of the vessel into the waters of this Province and disposing of cargo should the taking prove to have been a belligerent and not a piratical act." Vice-Admiralty court would allow all parties "to assert their claims there."[51]

From Halifax, Benjamin Wier forwarded a number of documents on the case to the Confederate agent at St. George's, Bermuda, Major Norman Walker. Walker advised Confederate Secretary of State Judah Benjamin that his government should either disassociate itself from the highjacking or recognize it as an act of war committed under a letter of marque. While personally disapproving of the "system of warfare" practised by Brain and Locke – an opinion shared by his wife, as well as by British Admiral and Lady Milne, in residence at St. George's – Walker believed that the Southern government should attempt to aid the prisoners. The *Ella and Annie*'s blunder at Sambro, he noted, had created strong sympathy for the captors in the British territories. Wier also forwarded an affidavit by H.A. Parr, explaining his status and role in the affair. This document, unfortunately, was lost. A Halifax lawyer who sympathized with the Confederacy had advised Wier that if they could produce proof of Parker's letter of marque, Brain's commission and Brain's and Parr's citizenship, then the South could make a claim for the impounded vessel and cargo. Wier even forwarded a proxy form for the Nova Scotia Admiralty court, to be signed by an agent of the Confederate government. The lawyer, J.W. Ritchie, also pointed out that without these proofs the highjacking was piracy. Wier commented that the expedition's leaders had erred by landing passengers and crew at Saint John, not arranging in advance for coal and not making it past Halifax. Nova Scotia's thinly populated eastern shore was not served by the telegraph and was close to Cape Breton's coal supplies.[52]

Rumours about the continued presence of highjackers in the region and intercepted Rebel dispatches made the consul at Halifax nervous. He now feared the *Chesapeake*'s seizure to be part of a new plot by Rebel sympathizers. Two coded letters addressed from New York to Alexander Keith were deciphered by American government telegraph clerks. The letters, intercepted by the New York postmaster, suggested that a large number of rifled muskets were being sent via Halifax, either for use by local insurgents or for shipment through the blockade. These rumours were serious enough to be made the subject of diplomatic correspondence. In a communiqué to Lord Lyons, Sir Charles Hastings Doyle wrote: "Fears are not entertained by the Government of her rescue by Confederates. Have taken proper precautions." These included mooring the steamer at the naval dockyard and placing armed sentries on board.[53]

In anticipation of the Admiralty case, the Nova Scotia government sent two confidential excise officers to the south shore to recover the *Chesapeake*'s missing cargo. A number of merchants made claims for their lost goods.[54] Officers J.V. Ross and J.W. Cragg returned to Halifax on 2 January 1864, having conducted a successful investigation. Despite the harsh weather, difficult travelling conditions and the lapse of time, they had recovered goods in Lunenburg and Shelburne counties to a value of several thousand pounds. Ross and Cragg had been assisted by the deputy sheriff for Lunenburg County and the collector of customs, who searched for illegally landed goods along the La Have River and seized a load of sugar. The Shelburne schooner *Anna Marin* brought two dozen bales of cotton from La Have; another schooner brought goods from Lunenburg. More cargo was reported to be on its way from Lunenburg and Bridgewater.[55]

In the Vice-Admiralty proceedings the Crown was represented by the attorney general in his capacity as advocate general. James William Johnston, in addressing the court, stated that he felt difficulty in bringing the case before Judge Alexander Stewart, C.B., as there was a pretence of the steamer being a lawful prize when there was prima facie evidence of piracy. Johnston was actually related to the Almons; he had married Amelia Elizabeth Almon, who was an aunt of Dr. W.J. Almon. In his opinion the vessel should have been returned to its owners without the expense and delay of Vice-Admiralty court. The State Department and a number of American journals had come to the same conclusion. But the Colonial Office and the lieutenant-governor could not overlook the wrongful actions of the *Ella and Annie* in entering colonial waters, boarding vessels with arms and seizing British subjects. The owner of the *Chesapeake*, H.B. Cromwell of New York, was represented by W.A.D. Morse, described by the U.S. consul as one of the few local attorneys who sympathized with the Union cause. Morse, born in Amherst in 1837, was later appointed a judge of probate and then a county court judge for Cumberland and Pictou. He was assisted by S.L. Shannon, a Tory barrister and member of the assembly. J.W. Ritchie, counsel for "the Confederates," argued that the seizure off Cape Cod was valid and that any citizen of the Confederacy, with or without a commission, had an absolute right to capture any vessel belonging to the Federals.[56]

John W. Ritchie, a key individual in the defence of the pirates, maintained a watching brief for the Confederacy in the Admiralty case. Ironically, the absent Mortimer M. Jackson had telegraphed his temporary replacement at the outbreak of the crisis, advising him to retain Ritchie as consul for the U.S. government. This legal luminary was described as "clean cut and distinguished" and possessing "an eagle-like face." He acted on his own initiative, or possibly at the urging of Almon, Wier, Keith and others with whom he was active socially. Born at Annapolis Royal in 1808, he was the son of Thomas Ritchie, who had attempted to secure legislation to protect the property of Nova Scotia slave owners. He also was the brother of the New Brunswick judge who liberated Collins, McKinney and Seely. John Ritchie was schooled at home and trained for law by an influential Tory uncle. He married Amelia Rebecca Almon, sister of Dr. W.J. Almon. Appointed clerk of the legislative council in 1837, he honed his legal skills and reputation throughout the 1840s. At mid-century he participated in the revision of the statutes of Nova Scotia.[57]

Politically and socially, Ritchie belonged to the Anglican elite.

His estate, Belmont, nestled along Halifax's North West Arm. He was a founder of the Union Bank and a member of the board of governors of Dalhousie College. In 1859 the Colonial Office appointed him to the commission investigating the land question on P.E.I. where his fellow commissioners were Joe Howe and John Hamilton Gray of Saint John. In May of 1864 he was nominated to the legislative council by the Conservative government of J.W. Johnston – his uncle and the prosecutor in the Vice-Admiralty case – and Charles Tupper. He entered the cabinet as solicitor general and government leader in the upper chamber. In the fall of 1864, Ritchie became Nova Scotia's chief advocate of colonial union, a stance that made him one of the province's Fathers of Confederation. A delegate to the 1866 London conference which put the finishing touches on the British North American Act, Ritchie, like Benjamin Wier, was rewarded for his pro-Confederation work with a seat in the Canadian Senate. In 1879 he attained a more prestigious goal: puisne judge of the Supreme Court of Nova Scotia.[58]

Judge Alexander Stewart, much to the consternation of Southern sympathizers, refused to entertain an application by the Confederates for the steamer. "No English court," he told Ritchie on the opening day, would do so. The *Chesapeake* had "divested itself of all Southern character" by violating Imperial neutrality regulations. Even if it had been commanded by genuine Southern officers, it would have been seized by Her Majesty's government.

Ritchie argued that belligerents on the high seas had the right to capture any enemy vessel which then became property of the state; the steamer's visit to Nova Scotia ports to obtain fuel was justifiable; witness the sheltering of C.S.S. *Sumter* under British guns at Gibraltar. Ritchie was convinced that the steamer no longer belonged to its former owner. The leader of the expedition, he explained, was a Southern officer who could not be safely brought before the court "as he would likely be arrested on a charge of piracy and murder, made by Federal agents." Local magistrates would probably hand him over to the Americans, who would hang him. So Ritchie had advised the leader to look to his own safety. One of the highjackers (Parr?) "was not long in the Confederate army and had distinguished himself by acts of daring and deeds of bravery" for which he had been promoted to lieutenant.[59]

Ritchie had hoped for time to secure documentation proving the validity of "Parker's" letter of marque and Brain's commission, but the court would not wait. Stewart reiterated that no British court could consider the *Chesapeake* a Confederate prize, to which Ritchie countered that no court could lawfully restore it to its owner.

According to the lieutenant-governor's papers, either before or after the *Chesapeake* decision the attorney general and Judge Stewart were shown pertinent dispatches from the Crown's legal advisers in London. The case of the C.S.S. *Tuscaloosa* at Cape Town had recently established the principle that any captured vessel brought into British waters before going through a Confederate prize court should be detained by the colonial authorities and surrendered to its original owners.[60]

Spectators were surprised that a judge of Vice-Admiralty would volunteer his opinions before any evidence had been taken or arguments conducted. The *Morning Chronicle* asked why the government had bothered to place the vessel into Admiralty in the first place. At the next session, 13 January, Stewart read a prepared statement which more carefully explained his earlier remarks. A large number of legal men and interested citizens were present. Stewart was primarily concerned with Britain's national sovereignty and with what had happened to the steamer after it entered Nova Scotia waters. The captors had "suffered judgement by default" because they had failed to appear on the return day of the arrest warrant, 12 January. Forfeiting the *Chesapeake* to the British authorities would be "derogatory to the royal authority." Restoring the vessel to its original owners was not a favour, but "an act of justice to the offended dignity of the Crown . . . fit punishment of the offenders and a warning to others." The *Chesapeake*, if a prize at all, was an uncondemned prize. For a neutral state to afford protection in this case "would be an act justly offensive to the other belligerent state." The steamer had been brought into several Nova Scotia ports under a false name and its captain had sold part of its cargo. Finally, "instead of vindicating the rights which it was asserted for them at the bar they possessed, they [the captors] have long since fled and are still fugitives from it [the law]."[61] Three days after the ruling, John Bourinot, assemblyman for Cape Breton, asked the government about Judge Stewart's decision to treat the captors as pirates before giving their counsel a chance to explain himself. Bourinot also demanded copies of all documents relating to extradition. The attorney general replied that a competent court had decided the matter and that the subsequent conduct of the captors had precluded them from enjoying any standing in the court. Provincial Secretary Tupper replied that diplomatic dispatches on the incident were confidential Imperial matters and could not be released to the House. According to writer Thomas Raddall, Judge Stewart was "upbraided and insulted" by a fellow member at the exclusive Halifax Club.[62]

The ruling, for Northern journals, was evidence of a shift in British opinion away from the Rebels and towards the Union. Halifax's *Express* described the outcome as bringing credit to both sides. Seward's apology, issued before it had been demanded, was "somewhat novel in American diplomacy." The Secretary of State "appreciated the enlightened and impartial spirit" of the Nova Scotia court, but William Seward was not totally enamoured by Stewart's decision; the State Department advised the ship's owners to pay the court costs under protest and privately Seward believed that the steamer should be delivered up unconditionally. The legal costs of the Admiralty case were a burden, but they were small compared the amount that salvage would have entailed.[63]

U.S.S. *Miami*, "a small, symmetrical gunboat, schooner rigged," arrived in Halifax from Saint John on St. Patrick's Day. Captain Willett, who had been in Halifax since mid-January, refused to sail without an armed escort. A month earlier, upon the *Chesapeake* being moved from the naval dockyard to Collins Wharf, the military guard had been removed and its cargo unloaded into a bonded warehouse. In recent weeks it had been under guard by off-duty policemen, including Lew Hutt. U.S. Consul Jackson had information from a Massachusetts skipper that Vernon Locke was in the vicinity of Sheet Harbour planning another raid against Northern shipping. With the arrival of the gunboat the *Chesapeake*'s freight was loaded and the vessel was coaled and made ready for sea. Escorted by the revenue cutter, it steamed out of Halifax harbour on 19 March, headed for Portland.[64]

PROFESSOR HOLCOMBE'S MISSION

On 15 February, the day of Stewart's decision in Halifax, Confederate Secretary of State Judah Benjamin appointed J.P. Holcombe, a University of Virginia professor of law and author of legal treatises, as a special commissioner to British North America. Benjamin sent a letter of introduction on to the lieutenant-governor of Nova Scotia. Holcombe's immediate assignment was to explain his mission: claiming the *Chesapeake* on behalf of the Southern government. If Nova Scotia's governor was not the proper official to approach, he was to contact the governor general of British North America, Viscount Monck. Jefferson Davis's government would request that the fate of the valuable steamer and cargo be decided not by a tribunal in a neutral nation but by a Confederate admiralty court. If Holcombe managed to secure the vessel he was to arrange for a captain and crew, as well as coal and supplies. First preference was to be given to "the officers who captured the Chesapeake." If the colonial authorities did not cooperate, Holcombe was instructed to lodge a protest and secure legal counsel to pursue the matter in the Nova Scotia Vice-Admiralty court. If rebuffed by the British authorities at this stage, he was to "plainly state that we hold Great Britain responsible for the whole value of the captured property and shall ever insist upon our demand for indemnity."[65]

The incident, judging by the complexity of the memorandum sent to Holcombe, had received considerable attention in the Confederate Department of State and no doubt was discussed in cabinet. Benjamin admitted that his sources were not entirely reliable and that his government was unaware of more recent developments in the case. He sent commissioner Holcombe a detailed synopsis of the affair and a legal and diplomatic discussion aimed at bolstering Confederate claims. The instructions were out of touch with the political and diplomatic realities in the Maritimes. Richmond was banking on the fact that Britain had recognized it as a belligerent, if not an independent, nation and had declared itself neutral in the contest between North and South. Holcombe was urged to point out that persons in the service of one belligerent could not be delivered by a neutral power to another belligerent with the certainty that the prisoners would be executed or subjected to "prolonged and cruel captivity." Holcombe also was to demand the release of any prisoners captured by the British authorities as the result of "frivolous and vexatious prosecutions" initiated by Federal authorities.[66]

Professor Holcombe was not destined to reach Nova Scotia in time to influence the Vice-Admiralty case. His storm-tossed steamer arrived on 23 March, four days after the *Chesapeake* left port. He had sailed from the Confederacy on the blockade runner *Caledonia* and transferred to the British mail steamer *Alpha* at Bermuda. After leaving the Gulf Stream the *Alpha* had encountered severe weather and was delayed. Upon reaching Nova Scotia the commissioner learned of Stewart's decision, which appeared to depart from the established rules of Admiralty. "I do not believe any judicial proceeding has taken place in a British court for a century and a half so discreditable to its dignity, its intelligence or its justice," he wrote. The news from New Brunswick was more heartening; three of the highjackers had been released on habeas corpus and, although wanted on a new warrant, they did not seem to be in any danger of being taken into custody. Their arrest, Holcombe reported, would be extremely embarrassing for the Confederacy. Nevertheless, the local population seemed to empathize with these men who were "mainly impelled by a general sympathy with our cause." For the time being, Holcombe chose not to lodge any protest but to maintain "a diplomatic reticence."[67]

Despite Holcombe's displeasure with the Vice-Admiralty ruling, he deemed it injudicious to intervene in any fashion. Neither the British government nor its courts, he reasoned, could entertain a Confederate claim. A demand for the vessel would be "doubtful in law and equivocal in morals," largely because only one of the fourteen captors had "any claim to the character of a Confederate citizen, or belonged in any way to its service" – Henry A. Parr, who had resided in Nashville, Tennessee. "Lieutenant" John C. Brain purported to have been in the Southern military, but this Holcombe doubted. Brain, furthermore, was not a Confederate citizen but a British subject. For Holcombe, proof of a military or naval commission was necessary to legalize the capture of a vessel on behalf of a belligerent state by neutrals. It was difficult to assess the finer points of the law regarding Captain Parker's commission, Holcombe wrote, because of the meagre resources of the Halifax Law Library. Letters of marque, he continued, went not with a master from ship to ship but conferred warmaking authority on the captain of a specific vessel. Parker, therefore, was only a private citizen with no power to enlist men or appoint officers. Added to these problems was evidence from the Saint John trials that suggested that Parker had violated the Foreign Enlistment Act. Finally, the peddling of the steamer's cargo, the appropriation of some of the profits for personal gain and doubts as to the character and motives of John Brain led Holcombe to conclude that the Confederacy should not press the issue.[68]

In his 1 April, 1864 report to the secretary of state, the commissioner added that his opinions were in accordance with "the judgement of our most discreet and intelligent friends in this place." In a follow-up report which reached Richmond in late May, Holcombe stated that local legal types continued to back his approach to the *Chesapeake* case. Given the nature of the highjacking and the blunders committed by the captors, any claim made for the vessel or for reparations would damage Confederate prestige and weaken its moral support in the British world. None of the captors had been taken into custody under the new warrant in New Brunswick: "It would embarrass the government here as much as it would the Confederate government to have the solution of the question forced upon them in reference to the captors." Holcombe also paid tribute to Halifax's Southern supporters – Almon, Wier, Keith and Ritchie. "They have given money, time and influence without reserve, as if our cause had been that of their own country." Ritchie and John Hamilton Gray, who had tendered their professional services gratis, were especially recommended for recognition.[69]

The Confederate government, in light of the new information on the *Chesapeake* affair, expressed satisfaction with the conduct of its commissioner in Nova Scotia and his success in upholding the principles of international law and diplomacy. The Davis administration disavowed the *Chesapeake* seizure, disapproved (to Holcombe at least) of any encroachment on British neutrality and disclaimed "all attempts to organize within neutral jurisdiction expeditions composed of neutral subjects for the purpose of carrying on hostilities against the United States." President Davis, the message continued, was much pleased that the "superior judicial authorities of New Brunswick have rejected the pretensions of the consul of the United States that the parties engaged in the capture should be surrendered."[70]

Holcombe visited Fredericton where he informally conferred with Provincial Secretary S.L. Tilley and discussed the subject of escaped Confederate prisoners of war who returned through the province from Canada. Southerners continued to trickle down the valley of the Saint John, but never to the degree envisioned by Holcombe, who had left funds with Wier to cover transportation costs. In March of 1864, for example, Captain D.V. Barsiza of the 4th Texas Regiment and two comrades reached Saint John. Captured at Gettysburg, Barsiza had jumped from a train in Pennsylvania en route to Maryland. He spoke of the harsh conditions and small rations endured by Rebel prisoners on Johnson's Island. Professor Holcombe reached Canada in May to meet with Confederate emissaries and promote his Halifax pipeline for escaped Rebel soldiers. Although no British North American official gave Holcombe any formal recognition, he reported that Nova Scotia's lieutenant-governor, like most British officers, favoured a Confederate victory.[71]

HALIFAX'S FRIENDS OF THE SOUTH

Halifax's Confederate sympathizers projected a genteel image, but equally prominent citizens held opposing views and others were neutral. A number of the pro-Confederates were members of the prestigious new Halifax Club, the first gentlemen's club in the lower colonies. Founded on Hollis Street in 1862, the club was used to entertain a number of prominent Confederates. In February, following the *Chesapeake* incident, ex-Marshall George Kane of Baltimore returned to Halifax via Saint John. In the Nova Scotia capital he was honoured with a seat in the legislative council chamber during the opening of the legislature where he chatted with various dignitaries. Given that the former Maryland police official had been named in a plot against President Lincoln in 1861, these honours hardly seem politic. On 8 February a sleighing party was held for visiting Southerners. On the following evening, Kane and several escaped Southern officers were honoured by a dinner at the Halifax Club before departing for Bermuda. Another prominent Rebel entertained at the club was Reverend Lynch, Roman Catholic Bishop of Charleston, who stopped in Halifax on his way to Europe in May 1864. Confederates seemed to be constantly passing through Halifax. In late 1863, courier H.D. Norrell spent several days in the city where he conferred with James A. Gray of Augusta. Early in 1864, Beverly Tucker of Virginia and Colonel J.G. Ward, former American minister to China, arrived from Bermuda. Jacob Thompson of Mississippi and Clement C. Clay of Alabama, part of a well-financed Confederate mission to British North America, reached Halifax a few weeks later.[72]

Equally revealing were the names of the ladies of the Halifax committee of the Southern Prisoners Relief Fund, which collected articles for sale at a bazaar in Britain to raise funds for Southern prisoners in Northern camps. Items to the value of $2,500 were forwarded from Nova Scotia in the fall of 1864. The captains of several blockade runners added a handsome sum. The committee consisted of Mrs. W.J Almon; Mrs. A.G. Jones, wife of a prominent merchant with an estate on North West Arm; Mrs. W.J. Stairs, wife of the banker; Miss Pilsbury, daughter of the former American consul and Dartmouth resident suspected of Rebel proclivities; Mrs. R. Hugonin, wife of a McNab's Island resident; and the former Mary Martha Fairbanks, daughter of the politician-judge Charles Fairbanks and now married to barrister H.C.D. Twinning.[73]

Of the various Halifax families that aided the Rebels, none surpassed in their determination the Almons, whose British loyalty was matched only by their anti-Yankee feelings. W.J. Almon personified Halifax's elite; he served on the board of governors of King's College and the council of the Nova Scotia Historical Society and was surgeon for the Halifax Volunteer Artillery and the St. George's Society. Almon, whose grandfather had served in the Revolutionary War, was fascinated by Major John Andre, the British officer who had been executed by the Patriots as a spy. He later came into possession of a walking stick that was purported to have belonged to Andre.[74] In late 1863 a reporter for the London *Telegraph*, on a brief stopover, described a Halifax physician who in all likelihood was Almon:

I accompanied an English friend to the boarding house where he habitually stayed; I was introduced to the heartiest and most English-looking doctor I ever met with – a doctor who had a sumptuous engraving of Her Majesty the Queen over the mantle piece in his consulting room; who was a thorough going Conservative; who held the United States, one and all, in a lively hatred, who regaled me with sherry, who offered me to drink of the famous bitters of Augstouras and gave me a copy of the "Life of Major Andre."[75]

Dr. Almon's son William Bruce, named after his grandfather who had died of typhus in 1840 as a result of duties as port medical officer, had departed for the South just prior to the *Chesapeake* ruckus. The Halifax *Citizen* reported in November that the "courageous young doctor" had left by steamer to report for duty in Richmond, Virginia. Although trained in a Northern medical school, William had volunteered as a Confederate military surgeon. Two months later, Consul M.M. Jackson reported that W.B. Almon II had been captured on a vessel attempting to run the blockade off Wilmington. If this was the case, Almon, like all citizens of neutral countries, would have been released. The Almon family scrapbook contains a military pass issued to William for the city of Charleston dated 26 January 1864. According to family history the arrival of the young volunteer from the distant British colony was such a rare event that for weeks he was suspected of being a Northern spy. At least three dozen Nova Scotians served as Union military surgeons (most of them recruited from Northern medical colleges). Almon appears to have one of the few in Southern service. Months later, in August, the Confederate army medical authorities appointed the Bluenose an assistant surgeon posted to the Lady's Hospital at Columbia, the inland capital of South Carolina. The city also contained a medical laboratory and a distillery for the production of alcoholic stimulants. By 1864 the tightening blockade made it difficult for hospitals to secure sufficient supplies of drugs such as opium, morphine and quinine, and Almon may have had to experiment with home remedies and natural medicines derived from indigenous plants. His duties would have included treating patients for diarrhea, smallpox, dysentery, malaria and various fevers, removing musket balls and dressing wounds and, in the case of shattered legs and arms or gangrene, amputating limbs.[76]

William B. Almon II, retreating before the advancing enemy, was captured in Florida and later paroled at Gainesville in the early summer of 1865 and allowed to return to Nova Scotia. When he died in Halifax of consumption two years later, he was only twenty-six years old. A number of Southerners resident in the city paid tribute to his aid "to our lost but glorious cause." The younger Almon carried his anti-Yankee bitterness to the grave. In 1865 he responded to press stories that condemned the harsh treatment of Northern prisoners in camps such as the infamous Andersonville, whose commandant was the only Confederate officer executed for war crimes. A Nova Scotia journal had dismissed negative accounts of Northern prisons such as Elmira and Johnson's Island as entirely groundless fabrications of Southern propaganda. In a letter to the press, Almon rebutted these assertions, based on his conversations with survivors of the Northern camps and observations of Yankee prisoners passing through Columbia. Southern prisoners had been robbed of personal possessions and put on meagre rations, "just barely enough to keep body and soul together." Returning prisoners claimed that they had lacked sufficient fuel to shelter from the Northern winters and had been "liable to be shot down like a dog through the caprice of a brutal sentry." As for Northern captives in the Confederacy, Almon had seen thousands on their way to Andersonville, and he claimed that most looked hale and hearty and were issued the same rations as Southern soldiers. The idea that Confederate prison camps were purposely cruel was simply "Yankee lies."[77]

THE HALIFAX PROSECUTIONS

At the insistence of the lieutenant-governor, warrants were issued for Smith, Almon and Keith on the charge of interfering with the police on 2 January 1864. The prosecution went very much against community feeling. The room in the municipal courthouse was crowded by "a large attendance of the respectability of the city." One of the accused, Alexander Keith, was a member of the legislative council.[78]

The proceedings were delayed several days at Almon's request so he could prepare a defence. He objected to the small size of the court room, demanding a hearing open to both press and public. It was up to the magistrate to decide whether the hearing would be held in open court; usually proceedings before justices of the peace were not. Many suspected that it would be impossible for Almon and his colleagues to receive an impartial hearing before any magistrates, given their social connections and prestige and the pro-Confederate opinion of many Haligonians. Halifax did not have a stipendiary magistrate; its lower criminal court was run by elected civic officials. The chief magistrate, who also supervised the police and night-watch, was Mayor Philip Carteret Hill, a lawyer member of the same "tory-Anglican-merchant establishment" which included the Almons. The mayor, a King's College graduate described as "cultivated, urbane, dignified," was better known for his charitable and community work than his legal skills. The mayor was assisted on the bench by fellow magistrate Alderman William Roche, a Lower Water Street merchant.[79]

The examination was somewhat exceptional in that the attorney general, at the request of the governor, was present and fielded questions about the Queen's wharf affair. On 11 January, Almon gave a lengthy account of the events, ridiculing the U.S. Navy, the Northern press and Yankees in general and abusing the American-owned telegraph company for operating on the Sabbath. He denounced the press for erroneously reporting that Wade had confessed to shooting Orin Schaffer, and he also boasted of having communicated with Wade since the escape. The doctor was allowed to cross-examine witnesses. Officer Hutt testified that Dr. Almon had grabbed his arm after the rowers had obeyed his command to halt in the Queen's name. Keith had tried to pull the pistol from his grip. "Those interfering," Hutt continued, "knew I was a policeman." Hutt recalled that the warrant, bearing fourteen names, had been put into his hands twenty minutes before one o'clock that day. He saw the sheriff, "who did not seem to be in much of a hurry," on the wharf. Dr. Almon, also on the wharf, had asked Hutt his business, which he had told freely. Almon allegedly examined the warrant, remarking that it was the mayor's and "That is a shame." Within minutes the prisoners had been landed from the American boat, and Hutt had stood on the slip waiting for the released Wade to step forward. Before he knew it, Wade was in a small boat manned by Holland and Gallagher, who were pulling away from the slip. When Hutt pulled his gun, he was tackled by Almon, Keith and Smith, who held him until the boat was out of sight. The officer claimed that he held the writ in his left hand and that he had not intended on firing the pistol. He saw one "Southerner" on the wharf, a Major Summers. At the hearing, Almon asked Hutt if he had been "in fun" when he pointed the pistol; the officer said the Colt had not been cocked.[80]

City Marshall Cotter testified that the American consul had passed the warrant into his hands. He had seen constables Hood and Burke on the wharf with Hutt prior to the fracas. The marshall claimed that Almon had left the wharf after speaking to Hutt and then returned. At Hutt's order the fleeing oarsmen had begun to return, but after Almon's interference they continued to pull away. Cotter also yelled for the boat to return and for the American boat to lend assistance, but his voice was drowned out in the confusion. Cotter's "instructions" to arrest Wade had come from the American consul's lawyer, yet he testified that he did not know the specific reasons why Wade could be extradited. Constable Hood testified that he saw Almon gesture to a nearby boat as the sheriff was releasing the prisoners. He attempted to go to Hutt's assistance but was restrained by Keith and Dr. P.W. Smith. Constable Burke saw Almon shake hands with one of the released men, then whisper something to George Wade. Witnessing the scuffle between Hutt and Almon, Burke had run to the end of the slip to try to jump into the departing whaler.[81]

The junior officer of the garrison who had been in charge of military security testified that he had not been sure that the man who rushed down the wharf wearing a "wide-awake" hat and brandishing a revolver was a policeman. Less than one hundred people had been allowed on the wharf, according to Lieutenant Reyne, and only a dozen or so were on the slip when Wade and the Henrys had been released. Reyne opined that Almon could have been shot and possibly killed in the struggle with Hutt if not for the quick action of Smith and Keith. By the time he returned to the slip with the rest of his guard the action was over. Sheriff Sawyer testified that he had told the three prisoners they were free and had advised Hutt to wait a few minutes before executing his warrant. He admitted that, from behind, Hutt had not looked like a police officer.[82]

J.W. Ritchie, who appeared for the defence, argued that the case was trivial and that Almon, Keith and Smith had intervened only to prevent bloodshed. Almon's actions had been not only justifiable but commendable: "He hoped his Worship would not send such a trumpery case as this to the Supreme Court." Smith and Keith spoke briefly, declaring the affair to be of a minor nature. Alderman Roche, one of the examining magistrates, declared that officer Hutt had acted improperly and that if he had been in Almon's place he would have done the same. Roche also declared that if he had been aware of the nature of the warrant, as a justice of the peace he would have stopped the arrest. He argued against his fellow magistrate, who held that the police court had complete jurisdiction over the matter.[83]

If Roche was inclined to see Almon's intervention as a humanitarian act, Mayor Hill believed that he must be governed by law. He explained that he was acting not as a police magistrate who could try the case summarily, but as a justice of the peace. The case would be tried by a judge and jury. Almon continued to appeal to the court's sense of fair play, claiming that he could not, as a Nova Scotian, "quietly allow a British subject to be dealt with by Yankees in British waters." The police, he feared, had driven Brain from the province to prevent him from making a claim against the impounded steamer. Wade, if arrested on the wharf, would have been sent "to a land where law is a mockery and where justice is denied, where judges have been imprisoned for giving a decision different from that of the man who sits on the throne in Washington, where the safeguard of civil liberty, the habeas corpus, is no longer in force."[84]

The report of Attorney General Johnson, prepared for the lieutenant-governor, tended to give Almon (Johnson's nephew) and his colleagues the benefit of the doubt. Hutt's testimony, he wrote, was questionable, as "the acting policeman was naturally excited and prone to exaggeration." Hutt's claim that he had invoked the Queen's name and announced that he had a warrant was not corroborated. The number of "unofficial civilians" on the wharf had been trifling. The landing of Wade and the two engineers in irons was "a cause of just offence," an ill-advised exhibition of illegal force, especially in the case of the Henry brothers. It was not clear, in Johnson's view, that Almon had offered any resistance until after Hutt had displayed his weapon. In the ensuing tussle, Keith and Smith had interferred because Almon appeared to be in bodily danger, with a revolver pointing at his face. The boatmen had not been pursued because, "being skilful oarsmen," they soon were beyond city limits "and the authority of the mayor's warrant and the policeman's authority." Although he agreed that Dr. Almon seemed to know that Hutt was a police officer and that a warrant had been prepared for Wade's arrest, the attorney general could see no premeditation; the escape "resulted from means that casually offered at an opportune moment." There were no grounds to describe the affair on the wharf as a riot, as it had involved only three individuals.[85]

The *Acadian Recorder* criticized the authorities for pursuing the case, accusing the magistrates of acting like "dark, prowling officers" and condemning police officers for threatening loyal subjects with weapons. Keith, Almon and Smith should not be "subjected to the ignominy of a committal for a trial" but immediately acquitted. The examination was not a trial, only a hearing to gather depositions. Almon entered a plea of not guilty and stated that there had been no complicity with Smith and Keith. The trio, bound over for two hundred pounds and sureties of one hundred pounds each, was ordered to appear before the spring session of the Supreme Court for Halifax County. The charge was not "rescuing a prisoner," as Wade, at the moment of his escape, had not been under arrest. Rather it was the less serious but still indictable infraction of interfering with a police officer.[86]

The Halifax *Reporter* surmised that the reasons behind the examination and committal were political – to prove to the United States government that the actions on the Queen's wharf had been spontaneous and had not involved any complicity by public officials. The prosecution reflected not public opinion but the lieutenant-governor's wishes. Although possibly pro-Southern, Doyle was a stickler for British neutrality. Reverend Nathaniel Gunnison, who had acted as U.S. consul, opined that the Halifax police were in service of the citizens who had prevented Wade's arrest. Halifax, he wrote, "is nearly as secesh as the city of Charleston, S.C., and justice may not be expected from this city only as it is found through Lord Lyons." The accused were expected to benefit from their social and political connections. Writing his counterpart in New Brunswick, Doyle noted that Dr. Almon was related to the attorney general. Doyle also suspected that Mayor Hill had been purposely lax in securing the apprehension of Wade and had been lukewarm in his decision to prosecute the three men. In a report to the Colonial Office the governor concluded that Keith and Smith seemed "but slightly implicated" in that they did not appear to have taken part in the affair until after Almon's interference. Doyle, after reading the attorney general's report, agreed that there was little evidence of premeditation.[87]

The May session of the Supreme Court reflected the continuing support in the province for the Southern cause and lingering resentment against the actions of the U.S. Navy at Sambro. With news of heavy military campaigning in Virginia, sympathy for the Confederacy continued to run high in the British colonies. The case never made it to a petit jury; the grand jury, whose duty it was to review all indictable cases prior to trial, refused to find a "true bill" against Almon, Keith and Smith on the grounds of insufficient evidence. Almon, just prior to the grand jury's ruling, had performed an amputation on the arm of a woman injured in a steam bakery's machinery. The testimony of Hutt, Reyne and others who had been on the wharf had created doubt as to the actual events of that afternoon. So although the Cromwell steamer was now safely back on its run between New York and Portland, the courts and legal authorities of New Brunswick and Nova Scotia had been exceedingly kind to the captors of the *Chesapeake* and their abettors. And John Brain and his colleague Henry Parr were still at large and intent on doing mischief.[88]

8 Summer of the *Tallahassee*

Despite our condition, the law, custom or sympathy, we were peremptorily ordered to sea.
– Confederate naval officer, Halifax *Chronicle*, 12 October 1864

In the spring of 1864, Major Smith Stansbury of the Confederate Ordnance Bureau, who had been posted to Bermuda in 1863, travelled to Nova Scotia in an attempt to recover his failing health. The Stansburys arrived in Halifax on the same steamer as Confederate diplomat J.R. Holcombe. Mrs. Smith Stansbury reportedly missed her friends in Richmond, Virginia, and had found Bermuda dull. Confederate diarist Georgiana Gholson Walker described Nova Scotia as a "land of ice and snow" but appreciated that its people were hospitable to Southerners. Hospitality, unfortunately, could not save Major Smith Stansbury, who died in a Halifax boarding house. Walker recorded: "Poor Mrs. Stansbury. What a sad fate is hers, to bury her husband in a strange land – and so sudden his death must have been. She says that he met his death with a great deal of fortitude and composure – but what a dissolute broken heart must be hers!"[1]

Personal tragedies such as that of the Smith Stansburys notwithstanding, by the summer of 1864, colonial supporters of the Confederacy believed they had grounds for optimism. The view from afar was that the Rebels, led by the indomitable Robert E. Lee, were holding their own. Confederate commerce raiders, until the sinking of the *Alabama* in June, roamed with seeming impunity and dozens of fleet, blockade-running steamers continued to cruise between the Caribbean and the Carolinas. In the North the peace wing of the Democratic party expected war-weariness to bring it victory in state, congressional and presidential elections.[2]

Despite some hard fighting and determined use of dwindling resources, the Confederacy was feeling the enemy's grip around its throat. Foreign governments such as Britain's had become more respectful of Northern power. Yet the Maritimes, more specifically the port of Halifax, remained openly sympathetic to the Confederacy. Local businessman John Allison Bell recorded in his diary: "The American Civil War drags along. The struggle has been gigantic for three years – but the South though showing pluck and best generalship has been losing ground during the past year. The resources of the North and West are so vast that it's now thought that the South will have to succumb."[3]

During the summer and autumn the war again made Nova Scotia the focus of international attention. Maritimers were beginning to take greater interest in the idea of Confederation. But at the same time the failure of the American union continued to present its tragic evidence by letter, telegram, newspaper and word of mouth. In the months following the *Chesapeake* incident, two events brought Nova Scotia back into international news coverage of the war: a raid against Northern shipping and Halifax's temporary displacement of Nassau and Bermuda as a base for blockade runners.

The cruise of the raider CSS *Tallahassee* began in an inauspicious fashion on 6 August 1864, hundreds of miles to the south of Nova Scotia on the Cape Fear River. Its captain, Commander John Taylor Wood, CSN, had been ordered to destroy enemy merchantmen off the coast of the Mid-Atlantic and New England states. The strategic benefits of such a raid were less important than the propaganda effect; the cruise of the *Tacony*, culminating in the raid on Portland in 1863, had caused an uproar along the northeastern seaboard.

Wood's craft, despite Northern criticisms, was not ordered from a British yard but was a wartime conversion. Formerly the block-ade-runner *Atalanta*, the twin-screw steamer was fast and manoeu-vrable. The *Atalanta* had been constructed as a packet by the firm of J. and W. Dudgeon on the Thames River, England. The hull was white, with a red bottom, and the rigging was of the fore-and-aft schooner variety. It had reached Bermuda in July 1864 and cleared for Nassau with seven hundred cases of preserved meat and fifty casks of bacon, all destined for the Confederate army. The craft was modified to carry an armament of one one-hundred-pound rifled gun amidships, a rifled thirty-two-pounder forward and a smooth-bore aft. Although no match for a Union gunboat, it would soon join the elite of the Southern raiders in numbers of prizes. Speed was its greatest asset.[4]

Wood, born at Fort Snelling, Minnesota, had grown up as a "base brat" on American army posts. In 1847 he enlisted in the navy and served during the Mexican War. Seven years later he graduated from the Naval Academy at Annapolis before continuing with active service. In 1860, Wood was appointed assistant instructor in naval tactics and gunnery at Annapolis. As grandson of President Zachary Taylor and former nephew of Jefferson Davis, Wood was well connected. Prior to the rebellion he owned slaves, and during the crisis of 1861 he was greatly troubled by the prospect of civil war. In the end he sided with the Confederacy, serving as an artillery officer on the James River in 1862. That spring he directed skirmishers and sharpshooters at the successful defence of Drewery's Bluff (Fort Darling) against Union ironclads and gunboats. Wood also commanded a pivot gun on the *Virginia* (*Merrimack*) at the engagement at Hampton Roads. He went on to take part in the defence of Port Hudson and Vicksburg, Mississippi, and distinguished himself in a number of small-boat raids that employed commando tactics to surprise and capture enemy gunboats. In the spring of 1864, Wood had been posted to the ram *Albermarle* on the Roanoke River. Partly through family connections and partly through gallantry, he was appointed naval aide-de-camp of President Davis. In short, he was a capable officer with a reputation for self-reliance.[5]

Wood's instructions from the secretary of the navy left much to his own discretion, although he was advised to pay particular attention to the coasts of New England and its valuable fishery. As the Confederacy had no easily accessible ports, its commerce raiders generally scuttled or burned their prizes, although it resorted to the more humane practice of issuing bonds of ransom if the cargo was owned by neutrals or if civilian prisoners required safe passage. The bonded party promised to pay the Rebel government the assigned amount after the termination of hostilities; when the South lost the war, the bonds became worthless. The Rebels were short of ocean-going warships; two steam rams built by the Laird firm in England for the Confederate navy had been seized by the British government in 1863. While recruiting for the *Tallahassee*, Commander Wood learned of the destruction of CSS *Alabama*. The day before he sailed, the U.S. Navy under Farragut fought its way into Mobile Bay. The cruise of the *Tallahassee*, following so closely on these reverses, would give the South a badly needed morale boost.[6]

The Confederacy's newest cruiser began its mission by leaving the cotton port of Wilmington, North Carolina. Near the river's mouth it grounded on an obstruction known as the Rip and had to be towed off by three blockade runners.[7] The *Tallahassee* carried a crew of roughly 120; few were able-bodied seamen and many hoped to desert at Nassau or some other neutral port. Although Wood had nineteen officers, it was difficult to keep things "shipshape." The extra coal supply created a grimy powder that coated clothing, equipment and decks. Freed from the Rip, the raiders steamed towards Fort Caswell, planning to exit by way of the western bar (Old Inlet). The steamship moored off Smithville until the boatswain piped "up anchor," and then it slipped into the channel. Beyond lay a cordon of heavily armed blockaders. The moon was down, according to plan, and the stars "shone dimly through a vapour that rose from the water." *Tallahassee* darted across the bar at 10 p.m. and soon had slipped between two unsuspecting patrol vessels. It would have escaped unnoticed if not for a streak of flame that burst from the smokestacks at an inopportune moment. Enemy ships flashed signals, but meeting no response they opened fire from both sides. The Rebels had passed so close to one blockader that they heard an officer bark orders to a gun crew. Fortunately the Union guns were aimed too high to inflict any serious damage and *Tallahassee*'s twin hundred-horsepower engines soon had her out of range of rockets and shells.[8]

The steamer ran south to avoid Frying Pan Shoals and then headed in an northeasterly direction for the world's richest sea lanes – the western approaches to the North Atlantic's "Great Circle" route. The waters off the Carolinas were thick with enemy cruisers, none of them cause for much worry. In addition to being powerful, the raider, with its low silhouette, white hull and relatively smokeless coal, was difficult to spot at sea. On the second day the Confederates were sighted by a Union gunboat and pursued for two hours. A second joined the chase, but neither was able to keep up. That morning officers discovered three stowaways, deserters from the Confederate navy, who were sent to the bunkers to help the stokers. A third gunboat appeared in the afternoon and dogged the Confederates until nightfall. As dark came, the *Tallahassee* almost collided with a fourth enemy warship, but once again Wood was saved by superior speed and manoeuvrability. The enemy's shells fell astern as the former blockade runner sped away.[9]

The third day of the cruise, in the swells of the Gulf Stream, proved uneventful. A lone vessel, the neutral German brig *Louise Wilhemine*, was encountered. On 9 August the raiders "spoke" the Bremen big *Santiago* and the Nova Scotia schooner *Fanny*. In the evening the *Tallahassee* overhauled and boarded a Yankee brig that proved to be "whitewashed, under British registry. In this case the "flight from the flag" saved both vessel and cargo. The next day the cruiser met a British barque and schooner and obtained recent

New York newspapers. After dark, Wood and his men sighted an unidentified vessel running without lights which they caught up to by putting up sail. One of the Southern officers recorded: "There is an ugly look about her when seen closely but we stand on until nearly alongside, when it is found that we have caught a tartar in the shape of a frigate." Not wishing to tangle with a more heavily armed vessel, the Confederates bore away from the unsuspecting warship with a full head of steam.[10]

At dawn on 11 August, two merchantmen were in sight. While the *Tallahassee* communicated with an English barque, a Yankee schooner, suspicious of the steamer's intentions, turned on the wind and ran. It was pursued for an hour and halted after the Confederates fired small arms. Wood had taken his first prize, the Boston schooner *Sarah Boyce* on its way to Philadelphia. Its crew and their provisions were transferred to the steamer and the vessel was scuttled. The pickings would be good; Wood was roughly twenty miles from Long Island, N.Y., with several sails in sight. An old privateering trick – flying false colours until within gun range of enemy merchantmen – allowed the raiders to quickly deploy a boarding party to secure and then scuttle a prize.[11]

Towards 9 a.m. the pilot boat *James Funk* approached, thinking it had a potential customer. American pilot craft, which raced miles off shore to meet new arrivals on a first-come, first-served basis, looked more like pleasure yachts than working vessels. The pilot came aboard from a small boat just as the Stars and Stripes were lowered and the Confederate ensign was raised. One of the *Tallahassee*'s officers, who wrote of the voyage under the name "Bohemian," described the pilot as "a large, well-dressed man, with a heavy watch guard, a massive ring on his little finger, and the air of a genuine New York butcher boy." The New Yorker turned pale with fright, his knees knocking. Wood ordered a prize crew under Acting Master Curtis aboard the handsome pilot boat, which for a time acted as a tender to the raider. The next victim, the brig *Carrie Estelle* of Boston, carrying lumber for New York, appeared at 11 o'clock. Its crew was removed, as were its charts and nautical instruments. Commander Wood, in imitation of other Rebel rovers, was making a collection of chronometers. The Northern press depicted the raiders as uncouth pirates who looted their victims of money, clothing and other items. But with the exception of chronometers, crews and passengers on Wood's prizes were allowed to keep their personal possessions.[12]

After the collier was set on fire, *Tallahassee* took on board the crew of the *Bay State*, hauling pine to Boston. The barque had been stopped by the prize crew on the *James Funk* who signalled for it to come alongside the steamer. As this was done, a gun was fired, the Rebel flag hoisted and two boats with armed men lowered. Captain T.C. Sparrow of the *Bay State*, which was in ballast, was accompanied by his wife, two children and nurse. Although their vessel was burned, the prisoners on the raider were treated civilly. In addition the Confederates destroyed pilot boat Number 22, the *William Bell*, after a thirty-minute chase, and the Maine brig *A. Richards* also was intercepted, searched and set ablaze. A short time later, two fishing schooners which happened on the scene were halted by a volley of blank cartridge. The *Tallahassee's* deck was now crowded with forty prisoners and their personal effects. Wood decided to bond the schooner *Carroll*, of East Machias, Maine, and place the prisoners on board. A second schooner, the *Atlantic*, hauling wood, was condemned and destroyed.[13]

Wood toyed with the idea of sneaking into New York harbour by way of the East River, disguised as a merchant vessel. From what he could tell, America's chief port was lightly defended by warships, leaving dozens of possible prizes to be burned. The *Tallahassee's* guns could inflict considerable damage on shore installations in a surprise attack. But the navigational obstacles around New York were formidable and the lightly constructed commerce raider was too valuable to be risked against shore batteries. The Richmond government would have regarded such a mission suicidal. In an article published in the 1890s, Wood recalled that the attack was not prosecuted because no Northern pilot would guide him in.[14]

The U.S. Navy Department was first alerted to the presence of a raider in northern waters by a telegram from Fire Island, where survivors had landed. An unidentified Confederate steamer was reported to have captured at least six vessels, including a pilot boat, with not a single Union gunboat in the area. A month earlier, Maine authorities had feared depredations by CSS *Florida*, and there were spurious reports of "Rebel steamers" off Grand Manan, burning "English coal." The governor of Maine had thanked the secretary of the navy for "alleviating fears" about the security of vessels sailing for Saint John but repeated his apprehensions about Southern raiders and highjackers.[15]

The navy came under immediate pressure from shipping and marine insurance interests to neutralize the *Tallahassee*. After receiving reports of burning ships off Sandy Hook, New Jersey, south of New York City, the commander of the Brooklyn navy yard dispatched three vessels to the area. By this point the Northern authorities knew that the "pirate" was commanded by John Taylor Wood, formerly of the U.S. Navy. Some of the Maine seafarers who encountered the raider mistakenly thought its captain was from Portland or perhaps Nova Scotia. A cable from New York identified the Rebel craft and its commander, adding that its deck was covered with barrels of turpentine for firing prizes. Bales of cotton supposedly protected its vulnerable boilers.[16]

The sloop USS *Dacotah*, which had been involved in the successful pursuit of the *Chesapeake*, was ordered ready for sea duty. The Brooklyn base dispatched the *Susquehanna* (a heavy sidewheeler launched in 1850), the *Grand Gulf* and the sidewheeler *Pontoosuc*, a gunboat built in Portland. *Grand Gulf* was ordered to Newfoundland's Grand Banks to protect Northern vessels homeward-bound from Europe. The Philadelphia navy yard sent out the *Yantic* and the armed tugs *Aster* and *Moccasin*. A number of naval training vessels also remained on the lookout for the raider. The *Pontoosuc*, in the control of Lieutenant-Commander George A. Stevens, cruised down the south coast of Long Island and the Nantucket shoals and then searched the shores of Maine as far as Eastport, where it stopped to check for telegraphic messages. On its way the gunboat boarded a dozen vessels, including the brig *Ocean Pearl* from Windsor, Nova Scotia, but Stevens could learn nothing of the raider.[17]

One naval report dated 14 August claimed that the *Tallahassee*'s crew was badly dressed and "of all nationalities." The report repeated the unfounded rumour that the Rebels stripped "everybody of everything valuable." By this point the Northern naval authorities quite reasonably expected that the cruiser, which had been out of Wilmington for several days, would attempt to reach neutral Bermuda. The sloop *Susquehanna* cruised to the British island colony, then westward to North Carolina before heading back to Cape Cod and on to Nova Scotia, consuming almost four hundred tons of coal in the process. USS *Juanita* patrolled off Cape Henry to the Delaware Capes, then on to Sandy Hook.[18]

As part of a pursuit force that soon numbered over a dozen craft, the *Dacotah* under A.G. Clary returned to the waters of the Maritimes. Clary had chased the raider once before, as the blockade runner *Atalanta*, and respected its swiftness. After leaving Boston the sloop reached the opening of the Bay of Fundy and the tell-tale remains of two recently burned schooners. A fishing vessel's captain claimed to have witnessed a steamer pursuing sailing craft and said that several merchant vessels, including a collier, had been burned or bonded near Seal Island off Cape Sable. Commander Clary, no doubt thinking of the flight of the *Chesapeake*, thought that the raider would

CSS *Tallahassee* burning the liner *Adriatic*.

attempt to find shelter and take on coal among the unfrequented anchorages of the Tusket Islands south of Yarmouth. Steering towards southwestern Nova Scotia, he encountered, late at night, a steamer which he suspected to be the *Tallahassee*. He later was reprimanded for not catching up to the mystery vessel. The sea was so heavy that the sloop, which Clary considered unfit for sea duty, took two days to steam "up" the Bay of Fundy (in the direction of Yarmouth). Under these conditions the warship could manage six knots at best. Thick fogs and strong tides delayed the *Dacotah*'s arrival at Seal Island, where the weather prevented it from securing an anchorage. Under ideal conditions it might have been possible to visit Yarmouth to check the telegraph and secure a local pilot, but with only enough coal in his bunkers for only a two-day cruise, Clary decided to head back to Boston.[19]

On the twelfth off Long Island's Montauk Point the *Tallahassee* had captured and bonded the barque *Suliote* of Belfast, Maine, returning from Cow Bay, Nova Scotia. Wood then overhauled one of his most valuable prizes, the ship *Adriatic*, which was crossing from Europe with roughly 250 German immigrants, including women and children. This substantial wooden liner, built by famous shipbuilder Donald McKay, formerly of Shelburne, Nova Scotia, was intercepted at 40° 40' N, 71° 40' W. The passengers were terrified when the "pirates" came alongside their giant vessel and even more so when the two craft collided, breaking one of the raider's two masts and entangling rigging around its propellers. The shock of the crash had also sprung the *Tallahassee*'s deck, causing heavy leaking. The Confederates managed to clear the props and placed the worried immigrants, together with the crew of the *James Funk*, aboard *Suliote*, which carried them to safety. Turpentine was applied and the majestic *Adriatic* went up in flames. That day Wood also burned the schooner *Spokane* and bonded the schooner *Robert E. Pecker* of Richmond, Maine. The *Spokane*'s captain, from Tremont, Maine, spent six hours on the raider. Also scuttled was the brig *Billow* of Salem, Massachusetts, loaded with bales of lathes. (The latter, inexplicably, was found dismasted at 40° 11' N, 71° 16' W, by the USS *Grand Gulf*.) The crews of the *Spokane* and *Billow* were placed on the *Pecker*, which put in at Holmes Hole harbour on the fourteenth. Wood allegedly warned Captain Reed of the *Billow* that "Honest Abe [had] better look out." The Confederate officer appeared to be quite affable, explaining that "he was doing what it was not pleasant for him to do."[20]

The sole victims of the thirteenth were the schooner *Lamont Dupont* and the *Glenaven*, sailing from Scotland. The later was a superbly crafted barque from Belfast, Maine, owned by its captain. His wife lamented the destruction of their investment, explaining to Wood that they had laboured thirty years to provide for their children. "Bohemian" wrote, somewhat chivalrously, "It seemed a pity to destroy such a noble craft and I looked upon our work with sorrow." He was less charitable towards one of the barque's passengers, a retired mariner's wife, a "horrible woman" who bothered the captors by distributing Bibles and religious tracts – a genuinely Yankee habit. Captain Watts of the *Glenaven* later disappointed his captors in a press interview by denouncing the crew as "a ragged, undisciplined set of cut throats."[21]

The *Tallahassee*, which burned or bonded over thirty vessels on its initial cruise, would become one of the Confederacy's most successful sea rovers. The North, which had just demonstrated its naval superiority in the Battle of Mobile Bay, seemed unable to police its nautical backyard, which by custom extended beyond Nova Scotia to Labrador. Maine vessel owners were heavy losers. Despite their own colourful history of privateering, the Northern states did not accept Wood's cruise as legitimate warfare. Even official sources referred to the commerce raider as a "pirate." A New York journal described the raid as a tale of "cowardly outrage," dismissing Commander Wood as "a fine specimen of a peace rebel." It was incensed by the fact that the Rebel commander had held Sunday services on his quarterdeck before destroying defenceless fishing schooners, an incongruous example of a "Christian pirate."[22]

Prisoners continued to accumulate. The crews of the *Lamont Dupont*, the ship *James Littlefield* of Bangor and the schooner *Mercy A. Howes* (of Chatham, Massachusetts) were placed on board the neutral schooner *Sophia* from Turk's Island on its way to Yarmouth with salt. This schooner's owner was Yarmouth merchant and Assembly member Thomas Killam who profited from the blockade. In 1863, Killam was owner or part owner of thirteen Yarmouth-based vessels, ranging from schooners to square riggers. The *Sophia*'s captain, J.R. Hilton, was persuaded to take the prisoners after being given extra provisions and half a keg of tobacco. The crews were landed at Yarmouth on 16 August. Contacted by telegraph, the U.S. consul in Halifax theorized that the raider was near Yarmouth and had been refuelled at sea by a blockade runner, intelligence that was immediately relayed to Washington.[23]

On the fifteenth, Wood encountered several more unfortunate Yankee vessels: the Maine schooner *S.B. Harris*, intercepted twelve miles west of Maine's Seal Island, was returning from Canso; the schooner *Howard* of New York was hauling Cape Breton coal; and the *Restless*, of Booth Bay, Maine, was loaded with 175 quintals of green cod taken in the Gulf of St. Lawrence. Two other Maine schooners, *Floral Wreath* and *Etta Caroline*, fell prey to the raider; in addition to forfeiting their vessels and fishing shares, the downeasters were required to sign paroles, promises not to take up arms against the Confederacy. "Bohemian" recorded: "These rough, hardy fishermen are a timid set and show much horror when taken on board. Several have actually shed tears and others, with faces deathly white, tremulously ask what will be done with them." The Confederates bonded the *Harris* for $8,000 and placed on board the crews from the schooners *Howard*, *Etta Caroline* and *Restless*. The prisoners, according to telegraphic accounts, were well treated.[24]

On Tuesday, 16 August, the *Tallahassee* was running down the coast of Maine in the direction of Penobscot Bay near the islands of Monhegan and Matinicus. The people of Thomaston claimed that the cruiser, manned principally by Nova Scotians, had sunk twenty-five vessels off Matinicus Rock alone.[25] The raiders passed close enough to these islands to view people on shore. Yarmouth was only 140 miles due east, and the island of Grand Manan lay 110 miles up the coast. At an early hour the raiders spoke a Nova Scotia ship. The barque *P.C. Alexander*, of Harpswell, Maine, was en route to Nova Scotia for coal when it was overhauled off Matinicus. The 280-ton vessel, worth $12,000, was torched. The schooner *Leopard* of Boston, loaded with wood from Kentville, Nova Scotia, was bonded and entrusted with the prisoners from the barque. The schooners *Magnolia* and *Pearl*, from Friendship, Maine, were returning from the Newfoundland fishing banks; and the next victim, the *Sarah Louise*, carried wood for Maine. The *Tallahassee* was again crowded with prisoners. Wood bonded the schooner *Sea Foam* and had the prisoners transferred on board. The latter, according to "Bohemian," displayed stereotypical Yankee traits, "speaking in a very loud tone of voice and with a nasal twang – cursing, using slang words, and very popular idioms they caused us no little amusement"; one peculiarity of Maine dialect, shared with Bluenoses, was the habit of using the word "to" instead of "at," as in "We were to home." The raiders had now reached the coastal frontier of the Pine Tree State. Wood's chief engineer reported that the fuel supplies were too low to enable them to return to the Confederacy. There was little choice but to head for a neutral port.[26]

Commander Wood decided to cross the Bay of Fundy and set a course for Halifax, where the Confederacy had an agent, B. Wier and Co. At dawn on the eleventh day out, the cruiser was on Brown's Bank, forty miles from Cape Sable. On the first leg of the run to

A raider refuels: CSS *Tallahassee* at Halifax, August 1864.

Halifax, it captured a New London, Connecticut, schooner returning from the banks. The Rebels helped themselves to a breakfast
of fresh halibut before scuttling the first prize of the day. At nine
in the morning they overtook the brig *Neva*, from East Machias,
hauling coal from Lingan Bay, Cape Breton. The prize could not
legally be taken into British waters to allow the Confederates to
load its badly needed coal. The latest batch of prisoners was placed
on board the collier which was bonded for $17,500, and the crew
was paroled.[27]

The *Tallahassee* made landfall above Cape Sable five hours after
encountering the *Neva* and began to skirt the shore. A large steamer,
most likely the liner *Franconia* on the Boston-Halifax-Charlottetown
run, was spotted out to sea, but Wood lacked sufficient coal to
go in pursuit. He also suspected that it might be a British man-
of-war. Later the Confederates nabbed the Rockland, Maine, schooner
Joseph Achorne, headed for Cape Breton for coal. A boat party removed
the schooner's crew and their baggage and used turpentine to set
it ablaze. Two small schooners further up the coast, seeing the
burning vessel, turned in for the safety of shore. Yankee fishermen
from the *Diadem* and *D. Ellis* of Massachusetts took to their boats
but were headed off. Wood decided that the prizes were within
Nova Scotia territorial waters. Anxious to avoid a breach of neutrality, he ordered the prisoners, who feared for their lives, to be
released. As dark came, the raider was running along the colony's
south shore, sixty miles from Sambro lighthouse. To conserve coal,
the vessel was kept "under easy steam to make it to daybreak."[28]

On Thursday the eighteenth, Bohemian recorded: "Morning came
in cold and wet – the dense fog that hung heavily over the water
lacking only the name to be a shower." After Sambro Head the
steamer cautiously edged towards Halifax by following the rocky
coast through the fog. Suddenly an angry Irish voice shouted a

warning about fishing nets; a red-haired fisherman climbed aboard and agreed to guide the Confederates until a pilot boat appeared. The *Tallahassee* entered the wide western or main channel into Halifax after dawn. The dark forest of Point Pleasant on the port side soon gave way to the cluster of wharves, warehouses and wooden residences, intermingled with stone and brick public and commercial buildings, that formed downtown Halifax. "Bohemian" penned the following description: "The houses are built principally of wood, and have an air of age, although the main portion of the town is comparatively new. Along the bay is the business portion, and back upon the hill the residences of the merchants and the military. The land upon which the city is built rises rapidly from the water into a hill, crowning which is a citadel, a strong and heavily armed fortress, protecting the town and commanding the harbour." Haligonians, for whom a Confederate warship was a novelty, rushed from their homes and places of work and gathered on wharves, roof-tops and Citadel Hill to catch a glimpse of the visitor. Wood, expecting all the privileges of a neutral belligerent, steered past George's Island and anchored off the Market wharf.[29]

The *Morning Chronicle* described the raider as "a strange armed vessel of rakish appearance." Contrary to adverse reports, the steamer appeared to be well officered, "and judging from the appearance of things, good discipline is maintained on board." The captain did not seem fearful of the enemy ships sent in pursuit. Wood's style of warfare, like that of the German submariners of World War I, was controversial, yet the Halifax *Journal* called on readers to remember "the treatment of defenceless Southern women and children by Yankee ruffians." The more hostile *Sun* predicted that the *Tallahassee* was the prototype of a new class of swift Southern raiders that could alter the course of the war. For the *Sun*, the captains of Confederate raiders were "thieves, felons and freebooters." The New York *Times* mistakenly believed many of its crew to be Bluenoses and predicted that they would be "coddled and feasted" in Nova Scotia. The Maritime colonies, it continued, possessing "a large seafaring population, needy, greedy, courageous, unscrupulous and anything but well-disposed towards the U.S.," could outfit fifty such vessels.[30]

The *Tallahassee* had arrived at an historic time. Two days earlier the "Canadian delegates," politicians visiting the Maritimes to discuss the prospects of colonial union, had embarked at Windsor to visit New Brunswick. For a number of days these future Fathers of Confederation had attended receptions, dinners and entertainments in their honour, repaying their Bluenose hosts with flowery speeches

and performances of French-Canadian folk songs. Within two weeks
the Canadians, joined by delegates from New Brunswick, Nova Scotia
and Prince Edward Island, would gather in Charlottetown for the
important conference that set the stage for the federal union of 1867.[31]

During the *Tallahassee* excitement, New Brunswick was visited
by another official delegation, a group of fifty prominent Republican politicians and journalists touring the Maine frontier. The select
Congressional committee and entourage, which included railway
promoter John A. Poor, had left Bangor, Maine, on 16 August on
a revenue cutter to inspect coastal defences, which the Americans
were gradually strengthening. The governor of New Brunswick, on
a visit to Grand Manan, had noticed "offensive" gun batteries on
an American island off Campobello and on Treat, or St. Croix, Island,
threatening Welshpool, Campobello. In late 1864 the battery on Treat
Island fired live practice rounds in the direction of a bluff on British
territory; one projectile ricocheted over the water, passed over a
house and landed in a barn yard in New Brunswick.[32]

The Congressional junket gave the Boston *Advertiser* an opportunity to reflect on Maine's security and relations with its neighbour. Although extensive fortifications were being constructed
around Portland and at the mouth of the Kennebec River, the state
felt vulnerable. What Mainers wanted most of all was peace, trade
and a railway to the New Brunswick border. On crossing that
boundary "the traveller already finds New Brunswick distinguished
by no outward sign from New England." Most New Brunswickers
opposed Northern war policies but looked to the U.S. "as the natural
seat of their commercial relations."[33] The cutter had left Eastport,
reaching Saint John when the *Tallahassee* was still thought to be
in Maritime waters. There they were enthusiastically welcomed by
the U.S. consul, American nationals and prominent citizens. The
excursionists visited Shediac on the Gulf coast by rail. At Fredericton
they met the mayor, Provincial Secretary Tilley, the solicitor general
and the chief justice. Although favouring Confederation, a policy
that would defeat his government in 1865, Tilley understood the
importance of good relations with the North.[34]

In keeping with protocol, Commander Wood manned his gig
and first paid his respects to the senior Royal Navy officer on the
station, Vice-Admiral Sir James Hope. The fifty-year-old admiral
had joined the navy as a boy but until recent years had seen little
action. During the Crimean War, he had commanded the battleship
Majestic in the Baltic. In 1859 he had been appointed senior officer
on the China station and had led the French and British expedition
that attempted to break the obstructions on the Peiho River and

reach Tientsin. The engagement had ended in disaster for the Europeans and much of the blame rested with Hope. The Allied gunboats and troopships expected little serious opposition but were mauled by hidden batteries and concentrated fire. Hope, on the gunboat *Plover*, was seriously wounded, having part of a thigh and a leg shot away. Nevertheless, he transferred to a second and then a third vessel, which also were seriously punished by the enemy. After an artillery duel which damaged a number of his vessels but did little to incapacitate the large sand forts, Hope made his biggest tactical blunder. Several hundred marines, sappers and sailors were landed, in the mud, in a wasteful direct assault on the forts. Half of them were killed, wounded or taken prisoner. The survivors were taken off by five gunboats and the forts were not captured until the following year when a two-hundred-vessel Allied squadron under Hope forced its way up river and landed troops who captured Tientsin and Peking, burning the Emperor's summer palace.[35]

The commander of the neutral American squadron observing the action on the Peiho had been Flag Officer Josiah Tattnall, a Georgian who became a prominent Confederate naval officer. Tattnall, as the new skipper of the ironclad *Virginia* in 1862, would order it blown up rather than risk it falling into enemy hands. When the Allied fleet ran into stiff opposition on the Peiho and Hope was wounded, it had been Tattnall who had come to their rescue. His barge towed boatloads of wounded British sailors and marines to safety and American bluejackets helped man the guns on the damaged British flagship. Tattnall later justifying his violation of neutrality on the grounds that "blood is thicker than water."[36]

A Canadian reporter had described the vice-admiral as possessing the "polished bearing of a man of family and the diplomatist." But if Wood expected the one-legged Hope to show appreciation for the Georgian's gallantry, he was mistaken. For one thing, in 1859, Tattnall had been a naval officer for the United States, not the Confederate States. Second, early in the year the British government had instructed naval commanders to refuse to salute, or return the salute of, Confederate war vessels entering Halifax or other ports. British officers had been accused of going out of their way to welcome and entertain Confederate naval officers, extending them the privileges of the wardroom. Naval commanders were ordered to remind Rebel captains that the Confederacy had been recognized by Britain not as a sovereign state but only as a belligerent. On boarding HMS *Duncan* shortly before noon, Wood realized that he was being denied the "customary courtesies," despite having borrowed parts of a proper uniform from junior officers on board the flagship.[37]

The *Duncan* was a massive ship of the line with a crew of nearly one thousand officers, sailors and marines. Its engines were capable of producing 800 h.p. Like most flagships it bristled with cannon, a number of them new Armstrong guns. Several days earlier Sir James Hope had hosted a "bonnet hop" in honour of the Canadian delegation, including Sir John A. Macdonald and George Etienne Cartier. Halifax belles had danced in the battleship's gunroom with officers of the fleet and garrison while the Canadians and the men of the lower decks looked on. Now Hope's responsibilities were more pressing and far less pleasant: containing a situation fraught with serious diplomatic consequences. The "fighting admiral" was coldly polite to Wood, informing him that he had only twenty-four hours to recoal and that no munitions of war could be purchased. The two men discussed the problem of American vessels that had been "whitewashed" (placed under British registry). Wood assured the vice-admiral that he would respect all ships flying British colours. With that, the interview was over.[38]

The lieutenant-governor in charge of Nova Scotia's foreign affairs was Sir Richard Graves MacDonnell, a youngish colonial administrator who preferred direct control of crown colonies over the more passive rule of self-governing dominions. MacDonnell, an Irish Protestant with a background in law, had served as governor on the Gambia River from 1849 to 1851, where he engaged in exploration and punished unruly tribes. He next administered the small Caribbean colony of St. Vincent before a seven-year term as governor of South Australia. When offered the chance to succeed the Earl of Mulgrave in Nova Scotia in 1864, MacDonnell had been unemployed for two years. An outspoken man with strong views, he would play a controversial role in the Confederation process. To his great relief and to the joy of pro-Confederation politicians, he was assigned the governorship of Hong Kong, where one of his "accomplishments" was a harsh penal code for Chinese law-breakers.[39]

Consul Mortimer Jackson, who had been absent during the *Chesapeake* crisis, endeavoured to aid the naval pursuit by telegraphing regular intelligence reports. He also attempted, in a series of notes to Provincial Secretary Tupper, to persuade the Nova Scotia authorities to detain the *Tallahassee* or at least prevent it from taking on coal. Everyone was aware that in 1863 the authorities at Nassau had stretched the rules for CSS *Florida*, allowing it to remain in port for thirty-six hours and take on coal for an extended cruise; five months later, fourteen additional Yankee prizes, including the brig *Clarence*, had been taken. Jackson hoped to supply proof that the raider had violated international and municipal law. In a cable to Washington the consul predicted that the Rebels would outfit more blockade runners to prey upon Union commerce.[40] The lieutenant-governor, suspecting that Jackson merely sought to delay Wood's departure until Federal gunboats arrived, replied that he had no jurisdiction in the matter. As long as Wood complied with British regulations for belligerents, he was free to go.[41]

In fact, as far as the Nova Scotia authorities were concerned, the sooner the raider departed, the better. In a report to the British colonial secretary, Lieutenant-Governor MacDonnell explained that he had attempted to deal with the *Tallahassee* as he would a Federal warship, remaining "sensible of the extreme importance of not only observing practically the most impartial neutrality, but also of convincing others that I am determined to do so." In a follow-up report, he justified his decision to limit Wood's coal intake. The raider, because of its speed, was "the most formidable adversary which the Federal commerce had yet encountered." MacDonnell reasoned that "every five tons of coal in excess of the amount strictly allowable might be regarded as a heavy loss to Federal shipping." Hence the Confederates could load only enough fuel to take them to their nearest home port. From Washington came a coded telegram from Lord Lyons, who advised that the U.S. government was "a good deal disturbed" by the *Tallahassee*'s visit. Lyons had at first refused to contact MacDonnell but had been convinced to do so by an agitated American secretary of state, who had announced that Alexander Keith had ordered a ship's compass and three thousand barrels of pork from New York, probably for the *Tallahassee*.[42]

Local sympathizers of the Confederacy viewed Wood's vessel as the new *Alabama*. A month earlier, First Officer John McIntosh Kell, Surgeon F.L. Galt and several of the crew of the famous raider, recently sunk off the coast of France, had arrived in Halifax on the steamship *Europa* on their way to Bermuda. Local interest in Wood's craft was high; even enemies of the South came out in small boats to view the steamer. On its last evening in port, one of the harbour ferries arranged an excursion, complete with the Halifax Volunteer Band playing secessionist airs such as "Bonnie Blue Flag" and "Dixie."[43]

The Halifax *Sun* was dismayed that a Rebel "shark" which had captured several vessels carrying Cape Breton coal had been "petted and comforted by our inhabitants." Such a stance, the *Sun* explained, was bad for the colony's export business. For "Bohemian," local sympathy for the Rebels was purely mercenary. With the exception of a handful of prominent individuals who opened their purses and homes to Confederates, the Bluenoses, he regretted, were doing little to advance the Southern cause. Bohemian noted that British army and naval officers were less enthusiastic towards the Rebels, owing to their increasing fear of Northern military might. He also contended that the former lieutenant-governor and the admiral's predecessor had been replaced for displaying sympathies for the South.[44]

Northerners were ready to believe that the raider's visit to the British colony was anything but coincidental; one Boston journal described it as a "Nova Scotia pirate" and mistakenly asserted that its crew included Bluenoses. Lord Lyons reported "a loud and universal outcry against the efficiency of the [American] Navy Department," as well as accusations and recriminations against England. The American secretary of state warned Lyons that Wood's raid would adversely affect public opinion towards Britain, particularly if the *Tallahassee* were resupplied at Halifax. Secretary Seward reminded Lyons of the *Chesapeake* highjacking and suspected that Wood's cruise to Nova Scotia was part of a larger conspiracy involving colonials such as Alexander Keith. The secretary of the navy, as late as December, believed that the *Tallahassee* was still owned and registered in Britain. Consul Jackson reported to the State Department that the Confederates maintained a fuel depot at Halifax, complete with Welsh coal, "which is best adapted to their purposes."[45]

The state of Maine had already been agitated by the threat of attacks launched from British territory. Only weeks earlier, three "Confederates," including the brother of one of the *Chesapeake* pirates, had attempted to raid a Calais bank. The authorities in that city had been made aware of the plot by the U.S. consul in Saint John, who was suspected of having helped to arrange for an agent provocateur to encourage the raid. Although the incident was minor and there was no bloodshed, for many Northerners it was additional proof of British favouritism toward the Rebels.[46]

The precise details of the Calais bank incident, an unsuccessful version of the more famous St. Alban's raid, are difficult to discern. According to the New Brunswick press, a federal detective or spy, working closely with the Saint John consul, had egged on the three conspirators. Consul J.Q. Howard's correspondence with the State Department refers to a William Daymond, a deserter from a New Jersey infantry regiment seeking an official pardon. In return he offered to perform intelligence work in Saint John, where he was working as a potter. Daymond supplied Howard with valuable information and "kept the authorities at Calais and the officers of the Calais Bank informed concerning the movements of the Confederate thieves." The consul had been apprised of a possible plot by Reverend John Collins of Maine, brother of one of the raiders. However, Howard did not warn the Saint John or New Brunswick authorities that a hostile operation was about to be launched from British territory, an omission that would embroil him in more controversy. The New Brunswick press, although embarrassed by the raid, trained most of its guns on the consul for having provoked it through the use of a spy.[47]

Howard compounded the problem by sending the governor of Maine a vague telegram warning of an impending raid from Saint John. The governor, envisioning a waterborne assault, frantically cabled Washington for gunboats. At Calais the militia turned out and the citizens remained awake all night, expecting the worst. The next day, four men entered the National Bank to exchange gold for cash. Before they could take any hostile action, they were surrounded by armed tellers and citizens. The bank and the sheriff had been tipped off by Howard's informer, who had accompanied the "raiders" to Calais. The men were arrested on suspicion; when searched they were found to be carrying incriminating documents and a Confederate flag. A letter on one of the prisoners suggested that they had planned to set buildings on fire. One account mentioned revolvers and bowie knives.[48]

The leader of what the consul described as a "disrespectful and desperate" band of characters – "Major" William Collins, a British subject – was in Howard's opinion a "Rebel spy." Collins, who claimed to be an officer in the Confederate army, had been residing in Saint John for a number of months. The *St. Croix Herald* described the ringleader as possessing a "countenance indicative of treachery and baseness." The Irish-born New Brunswicker was a brother of David Collins of *Chesapeake* notoriety. Incidentally, he had been warned by the pro-Southern editor of the Saint John *Telegraph* that New Brunswick would tolerate no attacks on America from its soil. Earlier, Collins had appeared in Toronto, ready for action; a Confederate commissioner had sent him to St. Jean, Canada East, where according to one tall tale he had killed two men. A second raider, Francis Jones, who probably used a pseudonym, claimed to be a Southerner whose wife and children had been murdered by Union guerrillas. He supposedly had been ordered to New Brunswick on "secret service" duties. Saint John resident "Phillips," the third raider, stated that he had been promised a chance to sail on a "piratical craft." The *New Brunswick Reporter* suspected that none of the men were actual Confederate soldiers.[49]

After their arrest, the prisoners, full of bravado, demanded to be treated as prisoners of war. Instead they were handled by the civil courts. The trio was conveyed by the Home Guard to the county jail at Machias where they were tried, convicted and sentenced to the state penitentiary for three years. Collins blamed their capture on the treachery of Daymond. Jones "confessed" to a wild plot aimed at Maine's coastal communities. Several authors, such as James D. Horan in *Confederate Agent*, have accepted the "Maine coast plot" at face value. The operation, which seems too fanciful to be taken seriously, supposedly involved sending fifty engineers and topographers, carried out of the South by blockade runners, to map the coasts of Maine. The military intelligence gathered by these spies was coordinated in Halifax. According to Jones, the *Tallahassee* and a number of blockade runners would land a sizeable body of raiders in Maine. Other rumours spoke of a second attack on the *Chesapeake*, which was back on the run to Portland.[50]

For a number of weeks people in border areas of Maine lived in fear of attack. The militia stayed alert to repel rumoured incursions from Canada East. Late into the year the provost marshall at Bangor worried about frontier security, particularly in view of the large number of draft dodgers and deserters who worked in lumber camps on both sides of the border. Many of these men, he feared, were Rebel sympathizers and could form the nucleus for hostile operations across the border, hence the need for a permanent frontier patrol. He claimed that raids had been contemplated "in the vicinity of Houlton, which is the great thoroughfare into the provinces." Collins managed to escape from penitentiary in December, but Jones and the guileless Phillips served out their sentences.[51]

Martial readiness on the New Brunswick side of the border was less apparent. The September militia muster at St. Stephen, for example, turned into a drunken revel. The Calais Home Guard, consisting mainly of local businessmen and clerks, was an object of mirth for the New Brunswick press. Yet border tensions were brought home by two incidents, one of them tragic. On the evening of 15 July, as the bridges over the St. Croix River were manned by armed guards, someone fired two rifle shots from Calais into St. Stephen. Journalist John Hay, whose anti-British opinions had forced him to relocate in Calais, apparently was involved in the gunplay. "British blood" began to quicken, a crowd assembled on the New Brunswick side of the line and a riot was narrowly averted only after an explanation and apology. In early August a nervous border sentry shot and killed a young New Brunswick millworker who was walking at night.[52]

The *Tallahassee*, Jones' revelations aside, was not linked to any raid on the Maine coast. Its captain was concentrating on escaping the imminent arrival of the U.S. Navy. A supply of coal was arranged by Wier and Co. from the Prussian brig *Marie Griefswald* and loading began at Woodside, on the Dartmouth shore. Royal Navy officers had inspected the vessel's state-of-the-art engines and estimated its fuel needs. The vice-admiral reckoned that the minimum amount of coal for a direct cruise back to Wilmington was sixty tons. As his crew was ragged in appearance, Wood authorized the issue of specie to buy a quantity of clothing. The Confederates also purchased a supply of coffee, flour and sugar. Twenty-seven men, almost a quarter of the crew, jumped ship while in Halifax. A ships's officer later blamed "Yankee emissaries" for the desertions. A number were locked up by the police, but none seem to have made it to court. These individuals no doubt wished to escape naval discipline and avoid combat with pursuing enemy gunboats. Or perhaps they were attracted to the high wages paid to experienced sailors on blockade-running steamers.[53]

Dr. W.J. Almon offered to find a new mast, which could be stepped, provided the rigging for the two small fore and aft auxiliary sails was ready. Given the scarcity of coal, Confederate vessels were expected to make as much use of sail as possible. The steamer continued to be an object of curiosity. Visitors to the *Tallahassee* included Almon; Wier; Alexander Keith, Jr.; Dr. Peleg Wisiwell Smith (of Queen's wharf notoriety); and W.A. Henry, attorney general in Charles Tupper's government and future Father of Confederation. "Bohemian" the ship's surgeon, also paid tribute to Albert Pilsbury, Dr. Slayter and Archbishop Connolly as true friends of the South (Pilsbury was part owner of the Dartmouth marine slip which repaired the hulls of blockade runners).[54]

Acting on a report that the Southern warship had loaded 180 tons of coal, the lieutenant-governor sent Wood firm instructions to abide by his earlier orders. The Confederate captain came ashore to Government House for twelve noon where the order was repeated in person. The raider had yet to ship a mainmast and the original deadline was about to expire. Wood requested three or four more hours to complete the coaling and to effect repairs. MacDonnell, in a fit of generosity, granted an additional twelve hours starting at 5:30 p.m., which gave the *Tallahassee* until dawn on Saturday. But at the same time he requested the vice-admiral to enforce the refuelling order. Unlike during the *Chesapeake* incident, with five American warships and not a single British frigate anchored in the harbour, the Nova Scotia authorities now had sufficient naval muscle. Sir James Hope despatched a number of launches and boats from the frigate HMS *Galatea* to Woodside. The boats, manned by armed marines and sailors, surrounded the steamer and its collier to ensure that it took on no contraband or extra fuel. Most of the Rebel officers were still on shore. Hope and a number of aides visited the raider and remained on board for some time. An officer later recounted the incident to a Southern journalist: "This was rather galling to our pride and entirely unnecessary, for a simple order from the Admiral would have been sufficient, without this armed display." MacDonnell, anxious to avoid wounding Wood's feelings, later removed all the boats except one. Wood recalled years later that the junior officer on board after the admiral's departure, possibly Lieutenant R.H. Thompson, offered his sympathies and enjoyed a glass of grog with the Confederates.[55]

Wood declined an offer of a naval escort to the three-mile limit, sensing that it would lead to a confrontation with one or more of the Union gunboats on his trail. He was thinking more like a blockade runner than a warship commander. Although he first thought that his bunkers held less than one hundred tons, Wood ordered the refuelling stopped. He would go to sea under the cover of darkness and avoid enemy craft by trying the seldom-used secondary harbour channel. The navigation of the tricky eastern passage would depend upon a skilful, knowledgeable pilot, probably secured by Wier. Although he would work as a harbour pilot until the 1890s, John "Jock" Flemming already knew every reef, channel and landmark from the treacherous waters near Sambro lighthouse to commodious Bedford Basin. Flemming, present at the thwarted refuelling of the *Chesapeake* in 1863, assured Commander Wood that he could guide the *Tallahassee* between McNab's Island and the Dartmouth shore with the bottom touching only eel grass. The island was about to become part of Halifax's defensive cordon through the erection of gun batteries. All vessels passing into the harbour through the main channel had to pass McNab's on the east and York Redoubt to the west. The eastern channel, unmarked by buoys or bells, was used only by light-draft coasters. The water over the bar at the channel's entrance was only nine or ten feet deep at flood. A British defence expert reported that the channel was "so narrow and shallow, and is besides so much sheltered from the action of the sea, that there would be no difficulty in stopping it up in time of war by means of a vessel filled with stone" – a local version of Charleston's stone fleet.[56]

The Confederates left their anchorage after midnight, taking advantage of the cover of darkness and the fog bank that hovered offshore. The steamer, according to a Virginia paper, moored until a guard party returned from a fruitless search for deserters. Consul Jackson had anticipated some movement and cabled his superiors in Washington prior to and immediately after the departure. A new mainmast supplied by the resourceful Dr. Almon lay on the deck. It had not been stepped or mounted because there had been no time to repair the rigging. The steamer passed Halifax landmarks such as the Ordnance Yard and Queen's wharf on the western side of the harbour, and George's Island. McNab's Island, two thousand yards from the gun batteries at Point Pleasant, was largely uninhabited and used as a sheep pasturage. The British authorities had purchased a site at Ive's Point on the northern tip of the island for a new defensive work, but for now McNab's was guarded solely by an aging tower (which doubled as a lighthouse) on Maugher's Beach opposite the main channel. The tower was armed with three twenty-four-pounders, suitable for close-range bombardment only. Lofty York Redoubt, on the far side of the main channel, appeared formidable because it was close to one hundred feet above the water. But it was only a signal station; its old rubble masonry tower and earthen battery were without artillery. The Fort Clarence "sea battery" on the Dartmouth shore guarded the northern end of the eastern passage. This work, in the process of being rebuilt, was unarmed.[57]

Flemming guided the steamer into the shallow waters of the passage. At one point, between McNab's and Lawler's islands, he lost the way and Wood put a small boat ahead to take soundings. After some careful navigating, the steamer cleared the treacherous bar at the outer end of the channel. If the raiders had been allowed to ship more coal, they would never have gotten over the bar. Far across the harbour, in the dark, Yankee gunboats, if any, would be standing guard. The final obstacle along the eastern shore of the harbour approaches was Devil's Island, site of a lighthouse and home to a few fishing families. When Devil's Island light was on their stern, the Confederates dropped pilot Flemming and two stowaways and made for open water. Wood actually had 120 tons of fuel when he left Halifax.[58]

Despite the romanticized version of the raider's visit presented in twentieth-century Nova Scotia school readers, Wood had not really outwitted anyone. The first Union warship to reach port, *Pontoosuc*, did not arrive until dawn, several hours after the Rebels had reached deep water. The gunboat had docked at Eastport at 4 a.m. on the seventeenth and had left the following day after receiving a telegram from Washington. On the morning after the departure of the Confederate vessel, the military telegraph indicated that a Federal man-of-war was anchored in the fairway opposite York Redoubt. *Pontoosuc*'s commander, unaware that his prey had sailed, sent several officers ashore in a whaleboat manned by armed sailors. The Yankees paid their respects to the governor but neglected to meet with Vice-Admiral Hope, even though the Royal Navy had made a tender available. The Americans returned to their vessel at noon after conferring with their consul. By now the *Tallahassee* had almost half a day's head start. In a final breach of diplomatic and naval etiquette, the gunboat suddenly put to sea, violating the British regulation requiring warships of one belligerent power to wait at least twenty-four hours before leaving port to pursue recently departed enemy vessels. This rule applied to Federal as well as Confederate naval vessels (such as CSS *Nashville* when it had reached Bermuda in 1862). That morning the Fort George signal station on Citadel Hill announced the approach of five American men-of-war, but only the *Pontoosuc* entered the harbour. The consul later explained to Washington that he sent a small boat out to the gunboat. At 9 a.m. the first officer and paymaster accompanied Jackson to Government House. The vessel's departure was delayed until 2 p.m. because the Americans required a coastal chart.[59]

Consul Jackson believed that the raider, having refuelled, would cruise "among the fishermen" in North Bay and other areas of the Gulf of St. Lawrence. These traditional haunts of the New England fishery were virtually unprotected. The *Pontoosuc*, having violated port regulations, steamed on for Cape Breton and passed through Canso Strait to Plaster Cove before patrolling "through the fishing fleet" off Prince Edward Island. New England schooners had long followed this route into "the Bay." The Confederate steamer did not appear to be in the area, so Commander Stevens pushed on to the Magdalen Islands and then cruised back to Cape Breton. The warship stopped at Sydney for coal before returning to New York. Another double-ender gunboat, the *Iosco*, was ordered to the Gulf of St. Lawrence by way of Canso Gut.[60]

The secretary of the navy, frustrated by the pursuit operation's delays, censured the commander of the New York navy yard for not immediately dispatching to Halifax a sloop recently arrived from Florida. The vessel, none other than the *San Jacinto*, which under Wilkes had twisted the tail of the British Lion in 1861, had turned out to have engine trouble and virtually empty bunkers. If it had departed on time, it would have reached Halifax before the enemy and probably stopped it from resupplying. *San Jacinto* eventually reached the Halifax area on 24 August where a pilot boat informed Lieutenant-Commander J.N. Quackenbush that the Rebel warship was long gone. The fog was so thick that Quackenbush decided to refrain from sending a boat into town to contact the consul. If this vessel, of *Trent* notoriety, had ventured into the harbour, the loyal residents of Halifax would have erupted in a storm of indignation.[61]

Rumour and a deliberate disinformation campaign threw the pursuers off track. From Washington the secretary of the navy attempted to assemble as many intercepter vessels as possible. New orders issued to the commandants of navy yards attempted to better coordinate such pursuit operations. Consul Jackson telegraphed the State Department on 26 August that the Rebel cruiser *Edith* had left Wilmington, North Carolina, and was headed for Nova Scotia. Jackson also reported that the Rebels planned an operation, inspired by the *Chesapeake* piracy, against civilian steamers on Lake Ontario. Commander Wood, according to waterfront gossip, had hired a pilot for Nova Scotia's eastern shore and a British brig had sighted the steamer off Cole Harbour. On the same day a schooner passed a mysterious steamer near Port Hood, Cape Breton. Pursuit vessels, Jackson recommended, should carry fishermen from Gloucester or Cape Ann as pilots. The Nova Scotia government, in keeping with British neutrality regulations, ordered customs officials at all ports in the colony to prevent the raider from receiving supplies for a period of three months.[62]

However, the *Tallahassee* was not among the mackerel fishermen in the Gulf or off the Newfoundland Banks but on a direct course for the Carolinas. With limited fuel, Wood had little choice but to avoid the prize-rich coastal waters of New England and the Mid-Atlantic states. His only capture on the return voyage was the Massachusetts vessel *Roan* headed for Glace Bay, taken on the twentieth. The next day was the sabbath and Wood conducted religious services on the quarterdeck. Three more stowaways, one a boy, were discovered and put to work. Thursday morning began with a chase by an unidentified warship. As late as 24 August, one day before Wood reached Confederate waters, the Navy Department was convinced that one or more Rebel raiders were off the northeast coast. A week later there were reports that the *Tallahassee* had been sighted near the Magdalen Islands. From Prince Edward Island came a rumour that it had burned two dozen Yankee fishermen off Cape North and was being chased by an American sloop. A Newport, Nova Scotia, schooner encountered an unidentified steamer off Liverpool which the captain took for a privateer.[63]

The raid had brought a dozen or more Federal warships to the Gulf of Maine, the Bay of Fundy, the coast of Nova Scotia and the Gulf of St. Lawrence. These patrols were arduous and expensive because rough seas forced commanders to remain under steam most of the time. The sailing vessel *Ino* was disguised as a merchantman and sent to the Newfoundland banks for a month in order to entrap Rebel "pirates." *Ino* left Hampton Roads on 2 September and patrolled Green, St. Peters and Banquereau banks, then skirted the Nova Scotia coast from Canso to Cape Sable before returning to base, a cruise of 4,186 miles. For several weeks the U.S. Navy was highly visible off Halifax and other areas of the colonies. Consul Jackson advised that two or three warships should be kept on station to counter raiders and blockade runners. At one point the provincial government sent customs officers to Ketch Harbour where the small blockade runner *Constance* from Bermuda was sheltering from Northern gunboats. The black-hulled, 163-ton sidewheeler, built in Greenoch and owned in London, had been repaired that summer at the Dartmouth marine works. Its captain had attempted to leave Halifax but had hugged the western shore until reaching Ketch Harbour and now was wisely biding his time. The officials were to prevent unauthorized unloading of cargo and the illegal shipment of munitions. *Constance*, under veteran blockade runner Captain Duncan Stewart, managed to depart for warmer climes but in early October struck an obstruction at the entrance of Charleston's harbour and sank.[64]

The increased presence of American gunboats, together with their commanders' ignorance of protocol, caused the Nova Scotia authorities to issue stricter port regulations in the form of an order in council. All visiting men of war, Confederate or Union, had to anchor in the inner harbour near the Naval Dockyard. Not all complied. The *Iosco*, which later coaled at Pictou, anchored within a mile of the city but then departed at night without communicating with the government or the naval authorities. Northern vessels could only remain in port for twenty-four hours, but those which followed the rules were treated with all due courtesy. When the double-ender USS *Tallapoosa* (with a rudder at either end) entered the harbour, it hoisted the British ensign and fired a twenty-one-gun salute which the Citadel artillerymen returned. The American visitor then fired a salute in honour of the admiral's pennant, which also was returned. USS *Shawmut*'s captain followed naval protocol when he visited Halifax in November, but part of his crew did not. When he was conferring with the American consul, his entire boat crew took "French leave" and was harboured by the locals. A minor but significant sign of the times was the reception of USS *Florida* in October, which had been violating port regulations by "blockading" Halifax harbour. While two of its officers met with Vice-Admiral Hope, the rest were entertained in the wardroom of HMS *Jason*. The *Florida* was in Nova Scotia waters for nine days and saw no blockade runners outside territorial waters.[65]

On the evening of 25 August, on patrol off New Inlet, North Carolina, USS *Monticello* encountered an intruder eight miles northeast of Fort Fisher. The long, low-silhouetted steamer, with twin stacks, appeared to be an English-built blockade runner heading inshore at a rate of twelve knots. The Federal guardian signalled a challenge and then fired off rockets to alert the rest of the squadron. The gun crews opened fire, but this time, instead of a regular turkey shoot, the encounter turned into a confused nighttime firefight, with much signalling from Rebel range lights on shore. The mystery craft, running close to shore, sheared and unexpectedly returned volleys of shell and grapeshot. The artillery flashes attracted the blockaders *Mercredita* and *Britannia*, one of which joined the fight. Shrapnel from the unidentified cruiser hit the latter's paddle box. The intruder, clearly visible in the burst of an exploding shell, was the *Tallahassee*. Its wheelhouse was damaged by shell or shrapnel, but Wood, still steaming at twelve knots, succeeded in crossing the bar. Confederate coastal batteries entered the fray, forcing the pursuers to keep their distance. "Bohemian" recorded: "As soon as the anchor was dropped, all hands were called to muster and Captain Wood read prayers, thanking God for having protected us through scenes of peril and for delivering us from the hands of our enemies, bringing us safe into our destined port." Next morning the crew of USS *Niphon* clearly observed a slightly battered *Tallahassee* anchored near the Mound battery. After rounding Confederate Point, Commander Wood steamed up the Cape Fear River to Wilmington where he was assigned to other duties.[66]

Wood's cruise and successful return to home base, for the Halifax *Morning Chronicle*, was "unprecedented in the history of naval warfare." The raid's real impact is difficult to assess. The South had scored a propaganda victory, one that appealed to British subjects with their own national memories of sea rovers such as Francis Drake. Fear of the *Tallahassee* drove up marine insurance rates, continued the flight from the flag and caused the U.S. Navy Department to redeploy vessels. Yet the August raid did little to alter the course of the war. If anything, as a number of prominent Confederates later lamented, it brought increased Northern pressure to the Cape Fear River, the South's last great supply conduit. Northern outrage at the destruction of unarmed sailing vessels helped rally political support for the storming of Fort Fisher. General Robert E. Lee, the governor of North Carolina and a number of Southern journalists blamed the *Tallahassee*, in part, for the eventual loss of Fort Fisher and Wilmington. Another Confederate general complained that the raider was not a "fighting ship" and that its guns and crew were more valuable on picket boats, shore batteries and the river guard. Strategically, the vessel would have better served the war effort as a smuggler than a raider. And a number of Confederate officers, such as the commander of the raider *Chickamauga*, were embarrassed by their navy's destruction of helpless fishing schooners and other small craft. Naval Secretary Mallory, however, defended his deployment of the raider.[67]

For several weeks the northeastern seaboard was alarmed by rumours that the *Tallahassee* was again on the loose. The raider seemed to be everywhere and nowhere. Paranoia crept into Consul Jackson's dispatches. On 30 August he warned of a new plot to seize a steamship on the Portland to Saint John run, either by disguised highjackers or a commerce raider. Another red herring held that the *Tallahassee* had burned twenty fishing boats off Cape Cod. In early September the captain and crew of an American packet had a fright when steaming between Seal Island and Cape Sable. The SS *Franconia* came across an unidentified steamer which appeared to give chase. The *Franconia*'s captain ordered up more sail to outrun the pursuer, which changed course only after the liner steamed close to the shore in the direction of Barrington Harbour. The mystery vessel was possibly the *Mary*, a Confederate merchantman (mentioned in the next chapter). The ten-gun *Massasoit* was ordered to patrol off the British colonies in early September in case John Taylor Wood was back in the neighbourhood; a faulty compass took the gunboat east of Seal Island where it sheltered off Port Medway for a day. On its way back to Cape Sable, the *Massasoit* spotted a steamer giving off black smoke, so the captain beat to quarters and gave chase. The unidentified craft, possibly the packet *Franconia*, disappeared from view. On 2 September the gunboat anchored off Saint John, from where it set a course for the Maine coast. USS *Susquehanna* was sent from Cape Cod to Cape Sable and on to Halifax. The *Iosco* reached Ship Harbour (Port Hawkesbury) in Canso Strait on 5 September. In late October the *Dacotah* was at Ship Harbour on a fisheries protection cruise. A Canso resident wrote that up to fifty Yankee fishing vessels were in the Strait of Canso, transferring cargoes destined for Boston, Cape Cod and Gloucester into the holds of British vessels – the New Englanders were convinced that the *Tallahassee* was in the area. Just in case, in late August the Navy Department dispatched USS *Maumee* to the vicinity of Halifax.[68]

The raider, under the name *Olustee*, did return to sea, but with a new commander. In late October it broke out of Wilmington, North Carolina, and took several prizes off the coast of Delaware despite being damaged by enemy fire as it had headed to sea. The Northern authorities also feared that the cruiser *Edith* was on the prowl. Renamed the *Chickamauga*, the former blockade runner had made a sortie from Wilmington a day before the *Olustee*'s outing. During this second panic on the eastern seaboard, Rear Admiral David Porter's orders in reference to the cruiser were blunt: "Sink her at all hazards." New York shipping interests were alarmed by reports that the *Tallahassee* had been lurking off Long Island in early November. The vessel in question was CSS *Chickamauga*, which captured several prizes off the coast of New Jersey and New York before steaming to Bermuda.[69]

The cruise of the gunboat USS *Shawmut* under Lieutenant-Commander George Morris reveals how much the *Chesapeake* and *Tallahassee* incidents had influenced Northern naval and consular thinking. The *Shawmut* touched at Eastport on 12 November and then steamed to Saint John where Morris met with Consul J.Q. Howard. In the absence of reliable intelligence, Howard advised cruising the Bay of Fundy between Grand Manan and Brier Island and checking St. Mary's Bay and the Yarmouth area. He thought that if the former *Tallahassee* reached the Gulf of Maine, it might rendezvous with a collier at Seal Cove, the Grand Manan harbour visited by the *Chesapeake* (British authorities had forbidden the vessel from entering their ports until 19 November). The *Shawmut* put in at Grand Manan on the sixteenth and then sailed for Yarmouth, where Consular Agent Merrill reported the presence of a suspicious steamer, possibly a tender for a raider, taking on coal. The consul in Halifax wired that there was a large white-hulled steamship at the mouth of the LaHave River. He advised the commander of USS *Yantic*, which reached Halifax on 1 November, that the object of the search "would not come to Halifax, as the summary and not over courteous manner with which she was ejected from that port during the late raid must be fresh in her memory." Although the most recent Confederate raider had burned two vessels from Maine, it had been nowhere near the Maritimes and returned to Cape Fear on 7 November.[70]

In December the Confederate authorities stripped the *Olustee* of its guns and assigned it to smuggling duties as the private vessel

Chameleon under Lieutenant John R. Wilkinson who had taken the *Robert E. Lee* to Halifax in 1863. Wilkinson had also commanded CSS *Chickamauga* on its November raid. At the end of the war, the *Chameleon*, which had narrowly escaped capture at Fort Fisher in January 1865, reached Liverpool where it was seized by the British government. The U.S. government acquired the vessel through an admiralty court proceeding.[71]

The Nova Scotia authorities had handled the *Tallahassee* in a skilful manner, and Governor MacDonnell was later commended by the Colonial Office.[72] Although local sympathies for the Confederacy had been manifest, the official reaction had been firm. The governor and the admiral, by limiting Wood's fuel supply and time in port, had discouraged other Confederate raiders from approaching the Bay of Fundy and Nova Scotia shores. The governor of Bermuda, faced with the arrival of the *Chickamauga* on 7 November 1864, adopted a similarly strict approach, effectively bringing its cruise to an end. Northern perceptions aside, British ports were rarely used by Rebel warships. If this did little to win Northern goodwill, at least it minimized the probability of further international incidents that would compromise British neutrality.[73]

9 Last Hurrah of the Blockade Runners

Now landed safe in Halifax, the dangers we have passed
Enhances all our pleasures – too dear, alas! to last.
From ladies' hearts and shopmens' arts, resistance is not made–
We spend our gold, like Timon old, while "Running the Blockade"
So fill our glass to every lass, of every hue and shade
Who takes her stand, for Dixie's land
And Running the Blockade.
 – "Running the Blockade," Halifax *Sun*, 7 November 1864

By 1864 it was not English-built commerce raiders but blockade runners that were keeping the Confederacy in the war.[1] The Rebel authorities had ordered smugglers to reserve space for government freight. In March, Richmond formed a Bureau of Foreign Supplies. The U.S. Secretary of the Navy Gideon Welles noted in his annual report that almost every specialized smuggler was British-built and British merchants were reaping enormous profits from illicit commerce. Charts used by U.S. Navy blockaders indicated the "Halifax line," running southeasterly along the Carolina coast to Cape Fear. Welles wrote that "the advantages of those triangular depots of blockade-runners and rebel supplies – the ports of Halifax, Bermuda and Nassau, ports which will always be in sympathy with the rebels – has induced them to engage in trade."[2] An intelligence report from early September 1864 contended that a regular line of smugglers was about to be established between Nova Scotia and Bermuda. Although the Maritimes was only marginally involved in the estimated eight thousand blockade violations, its trade links with the West Indies and its political sympathies worried both the American government and the navy.[3]

For Secretary Welles, British involvement in sustaining the slaveocracy of the South was on a moral plane with supplying opium to China. Yet, as in the period 1861–63, Northern merchants and exporters, either directly or indirectly, were also involved in the Confederate supply effort. The two sides remained each other's best customer.[4] The steamer *Frances* from Philadelphia was sold in Nova

Scotia for smuggling purposes. In another instance the authorities in Philadelphia seized a ship loaded with a pair of locomotives supposedly destined for New Brunswick. Federal detectives determined that the gauge did not match any colonial line and suspected the engines were destined for the Confederacy via the British colonies. Alexander Keith may have played a role in this transaction.[5]

Partly to stem this outflow, in 1862 and 1863, Washington outlawed the export of anthracite (suitable for blockade runners), arms, munitions, horses, mules and livestock. Congress approved legislation that allowed the secretary of the treasury to "refuse clearance to any vessel laden with a cargo destined for a foreign or domestic port if there was reason to suspect that the real terminus for the freight or part of it was in Confederate territory." The captain of the steamer *Alpha* who brought a cargo of coal to Halifax for commercial speculation was accused by a New York journal of operating a tender for the blockade-running squadron.[6]

Ex-Maritimer Louis M. Coxetter was heard of again, this time in the smuggling business. In the summer of 1862, in command of the steamer *Herald* out of Charleston, he had been chased into Nassau by USS *Adirondack*. The Yankee warship closed to within three hundred yards and fired a volley across Coxetter's bows; his response was to order up full steam. Next came a broadside of shell, solid shot and chain meant to cut masts and rigging. The *Herald*'s flag was shot away and a shell splintered its deck as the captain stood, bravely or foolishly, on the paddlebox, surveying the scene before reaching the safety of Nassau harbour. So aggressive had the Northern pursuit been that the colonial authorities sent out HMS *Greyhound* to protest. In 1863, Coxetter took the *Herald* (rechristened *General Beauregard*) into Charleston under enemy fire. He also commanded the *Fanny and Jennie*, which ran aground near the same port in February 1864.[7]

By the spring of 1864, Lord Lyons was so struck by the growth of the U.S. Navy, the size, speed and firepower of its newest vessels and the increasing professionalism of its officers that he was convinced that war was in the offing. The American buildup seemed aimed more at first-class naval powers than the Confederacy.[8] Increased American naval activity off Halifax in September caused Vice-Admiral Hope to station HMS *Jason* near Herring Cove to prevent breaches of international law by belligerent vessels. The officers of this corvette had entertained their counterparts of CSS *Alabama* at Jamaica a year earlier. The Nova Scotia executive further tightened regulations for visiting warships in October. American vessels had been anchoring beyond the three-mile limit and sending

boats into the harbour. The government forbade all communications from outside the harbour by small boats. But foreign naval
vessels were allowed to communicate with shore and leave without
anchoring "if they come openly to the proper part of the harbour."
The New York *Daily News* reported that as long as blockade runners
flew British flags, they would be under Royal Navy protection off
Halifax.[9]

Southerners were frequent visitors to Halifax in 1864 and typically received more press coverage than the more numerous Yankees. Beverly Tucker arrived from Richmond via Bermuda in
February on a supply mission for the Rebel government. While in
Nova Scotia a hand injury prevented him from writing dispatches
and letters, so Albert Pilsbury, the former consul, acted as his
secretary. Tucker developed a friendship with Dr. W.J. Almon, who
treated the injured Virginian by amputating part of his thumb. From
Canada, Tucker described Halifax as "the only place and its people
the only people that I have any heart for outside my dear old
Virginia." Almon had knowledge of various Southern agents arriving in Halifax by steamer and was sent mail on their behalf.
In one case he was forwarded a book of signals from New York.[10]

Although Gulf of St. Lawrence steam navigation was open part
of the year, most Southern travellers between Canada and the lower
provinces faced a long trek by wagon or coach. The majority travelled via the Temiscouta route, which, like the more circuitous
Matapedia-Bathurst-Newcastle road, was more passable in the winter
months than in spring. Preferred stopping places for Southerners
included Newcomb's at Tobique, Renfrew's of Woodstock,
Fredericton's Barker House, Hesslein's in Saint John and Halifax's
Waverly Hotel. There was little need to travel incognito. In June
and July, Judge Jackson noted the arrival from Montreal of two
dozen escaped prisoners, two of them in Confederate grey.[11]

Confederate Senator Clement C. Clay, on his way to Canada on
diplomatic business, reached Halifax in May. Too ill to accompany
colleague Jacob Thompson of Mississippi on the gruelling overland
trip to Canada East, he stayed in Halifax to recuperate. Clay received a letter of introduction to Catholic priests and bishops from
Archbishop Connolly, who wrote that the Confederate cause "commands the respect and sympathy of the world." While in Nova Scotia,
Clay encountered Lieutenant Bennett Young, a Kentuckian who
would lead the raid on St. Alban's, Vermont, in October. Clay passed
through Saint John on his way to Montreal, which inspired a veteran
of the Confederate army to offer his services to the U.S. consul
as a secret agent. The individual promised to "arrest" the Southern

diplomat in Canada. Consul Howard reported that his agent had travelled to Quebec "but did not keep his promises," possibly because he had been seduced back to the Rebel fold by a letter from home. Clay, together with Professor J.P. Holcombe, would constitute the unofficial Confederate peace mission at Niagara Falls, a tactic meant to influence the presidential elections of that fall. While in Canada, Clay and Thompson met with northern Copperheads, including Clement Vallandigham. Thompson also was linked to the Lake Erie plot of September which resulted in the capture of the American steamers *Island Queen* and *Philo Parsons*; and Clay and George Saunders were connected to the guerrilla operation against St. Alban's in October of 1864.[12]

In September, Holcombe, on behalf of the Confederacy, presented Halifax barrister J.W. Ritchie with a set of plate for services rendered in connection with the *Chesapeake*. A number of influential gentlemen, including Dr. Almon, A.G. Jones and Railway Commissioner James McDonald, gathered at the Halifax Hotel for the occasion. Holcombe, a flowery orator who cultivated his scholarly image by dressing in black and carrying a book of poetry, referred to Ritchie as a generous sympathizer of a "sorely tried country in her stern struggle for liberty." Ritchie, although accepting the gift in a private capacity, happened to be solicitor general in Charles Tupper's government. He alluded to "the noble devotion of the South and her patriotic cause."[13]

Among the Southern personalities who passed through Halifax during the later part of the Civil War, few were as intriguing as Rose O'Neal Greenhow, a Maryland native and influential Washington hostess. Greenhow, a persuasive and well connected widow, was a Southern partisan who had forwarded messages to the Rebels on Federal troop movements during the First Bull Run campaign. Under surveillance by detective Allen Pinkerton, she had been placed under house arrest but continued to spy. Next she had been confined, with her young daughter Rose, to the Old Capitol Prison. After six months in this "Union Bastille," and still suspected of operating an espionage ring, Greenhow was expelled behind the lines. In Richmond she was received as a heroine. Carrying letters to Confederate diplomats in Europe, the "wild rose of the Confederacy" departed from Wilmington on a blockade runner bound for Bermuda. From there she sailed to England without stopping at Nova Scotia. In Europe she moved in "society" as an informal Confederate lobbyist, was received by Queen Victoria and the Emperor of France and was proposed to by a British peer. Greenhow's *My Imprisonment and the First Year of Abolition Rule in Washington,* a book published in England, won considerable sympathy for the Southern cause.[14]

Greenhow returned to North America on the steamer *Condor*, which reached Halifax in September of 1864. The Glasgow-built, lead-coloured blockade runner, commanded by a former captain of the Royal Navy, was on its maiden voyage.[15] Of Greenhow's stay in Halifax little is known, although she possibly attended the bazaar for relief of Southern prisoners, described by one correspondent as the social event of the season. The *Condor*, a Confederate navy vessel, cleared port on 24 September carrying an additional passenger, Professor Holcombe, and clothing for the Rebel army. Holcombe had returned from Canada via New Brunswick where he had met a number of prominent politicians. He remained optimistic that if the Democrats nominated General G.B. McClellan for president, Lincoln would go down to defeat, an armistice would be negotiated between North and South and the Confederacy would obtain its independence.[16]

News of the *Condor*'s presence was relayed to Washington by Consul Jackson. The three-hundred-ton steamer encountered no difficulties until off Cape Fear where it was challenged by a gunboat which it managed to evade. But in so doing the freighter ran aground in sight of Fort Fisher. The USS *Niphon* was kept at bay by Confederate gunners – Colonel William Lamb, the fort's commander, deployed mobile, rifled Whitworth guns to protect incoming or stranded blockade runners. Greenhow, fearing capture, insisted on going ashore and a boat crew was readied. Holcombe chose to risk remaining on board, which was the wiser decision because the smaller boat capsized and Greenhow and the sailors were drowned. Her body washed ashore where it was looted of gold sovereigns by a Rebel soldier, but later it was conveyed to Richmond and interred with honours. The luckless *Condor* remained grounded for months until wrecked by Confederate gun crews.[17]

It was rare for Southern or British blockade runners to travel directly between the Confederacy and Nova Scotia before 1864. The arrival of the paddle-wheeler *Will o' the Wisp* in January presaged the next stage in the Rebel supply effort. The 275-foot shallow-draft steamer, built on the Clyde, required repairs to its leaking hull. The first "new" blockade runners were Scottish and English coastal or cross-channel steamers adapted for smuggling. The class that began to appear in 1864 was built purposely for evading blockaders: engines and boilers were protected, the length-to-beam ratio was high and decks were clear of excessive cabins, masts and other obstructions. Sidewheelers, although presenting bigger targets, were more manoeuvrable than single-screw propeller craft when crossing sand bars. *Will o' the Wisp* was beached until it could taken into Darmouth's marine works, which employed three steam-powered "railways" to pull vessels out of the water. Its cradles were capable of holding one fifteen-hundred-ton vessel, one of seven hundred tons and two of five hundred. In the spring the U.S. consul protested that the steamer was to be armed at Ketch Harbour as a commerce raider. The chief American representative protested to the British government the steamer's departure "under direction of agents now having harbour at Halifax." The Nova Scotia government, upon investigation, found the allegation to be groundless; the steamer was destined to be an unarmed smuggler.[18]

Among the vessels seeking repairs at the Chebucto Marine Railway was one of the war's most successful smugglers, the celebrated *A.D. Vance* or *Advance*, which arrived from the Bahamas in April.[19] The five-hundred-ton paddle-wheeler, capable of seventeen knots, was owned not by private interests but by the state of North Carolina, and its captain was an officer in the state navy. Crowds of waterfront workers cheered when it steamed to its mooring. Repairs to *A.D. Vance* would have pumped several thousand pounds into the local economy, but in the end the owners sought a British shipyard. Formerly the *Lord Clyde*, it made over thirty successful trips through the naval screen to and from Bermuda. On its third voyage, approaching Fort Fisher, it ran through the entire blockading squadron in broad daylight. *A.D. Vance*, under Captain Tom Crossan, was finally captured in September 1864 after making several unsuccessful attempts to exit the Cape Fear River. Crossan managed to elude the first line of enemy guardians but inadvertently encountered the swift USS *Santiago de Cuba* heading north for fuel. After a chase that lasted nearly ten hours, North Carolina's handsome blockade runner and its cargo of cotton were captured. The state governor blamed the fact that its high-quality "foreign" coal had been appropriated for the use of the *Tallahassee*.[20]

In August Major Norman Walker, CSA, visited Halifax from Bermuda on the blockade runner *Falcon*, a triple-stacker capable of eighteen knots. He recommended the Nova Scotia port as an alternative base for Confederate supply and then departed for Britain on official business. Consul Jackson suspected that Walker would attempt to secure a new commerce raider similar to the *Tallahassee*. Several Southern officers embarked on the sidewheeler *Helen* for Wilmington, North Carolina, in late August; the steel-hulled *Owl*, which Fraser, Trenholm and Co. turned over to the Confederate government, cleared for Nassau, carrying a large crew of one hundred, part of it possibly to man a second vessel. Another party of Southerners, including Dr. Luke Blackburn of Natchez, Colonel Carroll Bicks of Georgia, Dr. Fall, the former editor of the Vicksburg *Sentinel*, and several other gentlemen, arrived in September. In October a number of Rebel officers who had spent some time in the city departed by steamer. A large crowd gave them an ovation and the band of the Prince of Wales regiment supplied music.[21]

The ever-vigilant consul was greatly alarmed by the arrival of the well-known steamer *Mary*, barque-rigged, with "rakish masts, round stern, very straight stem." The 280-ton vessel had been built for Fraser, Trenholm and Co. by a British yard in 1863 to be converted into a gunboat. Named *Alexandra* in honour of the Princess of Wales, this supposed mate of the *Florida* had been seized by British customs authorities for violation of neutrality regulations, and considerable litigation had ensued; at one point the Russian government had been interested in the ship. Months later it was released and renamed *Mary* by owner Henry Lafone, a Confederate agent operating for the Importing and Exporting Co.[22]

Union officials feared that the vessel would be armed at Nassau or Bermuda after leaving Liverpool. In early 1864, *Mary* turned up at Liverpool, Nova Scotia, where Consul Jackson suspected that it would be equipped with guns. The lieutenant-governor declined to subject the vessel to any special surveillance but did arrange for its inspection by a naval officer. The *Mary*, although solidly built, was not suitable as a fighting ship, the Nova Scotia authorities concluded, because its top speed was under five knots. According to C.K. Prioleau, head of Fraser, Trenholm and Co. in Liverpool, the vessel required new boilers. After extensive repairs at Halifax, including a new propeller, it departed for Bermuda and then steamed to Nassau. There the U.S. consul succeeded in having her libelled in Vice-Admiralty court, effectively tying her up for the war's duration. Perhaps because of the stir created by the ship's visit, the Nova Scotia government published an order in council which repeated the Imperial edict against dismantling or selling belligerent vessels in British ports.[23]

Yellow fever among crews and passengers shipping out of the Bahamas and Bermuda worked to Halifax's advantage in the late summer of 1864. Prioleau, writing to a Confederate officer who journeyed to Nova Scotia in order to supervise repairs to the *Mary*, did not regard Halifax as "a practical place to carry on the trade from," even under normal circumstances. The fever changed this. By avoiding the British islands, blockade runners were spared the expensive one-month quarantine at Wilmington. Nova Scotia suddenly became a popular rendezvous for a colourful fleet of smugglers. Prior to this, Halifax had been mainly a refuelling stop and repair station for vessels with leaky hulls or fouled bottoms.[24] Stephen Wise, author of *Lifeline of the Confederacy*, has found that steam-powered smugglers completed less than a dozen round trips between Halifax and North Carolina and that no direct trips to South Carolina ports succeeded. Most of the freight consigned locally was handled by the firms of B. Wier and G.C. Harvey. The *Caroline* (six successful trips out of seven attempts) and *City of Petersburg*, which both cleared in mid-October, took cargoes consigned to Wier and Harvey, respectively. To expedite matters, Wier and Co. employed Gustave Alexandre, formerly a clerk in Confederate service in Bermuda.[25]

The American consul requested his own clerk assistant, owing to the more extensive operations carried on by the Confederates via Nova Scotia. Jackson, given his window on North Atlantic trade, relayed information not only on Halifax but also Bermuda, the Bahamas and the South. Several of his reports were issued as circulars to naval commanders on blockade duty. In early September, Jackson logged the presence of the graceful runners *Falcon*, *Old Dominion* and *Colonel Lamb*. The former cleared officially for Nassau on 9 September but was suspected of heading directly for New Inlet, North Carolina. The swift *Flamingo*, owned by Alexander Collie and Co., remained at anchor. On 12 September the consul communicated the arrival of *City of Petersburg* and *Annie*, bringing over twelve hundred bales of cotton. Crenshaw and Co.'s *Armstrong*, loaded with provisions for the Confederate Subsistence Bureau, reached port a few days later. Although poorly built, this steamer, under Captain Michael Usina, managed five successful runs. Jackson's hunch was that it would attempt to enter the Cape Fear River on a moonless night. *Armstrong*, after a second trip to Nova Scotia, was intercepted by three Union warships in December. *Flamingo*, Captain T. Aitkinson, cleared on 21 September, heavily laden with freight. *Ptarmigan*, a 284-ton sidewheeler in Confederate navy service, touched at Halifax with a cargo of cotton. *Askalon* was another September arrival.[26]

More blockade runners used the port's services in October, according to Consul Jackson's methodically filed reports. *Caroline*, a new 403-ton steamer built and registered in Glasgow, entered port in early October with machinery and other items. Its sister ship, the *Constance*, arrived a week later. *Old Dominion*, 518 tons, was making ready to clear for Southern waters. The Halifax *Express* reported on 12 October that the masters of several runners had recently paid out large disbursements to their crews. On 17 October,

Blockade runner *Little Hattie*, built in Scotland in 1864, made ten successful trips through the blockade.

a few days after the *Constance* was reported lost, *Caroline* cleared for Bermuda with cargo consigned to Wier and Co. Word arrived that the runner *North Heath*, which had visited Halifax in August for repairs, had reached North Carolina unmolested. Early in the New Year it was sunk as an obstruction in the Cape Fear River.[27]

Saint John, although not participating directly in illicit trade, continued its links with Confederate supply because of its proximity to Boston and New York. The pro-Northern *Globe* claimed that local merchants had not become involved in blockade running. However, the fact was that the port serviced vessels supplying the South through the Caribbean. In July 1863 the consul reported that a Captain Hamill of Charleston, "an unquestionable traitor," was negotiating with the firm J. and R. Wright for three steam vessels. The screw steamer *Douro* cleared port carrying flour, dry goods, alcohol, whiskey and gin. It had been nabbed exiting Wilmington in March with cotton, turpentine and tobacco. After being condemned and sold for a prize, the vessel returned to smuggling under the same name until destroyed by gunfire off New Inlet. The Confederacy's unofficial representative in New Brunswick, according to the consul, continued to be William H. Turlington, formerly of North Carolina. Howard suspected that he was financed by Major Norman Walker.[28]

Several Northern steamships, a number of them former blockade runners, were refitted in Saint John for feeder trade with Nassau. In 1863 and 1864 they included the small vessels *St. John* and *Union*, supposedly sold to Southerners or "their British allies." The *Laura* cleared for Nassau, always a suspicious destination in the opinion of the American consul, in late August. The *Flora*, one of four blockade runners with this name, was formerly the prize steamer

Blockade runner *Armstrong* called at Halifax in 1864 and was later captured by the U.S. Navy.

Rouen. Built at Millwood, London, in the 1850s, it had begun its smuggling career as the property of a Bermuda resident. Captured and released by the U.S. Navy, it reached Saint John on 4 September. Said to be owned by New Brunswickers, it docked at Nassau a few weeks later and eventually went to Cuba to test the blockade off Galveston where it was lost. Another worry for Union authorities were two new steamers built for river service in China. These vessels, the *Fong Soey* and *Fire Queen*, which were adaptable for naval purposes, showed up in the Bay of Fundy in July during the latest border scare. Many of the steamers described in consular or press accounts were not violators of the blockade but freighters that went no farther than Bermuda, Nassau or Cuba. Such was the case with the *Maria*, taking coal to Havana. A number arrived or departed in ballast.[29]

The *Acadian Recorder*, on the basis of information from "Southern friends," published a detailed examination of the smuggling business in August, noting that four recently arrived runners carried fatal cases of yellow fever. The iron-hulled *Ptarmigan*, which entered Halifax in late September, had lost twelve crew and passengers. It was of the *Condor* class, procured in Britain by Commander J.D. Bulloch, CSN. When it left Nova Scotia waters in October, its freight was consigned to G.C. Harvey. The odds of capture had increased, but smuggling remained profitable. The industry was controlled by large joint-stock companies which maintained a fleet of fifty steamers representing an investment of eight million pounds. The trading companies specialized in fast steamships which drew no more than eight feet of water when fully loaded and whose paddle boxes where muffled by canvas. Their metal hulls sported the first camouflage paint in the history of naval warfare. Each steamer carried a company agent; the well-paid captains usually were Southerners or Britons.

By 1864, able-bodied seamen were fetching from $100 to $150 per round trip, firemen double this amount. Engineers, upon whose skills rested the entire venture, were paid $800 to $1,000. Captains and pilots were remunerated on a greater scale. One-third of seamen's wages were paid in advance. In addition, each hand was allowed to bring out a quantity of cotton, turpentine or other Southern goods, for a high rate of profit. The chief inbound cargoes were machinery, shoes, clothes and cloth; the Confederacy was less dependent on imported weapons and ammunition.[30]

Although the colony abounded with experienced sailors, few Bluenoses appear to have served on these specialized craft. One reporter wrote, however, that a number of Haligonians, owing to "the thirst of adventure inherent among British subjects," had left profitable positions and signed on as clerks or stewards. Horatio Nelson Black, of River Philip, Nova Scotia, a veteran of the Rebel army, wrote from Savannah in May 1864 that he was about to ship out on a cotton schooner. The testimony of witnesses before the Nova Scotia Court of Vice-Admiralty in November reveals more about working conditions on board the smugglers. In this case the steward and chief cook on the *City of Petersburg*, owned in London, sued for back wages. The men were remunerated in gold, and a bonus was paid once the cargo was safely discharged. George Page, master of the sister vessel *Old Dominion*, testified that blockade runners kept a "liberal table." Wages were high, but the risk of capture was not as great, in his opinion, as the danger of running aground. There were more dangers in exiting port than going in. Captains were forbidden to leave crewmen behind in Wilmington or to ship Southerners.[31]

A Halifax correspondent to an American journal reported that the runners "added a miscellaneous population of a character hitherto unknown to the staid old city." Earlier in the war a minstrel and burlesque troupe had presented the successful farce "Running the Blockade." On 12 September, the day of the "colonial dinner" for delegates discussing Confederation, the steamer *Annie* arrived with 450 bales of cotton. Eight other runners rode at anchor in the harbour, all waiting for the moon to change and the nights to become darker. The press noted a large amount of cargo on wharves and in warehouses, most of it owned by British speculators, awaiting shipment. Halifax's hotels and boarding houses were full, and even "choice spots on bare floors" were in great demand. Warehouses, shops and taverns did a good business. One journal credited the fleet of smugglers for reviving an otherwise dull commercial season. "Jack ashore," as always, was high-spirited. Confederates, or men sailing under Confederate colours, were reported engaging in street brawls. A sailor from the *Old Dominion* was sent to penitentiary for stabbing a shipmate; another was robbed of his gold. Two Southerners fought a duel over a woman on the outskirts of town and both were slightly wounded. Another highly publicized incident was a scuffle between Benjamin Wier and the captain of the runner *Little Hattie*. Wier was never known to back away from a fight, and Captain Libby, in true Southern fashion, drew a knife.[32]

The blockade-running vessels, in addition to their glamorous reputations, were beautiful to behold and drew admiration from the local press. They represented the latest in marine architecture and technology.[33] The steel-hulled *Bat*, for example, 230 feet long and with a power plant capable of 280 h.p., drew under eight feet of water when loaded with coal and freight. The *Little Hattie*'s engine, on a trial run after repairs in Dartmouth, was clocked at an impressive 35 r.p.m. As it passed HMS *Duncan*, in the words of the *Journal*, "the beautiful banner of the Confederate States was courageously dipped." The vice-admiral's blue ensign was lowered in response – apparently the Imperial rule against saluting Confederates did not extend to civilian craft. *Little Hattie* succeeded in reaching Wilmington and clearing with several hundred bales of "white gold" for Bermuda in October.[34]

The captain and crew of the yacht-like *Florie* won many friends during their two-month Nova Scotia sojourn. The vessel's refit at Dartmouth included hull reinforcement and an engine overhaul. On a trial trip before departing for Bermuda, the *Florie*, carrying a pleasure party of ladies and gentlemen, was cheered from the Dartmouth shore. During one of its Halifax stops the owner of the steamer *Lucy* presented the captain with a silver service for having evaded the blockade eighteen times. When the vessel returned for hull repairs in December and sailed up the harbour flying a large Confederate flag, it was "cheered from wharf to wharf by labourers and others about the docks and warehouses." Another impressive specimen of marine design was the *Colonel Lamb*, a 1,788-ton steamer that made Halifax in nine days from Liverpool, England. This new vessel was named after the commander of North Carolina's Fort Fisher, an esteemed friend of the smugglers. The 281-foot screw steamer, which had been transferred to a Confederate agent in the Bahamas, cleared port on 25 October under Tom Lockwood after completing repairs. Its cargo, consigned to Alexander Keith and others, consisted of sugar, bluestones, shoes, shirts, hats, dry goods and liquor, goods that would find a ready market in the Confederacy. Keith, in light of travel restrictions, applied to the U.S. consul for a passport; this was refused on the grounds that he was a smuggler and Rebel agent.[35]

"No labour, no fighting and lots of prize money." So commented a New Brunswick journalist on life in the Union blockade squadron.[36] From 1 November 1863 to 1 November 1864 the navy captured or ran aground 324 runners, including 105 schooners, 88 steamers and 40 sloops. Condemned vessels and cargo were sold at public auction and the profits split between the government and naval personnel. Individual crewmen pocketed up to one thousand dollars per prize. Part of these monies were distributed to officers and men from Prince Edward Island, New Brunswick and Nova Scotia who officered and crewed Union vessels. Although steamers operating in and out of the Carolinas in 1864 enjoyed a high success rate, the Rebel government could not agree with Norman Walker's optimistic assessment of the port of Halifax. The secretary of the Confederate navy preferred supply vessels to utilize Nova Scotia as seldom as possible. In orders to J.N. Maffit of the *Owl*, Secretary S.A. Mallory advised that steamers should proceed to Bermuda rather than Nova Scotia because Halifax had less cargo available, the trip consumed more fuel and the risks of accident or capture were higher.[37]

In the late summer of 1864, two dozen smugglers were destroyed off Cape Fear and another twenty-six were captured. One was the Confederate government's brand-new 325-ton *Bat*, recently in Halifax; the 230-foot sidewheeler, under Captain A. Hora, carried shoes and machinery. Equipped with twin, vertical, double-oscillating engines, it was twice as fast as the typical gunboat. After a chase during which a shell mortally wounded a crewman, the *Bat* surrendered on 10 October 1864 and was taken to Boston for prize adjudication. There it was condemned and sold to private interests. Renamed the *Miramichi*, it worked in the Gulf of St. Lawrence–Newfoundland trade for thirty years. The *Annie* was destroyed off North Carolina following a chase by USS *Aster*. The loss of these vessels underscored Secretary Mallory's warning. *Old Dominion*'s signal officer, although sheltered below deck, was killed by shrapnel. The vessel itself survived to revisit Halifax in mid-October, having failed to reach Fort Fisher. All persons found on board captured blockade runners were detained until the captain, supercargo and part of the crew gave evidence before prize commissioners. Aliens were permitted to leave, but American citizens were jailed.[38]

As Halifax temporarily became a port of call for blockade runners, Nova Scotia naturally attracted more Federal warships. Their captains were expected to conduct themselves in a more professional and competent manner than had been exhibited during the hunt for the *Tallahassee*. In a 25 August 1864 diary entry, Secretary Welles described his gunboat commanders as "feeble and inefficient," suspecting a number of them of drunkenness, disloyalty and Rebel sympathies.[39] The Navy Department advised its cruisers to use Portland as their main coaling base in the surveillance of the Maritimes. USS *Vanderbilt*, which in 1863 had pursued the *Alabama* to South Africa and captured the *Peterhoff* off St. Thomas, spent a month in the vicinity of Halifax hoping to intercept blockade runners, or as the captain called them, "privateers." American naval commanders tended to view all runners as "Confederate," even when owned and registered in Britain. The navy had greater success further to the south, as on 28 October when two gunboats apprehended a burning *Lady Sterling*, which had touched at Halifax, off North Carolina.[40]

The Halifax press, a month after Wood's foray to Nova Scotia, reported that a Union warship had recently probed the harbour as far as Maugher's Beach light and then returned to sea. The following day a second warship passed the port heading in a southwesterly direction and a third anchored off Camperdown, a rocky bluff on the way to Sambro used as a signal station. Union warships, in the opinion of one journal, had an indisputable right to patrol the high seas, "but they are not justified by any acknowledged authority to blockade the ports of a British possession." This journal also complained that since the outbreak of the war several U.S. gunboats had entered the harbour, obtained supplies and "remained unmolested and undisturbed for several days," whereas the lone Confederate naval visitor had been treated brusquely. The commander of USS *Yantic*, which anchored at Halifax on 1 November reported that local "secessionists" greeted his ship's arrival with jeers and remarks "anything but complimentary." Blockade runners, Consul Jackson advised, usually escaped Halifax by hugging the western shore from George's Island to Sambro, then striking out to the south and southeast, outflanking Union gunboats. A correspondent to a New York newspaper reported that the Citadel displayed lanterns at night to warn off American cruisers. The lieutenant-governor asked Sir James Hope to secure the waters off Halifax. It was difficult, he wrote, "to draw any distinction between such proceedings and those of a hostile belligerent power blockading an enemy's ports."[41]

Halifax's celebrity as a smuggling centre was short-lived. It also distracted the American press from a more important pattern: Nova Scotia exports to the United States in 1864 (excluding new ships) were almost double that to the British West Indies, and nearly one-third of Nova Scotia's imports were American. And despite the Confederate cruiser threat, the volume of trade at Northern ports continued to rise.[42]

As 1864 drew to a close, steamers outfitted or built for evading the blockade were less frequent visitors to Maritime waters. The August to November arrivals were atypical of the industry's overall patterns; Nassau and, to a lesser extent, Bermuda were still the linchpins of Confederate supply. The cotton-laden *Old Dominion* returned from the Bahamas at Christmas, months after carrying freight to Nassau for Nova Scotia merchants. News arrived that the *Armstrong*, which had visited Halifax, had been apprehended after a seven-hour chase during which more than one-hundred shells had been fired. The steamer halted only because of a cabin fire. Vessel and cargo were said to be worth $350,000. The Gulf ports, such as Galveston, were still accessible, but the Maritimes were too distant to have much of a connection with this theatre. Although Halifax was visited by similar vessels in the New Year, by then the Confederacy's ambitious sea-borne supply effort had collapsed.[43]

BRAIN'S SECOND RAID

In the fall of 1864, John Brain, who had remained a fugitive from justice in Nova Scotia and New Brunswick, struck another blow against Northern shipping. Assisted once again by Henry Parr, he conducted an operation obviously inspired by the mission organized in New Brunswick in 1863. This time, however, Brain had taken the precaution of securing a provisional commission as "Acting Master" from the Confederate Navy Department. He later wrote his uncle in England (on stationery from the captured steamer *Roanoke*) that he spent the month of May in Richmond, before being ordered "out with my officers and crew to captain this ship." Brain had approached the secretary of the Confederate navy for a temporary commission, with a general plan to seize an enemy vessel and convert it into a privateer. Secretary Mallory, understanding that the expedition would board a Yankee steamer at New York and commandeer it en route to Cuba, acceded to Brain's request but gave "special and stringent instructions that the strictest regard must be had for neutral rights." Unlike the *Chesapeake* mission, any hostile expedition had to be organized in a Northern harbour – a dangerous undertaking for Brain.[44]

Despite his orders, Brain travelled not to enemy territory but neutral Cuba. His target was the thousand-ton sidewheeler *Roanoke*, a "hermaphrodite" brig-rigged steamer with two walking-beam engines and one stack, owned by the New York and Virginia Steamship Co. Once in Havana, Acting Master Brain boldly told Confederate agent Charles J. Helm that he had personally discussed his plan with President Davis, which was an outright lie. Helm, fearing that the Englishman would breach neutrality, refused to advance him any funds. In a detailed report to the Confederate government, Helm explained why he objected to the mission. The secretary of state, after reading the report, concurred. Brain had called at Helm's office, apprising him of his plan to seize one of three Northern steamers that plied the waters between Cuba and New York. Brain had first journeyed to Bermuda where he purchased a schooner and cleared for Matanzas, a port in northwestern Cuba, with a layover in Nassau. At Havana he claimed (falsely) to have been furnished with more than three thousand dollars by the Richmond authorities and one thousand by the Confederate agent in Nassau. Brain tried to hit Helm up for an additional fifteen hundred in order to recruit ten men and purchase revolvers, handcuffs, flags and other supplies. He also intimated that he planned to capture the *Roanoke* after it left Cuban waters. The agent realized that this would be a gross violation of Spanish neutrality and doubted if Brain grasped the seriousness of the consequences.[45]

In a letter to his superiors, Helm argued that a capture under these circumstances would jeopardize the Confederacy's good relations with Spain. Cuba's governor, after all, had exhibited a friendly neutrality towards the South, twice allowing CSS *Florida* to stop for coal and interfering in communications between Union agents on shore and the American navy. Helm particularly feared that any incident created by Brain would endanger the Confederacy's important trading rights with the Spanish colony and its favourable treatment of Southern refugees. He also doubted whether Brain could actually carry out a highjacking, given that Yankee vigilance had been redoubled since the *Chesapeake* attack. All passengers embarking on Northern steamers at Havana required a Spanish passport and a visa issued by the American consul. To obtain the latter, Americans had to swear allegiance to the republic. A group of ten or twelve strangers boarding at Havana, Helm concluded, would raise suspicions immediately. Brain's party of fourteen, he reported, was destitute and desired to return to the South. Thinking he had defused the situation, Helm paid the passage of a dozen of these men back to Nassau. The Spanish officer in charge of port security did not appear to be concerned about Brain's presence. But the resourceful Englishman simply recruited eight or nine adventurers from Havana's waterfront, probably promising them shares of the prize, and carried on.[46]

The Cuban highjacking bore a number of similarities to the expedition planned in Saint John a year earlier. The *Roanoke*, carrying mail, an assorted cargo and forty passengers, left Havana on 29 September 1864. Its crew was mostly Cuban. Few of the insurgent passengers had tickets or passports; they were smuggled on board or picked up from small boats after the steamer had left the dock. According to Captain F.A. Drew, it was customary for steamships to pick up passengers in this fashion, provided they had passports. Three men, one of then Brain alias Johnson, were taken from two boats; the purser, according to Drew, determined their papers to be in order. The purser later wrote that the captain had allowed two of the men to board even though they lacked passports. The officers of the *Roanoke*, according to Drew, had been warned about a highjacking attempt and were armed.[47]

Brain seized the ship after the captain and most of the crew had retired for the night. During the takeover the ship's carpenter was shot and killed, allegedly for threatening the captors with an axe, and the third engineer was wounded. The carpenter, according to the purser, had been handcuffed but had escaped to his room to fetch the axe. He was pursued into the engine room where he was shot through the hand and then the body. Weak from loss of blood, he climbed to the deck where he was shot several more times before expiring. His corpse was thrown over the side and the entire crew, except the firemen, was placed in irons. The party seemed to be led by Brain, Parr and a third individual. The Confederate agent at Havana speculated that the seizure was an inside job, given that the steamer's captain was a North Carolinian with two sons in the Rebel army. The *Roanoke* was more that a potential blockade runner; according to a police official in Bermuda, it carried several thousand dollars in gold and greenbacks.[48]

The pirates proceeded to Bermuda, contacting a pilot boat on the evening of 4 October and anchoring near Five Fathom Hole to the east of Saint George's. Brain departed in the pilot boat, possibly to confer with resident Confederate agent Norman Walker, and returned the next morning with four or five "Confederates." The steamer's officers were paroled during the day but placed in irons at night. The prize put to sea but returned to its anchorage in the evening. More men boarded before midnight; one of them was recognized as a British merchant from Saint George's. Witnesses later claimed that a number of the men who joined the highjackers off Five Fathom Hole had been armed. The *Roanoke*'s purser overheard that a brig would be arriving with coal and supplies for the highjackers. On the evening of the sixth there was a rendezvous eight or ten miles from shore with the brig *Village Girl*. Supplies were transferred and all of the following day was taken up with loading coal into the steamer's bunkers. Most of this labour was performed by forty men hired for the day who succeeded in transferring only fifteen tons. Brain and his "officers" informed the prisoners that a second vessel would carry them north to Halifax. A Danish brigantine, *Mathilde*, did appear and first the baggage, then the passengers and then most of the crew were placed on board. The brigantine attempted to sail for Saint George's, but the wind had died. When the *Mathilde* took its leave on 8 October, three crewmen remained on the steamer, still in irons.[49]

The owners of the *Roanoke*, meanwhile, suspected that it had been captured or destroyed by pirates or wreckers. Naval patrols were instructed to keep a sharp eye open for the missing vessel and for suspicious craft. The *Mathilde* landed passengers at Saint George's and sailed on to Halifax. According to a Bermuda police report, the vessel's consignee "Johnson" went along to Nova Scotia. Earlier in the week the authorities in Bermuda had heard reports from the U.S. consul of a Confederate vessel attempting to refuel in neutral waters. As yet there was insufficient evidence to justify government interference, but the police magistrate at Saint George's was instructed to watch out for violations of the Foreign Enlistment Act; revenue officers were reminded to enforce customs regulations; and the commander of the garrison was alerted of possible security breaches. Once the purser and chief officer of the missing steamer reached Saint George's and swore out depositions, the authorities began to act. The magistrate ordered the arrest of suspicious parties. Brain burned his prize on Sunday the ninth, but not before his men had helped themselves to its cargo of Cuban cigars. Thirteen were arrested on Saturday and an additional dozen on Sunday. Three of the highjackers wore Confederate uniforms. The U.S. consul sought their extradition on a charge of piracy. Revenue officers tracked down large quantities of cigars which had been landed and hidden in cellars and various nooks and crannies. The *Mathilde* later arrived in Halifax where its skipper denied any complicity in the crime.[50]

The prisoners, including John Brain, were brought before the police magistrate and a justice of the peace. In expectation of "disturbances," the government held the sailors and marines of HMS *Steady* in readiness. Already the governor in Hamilton had doubts as to the validity of the consul's extradition request. Revenue laws and the Foreign Enlistment Act, it seemed, had been flaunted. But were the prisoners pirates? The Bermuda *Mirror* reported that Brain had planned to steam to Wilmington but had run short of fuel. On the third day of the examination the court ruled that charges of piracy could not be sustained. Brain's commission appeared to be genuine, so the prisoners were liberated. British justice, once again, had clashed with Northern expectations. The attorney general of Bermuda reported to the Colonial Office that after their acquittal, the high-jackers "celebrated their escape with wine and noisy conviviality, openly boasting that very soon their exploit would be repeated." Colonial Secretary Cardwell endorsed the Bermuda government's course of action and agreed with the police magistrate that Brain, possessing a Confederate commission, was a genuine belligerent.[51]

The American government, once again, had cause for protest. The British colonial authorities had twice allowed an accused pirate and murderer to escape justice. Both incidents had a Maritime connection. The *Roanoke* news, moreover, broke at the same time as the much more serious St. Alban's raid: on 19 October, twenty rebels in civilian garb robbed three banks and killed a citizen of this Vermont border town and then fled into Canadian territory where several were apprehended. Brain, meanwhile, continued to be the subject of rumour. In Halifax in December the U.S. consul wrote that the notorious Rebel had been in town for a week in disguise before leaving by schooner for the Bahamas. Part of a "piratical gang" had departed on the steamer *Acadia* for Nassau and Cuba. Brain's comrade MacDonald, implicated in the *Chesapeake* incident, was reported to be in Canada. The dutiful Jackson gave notice of yet another fantastic plot by the Rebels, warning that a Confederate organization of a least three hundred had set its sights on unprotected Union steamers. The pirates would operate out of Nassau, Havana, Veracruz and California. From London the American consul communicated with the State Department that Brain was on his way to Scotland to take command of a Rebel steamer. The Bermuda *Advocate* published a more familiar story in January: "bold Captain Brain" had "hooked it," "victimizing hotel keepers and merchants to the tune of several hundred pounds."[52]

The departure of the small blockade-running fleet from Nova Scotia, like the outcome of the 1864 Presidential elections, marked a new and final stage in the war. The significance of Lincoln's re-election was not lost upon well-informed Maritimers. Merchant William Norman Rudolf recorded in his diary that the U.S. consul at Pictou had celebrated the Republican victory by flying an immense Union flag. "This means a continuation of the war and further shedding of blood, for that which seems an impossibility, the restoration of the Union," he wrote. The *Novascotian* saw it as a victory for "the exterminating party." Diehard Southern partisans shrugged off these developments, as they did the fall of Atlanta and the eventual capture of Fort Fisher. The Confederates, they vowed, would fight on in the hills and forests and would continue to command the respect and sympathy of British North America.[53]

Agitation against the Reciprocity Treaty had been on the rise in the Northern states since early 1864. The St. Alban's raid, following on a second plot against Johnson's Island in Lake Erie, would further jeopardize relations between the North and the colonies. Britain still maintained over ten thousand troops in British North America, thirty-five hundred of them in the Maritimes, yet Canada's government seemed frightened by American sabre rattling. In light of the Canadian authorities' initial mishandling of the fugitive St. Alban's raiders, bellicose Northern newspapers talked confidently of war with England.[54] The Canadian delegates who visited the Maritime colonies spoke on defence issues, arguing that a united British North America would be more secure militarily.[55]

Northern officials resented any British connections, real or imagined, to blockade evasion. Near the war's end, in summarizing colonial support for the Rebels, Frederick William Seward, who had visited the Atlantic colonies in 1857, admitted to a British official that Nova Scotia had not been a base for hostile raids. But the colony had served as a "naval station" for blockade runners, "a rendezvous for piratical cruizers" and "a postal dispatch station" for the Confederacy. Halifax merchants and shippers had been "willing agents and abettors of the enemies of the United States."[56]

Nova Scotia's links, although minor, were visible, and continued Confederate traffic through Halifax was a cause of concern. Major Norman Walker had returned to the colony in October 1864. He remained in Halifax until the early New Year until the fall of Fort Fisher and the effective closure of Wilmington ruined his plans for purchasing and arming a successor to the *Tallahassee*. By this time even ardent partisans were having doubts about Southern survival. Halifax merchants who had planned to expand trade with an independent South had to consider alternatives. The price of cotton began to fall after the Battle of Mobile Bay in August and Atlanta's capture in September. Sherman's march through Georgia and the Union victory at Nashville in December re-emphasized for outside observers that the Rebels were on their last legs.[57]

The rapidly changing military situation to the south and the growing public discussion of Confederation encouraged Maritimers to ponder their own political destiny. Charles Tupper urged Nova Scotia

to consider a colonial federation. But most colonists preferred independence over union with Canada. Economic indicators suggested
that the post-war era would be unsettling. By early 1865, New Brunswick's custom revenues were down, receipts for the government-
owned European and North American Railroad were falling and
shipbuilding activity had all but halted.[58]

Although annexation would become more of a tangible expression after 1867, many colonists, paradoxically, supported becoming
part of the United States. B.H. Norton, U.S. consul at Pictou, had
believed since early in his tenure that trade and investment would
eventually absorb Nova Scotia and all of British North America
into the republic. The benefits of leaving the British fold would
be prosperity – the goal that had drawn thousands of Maritimers
to America – and an escape from Canadian domination. The New
York *Daily News* summarized these conflicting sentiments: "There
are many, even of those who warmly espouse the cause of the South,
who lean kindly to Annexation to the States and regard that country
as a model for guidance and emanation."[59]

10 Echoes of War

There's no knowing now which had the right of it, for a brave man
makes a brave cause, and blood's the one colour, North or South.
But whichever jacket he wore, the Bluenose was an honest man
and a fighting man and a credit to Nova Scotia.
    – Thomas H. Raddall, "Blind McNair,"
    Tambour and Other Stories (1945)

In March 1866, several months after most of the huge Union army
had been disbanded, Charles Vaughan of Halifax turned out with
the members of his Nova Scotian volunteer militia battalion. This
was not a drill but a partial mobilization of volunteers in the event
of a possible attack. The colonial administrator had received a coded
telegram warning of belligerent action emanating from the United
States. Volunteer infantry and artillery manned defensive positions
around the harbour, and munitions were delivered to outlying
batteries. Colonists living along the New Brunswick and Canadian
borders were equally alarmed. Outstanding issues such as the
Alabama claims continued to irritate Anglo-American relations.
However, the colonial authorities and officers of the garrison feared
raids not by the American army or navy but by Fenians, Irish Americans bent on liberating Ireland from British rule. A significant number
of members of both branches of American Fenianism were Civil
War veterans. British military strength in North America had been
declining since January 1864, but there were still eight thousand
troops in Canada plus the detachments at Halifax and Fredericton.
The Royal Navy maintained nearly thirty vessels, mostly versatile
frigates, on the North America and West Indies station.[1]

Vaughan must have found his situation ironic. In May of 1861
the twenty-three-year-old Bluenose, then working as a barber in
South Boston, had enlisted in Company A of the 29th Massachusetts
Volunteer Infantry. The unit, under fire at Big Bethel two weeks
later, spent the winter of 1861–62 at Newport News, Virginia. During

the following summer the regiment was transferred to the Irish Brigade and saw action during the Peninsular campaign at Fair Oaks, Gaines Mills, Savage Station, Nelson's Farm and Malvern Hill. During the last battle, where Union gunners mauled Lee's troops, Vaughan had carried the brigade colours on the field. Discharged from the 29th Massachusetts in the fall after complaining of remittent fever and a back injury, he returned to his parents' home in Nova Scotia for most of the 1860s. In 1864 he married Bridget Mary Power at St. Mary's Cathedral. The veteran of the Army of the Potomac, despite a war injury, did not give up military pursuits but joined the local volunteers where his marksmanship was noted.[2]

As part of the Halifax Volunteer Battalion, in 1866 Vaughan was guarding against possible attack by former officers and men of the Irish Brigade. With elements of the British garrison being sent to New Brunswick, the governor had decided to call out five hundred volunteers. Fortifications were reinforced with palisades as the defenders prepared to repel Fenian ironclads. Trees obstructing Fort Olgivie at Point Pleasant were felled, and Armstrong guns, smooth-bores and mortars were positioned and sighted. The 3rd Regiment of the Halifax Militia was placed under oath and issued Enfields and sword bayonets. Possible landing places such as Eastern Passage and McNab's Island were guarded. The 8th Regiment of the county militia was assembled and armed at Bedford. Two hundred men over the age of forty-five volunteered as special constables to patrol the streets.[3]

To fully understand the nervousness of the Maritime colonies that spring, it is necessary to return to the final months of the American war. The year 1865 had opened with a Confederate loss, with direct repercussions for the port of Halifax. On 15 January, Fort Fisher was stormed; Wilmington fell within weeks, followed by the doggedly defended port of Charleston.[4] The developing military situation caused most colonial editors to accept the inevitability of Northern victory, but a number of regional journals such as Saint John's influential *Telegraph* stubbornly persisted in hoping for Southern independence. Cities had been evacuated, ports closed and entire armies destroyed, but there remained the possibility that the Rebels were capable of one last great battle. Perhaps they would arm the slaves. Halifax's Charles Pilsbury wrote a series of public letters predicting a punishing guerrilla war; he believed Lee, like Washington at Valley Forge, would fight on. Pilsbury did not regret the curtailment of blockade running, which at heart was a mercenary activity that exploited the South's isolation. In a letter to Dr. W.J. Almon, Confederate purchasing agent Major Norman

Walker opined that the loss of Fort Fisher would make little difference to the course of the war. Walker had cause to be less blasé. Smuggling by steamers had kept the Confederate armies armed, clothed and fed for most of 1864; by the spring of 1865, stockpiled supplies would fail to reach the surviving armies.[5]

In the last few months of the war, steamers specializing in running the blockade were increasingly rare in Nova Scotia waters. *Old Dominion* cleared for Bermuda in January, carrying the Walkers and their "little Bluenose," six-week-old Edith.[6] A month later, Consul Jackson was instrumental in a seizure by revenue officers of a dozen cases of revolvers and ammunition which had been forwarded from Boston for reshipment to the West Indies.[7] The *City of Petersburg*, which cleared soon thereafter, and the Universal Trading Co.'s *Helen*, in Consul Jackson's view, would probe the blockade off Galveston. The Texas coast was the last hope of companies engaged in Confederate supply. In February the mail steamer from Boston brought officers and crew of the captured runner *Charlotte* and fifty-four officers and men captured from CSS *Florida* who had been held in Fort Warren. The Confederates embarked for England after reaching Halifax. The *City of Petersburg*, consigned to G.C. Harvey, reached port the same month. In March a schooner from New Providence landed a Confederate major and several pilots and signalmen who had guided blockade runners. Later in the month came the steamers *Secret*, *Virginia*, *Chicora* and *Druid*, three of them with goods for B. Wier and Co. *Chicora*, owned by the Chicora Importing and Exporting Company of South Carolina, was the last steamer to exit Charleston before its evacuation. The Liverpool-built craft, sister to *Colonel Lamb* (and eventually renamed *Letter B)* completed all fourteen of its attempts through the blockade. It was sold at Halifax and ended up as a pleasure boat on the Great Lakes. *Druid* was an older Glasgow-built sidewheeler that had eluded the blockaders on eight occasions. The other vessels arrived in the western Atlantic after the Union navy had effectively closed Wilmington and Charleston. *Secret*, which never tested the blockade, was purchased at Halifax by the Quebec Steamship Co.[8]

At Nassau and Bermuda, merchants were stuck with millions of dollars worth of luxury goods, foodstuffs, clothing and military supplies. Part of this stock was dumped on the Maritime market in the spring and summer at cut-rate prices. The *Cape Breton News*, for example, advertised goods from Nassau such as cottons, prints and woolens. The cargoes landed at Halifax included drugs, shoes and boots, preserved meat and saddlery. As late as 1866, one newspaper was advertising a sizeable quantity of Confederate grey cloth. Trade patterns gradually normalized. The end of the blockade did not cut colonial commerce with the South. The volume of Maritime shipping entering Charleston, it turned out, grew substantially in the post-war years because cotton, a bulk commodity, could still be carried more cheaply by sail than by steam. Southern economic resurgence in the 1870s helped prolong the life of the large Maritime deep-sea sailing fleet.[9]

The colonial economic and political situation of 1865 was much affected by external forces. The U.S. Senate approved the abrogation of the Reciprocity Treaty in January, distressing news for producers and shippers of natural products but an encouraging development for promoters of colonial union.[10] From January to March the Canadian parliament debated the Confederation proposals framed at Quebec the previous year. Colonial federation was dealt a temporary blow by the defeat of the New Brunswick government in March; the colony's "Antis," represented by the Saint John *Globe* and *Freeman*, favoured independence and "Western Extension," the completion of the European and North American Railroad to the Maine border. They controlled thirty-four seats in the assembly but lacked unanimity. Opposition had developed over the specifics of the Quebec scheme, not the principle of union. The economy was the foremost political issue of the day; Confederation had been portrayed as an enormous tax grab.[11] New Brunswick's Anti-Confederates embraced a "pro-American economic policy," hoping for a new preferential trading arrangement. The exodus of young, single Maritimers to the States not only continued but heightened.[12]

The language of the American war, interestingly, affected the New Brunswick contest, often in confusing ways. The rebellion had infiltrated popular culture and everyday conversation. Confederate and Union war songs were more popular than ever. The *Globe* described politicians at the Quebec Conference as "Confederate delegates"; a Yarmouth journal spoke of "the new Confederacy." Anti leader Albert J. Smith had warned the electors of Westmoreland that forced union with Canada would end in rebellion; during the 1865 campaign he argued that New Brunswickers, once part of Confederation, would have no recourse but violent secession. The Saint John *Freeman* referred to an Anti gathering at Quaco as an "anti-slavery meeting" and noted that, in the excitement "for the struggle for independence for our country," New Brunswickers had barely noticed the fall of Charleston, South Carolina. The "Confederates" were described as secretly organizing for war upon the New Brunswick constitution.[13]

The imagery of war had filtered into political discourse. At a

Halifax banquet, Canada's John A. Macdonald was cheered when he suggested that British North America, with a population smaller than that of the white "Southern Republic," could ably defend itself. In speeches from Charlottetown to Toronto, Maritime delegates reflected the impact of the American war on popular consciousness. Pro-Confederation Charles Fisher recalled that New Brunswick's western border had been sacrificed to benefit "cotton spinners and tobacco growers." Anti-republican T. Heath Haviland of P.E.I. predicted a war of "civil and religious liberty" between Canada and America. Nova Scotia's Adams Archibald was confident that British North American union would succeed as American union had failed.[14]

Joseph Howe worked hard on behalf of Reciprocity in 1865, delivering a well-received speech to the Detroit Commercial Convention in July. Nova Scotians initially had resented the arrangement for granting Americans access to their fishery, but in the interim they had come to equate the treaty with commercial vitality. Howe told his business audience that British North America, appearances aside, had supported the Northern war effort and had engaged in very little direct trade with the Rebels. And hundreds of colonials returning from service in the war had left "scores of their companions behind to enrich the soil." Back home the press predicted dark days for Maritime shipping, lumbering, mining and agriculture should Reciprocity end. Four-fifths of Nova Scotia's valuable coal exports in the 1850s and early 1860s, for example, had been consumed in the United States.[15]

The issue of British North American union would not die, largely because of initiatives from Britain and Canada. By mid-summer the Canadian parliament was dominated by a coalition committed to Confederation. In Nova Scotia, Conservative leader Charles Tupper and a number of journalists and business leaders remained interested, but an American visitor in February was informed that most assembly members were opposed. Instead they debated Maritime Union. A series of Confederation meetings had been held on Prince Edward Island starting in late 1864 and the lieutenant-governor had endorsed the measure. The premier, however, had not, and the government vowed to resist British pressure. The Island's only response to outside political influence was a slight improvement in its militia system. By summer, politicians and the press were more preoccupied with Tenant League agitation and a local "land war." The language of combat was prominent in political discourse. One tenant meeting denounced the colony's "slave-holding system." Following a series of incidents involving tenant resistance to landlords, bailiffs and the courts, the government asked for assistance. Two companies of the 17th Regiment arrived from Halifax on the steamer *Merlin* in early August. In this case the "rebels" had not advocated their own country, merely a reform of the Island's distinct landholding system. A squad of redcoats left for the country with the Queen's County sheriff, a magistrate and several bailiffs. The *Islander* warned rebellious tenants that the law would be enforced even with "the bayonet or the minie ball."[16]

The Canadian government, following the embarrassment of the St. Alban's raid and evidence of partiality on the part of legal officials in the trials of the raiders, had enacted an Alien Act which tightly controlled the activities of Confederate plotters. As a reward, the passport system was rescinded for Canada on 8 March 1865. The Canadian treatment of the St. Alban's raiders and other Confederates incensed the Halifax *Reporter*, which saw it as a violation of the British tradition of political asylum. The Northern government pressured New Brunswick to pass similar legislation, but Governor Gordon saw little need, largely because of the political risks involved in instituting a policy perceived as pro-Northern. The Smith administration attempted to improve security by raising militia spending and lengthening the training period for volunteers. The Maritimes suffered the passport system until June, weeks after the cessation of hostilities.[17]

Most Maritime newspapers welcomed the news of Lee's surrender at Appomattox, although many paid tribute to Confederate honour and bravery. The Yarmouth *Tribune*, for example, concluded that although the rebellion had produced great evil, not all Southerners were villainous. Pictou diarist W.N. Rudolf acknowledged slavery's destruction but clung to a common Calvinist view of the war as providential punishment of both South and North. William J. Stairs, who had sympathized with the Rebels, agreed that God's will had reversed the tide of the South: "The North was the instrument of good and holy temper." John Allison Bell of Halifax wrote that abolition was only incidental to Union victory and that large sections of Northern society were hostile to the Negro. Intelligence of Lee's capitulation did not reach Prince Edward Island until 16 April. The following evening, unaware that his president had been shot, Consul J.H. Sherman entertained American residents and friends with illuminated windows, fireworks, rockets and band music. With the tables loaded with fruit, wine and champagne, national toasts pledged friendly relations between the powers. Recognizing the normalization of relations, the Nova Scotia government cleared up a minor grievance left over from Brain's raid;

it obtained the church bell given away at La Have and returned it to its rightful congregation in Maine.[18]

After Gettysburg, British military observers paid closer attention to American weapons and tactics. With victory the North was an impressive and seasoned military power. On 1 May 1865 there were more than one million soldiers in Union service. Six months later, 80 percent of the army had been disbanded.[19]

In 1865, Hastings Doyle, who as colonial administrator had beefed up Halifax's defences earlier in the war, personally toured the Union lines near Richmond. With the Rebel defeat, former critics of Yankee barbarity and inefficiency now paid tribute to the Anglo-Saxon pluck and endurance of the Northerners and the sagacity of generals such as Grant and Sheridan. That summer Doyle warned militiamen assembled at a Fredericton camp that the Americans "would make no mean enemy."[20] In May there was a grand review at Washington, D.C., of the armies of the Potomac, Tennessee and Georgia. The victorious legions included hundreds of Maritimers. One was Thomas Inglis of P.E.I., who had marched with Sherman through Georgia and faced down Lee at Appomattox. As the Americans were gearing towards peace some colonial administrators were thinking of war. The Nova Scotia lieutenant-governor continued to improve Halifax volunteer artillery units and Pictou's harbour battery finally received new ordnance.[21]

The Union navy, large and capable in 1865, was scaled down considerably a year later. Yet America's naval capability remained considerable. As if to prove the point, in May of 1866 the USS *Mainitomah* visited Halifax, the first American ironclad to do so. Although limited as a "blue water" combat craft, the 175-foot monitor, its deck less than two feet above the water line and its profile dominated by two turrets sporting twin fifteen-inch guns, had a deadly look. The officers of *Mainitomah* and its gunboat tender were entertained by Vice-Admiral Hope, Major-General Hastings Doyle, Lieutenant-Governor Fenwick Williams and Consul Jackson. A few weeks later the officers of the gunboat USS *Winooski*, which had helped contain the Fenians on the Maine border, were honoured in similar fashion. Speeches and toasts pledged mutual friendship and peace, but John Bull was not ignoring changing naval technology. During the protracted visit of America's "naval wonder," Halifax also hosted the "sullen, dangerous-looking" HMS *Favourite*, an armoured monitor that represented a new era for the Royal Navy.[22]

The termination of hostilities did not end colonial fascination with events to the south. Maritimers who consulted local and American newspapers, conversed with friends and co-workers or received letters from the States were well aware of the war's tremendous losses in lives and property. A New Brunswicker travelling to Iowa saw the famous Shenandoah Valley on his way west; the once-fair region was desolate and gloomy. A special correspondent to John Livingston's *Telegraph*, in Richmond by early August, described poverty, property destruction, commercial ruin and widespread anxiety about the future of Southern race relations. Writing from St. Louis in July, former Liberal premier of P.E.I. George Coles reported that he had spent an "agreeable half hour" with that practitioner of total war, General William Tecumseh Sherman. The brewer and the despoiler of Georgia discussed the war, trade relations and colonial fisheries.[23]

The assassination of President Lincoln was a cathartic event that caused Maritimers of all persuasions to accept the finality of Confederate defeat. Halifax's *Sun* lauded Lincoln as an "uncorrupted and incorruptible martyr." Even the pro-Southern *Reporter* found Booth's deed horrific. In the ensuing weeks the Northern authorities and press, convinced that Lincoln's death was part of a larger conspiracy, sought scapegoats at home and abroad. These included individuals with Nova Scotia connections, such as Jacob Thompson, Clement Clay, Beverly Tucker and George Sanders. All four Confederates had operated in Canada and passed through Halifax. British and American diplomatic correspondence continued to mention allegations of Nova Scotia–linked conspiracies until April 1865. Consul Jackson's monitoring of Southerners and anti-Union sentiment continued after the cessation of hostilities. Jacob Thompson, following Lee's surrender, was nearly arrested in Maine but released on Lincoln's order. He arrived in Halifax in Benjamin Wier's personal carriage on 14 April before departing for England. That evening the president was fatally wounded while attending the theatre in Washington.[24]

The assassination's effect on the colonies was immediate and electric; the Nova Scotia legislature adjourned and sent condolences to the president's widow. In most towns of the region, business came to a halt and flags flew at half-mast on both the morning of Lincoln's passing and the day of his interment. In Yarmouth the news produced "a spontaneous emotion of profound sorrow." At Charlottetown a special sermon was preached in the Baptist church. The governor's throne speech to the New Brunswick legislature expressed similar regrets. The funeral was commemorated in Saint John by a series of speeches at a local hotel. The city staged an elaborate memorial exercise a few weeks later on the day of mourn-

ing that had been ordered by President Johnson. The consul and
mayor were joined on the stage of the Mechanics Institute by several
clergy, politicians and officials. British and American flags were
interwoven and the walls of the hall were decorated with the words
"liberty, justice and peace." C.M. Ellis, a Massachusetts senator,
delivered a lengthy oration that commenced with the political history
of slavery and traced the rise of the Republican party. Ellis stressed
the parallels between the United States and Britain and applauded
their joint mission to spread the benefits of freedom, eulogized
Honest Abe and castigated the leaders of the rebellion as pawns
of the Devil. Another speaker proclaimed the crime a blow against
liberty, jurisprudence and right. Reverend Elder explained how
Maritimers were personally touched by the tragedy. Ultra-Protes-
tant John Boyd, who had met Lincoln, compared his historic legacy
to Cromwell's. On 4 July the *Globe* paid tribute to the Stars and
Stripes, noting that America's day of regeneration was at hand.[25]

Halifax, typically, could not escape controversy in the wake of
Lincoln's death. On 13 April the city had been in a festive mood
as citizens had welcomed New Brunswick's Confederation delegates
prior to their departure for London with their Nova Scotia counterparts. A number of vessels anchored in the harbour unwittingly
flew Confederate flags the day the telegraph relayed news of the
shooting. They included the *Chicora*, *Jewel* and English-built
sidewheeler *Dream*, which like the *Secret* and *Virginia* had reached
Nassau too late to safely enter Wilmington. Captain Tom Lockwood
on the *Colonel Lamb* was even bolder, carrying a number of ladies
and gentlemen on a pleasure excursion. The vessel, owned by John
Fraser and Co., was Lockwood's pride and joy. He personally had
supervised its construction with a resulting price tag of fifty-thou-
sand pounds. Following complaints from the U.S. consul and others,
the lieutenant-governor instructed the captain of HMS *Medea* to use
force, if necessary, to remove the offending banners. Lockwood
apologized to MacDonnell, insisting that he and his colleagues had
been unaware of the shocking news.[26]

The war had been an obvious theme for ministers' sermons. Generally they avoided explicit political commentary, played on Calvinist themes and urged colonists to give thanks for being spared
separation, destruction and brutality. One Confederate soldier in
four died; the Union ratio was one in six. But the loss of a single
individual to the assassin's hand now produced a sudden, focused
outburst of sorrow in neutral British territory. For many of the
undecided, it was an epiphany that placed them squarely on the
side of the North. A number of clergymen alluded to Lincoln during

their Easter sermons. Universalist Nathaniel Gunnison, who had acted as American consul in 1863–64, drew parallels with Christ's crucifixion. In both cases a redeemer had been sacrificed for the greater good. In a letter published in Boston, Gunnison criticized Haligonians for their lukewarm display of sympathy following the assassination. The uproar that followed drove the New Englander from the colony.[27] Union partisans in the city council attempted to secure a resolution of sympathy akin to that of the provincial government's, a move that produced only rancour. Alderman Roche, who in 1864 had openly sympathized with Almon, Keith and Smith for their interference on Queen's wharf, protested that nine-tenths of the city's inhabitants would not endorse the measure.[28]

Northern opinion was understandably touchy following the president's murder and prompted fears of vengeance in the colonies. The *Colonial Farmer* trusted America's political leaders but not the Yankee people.[29] Maine had suffered heavily from the depredations of Rebel raiders and, although certain areas resented military conscription, had contributed disproportionately to the war effort. Border security was a burning issue during the conflict. As late as the spring of 1865 a delegation had waited upon the secretary of the navy for a war steamer to patrol Maine's shores. According to officials, the state's French settlements, located in a number of the forty border counties, had experienced widespread draft evasion. Maine capitalists easily interpreted British neutrality as a plot to ruin Northern shipping and commerce. The Eastport *Sentinel* reported any colonial slights on American honour, such as the curt treatment of a U.S. revenue cutter at Saint John, and advised New Brunswickers that the punishment of Jefferson Davis was none of their business.[30] Bitter and somewhat exaggerated memories of British collusion with the rebels would shape American views for a half century.[31]

Consular officials remained alert in the wake of the so-called Lincoln conspiracy. J.Q. Howard recorded the presence of Southern insurgents in Saint John and recommended a man-of-war to patrol the coast of Maine. As late as December he feared that traitors such as Clement C. Clay would organize a new raid on Calais. From Charlottetown an angry Consul Sherman wrote that the people of the Maritimes, "without distinction, are our bitterest enemies." Several weeks after the assassination he advised the retention of the passport system owing to the character of individuals roaming the colonies intent on carrying out hostile acts against the United States. Charlottetown, which during the war had sheltered few Southern émigrés, was now frequented by a Confederate veteran who had uttered threats against the new President, Andrew Johnson. Passport controls on the Maine–New Brunswick border were not lifted until June.[32]

Colonial commentary on the assassination and its aftermath, largely because of latent anti-republicanism, was not uniformly sympathetic. The New Brunswick *Reporter* mourned Lincoln but was shocked by the summary treatment of a number of the alleged parties to the conspiracy; their trial, conviction and execution constituted little more than "judicial murder." A correspondent to Prince Edward Island's *Vindicator* charged the late president as a willing accomplice to "more butchery than could even be charged to Napoleon." Others were more concerned by the removal of a moderate leader who had held the more radical Republicans in check. A number of commentators lamented that Andrew Johnson, an alleged drunkard, was now in charge of the world's most powerful republic.[33]

The reaction of Maritime blacks to Northern victory, given the dearth of surviving written sources, can only be surmised. Lincolnville, a small black community in rural Guysborough County, may have been named in honour of the president associated with emancipation. Even the illiterate would have been acquainted with the war's highlights. Church activities were one forum for news and discussion, and the African minority had kin and friends in the Northern states (and presumably the South) and in the armed forces, particularly the navy. The negro volunteer regiments, and the U.S. Colored Troops, which included Maritime-born blacks, were important role models. In theory, the Northern victory allowed Maritime blacks to safely link up with long-lost relatives from the Chesapeake region. But seafaring jobs were more likely to take black males to Boston, New York and Philadelphia. Reconstruction, despite its mixed record, and Northern civil rights advances probably encouraged more colonial blacks to emigrate to New England.[34]

On Emancipation Day in 1865, Halifax's "coloured folk" embarked on a steamer to the Bedford Basin to view boat races and then sailed to the Northwest Arm for a picnic. One-third of the province's several thousand blacks lived in and around Halifax, offering opportunities for a small middle class, voluntary organizations and community life. By now most of the black residents of Hammonds Plains, Preston and Halifax proper were Nova Scotia–born. Both their community leaders and white authority figures taught the value of British institutions. The war had eradicated North American slavery but had not solved complex questions surrounding the social relations of the races. In 1866, Haligonians flocked to the melodrama "Octoroon, or Life in Louisiana" and applauded its anti-slavery message. The play, which contained a slave auction scene, had been a favourite at the Saint John Lyceum since 1860; a production of "Uncle Tom's Cabin" was another hit that year.[35]

The stage was a fitting setting for sentimental humanitarianism. But the streets, workshops, schools and public conveyances of the Maritimes proved impervious to radical change in racial attitudes. Fighting broke out at a dance held by the Halifax Abolition Society at the Masonic Hall, confirming white stereotypes of local blacks. Blacks, in the words of Winks, were somehow "unnatural to the Northern landscape."[36] Popular culture continued to suggest the placement of a wise gulf between the races. Social segregation, minstrel shows, "Rastus" jokes in the press and everyday expressions indicated that black Maritimers lived in a "bicultural world."[37]

The perceived experience of civil war and emancipation in America, like West Indies abolition a generation earlier, tempted many white Maritimers to make excuses for racial bondage.[38] Most accepted social inferiority for blacks as a given. William Smith, Collector of Customs at Saint John, advised that the Negro should

be treated like a child; he should be governed with firmness, decision and discipline as well as kindness, but, as far as my experience goes. . . . I am convinced that he is not capable of governing himself and political agitation will only excite him, and render him a dangerous element in the hands of demagogues.[39]

Another echo of the war with a Maritime connection was the Blackburn plot. Luke Blackburn, a Southern physician who had testified at the *Chesapeake* trial in Saint John, had offered his professional services to the authorities in Bermuda during an upsurge of yellow fever and in return had received the official thanks of the Admiralty. After Lincoln's death, the American consul general for Canada was informed that Dr. Blackburn had masterminded a scheme involving clothing contaminated with yellow fever. The infected garments supposedly were shipped from Maritime and Canadian ports for sale in unsuspecting Northern cities.[40] Maritimers were familiar with "yellow jack" because it had carried off a number of their sailors, captains and merchants in the tropics. The fever could not be transmitted by direct contact, but this was unknown to Victorian medical science. Contemporaries feared that Blackburn, a Southerner financed by the sale of cotton in Havana, was guilty of biological warfare against helpless civilians. A story in a Toronto newspaper focused on Blackburn's accomplice, J.W. Harris alias Hyman. Harris, who was working as a shoemaker in Toronto, allegedly had visited Halifax from Canada in 1864. Before leaving

Montreal for Riviere du Loup and Grand Falls, the Arkansas native had allegedly obtained funds from Professor Holcombe. In Halifax he met Alexander Keith who functioned as a messenger for Confederates on secret business. Also present was C.W. Hunley, a Southerner who took part in the St. Alban's raid. While in the city, Harris was shadowed by "detectives," either Union agents or employees of the consul. Blackburn, and the infected clothing, supposedly arrived in Halifax from Bermuda on 12 July 1864.[41]

Following so closely on Lincoln's assassination, the alleged plot shocked Northerners and British North Americans alike. Blackburn had spent time in both Saint John and Halifax and had been wined and dined in a manner fitting a Southern gentleman. A controversy now erupted: did Halifax medical men know of his scheme in advance? Drs. Slayter and Jennings signed affidavits denying prior knowledge and Dr. Charles Tupper, head of the government, issued a disclaimer. The trunks supposedly were carried to Boston on the bark *Halifax* (its captain denied this) and the garments were sold in Baltimore, Philadelphia and Washington. Like all Civil War spy stories, the yellow fever plot probably was nine-tenths fabrication. Yet a Canadian magistrate felt compelled to place Dr. Blackburn under arrest for violating British neutrality. Months later he was brought to trial but discharged due to lack of evidence. In the meantime, Halifax's prestige in the North was dealt another blow.[42]

Several prominent Confederates spent time in Halifax at the war's end; a number of them, such as John Taylor Wood, decided to settle there. Wood, after a series of adventures eluding Yankee pursuers in Florida, arrived on the blockade runner *Lark* from Cuba in early July. The steamer was consigned to Benjamin Wier, who shortly thereafter sold his share in the trading house Wier and Co. That month a Southern exile organized a relief effort for his devastated homeland; a local merchant, probably Wier, donated provisions and the use of a wharf and warehouse. Dr. Richard Randolph Stephenson, formerly in the Confederate service, established himself at Stewiacke, outside of Halifax. Like W.B. Almon II, he penned letters to the press that took issue with Northern accounts of Confederate prison camps. The Kentuckian was in a position to know – he had served as chief medial officer at the infamous Andersonville prison. Stephenson left the province in 1873 to practice medicine in Virginia and write an apologia for the Rebel prison system. He returned a number of years later, remarried and set up a practice at Little River.[43]

In May of 1865 the United States government lifted most of the blockade east of the Mississippi. At the same time the British government instructed the colonies to deny coal and supplies to Confederate vessels. One commerce raider, CSS *Shenandoah*, continued to destroy Yankee whalers and merchantmen in the Pacific for months after cessation of the war. The Nova Scotia authorities were warned by London not to assist the vessel.[44]

A number of former smugglers and Confederate naval officers straggled into Nova Scotia over that summer. The steamer *Foam*, formerly *Owl*, commanded by J.N. Maffitt of *Florida* fame, dropped anchor on 12 July. Maffitt had steamed from Galveston, still under Rebel control, to Havana and was now on his way to Liverpool. Two weeks later the *Rothesay Castle*, built in Scotland in 1861, followed. It was purchased by local capitalists for use as a coastal packet.[45]

Halifax and Saint John had been visited by a sizeable minority of the estimated 350 Civil War blockade-running steamers. The two ports had serviced at least fifty vessels of this class and their presence generally elicited public interest and support. But few of these craft had voyaged directly between the Maritimes and Confederate ports; most were on transatlantic cruises or runs from the Caribbean. Halifax's great attraction was repair facilities. At least some of the cargo carried between the West Indies and Nova Scotia by local barques and schooners was connected to the blockade. In addition, Halifax, Saint John and other ports such as Yarmouth had links with an unknown number of smaller, wind-powered craft which violated the blockade from Louisiana to the Carolinas. Yet a sense of perspective is needed – much more of the region's trade and shipping was with Northern ports such as Boston and New York than with Wilmington and Charleston or the entrepots at New Providence or Bermuda. New Brunswick's official exports to Nassau in 1864 were less than four percent of its total sales to the United States. Trade with the West Indies, furthermore, was perfectly legal.[46]

The list of Rebel refugees, travellers and settlers continued to grow. Captain T.J. Page, who had brought the French-built ram *Stonewall* across the Atlantic to attack a Union base in North Carolina, sold it to the Cuban government and paid off his crew; he and two other officers reached Halifax on the runner *Ptarmigan* in June and continued on to England.[47] John R. Wilkinson of the *Robert E. Lee* also found his way back to the Nova Scotia capital. In time he entered into business with John Taylor Wood. The partners proudly flew the Confederate flag at their waterfront establishment. Wood later went into business for himself and managed a line of steamships trading with Newfoundland. He served as secretary of the harbour pilotage commission and was active in the Church of

England and yachting circles. The skipper of the *Tallahassee* raised his family in Halifax and was regarded as a supporter of not only Canada but the British Empire. One of his sons became an officer in the Northwest Mounted Police and the other was killed in the Boer War.[48]

The former second lieutenant of the *Alabama*, R.F. Armstrong, also made Halifax his home, becoming a British subject and serving as general agent for the Grand Trunk Railroad in the Maritimes. Merchant William J. Stairs recorded that three other Confederate officers spent the summer of 1865 in the city; one, Captain Darney, was a guest at Stair's own home. Other officers who reached the colony included G.T. Sinclair, his son Lieutenant George T. Sinclair, Jr. and Lieutenant of Marines B.K. Howell (the last two both from the *Alabama*). Commodore Josiah Tattnall rounded out the migration of Confederate naval officers in 1866; he resided in Dartmouth for a period before returning to Georgia. Armstrong and fellow Southerners F.L. Page and B.H. Hornby purchased property in Dartmouth for the manufacture of tobacco. These individuals appreciated the conduct of local pro-Confederates. In August 1865, Dr. W.J. Almon was presented with a gift by Southern gentlemen for his services on behalf of their cause.[49]

Most of the *Chesapeake* pirates disappeared into obscurity, but several key participants were heard from again. Predictably, John Brain was unable to escape notoriety. In the declining days of the war, Master Brain led a small party in the capture by ruse of the Baltimore schooner *St. Mary's* in the Chesapeake region. The captors intercepted a second schooner, loaded on the crew of the *St. Mary's* and sailed to Nassau. There the U.S. consul requested the British authorities to intervene, but it was decided that the capture had been a belligerent act, not piracy. Brain was next reported at Kingston, Jamaica, where he abandoned his prize and booked passage for Liverpool. He was arrested in the United States for murder and piracy in 1866 and remained imprisoned, without trial, for three years. In a press interview he was described as "the last Confederate prisoner of war." After his release he went south, lecturing in Florida and Texas and living off his wits. In 1903, Brain was arrested for defrauding a Maryland hotel – old habits die hard. Three years later the leader of the *Chesapeake* expedition was dead.[50]

Vernon Locke remained in the States after the war and continued to follow the sea. Diplomatic correspondence in 1865 recorded that the former Bluenose had landed at Nassau in February where he was arrested on complaint of the American consul. The State Department was confident that Locke could be extradited on charges arising out of the *Chesapeake* incident. Earl Russell advised Charles Francis Adams that Locke first would be examined for offences alleged to have been perpetrated on British soil. He appears to have been cleared of any charges soon after. In the summer of 1890, Locke was skippering the sail boat *Marion* out of a Boston yacht club. On his final cruise off New Hampshire the vessel hit a rock, forcing the party to take to a small boat. This capsized and Locke and two others, unable to cling to the gunwales, perished. George Robinson died the same way when a boat overturned in Halifax harbour in 1865. Henry Parr acquired the status of a naturalized British subject at Yarmouth in 1867. In July of 1865, he had been reported as having sailed from Cuba to Nassau after taking part in the capture of the *St. Mary's*. The pirate-apothecary entered the drug and medicine trade, married locally and eventually branched out into dentistry. Years later he relocated his practice to New York where he prospered, despite the minor inconvenience of being arrested for the murder of Orin Schaffer.[51]

Linus Seely reappeared in Saint John early in 1865 at a time when authorities on both sides of the border were agitated by the St. Alban's raid. Several of the raiders, twice freed by Canadian courts, had disappeared in Canada East. The American State Department suspected that Bennett Young and other raiders may have fled to New Brunswick, whose governor came under immediate diplomatic pressure to issue a preliminary warrant of arrest.[52] Although Arthur Hamilton Gordon personally approved of a British government suggestion that the colony enact an Aliens Law, he deemed it politically inadvisable.[53]

Gordon also was notified by the U.S. consul that a number of the *Chesapeake* fugitives had reappeared in the vicinity of Saint John. The governor, who had been absent for several months, was anxious to cooperate. Provincial Secretary Tilley requested the county sheriff to execute the outstanding warrant. George Wade had arrived on the Boston steamer. The police watched his wife's residence and the sheriff placed his father under surveillance, but Wade somehow escaped this dragnet and trekked to Halifax where he shipped out as a sailor. The two Cox brothers, reported as making shingles in nearby woods, escaped because of problems in identification. Seely was apprehended by the county sheriff; Police Chief Marshall contended that if he had possessed Justice Parker's warrant he could have nabbed more of the pirates. Consul Howard feared that Seely's venereal disease was so advanced that he would be judged incompetent to stand trial. Yet he was pleased that public opinion in New Brunswick was "entirely changed."[54]

Seely was committed to trial after an examination by two judges. The Court for the Trial of Piracy and Offenses on the High Seas convened in May, in the midst of Northern hysteria about the Lincoln plot and the fate of Jefferson Davis. The accused could not be extradited, but the American government, eager that someone be punished, sent witnesses and a lawyer to aid the prosecution. The grand jury returned a true bill and the prisoner was committed to trial. Seely, a convicted felon with no friends or money, was defended once more by John Hamilton Gray and his colleague Weldon. Gray's basic defence was that his client had a weak mind and had honestly believed that Brain's mission was an act of war. The jury acquitted the prisoner, much to Consul Howard's disgust. Justice Ritchie's summation to the jury, in Howard's estimation, had prejudiced the court and secured a ruling that defied the authority of both the American and New Brunswick governments. The Imperial law officers in London concurred with the court's findings. A decade later Seely got into an argument with another man in a bar in Saint John's south end. The fight moved into the street, a shot rang out and the noted jailbird was mortally wounded. Seely, as the Victorians would say, was "launched into eternity" only blocks from where Brain and Locke had hatched the *Chesapeake* plot in 1863.[55]

THE FENIANS AND UNION

John A. Macdonald stretched the truth in 1865 when he described the seaboard colonies as "powerless, scattered, helpless communities." New Brunswick, Prince Edward Island and Nova Scotia were still protected by British seapower.[56] They also were protected, in the words of one Island commentator, by their insignificance.[57] Canada was the most vulnerable, and most valuable, target of any possible American assault on British North America. Yet the Maritimes were not beyond danger.

The cult of militarism and increased preparedness of the 1860s proved invaluable to New Brunswick after the Civil War when American Fenians became a source of consternation. Warned in December of 1865 by the British representative in Washington of possible trouble, Governor Gordon inspected the frontier and began to organize a defence. Detectives hired by the British consul in Washington surveyed a number of Maine towns but discovered little in the way of Fenian plotting. The attorney general conferred with Saint John police authorities and bankers who feared for their deposits. Local militia officers plotted defence strategy and all suspicious arrivals on the American steamer were monitored. Starting in January the Home Guard was on duty near Woodstock, New Brunswick. HMS *Pylades* left Halifax for the Bay of Fundy, carrying guns for the Negro Point battery opposite Saint John. Charlotte County residents had blamed recent militia reforms for drawing militia and volunteers away from their farms and jobs in the middle of the summer, but now they were organizing part-time home guard companies. St. Stephen, Milltown and Middle Landing mustered 250 home guards before Christmas. Companies also organized in Carleton County parishes.[58]

Governor Gordon suspected that St. Andrew's and the Fundy Isles would be the likely targets of Fenian raids. B.D. Killian, a Fenian leader in New York, had proposed an attack on the New Brunswick island of Campobello, more as a diversion that an actual invasion. The operation was dropped, but Killian's plan was revived in March of 1866. The British consul was alerted by an informer in the Fenian inner circle. The American government announced that it would tolerate no breaches of neutrality, but a number of American officials saw the Fenian complication as fitting punishment for colonial cupidity during 1861–65. Local relations between Americans and British colonists were relatively friendly and the Passamaquoddy was as an integrated economic region. The exact border in narrows between Lubec, Maine, and Campobello, however, was uncertain and gave Fenian leaders an possible base for harassing the colonies.[59]

By March of 1866, New Brunswick and its neighbours were swept by disturbing rumours of Fenian attacks, and ten thousand Canadian militia volunteers were called up. In Charlottetown, extreme Protestants stirred up panic by alleging that local Fenians would stage an uprising on St. Patrick's Day. The Island had proportionately the largest Catholic minority (much of it Scottish and Acadian) in the region. On the previous St. Patrick's Day the capital's tranquillity had been disturbed by Tenant League protestors. Now precautions were taken to secure the colony's store of public arms, which the government ordered moved from the arsenal to the barracks, and the concealment of weapons was outlawed. On the appointed day the Irish Society planned its customary parade to the Catholic chapel. The British garrison was confined to barracks on the nights leading up to 17 March, a field gun was placed in Barracks Square and fifty soldiers were issued with rounds of ball cartridge in case of rioting. The mayor called upon all magistrates to attend city hall on St. Patrick's Day and sent circulars to dozens of potential special constables. Edward Whelan, who interpreted the scare as a crass attempt on the part of the Conservatives to exploit sectarianism, alleged that local Orange lodges were meeting "full blast," their members purchasing handguns.[60]

Suspicions also fell upon Saint John's large and sometimes boisterous Irish Catholic population. The police chief investigated a report of a cache of pikes on Canterbury Street. The inherited lore of New Brunswick Orangemen automatically brought up images of the 1798 rising in Ireland. However, Chief Marshall worried more that depositors would make a run on local banks; letters from the States had warned residents to hide their gold. A bogus manifesto extolling republican virtues circulated in the city, but police detectives, working overtime, could find no Fenian circle.[61] All the same, artillery was mounted on the Martello tower at Carleton and an aged blockhouse was torn down and replaced with an earthwork whose cannon could sweep the approaches to Manawagonish Road and the suspension bridge. Guns were also placed on Partridge Island. Munitions in the Carleton tower were moved to a more secure spot across the harbour. Given the dearth of British regulars and the need to man the border, the government resorted to extreme measures, mobilizing volunteer and militia units in Charlotte, York and Saint John counties for a three-month term. Several hundred men of the New Brunswick Regiment of Artillery and the Saint John Volunteer Battalion were placed under the articles of war. St. Andrew's, which had been denuded of all armaments, was finally given a modern artillery piece to protect the harbour. Eastport's *Sentinel* and the Machias *Republican* clearly relished the predicament of Maine's neighbours.[62]

In early April, Killian and entourage reached Eastport where their activities worried authorities on both sides of the border. The Irish American filibusters were said to be well funded and to have acquired arms and ammunition for a raid in force. A Saint John detective monitoring Eastport was surprised to find them orderly, tight-lipped, "perfectly sober" and rarely on the streets past 9 p.m. The security of Campobello was jeopardized, causing many residents to flee into Maine until British troops and naval units arrived. The Fenian threat seemed to be mainly hot air until over one hundred cases of weapons were shipped in mid-April to Eastport, where they were impounded by the customs office. In all, Killian's party chartered three schooners. When the citizens of St. Stephen heard that a Fenian schooner was sailing upriver, the militia turned out, marched through the town behind the fife and drum and defied the enemy with three stout cheers for the Queen. Soon after, nocturnal raiders terrorized a New Brunswick customs collector on Indian Island and stole a British flag. They returned a week later to burn the customs house and a bonded warehouse – all the lost property there was owned by Americans. In a related incident, militia sentries on Marble Island, off Indian Island, exchanged fire with unidentified boat raiders.[63]

In a speech to the volunteer militia, Major-General Hastings Doyle vowed to give the invaders "two pence worth of powder" and attempted to stir morale by warning that the enemy intended to steal their gold and ravish their families. Doyle, an Irish Catholic, opined that the idea of an independent Ireland was preposterous and portrayed the Fenians, despite their Civil War experience, as militarily incompetent. In private he was more cautious, prepared to fall back from St. Stephen and St. Andrew's if the Irish Americans ventured across the frontier, then catch them in the open. Lieutenant Governor Gordon, however, insisted that the border be held at all costs. This would not be difficult; the would-be insurgents lacked heavy weapons and supplies and were outnumbered by the Crown forces five to one. And the Royal Navy commanded the waters of the area.[64]

The Fenians, more for show, drilled at Robbinston across the river from St. Andrew's and at Calais, setting off a momentary panic in St. Stephen where townsfolk sounded fire alarms. The militia officer who was appointed commander of the "Western frontier" employed two "secret service" men to gather intelligence. At night, sentinels and patrols watched the streets and volunteers slept with their weapons. By this time, volunteers on the New Brunswick frontier had been equipped with Enfields, and the Calais militia stood watch on the other end of the toll bridge over the St. Croix. An estimated one thousand Irishmen had gathered at Eastport and other border communities, and many of them wore parts of Civil War uniforms and carried revolvers.[65]

HMS *Pylades* made a brief call on 9 April, anchoring three miles down the bay from St. Andrew's. Its captain at first was incredulous of the seriousness of the situation. Despite the entreaties of the militia commander, the man-of-war was under orders to sail on. The Royal Navy's North American squadron was returning from duties in Jamaica, so no other vessels were available until four days later when a smaller warship, *Rosario*, reached St. Andrew's and helped secure seaward approaches to the town.[66]

Nova Scotia, although far from the "front lines," remained on alert. Halifax's military energies radiated outward. Several hundred rifled muskets were shipped to the militia of Lunenburg and Yarmouth. County militiamen, even when they lacked weapons, loyally turned out for drill across the province. The 9th Halifax

Regiment, commanded by William J. Stairs, harbourer of Confederate refugees, guarded the western approaches to the capital. Thirteen "late citizens of the Confederacy," including John Taylor Wood, notified the government that they would volunteer their services against the Fenians. The Halifax police tore down Fenian handbills and arrested one drunken Irishman who insisted that he was a member of the brotherhood. Otherwise, the streets were peaceful. In Saint John, Charlottetown and Halifax the phantom revolutionary circles failed to rise on the seventeenth.[67]

Fenian leader Killian addressed a public meeting at Calais on 16 April, disavowing any plan to invade British territory but promising to punish England for supporting the Rebels during the Civil War. His assistant, "Major" Patrick Sinnott, who claimed to be a native New Brunswicker, in the words of one journalist (who probably put words in his mouth), explained that the Irishmen wanted to "kill Confederation." The Calais authorities appealed to the state and federal governments for intervention. An American gunboat brought 350 U.S. Army Regulars to Eastport to await the arrival of the commander of the military division of the Atlantic, General Gordon Meade, of Gettysburg fame. The British also arrived on the scene. On 18 April six hundred men of the 17th Regiment (the Bengal Tigers), Royal Artillery and Royal Engineers disembarked at St. Andrew's from Vice-Admiral Hope's flagship HMS *Duncan*. The troopship *Simoon* and its corvette escort *Niger* docked at Saint John with a battalion of the 22nd (Chesire) Regiment which had been stationed at Malta. Other redcoats came from P.E.I. Vessels brought artillery and gunpowder from Nova Scotia. Halifax was reinforced by elements of the 17th Yorkshire East Regiment, transported from Malta on HMS *Tamar*.[68]

Despite this buildup, a number of minor incidents took place in late April and early May. During one escapade, Irishmen temporarily commandeered a Nova Scotia schooner. Another was arrested by Calais authorities after firing a revolver on the toll bridge. The Fenians, however, never launched their attack; their objectives in the east were mainly political. The decisive factors were the seizure of rifles by U.S. authorities and the arrival of the professional military. The St. Croix River and Passamaquoddy Bay were controlled by the Royal Navy and Federal forces. A correspondent to the *Globe* reported that while fifteen hundred redcoats and militia on the "British" side readied for war, the Fenians lounged in small groups, talking, smoking and pitching pennies. Meade, although ill, met Hastings Doyle at St. Andrew's prior to the second incident on Indian Island. The hero of Gettysburg promised that he would take the situation in hand. American soldiers were already at Eastport, a revenue cutter patrolled the St. Croix and a detachment of U.S. infantry guarded Treat's Island. Meade, who had already warned the Fenian leaders to behave, proceeded to Calais with a sizeable force; Killian left for Portland. The remaining Fenians, who expected to be paid for their services, began to drift out of Maine in small groups.[69]

On 21 April a New Brunswick journalist reported that all was quiet on the St. Croix. Yet with four British and three American warships in the vicinity, the authorities were taking few chances. The New Brunswick militia companies remained on active service until late June, taking one thousand citizen-soldiers away from their usual pursuits. Early that month another branch of the Fenians had launched an incursion into Canada West; at Ridgeway the Civil War veterans clashed with untested militia, killing nine and wounding others before withdrawing. Ridgeway proved that the Fenians were more than an amateurish, drunken rabble. Nova Scotia was in no danger, but the shedding of British blood in distant Ontario prompted spontaneous demonstrations of martial loyalty. Garrison troops were shipped to reinforce Canada, the Halifax Volunteer Battalion was called out for an additional month and enthusiastic volunteers drilled from one end of the colony to the other.[70]

The Fenian episode on the frontier of the Maritimes, anticlimatic in military terms, created political shock waves. The Western Extension railway had no hope of success without British aid. The Anti government of Albert J. Smith, crumbling from within and under pressure from the governor, resigned at the start of the Fenian crisis. During the general election of May and June, pro-Confederation politicians played the loyalty card, stressing the blessings of the British connection and the dangers of American republicanism. Allegations that the Antis were somehow connected to the Fenian enemy figured prominently in pro-Confederation electioneering. And public denunciations of Fenianism by leading churchmen helped snatch much of the Roman Catholic vote from the Antis. Father E.J. Dunphy of St. Stephen, for instance, labelled Fenianism "a mania and a delusion." The "Union" forces swept all the counties except Gloucester, Kent and Westmoreland – all Gulf of St. Lawrence constituencies which contained large Acadian majorities. To further control any possible Fenian conspiracies, the new government copied Canada and suspended habeas corpus.[71]

As in the 1865 contest, Civil War images and slogans were prominent. Opposition newspapers trumpeted the "Confederate" ticket and praised "friends of the Union." The government was tarred as "the enemy," allied to Fenians, annexationists and Americans in general. The St. Andrew's *Standard* called on Charlotte County voters to "Rally Round the Flag" of "the Union." The day after the telegraph brought news of the battle of Ridgeway, the Canadian-funded "Confederates" captured Saint John County Tilley's party, humiliated in 1865, was swept back to power, in large part because of the Fenians. The end of Reciprocity and disagreements about railway policy had also destroyed much of Smith's credibility. The Fenians, the New Brunswick elections and Archbishop Connolly's pronouncement in favour of Confederation in 1865 encouraged Tupper to secure passage of a pro-union resolution in the Nova Scotia Legislative Assembly; the question of union would not be submitted to the people. Howe, a strong opponent of union, reminded his readers that the untrustworthy Canadians had been rebels in 1837–38. The Antigonish *Casket* warned that the people of Nova Scotia risked becoming "Canadian slaves," and this analogy would be repeated often. The president of the Anti-Confederation League was W.J. Stairs, who had witnessed the sundering of the Union at Charleston in 1861. Antis in the three Maritime colonies in the period 1865–66 invoked fears of being drafted for military service in distant Canada and described the region's Fathers of Confederation as traitors.[72]

One of the more novel attempts to exploit Civil War themes was a letter by "Bluenose" to Halifax's *Morning Chronicle* in the midst of the Fenian scare. The writer envisioned Confederation as bringing economic ruin to Nova Scotia; the resulting "puny government" would be controlled by Canadians, the British garrison would be withdrawn and provincial shipping would dry up. In time, frustration and opposition would produce civil war: "resolute men had gathered to the Acadian standard, which was planted ever against Canada, on the banks of the Restigouche." In Bluenose's futuristic tale, the "Acadians" ask for and receive American assistance against their inland oppressors; "blue-coated soldiers" who had "trodden down the gallant legions of Johnson and Lee" lend a hand in battling the arrogant Canadians.[73]

As a result of the Civil War, the political elite of the colonies were quite conscious of the strengths and weaknesses of American federalism. But in Nova Scotia there was no correlation between Confederation sympathies and opinion on the American conflict. These issues divided the two political parties. Halifax's large Anti petition of 1866 was signed by John Tobin, J. Jennings, John F. Stairs, A.J. Ritchie and Alderman W. Roche, business and political leaders who lacked a consensus on the Civil War. Benjamin Wier saw the economic logic of political union and was rewarded with a seat in the Senate. Archbishop Connolly, another pro-Southerner, in 1867 urged local Catholics to vote "the whole union ticket." J.W. Ritchie, who had represented the Confederate government in the *Chesapeake* matter, and lawyer W.A. Henry, a probable Southern sympathizer, were part of the province's delegation to London in 1865–66 to advise on the British North American Act.[74]

In the immediate aftermath of Confederation, Maritimers" response to the neighbouring republic remained ambivalent, multi-faceted and somewhat unpredictable. Culturally, anglophone Maritimers were "British," but they admired much about the Americans. In societies without a clear sense of nationhood, loyalties were nebulous and at times conflicting. Smarting from the British and Canadian collusion that led to Confederation in 1867, Nova Scotia business and political leaders clamoured for "repeal." One wing of the Antis even advocated annexation to the United States as an alternative to the Canadian yoke, and an Annexation Society was founded in Halifax in 1869. In areas where anti-Northern sentiment had been strong in 1861–65, many flagstaffs flew the Stars and Stripes. As the annexation movement peaked in the province, Anglo-American relations were stirred up by the *Alabama* claims and trade and fisheries disputes. The 1871 Treaty of Washington, an attempt by Britain and the U.S. government to solve their Civil War differences, was a bitter pill for the Maritimes because it signed over inshore fishing rights without securing a preferential trade deal. In time, Maritimers reconciled themselves to Confederation far easier than Southerners accepted defeat, emancipation and Reconstruction, although there were still repeal rumblings in 1880s Nova Scotia.[75]

Prince Edward Island resisted Canadian blandishments as long as its tiny treasury allowed. Journalist Edward Whelan explained to a Canadian colleague that Anti politicians were exploiting "the asses of country people who can't see an inch beyond their noses." "Better terms," accepted by Nova Scotia in 1869, were rejected and the Island was rebuked in its attempt to pursue an independent commercial and fisheries policy. The Dominion of Canada grew concerned about the possibilities of a special relationship between P.E.I and the United States. Republican Congressman Benjamin F. Butler, a controversial "political" general during the Civil War, had led a fact-finding mission that had reported on the Island's prospects as a sphere for American trade and investment. Finally, impoverished by a grandiose railway building program and encouraged by the promise of funds for land reform, Islanders surrendered their independence to Canada in 1873.[76]

REMEMBRANCE

As the generation of young men of the 1860s grew old, memories of the region's immediate connections with the "war next door" faded. However, Maritimers did not stop travelling to the United States and, if anything, the pace of outmigration quickened. Their home region, however, began the uneven process of becoming Canadian. The Maritime press printed the occasional item on the war's more famous participants, and the educated classes no doubt read the flood of books and articles that the conflict unleashed. Much of this literature, such as the popular "battle papers" published in *The Century Magazine* in the 1880s after the failure of Reconstruction, glorified heroic combat and sought reconciliation through tales of mutual sacrifice.[77] Jefferson Davis spent time in Canada in 1867 and again in 1868. In 1866 his eldest daughter had been a student in a convent school in Montreal; Archbishop Connolly of Halifax was said to have played a hand in the arrangements. When Lee died in 1879, he was remembered in Canada as a gentlemanly father figure of Southern society.[78]

By the early twentieth century, Maritime connections with the Civil War were being forgotten. One exception was the story of the *Tallahassee* which ended up in a 1932 Nova Scotia reader; the raider's name also graced a school at Eastern Passage. In his story "Blind McNair," originally published in the *Saturday Evening Post*, novelist Thomas Raddall attempted to dramatize the region's ambivalence towards the American war. The protagonist, a Bluenose blinded in battle against the Yankees, spouts "reconciliationist" rhetoric about mutual bravery; the same tactic allowed individuals such as Almon, Keith, Wier, Ritchie and Gray and most Maritime journalists in the 1860s to downplay or ignore the Southern evil of slavery. The world-weary character McNair, furthermore, displays greater integrity than his foil, a colonial who enlisted in the Northern army for mercenary reasons. Raddall was writing at a time when American historians were blaming the war on extremist abolitionists and when race was invisible as an issue in Canadian society. His classic history *Halifax: Warden of the North* (1949) perpetuated the folk memory that Halifax, and by implication the entire province, had been sympathetic to the Confederacy.[79]

Many families in the region preserved Civil War lore, letters and objects of members who had participated. One Acadian family in Digby County was told that their cavalryman ancestor, although short in stature, was "a good shot."[80] C.W. Hall of the 43rd Massachusetts Regiment, a true Victorian, sent back poetry which was published in an Island newspaper: "A Sentinel's Reflection" dwelt on the theme of separation; the soldier longs for "the white wall of my Northern home" and the "much loved forms" of family. Robert A. McLeod, born and raised in the Maritimes, penned letters and poetry while recovering from wounds as a prisoner in the North. He confessed to a sister that the stern realities of soldiering were nothing like the romantic fancies of boyhood. Walter Wile of Kentville remembers family tales based on a series of old letters sent to his aunt from his four uncles, all of whom were in Union regiments. In addition to letters, families acquired photographs, uniforms, weapons and other military equipment. Mary (Wright) Bradshaw of Summerside came into possession of her great-great-uncle's sword. Such connections are uncovered regularly by family historians.[81]

Spouses, parents and siblings who lost loved ones in the conflict found comfort in letters describing their selfless acts, devotion to duty or pious utterances before expiring. A friend wrote that Watson Williams of Yarmouth, seriously wounded at Antietam, was "a Christian and a noble boy," who did his duty and was now dying without complaint. A Yarmouth County family was reassured that their son had brought down several of the enemy in battle before being shot. Other letters from officers and comrades, in almost ritualistic fashion, reassured families that the fallen had been well liked by the regiment or had lived exemplary lives under adverse conditions. Norman Wade's shipmates contacted a friend in Boston who broke the news of his passing to Wade's family back in Nova Scotia. Embellishment and exaggeration were bound to creep in, as when a colleague wrote about the death of Sergeant John J. MacDonald in the assault on the Rebel works at Secessionville, South Carolina. Thomas Kirwan's letter had the former Islander planting the regimental flag on the enemy's parapet before being sacrificed as a "soldier of liberty." In truth, MacDonald was killed in the charge, but his commanding officer's official report of the engagement makes it clear that the 28th Massachusetts Regiment got nowhere near its target. MacDonald's wife Clemmy, at home in Boston with two children, was first told that her spouse was missing in action, and then that he was dead and that the body could not be recovered.[82]

More pathetic were farewell messages written by the dying themselves on battlefields or in ambulances, hospital wards or prison camps. Thomas F. Goudey of Deerfield, Nova Scotia, suffered the misfortune of becoming ill in the filthy and crowded prison stockade at Andersonville, Georgia. In a final letter he promised to meet his sister in the next world: "They can torture our bodies, but they cannot shut out the bright and love of God from our Hearts."[83]

Peter Welsh, a New York carpenter born at Charlottetown, wrote his Irish-born wife on 15 May 1864, bragging that his regiment had "licked saucepans" out of the Rebels at Spottsylvania. He also noted that he had received a "flesh wound" but looked forward to a "furlow." Two weeks later, Welsh died of blood poisoning. Margaret (Pendergast) Welsh safeguarded dozens of letters from her spouse. After her death in 1892, family members in New York kept the Victorian writing case containing the letters, which, unlike most 1860s correspondence, ended up in an archives.[84]

In 1868 a young widow residing in Charlottetown, Laura Agnes Stevenson, published a brief "afterword" in her small book of humorous fiction, *The Ladies Benevolent and Industrial Sallymag Society*. The afterword was an edited and annotated version of a long letter written by her English-born husband, who had served in the Confederate forces. S. Wentworth Stevenson, who also was a veteran of the British 6th Dragoon Guards, died in 1865 of complications arising out of quinine treatment. The couple had lived in Missouri and Louisiana prior to the war. Wentworth had enlisted in a Missouri infantry regiment as a common soldier, mustering out after Corinth, Shiloh and Vicksburg because of health problems. After this he was a prisoner in St. Louis. For a time the Stevensons lived in Toronto. Laura Agnes Stevenson, who supported herself in P.E.I. by giving singing lessons, borrowed books from leading Charlottetown residents in order to complete her Civil War research.[85]

Family lore, especially when it involved the Civil War, could be inventive. The folkloric nature of these accounts suggests the extent to which the war was widely familiar throughout the region for two generations. In the 1920s, writer Clara Denis, who filled notebooks with information on Nova Scotia people and places, interviewed Gerry Lone Cloud, a well-known Mi'kmaq hunting and fishing guide. Lone Cloud was born in Maine in the mid-1850s; his parents were "medicine people," Mi'kmaq who worked in Indian medicine shows in New England. His father, Abraham Alexis Luxcy (also known as Bartlett), supposedly enlisted in a New York regiment at Plattsburgh. After his three-year service, he was paid five hundred dollars to substitute for a Vermonter. According to Denis's notes, Alexis was one of "eighteen who volunteered to capture Booth who shot Lincoln." (John Wilkes Booth was cornered in a barn near Port Royal, Virginia, by twenty-five men of the 12th New York Cavalry and two detectives.) Most accounts of Booth's capture credit Sergeant Boston King with the "kill" or suggest, as did officers leading the detachment, that Booth committed suicide. Lone Cloud claimed that his father had fired a shot that had wounded the fugitive in

Grave marker of Bernard Hogan, Corporal, 17th Maine Volunteer Infantry, of Cape Cove, Nova Scotia, who died of wounds suffered at Gettysburg in 1863.

the leg. (Booth was fatally wounded in the back of the head). Alexis told his son that the troopers took the prisoner, who in this account was still alive, "on an old fashion man-of-war boat . . . put him overboard way off the coast of Virginia. Killing other way was too good. They wouldn't give him the honour to hang him." While the family waited at Waterbury, Vermont, Abraham, the story goes, went to New York to claim his share of the reward, which totalled $18,000 in one interview and $100,000 in another. The father, possibly robbed and killed by "blacklegs," was never heard from again.[86]

In the late nineteenth century, Maritime newspapers printed notices of veterans" pensions and brief obituaries on their passing. Some death notices mentioned war service, but many did not. Halifax's Charles Robinson, for example, had served as boatswain mate on the gunboat *Baron de Kalb* in the western theatre. As a result of bravery during the hazardous Yazoo River expedition in December 1862, the Maritimer was awarded the Congressional Medal of Honour, the Union's highest decoration for valour. He returned to Nova Scotia and married a Prospect woman. When Robinson died in Halifax in 1891, after a peacetime career that included policeman and storekeeper, the press mentioned neither his Civil War service nor his rare achievement.[87]

Graveyards also conspired to cover up the past. Considerable numbers of the fallen had been buried in the field and in military, church and family plots in the United States.

Cabinetmaker John Birch, born in Charlottetown, had succumbed to typhus while serving with the 35th Massachusetts Infantry. He was buried in the Mississippi River National Cemetery at Memphis. Fellow Islander Archibald Buchanan, fatally wounded at the Wilderness, was interred at Mount Auburn.[88] A few veterans who found their final resting place in the Maritimes were commemorated in stone. Charles F. and George Balsor, born at Wilmot Springs, had served in Massachusetts cavalry regiments and survived the war; their headstones in Middleton, Nova Scotia, were provided by the U.S. Army. Steamships, railroads and embalming technology allowed families with the means to bring the departed home. Cavalryman Corporal Henry Evans, killed in 1862, was embalmed and shipped for burial at rural Westcock, outside Sackville, New Brunswick. Young James Wightman, son of a noted Prince Edward Islander, died of typhoid in a Washington hospital after being appointed assistant surgeon in the 2nd Massachusetts Regiment. His corpse was preserved in Boston and later interred in St. Andrew's Point Cemetery, Lower Montague.[89]

The experience of the region's Civil War veterans was a varied as their peacetime origins. The bulk remained in the States, became naturalized citizens, married and raised families. Typical was Henry Closson, a Digby native who emigrated to Boston at age seventeen. Working as a carpenter, he married in 1853 and started a family. Following service in the 9th Army Corp, he lived for over three decades in Fitchburg, Massachusetts. He died in 1901, survived by eight children.[90]

As they had before the war, many crossed the border more than once for work and personal reasons. The international border was a porous barrier.[91] Charles Vaughan had defended the Union in 1861–62 and stood up for the Union Jack at Halifax in 1866. A number of years later he was residing in Roxbury, Massachusetts, working as a tailor's pressman. Pensions became important to aging veterans and their dependents. In an 1881 application for a disability pension, Vaughan claimed to have been wounded during a Confederate cavalry charge at Malvern Hill. Affidavits on his behalf were filed from individuals in Nova Scotia and Massachusetts. A knee injury apparently contributed to the partial lameness that troubled the aging veteran. His last years were spent in Halifax, where he died in 1911. Bridget Mary received a widow's pension thereafter. Islander Thomas Billings Adams, in the ranks of the 17th Wisconsin at Vicksburg, began his disability pension in 1865. He claimed that arduous service had caused piles and rheumatism.[92]

Fred Howe survived his adventures in the Shenandoah Valley, followed his father's uncharacteristic advice to refrain from politics and ended up in Ontario working for the Grand Trunk Railway. W.F. McNutt, born at Truro, attended an American medical school before serving as head surgeon on the hospital ship *Red Rover*. He later moved to California where he taught at the state university. Dr. Hugh Cameron of St. Andrews, Nova Scotia, returned from Northern medical service to Mabou where he practised medicine, and Conservative politics, for several decades. Alexander MacPherson had lived at Baddeck as a boy. He endured almost twenty battles in Company K, 44th Massachusetts Regiment, before his discharge in 1864. Back on Cape Breton he established a mining and trucking company and kept up his American contacts through the Grand Army of the Republic. William Cundy, born and raised at Fredericton, followed a stint as a staff officer in the Army of the Potomac with a career as a real estate promoter and Massachusetts state assemblyman. Privateer and blockade runner Louis Coxetter resumed life as a steamer captain in South Carolina.[93]

Fighting for the Confederacy did not necessarily affect one's later career adversely. Jonas Howe emerged from the Confederate army unscathed, ran a manufacturing enterprise in his native Saint John, helped found the provincial historical society and contributed to the turn-of-the-century journal *Acadiensis*.[94] Island-born, New Brunswick–raised Robert McLeod, despite serving on the "wrong" side and losing an arm, achieved some prominence as a man of letters. During the war he studied the classics, carrying Caesar's writings in the trenches. In 1865 he returned to Baltimore and later entered Harvard, graduating in the class of 1869. In the process he was adopted by Boston's Brahmin class and recognized for his good character and breeding. Writing to McLeod's only daughter in the 1930s, a classmate attributed her father's decision to support the Rebels to his Scottish blood. He had enlisted "in the spirit of the Cavaliers of the "15 and the "45" Jacobite rebellions against Protestant rule. The writer praised McLeod for bravely enrolling at a "Roundhead" college. In 1871 McLeod departed for Europe where he travelled and wrote; one of his unpublished manuscripts was on the life of Cavour. In Paris he married a French widow. He was struck down with a throat ailment and died in Algiers in 1878.[95]

William Charles Archibald of Musquodoboit also took up the pen. His 1910 memoirs imitated contemporary American war chronicles by equating Christian soldiering with manhood. As one historian notes, by the 1890s the "carefully constructed memory" of veterans portrayed the war as "disciplined, heroic and strenuous."[96] Archibald's memoirs also reflected the spirit of reconciliation evident between aging Union and Confederate veterans and, to a lesser extent, Northern and Southern societies. His was a success story. Not every veteran smoothly readapted to civilian life. Traumatic stress or combat fatigue could be just as damaging as wounds and disease. At least three veterans, including Dr. A.L. Mitchell of Chester, Nova Scotia, and New Brunswicker Dr. Kitson Casey, killed themselves after returning to the region. Bluenoser Norman Upham shot himself in a barracks in 1864 after being discharged from a Massachusetts regiment. Others were destroyed by drink or ended up on the wrong side of the law.[97]

Most returning warriors followed humble pursuits, labouring on farms or ships, or in workshops, timber camps or stores. American government pensions cushioned the hardships of meagre resources and declining health. William McQuinn, after service with an artillery unit, headed back to Sackville, New Brunswick, where he assumed his pre-war occupation of shoemaker. Samuel Raymond of Woodstock, captured during the Cold Harbour campaign, survived imprisonment at Andersonville and then lived another fifty-four years, dying at Perth, New Brunswick. African Nova Scotian Ben Jackson ended up back near Hantsport. Hugh Munro, his left arm incapacitated during the siege of Charleston, was mustered out of his Maine regiment in 1864 and received his pension in later years at Welsford, Nova Scotia. Clemmy (Boswell) MacDonald, widow of John J., returned to P.E.I. with her children.[98]

Complicating any remembrance of Maritime participation in the American war was the fact that the region was British territory, did not celebrate Memorial Day and awarded no prestige or political attention to the Grand Army of the Republic and other Civil War veterans' organizations. Regimental histories were published south of the border and the tattered battle flags – such as the banner carried by John J. MacDonald at Secessionville in 1862 – hung in American town halls, state houses and armouries. Instead, Maritime society memorialized the gray-haired men who had been youthful volunteers during the Fenian scare of 1866. The growing articulation of British Imperialism as a form of English Canadian nationalism perpetuated ambivalence about the United States. In 1895, for example, a year of strained Anglo-American relations over Venezuela, Fenian Raid veterans gathered in Fredericton to commemorate their defence of the province. The volunteer artillery and infantry of 1866 – like the Loyalists in the 1780s, the militia who had suppressed the Northwest Rebellion in 1885 and Canadian volunteers in South Africa who had sailed from Halifax – had done their bit for the Empire.[99]

During the golden age of British Imperialism, many Maritimers

The Carleton Martello Tower in West Saint John (c. 1864) was armed to repeal Fenian invaders in 1866.

were grasping for evidence of martial patriotism. Statues honouring Canadian sacrifices in South Africa, and eventually Europe, appeared in villages such as Canning and cities such as Charlottetown and Saint John.[100] In 1912, nearly a half century after the crisis, the Dominion government made a bounty available to Fenian Raid volunteers and their widows. In Nova Scotia, thousands of alleged veterans of this bloodless affair applied for and received the bounty, over fourteen hundred in Pictou County alone. Nova Scotia had celebrated its Civil War–era heroes according to the rules of local patronage politics and forged a political myth in the process.[101]

In the late 1950s and the early 1960s, when America experienced a centenary revival of popular interest in the Civil War, Canadian historians, journalists, politicians, educators and communities prepared to celebrate their own centennial. In their view, one nation had almost destroyed itself; a second, built on French-English cooperation, had been forged without bloodshed. In the works of distinguished historians such as Donald Creighton, the American conflict presented both a threat and political opportunities for the far-sighted Fathers of Confederation. The war itself was a foreign occurrence of secondary importance, a topic for external relations specialists or military history buffs. Nationalist history tended to suggest that Confederation was the only logical outcome of 1860s pressures. Since the 1970s, revisionist Maritime historians have been obsessed with the economic and political consequences of Canadian union for the region, but once again the Civil War is background and not central to the main story of regional history.[102]

This book is about recapturing memory. For New Brunswickers, Prince Edward Islanders and Nova Scotians, the Civil War was an event of North American, not simply American, significance. The reactions of Maritimers were complex, contingent and constantly shifting – in short, typical of the overall pattern of Canadian-American relations. War, as it had been in 1812, was good for business. The *Trent* and *Tallahassee* incidents became important in local historical memory. Significant numbers of American warships entered Maritime waters and several thousand men from the region enlisted in the Union armed forces. Maritimers reacted to the neighbouring rebellion as individuals, family members, members of economic classes, and residents of their towns, counties or colonies, and as subjects of the British Empire. At home most adopted a sentimental attachment to the underdog, slavery notwithstanding. Abroad, Maritimers rallied round the flag of the Union. War and Reconstruction produced unprecedented attention to racial issues but few tangible improvements for Maritime blacks. A century later a sociological study described Nova Scotia blacks as "a people trapped in the wasteland of economic deprivation and social neglect."[103]

The American rebellion cannot be said to have dominated political or personal life in the colonies, and it possibly bypassed many locales and internal minorities such as the Acadians. But international boundaries did not insulate the colonies from the pressures of war. For nearly five years, Maritimers lived in Armageddon's shadow and it touched many of their lives deeply.

Notes

ABBREVIATIONS

CNSHS   *Collections of the Nova Scotia Historical Society*
CSA   Confederate States Army
CSN   Confederate States Navy
CWD   *Civil War Dictionary*
CWNC   *Civil War Naval Chronology*
DCB   *Dictionary of Canadian Biography*
HT   *Historical Times Illustrated Encyclopedia of the Civil War*
JHA   *Journal of the House of Assembly*
NBMA   New Brunswick Museum Archives
ORA   *Official Records of the Union and Confederate Armies*
ORN   *Official Records of the Union and Confederate Navies*
PANB   Provincial Archives of New Brunswick
PANS   Provincial Archives of Nova Scotia
USCD   United States Consular Dispatches

PREFACE

1 PANS, MG5, vol. 3045, Camp Hill Cemetery Register, 1864; *ORA*, series IV, vol. II, 85, 243, and series I, vol. XI, 510–11; Goff, *Confederate Supply*.
2 Halifax *Morning Journal*, 29 April 1864; Stansbury's letterbook for June–Nov. 1863 is reproduced in Vandiver, *Confederate Blockade Running*, 71–103.
3 Marble, "William Johnston Almon," 16–17; Sutherland, "Benjamin

Wier," 838–40. The author wishes to thank the staff of the Camp Hill Cemetery for assistance in locating Stansbury's resting place.

4   Holy Cross Cemetery Register, 1864; Halifax *Acadian Recorder*, 30 April 1864; *Halifax Business Directory for 1863*; Dyer, *Compendium of the War of the Rebellion*, vol. 3. For a preliminary treatment of British North Americans in the war, see Jenkins, "British North Americans Who Fought in the American Civil War."

5   Levine, *Half Slave and Half Free*; McPherson, *Battle Cry of Freedom*; Gallmam, *The North Fights the Civil War*.

6   The classic account of the war's impact on British North America remains Winks, *Canada and the United States*.

7   Waite, *Life and Times of Confederation*; Martin, *Causes of Canadian Confederation*; Buckner and Reid, *Atlantic Region to Confederation*.

8   Saint John *Globe*, 9 July 1863; Charlottetown *Examiner*, 25 Jan. 1864; Charlottetown *Protestant and Evangelical Witness*, 23 Jan. 1864; Halifax *Morning Journal*, 13 Dec. 1861, 21 Nov. 1862.

9   Thurston, *Tallahassee Skipper*, 207; Yarmouth *Tribune*, 3 and 31 Aug., 21 Sept. 1864; Halifax *Reporter*, 20 July 1865.

10 Marquis, "Soldiers of Liberty," 2–8.

11 Charlottetown *Examiner*, 12 Aug., 9 Sept. 1861; Halifax *Citizen*, 15 April 1864.

12 Bailey, *Letters of James and Ellen Robb*, 115.

13 Brookes, "Out-Migration from the Maritimes," 26–55; Wynn, "New England's Outpost," 64–90.

14 Bourne, *Britain and the Balance of Power*; Winks, *Canada and the United States*; Haliburton, *Sam Slick*.

15 Hill, *The United States and British Provinces*. For Hill, see Beck, "Phillip Cartaret Hill," 1–16.

16 Hill, *The United States and British Provinces*.

CHAPTER ONE

1   Halifax *Evening News*, 16–17 Nov. 1860; Halifax *Acadian Recorder*, 3 Nov., 1 Dec. 1860; Charlottetown *Ross's Weekly*, 7 Jan. 1861.

2   Woodstock *Carleton Sentinel*, 11 Nov. 1859.

3   Eastport *Sentinel*, 19 June 1861.

4   Gunn, "New Brunswick Opinion on the American Civil War"; Winks, *Canada and the United States*; Saint John *Morning Freeman*, 25–27 April 1861; Halifax *Morning Sun*, 4 and 9 Jan. 1861.

5   *Freeman*, 7 May 1861.

6   Wallace, "Sir Leonard Tilley," 124.

7   Halifax *Novascotian*, 28 Jan. 1861; *Sun*, 1 Feb. 1861; *Acadian Recorder*, 16 Feb. 1861. See also Morse, *Local History of Paradise*, 31–32.

8   Halifax *Christian Messenger*, 20 Feb. 1861, 22 May 1861.

9   *Acadian Recorder*, 23 Feb. 1861.

10 Halifax *Church Record*, 12 Feb. 1862; PANS, RG7, Provincial Secretary's Correspondence, John Munro to Joseph Howe, 27 March 1862.

11 Parker, *Daniel McNeill Parker*, 17–20.

12 "Report from Our Man in Savannah," *Atlantic Advocate*, 59. To allay Southern suspicions and prove that they were British subjects, the Nova Scotia tourists secured "protective papers" from the British consul.

13 Parker, *Daniel McNeill Parker*, 148, 153, 172–74, 199, 201.

14 "Report from Our Man in Savannah," 60.

15 Parker, *Daniel McNeill Parker*, 176–77, 184–85, 194–95.

16 *Sun*, 15 April 1861.

17 PANS, RG1, Public Records of Nova Scotia, vol. 104, Russell to Dundas, no. 75, 14 May, 15 June 1861; Marquis, "Soldiers of Liberty," 3; *Sun*, 1 May 1861.

18 PANS, RG1, vol. 126, Mulgrave to Newcastle, 2 Oct. 1861; *Sun*, 29 May 1861; Pictou *Eastern Chronicle*, 25 July 1861. The schooner *Susan* from Halifax was denied access to Hampton Roads on 14 May 1861; the other vessel was the *Promoter*.

19 *Acadian Recorder*, 18 May 1861; Winks, *Canada and the United States*, 62–63, 208.

20 *Acadian Recorder*, 1 and 15 June 1861.

21 Pictou *Colonial Standard*, 6 Aug. 1861; *Novascotian*, 5 Aug. 1861.

22 Charlottetown *Examiner*, 16 Sept. 1861.

23 *Acadian Recorder*, 24 Aug. 1861; *Novascotian*, 29 July, 2 Sept. 1861.

24 *Freeman*, 30 July 1861; Warder and Catlett, *Battle of Young's Branch*. Howe's personal copy of the Warder and Catlett book is now owned by Tim Lowery of Quispamsis, N.B.: Tim Lowery to author, 1 Dec. 1993.

25 Halifax *Evening Reporter*, 13 Aug. 1861; *Sun*, 25 Sept. 1861; Yarmouth *Herald*, 29 Aug. 1861; Saint John *Morning News*, 25 Sept. 1861.

26 Fladeland, "Alias Frank Thompson," 435–62. Edmunds is also discussed in Wheelwright, *Amazons and Military Maids*.

27 Halifax *Evening Reporter*, 10 and 13 Aug. 1861.

28 "British Feelings on the American Civil War," 171–72; Crook, *The North, the South and the Powers*; Jenkins, *Britain and the War for Union*, 100–1.

29 Fredericton *New Brunswick Reporter*, 27 March 1863.

30 *Morning News*, 23 Dec. 1861; *Freeman*, 4 Jan., 5 July, 23 Aug. 1862; Saint John *Globe*, 30 Jan. 1863.

31 Raddall, *Halifax: Warden of the North*; Johnson, *Defending Halifax*, 20–40.

32 *Freeman*, 28 Dec. 1861; Halifax *Express*, 21 Feb. 1862; *Acadian Recorder*, 6 Dec. 1861; PANS, William Norman Rudolf Diaries (micro R-10980), 8

April 1862; Saint John *Globe*, 15 July 1864; *Carleton Sentinel*, 16 Aug. 1862; Yarmouth *Tribune*, 1 Oct. 1861; Antigonish *Casket*, 5 Dec. 1861.

33 Charlottetown *Examiner*, 14 Oct. 1861; *New Brunswick Reporter*, 20 Feb. 1863; Saint John *Globe*, 11 June 1862; *Novascotian*, 15 Oct. 1861; Winks, *Canada and the United States*, ch. 2; Owsley, *King Cotton Diplomacy*.

34 *Sun*, 13 Sept. 1861; *Carleton Sentinel*, 10 Jan. 1863; Halifax *Presbyterian Witness and Evangelical Advocate*, 21 Sept. 1861. This was an established theme in North American Protestant culture: see Miller, "From Covenant to the Revival," 322–68.

35 Charlottetown *Ross's Weekly*, 17 June, 22 July 1861; *Carleton Sentinel*, 5 Nov. 1864; Fredericton *Colonial Farmer*, 14 Sept. 1865; Hallock, *Sketches of Stonewall Jackson*; Pollard, *Southern History of the Great Civil War*. For minstrel shows and blackface entertainments, see Roediger, *Wages of Whiteness*.

36 *Freeman*, 9 May 1862, 20 Aug. 1863.

37 Stacey, *Canada and the British Army*; Bourne, *Britain and the Balance of Power*; MacNutt, *New Brunswick*; Chapman, *Career of Arthur Hamilton Gordon*, chs. 1–2.

38 Preston, "General Sir William Fenwick Williams," 605–22. For British strategic thinking and policy towards the United States, see Preston, *Defence of the Undefended Border*.

39 PANS, RG1, vol. 127, MacDonnell to Cardwell, 22 Nov. 1864.

40 Bourne, "British Preparations for War," 600–32; Saint John *Freeman*, 12 Dec. 1861; Tallman, "Warships and Mackerel," ch. 2.

41 Halifax *Morning Chronicle*, 10 Nov. 1863; Halifax *Express*, 18 June 1861; *Citizen*, 10 Nov. 1863.

42 *Sun*, 25 Oct. 1861; Saint John *Morning News*, 23 June 1862.

43 Halifax *Express*, 12 May 1862; Halifax *Evening Reporter*, 31 May 1862; Pictou *Eastern Chronicle*, 15 May 1862.

44 Story, "H.M. Navy Yard, Halifax," 43–47; Halifax *Express*, 18 June 1861; *Ross's Weekly*, 3 Oct. 1861.

45 Preston, "General Sir William Fenwick Williams"; Bourne, "British Preparations for War."

46 Piers, *Evolution of Fortress Halifax*; Johnson, *Defending Halifax*; MacKinnon, "Imperial Fortresses in Canada," chs. 1–2.

47 Saint John *Globe*, 20 July 1864.

48 PANS, RG7, Provincial Secretary's Correspondence, Milne to Administrator of Government, 29 Aug. 1862; *Freeman*, 27 May 1862.

49 *Sun*, 23 May 1862; 17 April, 1 May 1863; Halifax *Provincial Wesleyan*, 11 Oct. 1856. For plebeian leisure pursuits in Halifax see Fingard, *Dark Side of Life in Victorian Halifax*.

50 *Ross's Weekly*, 4 Sept. 1863.

51 Sun, 17 and 19 June 1861; United States Consular Dispatches, Halifax,

C. Pilsbury to Seward, 20 June 1861; Milne to Pilsbury, 18 June 1861; Pilsbury to Milne, 19 June 1861.

52 PANS, C.O. 188 (N.B.), vol. 133, Major General Charles Trollope to Secretary of State, 9 June 1860; PANS, MG12, British Army, Halifax, vol. 58, Head Quarters Orders, 3 Aug. 1864.

53 Raddall, *Halifax: Warden of the North*; Halifax *Evening Express*, 2 Sept. 1864; Gobineau, *A Gentleman in the Outports*, 37.

54 Facey-Crowther, *New Brunswick Militia*; Jones, "Anglophobia and the Aroostook War," 526; Desmond et al., "Defending Maine and the Nation," 342–69; Scott, *Ties of Common Blood*.

55 Arndt, "Maine in the Northeastern Boundary Controversy," 205–23.

56 Charlottetown *Examiner*, 21 Sept., 26 Oct. 1863; Saint John *Globe*, 4–5 Sept. 1864; *Carleton Sentinel*, 31 Dec. 1859; 12 and 19 Sept. 1863.

57 PANS, RG1, vol. 126, Mulgrave to Newcastle, 24 Dec. 1861.

58 McDonald, "Public Career of Sir Charles Hastings Doyle," ch. 1; Halifax *Citizen*, 24 Nov. 1863; Yarmouth *Tribune*, 9 Aug., 4 Oct. 1865; *Ross's Weekly*, 17 Sept. 1863; Facey-Crowther, *New Brunswick Militia*; Edwards, "Militia of Nova Scotia," 63–109;

59 PANS, MG24, B29, Howe Papers, vol. 8, Howe to Mulgrave, 15 April 1862.

60 Nova Scotia, "Report of the Adjutant General of Militia, 1863," *Journal of the House of Assembly*, 1864"; MacNutt, *New Brunswick*, ch. 15.

61 PANS, Rudolf Diaries, 20 Feb. 1862.

62 *Sun*, 6 March 1861. See also Kennedy, *Rise and Fall of British Naval Mastery*, 150–75.

63 *Carleton Sentinel*, 11 June, 31 Dec. 1859; *Sun*, 24 and 26 July 1861; Seward, *Reminiscences of a War-Time Statesman and Diplomat*, 183.

64 Morton, *Military History of Canada*, 81–87; Halifax *British Colonist*, 12 Dec. 1861.

65 Saint John *Morning News*, 3 Jan. 1863; Facey-Crowther, *New Brunswick Militia*; Edwards, "Militia of Nova Scotia," 63–109.

66 Facey-Crowther, *New Brunswick Militia*, 91–101; Charlottetown *Examiner*, 7 and 21 July 1861; *Ross's Weekly*, 7 and 22 Aug. 1861. For the Island militia, see Webber, *One Thousand Young Men*.

67 *Novascotian*, 25 Feb. 1861; Halifax *Church Record*, 28 May 1862; Thomas Egan, *Halifax Volunteer Battalion and Volunteer Companies*, 1–3; Edwards,"Militia of Nova Scotia."

68 Jenkins, *Britain and the War for the Union*, vol. 1; Bourne, *Britain and the Balance of Power*; Ferris, *The Trent Affair*; Warren, *Fountains of Discontent*. For a contemporary account, see Fairfax, "Captain Wilkes's Seizure of Mason and Slidell," 135–42.

69 Adams, *Great Britain and the American Civil War*, vol. 1, 217–18; Winks, *Canada and the United States*, 95–96; Halifax *Evening Reporter*, 21 Nov.

1861.

70 Nova Scotia, "Report of the Adjutant General of Militia, 1861," *Journal of the House of Assembly*, 1862.

71 PANS, MG24, B29, Howe Papers, vol. 3, Howe to Lord Mulgrave, 30 Nov. 1861. For Howe see Beck, *Joseph Howe*.

72 Howe to Mulgrave, 30 Nov. 1861.

73 Halifax *Morning Chronicle*, 7 Dec. 1861; Jenkins, *Britain and the War for the Union*, vol. 1, 41–50. An anonymous officer or official studied the weak points of Halifax harbour in 1861 and made notes on the back of a Bayfield chart. The report noted that the guns at York Redoubt were "too high" and that most Point Pleasant guns were in barbette: Maritime Museum of the Atlantic, Chart M-67101; thanks to Dan Conlin.

74 Halifax *Provincial Wesleyan*, 30 Dec. 1861, 8 Jan. 1862; Sydney *Cape Breton News*, 1 Feb. 1862; Saint Andrew's *Standard*, 22 Jan., 23 April 1861. For a list of the forces sent to British North America, see Stacey, *Canada and the British Army*, 120–22.

75 Saint John *Morning News*, 17 Jan. 1862; Chapman, *Career of Arthur Hamilton Gordon*; PANB, RS348, A.3, Lieutenant Governor's Correspondence, Gordon to Lord Lyons. Gordon was not apprised that the Imperial government was satisfied with the outcome of the crisis until late January.

76 Saint John *Morning News*, 3 and 13 Jan., 10 Feb. 1862.

77 *Provincial Wesleyan*, 19 March 1862; Fredericton *Reporter*, 17 Jan., 14 March 1862; Crook, 143–45.

78 Bourne, "British Preparations," 145–46; Warren, *Fountains of Discontent*, 124–37; Crook, *The North, the South and the Powers*; Charlottetown *Protestant and Evangelical Witness*, 11 Jan. 1862; Adams, *Great Britain and the American Civil War*, vol. 1, 131–32. In 1814, over one hundred Royal Navy vessels blockaded American ports.

79 *Carleton Sentinel*, 11 and 18 Jan., 1 and 8 Feb. 1862.

80 Stanley, *War of 1812*, ch. 13; Preston, *Defence of the Undefended Border*, 26–27.

81 Saint John *Morning News*, 15 Jan. 1862. Portland's defences are described in Smith, *Confederates Downeast*, ch. 9, and Desmond et al., "Defending Maine," 353–67.

82 Eastport *Sentinel*, 21 Jan. 1863; ORA, series III, vol. 1, 588–90, 627, 670–71, 783, 924–25, 956, vol. 2, 5–9.

83 PANB, RS348, A.3, B. Robinson to A.H. Gordon, Jan. 1862.

84 Winks, *Canada and the United States*, 110. See also McDonald, "The Public Career of Sir Charles Hastings Doyle"; Preston, "General Sir William Fenwick Williams."

85 Saint John *Morning News*, 3 Jan. 1862; Ferris, *The Trent Affair*; Winks, *Canada and the United States*, ch. 6. Gordon had little faith in the New

Brunswick militia: PANS, C.O. 188, vol. 135, Gordon to Newcastle, 23 Dec. 1861. See also "Defence of Canada," 228–58.

86 *Provincial Wesleyan*, 2 April 1862. The battle also captured the imagination of the British public, but it did little to change naval tactics in the short run: Adams, *Great Britain and the American Civil War*, vol. 1, 276–77.

87 McPherson, *Ordeal by Fire*, 230–31. Governor Gordon believed that his colony was vulnerable from attack from Maine via inland river systems: PANS, C.O. 188 (N.B.), vol. 14, Gordon to Newcastle, 25 Nov. 1861.

88 *Ross's Weekly*, 3 and 10 April 1862.

89 Ibid.

90 Facey-Crowther, *New Brunswick Militia*, 100–10; *Ross's Weekly*, 10 April 1862; Charlottetown *Examiner*, 21 July 1862; Saint John *Freeman*, 14–19 Oct. 1865.

91 Saint John *Globe*, 20 Aug. 1863.

92 PANS, RG1, vol. 127, Mulgrave to Newcastle, 22 Jan. 1863; vol. 127, Doyle to Newcastle, 18 Feb. 1864; Nova Scotia, "Report of the Adjutant General of Militia," 1863–64; Pictou *Colonial Standard*, 7 July 1863.

93 Nova Scotia, "Report of the Adjutant General of Militia, 1865;" Edwards, "The Militia of Nova Scotia."

94 Saint John *Freeman*, 17 Oct. 1863; *Report on the Defence of Canada*, (Jervois Report); Stacey, *Canada and the British Army*.

95 PANS, C.O. 188 (N.B.), vol. 133, J.H.T. Manners-Sutton to Under Secretary of State, War Office, 29 Jan. 1861.

96 Ibid.

97 Jervois Report; *Protestant and Evangelical Witness*, 12 Aug. 1865; *Ross's Weekly*, 26 June 1862. For 1860s P.E.I., see Bolger, *Prince Edward Island and Confederation*, and Robertson, *Tenant League of Prince Edward Island*, 105–6. Because much of the P.E.I. militia belonged to the Tenant League, it could not be trusted to aid the civil power in 1864–65.

98 PANS, RG1, vol. 127, Charles Hastings Doyle to Cardwell, 22 Nov. 1864; MacKinnon, "The Imperial Fortresses"; Tennyson, "Early Fortifications in Sydney Harbour," 1–32.

99 *Novascotian*, 26 Aug. 1861; *Colonial Standard*, 21 Jan. 1862; Halifax *Express*, 6 Dec. 1861; Halifax *Christian Messenger*, 2 April 1862; Baker, *Timothy Warren Anglin*, 46–50.

100 Roberts, *History of Canada*, 340; PANS, MG1, vol. 427, no. 193, Harrison Papers, W.H. Harrison to Edward Harrison, 28 Feb. 1862.

101 PANS, Howe Papers, vol. 8, Howe to C.B. Adderley, 24 Dec. 1862.

102 Barnes and Barnes, *Private and Confidential*; PANS, MG1, Thomas Connolly Papers, Clement C. Clay to Hon. J.P. Benjamin, 14 June 1864; *Sun*, 16 Dec. 1863.

103 Baker, *Sam Slick*; Chittick, *Thomas Chandler Haliburton*. See also Winks, *Canada and the United States*, 216, 635–37.

CHAPTER TWO

1 PANS, RG1, *Public Records of Nova Scotia*, vol. 126, Mulgrave to Newcastle, 20 March 1862; Halifax *Reporter*, 4 July 1861.
2 Halifax *Evening Reporter*, 10 June 1865; *Novascotian*, 31 June 1861; Saint John *Telegraph*, 5 May 1864, 19 Dec. 1865; Overholtzer, "Nova Scotia and the United States Civil War," ch. 2. According to Abraham Gesner, in the early 1860s large numbers of Nova Scotians worked on the migratory New England fishing fleet off Cape Breton for wages or shares: Fergusson, *Uniacke's Sketches of Cape Breton*, appendix J, 176.
3 Halifax *Journal*, 3 Oct. 1831, 8 July 1833, 11 Feb. 1834; Halifax *Acadian Recorder*, 8 Oct. 1831; Marquis, "Haliburton, Maritime Intellectuals and the Race Question."
4 Owsley, *King Cotton Diplomacy*, ch.1; Fraser, *By Favoured Winds*, 95; *Eastern Chronicle*, 18 Nov. 1862; Halifax *Chronicle*, 21 Oct. 1862, 2 Sept. 1864; *Acadian Recorder*, 1 Nov. 1862; St. Andrew's *Standard*, 13 April 1864.
5 Nelson et al., "Canadian Confederation," 50–85; Wynn, *Timber Colony*; Judd, *Aroostook*, 20–45; Davis, *International Community on the St. Croix*.
6 Halifax *Journal*, 11–18 Aug. 1862; *Novascotian*, 2 March, 23 April 1863; Saint John *Morning News*, 10 Aug. 1863; Overholtzer, "Nova Scotia," 67; Clark, *Three Centuries and the Island*, 116–17.
7 *Provincial Wesleyan*, 27 Aug. 1862; *Eastern Chronicle*, 19 Sept. 1861; Halifax *Journal*, 12 Feb. 1862; Sackville *Borderer*, 15 Sept. 1865; Whitelaw, *Maritimes and Canada Before Confederation*, 133–35; Hornsby, *Nineteenth-Century Cape Breton*, 170–71; Cameron, *Pictonians in Arms*, 63.
8 *Novascotian*, 4 March 1861, 12 Oct. 1863; Saunders, *Economic History of the Maritime Provinces*; Sager with Panting, *Maritime Capital*, ch. 5. Sager concludes that most shareholders in Saint John and Halifax were not merchants, but that merchants owned the larger vessels.
9 Yarmouth *Herald*, 2 Jan. 1861; Yarmouth *Tribune*, 1 Jan. 1864; Lawson, *Record of the Shipping of Yarmouth, N.S.*
10 *Novascotian*, 12 Oct. 1863; Saint John *Globe*, 16 Oct. 1863; Sager, *Seafaring Labour*, ch. 9.
11 PANS, W.H. Harrison to Edward Harrison, 25 March 1864; Halifax *British Colonist*, 7 Nov. 1863; McPherson, *Battle Cry of Freedom*, ch. 12; Dalzell, *Flight from the Flag*; Blume, "Flight from the Flag," 44–55; Nealy, "Perils of Running the Blockade," 101–18. The tonnage of the American cod fishing fleet declined by over two-thirds between 1860 and 1866:

Masters, *Reciprocity Treaty of 1854*, 150. According to O'Leary et al., "Age of Monopoly," 391–419, Maine's fishing fleet declined because of inflation, higher costs for supplies and the repeal of the fishing bounty in 1866.

12 Saint John *Freeman*, 9 Aug. 1862; Eastport *Sentinel*, 1 Jan. 1862; Nash, *Naval History of the Civil War*, ch. 15; Crook, *The North, the South and the Powers*; Hearn, *Gray Raiders of the Sea*; Robinson, *Shark of the Confederacy*, ch. 14; Martell, "Intercolonial Communications," 179–201. The *Empress* was owned by King Brothers.

13 Eastport *Sentinel*, 9 Aug. 1865; "Maine," in Faust, *Historical Times Illustrated Encyclopedia of the Civil War (HT)*, 469; O'Leary and Allin, "Maine's Maritime Trades," 289–307; United States, "American Vessels Transferred to Foreign Registry, 1863;" U.S., *Foreign Relations*, 1864. The *Alabama* sank, burned or captured sixty-nine vessels.

14 Duncan, *Coastal Maine*, 327.

15 *Sun*, 6 July, 21 Sept. 1864; Saint John *Globe*, 7 July 1864; Saint John *Telegraph*, 11 July 1864; Charlottetown *Protestant and Evangelical Witness*, 30 July 1864.

16 Early in the war the British government, in keeping with its policy of neutrality, decided that Confederate privateers would not be treated as pirates: Adams, *Great Britain and the American Civil War*, vol. 1, 89–91. For early American privateering, see Hearn, *George Washington's Schooners*.

17 *New York Times*, 4 Sept. 1861; Saint John *Morning News*, 26 July 1861; U.S. Navy, *CWNC*, I-18-22; Browning, *From Cape Charles*, 7–8; *ORN*, series I, vol. 1, 37–42; vol. 17, 288.

18 *Morning News*, 31 July, 26 Aug. 1861; *British Colonist*, 29 Aug. 1861; Halifax *Journal*, 26 July 1861; Eastport *Sentinel*, 7 and 17 July 1861; Yarmouth *Tribune*, 20 Aug. 1861; U.S. Navy, *CWNC*, VI-238, 256; *ORN*, series I, vol. 5, 787, 793–94; vol. 6, 59; vol. 7, 684; vol. 12, 622–23; series II, vol. 1, 257. Despite Northern views on the subject, no Confederate privateer operated out of a foreign port or visited a British port: Adams, *Great Britain and the American Civil War*, vol. 1, 171, fn. 1.

19 West, *Mr. Lincoln's Navy*, 45.

20 Halifax *Evening Express*, 9 Feb. 1863; Halifax *Journal*, 30 June 1862; Halifax *Chronicle*, 24 Sept. 1861; *Acadian Recorder*, 7 Feb. 1863; Saint John *Globe*, 10 Oct. 1861; Saint John *New Brunswick Courier*, 3 Aug. 1861.

21 Halifax *Sun*, 10 Jan. 1862; *Carleton Sentinel*, 18 Jan. 1862; *Ross's Weekly*, 14–15 July 1864; Charlottetown *Examiner*, 20 Jan. 1862; Halifax *Evening Express*, 21 Feb. 1862; "Convulsions of America," *Blackwood's Magazine*, XCI (Jan. 1862), 123–25; Adams, *Great Britain and the American Civil War*, vol. 1, 253–56. For the defence of Charleston, see Burton, *Siege of Charleston*.

22 Charlottetown *Protestant and Evangelical Witness*, 12 March 1864; *Ross's Weekly*, 17 March 1864. According to *Ross's Weekly*, Currie spent most of his talk justifying slavery.

23 *Nova Scotian*, 2 Sept. 1861; Halifax *Journal*, 12 Feb., 10 March, 19 Sept. 1862; *British Colonist*, 8 Feb. 1862; Halifax *Express*, 5 Aug. 1861; *Colonial Standard*, 6 Aug. 1861.

24 Chisolm, *Speeches and Public Letters of Joseph Howe*, vol. 2, 450–53.

25 Overholtzer, 67–68; Charlottetown *Examiner*, 12 Jan. 1862; *The Acadia Powder Company and Its Works at Waverly, 1862–1910* (Halifax, 1988); The total tonnage of vessels clearing Nova Scotia for the U.S. surpassed British West Indies–bound tonnage by a magnitude of six to seven during the 1860s. See Sager, *Maritime Capital*, 105.

26 Overholtzer, "Nova Scotia and the United States Civil War," 52. Nova Scotia trade with the West Indies had been on the rise since before the war: Sager with Panting, *Maritime Capital*, 103.

27 Masters, *Reciprocity Treaty*, 105.

28 Halifax *Christian Messenger*, 27 Jan., 23 March, 20 April 1864.

29 *ORN*, series I, vol. 9, 125; Goff, *Confederate Supply*; Cochran, *Blockade Runners of the Confederacy*; Wise, *Lifeline of the Confederacy*. Britain, as a maritime nation, officially accepted the legitimacy of the blockade but expected merchants and shipowners to attempt to violate it: Adams, *Great Britain and the American Civil War*, vol. 1, 263.

30 *Provincial Wesleyan*, 8 Feb. 1865; United States Consul's Dispatches, Saint John, 12 Nov. 1862; Chisolm, *Speeches and Public Letters of Joseph Howe*, 450; Wise, *Lifeline of the Confederacy*; Taylor, *Running the Blockade*; Browning, *From Cape Charles*, 7; Bulloch, *Secret Service of the Confederate States*, vol. 1, 81. In 1863 the Confederate agent at Bermuda purchased several tons of hemp twine, for fixing field ammunition, from Halifax. But most of the war materiel brought into Bermuda came directly from Europe: Vandiver, *Confederate Blockade Running*, 79–80.

31 *ORN*, series I, vol. 6, 165, 189, 205. The vessels were the *Adelaide, Susan Jane* and *Argyle*. See Halifax *Evening Express*, 1–7 Aug. 1861. *Adelaide* and a second topsail schooner, *Argyle*, reportedly were manned by American captains and crews. Both were built in North Carolina and owned by Nehemiah K. Clements of Yarmouth. *Argyle* was lost near Shelburne, N.S., in 1871.

32 *Evening Express*, 23 Aug., 16 Sept., 23 Oct., 25 Nov. 1861; *Sun*, 18 Nov. 1861; United States Consular Dispatches (Halifax), 9 Nov. 1861; *ORN*, series I, vol. 6, 210; PANS, RG12 A1, Shipping Registers, Halifax, vol. 52B (micro-R-14540). *Emery* brought turpentine that sold for $1.10 per gallon. Barss was a part owner of the *Beverly*, built at Salisbury, Mass. Pitch, turpentine and other naval stores had been delivered by New Englanders to Saint John and Halifax during the War of 1812 under a

system of British licenses: Stanley, *War of 1812*, 363.

33 CWNC, I-26–27; Halifax *Chronicle*, 28 Sept. 1861; *Evening Express*, 27 Sept. 1861; Liverpool *Transcript*, 10 Oct. 1861; *Acadian Recorder*, 12 Oct. 1861.

34 Liverpool *Transcript*, 9 Jan. 1862; Lawson, *Record of the Shipping of Yarmouth*; ORN, series I, vol. 5, 782; vol. 6, 89.

35 Saint John *Morning News*, 28 Oct. 1861; ORN, series I, vol. 6, 354.

36 Stuart Allison Pye to author, 18 Feb. 1994; *Ross's Weekly*, 26 June 1862.

37 *Acadian Recorder*, 12 Oct. 1861; Halifax *Evening Express*, 27 Sept. 1861; 9 April 1862; Halifax *Chronicle*, 14 April 1863; ORN, series I, vol. 12, 543. *Fairplay* was captured by the blockading squadron. *Magnet* left Halifax before Christmas 1861.

38 Shipping Register, Halifax. The fifty-ton schooner, built at Tatamagouche, was sold to Fraser on 24 Jan. 1863.

39 PANS, Rudolf Diaries, 5 March, 8 March 1862, 16 Sept. 1863; ORN, series I, vol. 12, 536, 793; vol. 13, 43; Miller, *Live: A History of Church Planting*, 131; Charlottetown *Monitor*, 29 Oct. 1863; Liverpool *Transcript*, 19 Nov. 1863. One month prior to the capture of *Magnet*, USS *Keystone State* had taken the Halifax schooner *Mars*, loaded with salt, near Fernandina.

40 Halifax *Chronicle*, 17 Oct. 1861; Nelson et al., "Canadian Confederation"; Saunders, *Economic History*.

41 Saint John *Freeman*, 2 Aug. 1862; PANS, C.O. 188 (N.B.), vol. 135, Gordon to Newcastle, 16 Dec. 1861; U.S. Consular Dispatches, Saint John, 12 Nov. 1862; 29 July 1863. Saint John was also a favourite fictitious destination for runners clearing customs in the Bahamas; see Blume, "Flight from the Flag," 49.

42 *Morning News*, 19 Aug. 1861; CWNC, II-50, VI-221–22; PANS, C.O. 188 (N.B.), vol. 135, William Smith to Gordon, 21 Dec. 1861; Gordon to Newcastle, 23 Dec. 1861; U.S. Consul Dispatches, Saint John, 13 Dec. 1861; ORN, series I, vol. 4, 782; vol. 6, 96–98, 259, 482; Tebeau, *History of Florida*, 207; *New York Times*, 7 Sept. 1861. The case of the *Kate Hale* drew the attention of the U.S. consul, Lord Lyons, and the New Brunswick and British governments: PANB, RS348 A, William Smith to Captain Moody, 11 Jan. 1862; Arthur Hamilton Gordon to W. Smith, 22 March 1862. The New Brunswick authorities also were concerned about the ownership of the vessel *Adelso*, formerly the *A.L. Hyde* of Maine, seized off Rhode Island on 17 August 1861.

43 Saint John *Globe*, 29 July 1864; Halifax *Reporter*, 27 June, 15 August, 5 and 17 Sept. 1861; Halifax *Evening Express*, 27 March 1865; USCD (Saint John), 9 Aug. 1861; ORN, series I, vol. 6, 96–98, 201, 224–25, 726; vol. 7, 282; Eastport *Sentinel*, 7 Aug. 1861; CWNC, II-56, IV–42; Wise, *Lifeline*, 64–65. *Gold Hunter*, according to the Halifax shipping register,

was sold by Wier and Co. to T.C. Kinnear and Alfred Jones in March 1862. The U.S. Navy captured a "British" blockade-running schooner of the same name off Texas in December 1864.

44   Cougle, *Canadian Blood*, 9–10.

45   St. Stephen *St. Croix Courier*, 17 Feb. 1866; Saint John *Globe*, 21 Oct. 1862; Masters, *Reciprocity Treaty*; Gunn, "New Brunswick Opinion"; Saunders, *Economic History*.

46   Nelson et al., "Canadian Federation"; Bolger, *Prince Edward Island*; Saunders, *Economic History*; Sager, *Maritime Capital*, 51.

47   U.S. Consular Dispatches (Charlottetown), Sherman to F.W. Seward, 6 Jan. 1863; Dundas to Lord Lyons, 2 April 1864; United States, *Foreign Relations of the United States*, 1864, pt. 2, 562–63; *Ross's Weekly*, 8 Jan. 1863; Marquis, "Soldiers of Liberty"; Beck, "Song for the Heather Belle," 12–14.

48   *CWNC*, I-26; Halifax *Chronicle*, 19 and 24 Sept. 1861; Liverpool *Transcript*, 10 Oct. 1861; *Acadian Recorder*, 12 Oct. 1861. Consul Jackson reported on the schooners *Argyle, Adelaide* and *Susan Jane* in August and September: USCD (Halifax), 7–8 Aug., 23 Sept. 1861. The forts guarded the entrance to Pamlico Sound, an inland waterway fed by the Neuse and Pamlico rivers and leading to Albermarle Sound: Hawkins, "Early Coast Operations in North Carolina," 632–59. The barque *Herald*, owned in Hants Border, N.S., was impounded after being searched by an American frigate. It was hauling pitch and turpentine from Beaufort, S.C: Chittick, *Hantsport on Avon*, 17–18.

49   *CWNC*, II-110; Halifax *Express*, 1 Dec. 1862; *ORN*, series I, vol. 6, 195, 205; vol. 8, 231; Browning, *From Cape Charles*, ch. 12.

50   Cousins, *An Annapolis Valley Youth in the Union Navy*, 15–16.

51   Halifax *Reporter*, 23 July 1861; *Acadian Recorder*, 7 Feb. 1863; Saint John *Telegraph*, 4 July 1864.

52   Browning, *From Cape Charles*, 251.

53   Chittick, *Thomas Chandler Haliburton*, 635–37. Haliburton's published correspondence is thin on the Civil War: Davies, *Letters of Thomas Chandler Haliburton*.

54   Halifax *Reporter*, 25 June 1863; *Sun*, 26 June 1863; *Acadian Recorder*, 1 Aug. 1863; U.S., *Foreign Relations*, 1861, 284–85; 1864, pt. 2, 385–87; Bernath, "British Neutrality and the Civil War Prize Cases," 320–31; Blume, "Flight from the Flag," 55; Shipping Register, Halifax. *Isabella Thompson* was a 104-ton schooner brigantine built at St. Martin's, N.B.

55   *New York Times*, 30 Aug. 1861; Beale, *Diary of Gideon Welles*, vol. I, 283; *Acadian Recorder*, 17 Feb. 1863; *Evening Express*, 28 May 1862; USCD (Halifax), 29 July 1862; Halifax *Chronicle*, 13, 19 and 24 August 1864; Goff, *Confederate Supply*. The steamer *Edward Hawkins*, with its masts shot away, put into Halifax for fuel and repairs early in 1863. It carried

1,500 bales of cotton from Matamoras according to the consul: USCD (Halifax), 21 Feb. 1863.

56 PANS RG5, series GP Misc. A, Petitions to the N.S. Legislative Assembly, vol. 4, petition re seizure of the *Will o' the Wisp*, 18 Aug. 1862; *CWNC*, II-10, 68; IV–11; *Acadian Recorder*, 1 Aug. 1863; Halifax *Evening Express*, 28 June 1863; *Sun*, 29 June 1863; Halifax *Chronicle*, 11 June 1864; Shipping Register, Halifax. Beaufort was captured by the Burnside expedition in April 1862: Barrett, *Civil War in North Carolina*. Wier and Co. had sold the seventy-six-ton schooner *Racer* to Charles Annand in November 1863. It was to be resold in Mexico or the West Indies.

57 U.S., *Foreign Relations*, 1863, 6–7; Lord, *They Fought for the Union*, 283. The schooner *Concordia* called at Halifax in May 1863. Its agents purchased blockade goods from New York and the vessel cleared customs for Mexico, but Consul Jackson predicted that it would test the blockade. Later that year a blockade runner with the same name was scuttled at Calcasieu Pass, La., before it could fall into the hands of the U.S. Navy: USCD (Halifax), 9 May 1863; *CWNC*, III-144.

58 Yarmouth *Herald*, 12 Nov. 1863; Liverpool *Transcript*, 19 Nov. 1863; Wise, *Lifeline of the Confederacy*, 64.

59 USCD (Halifax), 9 July 1863; USCD (SJ), 31 Nov. 1863; Saint John *Globe*, 3 March 1864; Shipping Register, Halifax. The U.S. Navy grounded and captured a 450-ton steamer named *Caledonia* in May 1864 near the lighthouse on Bald Head Point off Cape Fear.

60 Saint John *Globe*, 13 Oct. 1862; U.S., *Foreign Relations*, 1863, 404; *CWNC*, II-99.

61 West, *Mr. Lincoln's Navy*, 229.

62 Wise, *Lifeline of the Confederacy*, Appendix; Overholtzer, "Nova Scotia and the United States Civil War," 70–71; Halifax *Church Record*, 24 Dec. 1862; Halifax *British Colonist*, 12 Sept. 1863; USCD (Halifax), 5 Sept. 1862, 24 July 1863; Saint John *Globe*, 13 Aug., 4 Sept. 1863; *ORN*, series I, vol. 13, 507; McPherson, *Ordeal by Fire*, 196; Halifax *Chronicle-Herald*, 18 Sept. 1959. The alleged blockade runner *L.L. Boyd*, which stopped at Halifax, had its hull painted a new colour. Information on the number of runs completed by vessels, unless otherwise noted, is taken from Wise's appendices.

63 USCD (SJ), 1863; Wise, *Lifeline of the Confederacy*, Appendix; *CWNC*, *Eastern Chronicle*, 29 Oct. 1863; Saint John *Globe*, 20 Oct. 1863; *ORN*, series I, vol. 9, 128; U.S., Record of United States Vessels, 1863, *Foreign Relations*, 1864, pt. 1.

64 *CWNC*, IV-10; Saint John *Globe*, 12 April, 23 May, 11 Sept., 30 Oct. 1863, 11 Jan. 1864; Halifax *Journal*, 5 Feb. 1864. *Laura Jane* was captured in 1864, possibly off Florida's Ocklockonee River.

65 Saint John *Globe*, 11 Sept., 30 Oct. 1863.

66 *Sun*, 1 July 1864; Marion McWhinnie to author, 25 Jan. 1994.
67 Saint John *Globe*, 27 Nov. 1863; U.S., *Foreign Relations*, 1864, pt. 2, 509–10, 610–14; *ORN*, series I, vol. 9, 311.
68 Overholtzer, "Nova Scotia and the United States Civil War, 60–66; Saint John *Globe*, 9 July 1863; Barton, "First Blockade Runner," 45–64; Browning, *From Cape Charles*, 265. An estimated 350,000 bales of cotton were exported from the Confederacy between 1861 and 1865.
69 *Acadian Recorder*, 27 Aug. 1864.
70 Saint John *Globe*, 2 July, 20 Aug. 1863; USCD (Halifax), 9 and 27 June, 21 July 1863; USCD (SJ), 15 April 1863. During the capture of the *Scotia* in 1862, John Martin of Halifax, a sailor on *Restless*, had drowned.
71 *Sun*, 5 June 1863; Halifax *Reporter*, 27 June 1863; Liverpool *Transcript*, 9 July 1863; *CWNC*, III; Wise, *Lifeline of the Confederacy*; PANS, Shipping Registers, Halifax (micro-R 2424), 26 June 1863. Fergusson, who emigrated from Scotland to Canada East in 1849, was a South Carolina master mariner/merchant who had chartered the steamer *Chesterfield* to the Rebel government in 1861. He appears to have had Halifax business or personal connections: *CWNC*, VI-211. The author is indebted to Edward D. Sloan, of Greenville, S.C., for sharing his research on the *Fannie and Jennie*: Sloan to author, 13 Oct. 1995.
72 Halifax *Reporter*, 13 Oct. 1863; *Acadian Recorder*, 17 Oct. 1863; *Citizen*, 7 Nov. 1863; USCD (Halifax), 13 Oct. 1863; Overholtzer, "Nova Scotia and the United States Civil War," 60; Vandiver, *Confederate Blockade Running*, 73–75; Wilkinson, *Narrative of the Blockade Runner*, 26–27; Winks, *Canada and the United States*, 145–54; Hill, *Seadogs of the Sixties*, ch. 4. John R. Wilkinson, who brought the *Lee* to Halifax, had served on the "iron floating battery" *Louisiana* in the unsuccessful defence of New Orleans against Farragut's fleet. The *Lee* was captured after leaving Halifax and several local investors, including Charles Hallock, suffered heavy losses in cargo.

CHAPTER THREE

1 Mahant and Mount, *Introduction to Canadian-American Relations*, 54.
2 Winks, *Blacks in Canada*, 51–53; Hart, *History of the County of Guysborough*, 62–63, 187–89, 246–47; Condon, *Envy of the American States*, 190–93. Most black Loyalists came from Virginia and South Carolina. Several hundred blacks, including an unknown number of slaves, lived in Nova Scotia prior to the Loyalist influx.
3 Condon, "Loyalist Arrival, Acadian Return and Imperial Reform"; Walker, *Black Loyalists*.
4 Winks, *Blacks in Canada*, ch. 3.
5 Pickart, "Trelawny Town Maroons."

6 Spray, *Blacks in New Brunswick*; Fergusson, *Negroes in Nova Scotia*, 106; McKerrow, *Coloured Baptists of Nova Scotia*; Winks, *Blacks in Canada*, ch. 5.

7 McCulloch, *Mephiboseth Stepsure Letters*, 13, 172.

8 Hornby, *Black Islanders*, 45–72; Canada, Census of 1871.

9 *Acadian Recorder*, 19 July 1818.

10 Winks, *Blacks in Canada*, 340–47; Sun, 19 July 1861; Moody, *Repent and Believe*. Haliburton's Sam Slick tales included "The Black Brother," an unflattering caricature of a self-taught American Negro minister, "Dr. Query." Although the story is set in the United States and is narrated by Sam Slick of Connecticut, Query was possibly inspired by Preston.

11 Fingard, "Race and Respectability in Victorian Halifax," 169–95; *British Colonist*, 17 Oct. 1863; Hornby, *Black Islanders*, 11.

12 Penner, *Chignecto "Connexion,"* 6–7.

13 Winks, *Blacks in Canada*, 106–7; Hornby, *Black Islanders*, 1–44; Fergusson, *Negroes in Nova Scotia*, 8–9; Litwack, *North of Slavery*; Stouffer, *Light of Nature and the Law of God*.

14 Halifax *Morning Post*, 27 May 1843; Winks, *Blacks in Canada*, ch. 5; PANS, RG2, Governor's and Lieutenant-Governor's Papers, vol. 305, Seth Coleman to William Sabatier, 6 Feb. 1815.

15 *Sun*, 28 Sept. 1863, 4 Aug. 1865.

16 Cap. LXVIII, "An Act to Prevent the Clandestine Landing of Liberated Slaves and Other Persons Therein Mentioned, from Vessels Arriving in This Province," *S.N.S.* (1834); Winks, *Blacks in Canada*, 129.

17 *Presbyterian Witness*, 25 Oct. 1862; Halifax *Reporter*, 28 Feb. 1865; Saint John *Religious Intelligencer*, 7 May 1858; Halifax *Reporter*, 28 Feb. 1865. McArthur, who had trained in Nova Scotia, was possibly from Demerara. Sheffield, a pre-Loyalist Yankee settlement, had a Congregational or "Puritan" church as early as the 1760s.

18 *Monitor*, 30 April 1862; *Presbyterian Witness*, 1 Nov. 1862.

19 *Novascotian*, 21 Jan. 1841; Halifax *British Colonist*, 8 Aug. 1850.

20 Saint John *Globe*, 21 Oct. 1863; Winks, *Blacks in Canada*, 153; Facey-Crowther, *New Brunswick Militia*.

21 *Novascotian*, 25 Feb. 1861; Reid, *Sketches in America*, 164; Ruck, *Black Battalion*; Halifax *Mail-Star*, 23 Dec. 1993; "Truro's Humble Giant Had to Fight to Fight," Halifax *Daily News*, 11 Nov. 1995.

22 Campbell, *History of Yarmouth*, 145–46; Liverpool *Transcript*, 6 July 1865; Halifax *Bullfrog*, 4 Feb. 1865.

23 Saint John *Telegraph*, 12 Aug. 1864.

24 Saint John *Morning News*, 6 Feb. 1863.

25 Haliburton, *Rule and Misrule of the English in America*; Winks, *Canada and the United States*, 216–17; Clarke, "In Defence of Giving Haliburton Hell," Halifax *Mail-Star*, 15 Oct. 1993; Adams, *Great Britain and the*

American Civil War, vol. 2, 192–93.

26 Reid, *Sketches*, 155–56. Reid had provided a testimonial for his former student James McArthur, the black missionary who also studied at Gorham College and the Old Presbyterian College in Nova Scotia before his ordination in 1858: *Religious Intelligencer*, 7 May 1858.

27 Reid, *Sketches in North America*, 156–57. For biological determinism and race, see Stephan, *Idea of Race in Science*.

28 Reid, *Sketches*, 291. "Negro songs" were popular entertainment as early as the 1840s: Halifax *British American*, 14 Sept. 1850; *Sun*, 17 Oct. 1864; Fraser, *By Favoured Winds*, 189; Hornby, *Black Islanders*, 79–88. For more on minstrel shows and blackface, see Roediger, *Wages of Whiteness*. Reid's views closely resemble the racial conservatism of his better-known contemporary Trollope, *West Indies and Spanish Main* (1859).

29 *Examiner*, 7 June 1861.

30 Halifax *Citizen*, 5 Nov. 1863; *Christian Messenger*, 23 Feb. 1859.

31 *Religious Intelligencer*, 4 June 1858, 15 and 22 June 1860, 25 Jan. 1861, 23 Feb. 1861, 1 March 1861.

32 Saint John *Globe*, 16 April 1863; *Citizen*, 21 Jan. 1864; *Sun*, 2 Jan. 1861; Halifax *Reporter*, 29 Jan. 1861; *Provincial Wesleyan*, 27 Feb. 1861; MacNutt, *New Brunswick*, 394; Patrick Brode, *Odyssey of John Anderson*.

33 Blockson, *Hippocrene Guide to the Underground Railroad*, 334; Spray, "Robert Patterson," 677–78. A number of mariners from the Caribbean also joined the African Nova Scotian community in and around Halifax.

34 Haliburton, *Sam Slick*, 168–175.

35 Robertson, *Book of the Bible Against Slavery*; Levine, *Half Slave and Half Free*, 165.

36 *Experience of Thomas Jones*. This pamphlet, written by an educated, presumably white friend in New Brunswick, was republished in Springfield, Mass., in 1854. See Ripley, *Black Abolitionist Papers*, 134–35.

37 *Experience of Thomas Jones*, 1–34.

38 Ibid., 35–47.

39 Ripley, *Black Abolitionist Papers*, 134–35. During his Maritime sojourn, Jones sold subscriptions to Garrison's *The Liberator*. The Halifax *Wesleyan* (21 June 1851) recorded that Jones visited Halifax in 1851.

40 Jones eventually settled at Worcester, Mass.

41 Fergusson, *Negroes in Nova Scotia*, 1–7; *British Colonist*, 8 Aug. 1850; Halifax *Journal*, 3 Aug. 1863; Winks, *Blacks in Canada*, 340. The Colonist was shocked by Howe's attendance at the Abolition Society's picnic, suggesting that the organization was racially exclusive.

42 Halifax *Journal*, 3 Aug. 1863; Saint John *Morning News*, 5 Aug. 1863.

43 *Presbyterian Witness*, 20 Feb. 1856, 3 Aug. 1861, 4 May 1862; Saint John *Globe*, 22 Aug. 1864; Saint John *Religious Intelligencer*, 8 July 1864.

44 The Free Baptist organ in New Brunswick was the *Religious Intelligencer*.

45 *Sun*, 30 Jan. 1865; Somerville, *Southern Slavery*. For the Bible and slavery, see Davis, *Problem of Slavery*, ch. 11.

46 *Eastern Chronicle*, 21 May 1863; *Citizen*, 17 Nov. 1863, 18 Jan. 1864; *Sun*, 2 Feb. 1863; *Morning News*, 2 June 1862.

47 *Wesleyan*, 23–24 Jan. 1863; Saint John *Globe*, 15 July 1865; Yarmouth *Herald*, 9, 23 and 30 Jan. 1862; Charlottetown *Examiner*, 23 Jan. 1864; *Protestant and Evangelical Weekly*, 24 Jan. 1863, 23 Jan. 1864.

48 *Carleton Sentinel*, 10 Jan. 1863; *Church Record*, 13 Feb. 1861; *Sun*, 11 Feb. 1861. Reverend Spurdon, lecturing on "Cotton" at the Fredericton Temperance Hall in 1864, discussed the war's "providential design": *Religious Intelligencer*, 15 Jan. 1864.

49 *Sun*, 11 Feb. 1861; *Protestant and Evangelical Witness*, 7 Jan. 1865; Saint John *Globe*, 25 June, 6 July 1864; Higgins, *Life of J.M. Cramp*, D.D.; *Sun*, 5 May 1865; Winks, *Blacks in Canada*, 347. Cramp was president of Acadia College from 1851 to 1853 and 1855 to 1869.

50 Winks, *Blacks in Canada*, ch. 10; Stouffer, Law of Nature.

51 *Ross's Weekly*, 22 July 1861; Sun, 28 Sept. 1863.

52 Knight, *American War*; Halifax *Journal*, 5 Oct. 1864; *Novascotian*, 9 Dec. 1861; Parker, *Daniel McNeill Parker*, 200–2; Haliburton, *Sam Slick*, 172; *Novascotian*, 9 Dec. 1861; Foner, *Politics and Ideology in the Age of the Civil War*. Knight argued that slavery was not a "proximate" cause of the war. See also "Canada's Interest in the American Civil War" (1861) in Murphy, *D'Arcy McGee*, 190.

53 *News*, 2 Nov. 1863; *Journal*, 26 Sept. 1860, 14 April 1861.

54 Gunnison and Gunnison, *Autobiography of Rev. Nathaniel Gunnison*, 27

55 PANS, MG1 (micro 10180), Thomas Connolly Papers, Connolly to Father Heckler, 26 April 1861; Allen, *Making of the White Race*, vol. 1, 181–92. In 1866, Connolly signed a petition and wrote a public letter on behalf of Harry Dowcey, a black cook condemned for murdering the captain of the Zero. A white co-accused was convicted but escaped the gallows owing to executive clemency. Connolly argued that a "poor, uneducated and friendless negro" had been sacrificed on racial grounds. Yet Dowcey was also a Catholic, and religion, not race, probably sparked the cleric's protest: *Novascotian*, 29 Jan. 1866

56 *Freeman*, 25–27 April 1861; *Liverpool Transcript*, 6 July 1865. Republicans criticized the Catholic hierarchy for its soft support of the war and its alleged toleration of slavery. Anglin responded by pointing out that Southern Catholics were too few in number to influence the political debate on slavery: *Freeman*, 25 Aug. 1863

57 Parker, *Daniel McNeill Parker*, 199–200.

58 *Christian Messenger*, 22 May 1861, 10 Sept. 1862; *Wesleyan*, 1861–65.

59 *News*, 7 Sept. 1863; Reid, *Sketches in North America*, 162. See also Halifax *Journal*, 9 Nov. 1860 and 22 Nov. 1861.

60 Saint John *Globe*, 13 Aug. 1863; *Provincial Wesleyan*, 14 June 1856; Halifax *Examiner*, 27 Sept. 1861; Winks, *Canada and the United States*, 184–85.

61 *New Brunswick Reporter*, 25 Nov. 1859; *Christian Messenger*, 1 Jan. 1860.

62 Reid, *Sketches in America*, 96–100. See also *Religious Intelligencer*, 9 Dec. 1859; Charlottetown *Examiner*, 25 Jan. 1864.

63 *News*, 21 Nov., 7 Dec. 1859; *Headquarters*, 14 Dec. 1850; Yarmouth *Tribune*, 26 Nov. 1861.

64 *Carleton Sentinel*, 28 Jan. 1860; *New Brunswick Reporter*, 22 Nov. 1860; *Headquarters*, 15 Jan. 1860.

65 *Christian Messenger*, 20 Feb. 1861; *Presbyterian Witness*, 16 Feb. 1861; *Carleton Sentinel*, 1 Dec. 1860; Halifax *Sun*, 12 Aug. 1861.

66 *Sun*, 9 Nov. 1864.

67 *Ross's Weekly*, 12 March 1864; *Morning News*, 13 April 1864; *Novascotian*, 31 Oct. 1864.

68 *Sun*, 26 Nov. 1862.

69 *Sun*, 5, 21 and 22 July 1861; Yarmouth *Herald*, 9 Jan., 23 Dec. 1862, 11 Jan. 1865; Liverpool *Transcript*, 25 April 1861; *Carleton Sentinel*, 20 Sept. 1860; *Headquarters*, 30 Oct., 21 Nov. 1861; Saint John *Globe*, 14 Sept. 1864; *Provincial Wesleyan*, 4 Feb. 1863. The editor of the *Transcript* was Samuel James MacIntosh Allen, born in Eastport.

70 *Provincial Wesleyan*, 11 Sept. 1861; *New Brunswick Reporter*, 6 Jan., 25 April 1862, 15 May 1863; *Carleton Sentinel*, 6 Aug. 1862; Saint John *Telegraph*, 11 Jan. 1865; *Reporter*, 29 Aug. 1861.

71 *Reporter*, 10 June 1862.

72 Reid, *Sketches in North America*, 161; *Casket*, 5 Dec. 1861, 16 Jan. 1862. See also Halifax *Journal*, 11 Aug., 12 Sept. 1862.

73 Saint John *Globe*, 13 Aug. 1863; *Express*, 12 Sept. 1862, 17 April 1865; Yarmouth *Herald*, 24 July 1863. During the New York riots a Royal Navy vessel was sent to the city to evacuate, if necessary, "British negroes." An eyewitness informed the *Religious Intelligencer* that the rioters were all "Irishmen and Papists of the deepest dye": *Religious Intelligencer*, 24 July 1863.

74 Adams, *Great Britain and the American Civil War*, vol. 2, ch. 12; Journal, 10 Oct. 1862

75 *Acadian Recorder*, 1 Dec. 1860, 4 Oct. 1862; Halifax *Reporter*, 11 Oct. 1862.

76 *New Brunswick Reporter*, 23 Jan. 1863; *Christian Messenger*, 6 Jan. 1863; Halifax *Examiner*, 10 Oct. 1862; Overholtzer, "Nova Scotia and the United States Civil War," 28.

77 *Provincial Wesleyan*, 22 Oct. 1862; *Express*, 6 Dec. 1861; *Colonial Standard*, 3 Feb. 1863.

78 *Church Record*, 8 Oct. 1862; *Carleton Sentinel*, 10 Jan. 1863; *Ross's Weekly*, 9 Oct. 1862; *Sun*, 28 Jan. 1863; *Eastern Chronicle*, 16 Oct. 1862; *Provincial Wesleyan*, 28 Jan. 1864.
79 *Novascotian*, 14 Nov. 1864; *British Colonist*, 3 Sept., 22 Nov. 1864.
80 Halifax *Journal*, 12 Sept. 1862; Halifax *Chronicle*, 7 and 14 Nov. 1864; Halifax *Reporter*, 13 Aug. 1864.
81 *Provincial Wesleyan*, 15 Dec. 1862 ; Jenkins, "British North Americans," 57.
82 Edmonds, *Nurse and Spy in the Union Army*, 383.
83 *Ross's Weekly*, 14 Aug. 1863.
84 *Sun*, 3 Oct. 1864; *Express*, 13 Aug. 1862; Black, "Soldier of Misfortune," 76–84; "Life of Robert Alder McLeod, from the Records of the Class of 1869, Harvard College" (typescript, n.d.). The last item was provided by Edward MacDonald, the P.E.I. Museum and Heritage Foundation.
85 Jenkins, "British North Americans"; Tom Brooks, communication to author, 22 Nov. 1995; Duncanson, "Ben Jackson," 10–11. Brooks has identified several hundred Canadian-born blacks in Northern regiments.
86 *Eastern Chronicle*, 24 Dec. 1863; William Drake to Family, 21 Nov. 1865 (photocopy provided by Edward MacDonald).
87 *Casket*, 5 Dec., 2 Oct. 1861, 16 Jan. 1862; *Provincial Wesleyan*, 21 Dec. 1861; *Telegraph*, 31 July 1865; *Sun*, 28 July, 4 Aug. 1865, 6 July 1866. See also Halifax *Express*, 3 July 1865.
88 Corey, *History of the Richmond Theological Seminary*.
89 Ibid.
90 PANS, MG1, vol. 3250, series A, W.J. Stairs Journal, 1865; Stairs, *Stairs Family*. Stairs, despite his sympathies with the South, did not endorse slavery.
91 *Reporter*, 14 Jan. 1862, 25 May 1865.
92 Saint John *Globe*, 24 and 29 Aug. 1865. See, for example, Justice Wilmot's address to the fall term of the Charlotte County, N.B., circuit court in 1864: St. Andrew's *Standard*, 2 Aug. 1864.
93 *British Colonist*, 1 Nov. 1865; *Reporter*, 26 Oct., 7 Nov., 30 Nov., 21 Dec. 1865; *Novascotian*, 25 Dec. 1865. At this time a ship on the Halifax station was involved in operations against the anti-British faction in Haiti. Jamaica's "Governor Eyre Controversy," which revived issues similar to the Indian Mutiny, divided British intellectuals on racial questions: Rich, *Race and Empire*, ch. 1
94 *Examiner*, 11 Dec. 1865; *Novascotian*, 15 Jan. 1865; *Freeman*, 16 Dec. 1865; Erickson, "Empire or Anarchy?" 99–129. For contemporary observations on Jamaica, see PANS, C.O. 188 (N.B.), vol. 146, William Smith to Cardwell, 29 June 1866. Smith, New Brunswick's representative on the West Indies Trade Committee in 1865–66, recommended that Jamaica's

blacks be denied political privileges and placed under a strong court and police system.

95 *Census*, 1871. The relative importance of the Maritimes in the national total was a result of the outmigration of blacks from Ontario in the 1860s and 1870s. The actual totals in the Maritimes probably were higher.

96 Winks, *Blacks in Canada*, ch. 10; Walker, *Racial Discrimination in Canada*; Smedly, *Race in North America*, chs. 10–11; Westcott and Schriver, "Reform Movements and Party Reformation," 203–6; Marquis, "Haliburton, Maritime Intellectuals and the Race Question."

CHAPTER FOUR

1 The most popular route for travel between Lower Canada and the Maritimes was through Portland, Maine: Martell, "Intercolonial Communications."

2 Halifax *Unionist*, 23 Jan. 1865. See also *British Colonist*, 8 Nov. 1864.

3 *Eastern Chronicle*, 23 May 1861. Less than 10 percent of the Loyalists who moved north of the Bay of Fundy were Southerners: Condon, *Envy of the American States*, 85.

4 Overholtzer, "Nova Scotia and the American Civil War," 18–19; Morton, *Monck Letters and Journals*, 11 April 1865, 258. Monck himself, according to his wife, was a Northern sympathizer.

5 *Telegraph*, 5 May 1864.

6 *Colonial Standard*, 6 Aug. 1861, 21 Jan. 1862; Saint John *Morning News*, 24 July 1863. For excessive romanticism and underdog ideology, nothing matches the prose of a Canadian sympathizer who attempted to capture the last thoughts of Confederate saboteur John Y. Beall, executed in 1865: *Memoir of John Yates Beall*, 87. According to Harry Arthur Thurston, shipowner and blockade runner N.K. Clements "established a plantation-style estate near Yarmouth complete with black servants": Thurston to author, 10 Oct. 1993.

7 *Unionist*, 23 Jan. 1865; Saint John *Freeman*, 13 July 1861

8 In reality, the Confederacy had important internal tensions and political conflicts. Like the North, it also introduced conscription and suspended civil liberties: Rable, *Confederate Republic*.

9 Saint John *Globe*, 24 Sept. 1862. Rable, *Confederate Republic*, 47, suggests that Southern secession in 1861 appealed to the abstract right of revolution, part of English political culture.

10 Saint John *Globe*, 24 Sept. 1862; *Eastern Chronicle*, 5 Feb. 1862; *News*, 15 June 1863; *Carleton Sentinel*, 22 Sept. 1860, 18 July 1863; Hatch, *Maine*; *Eastport Sentinel*, 17 April 1861; Hernon, "British Sympathies in the American Civil War," 356–67.

11 Reid, *Sketches in North America*, 39–40.

12 *Casket*, 24 May 1861; *Acadian Recorder*, 1 Dec. 1860.

13 *Citizen*, 17 Nov. 1863.

14 *Morning News*, 5 Aug. 1863; *Sun*, 16 Nov. 1864; *British Colonist*, 10 Nov. 1864; *Telegraph*, 17 May 1865.

15 *Morning News*, 13 April 1863, 2 May 1864; *Sun*, 11 May 1864; *Monitor*, 28 Jan. 1864. Adams, *Great Britain and the American Civil War*, vol. 1, 302–3.

16 *Colonial Standard*, 7 Jan. 1862. See also *British Colonist*, 14 July 1863.

17 "John McNeil," in Warner, *Generals in Blue*, 306.

18 Fellman, *Inside War*.

19 ORN, series I, vol. 8, 211–15; vol. 12, 816–19, 860–66; Saint John *Globe*, 6 Dec. 1862; *Morning News*, 8 Dec and 17 Dec. 1862; Yarmouth *Herald*, 11 Jan. 1863; Saint John *Telegraph*, 17 May 1864; *Reporter*, 20 Nov. 1862, 6 Jan. 1863; *Morning Chronicle*, 16 Dec. 1862; *Provincial Wesleyan*, 1862; Boatner, "John McNeil," *Cassell's Biographical Dictionary of the American Civil War, 1861–65*.

20 *Eastern Chronicle*, 30 Oct. 1862; Halifax *Examiner*, 12 Nov. 1862; USCD (Halifax), Jackson to Seward, 11 and 25 Nov. 1862; "Matthew Fontaine Maury," *CWD*, 520; Morgan, *Recollections of a Rebel Reefer*, 103.

21 USCD (Halifax), Jackson to Seward, 2 July 1862; Owsley, *King Cotton Diplomacy*, 364; Jones, *Life of Commodore Josiah Tattnall*; *Journal*, 13 Jan. 1865.

22 *Cape Breton News*, 4 July 1863. This same individual appears to have carried documents to Montreal in 1865 for the legal defence of the St. Alban's raiders: *New York Times*, 15 and 19 Feb. 1865.

23 *Memoir of John Yates Beall*; Winks, *Canada and the United States*. From Halifax, travellers took the train and steamer or sailing vessel to Saint John with connections for Maine or Lower Canada; took the train to Truro with connections to Gulf steamers from Pictou; or rode the stage coach from Truro to the Bend (Moncton). The overland route depended on wagons in the warm months and sleighs in the winter: Martell, "Intercolonial Communications."

24 *Telegraph*, 10 Dec. 1863; *Citizen*, 10 Dec. 1863; Saint John *Globe*, 27 Nov. 1863. Cougle, *Canadian Blood*, accepts contemporary press claims on the presence of Wheeler and Morgan. "Wheeler" was erroneously linked to the Chesapeake conspiracy by the Saint John *Globe* and other papers.

25 Yarmouth *Herald*, 17 Dec. 1864; *Telegraph*, 10 Dec. 1863; *Novascotian*, 14 Dec. 1863; Kinchen, *Confederate Operations*, 227–39; Wilkinson, *Narrative*; U.S. *Foreign Relations*, 349. Among the passengers on the steamer *Caledonia* from Quebec to Nova Scotia in the fall of 1863 was Francis Xavier Jones, a veteran of the 2nd Regiment of Missouri Volunteers and the First (Confederate) Missouri Regiment: Smith, *Confederates*

Downeast, ch. 4.

26   Liverpool *Transcript*, 19 Sept. 1861; Halifax *Express*, 22 April 1864.

27   PANS, MG1, Connolly Papers, Connolly to whom it may concern, 10 May 1864; Clement Clay to Judah P. Benjamin, 14 June 1864; Saint John *Freeman*, 19 Nov. 1861; Horan, *Confederate Agent*, ch. 4; Trombley, "Thomas Louis Connolly," 312–13; Kinchen, *Confederate Operations*, 46.

28   Henderson, *Private Journal of Georgiana Gholson Walker*, 91; Bulloch, *Secret Service*, 232; *Sun*, 4 May 1864.

29   *Private Journal*, 19–22, 108–19.

30   *Sun*, 28 Oct. 1862, 11 Nov. 1864, 9 Jan. and 17 Feb. 1865; "William Preston," *CWD*, 668.

31   *Reporter*, 14 Dec. 1861, 26 Feb., 4 June, 30 June 1863; *Express*, 13 Dec. 1861; USCD (Halifax), Jackson to Seward, 20 Feb. 1863, Kinchen, *Confederate Operations*, 41.

32   *Christian Messenger*, 13 April, 6 May 1864; Saint John *Globe*, 6, 9 and 11 May 1864; *Reporter*, 16 April 1864; *Carleton Sentinel*, 14 May 1864.

33   Hallock, "Aroostook and Madawaska," 688–98; Saint John *Globe*, 22 Oct., 6 and 27 Nov. 1863; Telegraph, 3 June 1864; Halifax *Reporter*, 21 Oct. 1863; *Journal*, 15 Jan. 1863, 23 Nov. 1864; Sun, 28 and 30 Oct. 1863. After the war Hallock published *The Fishing Tourist*, which featured a chapter on Nova Scotia.

34   *Colonial Standard*, 30 Jan. 1863; *Telegraph*, 1 March 1864. Photographs of Grinnell and other Southern heroines are found in the Almon Family Scrapbook at PANS.

35   Halifax *Bullfrog*, 4 Feb. 1865.

36   USCD (Halifax), 7 July 1863; *Eastern Chronicle*, 6 Aug. 1863; *Eastport Sentinel*, 15 July, 26 Aug. 1863; Saint John *Globe*, 9 July 1863; *Carleton Sentinel*, 29 Aug. 1863; Horan, *Confederate Agent*, 18–21; Winks, *Canada and the United States*, 143.

37   *Journal*, 7 and 19 Nov. 1862; *Telegraph*, 23 Jan., 27 Oct. 1864; *Sun*, 9 July 1862.

38   Gallman, *The North*, ch. 4; Punch, "Nova Scotians in the U.S. Civil War," 27.

39   PANS, RG7, vol. 50, Provincial Secretary's Correspondence, Petition of Port Mulgrave for Appointment of Stipendiary Magistrate, 17 March 1865; PANS, C.O. 188 (N.B.), vol. 140. Robert Shives to S.L Tilley, Feb. 1864; *Citizen*, 26 Dec. 1863; *Christian Messenger*, 1 Oct. 1862; *Carleton Sentinel*, 16 Jan. 1864; *Telegraph*, 14 Sept. 1861.

40   Saint John *Globe*, 20 May 1863; *Telegraph*, 14 Sept. 1864; *Carleton Sentinel*, 5 Sept. 1863; *News*, 20 May 1864..

41   *Telegraph*, 18 Oct. 1864.

42   Wilkinson, *Narrative of a Blockade Runner*, 181; Winks, *Canada and the United States*, ch. 10.

43 *Telegraph*, 20 July 1864; Geary, "Civil War Conscription," 208–28.

44 Burroughs, "Tackling Army Desertion," 28–60.

45 St. Andrew's *Standard*, 28 Dec. 1864; *Colonial Farmer*, 14 Sept. 1863; Robertson, *Soldiers Blue and Grey*; Wiley, *Life of Billy Yank*; Rorabaugh, "Who Fought for the North," 695–701.

46 *Colonial Farmer*, 14 and 17 Sept. 1863; *Carleton Sentinel*, 1 and 8 Feb. 1863; *Freeman*, 10 Oct. 1863.

47 PANS, RG42 (D), Halifax Police Court Minutes, vol. 19, 3 Aug. 1864.

48 *Citizen*, 22 and 27 Oct. 1864. In 1855 the U.S. Secretary of State viewed a scheme to recruit Americans via Halifax for the Crimean War as "an invasion of our national sovereignty." See Manning, *Diplomatic Correspondence of the United States*, vol. 4, 119.

49 PANS, C.O. 188 (N.B.), vol. 135, Gordon to Newcastle, 9 Dec. 1861; vol. 140, Jan. 1864; vol. 141, Col. J. Cole to Provincial Secretary, 5 Dec. 1862; Gordon to Cardwell, 12 Sept. 1864. In 1864, Gordon reported that "crimps are said to openly ridicule a fine of $80."

50 Liverpool *Transcript*, 17 March 1864; Lovesay, *To Be a Pilgrim*. The notebooks of early twentieth-century Nova Scotia travel writer Clara Denis contain references to Civil War participation by the father of Jerry Lone Cloud, an Indian guide and trapper: PANS, MG1, vol. 2867, Clara Denis Papers, Notebooks on Micmacs, no. 2. The author wishes to thank Dan Conlin for bringing this to his attention.

51 Thanks to Tom Brooks for this reference.

52 PANS, C.O. 188 (N.B.), vol. 135, Gordon to Newcastle, 9 Dec. 1861; vol. 138, 20 July 1863; vol. 140, Jan. 1864.

53 *Citizen*, 21 April, 12 and 25 June 1864.

54 NBMA, Charles Humphrey, Jr. to Charles Humphrey, Sr., 4 May 1862.

55 *Freeman*, 4 Oct. 1862; 5 and 17 Sept., 8 Oct. 1863, 21 Jan. 1864; Landon, in *Western Ontario and the American Frontier*, 225–27, believed that bounty jumping was rare.

56 Marquis, "Mercenaries"; *Freeman*, 3 Dec. 1863; *Telegraph*, 2 April 1864; Yarmouth *Herald*, 19 May 1864.

57 *Citizen*, 12 Jan. 1864; *Monitor*, 20 Oct. 1864.

58 *Freeman*, 3 Dec. 1863, 11 Oct. 1864; Marquis, "Mercenaries"; PANS, RG7, Provincial Secretary's Papers, vol. 48, William Fudge to Charles Tupper, 25 July 1863; see also vol. 47, Charles D. Boggs to J. Howe, 20 Sept. 1862.

59 *News*, 22 Nov. 1861; *Eastern Chronicle*, 26 Sept. 1861; *Journal*, 15 Feb. 1864; *Reporter*, 19 Sept. 1861, 25 Jan. 1862; *Telegraph*, 23 July 1864; Eastport *Sentinel*, 5 April 1865; Hansen, *Mingling of the Canadian and American People*, 156; Seward, *Reminiscences*, 213; *New Brunswick Royal Gazette*, 8 Jan. 1865.

60 PANS, C.O. 188 (N.B.), vol. 143, Gordon to Cardwell, 10 April 1865.

61 Bates, "A Rebel Cypher Despatch," 105–9.
62 McPherson, *Ordeal*, 294–95; PANS, MG2, Young Papers, vol. 741, Daniel Lord to Chief Justice Young, 14 March 1864.
63 *Reporter*, 30 Jan. 1862.
64 PANS, RG1, Public Records of Nova Scotia, vol. 126, Mulgrave to Lyons, 18 Sept. 1861; *Eastern Chronicle*, 12 Sept. 1861; *Express*, 4 and 27 Sept. 1861; Eastport *Sentinel*, 11 Sept. 1861; *New York Times*, 30 Aug., 7 Sept. 1861; *Reporter*, 29 Aug. 1861; *News*, 20 Oct. 1863. The Confederacy, contrary to this opinion, suspended habeas corpus from 1862 to 1863 and from 1864 to 1865. Local military commanders in the South regularly flouted civil liberties: McPherson, Ordeal, 366–67.
65 *Sun*, 24 July 1861.
66 *Express*, 2 and 9 Sept. 1861; *News*, 11 Oct. 1861; *Sun*, 16 Oct. 1861; Winks, *Canada and the United States*, 30–31, 42, 48–49; Smith, *Confederates Downeast*, 2; Overholtzer, "Nova Scotia and the United States Civil War," 15–17.
67 USCD (Charlottetown), 11 Oct.–24 Dec. 1861. Caitlin, from Massachusetts, was appointed in 1858. Norton was consul at Pictou, a busy harbour for American shipping, from 1849 to 1869.
68 Winks, *Canada and the United States*, 66.
69 USCD (Halifax), 18 March 1860–16 Sept. 1861, 3 Feb. 1863; Smith, *Confederates Downeast*, 20; *Reporter*, 30 Jan. 1862.
70 *Telegraph*, 23 and 28 July 1864. The Saint John police, reporting to the provincial government, also kept tabs on Confederate activities: Smith, *Confederates Downeast*, 33.
71 *Journal*, 7 March 1864; ORN, series I, vol. 9, G. Welles to S.P. Lee, 5 Feb. 1864, 461–63; *Telegraph*, 2 and 9 March 1864; *Rules and Regulations of the Halifax Club*. The club's management committee and shareholders included influential pro-Confederates such as W.J. Almon, B. Wier, Alexander Keith, W.J. Stairs and Dr. McNeill Parker, but also Union sympathizers such as John Tobin: PANS, RG7, vol. 48, Halifax Club Shareholders, 10 June 1863.

CHAPTER FIVE

1 *Freeman*, 19 Nov. 1861, 17 July, 1862; Saint John *Globe*, 19 July 1862; Halifax *Express*, 14 July 1862; G. Wayne Dow to author, 30 July 1994; PANB, Diaries of Wentworth Dow (microfiche); Lohn, *Foreigners in the Union Army and Navy*, 116–17; Warner, *Generals in Blue*, 306.
2 Marcus Lee Hansen, whose manuscript was published in the 1940s, concluded that there was "little evidence" that the Maritimes "sent any considerable number of their sons into the conflict": *Mingling of the Canadian and American People*, vol. I, 156. Robertson, *Soldiers Blue and*

Gray, 27–28, estimates that fifteen thousand Canadians served.

3 Winks, *Canada and the United States*, ch. 10; "Creation of a Myth," 33–43; Wiley, *Life of Billie Yank*, 309; Cougle, *Canadian Blood*; Jenkins, "British North Americans," ch. 1; Tom Brooks, communication with author, 22 Nov. 1995; Marquis, "Soldiers of Liberty." Cougle and Jenkins refer to the work of Saint John genealogist Daniel Johnson, who has found 2,600 Atlantic Canadian–born men in Maine volunteer regiments alone. Jenkins estimates that 34,000 British North Americans living in the U.S. enlisted.

4 Marquis, "Soldiers of Liberty."

5 Handlin, *Boston's Immigrants*, 52–53, 246, 257; Ernst, *Immigrant Life in New York City*, 66, 70–74, 83, 195–98, 201–4, 213, 236.

6 Yarmouth *Herald*, 5 Sept. 1861; Wiley, *Life of Billie Yank*, 109–23.

7 Marquis, "Soldiers of Liberty"; Charlottetown *Examiner*, 7 and 14 Oct. 1861. Additional information on MacDonald was provided by Bill Norin of the University of LaVerne, California.

8 *New York Times*, 19 July 1864; Halifax *Journal*, 22 Nov. 1861; NBMA, Humphrey Family Papers, Charles Humphrey, Jr. to Charles Humphrey, Sr., 29 Oct. 1861, 4 May 1862.

9 Tom Brooks to author, 13 Aug. 1997.

10 Hamilton, *History of King's County, Nova Scotia*, 154–55; *Morning News*, 4 May 1866; *Citizen*, 5 Nov. 1863; *Religious Intelligencer*, 10 Oct. 1862, 13 Feb., 27 Nov. 1863; McPherson, *Ordeal*, 382–83; Allen Marble to author, 4 April 1995.

11 "Life of Robert Alder McLeod."

12 PANB, RS348 A, Beardsley to A.H. Gordon, 22 Feb. 1862. Beardsley was captured six months later during the battle of Cedar Mountain. For the 10th Maine, see Kallgren and Crouthamel, *Dear Friend Annie*. For Canadian militarism, see Berger, *Sense of Power*, ch. 10.

13 Arsenault, *Island Acadians*, 209–10; Allen, "Franco-Americans in Maine," 32–66; Albert, *Histoire du Madawaska*, 254–55; Devlin, "Survey of Franco-American Participation in Maine Regiments"; Barry Rodrigue to author, 27 July 1995; Doty, *First Franco-Americans*; Brault, *French-Canadian Heritage in New England*, ch. 2. Charles White, from the Clare district of Nova Scotia, was an Acadian sailor who reportedly served in the U.S. Cavalry: Charles Handspiker to author, 31 Jan. 1994.

14 Webber, *One Thousand Men*, 40.

15 Andrew, *Development of Elites in Acadian New Brunswick*, 182–84.

16 Cornish, *Sable Arm*; McPherson, *Negro's Civil War*; Berlin, *Freedom*, 14–18; the list of Maritime-born men in U.S. Colored Troops was provided by Tom Brooks. Brooks has found Maritime-born men in the United States Colored Troops/Heavy Artillery and the U.S. Navy, as well as "Negro" regiments.

17 One British officer, who spent a year in the Confederacy, wrote that there were few foreigners or "soldiers of fortune" in the South. The Union forces, by contrast, were "crowded with adventurers," partly because of the inaccessibility of the South: "A Visit to the Cities and Camps of the Confederate States," 164.

18 Halifax *Chronicle*, 2 Feb. 1867; PANS, Almon Family Scrapbook; *Sun*, 24 May 1861; *News*, 13 Dec. 1863; Smith, *Confederates Downeast*, 18–21. The Union armies were 26 percent foreign-born; the proportion in the Confederacy was 9–10 percent: McPherson, *Ordeal by Fire*, 358. The Confederacy's 10th Louisiana Regiment contained a large number of Irish and German immigrants, but only nine Canadians: Brooks and Jones, *Lee's Foreign Legion*.

19 St. Andrew's *Standard*, 4 Feb., 9 Dec. 1863; *News*, 17 April 1864; New Brunswick *Colonial Farmer*, 4 April 1864; Saint John *Telegraph*, 17 April 1865.

20 Marquis, "Soldiers of Liberty"; Liverpool *Transcript*, 3 July 1862; *British Colonist*, 22 May 1862; Halifax *Express*, 7 July 1862; *Sun*, 7 July 1862.

21 *Wesleyan*, 16 Nov. 1863; Black, "An Astonishing Career," (*United Churchman*, 10 Feb. 1960, 3; 24 Feb. 1960, 3; Black, "Soldier of Misfortune," 76–85; J.W.J. to Robert A. McLeod, 24 Aug. 1863; "The Life of Robert A. McLeod," R.A. McLeod Correspondence (photocopies provided by Edward MacDonald, P.E.I. Museum and Heritage Foundation); Boatner, "Fort Wagner," *CWD*, 301.

22 *Wesleyan*, 16 Nov. 1863; McLeod Correspondence, R.A. McLeod to brother, 25 Aug. 1864, 23 Sept. 1864; R.A. McLeod to father, 1 Nov. 1864; R.A. MacLeod to sister, 6 Feb. 1864.

23 Halifax *Reporter*, 4 Sept. 1861; Saint John *Globe*, 18 Sept. 1862.

24 Dalhousie University Archives, MS1 A–1, Minutes of the Governors of Dalhousie College, 29 Nov. 1855, 10 Jan. 1856, 3 Feb. 1857, 14 Feb. 1860; Waite, *Lives of Dalhousie University, Vol. 1: 1818–1925*, 81–82; Halifax *Citizen*, 26 Dec. 1861.

25 *Sun*, 7 June 1861; *Journal*, 3 Feb. 1862; *Freeman*, 8 June 1861; *Express*, 6 Nov. 1861.

26 *New York Times*, 19 Sept. 1861; *Journal*, 31 July 1861; Halifax *Express*, 29 Nov. 1861; *ORA*, series I, vol. 12, Testimony of Military Commission, 25 Sept. 1862, 786–87; vol. 19, 527, 549, 585, 592, 595–605, 628, 665.

27 Liverpool *Transcript*, 4 July 1863; *Express*, 8 Sept. 1865; *Acadian Recorder*, 19 April, 13 and 17 June 1862.

28 Cougle, *Canadian Blood*, ch. 4; Hall, *Patriots in Disguise*, chs. 4–7; Fladeland, "Alias Frank Thompson"; Saint John *Telegraph Journal*, 5 Dec. 1959.

29 Cougle, *Canadian Blood*, ch. 4; Hall, *Patriots in Disguise*, chs. 4–7; Fladeland, "Alias Frank Thompson"; Saint John *Telegraph Journal*, 5 Dec. 1959.

30 Fladeland, "Alias Frank Thompson"; Hall, *Patriots in Disguise*; Cougle, *Canadian Blood*.

31 Edmonds, *Union Nurse*, 17–19.

32 Faldeland, "Alias Frank Thompson"; Hall, *Patriots in Disguise*. Seeleye died in Saint John during World War I. Reportedly he had been working on a revised manuscript of his late wife's book.

33 Gallman, *The North*, 105–7; Archibald, *Home-making*, 293–94. Margaret Gray Lord, the eighteen-year-old daughter of a P.E.I. politician, made no reference to the war in her 1863 diary: Macleod, *One Woman's Charlottetown*.

34 Punch, "Nova Scotians," 27.

35 Shaw, *Tell Me the Tales*; *Protestant and Evangelical Witness*, 25 June 1864.

36 *Protestant and Evangelical Witness*, 25 June 1864.

37 *Protestant and Evangelical Witness*, 25 June 1864; *Carleton Sentinel*, 13 Sept. 1862; *ORA*, series I, vol. 12, 258, 413, 438–41.

38 Palfrey, *Antietam and Fredericksburg*.

39 *Protestant and Evangelical Witness*, 25 June 1864; McPherson, *Ordeal*, 303–7.

40 *Carleton Sentinel*, 3 Jan. 1863.

41 *Protestant and Evangelical Witness*, 25 June 1864; *ORA*, vol. 27, 160, 178, 542–49; Pfanz, *Gettysburg*, 7, 138, 146, 305, 322, 366–77. For other examples of evangelical feeling in relation to battlefield death, fatal wounds and disease, see Liverpool *Transcript*, 21 Oct. 1862, and Marquis, "Mercenaries or Killer Angels?"

42 Archibald, *Home-making*.

43 Ibid.

44 Archibald, *Home-making*, ch. 1; Betty Langille to author, 16 Nov. 1993.

45 Archibald, *Home-making*, 227–28; 283–88.

46 Ibid., 232–33.

47 Ibid., 231–32.

48 Denison, "Cavalry Charges at Sedan," 52; Archibald, *Home-making*, 228–31.

49 Archibald, *Home-making*, 228–29, 231. For the static war in eastern Virginia, see Donovan, *West Point Military History*.

50 Archibald, *Home-making*, 235–36; *Carleton Sentinel*, 3 May 1862. For cavalry operations and tactics, see Rowell, *Yankee Cavalrymen*.

51 Starr, "The Wilson Raid," 218–41; Archibald, *Home-making*, ch. 2.

52 Archibald, *Home-making*, ch. 2.

53 Yarmouth *Herald*, 2 Feb. 1865. The 1st Maine "Heavies" were recruited primarily from the Penobscot Valley.

54 *Citizen*, 10 Nov. 1863.

55 Archibald, *Home-making*, ch. 2.

56 Archibald, *Home-making*, ch. 2; "Wilson-Kautz Raid," *HT*, 833.

57 The details of the Petersburg-Richmond campaign are found in Freeman, *Robert E. Lee*, vols. III–IV; the New Brunswicker's account is found in the Saint John *Freeman*, 30 Sept. 1864.

58 Archibald, *Home-making*, ch. 3.

59 Ibid., chs. 4–5.

60 Archibald, *Home-making*, ch. 4; "Hatcher's Run," *HT*, 350.

61 Gallman, *The North*, 195–96.

62 Yarmouth *Herald*, 21 July 1864; Liverpool *Transcript*, 28 Nov. 1861; R.A. McLeod to sister, 6 Feb. 1864; Wiley, *Life of Billie Yank*, 262–72; Robertson, *Soldiers*, ch. 9.

63 Archibald, *Home-making*, ch. 5; Robertson, *Soldiers*, ch. 3; Billings, *Hardtack and Coffee*.

64 Archibald, *Home-making*, ch. 4.

65 *Freeman*, 23 Dec. 1862, 20 Sept. 1864; *Carleton Sentinel*, 3 Jan. 1865. See also Saint John *Globe*, 23 Dec. 1864.

66 Archibald, *Home-making*, 258–59.

67 Archibald, *Home-making*, ch. 6; "Battle of Five Forks," *HT*, 261.

68 Archibald, *Home-making*, chs. 7–8.

69 Ibid., ch. 9.

70 West, *Mr. Lincoln's Navy*, 60; Lord, *They Fought for the Union*, ch. 17.

71 *Sun*, 20 Jan. 1865; *Journal*, 4 June 1862; Amherst *Daily News*, 18 Sept. 1918; Hayes, *Samuel Francis Dupont*, 274, 289, 376–78; Inez M. Moore to author, 7 March 1994; Marquis, "Soldiers"; Tom Brooks files.

72 Cousins, *An Annapolis Valley Youth*, 21; *Acadian Recorder*, 22 Nov. 1862; *News*, 10 June 1862; Saint John *Globe*, 9 June 1864; Marquis, "Soldiers."

73 Browning, *From Cape Charles*, ch. 13.

74 *Telegraph*, 6 Jan. 1864.

75 *Telegraph*, 30 Jan. 1865. For the battle, see Gragg, *Confederate Goliath*; Selfridge, "Navy at Fort Fisher," 655–61.

76 *ORN*, series I, vol. 21, Report of U.S. Steam Sloop *Lackawanna*, 6 Aug. 1864, 466–67; vol. 29, 4, 52, 148, 166–67, 253; Shelburne *Budget*, 16 July 1890.

77 Edmonds, *Union Nurse*, 239.

78 Marquis, "Soldiers"; Kohl and Richard, *Irish Green and Union Blue*.

79 Edmonds, *Nurse and Spy*, 386.

80 *Chronicle*, 24 May 1865; Chisolm, *Speeches and Letters*, 409.

81 Adams, *Great Britain and the American Civil War*, vol. 1, ch. 9.

CHAPTER SIX

1 Cox, "Sidelights on the *Chesapeake* Affair", 124–37; Jones, "Treason and Piracy"; Winks, *Canada*, ch. 12; Smith, *Confederates Downeast*, chs. 12–14.

2 J. Howe to A. Wier, 8 July 1863, Howe Papers. Howe was in Washing-

ton, Baltimore and Philadelphia during the rebel invasion of Pennsylvania in 1863. For the first three years of the conflict, British public opinion tended to view the war as a stalemate: Adams, *Great Britain*, vol. 2, ch. 16.

3 *ORN*, series I, vol. 11, 24–25.

4 Punch, "Nova Scotians", 29; microfilm R–14575, Shipping Registers, Pictou; Winks, *Canada*, 243; Rudolf Diaries, 10 Dec. 1863. One Union informant wrote of Locke and the Ragged Islands: "His family rules in that vicinity"; Smith, *Confederates Downeast*, 162.

5 *ORN*, vol. 2, 185–88; *British Colonist*, 21 Feb. 1863. Locke was rumoured to have served under Louis Coxetter on the privateer *Jefferson Davis*.

6 *ORN*, vol. 2, 65, 85.

7 *ORN*, vol. 3, J. Jewett to S.P. Chase, 27 June 1863, 322–25; Hill, *Sea Dogs of the Sixties*; Smith, *Confederates Downeast*, ch. 8.

8 *ORN*, vol. 3, G.L. Andrews to E.M. Stanton, 27 June 1863, 329; *Novascotian*, 20 July 1863; *Reporter*, 2 July 1863; *Sun*, 10 July 1863; Smith, *Confederates*, ch. 9; Hill, *Sea Dogs*.

9 *ORN*, J. Jewett to S.P. Chase, vol. 3, 322–35; *News*, 10 July 1863; *Chronicle*, 4 July 1863; *Novascotian*, 20 July 1863; Smith, *Confederates*, ch. 9; Hill, *Sea Dogs*.

10 *ORN*, vol. 3, J.H. Merryman to S.P. Chase, 325–26; E. Collins to Capt. N. Prime, 28 June, 1863, 328–29; Smith, *Confederates*, ch. 10; Hill, *Sea Dogs*.

11 *ORN*, vol. 3, Merryman to Chase, 325–26; Capt. N. Prime to G.L. Andrews, 27 June 1863, 327–28. Read was sent to Fort Warren and exchanged a year later for a Northern prisoner.

12 *ORN*, vol. 3, George L. Andrews to Major C.T. Christensen, 29 June 1863, 326–27. Because the *Florida* had been launched in Britain, the U.S. government later added the cost of the *Caleb Cushing* to reparations demanded as part of the *Alabama* claims.

13 Most published and contemporary accounts use the spelling Braine. I have decided to spell the name without the e, based on Brain's letters to his uncle in Britain: Hay and Hay, *Last of the Confederate Privateers*.

14 Hay and Hay, *Last of the Confederate Privateers*; Winks, *Canada*, 245–46.

15 McDonald, "Second *Chesapeake* Affair", 675–76; Yarmouth *Herald*, 17 Dec. 1863; *Novascotian*, 21 Dec. 1863; Halifax *Reporter*, 15 March 1862.

16 *Citizen*, 5 Jan. 1864; Saint John *Globe*, 16 Oct. and 11 Dec. 1863; 3 Feb. 1864; *Novascotian*, 21 Dec. 1863.

17 *ORN*, vol. 3, Testimony of Isaac Willett, 535–36; *Citizen*, 19 Dec. 1863; *Chesapeake:*, 6–7.

18 *ORN*, Willett Testimony, 536; Saint John *Globe*, 9 Dec. 1863; *Chronicle*, 7 Jan. 1864; *Chesapeake*, 6–7; Winks, *Canada*, 247. Unlike other accounts such as Smith's *Confederates Downeast*, this chapter does not claim to be a completely accurate portrayal of events on board the *Chesapeake*. The

full circumstances of Schaffer's death will never be known.

19 Willett Testimony, 536; *Sun*, 30 Dec. 1863.

20 *Sun*, 30 Dec. 1863; *Chesapeake*, 9–10.

21 *Chesapeake*, 6–13.

22 *Novascotian*, 21 and 28 Dec. 1863; *Sun*, 30 Dec. 1863; *Chesapeake*, 12–13.

23 *Sun*, 30 Dec. 1863; *Chesapeake*, 12–13.

24 *ORN*, vol. 3, John Parker to John Clibbon Braine, 2 Dec. 1863; *Chronicle*, 7 Jan. 1863; Jones, "Treason and Piracy."

25 *ORN*, vol. 3, Willett Testimony, 536–38.

26 Ibid.

27 *Chronicle*, 15 Dec. 1863; Willett Testimony, 537; *Globe*, 9 Dec. 1863; *Telegraph*, 10 Dec. 1863; *Novascotian*, 21 Dec. 1863; *Chesapeake*, 8–13; Jones, "Treason and Piracy."

28 Willett Testimony, 17 Dec. 1863; Yarmouth *Herald*, 17 Dec. 1863; *Telegraph*, 10 and 24 Dec. 1863; *Novascotian*, 21 Dec. 1863; *Chesapeake*, 8–13; Winks, *Canada*, 247.

29 Willett Testimony, 537; Yarmouth *Herald*, 17 Dec. 1863; Saint John *Globe*, 9 Dec. 1863; *Telegraph*, 10 Dec. 1863; *Chronicle*, 7 Jan. 1864; PANS, RG2, vol. 3, doc. 375, William Seward to Lord Lyons, 18 Dec. 1863; *Chesapeake*, 12–13. In Winks' account, *Canada*, 247–48, the highjackers attempted to refuel near Saint John.

30 USCD (SJ) Howard to F.W. Seward, 9 Dec. 1863, 18 Jan. 1864; *News*, 28 Dec. 1863; *Telegraph*, 24 Dec. 1863; Carleton *Sentinel*, 2 Jan. 1864; Charlottetown *Monitor*, 21 Jan. 1864; Smith, *Confederates Downeast*, ch. 13.

31 USCD(SJ) Howard to F.W. Seward, 9 Dec. 1863.

32 Saint John *Globe*, 10 Dec. 1863; *News*, 11–12 Dec. 1863; Kingston (C.E.) *Daily News*, 14 Dec. 1863; Charlotetown *Semi-Weekly Advertiser*, 22 Dec. 1863; *Freeman*, 10–12 Dec. 1863; *Telegraph*, 17 Dec. 1863.

33 *Colonial Standard*, 5 Jan. 1864; *Telegraph*, 17 and 31 Dec. 1863, 9 Jan. 1864; Winks, *Canada*, ch. 12.

34 *Ross's Weekly*, 22 Dec. 1863; *Eastern Chronicle*, 24 Dec. 1863; *Express*, 23 and 30 Dec. 1863; *New Brunswick Courier*, 18 Dec. 1863; *Freeman*, 10 Dec. 1863.

35 *Semi-Weekly Advertiser*, 22 Dec. 1863; *Colonial Standard*, 29 Dec. 1863; *New Brunswick Reporter*, 18 Dec. 1863; Montreal *Gazette*, 18 Dec. 1863. See also, *Novascotian*, 21 Dec. 1863.

36 *ORN*, vol. 3, H. Paulding to G. Welles, 11 Dec. 1863, 519–20; J.B. Montgomery to G. Welles, 9 Dec. 1863, 513; Montgomery to Welles, 11 Dec. 1863, 521; John A. Andrews to Gideon Welles, 9 Dec. 1863, 514; J.Q. Howard to W.H. Seward, 9 Dec. 1863, 515; Howard to Seward, 10 Dec. 1863, 517.

37 Morrison, *"Old Bruin"*, 28–82; Manning, *Diplomatic Correspondence*, vol.

4, 523–29. Following his cruise to the Maritimes, Perry was appointed commander of the East Indies squadron and took the *Mississippi* and three other warships to open Japan to American commerce.

38 Halifax *Reporter*, 2 July, 1863; *Acadian Recorder*, 4 July, 1863; *British Colonist*, 2 July, 1863; *Sun*, 3 July, 1863.

39 Bulloch, *Secret Service*, vol. 2, 181.

40 Rudolf Diaries, 20 Sept. 1864; Wise, *Lifeline*, appendix. Later in the war, Yarmouth was visited by the USS *Shawmut*, a gunboat commanded by the former captain of the *Cumberland*, destroyed by the *Virginia* at Hampton Roads.

41 *News*, 16 Nov. 1863; *Ross's Weekly*, 9 Oct. 1863; Charlottetown *Examiner*, 19 and 31 Aug. 1863; Marquis, "Soldiers"; Tuck, *Island Family Harris*, 126.

42 *Protestant and Evangelical Witness*, 17 Oct. 14 Nov. 1863; Charlottetown *Examiner*, 26 Sept. 1864.

43 *ORN*, vol. 3, Charles Steedman to Gideon Welles, 21 Dec. 1863, 525–26.

44 *CWNC*, VI–237–38, 290–91, 304. Earlier in the war, the *Niagara* had taken part in blockade duty and had bombarded Fort McRae, the Pensacola Navy Yard and Rebel positions around Warrenton, Florida. Commodore Thomas F. Craven and his vessel were to become better known later in the war on the European station. In the summer of 1864, the *Niagara* would cruise off Cherbourg against CSS *Rappahonnock*. Later it would capture, off the coast of Portugal, the steamer *Georgia*, formerly the CSS *Georgia* then owned by a British merchant. Early in 1865 Craven would blockade the ominous-looking Rebel ram *Stonewall* outside the Spanish town of Ferrol. When the CSS *Stonewall* later left port in an attempt to engage the *Niagara* and the USS *Sacramento*, Craven would choose not to sacrifice his vessels and to take refuge in the harbour of Coruna. For this action he would be tried by a court martial.

45 Contacting shore once again, Craven learned that a steamer matching a description of his prey had passed between Yarmouth and Shelburne earlier in the week. A telegram relayed the news that the *Chesapeake* was at LaHave "blockaded by one of the gunboats." *Niagara* got under way before dawn on 18 December, unaware that the wanted vessel had already been recaptured. Craven reached the mouth of the LaHave River in a blinding snowstorm and sent a boat to West Ironbound Island where the lightkeeper confirmed that the *Chesapeake* had departed on the morning of Wednesday, 16 December to the east. The commodore at first doubted the veracity of this information, but it was corroborated by other parties. *ORN*, vol. 3, Thomas Craven to Gideon Welles, 23 Dec. 1863, 534–35.

46 *Chesapeake*, 13; PANS, RG1, Public Records of Nova Scotia, vol. 127,

Doyle to Newcastle, 23 Dec. 1863; *ORN*, vol. 3, I. Washburn to W.H. Seward, 11 Dec. 1863, 520; C. White to W.H. Seward, 15 Dec. 1863, 523–24; Doyle to Newcastle, Dec. 1863, Great Britain, Sessional Papers, 1865, North American No. 9 (1864), "Papers Relating to the Seizure of the U.S. Steamer *Chesapeake*," 252–57; Winks, *Canada*, 248–49; Jones, "Treason and Piracy," 474–75. Doyle's account printed in the British Sessional Papers is the single best source for the Nova Scotia events.

47 PANS, RG2, vol. 3, doc. 375, Lyons to Seward, 18 Dec. 1863; Hastings Doyle to Lyons, 12 and 19 Dec. 1863, Correspondence on the Matter of the *Chesapeake*; McDonald, "The Public Career of Sir Charles Hastings Doyle," ch. 2.

48 W. Seward to Lord Lyons, 20 Dec. 1863; Doyle to Newcastle, 6 Jan. 1864, Great Britain Sessional Papers, 1865, North America No. 9, (1864) "Papers Relating," 252–53; USCD (Halifax), Jackson to F.W. Seward, 19 Jan. 1864; "Papers Relating," 253–56; Yarmouth *Herald*, 31 Dec. 1862; *Telegraph*, 24 Dec. 1863; *ORN*, vol. 3, Gunnison to W.H. Seward, 14 Dec. 1863, 523; Winks, *Canada*, 249–51; Cox, "Sidelights," 127–28; McDonald, "Second *Chesapeake*," 676.

49 *ORN*, vol. 3, Gunnison to Seward, 14 Dec. 1863; "Papers Relating."

50 *Chesapeake*, 13; "Papers Relating," 258; Affidavit of Patrick Connor, 6 Jan. 1864; Affidavit of Charles Edwin Kaulbeck, Deputy Sheriff, Lunenburg, 10 Feb. 1864; *Burning Bush*, 24 Dec. 1863; Yarmouth *Herald*, 14 Jan. 1864; PANS, RG40, Court of Vice Admiralty, 1864, Ships C–Z, vol. 23, The Ship *Chesapeake*. The loss of the cotton was bad news for the Bates Mill at Lewiston, Maine, which laid off thirty hands within days of the capture. John Heatherington Drumm, a former resident of Lunenburg who served as a chaplain in the Union army, wrote President Lincoln with information on both Locke and McKenny: Smith, *Confederates Downeast*, 162.

51 J. Harley to Receiver General of Nova Scotia, 14 Dec. 1863, "Papers Relating," 258–57.

52 *Chesapeake*, 13; *Provincial Wesleyan*, 23 Dec. 1863; Jones, "Treason and Piracy," 474.

53 USCD (Halifax), Jackson to Gunnison, 10 Dec. 1863; Gunnison to F.W. Seward, 9 and 14 Dec. 1863. See Gunnison and Gunnison, *Autobiography*, for the consul's version of the events.

54 USCD (Halifax), Jackson to F.W. Seward, 19 Jan. 1864; "Papers Relating;" Cox, "Sidelights," 127–28; McDonald, "Second *Chesapeake*;" Winks, *Canada*, 248–254. Davis was paid $450 for swearing out an affidavit against Brain.

55 J. Harley to Receiver General of Nova Scotia, 18 Dec. 1863, "Papers Relating," 258.

56 *ORN*, vol. 3, A.G. Clary to Gideon Welles, 14 and 18 Dec. 1863, 522–29.

57 *Ella and Annie*, a captured blockade runner, had been provisionally commissioned USS *Malvern* at Boston. It went on to important war service, serving as Admiral Porter's flagship at the storming of Fort Fisher and temporary home to President Lincoln two weeks before his death, on a cruise up the James River. *ORN*, vol. 3, J.F. Nickels to C. Stringham, 22 Dec. 1863, 526–27; vol. 9, Rear Admiral S.P. Lee to Gideon Welles, 12 Nov. 1863, 291–92; Smith, *Confederates Downeast*, ch. 14.

58 *Novascotian*, 21 Dec. 1863; *ORN*, vol. 3, Nickels to Stringham, 22 Dec. 1863; Smith, *Confederates Downeast*, ch. 14.

59 *Burning Bush*, 24 Dec. 1863; *ORN*, vol. 3, Nickels to Stringham, 22 Dec. 1863.

60 *Chesapeake*, 14; *Burning Bush*, 24 Dec. 1863; *ORN*, vol. 3, Nickels to Stringham, 527; PANS, RG40 vol. 23, Affidavit of Patrick Connor, 6 Jan. 1864; Cox, "Sidelights," 127–28. The *Chesapeake*, according to a slightly different south shore version, passed its pursuer "within gunshot" near Lunenburg. Given the aggressive nature of Nickels' patrol, this scenario is less likely.

61 *ORN*, vol. 3, A.G. Clary to Gideon Welles, 14 and 18 Dec. 1863, 522–29.

62 *Chesapeake*, 14; *Burning Bush*, 24 Dec. 1863; Hepworth, *Starboard and Port*. The highjackers had secured the services of local pilot A.M. Flynn.

63 PANS, RG40, vol. 23, Affidavit of Thomas Holt, Master Mariner, 6 Jan. 1864; and Affidavits of William and Alexander Henry, 6 Jan. 1864.

64 PANS, RG 40, vol. 23, Affidavits of William and Alexander Henry, 6 Jan. 1864.

65 Yarmouth *Herald*, 17 Dec. 1863.

66 McDonald, "Second *Chesapeake*," 676; Cox, "Sidelights," 127–28; Halifax *Herald*, 23 Dec. 1896; Winks, *Canada*, 249.

67 *ORN*, vol. 3, Nickels to Stringham, 527.

68 *ORN*, vol. 3, A.G. Clary to G. Welles, 14 Dec. and 18 Dec. 1863, 522–29.

69 *Novascotian*, 21 Dec. 1863; PANS, RG40, vol. 23, Affidavits of William and Alexander Henry, 6 Jan. 1864; Cox, "Sidelights," 129–31.

70 *Eastern Chronicle*, 24 Dec. 1863; USCD (Halifax), Jackson to F.W. Seward, 15 Jan. 1864; *Telegraph*, 24 Dec. 1863; *Chronicle*, 4 Feb. 1864.

71 *ORN*, vol. 3, Nickels to Stringham, 527; Affidavit of Patrick Connor, 6 Jan. 1864; PANS, RG40, vol. 23, Affidavit of Thomas Holt, 6 Jan. 1864; PANS, RG40, vol. 23, Affidavits of William and Alexander Henry, 6 Jan. 1864.

72 *Novascotian*, 31 Dec. 1863; PANS, RG40, vol. 23, Affidavit of Thomas Holt, and Affidavits of William and Alexander Henry.

73 *Church Record*, 22 Apr. 1864; *Telegraph*, 24 Dec. 1863; Liverpool *Transcript*, 20 Apr. 1864; Cox, "Sidelights."

74 *Church Record*, 22 April, 1864; *Novascotian*, 31 Dec. 1863; *ORN*, vol. 3,

A.G. Clary to G. Welles, 17 Dec. 1863, 524; McDonald, "Second *Chesapeake*," 677; Smith, *Confederates Downeast*, ch. 14; Seward to Lyons, 18 Dec. 1863; "Papers Relating," 249.

75 *Telegraph*, 24 Dec. 1863; *Chronicle*, 19 Dec. 1983; McDonald, "Sir Charles Hastings Doyle," 278–81; Jones, "Treason and Piracy," 475.

76 *Telegraph*, 24 Dec. 1863; Lyons to John Russell, 26 Dec. 1863, "Papers Relating," 246–47; PANS, RG2, Vol. 3, doc. 375, Seward to Lyons, 18 Dec. 1863.

77 *Telegraph*, 24 Dec. 1863; Johnson, *Defending Halifax: Ordnance*; Jones, "Treason and Piracy," 476, 482–83. For defence policy, see Preston, *Defence of the Undefended Border*, ch. 1.

78 USCD (Halifax), Gunnison to F.W. Seward, 17 and 21 Dec. 1863; *ORN*, vol. 3, C. Tupper to Officer Commanding U.S. Ships of War, 17 Dec. 1863; A.G. Clary to Provincial Secretary, 17 Dec. 1863, 530–31; RG1, vol. 127, Hastings Doyle to Newcastle, 23 Dec. 1863.

79 USCD (Halifax), Gunnison to F.W. Seward, 21 Dec. 1863; PANS RG1, vol. 127, Hastings Doyle to Newcastle, 23 Dec. 1863; Jackson to F.W. Seward, 3 Feb. 1864; *Chronicle*, 19 Dec. 1863; *Novascotian*, 21 Dec. 1863; Winks, *Canada*, 250; Sutherland, "James William Johnston," 381–88. Johnston, grandson of a British officer who left Georgia as a Loyalist, epitomized the colony's legal and political establishment. His first wife was Amelia Elizabeth Almon, which made him a relative of a chief Halifax supporter of the Confederacy.

80 *Chronicle*, 19 Dec 1863; *Novascotian*, 21 Dec. 1863; Winks, *Canada*, 250. Winks asserts that Brain was in Halifax when the arrest attempt was made.

81 Hastings Doyle to Newcastle, 23 Dec. 1863; *ORN*, vol. 3, Charles Tupper to A.G. Clary, 18 Dec. 1863; A.G. Clary to Charles Tupper, 18 Dec. 1863, 531–32; USCD (Halifax), Gunnison to F.W. Seward, 21 Dec. 1863; *Novascotian*, 28 Dec. 1863; McDonald, "Second *Chesapeake*," 678–79; Jones, "Treason and Piracy," 475.

82 *ORN*, vol. 3, Charles Tupper to A.G. Clary, 18 Dec. 1863, 532–33;*Telegraph*, 2 and 9 March 1864.

83 Beale, *Diary of Gideon Welles*, 490.

84 *Telegraph*, 24 Dec. 1863; Saunders, *Sir Charles Tupper*, 91.

85 *Telegraph*, 24 Dec. 1863; PANS, RG1, vol. 127, Hastings Doyle to Vice-Admiral Sir James Hope; Jones, "Treason and Piracy," 482–83. In March, Doyle wrote to Hope that he was prepared to use his "best efforts" to prevent the American vessels from leaving "by day". Lacking a man-of-war, the governor was helpless at night. As Jones notes, the senior naval officer at Bermuda sent the sloop HMS *Styx* to Halifax in January, 1864.

86 USCD (Halifax), 21 Dec. 1863; *Sun*, 23 Dec. 1863; Hastings Doyle to

Newcastle, 23 Dec. 1863; Saint John's *Day Book*, 14 Jan. 1864. Nickels, for some reason, described George Wade as "a noted New York thief".

87 Born in 1819, as a young man Hutt had apprenticed with a Nova Scotia sailmaker and then headed for the United States where he joined the navy in time to participate in the war with Mexico on the frigate USS *Cumberland*. Returning to Halifax, he secured a position in the Royal Dockyard, then shipped on brigs on the Boston run. Hutt was appointed to the police force in the 1860s. He was promoted to sergeant following the *Chesapeake* affair and became one of the city's first detectives. *Acadian Recorder* 3 Oct. 1882.

88 Jones, "Treason and Piracy"; Marble, "William Johnston Almon", 16–17.

89 *Church Record*, 22 July, 1863; MacKenzie, "The Almons," 754–55; PANS, Almon Family Scrapbook; PANS, L. Blackburn to My Dear Friend, 26 Jan. 1862, W.J. Almon Correspondence, Almon Papers. A personal photograph of General William Preston, CSA, who passed through Halifax, is inscribed: "To W.J. Almon, M.D. with kind regards." Almon, Alexander Keith and Archbishop Connolly contributed a total of 600 pounds to the Lancashire relief fund in 1862: *Acadian Recorder*, 1 Nov. 1862.

90 Sutherland, "Benjamin Wier," 838–40; Halifax *Express*, 15–16, 21 April, 1862; B. Wier to J. Howe, 14 Nov. 1861, Howe Papers.

91 *ORN*, vol. 3, B. Wier to N. Walker, 5 Jan. 1864, 544; Wilkinson, *Narrative of a Blockade Runner*.

92 There are suggestions that the American authorities may have confused Keith with another individual.

93 Pryke, "Alexander Keith, Jr." 395–96.

94 PANS, RG5, series GP, misc. A, vol. 4, Petition of Alexander Keith the Younger, 20 Sept. 1864; Shipping Register, Halifax, 1863–64.

95 Hastings Doyle to Newcastle, 23 Dec. 1863; *Reporter*, 19 Jan. 1864; *Acadian Recorder*, 16 Jan. 1864; Winks, *Canada*, 251–52.

96 *Reporter*, 19 Jan. 1864; *Chronicle*, 22 Dec. 1863; *Telegraph*, 24 Dec. 1863.

97 *Novascotian*, 28 Dec. 1863; *Reporter*, 19 Jan. 1864; *Chronicle*, 22 Dec. 1863; *Acadian Recorder*, 16 Jan. 1864; Winks, *Canada*, 252–53.

98 Gunnison and Gunnison, *Autobiography*; Hastings Doyle to Newcastle, 23 Dec. 1863; *ORN*, vol. 3, T. Craven to G. Welles, 23 Dec. 1863, 535; Winks, *Canada*, 252–54. Greely's *The American Conflict* depicted Wade as being "rescued by a mob".

99 *Telegraph*, 31 Dec. 1863; *Citizen*, 22 and 29 Dec. 1863; *Eastern Chronicle*, 24 Dec. 1863; *Colonial Standard*, 29 Dec. 1863; *Novascotian*, 19 Jan. 1864.

100 *Sun*, 4 Jan. 1864.

101 *Chronicle*, 26 Dec. 1863; Yarmouth *Herald*, 31 Dec. 1863; *Novascotian*, 28 Dec. 1863; *Telegraph*, 24 Dec. 1863. Brain was mistaking J. Davis for Pitcher.

102 *Telegraph,* 25 Dec. 1863, 2 Jan. 1864; *Citizen,* 9 Jan. 1864.
103 *Chronicle,* 31 Dec. 1863; Lord Lyons to W. Seward, 30 Jan. 1864; Hastings Doyle to Newcastle, 6 Jan. 1864; "Papers Relating," 269, 301.
104 USCD (Halifax), Gunnison to F.W. Seward; Saint John *Globe,* 24 Dec. 1863. Both Winks and McDonald, in his 1969 M.A. thesis, err by stating that Brain was arrested in New Brunswick.
105 Montreal *Gazette,* 26 Jan. 1863; Halifax *Herald,* 23 Dec. 1896; McDonald, "The Career," 680–81.

CHAPTER SEVEN

1 PANS, C.O. 188 (N.B.), vol. 140, Memorial of the Saint John Chamber of Commerce, 28 March 1864.
2 U.S., *Foreign Relations,* 1864, pt. 2, 525–27; Barnes and Barnes, *Private and Confidential,* 338–39; *Telegraph,* 19 Jan. 1864; Saint John's *Day Book,* 14 Jan. 1864; Jenkins, *Britain and the War,* vol. II, 351–52; Winks, *Canada,* ch. 12.
3 Beale, *Diary of Gideon Welles,* vol. 1, 490, 518–19; Dalhousie University, micro, *John Hay Diaries, 1860–70,* 17 and19 Dec. 1863; Barnes and Barnes, *Private and Confidential,* 339; Lyons to Russell, 31 Dec. 1863, Great Britain, Sessional Papers, North America No. 9.
4 Barnes and Barnes, *Private and Confidential,* 339; J. Woodward to A.H. Gordon, 11 March 1864, U.S., *Foreign Relations,* 1864, pt. 2, 583–84; *New York Times,* 8 March 1864.
5 Lyons to Russell, 31 Dec. 1863; *Reporter,* 3 March 1864.
6 *Chronicle,* 5 Jan. 1864; *Citizen,* 31 Dec. 1863.
7 *Sun,* 16 and 21 Dec. 1863; 1 and 16 Jan. 1864; PANS, RG1, Public Records of Nova Scotia, vol. 128, Newcastle to Hastings Doyle, 17 March 1864; U.S., *Foreign Relations,* 1865, pt. 1, 126–28; Adams, *Great Britain and the American Civil War,* vol. 2, 107–8.
8 Memorial to His Excellency Abraham Lincoln, U.S., *Foreign Relations,* 1865, pt. 1, 126–28; USCD (Halifax), Jackson to William Seward, 1864.
9 *Sun,* 1 Jan. 1864; *Citizen,* 21 Jan. 1864; Gunnison and Gunnison, *Autobiography.*
10 Perry *Consolidated Treaty Series,* vol. 93, 1842, 422–23; Brode, *Odyssey of John Anderson; Chesapeake,* 53–54. For an early attempt to extradite New Brunswick robbers from Maine, see Manning, *Diplomatic Correspondence,* vol. 4, 429–30.
11 A.H. Gordon to Duke of Newcastle, 1 Jan. 1864, Gordon to Lyons, 28 Dec. 1863, Great Britain, Sessional Papers, North America No. 9; *Chesapeake,* 55–56; PANS, C.O. 188 (N.B.), vol. 140, Gordon to Newcastle, 1 Jan. 1864; Attorney General J.M. Johnston to S.L. Tilley, 30 Dec. 1863; Solicitor General Charles Watters to S.L. Tilley, 2 Jan. 1864.

Gordon's warrant was issued under Act of Parliament, 6 and 7 Vic., cap. 76. Johnston opined that no warrant could be issued because the alleged offence did not take place in New Brunswick; Watters argued that a warrant could be issued only after the suspects reached New Brunswick.

12 Saint John *Globe*, 7 Jan. 1864; *Morning News*, 28 Dec. 1863; *Chronicle*, 31 Dec. 1863. Another brother, John, was a Wesleyan minister, with Yankee sympathies, at York, Maine: Smith, *Confederates Downeast*, 27.

13 *Freeman*, 28 Dec. 1863; *British Colonist*, 3 Jan. 1864; *Telegraph*, 29 Dec. 1863; Toronto *Globe*, 12 Jan. 1864; *Sun*, 1 Jan. 1864; *New Brunswick Courier*, 2 Jan. 1864; *Telegraph*, 15 March 1864; Gordon to Newcastle, 1 Jan. 1864, "Papers Relating"; Winks, *Canada*, 256–57 and McDonald, "Second Chesapeake Affair," 682, mistakenly claim that Locke and Parr were arrested in New Brunswick.

14 Gordon to Newcastle, 18 Jan. 1864, "Papers Relating".

15 *British Colonist*, 4 Feb. 1864.

16 *British Colonist*, 4 Feb. 1864; *Chesapeake*, preface; Acheson, "Andrew Rainsford Wetmore," 1096–98.

17 *ORN*, vol. 3, Turlington to G.A. Davis, 4 Jan. 1864, 539–41; *Morning News*, 28 Dec. 1863; *Monitor*, 21 Jan. 1864; Winks, *Canada*, 257.

18 Wallace, "John Hamilton Gray," 372–76; *Monitor*, 21 Jan. 1864; *News*, 6 Feb. 1863. Gray had also served as an umpire in the Anglo-American fisheries disputes in 1859.

19 *ORN*, series I, vol. 3, 651–60, 687, 703–4; vol. 4, 380, 391; vol. 8, 126–29, 138–41, 144–48, 774–75, 800; vol. 15, 810; vol. 52, 258; Boatner, *CWD*, "New Madrid and Island No. 10," 587–88; Walke, "Western Flotilla," 430–52; Walke, "Opposing Forces," 463.

20 *Monitor*, 24 Jan. 1864; *Chronicle*, 7 Jan. 1864; *Chesapeake*, 6, 56–8; Gray to Gordon, 14 Jan. 1864, "Papers Relating"; *Reporter*, 7 Jan. 1864.

21 *Chronicle*, 7 Jan., 2 Feb. 1864; *Telegraph*, 12 Jan. 1864; *Chesapeake*, 5–11, 56–58.

22 *Chesapeake*, 12–15; *Telegraph*, 9 Jan. 1864.

23 *ORN*, vol. 3, Turlington to Davis, 4 Jan. 1864, 539–41.

24 *Chronicle*, 2 Feb. 1864; *Telegraph*, 12 Jan. 1864; *Chesapeake*, 15–18.

25 *British Colonist*, 4 Feb. 1864; *Chronicle*, 4 Feb. 1864; *Telegraph*, 2 Feb. 1864; *Chesapeake*, 18–19.

26 *British Colonist*, 4 Feb. 1864; *Telegraph*, 2 Feb. 1864; *Chesapeake*, 19–20.

27 *British Colonist*, 4 Feb. 1864; *Chesapeake*, 20–21, 59–60; *Telegraph*, 12 and 14 Jan. 1864, 2 and 11 Feb. 1864.

28 *New York Times*, 13 and 25 Oct. 1861; *Telegraph*, 16 Feb. 1864; Rice, "Pirates or Patriots?" 46–52; Nash, *Naval History*, 292–95.

29 *CWNC*, I-18, 20, III-45, VI-328; Chandler, "Release of the *Chapman* Pirates," 129–43; Clarke, *Treatise upon the Law of Extradition*, 140–43.

30 *Memoir of John Yates Beall.*
31 *New York Times,* 7 Jan. 1864.
32 Saint John *Globe,* 27 Feb., 7 March 1864; *Sun,* 26 Feb. 1864; *Novascotian,* 29 Feb. 1864; *Chesapeake,* 22–23.
33 *Telegraph,* 25–27 Feb. 1864; *News,* 7 March 1864; *Sun,* 29 Feb. 1864; *Chesapeake,* 60–62.
34 *Reporter,* 19 March 1864; *New York Times,* 4 March 1864; *News,* 9 and 11 March 1864. For the Revenue Cutter Service, see Salter, "Guardians of the Coast," 34–40.
35 *New York Times,* 5 and 13 March 1864.
36 Bale, *William Johnstone Ritchie;* Bale and Mellett, "William Johnstone Ritchie," 895–900; Fenety, *Political Notes.*
37 *Chesapeake,* 23–24, 26–35. Ritchie's ruling was also printed in the pamphlet, Day, *Judgement.*
38 *Chesapeake,* 25, 36–39.
39 *Telegraph,* 12 March 1864.
40 *Chesapeake,* 40–48; Day, *Judgement,* 8–10.
41 *Chesapeake,* 44–45.
42 Day, *Judgement,* 12–14; *Chesapeake,* 49–50; *Telegraph,* 12 March 1864.
43 *Chesapeake,* 47–52; *Citizen,* 24 March 1864; Day, *Judgement,* 11–15.
44 *Telegraph,* 12 and 19 March 1864; *Reporter,* 15 March 1864. At this time the word on the streets of Saint John was that Brain had reached Wilmington and Parr had departed from Richmond carrying dispatches concerning the *Chesapeake.*
45 PANS, C.O. 188 (N.B.), vol. 140, Gordon to Newcastle, 4 Jan. 1864.
46 Ibid.
47 *News,* 11 March 1864; MacNutt, *New Brunswick,* 399.
48 *News,* 28 March 1864; USCD (SJ), Howard to F.W. Seward, 3, 4 and 10 March, 7 July 1864; *New York Times,* 8, 11 and 14 March 1864; William Seward to Lord Lyons, 21 March 1864, U.S., *Foreign Affairs,* 1864, pt. 2; Earl Russell to Lord Lyons, 11 March 1864, "Papers Relating". Seward, much to the ire of the British colonial secretary, continued to refer to the *Chesapeake* captors as "pirates."
49 *Telegraph,* 12 March 1864; *Freeman,* 15 March 1864.
50 *Telegraph,* 15 March 1870; Saint John *Globe,* 10 and 16 March 1864; *Express,* 16 March 1864. The case was later mentioned in Clarke's *Treatise upon the Law of Extradition,* 136–39.
51 PANS, RG1, vol. 127, Hastings Doyle to Lord Lyons, 23 Dec. 1863; Hastings Doyle to Newcastle, 17 March 1864; Hastings Doyle to Newcastle, 26 Dec. 1863; Hastings Doyle to Lyons, 6 Jan. 1864, "Papers Relating"; *New York Times,* 1 Jan. 1864; *Novascotian,* 18 Jan. 1864.
52 *ORN,* vol. 3, Wier to Walker, 5 Jan. 1864, 542–44; Henderson, *Private Journal,* 61.

53 USCD (Halifax), Jackson to F.W. Seward, 4 Feb. 1864; PANS, RG1, vol. 126, Hastings Doyle to Lyons, 6 Jan. 1864; Lyons to Russell, 8 Jan. 1864, "Papers Relating"; Bates, "Rebel Cypher Despatch."

54 The merchants included Charles Samson, Henry Charlotte, James Ross and John Ross of Quebec; E.J.S. Maitland and R.S. Taylor of Montreal; and James McSorley of Saint John.

55 *Novascotian*, 18 Jan., 15 Feb. 1864; *Express*, 8 Jan. 1864; USCD (Halifax), Jackson to F.W. Seward, 15 Jan. 1864; PANS, RG40, Court of Vice Admiralty, vol. 23, 1864, Ships C–Z, "Chesapeake." The expenses of the revenue officers amounted to $1500.

56 *New York Times*, 10 Jan. 1864; *Novascotian*, 18 Jan. 1864; Sutherland, "James William Johnston," 381–88.

57 Neil J. MacKinnon, "John William Ritchie," *DCB* XI: 754–55; Power, "Our First President," 1–15; Stayner, "John William Ritchie," 183–277.

58 Power, "Our First President," 1–15; Stayner, "John William Ritchie," 183–277.

59 *Novascotian*, 18 Jan. 1864; *Reporter*, 14 Jan., 11 Feb. 1864; *Sun*, 15 Jan. 1864; *Chronicle*, 12 Jan. 1864; Townshend, "Alexander Stewart," 1–114.

60 PANS, RG1, vol. 127, Hastings Doyle to Newcastle, 17 March 1864; *Chronicle*, 12 Jan. 1864; *New York Times*, 6 March 1864; *ORN*, vol. 2, Diplomatic Correspondence re *Tuscaloosa*, 710–20; Jenkins, *Britain*, vol. 2, 330–33. *Tuscaloosa*, formerly the barque *Conrad*, had been captured by the *Alabama* and armed to cruise the coast of Africa. In December 1863, after returning from a cruise to Brazil, it had been seized by British colonial authorities as an uncondemned prize violating neutrality.

61 *Chronicle*, 1 Feb. 1864; *New York Times*, 7 Feb. 1864; *Novascotian*, 18 Jan. 1864; *Sun*, 12 and 15 Jan. 1864; *Reporter*, 14 Jan., 11 Feb., 1864; *ORN*, vol. 3, 556–60; Townshend, "Alexander Stewart," 1–114; Winks, *Canada*, 259–60.

62 *Reporter*, 18 Feb. 1864; Raddall, *Halifax*, 201–2.

63 *Express*, 18 March 1864; William Seward to M. Jackson, 24 Feb. 1864, Great Britain, Sessional Papers, North America No. 9. During the *Alabama* arbitration, the U.S. made a claim upon Britain for the cost of sending gunboats in pursuit of the *Chesapeake*: Great Britain, Sessional Papers, "Report of the Committee Appointed by the Board of Trade," North American No. 4 (1872), 87.

64 *Reporter*, 12 and 19 March 1864; *New York Times*, 18 March 1864.

65 *ORN*, vol. 3, J. Benjamin to H.P. Holcombe, 15 Feb. 1864, 544–50; Horan, *Confederate Agent*, 81–88; Kinchen, *Confederate Operations*, 47–48; 92–93.

66 *ORN*, vol. 3, Benjamin to Holcombe, 15 Feb. 1864.

67 Jenkins, *Britain*, vol. 2, 354; *ORN*, vol. 3, Holcombe to Benjamin, 1 April

1864.

68 Ibid.
69 *ORN*, vol. 3, Holcombe to Benjamin, 1 and 24 April 1864.
70 *ORN*, vol. 3, Benjamin to Holcombe, 20 April 1864, 554–56.
71 Jenkins, *Britain*, vol. 2, 354; *Telegraph*, 15 March 1864.
72 *Journal*, 5 Feb. 1864; *British Colonist*, 27 Feb. 1864; *Express*, 22 April 1864; *Sun*, 28 Oct. 1863; *Telegraph*, 2 and 9 Feb. 1864.
73 *Telegraph*, 2 Sept. 1864; *Halifax City Directory, 1863*.
74 *Reporter*, 11 Feb. 1864.
75 *Chronicle*, 14 Sept. 1863.
76 *Citizen*, 14 Nov. 1863; PANS, Almon Family Scrapbook; *ORA*, series IV, vol. 1, 1041; vol. 3, 402, 713; Billings, *Hardtack and Coffee*, ch. 16; Wiley, *Life of Johnny Reb*, ch. 13. The author wishes to thank Allan Marble for a list of Nova Scotian physicians who served in the war.
77 *Reporter*, 30 Sept. 1865; PANS, Almon Family Scrapbook.
78 USCD (Halifax), Jackson to F.W. Seward, 2 Jan. 1864; *Novasotian*, 18 Jan. 1864; *New York Times*, 13 Jan. 1864.
79 Beck, "Philip Carteret Hill," 1–16.
80 *Reporter*, 12 and 19 Jan. 1864; *Acadian Recorder*, 16 Jan. 1864; *Novascotian*, 18 Jan. 1864; PANS, RG2, vol. 3, 398, Attorney General's Report on Examination of Messrs. Almon, Keith and Smith, 13 Jan. 1864.
81 PANS, Attorney General's Report; *Novascotian*, 18 Jan. 1864; *Reporter*, 12 and 19 Jan. 1864.
82 *Novascotian*, 18 Jan. 1864; *Reporter*, 19 Jan. 1864.
83 *Sun*, 16 Jan. 1864; *Citizen*, 16 Jan. 1864; *Novascotian*, 18 Jan. 1864; *Reporter*, 19 Jan. 1864; PANS, Attorney General's Report.
84 *Novascotian*, 19 Jan. 1864; *Citizen*, 16 Jan. 1864; *Sun*, 16 Jan. 1864; *Reporter*, 19 Jan. 1864.
85 PANS, Attorney General's Report.
86 *Acadian Recorder*, 16 Jan. 1864; *Novascotian*, 18 Jan. 1864.
87 *Reporter*, 12 and 19 Jan. 1864; PANS, RG1, vol. 127, Hastings Doyle to Newcastle, 20 Jan. 1864.
88 *Telegraph*, 10 March 1864; *Acadian Recorder*, 10 Jan. 1864; Winks, *Canada*, ch. 12; Jones, "Treason and Piracy," 472–87.

CHAPTER EIGHT

1 Henderson, *Private Journal of Georgiana Gholson Walker*, 91.
2 Bourne, *Balance of Power*.
3 PANS, micro 10076, Bell Diaries, 4 Jan. 1864.
4 Thurston, *Tallahassee Skipper*, ch. 23; Shingleton, *John Taylor Wood*, 118–20; Wood, "Tallahassee," 219–29.
5 Shingleton, *John Taylor Wood*, 48–53; Thurston, *Tallahassee Skipper*.

6 Thurston, *Tallahassee Skipper*, ch. 24. Hearn, *Gray Raiders of the Sea*, concluded that the *Tallahassee* was a fine blockade runner but a poor choice as a cruiser because of its dependence on engines.
7 Wood, "Tallahassee," 221.
8 *New York Times*, 29 Sept. 1864; Wood, "Tallahassee," 221; Thurston, *Tallahassee Skipper*, ch. 24; Shingleton, *John Taylor Wood*, 122–25; Smith, *Confederates Downeast*, ch. 6.
9 Wood, "Tallahassee," 222; *New York Times*, 29 Sept. 1864; Thurston, *Tallahassee Skipper*, ch. 24; Smith, *Confederates Downeast*, ch. 6.
10 *New York Times*, 29 Sept. 1864.
11 Ibid.
12 Thurston, *Tallahassee Skipper*, ch. 24; Wood, "Tallahassee," 223–24; *New York Times*, 15 Aug., 29 Sept. 1864; Smith, *Confederates Downeast*, 49–51. In some accounts the pilot boat is named *James Finch*.
13 Thurston, *Tallahassee Skipper*, ch. 24; *New York Times*, 17 Aug. 1864.
14 Wood, "Tallahassee," 224–25.
15 *ORN*, series I, vol. 34, W.H. Ludlow to G. Welles, 12 Aug. 1864, 137; S. Corry to G. Welles, 18 July 1864, 119.
16 Saint John *Globe*, 23 Aug. 1864; *ORN*, vol. 3, H. Paulding to G. Welles, 12 Aug. 1864; H. Paulding to G.R. Ranson, 13 Aug. 1864, 137, 142; *Religious Intelligencer*, 2 Sept. 1864.
17 *ORN*, vol. 3, A.G. Clary to S.H. Stringham, 19 Aug. 1863, 154; G.A. Stevens to G. Welles, 15 Aug. 1864, 148; C.K. Stringham to G. Welles, 13 Aug. 1864.
18 *ORN*, vol. 3, H. Paulding to G. Welles, 14 Aug. 1864, 144; W.R. Taylor to Welles, 20 Aug. 1864, 160; W.R. Taylor to Welles, 14 Aug. 1864, 147; S.W. Godon to G. Welles, 24 Aug. 1864, 167–68.
19 *ORN*, vol. 3, A.G. Clary to G. Welles, 9 Sept. 1864, 183–84.
20 *ORN*, vol. 3, A.G. Clary to S.H. Stringham, 19 Aug. 1864, 153; H. Paulding to Welles, 14 Aug. 1864, 145; G.M. Ransom to G. Welles, 14 Aug. 1864, 145; Wood, "Tallahassee," 225; *New York Times*, 15–17 Aug., 29 Sept. 1864; Thurston, *Tallahassee Skipper*, ch. 24; Smith, *Confederates Downeast*, 52–53.
21 Wood, "Tallahassee," 226; *New York Times*, 16–17 Aug., 29 Sept. 1864; *ORN*, vol. 3, G.S. Blake to G. Welles, 15 Aug. 1864, 149.
22 *New York Times*, 29 Sept. 1864. Quarterdeck prayers were common in the antebellum navy, as Herman Melville explained in his semi-fictional *White-Jacket, Or the World of a Man of War* (1851).
23 Thurston, *Tallahassee Skipper*, ch. 26; Wood, "Tallahassee." The *James Littlefield*, which carried Welsh coal, at one point towed the raider through the fog.
24 *New York Times*, 29 Sept. 1864; Thurston, *Tallahassee Skipper*, ch. 24.
25 *New York Times*, 18–20 Aug. 1864.

26 *New York Times*, 29 Sept. 1864; Thurston, *Tallahassee Skipper*, ch. 25; Smith, *Confederates Downeast*, 54.

27 *New York Times*, 29 Sept. 1864; Thurston, *Tallahassee Skipper*, ch. 25.

28 Thurston, *Tallahassee Skipper*, ch. 27; *Citizen*, 20 Aug. 1864. Wood later wrote that the raiders had found Halifax only by "constant use of the lead": *"Tallahassee,"* 227.

29 Wood, *"Tallahassee"*; Thurston, *Tallahassee Skipper*, ch. 26; *New York Times*, 29 Sept. 1864; *Novascotian*, 12 Sept. 1864; Saint John *Globe*, 22 Aug. 1864.

30 *Chronicle*, 19 Aug. 1864; *Reporter*, 18 Aug. 1864; *Sun*, 19 Aug. 1864; *Novascotian*, 12 Sept. 1864; *New York Times*, 18–19 Aug. 1864; *Freeman*, 18 Aug. 1864; *Telegraph*, 22 Aug. 1864. Lord Lyons reported that the American press called the raider an "Anglo-Rebel pirate": Barnes and Barnes, *Private and Confidential*, 347.

31 *Chronicle*, 5 and 11 Aug., 5, 13 and 14 Sept. 1864; *Novascotian*, 15 Aug. 1864; *News*, 11 Aug. 1864.

32 St. Andrew's *Standard*, 24 Aug. 1864; *News*, 23 Aug. 1864; Winks, *Canada*, 134, 287; U.S., *Foreign Relations*, 1865, pt. 2, A.H. Gordon to J.H. Burnley, 11 Aug. 1864; PANS, C.O. 188 (N.B.), vol. 138, Gordon to Newcastle, 14 Sept. 1863; vol. 144, Gordon to Cardwell, 31 Dec. 1865. According to Gordon, these works and a battery near Eastport had been built for "electioneering purposes."

33 Quoted in *New York Times*, 4 Sept. 1864.

34 *New York Times*, 20 Aug., 4 Sept. 1864; Saint John *Globe*, 26 Aug. 1864; St. Andrew's *Standard*, 7 and 14 Sept. 1864; *Carleton Sentinel*, 27 Aug. 1864; *Telegraph*, 12 Aug. 1864; USCD (SJ), J.Q. Howard to F.W. Seward, 23 Aug. 1864.

35 Graham, *China Station*; *Reporter*, 22 Oct. 1864; *New York Times*, 29 Sept. 1864.

36 Curtis, "Blood Is Thicker Than Water," 157–76; Farley, "Josiah Tattnall," 172–80; Hagan, *People's Navy*, ch. 5; Shingleton, *John Taylor Wood*, 136; Jones, *Commodore Josiah Tattnall*, 82–90. Wood's commander on the *Virginia* had also been present in the U.S. squadron on the Peiho River.

37 Thurston, *Tallahassee Skipper*, chs. 25–30; Wood, *"Tallahassee."*

38 *Novascotian*, 15 Aug. 1864; Thurston, *Tallahassee Skipper*, ch. 256; Shingleton, *John Taylor Wood*, 136–37; Smith, *Confederates Downeast*, 55. The North American and West Indies Squadron comprised ten medium and large warships and twenty-one smaller ones.

39 Burroughs, "Sir Richard Graves MacDonnell," 555–56 .

40 USCD (Halifax), M. Jackson to F.W. Seward, 16 Aug. 1864; Jackson to C. Tupper, 18 Aug. 1864; Tupper to Jackson, 18 Aug. 1864; Jackson to William Seward, 19 Aug. 1864.

41 *Reporter*, 20 Aug. 1864.

42 USCD (Halifax), Jackson to G. Welles, 18 Aug. 1864; PANS, RG1, vol. 127, R.G. MacDonnell to Cardwell, 18 Aug. 1864; PANS, micro 14645, F.O. 3, vol. 1094, R.G. MacDonnell to Cardwell, 18 and 22 Aug. 1864; Lyons to Earl of Russell, 19 Aug. 1864; Shingleton, *John Taylor Wood*, 137; Thomas, "CSS *Tallahassee*," 149–52; *Reporter*, 20 Aug. 1864.

43 *Sun*, 22 Aug. 1864; *Journal*, 18 July, 7 Sept. 1864; USCD (Halifax), M. Jackson to F.W. Seward, 22 July 1864; Semmes, *Memoirs of a Service Afloat*.

45 PANS, micro 14645, F.O. 3, vol. 1094, Lyons to Russell, 19 Aug. 1864; USCD (Halifax), Jackson to W. Seward, 18–19 Aug. 1864.

46 *Chronicle*, 28 July 1864; *Telegraph*, 23 and 24 July 1864; USCD (SJ), Howard to F.W. Seward, 21 July 1864; Horan, *Confederate Agent*, 113–20; Smith, *Confederates Downeast*, chs. 1–5.

47 USCD (SJ), Howard to F.W. Seward, 26 Aug. 1864; *Chronicle*, 28 July 1864; *New Brunswick Reporter*, 22 July 1864; *Telegraph*, 24 July 1864; Smith, *Confederates Downeast*, chs. 1–5.

48 Saint John *Globe*, 29 July 1864; *Freeman*, 19 July 1864; *Sun*, 18 July 1864; Horan, *Confederate Agent*, 227–28.

49 *New Brunswick Reporter*, 22 July 1864; Saint John *Globe*, 25 July 1864; Horan, *Confederate Agent*; Winks, *Canada*, 285–86; Smith, *Confederates Downeast*, chs. 4–5.

50 *Religious Intelligencer*, 28 Oct. 1864; *ORN*, series III, vol. 4, S. Conly to E. Stanton, 623–34; Winks, *Canada*, 285; Horan, *Confederate Agent*, 114–17, 227–28; Shingleton, *John Taylor Wood*, 143–44. According to Hatch, *Maine*, ch. 22, the Confederate sea rovers inflicted serious damage on Maine. Nearly half of the two hundred Northern vessels captured had been built in the state. From 1861 to 1864, the state registered less than 150 new vessels.

51 *ORN*, series III, vol. 5, E. Low to Acting Provost Marshall General, 6 Jan. 1865, 1038–39; *Telegraph*, 4 Aug. 1864; *Freeman*, 6 Dec. 1864; Charlottetown *Examiner*, 1 Aug. 1864; Winks, *Canada*, 286; Hatch, *Maine*, 494–96; Smith, *Confederates Downeast*, ch. 7.

52 *Carleton Sentinel*, 30 July, 6 Aug. 1864; *New Brunswick Reporter*, 1 Jan., 15 and 22 July 1864; *Telegraph*, 17 Sept. 1864; *Protestant and Evangelical Witness*, 20 Aug. 1864.

53 *Chronicle*, 19 Aug., 12 Oct. 1864; *New York Times*, 29 Sept. 1864; *Reporter*, 20 Aug. 1864.

54 *New York Times*, 29 Sept. 1864; *Sun*, 14 Oct. 1864.

55 PANS, RG1, vol. 127, R.G. MacDonnell to Edward Cardwell, 23 Aug. 1864; *Chronicle*, 12 Oct. 1864; PANS, micro 14645, F.O. 5, vol. 1094, "Case of the *Tallahassee*," Vice-Admiral Sir James Hope to Admiralty, 19 Aug. 1864; Vice-Admiral James Hope to R.G. MacDonnell, 20 Aug. 1864; Thomas, "CSS *Tallahassee*," 150–51.

338 Notes to pages 233–237

56 Thurston, *Tallahassee Skipper*, ch. 28; *Jervois Report* (1865), 39.

57 Hope to MacDonnell, 20 Aug. 1864; Saint John *Globe*, 6 Sept. 1864; *Chronicle*, 12 Oct. 1864; *Reporter*, 20 Aug. 1864; Johnston, *Defending Halifax*, 20–31.

58 *New York Times*, 29 Sept. 1864; Thurston, *Tallahassee Skipper*, ch. 28. Despite its romanticization in Nova Scotia, the pilot's role in the "escape" was not mentioned in the account of the incident that appeared in a Richmond journal: *Chronicle*, 12 Oct. 1864.

59 *ORN*, vol. 3, Gideon Welles to George Stevens, 18 Aug. 1864, 153; F.O. 5, vol. 1094, MacDonnell to Cardwell, 31 Aug. 1864; *Reporter*, 20 Aug. 1864; USCD (Halifax), Jackson to F.W. Seward, 31 Aug. 1864.

60 USCD (Halifax), Jackson to W.H. Seward, 19–20 Aug. 1864; *Citizen*, 20 Aug. 1864; Thomas, "CSS *Tallahassee*," 151–52; *ORN*, vol. 3, G.A. Stevens to G. Welles, 30 Aug. 1864, 176–77; *Chronicle*, 27 Aug., 1 Sept. 1864; *New York Times*, 31 Aug. 1864; Charlottetown *Examiner*, 19 Sept. 1864; USCD (Charlottetown), Sherman to F.W. Seward, 24 Aug. 1864.

61 *ORN*, vol. 3, G. Welles to H. Paulding, 20 Aug. 1864, 159–60; J.N. Quackenbush to G. Welles, 30 Aug. 1865, 176; Beale, *Diary of Gideon Welles*, vol. 2, 111–13.

62 *ORN*, vol. 3, G. Welles to W.R. Taylor, 23 Aug. 1864; USCD (Halifax), M. Jackson to W.H. Seward, 23 and 30 Aug. 1864; Saint John *Globe*, 23 Aug., 6 Sept. 1864; *Chronicle*, 22 and 27 Aug. 1864; *Express*, 26 Aug., 31 Oct. 1864.

63 *ORN*, vol. 3, M. Jackson to W.H. Seward, 30 Aug. 1864, 177; USCD (Halifax), Jackson to W.H. Seward, 30 Aug. 1864; *Chronicle*, 12 Oct. 1864; *Citizen*, 30 Aug. 1864; *News*, 30 Aug. 1864.

64 *ORN*, vol. 3, G. Welles to Charles A. French, 30 Aug. 1864, 178; French to Welles, 24 Oct. 1864, 306–7; *Novascotian*, 26 Sept. 1864; *Citizen*, 23 Aug. 1864; *News*, 11 Oct. 1864.

65 *ORN*, vol. 3, J.A. Drake to G. Welles, 1 and 5 Sept. 1864, 180–83; Extract from Minutes of Executive Council, 29 Aug. 1864, 295; Joseph E. DeHaven to Welles, 1 Nov. 1864, 313; Report of Captain E.P.B. Von Donop, 2 Oct. 1864, 294–96; vol 10, Abstract of Log of USS *Florida*, 297; PANS, RG1, vol. 127, MacDonnell to Cardwell, 31 Aug., 3 Oct. 1864; *Reporter*, 20 Sept. 1864; *Sun*, 23 Nov. 1864; *Chronicle*, 3 Oct., 2 Nov. 1864; Yarmouth *Herald*, 24 Nov. 1864; *Citizen*, 20 Sept. 1864; *Novascotian*, 26 Sept. 1864; *Express*, 16 Sept. 1864; *News*, 20 Sept., 1 Nov. 1864.

66 *ORN*, vol. 3, S.P. Lee to G. Welles, 26 Aug., 3 Sept. 1864, 170–72; H.A. Phelon to S.P. Lee, 26 Aug. 1864, 172; O.S. Glisson to S.P. Lee, 29 Aug. 1864, 172–73; S. Huse to S.P. Lee, 26 Aug. 1864, 173; J.R. Breck to S.P. Lee, 26 Aug. 1864, 174; vol. 10, W.H.C. Whitting to S. Mallory, 6 Oct. 1864, 774; *Chronicle*, 12 Oct. 1864; Saint John *Globe*, 3 Sept. 1864; *New York Times*, 29 Sept., 9 Oct. 1864; Wilkinson, *Narrative*, 222; Thurston,

Tallahassee Skipper, ch. 29. The Halifax *Journal* identified "Bohemian" as Dr. Schepardson.

67 *Chronicle*, 5 Sept. 1864; *ORN*, vol. 10, Major General W.H.C. Whiting to J.A. Seddon, 11 Oct. 1864, 781–82; Z.B. Vance to Jefferson Davis, 14 Oct. 1864, 783; *New York Times*, 10 Dec. 1864; *Citizen*, 15 Oct. 1863; *News*, 15 Oct. 1864; Wilkinson, *Narrative*; Robinson, *Shark of the Confederacy*, ch. 14.

68 USCD (Halifax), Jackson to G. Welles, 30 Aug. 1864; *Chronicle*, 7, 17 and 21 Sept. 1864; *Novascotian*, 19 Sept. 1864; *Citizen*, 10 Sept. 1864; *Express*, 31 Oct., 4 Nov. 1864; *News*, 10 Sept. 1864; *Freeman*, 8 Sept. 1864; *ORN*, vol. 3, G. Welles to S. Stringham, 24 Aug. 1864, 166–67; R.T. Renshaw to G. Welles, 4 Sept. 1864, 182–83; G. Welles to S.W. Godon, 1 Sept. 1864, 187; 24 Aug. 1864, 167–68; A.J. Drake to G. Welles, 28 Aug. 1864, 175–76.

69 *ORN*, vol. 10, S.P. Lee to G. Welles, 2 Sept. 1864, 416; David Porter to James Parker, 26 Oct. 1864, 603; USCD (Halifax), Jackson to F.W. Seward, 26 Aug. 1864; *New York Times*, 26 Oct. 1864; *Novascotian*, 3 Oct. 1864; *Chronicle*, 2 Nov. 1864; *Reporter*, 29 Nov. 1864; Wilkinson, *Narrative*, ch. 15; Dalzell, *Flight from the Flag*, 183–88; Thurston, *Tallahassee Skipper*, ch. 30.

70 *ORN*, vol. 3, J.Q. Howard to G.U. Morris, 14 Nov. 1864, 336; Morris to Gideon Welles, 10 Nov. 1864, 331; T.C. Harris to Rear-Admiral D. Porter, 6 Nov. 1864, 320; *Chronicle*, 9 Nov. 1864; *British Colonist*, 10 Nov. 1864; *Novascotian*, 21 Nov. 1864; *Sun*, 9 Nov. 1864.

71 *Journal*, 13 Jan. 1865; Thomas, "CSS *Tallahassee*," 155–59; Thurston, *Tallahassee Skipper*, ch. 30.

72 *British Colonist*, 16 March 1865.

73 *CWNC*, VI-211; Higginbottom, "A Raider Refuels," 208–28; Bernath, *Squall Across the Atlantic*. In a submission to the arbitration tribunal at Geneva in 1872, the U.S. government expressed favour in regards to the actions of Hope and MacDonnell in limiting the *Tallahassee*'s port time and fuel intake: "The Case of the United States to Be Laid Before the Tribunal of Arbitration to be Convened at Geneva, 1872," Great Britain, Sessional Papers, North America No. 2, 1872, 111–12.

CHAPTER NINE

1 As Robinson points out, the Confederacy's real problem was not the blockade, but the logistical difficulties of distributing supplies once they had been landed: *Shark of the Confederacy*, ch. 14.

2 *New York Times*, 8 Dec. 1864; *ORN*, vol. 3, S.P. Lee to Pierce Crosby, 20 Sept. 1864, 471.

3 Beale, *Diary of Gideon Welles*, vol. 2, 185; *ORN*, vol. 10, G. Welles to S.P.

Lee, 2 Sept. 1864, 416. For the blockade, see Marquis, "Ports of Halifax and Saint John," 1–19.

4   Adams, *Great Britain and the American Civil War*, vol. 1, 269, n. 2.

5   *Chronicle*, 22 Sept. 1864.

6   USCD (SJ), J. Howard to F.W. Seward, 6 Feb. 1863; *Chronicle*, 23 Sept. 1864; Winks, *Canada*, 137–39.

7   *New York Times*, 3 Dec. 1861; Saint John *Globe*, 6 June 1863; Nepveaux, *George Alfred Trenholm*, 60–61; *ORN*, vol. 13, 288, 447; Cochran, *Blockade Runners*, 159–61; Wise, *Lifeline*, 57, 68, 115, 338. The *Herald*, first owned by Fraser, Trenholm and Co., was sold to the (Chicora) Importing and Exporting Co. of South Carolina. *Fanny and Jennie* was grounded near Wrightsville Beach. Coxetter's "coloured" cabin boy and steward were drowned: Heyl, *Early American Steamers*, vol. 3, 157–58.

8   Basoco, "British View of the Union Navy," 30–45.

9   *ORN*, vol. 3, E.P.B. Von Donop to Lieutenant-Commander Magaw, 2 Oct. 1864, 296; PANS, RG1, vol. 127, R.G. MacDonnell to E. Cardwell, 3 Oct. 1864; U.S., *Foreign Relations*, 1864, pt. 2, J.H. Burnley to W.H. Seward, 1 Oct. 1864, 717.

10 PANS, MG1, D (micro 809), Correspondence of W.J. Almon, B. Tucker to W.J. Almon, 13 April 1864; U.S. *Foreign Relations*, 1865, pt. 1, Confederate correspondence, 14–7; Winks, *Canada*, 272–73, 297.

11 Winks, *Canada*, 141; USCD (Halifax), M. Jackson to F.W. Seward, 14 July 1864; Saint John *Globe*, 8 March 1864; USCD (SJ), Jackson to F.W. Seward, 8 June, 21 July 1864.

12 Trombley, "Thomas Louis Connolly," 312–13; PANS, Connolly Papers, Connolly to whom it may concern, 20 May 1864; C.C. Clay to Hon. J.P. Benjamin, 14 June 1864; USCD (SJ), J. Howard to F.W. Seward, 2, 17 June 1864; Kinchen, *Confederate Operations*, 36–39, 46, 127–28; *New York Times*, 21–22 July 1864; Jenkins, *Britain*, vol. 2, 355–57; Winks, *Canada*, 266–69, 273–75; Horan, *Confederate Agent*, ch. 4. Thompson was a former member of President Buchanan's cabinet.

13 Saint John *Globe*, 8 Sept. 1864; *Citizen*, 8 Sept. 1864; *Journal*, 8 Sept. 1864; Almon Family Scrapbook, J. Holcombe to W.J. Almon, 23 May 1864; Horan, *Confederate Agent*, 85. Most of the silver service is in the possession of a descendent of Ritchie in British Columbia.

14 *Journal*, 14 and 17 Oct. 1864; Horan, *Confederate Agent*, 111–12; Massey, *Bonnet Brigade*, 90–95.

15 Wise, *Lifeline*, 196–97.

16 *ORN*, vol. 10, M. Jackson to W.H. Seward, 26 Sept. 1864, 484; Horan, *Confederate Agent*, 111–12. The vessel, when it cleared Halifax, carried general cargo consigned to G.C. Harvey. *Condor*, *Falcon*, *Flamingo* and *Ptarmigan*, which all reached Halifax in 1864, were built at Govan, Scotland, by Randolph, Elder and Co. for Alexander Collie and Co.:

Wise, *Lifeline*, appendix 22.

17 USCD (Halifax), M. Jackson to F.W. Seward, 26 Sept. 1864; *Journal*, 4 Nov. 1864; *Novascotian*, 31 Oct. 1864; Kinchen, *Confederate Operations*, 92–3; Horan, *Confederate Agent*, 111–12.

18 PANS, RG1, vol. 127, Hastings Doyle to Newcastle, 17 and 21 March 1864; USCD (Halifax), M. Jackson to F.W. Seward, 22 Jan. 1864; *ORN*, vol. 10, Welles to S.P. Lee, 5 Feb. 1864, 461; Wise, *Lifeline*, 162–63. Doyle, in a letter to Vice-Admiral Hope, referred to the *Trent* and *Chesapeake* incidents and the difficulties in enforcing neutrality regulations to prove the necessity of a year-round, as opposed to seasonal, naval presence at Halifax: Hastings Doyle to Hope, 29 March 1864. *Will o' the Wisp* made six round trips through the blockade and was hit by artillery on its final run into the Cape Fear River.

19 *Sun*, 6 May 1864; USCD (Halifax), M. Jackson to F.W. Seward, 27 April 1864; *Citizen*, 28 April 1864. *Advance* joined the runner *Constance Decimo*.

20 *British Colonist*, 12 Sept. 1863; *Sun*, 29 April, 6 May 1864; *Citizen*, 28 April 1864; *Reporter*, 21 May 1864; *Novascotian*, 2 May 1864; *ORN*, vol. 10, S.P. Lee to G. Welles, 14 Sept. 1864, 453–54; Wise, *Lifeline*, 106, 157–58. In 1871 the Chebucto Marine Railway was capitalized at $100,000: PANS, micro 13627, 1871 Manuscript Census, Dartmouth, Schedule 6, Industrial Establishments. *A.D. Vance*, after its capture, was used as a gunboat in the North Atlantic Blockading Squadron. Renamed *Frolic*, it was sent to the European squadron in 1865: Heyl, *Early American Steamers*, vol. 3, 153–55.

21 *Sun*, 24 Aug. 1864; USCD (Halifax), M. Jackson to F.W. Seward, 8, 23, 31 Aug. 1864; Wise, *Lifeline*, 198–99; *Journal*, 14 Sept. 1864. *Helen* brought tobacco and cotton to Halifax. It returned in the fall for repairs which were completed in December. Walker, earlier in the war, had carried $2 million in bonds to Europe for the Confederate mission: "The Case of the United States to be Laid Before the Tribunal of Arbitration to be Convened at Geneva, British Parliament," Great Britain, North America No. 2, 1872, Sessional Papers, 64.

22 Bulloch, *Secret Service*, vol. 1, 330–32, 351–53; vol. 2, 176, 354; Jenkins, *Britain*, vol. 2, 199, 252, 281, 297, 303, 323, 330.

23 *Reporter*, 5 Nov. 1864; PANS, RG1, vol. 127, R.G. MacDonnell to E. Cardwell, 15 and 29 Sept. 1864; *ORN*, vol. 10, U.S. Consul, Bermuda, 25 Oct. 1864, 601; Adams, *Great Britain and the American Civil War*, vol. 2, 136, 196; U.S., *Foreign Relations*, 1864, pt. 2, R.G. MacDonnell to J.H. Burnley, 30 Sept. 1864, 738; Charles Kuhn Prioleau to Lieutenant J.R. Hamilton, 29 July 1864, Fraser, Trenholm and Co. Papers (photocopy supplied by Ethel Nepveux); Nepveux, *George Alfred Trenholm*; USCD (Halifax), M. Jackson to F.W. Seward, 9 Sept., 29 Oct. 1864; The vessel's

consignee was DeWolfe and Co. Jackson reported a rumour that an armed *Mary* would be commanded by John Brain.

24 Yarmouth *Herald*, 12 Nov. 1863; *Reporter*, 16 Aug. 1863; Saint John *Globe*, 15 Sept. 1864.

25 C.K. Prioleau to Lieutenant J.R. Hamilton, 2 Sept. 1864; C.K. Prioleau to C. Huse, 2 Sept. 1864, Fraser, Trenholm and Co. Papers; USCD (Halifax), M. Jackson to F.W. Seward., 29 March, 30 Aug. 1864; *Sun*, 29 April 1864; Wise, *Lifeline*, appendixes 5–8, 19, 22; *ORN*, vol. 10. S.P. Lee to G. Welles, 2 Sept. 1864, 416; Henderson, *Private Journal*, 110–12. *City of Petersburg* had visited Halifax in March for repairs.

26 USCD (Halifax), M. Jackson to F.W. Seward, 23 Aug., 9, 12, 13 and 17 Sept. 1864; *Sun*, 5 Aug., 21 Sept. 1864; *Chronicle*, 6 Oct. 1864; *Reporter*, 13 Sept., 29 Nov. 1864; *Novascotian*, 22 Oct. 1864; Rudolf Diaries, 20 Sept. 1864; *ORN*, vol. 10, Thomas Dunn to S.P. Lee, 6 Sept. 1864, 427; Circular, 13 Oct. 1864, 562–63. *Annie*, clearing for Nassau in early October, carried general cargo consigned to G.C. Harvey. *Ptarmigan* required repairs.

27 USCD (Halifax), M. Jackson to F.W. Seward, 17 Aug., 7, 10 and 17 Oct. 1864; *ORN*, vol. 10, Lee to Welles, 2 Sept. 1864, 416; *Novascotian*, 15 and 24 Oct. 1864; *Citizen*, 11 Oct. 1864; *Chronicle*, 17 Oct. 1864; *Express*, 12 Oct. 1864; Saint John *Globe*, 15 and 19 Oct. 1864; Wise, *Lifeline*, 208. *Old Dominion* left port in October, failed to enter the Cape Fear River and was pursued back to Nova Scotia by Federal warships. The consul cabled that a Federal detective who had been on assignment in Halifax was returning in early October.

28 Saint John *Globe*, 29 July 1864; USCD(SJ), J. Howard to F.W. Seward, 4 July, 31 Aug., 8 Dec. 1863; *Ross's Weekly*, 21 Aug. 1863; *CWNC*, III-49, 145, 147. For the Wrights, see Rice, "Wrights of Saint John," 317–37. W. and R. Wright were involved in a cargo carried to Nassau in 1862 for J.R. Armstrong of Liverpool: "Case Presented on the Part of the Government of Her Britannic Majesty to the Tribunal of Arbitration, 1871," North American No. 1 (1872), Sessional Papers, 174.

29 USCD (SJ), J. Howard to F.W. Seward, 28 and 31 Aug., 14 Sept. 1863; 26 Aug. 1864; Saint John *Globe*, 20 Oct. 1864; *Express*, 5 Sept. 1864; *Chronicle*, 22 Sept. 1864; *Telegraph*, 21 July 1864; *CWNC*, IV–84; *ORN*, vol. 10, Report of U.S. Consul, Nassau, 1 Nov. 1864, 604. *Laura Jane*, refitted and registered in Saint John, was captured early in 1864: Saint John *Globe*, 9 Feb. 1864.

30 *Acadian Recorder*, 27 Aug. 1864; USCD (Halifax), M. Jackson to F.W. Seward, 24 Oct. 1864; *CWNC*, VI-189, 287; Saint John *Globe*, 26 Sept. 1864; *Sun*, 24 March 1865; Wise, *Lifeline*, ch. 7; Gragg, *Confederate Goliath*, 8. After leaving Halifax, *Ptarmigan* was painted white and renamed *Evelyn*.

31 *Express*, 21 Oct. 1864; PANS, RG40, Vice-Admiralty Court, vol. 23, Steamship *City of Petersburg*, 1864. Most steam blockade runners were crewed by men born in the South, Britain and the Caribbean.

32 Saint John *Globe*, 26 Sept. 1864; *Chronicle*, 6 Aug., 24 Sept., 20 Oct. 1864; *Express*, 29 Aug., 12 Oct., 2 Nov. 1864; *Novascotian*, 22 Oct. 1864; *Sun*, 26 Sept. 1864, 24 March 1865; USCD (Halifax), M. Jackson to F.W. Seward, 13 Sept. 1864. For "Jack ashore," see Fingard, *Jack in Port*.

33 Foster, "Builders vs. Blockaders," 85–90.

34 *Journal*, 19 Sept. 1864.

35 *Sun*, 24 and 26 Oct. 1864; *Reporter*, 24 May 1864; *Chronicle*, 14 and 23 Sept., 26 Oct. 1864; Saint John *Globe*, 17 Nov. 1864; *Novascotian*, 25 Oct. 1864; *ORN*, vol. 10, U.S. Consul, Nassau to State Department, 7 Nov. 1864, 602; USCD (Halifax), M. Jackson to F.W. Seward, 29 March, 6 and 25 Oct., 30 Dec. 1864; Nepveaux, *George Alfred Trenholm*, 69–71; Wise, *Lifeline*, 165. *Colonel Lamb*, which was leased to the Confederate government, survived the war. One reporter claimed that local speculators, including A. Pilsbury, had loaded the brig *Africa* with blockade goods destined for Nassau. The ship was wrecked at Herring Cove in late 1864: *Sun*, 23 Dec. 1864.

36 Saint John *Globe*, 20 June 1864. For the blockade, see Browning, *From Cape Charles*.

37 *New York Times*, 8 Dec. 1864; Gragg, *Confederate Goliath*, 11; Bernath, *Squall Across the Atlantic*; Price, "Ships That Tested the Blockade of the Carolina Ports," 196–241; *ORN*, vol. 10, S.R. Mallory to J.N. Maffitt, 14 Sept. 1864, 741–42; Wise, *Lifeline*, 148.

38 *Express*, 21 and 26 Oct. 1864; *New York Times*, 18 Oct. 1864; Nepveux, *George Alfred Trenholm*, 51. Lord Lyons informed the secretary of state that the British government disapproved of its subjects violating the blockade but expected them to "be given rights under international law": U.S. *Foreign Relations*, 1864, pt. 2, Lyons to Seward, 22 May 1864, 613.

39 Saint John *Globe*, 15 Sept. 1864; Beale, *Diary of Gideon Welles*, vol. 2, 119.

40 *Citizen*, 4 Oct. 1864; *Sun*, 22 Nov. 1864; *ORN*, vol. 3, C.H. Baldwin to Rear-Admiral D.D. Porter, 13 Oct. 1864, 299; vol. 11, 90. *Lady Sterling*, built at Millwall, Great Britain, owned by a London resident, became USS *Lady Sterling* after its capture. As the merchant steamer *Hornet*, it returned to Halifax in 1869 under suspicion that it was linked to anti-Spanish filibustering. The Nova Scotia authorities authorized its departure for Ireland in September 1869. *Hornet* was later involved in landing filibusters in Cuba: Heyl, *Early American Steamers*, vol. IV, 171–74.

41 *Chronicle*, 19 Sept. 1864; *Citizen*, 20 Sept. 1, Nov. 1864; *Novascotian*, 26 Sept. 1864; *Telegraph*, 12 Oct. 1864; *ORN*, vol. 3, T.C. Harris to Rear-

Admiral D.D. Porter, 6 Nov. 1864, 320–21; vol. 10, M. Jackson to F.W. Seward, 12 Sept. 1864, 468; PANS, RG1, Public Records of Nova Scotia, vol. 127, R.G. MacDonnell to E. Cardwell, 29 Sept. 1864.

42 Saunders, *Economic History*, 100. See also Muise, "The 1860s," 18–26.

43 *Sun*, 14 Nov. 1864; *Reporter*, 22 Dec. 1864; *Express*, 21 Dec. 1864; *Citizen*, 20 Sept. 1864; *Chronicle*, 21 Oct. 1864, 26 Jan. 1865; *Novascotian*, 14 Nov., 26 Dec. 1864; *New York Times*, 1 Dec. 1864. One of the few steamers that visited Nova Scotia and then ended up in the Gulf was *Flamingo*, which completed two runs into Galveston: Price, "Ships That Tested the Blockade of the Gulf Ports," 262–90.

44 Hay and Hay, *Last of the Confederate Privateers*, ch. 9; *ORN*, vol. 3., S.R. Mallory to J.C. Braine, 26 May 1864, 238; J.P. Benjamin to Charles Helm, 20 Oct. 1864, 240–41.

45 *ORN*, vol. 3, Report of Charles J. Helm to J.P. Benjamin, 17 Aug. 1864, 233–37; Braine to C.J. Helm, 12 Aug. 1864; Helm to Braine, 16 Aug. 1864, 238–39. Hay and Hay make no mention of Helm's objections and even hypothesize that Brain might have been attempting to find a replacement for the *Alabama*.

46 *ORN*, vol. 3, C. Helm to Don Domingo Dulce, 21 Nov. 1864, 242–43; C. Helm to Benjamin, 17 Aug. 1864. The party, aside from Brain, included no British subjects.

47 *New York Times*, 6 Dec. 1864; Hay and Hay, 101.

48 *New York Times*, 23 Oct., 2 Nov. 1864; *ORN*, vol. 3, E.D. Nichols to F.E. Hawly, 8 Oct. 1864; *Reporter*, 2 Oct. 1864.

49 *New York Times*, 2 Nov. 1864; "Affidavit of *Roanoke*'s Chief Officer and Purser," U.S., *Foreign Relations*, 1864, pt. 2, 364–65; *Reporter*, 22 Oct. 1864.

50 *ORN*, vol. 3, Ludlam, Heineken and Co. to G. Welles, 8 Oct. 1864; Francis Skeddy to S. Draper, 11 and 13 Oct. 1864, 232–33; W.G. Hamly to E. Cardwell, 28 Oct. 1864, 243–44; S. Brownlow Gray to Lt. Gov. W.G. Hamly, 24 Oct. 1864, 244–47; "Affidavit of *Roanoke*'s Chief Officer and Purser," U.S., *Foreign Relations*, 1864, pt. 2, 364–65; *Citizen*, 20 and 25 Oct. 1864; *Chronicle*, 25 Oct. 1864. Word also arrived in Halifax via the steamer *Mavrocordatos*.

51 *Reporter*, 25 Oct. 1864; Saint John *Globe*, 12 Oct., 17 Nov. 1864; *Citizen*, 25 Oct. 1864; *Telegraph*, 26 Oct. 1864; U.S., *Foreign Relations*, 1864, pt. 2, W. Seward to Charles F. Adams, 24 Oct. 1864, 338–40; *ORN*, vol. 3, Gray to W.G. Hamly, 24 Oct. 1864; E. Cardwell to W.G. Hamly, 16 Jan. 1864, 247–48.

52 *Christian Messenger*, 26 Jan. 1865; USCD (Halifax), M. Jackson to F.W.S., 15 Dec. 1864; *ORN*, vol. 3, F.H. Morse to W.H. Seward, 30 Dec. 1864, 456; Winks, *Canada*, ch. 14. The Montreal police magistrate who initially heard the St. Alban's case, who was familiar with the

Chesapeake incident, dismissed the prisoners on the grounds of their being belligerents. Justice Smith also ruled that the raid was an act of war. A defence lawyer referred to the *Roanoke* precedent: Benjamin, *St. Alban's Raid*, 115–16, 434, 461–76.

53 PANS, Rudolf Diaries, 10 Nov. 1864; *Novascotian*, 31 Oct., 5 Dec. 1864; *Reporter*, 26 Jan., 31 Dec. 1864; *Presbyterian Witness*, 29 Oct. 1864; *British Colonist*, 8 Nov. 1864.

54 *Citizen*, 11 April 1865; *New York Times*, 16 Dec. 1864; *Reporter*, 3 Nov., 17 Dec. 1864; *Sun*, 21 Oct. 1864; Jenkins, *Britain*, vol. 2, 359–65.

55 Jenkins, *Britain*, vol. 2, 353, 372, 388–89.

56 U.S. *Foreign Relations*, 1865, pt. 2, F.W. Seward to J.H. Burnley, 14 March 1865, 96

57 Price, "Ships That Tested the Blockade of the Carolina Ports," 201; Henderson, *Private Journal*; *Sun*, 16 Nov. 1864, 25 March 1865; *Unionist*, 25 June 1865; Lamb, "Defence of Fort Fisher," 642–54.

58 USCD (Halifax), Jackson to F.W. Seward, 13 April 1864; *British Colonist*, 5 Dec. 1864; Saint John *Globe*. 9 Dec. 1864; Baker, *Timothy Warren Anglin*, ch. 10.

59 Manning, *Diplomatic Correspondence*, vol. 4, B.H. Norton to John M. Clayton, 21 Nov. 1849; Norton to W.L. Marcy, 20 March 1854.

CHAPTER TEN

1 *Novascotian*, 24 March 1866; *Chronicle*, 19 March 1866; Cameron, "Fenian Times," 103–52.

2 *Sun*, 6 April 1866; Vaughan's service and military files were kindly supplied by Colleen Murphy of Dartmouth. For Malvern Hill, see Porter, "Battle of Malvern Hill," 406–27.

3 *Sun*, 9 Feb., 12 and 19 March, 16 April 1866; *Chronicle*, 19–22 March, 17 April 1866; *Novascotian*, 12 and 18 March 1866; Johnston, *Defending Halifax*, 32–33.

4 USCD (Halifax), M. Jackson to F.W. Seward, 26 Jan. 1865.

5 *Telegraph*, 10 Jan. 1865; *Reporter*, 26–28 Jan. 1865; Almon Correspondence, Walker to Almon, 10 Feb. 1865; *Sun*, 2 Jan. 1865; Browning, *From Cape Charles*, 304–5; Waite, *Life and Times*, 237. By February, Walker reported the Bermuda base to be "in complete disrepair," with tons of supplies piled up: Fraser, Trenholm and Co. Papers, C.N. Prioleau to Caleb Huse. Prioleau noted that Lieutenant-Colonel M.J. Smith had arrived in Halifax with 127,000 pounds for the commissary department and orders "to spend it as rapidly as possible." The tendency to exaggerate Southern strength and deprecate Northern victories typified the London *Times* and its many imitators in 1864 and 1865: Adams, *Great Britain and the American Civil War*, vol. 2, 220.

6 Henderson, *Private Journal*, 12 Jan., 18 March 1865.

7 USCD (Halifax), M. Jackson to F.W. Seward, 11 Feb. 1865; *Sun*, 17 Feb. 1865.

8 *Novascotian*, 6 Feb. 1865; *Sun*, 17 Feb., 6, 8, 26, 27, 29 and 31 March 1865; *Reporter*, 30 March 1865; Wise, *Lifeline*, appendix 22; Heyl, *Early American Steamers*, vol. 5, 45–7; Horan, *Confederate Agent*, 264. *Chicora*, in service until 1914, was chartered in 1870 to carry troops west to Red River.

9 *Cape Breton News*, 10 June 1865; *Citizen*, 16 March 1865; *Express*, 20 and 24 March, 10 April, 5 May 1865; *Citizen*, 16 March 1865; Fischer, "Southern Alternative," 91–101.

10 Tennyson, "Economic Nationalism," 134.

11 Saint John *Globe*, 10 March 1864; Bailey, "Opposition to Confederation," 367–83; Waite, *Life and Times*, chs. 3 and 14. One of the defeated Assemblymen was John Hamilton Gray, who had been a delegate to the Quebec conference.

12 Winks, *Canada*, 350; Hansen, *Mingling*, 162.

13 Yarmouth *Tribune*, 30 Oct. 1862; Saint John *Globe*, 29 Nov. 1864; *Novascotian*, 2 Oct. 1865, 23 April 1866; *Freeman*, 25 Feb., 9 March, 14 Oct. 1865; Martin, "Case Against Canadian Confederation," 19–49; Muise, "The 1860s," 39.

14 Whelan, *Union of the Provinces*, 11, 43, 114–16, 173.

15 Chisolm, *Joseph Howe*, vol. 2, 438–55; *Sun*, 29 Jan., 5 Feb. 1865; USCD (Halifax), Jackson to F.W. Seward, 13 Dec. 1865; Tennyson, "Economic Nationalism," 134. Total exports from the region to the United States increased by 36 percent from 1861 to 1865: Marr and Patterson, *Canada: An Economic History*, Table 5.2.

16 *Islander*, 18 April 1864, 10 Oct. 1865; *Novascotian*, 2 Oct. 1865; Charlottetown *Examiner*, 17 Aug., 2 Oct. 1865; Bolger, *The Island*, 113–30; Peter McGuigan, "Tenants and Troopers," 22–28; Waite, *Life and Times*, 188–89. For the land issue, see Robertson, *The Tenant League*.

17 *Citizen*, 14 Feb., 9 March, 11 April 1865; *Reporter*, 14 Jan., 14 Feb. 1865; *News*, 9 Jan. 1865; *Examiner*, 6 Feb. 1865; New Brunswick *Royal Gazette*, 18 Jan. 1865; *Protestant and Evangelical Witness*, 10 June 1865; Waite, *Life and Times*, ch. 3; Winks, *Canada*, ch. 14; Morton, *The Critical Years*, 163–64.

18 *Novascotian*, 17 and 24 April 1865; *Citizen*, 15 April 1865; Yarmouth *Tribune*, 12 April 1865; *Religious Intelligencer*, 19 May 1865; PANS, MG1, Rudolf Diaries, 10 April 1865; PANS, MG1, vol. 3250, series A, W.J. Stairs Journal, 30 Nov. 1865; PANS, Bell Diaries, Good Friday, 28 June 1865; *Sun*, 7, 12, 19 and 28 April 1865; *Examiner*, 17 April 1865; Saint John *Globe*, 4 July 1865.

19 Preston, *Defence*, 38–39.

20 Saint John *Globe*, 20 July 1865.

21 *Sun*, 10 May 1865; Gallman, *The North*, 180–81; author's file of Prince Edward Islanders in the Civil War.

22 *Sun*, 11, 18 and 21 May, 6 June, 4 July 1866; *Novascotian*, 14 May 1866.

23 *Telegraph*, 17 and 26 Aug. 1865; *Examiner*, 31 July 1865.

24 *Sun*, 17 and 26 April, 8 May 1865; *Express*, 17–19, April 1865; *Unionist*, 2 June 1865; USCD (Halifax), M. Jackson to W.H. Seward, 5 May, 27 June 1865; Kinchen, *Confederate Operations*, 211; Horan, *Confederate Agent*, 265–69; Winks, *Canada*, ch. 16; Landon, *Western Ontario*, 228–29; Roscoe, *Web of Conspiracy*, 91–92, 449–53.

25 *New York Times*, 7 May 1865; Yarmouth *Herald*, 27 April 1865; *Sun*, 4, 19 and 21 April 1865; *Freeman*, 20 April, 3 June 1865; *Telegraph*, 1 June 1865; Saint John *Globe*, 17 and 19 April, 4 July 1864; *Islander*, 21 April 1865.

26 *Sun*, 19 April 1865; PANS, RG1, vol. 127, R.G. MacDonnell to E. Cardwell, 27 April 1865.

27 *Journal*, 7 June 1865; Gunnison and Gunnison, *Autobiography*, 35–38.

28 *Sun*, 19 April, 1 and 5 May, 9 June 1865; Gunnison and Gunnison, *Autobiography*, 37–38.

29 *Colonial Farmer*, 10 April 1865.

30 Eastport *Sentinel*, 5 April, 14 June 1865; *ORA*, series III, vol. 5, Provost Marshall E. Low to Acting-Assistant Provost Marshall General, 6 Jan. 1865, 1038–39. Maine, with over seventy thousand men in the Union Army and several thousand in the Navy, suffered the second highest number of casualties, in proportion to population, of the Northern states: Desmond, "Defending Maine," 358.

31 Adams, *Great Britain and the American Civil War*, vol. 2, 305.

32 USCD (SJ), J. Howard to F.W. Seward, 24 April, 8 and 11 Dec. 1865; USCD (Charlottetown), Sherman to F.W. Seward, 22 and 25 May 1865; USCD (Halifax), Jackson to F.W. Seward, 13 and 27 Feb., 13 March 1865, 11 Oct. 1866; PANS, RG1, vol. 127, R.G. MacDonnell to E. Cardwell, 30 March 1865; *Express*, 3 May 1865; *Islander*, 18 Aug. 1865. Sherman died at Charlottetown on 11 Aug. 1865.

33 *Reporter*, 26 May 1865; *Express*, 10 June 1865.

34 Fergusson, *Place-Names*, 354; Winks, *Blacks in Canada*, 288. Tom Brooks has found several dozen Maritime-born blacks in the U.S. Navy and U.S. Colored Troops.

35 *Reporter*, 3 Aug. 1865; *Sun*, 4 Aug., 8 June 1865; Saint John *Globe*, 5 and 8 July 1865; *Telegraph*, 5 Sept. 1865; Fingard, "Race and Respectability."

36 *Sun*, 1 Aug. 1866; *Acadian Recorder*, 5 Aug. 1866; Winks, *Blacks in Canada*, 289.

37 *St. Croix Courier*, 27 Jan. 1866; Hornby, *Black Islanders*, 79–80; Morton, "Separate Spheres, 61–83; Brown, "Black Faces," 15; Winchester, "Last

Minstrel Show," 13–14.

38 Marquis, "Haliburton."

39 PANS, C.O. 188 (N.B.), vol. 145, William Smith to Edward Cardwell, 29 June 1862. Although Smith was writing of conditions in Jamaica, his views on race relations would have found wide acceptance amongst Maritime whites.

40 *New York Times*, 11 and 21 May 1865; *Reporter*, 27 June 1865.

41 *Citizen*, 24 June 1865; *Sun*, 19, 21 and 29 May 1865; *Journal*, 5 June 1865; Winks, *Canada and the United States*, 368–69.

42 *Novascotian*, 3 July 1865; *Reporter*, 30 May, 27 June 1865; *Sun*, 19, 29 and 31 May, 26 June 1865; *Express*, 29 May, 5, 14 and 28 June, 20 Oct. 1865; *Citizen*, 29 June 1865; USCD (Halifax), Jackson to W.H. Seward, 10 June 1865.

43 *Reporter*, 13 July, 23 Sept. 1865; *Presbyterian Witness*, 30 Sept. 1865; *Sun*, 3 and 31 July 1865; PANS, Almon Family Scrapbook.

44 Adams, *Great Britain and the American Civil War*, vol. 2, 266; Morgan, *Confederate Raider*.

45 *Express*, 12 July, 18 Aug., 6 Sept. 1865.

46 Overholtzer, "Nova Scotia and the United States Civil War," 52–54; *Sun*, 24 March 1865; *Novascotian*, 9 Oct. 1865; Marquis, "Ports of Halifax and Saint John."

47 *Stonewall*, an iron ram initially sold to Denmark, mounted a three-hundred-pounder Armstrong and two seventy-pounder guns in turret.

48 *Sun*, 3 July 1865; USCD (Halifax), M. Jackson to W.H. Seward, 23 June 1865, Jackson to W.H. Hunter, 27 June 1865; Wise, *Lifeline*, appendix 22; Wilkinson, *The Narrative*, 249–50; Hill, *Sea Dogs*, ch. 4; Thurston, *Tallahassee Skipper*, 360–63; Shingleton, *John Taylor Wood*, 200–4; Bulloch, *Secret Service*, vol. 2, 99–100.

49 *Sun*, 6 April 1866; *Novascotian*, 14 Aug. 1865; PANS, 1871 Census, Dartmouth; PANS, Stairs Journal, 30 Nov. 1865; Martin, *Story of Dartmouth*, 58; Thurston, *Tallahassee Skipper*, 357–63; information on Hornby, Armstrong and Sinclair supplied by Terry Punch. George Norfolk later presented Almon a copy of a book on the 1865 imprisonment of Jefferson Davis, now in the Killam Library. Howell was a brother-in-law of Davis.

50 *News*, 16 Aug. 1867, 6 June 1868; *ORN*, vol. 27, T. Kirkpatrick to Admiral C.K. Stribling, 22 April 1865, 835; Saint John *Sun*, 9 March 1903; Hay and Hay, *Last of the Confederate Privateers*, chs. 10–11.

51 *Sun*, 20 Sept. 1865; *Express*, 12 July 1865; *Acadian Recorder*, 15 July 1890; PANS, RG18, Immigration, series A, vol. 1, Naturalization Oath of Henry A. Parr, 18 Sept. 1867; Yarmouth *Herald*, 9 Aug. 1932; Punch, "Nova Scotians in the American Civil War," 29.

52 Benjamin, *St. Alban's Raid*, 461–76; PANS, C.O. 188 (N.B.), vol. 143,

W.H. Seward to J.H. Burnley, 19 Dec. 1864; vol. 144, Gordon to J.H. Burnley, 21 Jan. 1865.

53 PANS, C.O. 188 (N.B.), vol. 144, Gordon to Foreign Secretary, 19 May 1865.

54 *Express*, 3 Feb., 24 March 1865; USCD (SJ), J. Howard to F.W. Seward, 20 Feb. 1865; U.S., *Foreign Relations*, 1865, pt. 2, A.H. Gordon to J.H. Burnley, 29 Dec. 1864; W. Seward to J.H. Burnley, 25 Jan. 1865, 42; Gordon to Burnley, 7 Feb. 1865, 74–75; J.A. Harding to S.L. Tilley, 8 Feb. 1865, 82.

55 *Reporter*, 9 June 1865; *News*, 31 May, 2 and 5 June 1865, 6 May 1875; USCD (SJ), J. Howard to F.W. Seward, 9 June 1865; U.S., *Foreign Relations*, 1865, pt. 2, 89–94; PANS, C.O 188 (N.B.), vol. 143, W. Parker to Gordon, 9 March 1865; vol. 145, Cardwell to Gordon, 1 Aug. 1865. A British official had warned the State Department that extradition was ruled out by the *Chesapeake* and *Garrity* precedents. Isaac Treadwell, one of the pirates, died at Saint John in 1909: Saint John *Globe*, 30 Nov. 1909.

56 Kennedy, *Documents of the Canadian Constitution*, 604.

57 Webber, *One Thousand Young Men*, 109.

58 PANB, RS8, Regular Army: Governor's Papers Respecting Fenian Troubles, Archibald to Gordon, 27 Dec. 1865; *News*, 3 April 1865; *Unionist*, 30 Jan. 1865; *St. Croix Courier*, 9 Dec. 1865; *Telegraph*, 1 June, 12 and 19 Dec. 1865; St. Andrew's *Standard*, 2 Jan. 1866; Saint John *Globe*, 9 Jan. 1866; Senior, *Last Invasion*, chs. 3–4; Davis, *An International Community*, 197–98; Winks, *Canada and the United States*, 370–71.

59 PANS, C.O. 188 (N.B.), vol. 145, Gordon to Cardwell, 12 March 1866; Davis, *An International Community*, 198; Davis, "Fenian Raid on New Brunswick," 316–34; Senior, *Last Invasion*, ch. 4; Walker, "Passamaquoddy Boundary Affair," 46–53.

60 Saint John *Globe*, 31 March 1866; *Examiner*, 19 March 1865; Webber, *One Thousand Young Men*, 102, n. 51. The crisis prompted the P.E.I. government to reactivate the militia.

61 PANB, Regular Army: Governor's Papers Respecting Fenian Troubles, Marshall to Gordon, 9 and 10 March 1865; 11, 16 and 28 April 1865; PANS, C.O. 188, vol. 145, Gordon to Cardwell, 25 March 1866.

62 PANS, C.O. 188 (N.B.), vol. 145, Gordon to Cardwell, 25 March 1866; *Chronicle*, 16 and 18 April 1866; *Telegraph*, 3 and 14 April 1866; Saint John *Globe*, 31 March, 11, 12 and 13 April 1866; Eastport *Sentinel*, 13 Dec. 1865; Senior, *Last Invasion*, ch. 4; Facey-Crowther, *New Brunswick Militia*; MacDonald, *Troublous Times in Canada*, ch. 2: the Fenian "secretary of war" associated with the 1865 Ohio convention was General T.W. Sweeny, still commander of the 16th U.S. Infantry. The assault on British North America would include the occupation of the

head of Passamaquoddy Bay to launch expeditions to "reduce Saint John and Halifax" (p. 14).

63 PANS, C.O. 188 (N.B.), vol. 145, D. Wilson to Col. Anderson, 27 May 1866; St. Andrew's *Standard*, 7, 14 and 21 March, 4, 11 and 18 April 1866; Saint John *Globe*, 11 and 13 April 1866; *Sun*, 12, 16 and 20 April 1866; *Telegraph*, 17 and 21 April 1866; Davis, *An International Community*, 198–99; Davis, "Fenian Raid"; Senior, *Last Invasion*, ch. 4.

64 PANS, C.O. 188 (N.B.), Gordon to Cardwell, 18 April 1866; St. Andrew's *Standard*, 25 April, 2 May 1866; Davis, "Fenian Raid."

65 Saint John *Globe*, 24 April 1866; *Telegraph*, 20 April 1866; *Colonial Farmer*, 21 and 23 March 1866; St. Andrew's *Standard*, 9 and 16 May 1866; Davis, *An International Community*, 199–200; Senior, *Last Invasion*, ch. 4. A detailed account of defence measures prior to 20 April is found in PANS, C.O. 188 (N.B.), vol. 145, Colonel Anderson to Gordon, 26 Sept. 1866.

66 PANS, C.O. 188 (N.B.), vol. 145, Anderson to Gordon, 26 Sept. 1866.

67 *Sun*, 16 April 1866; *British Colonist*, 20 March 1866; *Chronicle*, 26 March, 3, 11, 17, 18, 20 and 26 April 1866; *Novascotian*, 12, 18 and 24 March 1866; Cameron, "Fenian Times," 130–31; Thurston, *Tallahassee Skipper*, 358–61; Preston, "General Sir William Fenwick Williams," 629.

68 *Sun*, 25 April 1866; *Chronicle*, 18 April 1866; Saint John *Globe*, 16, 19 and 21 April 1866; PANS, C.O. 188 (N.B.), vol. 145, Doyle to Gordon, 3 May 1866; Davis, *An International Community*, 200–1; Davis, "Fenian Raid," 328–32. The 15th Regiment was on its way to Bermuda and the 16th to Barbados. Doyle was worried that if these units departed too late in the season, the troops would not be acclimatized and would be hard hit by yellow fever.

69 *Novascotian*, 14 May 1866; Saint John *Globe*, 21 and 24 April 1866; *Sun*, 20 and 30 April 1866; Senior, *Last Invasion*, ch. 4; Davis, "Fenian Raid."

70 *Novascotian*, 30 July 1866; *Chronicle*, 9 and 11 April 1866; *British Colonist*, 20 March 1866; Saint John *Globe*, 24 and 26 April 1866; *Telegraph*, 21 and 28 April 1866; Senior, *Last Invasion*, ch. 5.

71 Davis, *An International Community*, 201–2; Baker, *Timothy Warren Anglin*, 110–15; Waite, *Life and Times*, ch. 15; Hannay, *Wilmot and Tilley*, 247–52; Senior, *Fenians and Canada*, 133–34; Davis, "Fenian Raid," 320; Morton, *Critical Years*, 190–202. A second Fenian threat surfaced in 1870 when General John O'Neill led two hundred men from Vermont into Canada East to exchange fire with militia. Fenians also skirmished across the border from Malone, New York.

72 St. Andrew's *Standard*, 23 May 1866; *Novascotian*, 16 and 23 April, 30 July 1866; *Freeman*, 4 Oct. 1865; *Telegraph*, 1, 24 and 29 May 1866; Morton, *Critical Years*, 205; Sturgis, "Opposition to Confederation," 114–29.

73 *Chronicle*, 17 April 1866.

74 *Express*, 2 Jan. 1865, 15 and 21 April 1868; *Novascotian*, 23 July, 6 Aug. 1866; Sturgis, "Opposition to Confederation"; Overholtzer, "Nova Scotia," ch. 3. Waite, *Life and Times*, 202, suggests that the *Sun*'s unpopular pro-Northern opinions of 1861–65 undermined local Confederation support.

75 *Sun*, 13 June 1866; Morton, *Critical Years*, 220–22, 229–30; Pryke, *Nova Scotia and Confederation*; Overholtzer, "Nova Scotia," 86–87. Howe and other Antis raised the spectre of the Maritime militia being conscripted beyond its own borders at the whim of the Canadians: Joseph Howe's "Speech at Dartmouth, 22 May 1867," in Chisolm, *Joseph Howe*, vol. 2, 508–20. The 1871 Washington Treaty was controversial for many Maritimers because it granted Americans inshore fishing rights without securing a preferential trade deal in return. The extravagant demands America made on Britain for reparations prior to 1871 caused renewed resentment in Britain's dominions: Gardner, LaFeber and McCormack, *Creation of the American Empire*.

76 Bolger, *The Island and Confederation*, 174–75; Buckner, "Maritimes and Confederation," 100–2; Waite, *Life and Times*, ch. 12; Morton, *Critical Years*, 231. For an early statement on P.E.I. as a field for "American enterprise and capital," see Albert Caitlin to Lewis Cass, 1 Oct. 1859, in Manning, *Diplomatic Correspondence*, vol. 4, 808–10.

77 The *Century Magazine* series was expanded into the influential four-volume series, *Battles and Leaders of the Civil War*, edited by R.U. Johnson.

78 Thurston, *Tallahassee Skipper*, 371; Strode, *Jefferson Davis*, 315, 330–35.

79 Raddall, "Blind McNair," 371–88. Another fictional work based on Nova Scotia's Civil War connection is John, *Night-hawk*, written by Alice Jones, who published under the name Alix John and lived from 1853 to 1933.

80 Gerald Handspiker to author, 31 Jan. 1994.

81 Walter Wile to author, 5 Dec. 1993; Joseph Cox to author, 24 Jan. 1994; *Ross's Weekly*, 25 Dec. 1862; Semple, "Islanders in the American Civil War"; R.A. McLeod correspondence.

82 Yarmouth *Herald*, 30 June 1865; Liverpool *Transcript*, 6 Nov. 1862; *Colonial Standard*, 28 Oct. 1862; *Sun*, 14 July 1865; Cousins, *Annapolis Valley Youth*, 28–29; Marquis, "Soldiers of Liberty."

83 Yarmouth *Herald*, 19 Jan. 1865.

84 Information on the MacDonald family supplied by Bill Norin; Kohl and Richard, *Irish Green and Union Blue*, Preface, Introduction, 156, Epilogue.

85 Stevenson, *Ladies Benevolent and Industrial Sallymag Society*.

86 PANS, Clara Denis papers, Notebook on Micmacs, no. 1. Lone Cloud

joined the Kickaboo Medicine Company in Boston and travelled for four years. He later was known as the Indian Doctor of Liscomb Mills, N.S. The reward for the capture of Booth, $18,000, was shared largely by two officers: Hanchett, *Lincoln Murder Conspiracies*; Eisenschiml, *Why Was Lincoln Murdered?*, 125; Kunhardt and Kunhardt, *Twenty Days*, 176–82.

87   File on Robinson courtesy of Holy Cross Cemetery, Halifax, N.S.; Milligan, *Gunboats Down the Mississippi*, 107–8, 117.

88   Information supplied by Tom Brooks.

89   Wayne Baltzer to author, 6 Dec. 1993; *Eastern Chronicle*, 30 Oct. 1862; *News*, 3 Nov. 1862; *Protestant and Evangelical Witness*, 4 July 1863; Milner, *History of Sackville, New Brunswick*, 153; Ed MacDonald to author, 18 Oct. 1994.

90   Punch, "Nova Scotians in the U.S. Civil War," 27.

91   Jenkins, "British North Americans," 24–26; Handlin, *Boston's Immigrants*, 212.

92   Charles Vaughan, Pension File; Robert L. Adams to author, 19 Jan. 1994; Gallman, *The North*, 183.

93   Antigonish *Casket*, 16 May 1918; *News*, 15 April 1870; Allison, *History of Nova Scotia*, vol. 3, 517–18; Author's file on Nova Scotia surgeons in the Civil War; Dearing, *Veterans in Politics*.

94   Winks, *Blacks in Canada*, 297–98.

95   *Protestant and Evangelical Witness*, 16 Nov. 1863; McLeod Papers, Henry Richards to Roberta McLeod, 24 Dec. 1936; Life of Robert Alder McLeod; Black, "Soldier of Misfortune," 3.

96   Archibald, *Home-making*; Gallman, *The North*, 197.

97   *Christian Messenger*, 20 April 1864; *News*, 29 Aug. 1866, 14 Oct. 1868; *New Brunswick Courier*, 7 May 1864.

98   Beatrice McCallum to author, 21 Nov. 1993; Raymond information supplied by Paul B. Raymond of Tacoma, Washington; William McQuinn file courtesy of Don McQuinn of Riverview, N.B.; MacDonald newsletter, vol. 1 (Summer 1987): 1–7, courtesy Bill Norin; Duncanson, "Ben Jackson."

99   Fredericton *Daily Gleaner*, 16 April 1895; Preston, *Defence*, ch. 5.

100 Berger, *Sense of Power*, 235–38.

101 Cameron, "Fenian Times," 139–43.

102 Creighton, *Road to Confederation*.

103 Henry, *Forgotten Canadians*, vii.

Bibliography

ARCHIVAL SOURCES

PUBLIC ARCHIVES OF NOVA SCOTIA (PANS)

Almon Family Papers. MG1, vol. 11; Scrapbook, MG1, vol. 14.
Britain. Public Records Office, W.C.1 F.O.3, no. 311, Case of the
    Tallahassee, 1864.
British Army (Halifax). Headquarters Orders. MG12, vol. 58, 1864.
Camp Hill Cemetery Register, MG5, vol. 3045.
Canada, Census of, 1871, Halifax County. Manuscript. (micro: 13267).
City of Halifax. Police Court Minutes. RG42 D. 1864.
Clara Denis Papers. MG1, vol. 2857.
John Allison Bell Diaries. MG1 (micro: 10074).
John William Ritchie Correspondence. MG1 (micro: 809).
Joseph Howe Papers. MG1, vol. 1706.
List of Nova Scotians Who Served in the American Civil War.
    MG100, vol. 101, no. 49.
New Brunswick. C.O. 188. Lieutenant Governor's Dispatches to
    Colonial Office.
Nova Scotia. Governor's and Lieutenant-Governor's Papers. RG2.
– Provincial Secretary's Correspondence. RG7.
– Court of Vice-Admiralty Records. RG40, vol. 23, Ships "C-Z," 1864.
– Immigration. RG18, series A.
– Official Papers Dealing With the Case of the *Tallahassee* (micro:
    Ships: Tallahassee).
– Public Records of Nova Scotia. RG1.

Thomas Connolly Papers. MG1 (micro: Biography: Connolly).
W.H. Harrison Letters. MG1, vol. 247.
William J. Stairs Journal. MG1, vol. 3250, series A.
William Norman Rudolf Diaries. MG1 (micro: 10980).
William Young Papers. MG100, vol. 742.

KILLIAM LIBRARY, DALHOUSIE UNIVERSITY

Dalhousie College. Minutes of the Proceedings of the Board of
    Governors (Dalhousie University Archives).
John Hay Diaries, 1860–70. Microfilm.
Memoir of John Yates Beall. Montreal: J. Lowell, 1865. Microfilm.
United States. Dispatches of the U.S. Consul, Halifax, 1860–66.
    Microfilm.

NEW BRUNSWICK MUSEUM ARCHIVES (NBMA)

Humphrey Family Papers. CB doc. 2030.

PROVINCIAL ARCHIVES OF NEW BRUNSWICK (PANB)

Lieutenant Governor's Correspondence. RS348, A.3.
Regular Army: Lieutenant Governor's Correspondence. RS8.
United States. Dispatches of the U.S. Consul, Saint John, 1861–65.

UNIVERSITY OF PRINCE EDWARD ISLAND LIBRARY

United States Dispatches of the U.S. Consul, Charlottetown, 1861–65.

NATIONAL ARCHIVES AND RECORDS ADMINISTRATION
    (NARA), WASHINGTON, D.C.

Military Service and Pension Files:
    Thomas Billings Adams
    John Andrew MacDonald
    William McQuinn
    Charles Robinson
    Charles Vaughan
Research files compiled from Military service and pension records of
    the NARA. Supplied by Tom Brooks.

OTHER

Burial Register. Holy Cross Cemetery, Halifax.
Correspondence of Robert Alder McLeod. Photocopied material.
C.K. Prioleau Letterbook, Fraser, Trenholm and Co. Papers, National
    Museum and Galleries, Merseyside, U.K.

NEWSPAPERS

NEW BRUNSWICK

Fredericton
  Colonial Farmer
  Daily Gleaner
  Head Quarters
  Reporter
Sackville
  Borderer
  Chignecto Post-Borderer
Saint Andrew's
  Standard
Saint John
  Globe
  Morning Freeman
  Morning News
  Morning Telegraph
  New Brunswick Courier
  Religious Intelligencer
  Telegraph Journal
Saint Stephen
  St. Croix Herald
Woodstock
  Carleton Sentinel

NOVA SCOTIA

Antigonish
  Casket
Halifax
  Acadian Recorder
  British Colonist
  Bullfrog
  Burning Bush

Christian Messenger
Church Record
Citizen
Evening Express
Evening Mail
Herald
Morning Chronicle
Morning Journal
Morning Sun
Novascotian
Presbyterian Witness
Provincial Wesleyan
Reporter
Unionist
Liverpool
Transcript
Pictou
Colonial Standard
Eastern Chronicle
Shelburne
Budget
Sydney
Cape Breton News
Yarmouth
Herald
Tribune

PRINCE EDWARD ISLAND

Charlottetown
Examiner
Islander
Monitor
Protestant and Evangelical Witness
Ross's Weekly
Vindicator
Summerside
Journal-Pioneer

OTHER

Calais (Maine)
Saint Croix Courier

Eastport (Maine)
  Sentinel
Kingston (Ontario)
  Daily News
London (England)
  Times
Montreal
  Gazette
New York
  New York Times
Saint John's (Newfoundland)
  Day Book
Toronto
  Globe

OTHER PRINTED SOURCES

Acadia Powder Co. and Its Works at Waverly, 1862–1910. Halifax, n.p., 1988.

Acheson, T.W. "Andrew Rainsford Wetmore." *Dictionary of Canadian Biography* XII: 1096–98.

– *Saint John: The Making of a Colonial Urban Community.* Toronto: University of Toronto Press, 1985.

Adams, E.D. *Great Britain and the American Civil War.* 2 vols. New York: Russell and Russell, 1958.

Albert, l'Abbé Thomas. *Histoire du Madawaska.* Québec: Imprimerie Franciscaine Missionaire, 1920.

Allen, Theodore W. *The Making of the White Race: Vol. I. Racial Oppression and Social Control.* New York: Verso Books, 1994.

Allison, David. *History of Nova Scotia.* 3 vols. Halifax: A.W. Bowen, 1916.

Andrew, Sheila M. *The Development of Elites in Acadian New Brunswick, 1861–1881.* Montreal: McGill-Queen's University Press, 1996.

Archibald, William Charles. *Home-making and Its Philosophy.* Boston, 1910.

Arndt, Chris. "Maine in the Northeastern Boundary Controversy: States' Rights in Antebellum New England." *New England Quarterly* 62 (June 1989): 205–23.

Arsenault, Georges. *The Island Acadians, 1720–1980.* Charlottetown: Ragweed Press, 1989.

Bailey, A.G. "The Basis of Persistence of Opposition to Confederation in New Brunswick." *Canadian Historical Review* 23 (1942): 367–83.

–, ed. *The Letters of James and Ellen Robb*. Fredericton: Acadiensis Press, 1993.

Baker, Willam M. *Timothy Warren Anglin, 1822–96: Irish Catholic Canadian*. Toronto: University of Toronto Press, 1977.

Bale, Gordon *Chief Justice Sir William Johnstone Ritchie: Responsible Government and Judicial Review*. Ottawa: Supreme Court of Canada Historical Society, 1991.

– and Bruce Mellett. "Sir William Johnstone Ritchie." *Dictionary of Canadian Biography* XII: 895–900.

Barnes, James J., and Patricia Barnes, eds. *Private and Confidential: Letters From British Ministers to the Foreign Secretary in London, 1844–67*. Toronto: Selingrove, 1993.

Barrett, John. *The Civil War and North Carolina*. Chapel Hill: University of North Carolina Press, 1963.

Barton, Peter. "The First Blockade Runner and 'Another Alabama': Some Tees and Hartlepool Ships That Worried the Union." *Mariner's Mirror* 81 (Feb. 1995): 45–64.

Basoco, Richard, et al. "A British View of the Union Navy, 1864: A Report Addressed to Her Majesty's Minister at Washington." *American Neptune* 27 (Jan. 1967): 30–45.

Bates, David Homer. "A Rebel Cypher Despatch." *Harper's New Monthly Magazine* 47 (1898): 105–9.

Beale, Howard K., ed. *The Diary of Gideon Welles*. 2 vols. New York: W.W. Norton, 1960.

Beck, Boyde. "Song for the Heather Belle." *Island Magazine* 17 (Spring–Summer 1985): 12–14.

Beck, J. Murray. *Joseph Howe: Vol. II. The Briton Becomes Canadian, 1848–1873*. Montreal: McGill-Queen's University Press, 1983.

– "Phillip Cartaret Hill: Political Misfit." *Collections of the Royal Nova Scotia Historical Society* 42 (1986): 1–16.

– *The Politics of Nova Scotia: Vol. I. 1710–1896*. Tantallon: Four East Publications, 1988.

Benjamin, L.N., ed. *The St. Alban's Raid; or, Investigations into the Charges against Lieut. Bennett H. Young and Command*. Montreal, 1865.

Berger, Carl. *The Sense of Power: Studies in the Ideas of Canadian Imperialism, 1867–1914*. Toronto: University of Toronto Press, 1970.

Berlin, Ira, ed. *Freedom: A Documentary History of Emancipation, 1861–67: Series II. The Black Military Experience*. New York: Cambridge University Press, 1988.

Bernath, Stuart W. "British Neutrality and the Civil War Prize Cases." *Civil War History* 15 (Dec. 1969): 320–31.

– *Squall Across the Atlantic: American Civil War Prize Cases and Diplomacy*. Berkely: University of California Press, 1970.

Billings, J.D. *Hardtack and Coffee: The Unwritten Story of Army Life*. Chicago: R.K. Donnelly, 1965.

Black, Harold Garnet. "An Astonishing Career." *United Churchman* (10 and 24 February 1960): 3.

– "Soldier of Misfortune." *Dalhousie Review* 42 (1962): 76–85.

Blakeley, Phyllis. "William Alexander Henry." *Collections of the Nova Scotia Historical Society* 36 (1968): 96–140.

Blockson. C.L. *The Hippocrene Guide to the Underground Railroad*. New York: Hippocrene Books, 1994.

Blume, Kenneth. "The Flight from the Flag: The American Government, the British Caribbean and the American Merchant Marine." *Civil War History* 30 (March 1986): 44–55.

Boatner, Mark M., ed. *Cassell's Biographical Dictionary of the American Civil War, 1861–65*. London: Cassell, 1973.

– *The Civil War Dictionary* [CWD]. New York: Van Rees Press, 1967.

Bolger, F. *Prince Edward Island and Confederation, 1863–1873*. Charlottetown: St. Dunstan's University Press, 1964.

Bourne, Kenneth. *Britain and the Balance of Power in North America, 1815–1908*. London: Longmans, 1967.

– "British Preparations for War with the North, 1861–62." *English Historical Review* 76 (Oct. 1961): 600–32.

Brault, Gerard J. *The French Canadian Heritage in New England*. Montreal: McGill-Queen's University Press, 1986.

"British Feelings on the American Civil War." *Chamber's Journal* 17 (March 15, 1862): 171–72.

Brode, Patrick. *The Odyssey of John Anderson*. Toronto: Osgoode Society, 1989.

Brookes, Alan A. "Out Migration from the Maritimes, 1860–1900." *Acadiensis* 5 (Spring 1976): 26–55.

Brooks, Tom Walter, and Michael Dan Jones. *Lee's Foreign Legion: A History of the 10th Louisiana Regiment*. Gravenhurst, Ont.: Watts Printing, 1995.

Brown, S. "Black Faces Should be Red Faced." In *New Brunswick Reader*. 5, No. 15 (1998): 15.

Browning, Robert Jr. *From Cape Charles to Cape Fear: The North Atlantic Blockading Squadron During the Civil War*. Tuscaloosa: University of Alabama Press, 1993.

Buckner, Phillip. "The Maritimes and Confederation: A Reassessment." In *The Causes of Canadian Conferation*, edited by Ged Martin, 86–113. Fredericton: Acadiensis Press, 1990.

Buckner, Phillip, and John Reid, eds. *The Atlantic Region to*

Confederation. Toronto: University of Toronto Press, 1994.

Bulloch, James D. *The Secret Service of the Confederate States in Europe.* 2 vols. New York: Sagamore Press, 1959.

Burroughs, Peter. "Sir Richard Graves MacDonnell." *Dictionary of Canadian Biography* XI: 555–56.

– "Tackling Army Desertion in British North America." *Canadian Historical Review* 61 (1980): 28–60.

Burton, E. Milton. *The Siege of Charleston, 1861–65.* Columbia: University of South Carolina Press, 1974.

Cameron, James M. *Pictonians in Arms: A Military History of Pictou County, Nova Scotia.* Fredericton, 1969.

– "Fenian Times in Nova Scotia." *Collections of the Nova Scotia Historical Society* 37 (1970): 103–54.

Campbell, J.R. *History of Yarmouth County.* Saint John: J. and A. MacMillan, 1876.

Canada. *Census of Canada, 1871.* Ottawa: Queen's Printer, 1871.

Chandler, Robert J. "The Release of the *Chapman* Pirates: A California Sidelight on Lincoln's Amnesty Policy." *Civil War History* (June 1977): 129–43.

Chapman, J.K. *The Career of Arthur Hamilton Gordon: First Lord Stanmore, 1829–1912.* Toronto: University of Toronto Press, 1964.

Chesapeake: The Case of David Collins et al. on a Charge of Piracy. Saint John: J. and A. McMillan, 1864.

Chisolm, Joseph A., ed. *The Speeches and Public Letters of Joseph Howe.* 2 vols. Halifax: Chronicle Publishing, 1909.

Chittick, Hattie. *Hantsport on the Avon.* Hantsport: Hantsport Women's Institute, 1964.

Chittick, V.L.O. *Thomas Chandler Haliburton (Sam Slick): A Story in Provincial Toryism.* New York: AMS Press, 1966.

Clark, Andrew Hill. *Three Centuries and the Island: A Historical Geography of Settlement and Agriculture on Prince Edward Island, Canada.* Toronto: University of Toronto Press, 1959.

Clarke, Sir Edward. *A Treatise upon the Law of Extradition.* London: Stevens and Haynes, 1888.

Cleaves, B. Freeman. *Meade of Gettysburg.* Norman: University of Oklahoma Press, 1960.

Cochran, Hamilton. *Blockade Runners of the Confederacy.* Westport: Greenwood Press, 1973.

Cochran, Rev. J.C. *New Year's Address of the Congregation of Bishop's Chapel, Halifax, Nova Scotia.* Halifax: J. Bowes and Son, 1865.

Condon, Anne Groman. *The Envy of the American States: The Loyalist Dream for New Brunswick.* Fredericton: New Ireland Press, 1984.

– "Loyalist Arrival, Acadian Return and Imperial Reform." In *The*

Atlantic Region to Confederation: A History, edited by Phillip Buckner and John G. Reid, 184-209. Toronto: University of Toronto Press, 1994.

"Convulsions of America, The." *Blackwood's Magazine* 41 (Jan. 1862): 123–25.

Cordner, John. *The American Conflict*. Montreal: J. Lovell, 1864.

Corey, Charles Henry. *A History of the Richmond Theological Seminary, with Reminiscences of Thirty Years Work Among the Colored People of the South*. Richmond: J.W. Randolph, 1895.

Cornish, Dudley Taylor. *The Sable Arm: Black Troops in the Union Army, 1861–65*. Lawrence: University of Kansas Press, 1987.

Cougle, Jim. *Canadian Blood, American Soil: The Story of Canada's Contribution to the American Civil War*. Saint John: Civil War Heritage Society, 1994.

Cousins, Leone Banks, ed. *An Annapolis Valley Youth in the Union Navy: The Letters of Norman Wade*. Halifax: McCurdy Printing, n.d.

Cox, Dr. George. "Sidelights on the Chesapeake Affair, 1863–64." *Collections of the Nova Scotia Historical Society* 29 (1951): 124–37.

Creighton, Donald. *The Road to Confederation: The Emergence of Canada, 1863–1867*. Toronto: MacMillan, 1964.

Crook, D.P. *The North, the South and the Powers, 1861–65*. Toronto: John Wiley and Sons, 1974.

Curtis, Edith Roelker. "Blood Is Thicker Than Water." *American Neptune* 27 (July 1967): 157–76.

Dalzell, George W. *The Flight from the Flag*. Chapel Hill: University of North Carolina Press, 1940.

Davies, R. A., ed. *Letters of Thomas Chandler Haliburton*. Toronto: University of Toronto Press, 1988.

Davis, David Brian. *The Problem of Slavery in the Age of Revolution, 1770–1823*. Ithaca: Cornell University Press, 1990.

Davis, Harold. *An International Community on the St. Croix, 1604–1930*. Orono: University of Maine, 1950.

– "The Fenian Raid on New Brunswick." *Canadian Historical Review* 36 (Dec. 1955): 316–34.

Davis, Richard, ed. *The Letters of Thomas Chandler Haliburton*. Toronto: University of Toronto Press, 1988.

Day, George. *Judgement of the Honourable Judge Ritchie in the Case of the Capture of the American Steamer Chesapeake*. Saint John: George Day, 1864.

Dearing, Mary. *Veterans in Politics: The Story of the Grand Army of the Republic*. Baton Rouge: Louisiana State University Press, 1952.

"Defence of Canada, The." *Blackwood's Magazine*, vol. 91 (Feb. 1862): 228-58.

Denison, George. "Cavalry Charges at Sedan." *Canadian Monthly* 1 (Jan. 1872): 47–53.

Desmond, Jerry, et al. "Defending Maine and the Nation." In *Maine: The Pine Tree State from Prehistory to the Present*, edited by Richard W. Judd, Edwin A. Churchill and Joel W. Eastman, 342–69. Orono: University of Maine Press, 1995.

Devlin, Bernard. "Survey of Franco–American Participation in Maine Regiments during the Civil War." Unpublished paper, 1995.

Donovan, T.H., ed. *West Point Military History of the American Civil War*. Wayne, N.J.: Avery Publishing, 1987.

Doty, C. Stewart. *The First Franco-Americans: New England Life Histories from the Federal Writers Project, 1938–39*. Orono: University of Maine Press, 1985.

Duncan, Fraser. *Our Garrisons in the West, or Sketches in British North America*. London: Chapman and Hall, 1864.

Duncan, Roger. *Coastal Maine: A Maritime History*. New York: Norton, 1992.

Duncanson, John V. "Ben Jackson." *Nova Scotia Geneaologist* 5 (1987): 10–11.

Dyer, Frederick H. *A Compendium of the War of the Rebellion*. 3 vols. New York: Thomas Yeseloff, 1959.

Edmonds, S. Emma. *Nurse and Spy in the Union Army: The Adventures and Experiences of a Woman in Hospitals, Camps and Battle-Fields*. Hartford: Messrs. Williams and Co., 1865.

Edwards, Joseph Plimsoll. "The Militia of Nova Scotia, 1749–1867." *Collections of the Nova Scotia Historical Society* 17 (1913): 63–109.

Egan, Major Thomas J. *History of the Halifax Volunteer Battalion and Volunteer Companies 1859–1887*. Halifax: A. and W. Mackinly, 1888.

Eisenschiml, Otto.*Why Was Lincoln Murdered?* London: Faber and Faber, 1958.

Ellis, Charles M. *The Memorial Address on Lincoln Delivered at the Mechanic's Institute, Saint John, N.B., June 1, 1865, at the Invitation of the Citizens*. Saint John, 1865.

Erickson, Aruel B. "Empire or Anarchy? The Jamaica Rebellion of 1865." *Journal of Negro History* 44 (April 1959): 99–122.

Experience of Thomas Jones, Who Was a Slave for Forty-Three Years. Saint John: J. and A. McMillan, 1853.

Ernest, Robert. *Immigrant Life in New York City, 1825–1865*. Syracuse: Syracuse University Press, 1994.

Facey-Crowther, David. *The New Brunswick Militia, 1787–1867*. Fredericton: New Ireland Press, 1990.

Fairfax, D.M. "Captain Wilkes's Seizure of Mason and Slidell." In *Battles and Leaders of the Civil War*, vol 4. New York: Century, 1887.

Farley, M. Foster. "Josiah Tattnall – Gallant American." *Georgia Historical Quarterly* 58 (1974): 172–80.

Faust, P., ed. *Historical Times Illustrated Encyclopedia of the Civil War.* New York: Harper Collins, 1992.

Fellman, Michael. *Inside War: The Guerilla Conflict in Missouri During the American Civil War.* New York: Oxford University Press, 1989.

Fenety, G.E. *Political Notes and Observations.* Fredericton: S.R. Miller, 1867.

Fergusson, C.B., ed. *A Documentary Study of the Establishment of the Negroes in Nova Scotia.* Halifax: Public Archives of Nova Scotia, 1948.

– *Place-Names and Places of Nova Scotia.* Belleville: Mika Publishing, 1974.

– *Uniacke's Sketches of Cape Breton and Other Papers Relating to Cape Breton Island.* Halifax: PANS, 1958.

Ferris, Norman B. *The Trent Affair: A Diplomatic Crisis.* Knoxville: University of Tennessee Press, 1977.

Fingard, Judith. *The Dark Side of Life in Victorian Halifax.* Porter's Lake, N.S.: Pottersfield Press, 1989.

– *Jack in Port: Sailortowns of Eastern Canada.* Toronto: University of Toronto Press, 1982.

– "Race and Respectability in Victorian Halifax." *Journal of Imperial and Commonwealth History* 20 (May 1992): 169–95.

Fischer, Lewis. "The Southern Alternative: Canadian and British Shipping and the Port of Charleston, 1863-1912." In *Global Crossroads and the American Seas,* edited by Clark G. Reynolds. Missoula: Pictorial Histories Publishing, 1988: 91-101.

Fladeland, Betty. "Alias Frank Thompson." *Michigan History* 42 (Sept. 1958): 435–62.

Flemming, David B. "Thomas Louis Connolly." *Dictionary of Canadian Biography* X: 191–93.

Foner, Eric. *Politics and Ideology in the Age of the Civil War.* New York: Oxford University Press, 1980.

Forbes, E.R., and D.A. Musie, eds. *The Atlantic Provinces in Confederation.* Toronto: University of Toronto Press, 1993.

Foster, Kevin. "Builders vs Blockaders: The Evolution of the Blockade–running Steamship." In *Global Crossroads and the American Seas,* edited by Clark G. Reynolds. Missoula: Pictorial Histories Publishing, 1988.

Fraser, James A. *By Favoured Winds: A History of Chatham, New Brunswick.* Chatham: Town of Chatham, 1975.

Gallman, Matthew. *The North Fights the Civil War: The Home Front.* Chicago: Ivan R. Dee, 1994.

Gardner, L.C., W.F. LeFeber, and Thomas McCormack. *Creation of the American Empire: United States Diplomatic History*. New York: Rand and McNally, 1973.

Geary, James W. "Civil War Conscription in the North: A Historiographical Review." *Civil War History* 32 (Sept. 1986): 208–28.

Gobineau, J. Arthur comte du. *A Gentlemen in the Outports: Gobineau and Newfoundland*. Ottawa: Carleton University Press, 1993.

Goff, Richard D. *Confederate Supply*. Durham: Duke University Press, 1969.

Gragg, Rod. *Confederate Goliath: The Battle of Fort Fisher*. New York: Harper Perennial, 1991.

Graham, Gerald Sandford. *The China Station: War and Diplomacy, 1830–1860*. New York: Clarendon Press, 1978.

Great Britain. House of Commons. *State Papers* (Sessional Papers), 1861–66.

Greely, Horace. *The American Conflict: A History of the Great Rebellion of the United States of America*. Hartford: O.D. Case, 1866.

Gunn, Gertrude. "New Brunswick Opinion on the American Civil War." M.A. thesis, University of New Brunswick, 1956.

Gunnison, Foster N., and Herbert Foster Gunnison, eds. *An Autobiography of Rev. Nathaniel Gunnison*. Brooklyn, N.Y., 1910.

Hagan, Kenneth J. *The People's Navy: The Making of American Sea Power*. Toronto: Free Press, 1991.

Hale, Richard. *Patriots in Disguise: Women Warriors of the Civil War*. New York: Marlowe, 1994.

Haliburton, Thomas Chandler. *Rule and Misrule of the English in America*. New York: Harper and Brothers, 1859.

– *Sam Slick the Clockmaker: His Sayings and Doings*. E.A. Baker, ed. Toronto: Musson Books, 1929.

Halifax City Business Directory for 1863. Halifax: E.M. MacDonald, 1863.

Hall, Richard. *Patriots in Disguise: Women Warriors of the Civil War*. New York: Marlowe, 1994.

Hallock, Charles. "Aroostook and Madawaska." *Harper's New Monthly Magazine* 27 (Oct. 1863): 688–98.

– *Sketches of Stonewall Jackson, Giving the Leading Events of His Life and Military Career, His Dying Moments and the Obsequies at Richmond and Lexington*. Halifax: J. Bowes, 1864.

Hamilton, A.W.H. *History of King's County, Nova Scotia* [1910]. Belleville: Mika, 1972.

Hanchett, William. *The Lincoln Murder Conspiracies*. Chicago: University of Illinois Press, 1983.

Handlin, Oscar. *Boston's Immigrants, 1790–1880*. Cambidge: Harvard University Press, 1981.

Hannay, James. *History of New Brunswick*. 2 vols. Saint John: J. and A. Bowes, 1909.

– *Wilmot and Tilley*. Toronto: Morang, 1910.

Hansen, Marcus Lee. *The Mingling of the Canadian and American People: Vol. I. Historical*. New York: Russell and Russell, 1970.

Hart, H.C.. *History of the County of Guysborough* [1877]. Belleville: Mika, 1975.

Hatch, Louis Clinton, ed. *Maine: A History*. Somersworth: New Hampshire Publishing, 1974.

Hawkins, Rush C. "Early Coast Operations in North Carolina." In *Battles and Leaders of the Civil War*, vol 1. New York: Century, 1887.

Hay, David and Joan. *The Last of the Confederate Privateers*. Edinburgh: Paul Harris, 1977.

Hayes, John D., ed. *Samuel Francis Dupont: A Selection from His Civil War Letters*. New York; Cornell University Press, 1969.

Hearn, Chester. *George Washington's Schooners*. Annapolis: Naval Institute Press, 1995.

– *Grey Raiders of the Sea: How Eight Confederate Warships Destroyed the Union's High Seas Commerce*. Camden: International Marine Publishing, 1992.

Henderson, Dwight F., ed. *The Private Journal of Georgiana Gholson Walker, 1862–1865*. Tuscaloosa: University of Alabama Press, 1963.

Henry, Frances. *Forgotten Canadians: The Blacks of Nova Scotia*. Don Mills: Longmans Canada, 1973.

Hepworth, G.M. *Starboard and Port: The Nettie Along Shore*. New York: Harper and Brothers, 1876.

Hernon, Joseph M. "British Sympathies in the American Civil War: A Reconsideration." *Journal of Southern History* 33 (Aug. 1967): 356–67.

Heyl, Erik. *Early American Steamers*. Vols. III-IV. Buffalo: Erik Heyl, 1965.

Higginbottom, Don. "A Raider Refuels: Diplomatic Repercussions." *Civil War History* 4 (1958): 129–41.

Higgins, T.R. *Life of J. M. Cramp, D.D., 1796-1866*. Montreal: W. Drysdale, 1887.

Hill, Jim Dan. *Sea Dogs of the Sixties*. Minneapolis: University of Minnesota Press, 1935.

Hill, Phillip Carteret. *The United States and British Provinces Contrasted From Personal Observations*. Halifax: James Barnes, 1859.

Horan, J.D. *Confederate Agent: A Discovery in History*. New York:

Crown Publishing, 1954.

Hornby, Jim *Black Islanders: Prince Edward Island's Historical Black Community*. Charlottetown: Institute of Island Studies, 1991.

Hornsby, Stephen J. *Nineteenth-Century Cape Breton: An Historical Geography*. Montreal: McGill-Queen's University Press, 1992.

Jenkins, Brian. *Britain and the War for the Union*. 2 vols. Montreal: McGill-Queen's University Press, 1980.

Jenkins, Danny. "British North Americans Who Fought in the American Civil War." M.A. thesis, Ottawa University, 1993.

John, Alix [Alice Jones]. *The Night-hawk: A Romance of the '60s*. Toronto: Copp, Clark. c. 1901.

Johnson, A.B. *Defending Halifax: Ordnance, 1825–1906*. Ottawa: Parks Canada, 1981.

Johnson, D.F. *Vital Statistics from New Brunswick Newspapers*. Vols. 18–31. Typescript. Saint John, 1987–89.

Johnson, Robert Underwood, ed. *Battles and Leaders of the Civil War*. 4 vols. New York: Century Co., 1887.

Jones, Charles C. *Commodore Josiah Tattnall*. Savannah: Morning News Printing House, 1878.

Jones, Francis I.W. "Treason and Piracy in Civil War Halifax: The Second Chesapeake Affair Revisited." *Dalhousie Review* 71 (Winter 1991–92): 472–87.

Jones, Howard "Maine Anglophobia and the Aroostook War." *New England Quarterly* 48 (Dec. 1975): 519–39.

Judd, Richard. *Aroostook: A Century of Logging in Northern Maine*. Orono: University of Maine Press, 1989.

–, Edwin A. Churchill, and Joel W. Eastman. *Maine: The Pine Tree State from Prehistory to the Present*. Orono: University of Maine Press, 1995.

Kallgren, B., and L. Crouthamel. *Dear Friend Annie: The Civil War Letters of a Common Soldier from Maine*. Orono: University of Maine Press, 1992.

Kennedy, Paul. *The Rise and Fall of British Naval Mastery*. London: Trinity Press, 1976.

Kennedy, W.P.M., ed. *Documents of the Canadian Constitution*. Toronto: University of Toronto Press, 1918.

Kinchen, Oliver. *Confederate Operations in Canada and the North*. North Quincy, Mass.: Christopher, 1970.

Knight, Thomas. *The American War with Some Suggestions Toward Effecting an Honourable Peace*. Halifax, 1864.

Kohl, L.F., and M.C. Richard, eds. *Irish Green and Union Blue: The Civil War Letters of Peter Welsh*. New York: Fordham University Press, 1986.

Kunhardt, Dorothy Meserve, and Philip B. Kundhart. *Twenty Days.* New York: Harper and Row, 1965.

Lamb, William. "The Defence of Fort Fisher." In *Battles and Leaders of the Civil War*, vol. 4. New York: Century, 1887.

Landon, Fred. *Western Ontario and the American Frontier.* New York: Russell and Russell, 1941.

Lawson, J. Murray. *Record of Yarmouth Shipping.* Saint John: J. and A. MacMillan, 1876.

Leech, Margaret. *Reveille in Washington.* New York: Harper and Brothers, 1941.

Levine, Bruce. *Half Slave and Half Free: The Roots of the Civil War.* New York: Noonday Press, 1992.

Linderman, Gerald. *Embattled Courage: The Experience of Combat in the American Civil War.* New York: Free Press, 1987.

Litwack, Leon F. *North of Slavery: The Negro in the Free States, 1790–1860.* Chicago: University of Chicago Press, 1961.

Lohn, Ella. *Foreigners in the Confederacy.* Chapel Hill: University of North Carolina Press, 1940.

Long, Eugene. *The Civil War Day by Day: An Almanac, 1861–65.* Garden City, N.Y: Doubleday, 1971.

– *Foreigners in the Union Army and Navy.* Baton Rouge: Louisiana State University Press, 1951.

Lord, Francis. *They Fought for the Union.* Westport: Greenwood Press, 1960.

Lovesay, Dorothy May. *To Be a Pilgrim: A Biography of Silus Tertius Rand, 1810–1889.* Hantsport, N.S.: Lancelot Press, 1992.

MacDonald, Captain John A. *Troublous Times in Canada: A History of the Fenian Raids of 1866 and 1870.* Toronto: W.S. Johnston, 1910.

MacDougall, J.L. *History of Inverness County* [1922]. Belleville: Mika, 1972.

MacKenzie, Kenneth A. "The Almons." *Nova Scotia Medical Bulletin* 30 (Feb. 1951): 31–36.

MacKinnon, Neil J. "John William Ritchie." *Dictionary of Canadian Biography* XI: 754–55.

MacKinnon, Stuart. "The Imperial Fortresses in Canada: Halifax and Esquimault, 1871–1906." Ph.D. thesis, University of Toronto, 1965.

MacLean, Raymond, ed. (Ronald MacGillivray). *History of Antigonish.* Antigonish, N.S.: Casket, 1976.

Macleod, E.J., ed. *One Woman's Charlottetown: The Diaries of Margaret Gray Lord, 1863, 1876, 1890.* Hull: Canadian Museum of Civilization, 1988.

MacNutt, W.S. *New Brunswick, A History, 1784–1867.* Toronto: University of Toronto Press, 1963.

Mahant, Edelgard E., and Graeme Mount. *An Introduction to Canadian-American Relations*. Toronto: Methuen, 1984.

Manning, William R., ed. *Diplomatic Correspondence of the United States: Canadian Relations, 1784–1860*. Washington: Carnegie Endowment of International Peace, 1940–45.

Marble, Allan E. "William Johnston Almon." *Dictionary of Canadian Biography* XIII: 16–17.

Marquis, Greg. "Haliburton, Maritime Intellectuals and the Race Question." Paper delivered to T.C. Haliburton Bi-Centennial Symposium, Acadian University, Sept. 22, 1996.

– "Mercenaries or Killer Angels? Nova Scotians in the American Civil War." *Collections of the Royal Nova Scotia Historical Society* 44 (1996): 83–104.

– "The Ports of Halifax and Saint John and the American Civil War." *The Northern Mariner* 8, no. 1 (Jan. 1998): 1–19.

– "Soldiers of Liberty: Islanders and the Civil War." *The Island Magazine* 36 (Fall–Winter 1994): 2–8.

Marr, William, and Donald G. Patterson. *Canada: An Economic History*. Toronto: Gage, 1980.

Martell, J.S. "Intercolonial Communications, 1840–1867." In *Historical Essays on the Atlantic Provinces*, edited by G. A. Rawlyk. Toronto: McClelland and Stewart, 1967.

Martin, Ged. "The Case Against Canadian Confederation." In *The Causes of Canadian Confederation*, edited by Ged Martin. Fredericton: Acadiensis Press, 1990.

–, ed. *The Causes of Canadian Confederation*. Fredericton: Acadiensis Press, 1990.

Martin, John Patrick. *The Story of Dartmouth*. Dartmouth: n.p., 1957.

Massey, Mary Elizabeth. *Bonnet Brigade*. New York: Alfred Knopf, 1966.

Masters, D.C. *The Reciprocity Treaty of 1854*. Toronto: University of Toronto Press, 1957.

McCormack, L. Shirley. *Vital Statistics from the Presbyterian Witness, 1858–1864*. Typescript. Middleton, N.S., 1986.

McCulloch, Thomas. *The Mephiboseth Stepsure Letters*. Davies, Gwendolyn, ed. Ottawa: Carleton University Press, 1990.

McDonald, Ronald H. "The Public Career of Sir Charles Hastings Doyle, 1861–1873." M.A. thesis, Dalhousie University, 1969.

– "Second Chesapeake Affair." *Dalhousie Review* 54. (Winter 1974–75): 674–84.

– "Sir Charles Hastings Doyle." *Dictionary of Canadian Biography* XI: 278–81.

McGuigan, Peter. "Tenants and Troopers: The Hazel Grove Road, 1865–68." *Island Magazine* 32 (Fall–Winter 1992): 22–28.

McKerrow, Peter. *A Brief History of the Coloured Baptists of Nova Scotia*. Halifax: Nova Scotian Printing Co., 1895.

McPherson, James M. *Battle Cry of Freedom: The Civil War Era*. Toronto: Oxford University Press, 1988.

– *The Negro's Civil War*. New York: Ballantine Books, 1991.

– *Ordeal by Fire: The Civil War and Reconstruction*. New York: Randon House, 1982.

Melville, Herman. *White-Jacket, or the World of a Man of War* [1851]. Evanston, Ill.: Northwestern University Press, 1970.

Menefee, Samuel Pyeatt. "Piracy, Terrorism and the Insurgent Passenger: A Historical and Legal Perspective." In N. Ronzetti, ed., *Maritime Terrorism and International Law*. Netherlands: Kluwer Academic Publishers, 1990, 43–68.

Miller, J. Graham. *Live: A History of Church Planting in the New Hebrides, Book I*. Sydney, Australia: Bridge Publications, n.d.

Miller, Perry. "From Covenant to the Revival." In James Ward Smith and A. Leland Jamison, eds., *The Shaping of American Religion*. Princeton: Princeton University Press, 1961, 322–68.

Milligan, John D. *Gunboats Down the Mississippi*. Annapolis: U.S. Naval Institute, 1965.

Milner, W.C. *History of Sackville, New Brunswick*. Sackville: Tribune Press, 1934.

Moody, Barry, ed. *Repent and Believe: The Baptist Experience in Maritime Canada*. Hantsport: Lancelot Press, 1980.

Moore, D.R. *History of H.M.C. Dockyard, Halifax, N.S.* Typescript. Halifax, n.d.

Morgan, James Morris *Recollections of a Rebel Reefer*. New York: Houghton Mifflin, 1917.

Morgan, Murray. *Confederate Raider in the North Pacific: The Saga of C.S.S. Shenandoah*. Pullman: Washington State University Press, 1996.

Morrison, Samuel Eliot. *Old Bruin: Commodore Matthew C. Perry, 1794–1858*. Toronto: Little, Brown and Co., 1967.

Morse, William Inglis, ed. *Supplement to Local History of Paradise, Annapolis County, Nova Scotia*. Boston: Nathan Sawyer and Sons, 1938.

Morton, Desmond. *A Military History of Canada*. Edmonton: Hurtig, 1985.

Morton, Suzanne. "Separate Spheres in a Separate World: African Nova Scotian Women in Late 19th-Century Halifax County." *Acadiensis* 22 (Spring 1993): 61–83.

Morton, W.L., ed. *The Critical Years: The Union of British North America, 1857–1873*. Toronto: McClelland and Stewart, 1977.

– *Monck Letters and Journals, 1863–68*. Toronto: McClelland and Stewart, 1970.

Muise, D.A. "The 1860s: Forging the Bonds of Union." In *The Atlantic Provinces in Confederation*, edited by E. R. Forbes and D. A. Muise. Toronto: University of Toronto Press, 1993.

Murphy, Charles, ed. *D'Arcy McGee: A Collection of Speeches and Addresses*. Toronto: Macmillan, 1937.

Nash, Howard P. *A Naval History of the Civil War*. South Brunswick: A.S. Barnes, 1975.

Neely, Mark E., Jr. "The Perils of Running the Blockade: The Influence of International Law in an Era of Total War." *Civil War History* 32 (June 1986): 101–18.

Nelson, Ralph C., et al. "Canadian Confederation, As a Case Study in Community Formation." In Ged Martin, ed., *The Causes of Canadian Confederation*. Fredericton: Acadiensis Press, 1990.

Nepveux, Ethel. *George Alfred Trenholm and the Company That Went to War*. Charleston: Electric City Printing, 1994.

New Brunswick. *Journals of the House of Assembly*.

New England Quarterly 48 (Dec. 1975): 519–39.

Nova Scotia. *Journals of the House of Assembly*.

– *Statutes*, 1834.

Nova Scotia Genealogist, 1983–1995.

O'Leary, Wayne, et al. "The Age of Monopoly." In *Maine: The Pine Tree State from Prehistory to the Present*, edited by Richard W. Judd, Edwin A. Churchill, and Joel W. Eastman. Orono: University of Maine Press, 1995.

O'Leary, Wayne and Lawrence C. Allin. "Maine's Maritime Trades in the Period of Ascendancy." In *Maine: The Pine Tree State from Prehistory to the Present*, edited by Richard W. Judd, Edwin A. Churchill, and Joel W. Eastman. Orono: University of Maine Press, 1995.

Oliver, Pearleen. *A Brief History of the Coloured Baptists of Nova Scotia, 1782–1953*. Halifax: African United Baptist Association of Nova Scotia, 1954.

Overholtzer, Harry A. "Nova Scotia and the United States Civil War." M.A. thesis, Dalhousie University, 1965.

Owsley, Frank. *King Cotton Diplomacy: Foreign Relations of the Confederate States of America*. Chicago: University of Chicago Press, 1959.

Palfrey, Francis W. *Antietam and Fredericksburg*. New York: Jack Brussel, n.d.

Parker, William Frederick. *Daniel McNeill Parker, M.D.: His Ancestry and His Life*. Toronto: William Briggs, 1910.

Penner, Peter *The Chignecto "Connexion": The History of the Sackville Methodist/United Church, 1772–1990*. Sackville: Tribune Press, 1990.

Perry, Clive, ed. *Consolidated Treaty Series*. 93, 1842. Dobb's Ferry, N.Y.: Oceana Publications 1969.

Pfanz, Hary W. *Gettysburg: The Second Day*. Chapel Hill: University of North Carolina Press, 1987.

Pickart, Lennox O'Reily. "The Trelawny Town Maroons and Sir John Wentworth: The Struggle for Their Culture." M.A. thesis, University of New Brunswick, 1993.

Piers, Harry. *Evolution of Fortress Halifax, 1749–1925*. Halifax: PANS, 1947.

Pollard, E.A. *Southern History of the Great Civil War in the United States*. Toronto: P.R. Randall, 1863.

Porter, Fitz-John. "Battle of Malvern Hill." In *Battles and Leaders of the Civil War*, vol. 2. New York: Century, 1887.

Power, L.G. "Our First President: The Honourable John William Ritchie, 1808–1890." *Collections of the Nova Scotia Historical Society* 19 (1918): 1–15.

Preston, Adrian "General Sir William Fenwick Williams, The American Civil War and the Defence of Canada, 1859–65." *Dalhousie Review* 41 (Fall–Winter 1976–77): 605–22.

Preston, Richard A. *The Defence of the Undefended Border: Planning for War in North America, 1867–1939*. Montreal: McGill-Queen's University Press, 1977.

Price, Marcus. "Ships That Tested the Blockade of the Carolina Ports, 1861–1865." *American Neptune* 8 (July 1948): 196–241.

– "Ships That Tested the Blockade of Gulf Ports, 1861–65." *American Neptune* 11 (Oct. 1951): 262–90.

Prince Edward Island. *Journals of the House of Assembly*.

Pryke, Kenneth G. "Alexander Keith." *Dictionary of Canadian Biography* X: 395–96.

– *Nova Scotia and Confederation, 1864–74*. Toronto: University of Toronto Press, 1979.

Punch, Terry. "Nova Sccotians in the U.S. Civil War." *Nova Scotia Geneaologist* 5 (1987): 29.

Rable, George C. *The Confederate Republic: A Revolution Against Politics*. Chapel Hill: University of North Carolina Press, 1994.

Raddall, Thomas H. *Halifax: Warden of the North*. Toronto: McClelland and Stewart, 1949.

– "Blind McNair." In*Tambour and Other Stories*. Toronto: McClelland and Stewart, 1945.

Rawlyk, G.A., ed. *Historical Essays on the Atlantic Provinces*. Toronto:

McClelland and Stewart, 1967.

Rayburn, Allan. *Geographical Names of New Brunswick*. Ottawa: Canadian Permanent Committee on Geographical Names, 1975.

Reid, Hugo. *Sketches in North America, With Some Account of the Congress and the Slavery Question*. London: Longman, Green, Longman and Roberts, 1861.

"Report from Our Man in Savannah," *Atlantic Advocate* 54 (Jan. 1964): 59–60.

Report on the Defence of Canada, Made to the Provincial Government on the 10th November 1864 and of the British Naval Stations in the North Atlantic. London, 1865.

Reynolds, Clark G., ed. *Global Crossroads and the American Seas*. Missoula: Pictorial Histories Publishing, 1988.

Rice, Charles. "Pirates or Patriots?" *America's Civil War* 7, no. 4. (Sept. 1994): 46–52.

Rice, Richard. "The Wrights of Saint John: Study of Shipbuilding and Shipowning in the Maritimes, 1839–1885." In David MacMillan, ed., *Canadian Business History: Selected Essays, 1493–1971*. Toronto: University of Toronto Press, 1972, 317–32.

Rich, Paul B. *Race and Empire in British Politics*. New York: Cambridge University Press, 1986.

Ripley, Peter, ed. *The Black Abolitionist Papers II: Canada, 1860–65*. Chapel Hill, University of North Carolina Press, 1986.

Roberston, John William. *The Book of the Bible Against Slavery*. Halifax?, n.p., n.d.

Roberts, Charles G.D. *A History of Canada*. Boston: Lamson and Wolffe, 1897.

Robertson, Ian Ross. *The Tenant League of Prince Edward Island, 1864–1867: Leasehold Tenure in the New World*. Toronto: University of Toronto Press, 1996.

Robertson, James I. *Soldiers Blue and Grey*. Columbia: University of South Carolina Press, 1988.

Robinson, Charles M. *Shark of the Confederacy: The Story of C.S.S. Alabama*. Annapolis: Naval Institute Press, 1994.

Roediger, David R. *The Wages of Whiteness: Race and the Making of the American Working Class*. New York: Verso, 1991.

Roller, David, and Robert Twyman, eds. *The Encyclopedia of Southern History*. Baton Rouge: Louisiana State University Press, 1979.

Rorabaugh, W.J. "Who Fought for the North in the Civil War? Concord, Massachusetts Enlistments." *Journal of Social History* (Dec. 1986): 695–701.

Roscoe, Theodore *The Webb of Conspiracy*. Englewood Cliffs, N.J.: Prentice Hall, 1960.

Rowell, John W. *Yankee Cavalry Men: Through the Civil War with the Ninth Pennsylvania Cavalry.* Knoxville: University of Tennessee Press, 1975.

Ruck, Calvin. *The Black Battalion: Canada's Best-Kept Military Secret.* Halifax; Nimbus, 1987.

Rules and Regulations of the Halifax Club. Halifax: James Bowes and Son, 1863.

Sager, Eric W. *Seafaring Labour: The Merchant Marine of Atlantic Canada, 1820–1914.* Montreal: McGill-Queen's University Press, 1989.

– with Gerald Panting. *Maritime Capital: The Shipping Industry in Atlantic Canada, 1820–1914.* Montreal: McGill-Queen's University Press, 1990.

Salter, Remo. "Guardians of the Coast." *America's Civil War* 7, no. 1 (March 1994): 34–40.

Saunders, Edward Manning, *The Life and Letters of the Rt. Hon. Sir Charles Tupper, Bart., KCMG.* Toronto: Cassell, 1916.

– *Three Premiers of Nova Scotia.* Toronto: William Briggs, 1909.

Saunders, S.A. *The Economic History of the Maritime Provinces.* Fredericton: Acadiensis Press, 1984.

Scott, Geraldine Tidd. *"Ties of Common Blood": A History of Maine's Northeastern Boundary Dispute with Great Britain, 1783–1842.* Bowie, Md.: Heritage Books, 1992.

Selfridge, Thomas. "The Navy at Fort Fisher." In *Battles and Leaders of the Civil War,* vol. 4. New York: Century, 1887.

Semmes, Raphael. *Memoirs of a Service Afloat.* London: Richard Bentley, 1869.

Semple, Bill. "Islanders in the American Civil War." Summerside: *Journal-Pioneer,* Jun. 8–10, 1994.

Senior, Hereward. *The Fenians and Canada.* Toronto: Macmillan, 1978.

– *The Last Invasion of Canada: The Fenian Raids, 1866–1870.* Toronto: Dundurn Press, 1991.

Seward, Frederick William *Reminiscences of a War-Time Statesman and Diplomat, 1830–1915.* New York: Knickerbocker Press, 1916.

Shaw, Walter. *Tell Me the Tales.* Charlottetown: Square Deal Publications, 1975.

Shingleton, Royce Gordon. *John Taylor Wood, Sea Ghost of the Confederacy.* Athens: University of Georgia Press, 1979.

Smedley, Audrey. *Race in North America: Origins, Evolution and World View.* Boulder, Colo.: Westview Press, 1993.

Smith, Mason Philip. *Confederates Downeast: Confederate Operations in and Around Maine.* Portland: Provincial Press, 1985.

Sommerville, William. *Southern Slavery Not Founded on Scripture*

Warrant. Saint John, 1864.

Spray, W.A. *The Blacks in New Brunswick.* Fredericton: Brunswick Press, 1972.

Spry, W. "Robert Patterson." *Dictionary of Canadian Biography* XI: 677–78.

Stacey, C.P. *Canada and the British Army, 1846–71.* Toronto: University of Toronto Press, 1963.

Stairs, William. *The Stairs Family.* Halifax: McAlpine Publishing, 1906.

Stanley, G.F.G. *The War of 1812: Land Operations.* Toronto: Macmillan of Canada-National Museum of Man, 1991.

Starr, Stephen Z. "The Wilson Raid, June 1864: A Trooper's Reminiscences." *Civil War History* 21 (1975): 218–41.

Stayner, Charles St. C. "John William Ritchie: One of the Fathers of Confederation." *Collections of the Nova Scotia Historical Society* 36 (1968): 183–277.

Stephan, Nancy *The Idea of Race in Science: Great Britain, 1800–1960.* Hemden: Archon Books, 1982.

Stern, Phillip van Doren. *Secret Missions of the Civil War.* New York: Rand McNally, 1959.

Stevenson, Laura Agnes. *The Ladies Benevolent and Industrial Sallymag Society.* Charlottetown: W.H.Bremner, 1868.

Stewart, Alice "The State of Maine and Canadian Confederation." *Canadian Historical Review* 23 (June 1952): 148–64.

Story, D.A. "H.M. Navy Yard, Halifax, in the Early Sixties." *Collections of the Nova Scotia Historical Society* 22 (1923): 43–47.

Stouffer, Allan. *The Light of Nature and the Law of God: Anti-Slavery in Ontario, 1833–1867.* Montreal: McGill-Queen's University Press, 1993.

Strode, Hudson. *Jefferson Davis: The Last Twenty-Five Years.* New York: Harcourt, Brace and World, 1964.

Sturgis, James L. "The Opposition to Confederation in Nova Scotia, 1864–1868." In *The Causes of Canadian Confederation*, edited by Ged Martin. Fredericton: Acadiensis Press, 1990.

Sutherland, David. "Benjamin Wier." *Dictionary of Canadian Biography* IX: 838–40.

– "James William Johnston." *Dictionary of Canadian Biography* X: 381–88.

Tallman, R. "Warships and Mackerel: The North Atlantic Fisheries in Canadian-American Relations 1867–1877." Ph.D. thesis, University of Maine, 1973.

Taylor, Thomas *Running the Blockade.* London: John Murray, 1896.

Tebeau, Charlton A. *A History of Florida.* Miami: University of Miami Press, 1971.

Tennyson, Brian. "Early Fortifications in Sydney Harbour." *Nova Scotia Historical Review* 15 (1995): 1–32.

– "Economic Nationalism, Confederation and Nova Scotia." In *The Causes of Canadian Confederation*, edited by Ged Martin. Fredericton: Acadiensis Press, 1990.

Thomas, Mary Elizabeth. "The C.S.S. *Tallahassee*: A Factor in Anglo-American Relations, 1864–66." *Civil War History* 21 (June 1975): 148–59.

Thurston, Harry Arthur. *Tallahassee Skipper*. Yarmouth, N.S.: Lescarbot Press, 1981.

Townshend, C.J. "Life of Alexander Stewart." *Collections of the Nova Scotia Historical Society* 15 (1914): 1–15.

Trollope, Anthony. *The West Indies and the Spanish Main* [1859]. London: Dawsons of Pall Mall, 1968.

Trombley, R. Fay. "Thomas Louis Connolly (1815–1876): The Man and His Place in Secular and Ecclesiastical History." Ph.D. thesis, Catholic University of Louisiana, 1983.

Tuck, R.C. *The Island Family Harris*. Charlottetown: Ragweed Press, 1983.

United States. Department of the Navy. *Civil War Naval Chronology, 1861–65*. Washington: Naval History Division, 1971.

United States. Department of State. *Papers Relating to the Foreign Relations of the United States*. Washington: Government Printing Office, 1861–68.

– *The War of the Rebellion: A Compilation of the Official Records of the Union and Confederate Armies* [*ORA*]. 130 vols. Washington, D.C.: U.S. Government Printing Office, 1880–1901.

– *War of the Rebellion: A Compilation of the Official Records of the Union and Confederate Navies* [*ORN*]. 30 vols. Washington, 1894–1922.

Vandiver, Frank E. *Confederate Blockade Running Through Bermuda, 1861–1865*. Austin: University of Texas Press, 1947.

– *Their Tattered Flag: The Epic of the Confederacy*. New York: Harper's Magazine Press, 1970.

"Visit to the Cities and Camps of the Confederate States, 1863–64." *Blackwood's Magazine* 47 (Feb. 1865): 162–64.

Waite, P.B. *The Life and Times of Confederation, 1864–1867*. Toronto: University of Toronto Press, 1963.

– *The Lives of Dalhousie University, Vol. 1, 1818–1925*. Montreal: McGill-Queen's University Press, 1994.

Walke, Henry. "Opposing Forces at New Madrid (Island Number Ten), Fort Pillow, and Memphis." In *Battles and Leaders of the Civil War*, vol. 1. New York: Century, 1887.

– "The Western Flotilla at Fort Donelson, Island Number Ten, Fort

Pillow and Memphis." In *Battles and Leaders of the Civil War*, vol. 1. New York: Century, 1887.

Walker, Carl George. "A Note on the Passamaquoddy Boundary Affair." *Canadian Historical Review* 34 (March 1953): 46–53.

Walker, James W. St. G. *The Black Loyalists: The Search for a Promised Land in Nova Scotia and Sierra Leone*. New York: Africana Publishing Co., 1976.

– *Racial Discrimination in Canada: The Black Experience*. Ottawa: Canadian Historical Association, 1985.

Wallace, Carl. "John Hamilton Gray." *Dictionary of Canadian Biography* XI: 372–76.

– "Sir Leonard Tilley: A Political Biography." Ph.D. thesis, University of Alberta, 1972.

Warder, T.B., and James M. Catlett. *Battle of Young's Branch or Manassas Fought July 21, 1861*. Richmond: Enquirer Book and Job Press, 1862.

Warner, Ezra. *Generals in Blue: Lives of the Union Commanders*. Baton Rouge: Louisiana State University Press, 1964.

Warren, Gordon H. *Fountains of Discontent: The Trent Affair and the Freedom of the Seas*. Boston: Northeastern University, 1981.

Webber, David. *One Thousand Young Men: The Colonial Volunteer Militia of Pronce Edward Island*. Charlottetown: P.E.I. Museum and Heritage Foundation, 1990.

West, Richard S., Jr. *Mr. Lincoln's Navy*. Greenwood, Conn.: Greenwood Press, 1976.

Wheelright, Julie. *Amazons and Military Maids: Women Who Dressed as Men in Pursuit of Life, Liberty and Military Happiness*. London: Pandora, 1989.

Whelan, Devlin. "A Survey of Franco-American Participation in Maine Regiments During the American Civil War." Unpublished paper, University of Laval, n.d.

Whelan, Edward, ed. *The Union of the Provinces*. Charlottetown: G.T. Hazard, 1865.

Whitelaw, E.M. *The Maritimes and Canada Before Confederation*. Toronto: Oxford University Press, 1934.

Wiley, B.I. *The Life of Billy Yank: The Common Soldier of the Union*. Indianapolis: Bobbs-Merrill, 1952.

– *The Life of Johnny Reb: The Common Soldier of the Confederacy*. Indianapolis: Bobbs-Merrill, 1943.

Wilkinson, J.R. *The Narrative of a Blockade Runner*. New York: Sheldon and Co., 1877.

Winks, Robin. *Canada and the United States: The Civil War Years*. New York: University Press of America, 1988.

– *Blacks in Canada: A History*. Montreal: McGill-Queen's University Press, 1971.
– "The Creation of a Myth: 'Canadian' Enlistments in the Northern Armies during the American Civil War." *Canadian Historical Review* 29 (March 1958): 33–43.
Winchester, Dawson. "The Last Minstrel Show." *New Brunswick Reader* 5, no. 15 (1998): 13–14.
Wise, Stephen R. *Lifeline of the Confederacy: Blockade Running During the Civil War*. Columbia: University of South Carolina Press, 1988.
Wood, John Taylor. "The *Tallahassee* Terrifies New England." In *Secret Missions of the Civil War*, by Stern, Phillip van Doren. New York: Rand McNally, 1959.
Wynn, Graeme. "New England's Outpost in the 19th-Century." In Stephen Hornsby, Victor A. Conrad and James J. Herlan, eds., *The Northeastern Borderlands: Four Centuries of Interaction*. Fredericton: Acadiensis Press, 1989, 64–90.
– *Timber Colony: A Historical Geography of Early Nineteenth-Century New Brunswick*. Toronto: University of Toronto Press, 1981.

Index